750 best muffin recipes

Everything from breakfast classics to gluten-free, vegan & coffeehouse favorites

Camilla V. Saulsbury

Robert
ROSE

Design and Production: Daniella Zanchetta/PageWave Graphics Inc.
Editors: Sue Sumeraj and Jennifer MacKenzie
Proofreader: Sheila Wawanash
Indexer: Gillian Watts
Photography: Colin Erricson
Associate Photographer: Matt Johannsson
Food Styling: Kathryn Robertson
Prop Styling: Charlene Erricson

Cover image: Peach Melba Muffins (page 222)

We acknowledge the financial support of the Government of Canada through the Book
Publishing Industry Development Program (BPIDP) for our publishing activities.

Published by Robert Rose Inc.
120 Eglinton Avenue East, Suite 800, Toronto, Ontario, Canada M4P 1E2
Tel: (416) 322-6552 Fax: (416) 322-6936
www.robertrose.ca

Printed and bound in Canada

1 2 3 4 5 6 7 8 9 CPL 18 17 16 15 14 13 12 11 10

To Nicholas Daniel West, for changing my life forever.

Contents

● ●

Acknowledgments

To my publisher at Robert Rose, Bob Dees. It's funny how life (or, more precisely, cake mix) throws two people together. Thanks for the encouragement, advice and good faith. Here's to a long relationship.

To my unequivocally fabulous editors, Sue Sumeraj and Jennifer MacKenzie. I must have done something very good to deserve to work with such dedicated, talented and fun women.

To Kevin, my rock.

To Nick, the best little boy in the world and an excellent muffin taste-tester.

To my parents for being the most supportive, loving people ever.

To Lindsey and Becca for helping me keep my perspective.

To Miss Tammy and Miss Karen at the Early Childhood Lab at Stephen F. Austin University. This book could not have been written if Nick didn't love being in your classroom.

Introduction

I made my first muffins at the age of six. The recipe came from my first cookbook, a Christmas present from my parents, and the instructions were set to the tune of "She'll Be Coming 'Round the Mountain." Making them was easy (and fun, thanks to the singing), and the results were scrumptious; I was thrilled to have made 12 cinnamon-sugar-topped treats with my own two hands and a short list of ingredients from my mother's pantry. I've been a muffin fan, and proponent, ever since.

So when the opportunity for this project landed in my lap, I was nothing short of delighted. Muffins are a symbol of honest effort and are delicious anytime, anywhere. The fact that they are so easy to make is a huge plus for home cooks of all levels of experience these days. Thirty minutes in the kitchen pays dividends for several days.

Home baking is more popular than ever, and muffins are the perfect choice when the urge to bake strikes. Ever mindful of how home cooks are baking today, for this book I've created a modern collection of delicious muffin options. The chapter titles reflect my approach: The Top 25 Classics, Breakfast Muffins, Coffeehouse Muffins, Lunch and Supper Muffins, Farmers' Market Muffins, Global Muffins, Superfood Muffins, Gluten-Free Muffins and Vegan Muffins.

These are recipes you will want to make and enjoy again and again. The ingredients are simple and fresh, the flavors fantastic and the finished results beautiful. No esoteric baking equipment is required, though I have suggested a short list of tools that are handy to have around. I use the grocery stores in my small Texas town to determine the availability of ingredients: if it's not at one of my local supermarkets, it's not in these pages.

You'll find it hard to believe that breads so beautiful and delicious can be so quick and easy to make, but muffins prove that it's possible. And in the end, what could be more satisfying than buttering up, and blowing away, your beloveds with a basket of dark chocolate muffins, browned butter raspberry muffins or herbed ricotta supper muffins?

I hope you experience as much pleasure baking (and nibbling) your way through this cookbook as I did creating it; it was a labor of love, and I enjoyed every minute of it. And while the recipes aren't set to song (perhaps in the second printing?), I know you'll still have plenty of fun along the way.

Muffin Mastery

A major part of the appeal of making muffins is their quick and straightforward preparation. The primary method can be broken down into a short list of simple steps:

1. **Preheat the oven.** Preheat to the temperature specified in the recipe.

2. **Prepare the muffin pan.** Line the cups with paper liners, or grease them with solid vegetable shortening, as specified in the recipe. To grease muffin cups, lightly but thoroughly coat the bottoms and sides, using a paper towel for ease of spreading (and to keep your fingers clean).

3. **Whisk the dry ingredients.** Whisking the dry ingredients distributes the baking powder, baking soda, salt and spices in the flour. If the leavening is not evenly distributed, the muffins may have a bitter taste.

4. **Whisk the wet ingredients.** Whisk the wet ingredients, such as milk, eggs, oil and melted butter, until thoroughly combined. Sugar is sometimes also whisked in with the wet ingredients.

5. **Combine the dry and wet ingredients.** Add the wet ingredients to the dry ingredients all at once. *Stir just until the dry ingredients are moistened and the batter is combined.* A few lumps are okay. Overmixing the batter develops the gluten in the flour, causing the baked muffins to have tunnels and a tough and/or gummy texture.

6. **Add any extra ingredients.** Gently stir or fold in any extra ingredients, such as berries or chocolate chips. As in step 5, the aim is to avoid overmixing.

7. **Fill the muffin pan.** Spoon the batter into the prepared muffin cups (or use a large, spring-loaded cookie or ice cream scoop). Place the muffin pan on the middle rack of the preheated oven.

8. **Bake and test for doneness.** Check for doneness using the method described in the recipe when the minimum baking time specified in the recipe has elapsed.

9. **Remove the muffins from the pan.** Let the muffins cool in the pan for a few minutes, as specified in the recipe, then remove to a wire rack to cool further. If you leave the muffins in the pan to cool, the bottoms will get soggy.

Creamed Muffins

A small number of recipes in this collection direct you to cream the butter and sugar with an electric mixer before adding the other wet ingredients. As with the primary method above, take special care in combining the dry ingredients with the creamed mixture to avoid overmixing.

Transforming Standard Muffins into Loaves, Mini Muffins and Jumbo Muffins

All of the recipes in this collection are written for use with a standard-size muffin pan. But refashioning any of the recipes (with the exception of the gluten-free muffin recipes) into loaves, mini muffins or jumbo muffins is easy. Preheat the oven and prepare the batter as specified in the recipe, then follow the guidelines below for the desired type of pan or pan.

Loaves

Grease and flour a light-colored metal loaf pan or pans to prevent the loaf from sticking (due to the longer bake time required by a loaf). Spread the batter in the prepared pan, smoothing the top with a rubber spatula so that the loaf rises and browns evenly during baking. Place the pan in the preheated oven and bake for 5 to 20 minutes longer than the specified muffin baking time (the timing will depend on what size loaf pan you use). Test for doneness in the same manner as described for testing muffins. Let the loaf cool in the pan for 10 minutes. Run a butter knife around the sides of the loaf and unmold. Transfer the loaf, upright, to a wire rack to cool further.

Mini Muffins

Prepare the mini muffin pan as specified for the standard muffin pan in the recipe (i.e., greased or lined with paper liners). In general, a recipe with a yield of 12 standard muffins will yield 24 mini muffins. Fill the prepared muffin pans, then place in the oven. Reduce the baking time by 5 to 15 minutes, checking for doneness at the earliest time. Test for doneness in the same manner as described for testing the standard-size muffins. Let cool in the pan for the same amount of time as specified in the standard muffin recipe, then remove to a wire rack to cool further.

Jumbo Muffins

Prepare the jumbo muffin pan as specified for the standard muffin pan in the recipe (i.e., greased or lined with paper liners). In general, a recipe with a yield of 12 standard muffins will yield 6 jumbo muffins. Fill the prepared muffin pans, then place in the oven. Increase the baking time by 5 to 15 minutes, checking for doneness at the earliest time. Test for doneness in the same manner as described for testing the standard-size muffins. Let cool in the pan for the same amount of time as specified in the standard muffin recipe, then remove to a wire rack to cool further.

> If a recipe makes fewer muffins than the number of cups in the tin, fill the empty cups one-third full with water. This will prevent the pan from buckling — and potentially spilling some of the batter — in the oven.

Measuring Ingredients

Television baking shows give the illusion that baking is a freestyle event — a pinch of this here, a dash of that there, and voila! Perfect cookies, cakes and muffins. In reality, baking is much more like a chemistry experiment (albeit a delicious one) than a magic show. Accurate measurements are essential for creating the perfect balance of flour, liquids, leaveners and fats, and achieving consistent results time and again. Too much flour makes muffins taste dry and flavorless, too little baking powder makes them flat, and an excess of salt renders them inedible. So take both time and care as you measure; the success of your muffins depends on it.

Measuring Dry Ingredients

When measuring a dry ingredient, such as flour, cocoa powder, sugar, spices or salt, spoon it into the appropriate-size dry measuring cup or measuring spoon, heaping it up over the top. Slide a straight-edged utensil, such as a knife, across the top to level off the extra. Be careful not to shake or tap the cup or spoon to settle the ingredient, or you will have more than you need.

Measuring Moist Ingredients

Moist ingredients, such as brown sugar, coconut and dried fruit, must be firmly packed in a measuring cup or spoon to be measured accurately. Use a dry measuring cup for these ingredients. Fill the measuring cup to slightly overflowing, then pack down the ingredient firmly with the back of a spoon. Add more of the ingredient and pack down again until the cup is full and even with the top of the measure.

Measuring Liquid Ingredients

Use a clear plastic or glass measuring cup or container with lines up the sides to measure liquid ingredients. Set the container on the counter and pour the liquid to the appropriate mark. Lower your head to read the measurement at eye level.

Ingredients

Muffins have long been baking favorites because, in addition to their ease of preparation and quick baking time, the essential ingredients for preparing them are familiar and typical to most home pantries and refrigerators. Do you have all-purpose flour, baking powder, salt, sugar, butter or oil, milk and eggs? Then you have what you need to make a basic muffin that can be dressed up or down with an endless array of mix-ins, from fruit (fresh or dried) to nuts to chocolate. Craving a whole-grain muffin? Swap some or all of the all-purpose flour for whole wheat flour. Cutting back on refined sugar? Use an alternative sweetener — agave nectar, turbinado sugar, honey, molasses, maple syrup — in place of the granulated sugar. What follows are the key ingredients to keep on hand for a wealth of muffin recipes.

Flours, Grains and Nuts

All-Purpose Flour

Made from a blend of high-gluten hard wheat and low-gluten soft wheat, all-purpose flour is a fine-textured flour milled from the inner part of the wheat kernel and contains neither the germ nor the bran. All-purpose flour comes either bleached or unbleached; they can be used interchangeably.

Whole Wheat Pastry Flour

A fine-textured, soft wheat flour that includes the wheat germ, whole wheat pastry flour can be used interchangeably with all-purpose flour in most recipes. In many recipes in this book, I've used it in combination with all-purpose flour, but feel free to up the proportion of whole wheat pastry flour to replace more or all of the all-purpose flour.

It is extremely important not to substitute regular whole wheat flour for the whole wheat pastry flour; the results will be coarse, leaden and possibly inedible.

You can find whole wheat pastry flour at well-stocked supermarkets and at natural food stores. Store it in a sealable plastic bag in the refrigerator.

Whole Wheat Flour

Whole wheat flour is milled from hard red wheat; it has a fuller flavor and is far more nutritious than all-purpose flour because it contains the wheat bran and sometimes the germ. Because of its higher fat content, it should be stored in the refrigerator to prevent rancidity.

Cake Flour

This finely ground, soft white flour is low in protein, which means it will develop less gluten during mixing and will yield particularly tender baked goods. For a quick substitute for cake flour, replace 2 tbsp (30 mL) of each cup (250 mL) of all-purpose flour with cornstarch.

Cornmeal

Cornmeal is simply ground dried corn kernels. There are two methods of grinding. The first is the modern method, in which milling is done by huge steel rollers, which remove the husk and germ almost entirely; this creates the most common variety of cornmeal found in supermarkets. The second is the stone-ground method, in which some of the hull and germ of the corn is retained; this type of cornmeal is available at health food stores and in the health food sections of most supermarkets. The two varieties can be used interchangeably in most of the recipes in this collection, but I recommend sticking with the stone-ground variety where specified, as it has a much deeper corn flavor and is far more nutritious.

Rolled Oats

Two types of rolled oats are called for in these recipes: large-flake (old-fashioned) rolled oats are oat groats (hulled and cleaned whole oats) that have been steamed and flattened with huge rollers; quick-cooking rolled oats are groats that have been cut into several pieces before being steamed and rolled into thinner flakes. For the best results, it is important to use the type of rolled oats specified in the recipe.

Ground Flax Seeds (Flaxseed Meal)

Flax seeds are highly nutritious, tiny seeds from the flax plant. They have gained tremendous popularity in recent years thanks to their high levels of omega-3 fatty acids. But to reap the most benefits from the seeds, you must grind them into meal. Look for packages of ready-ground flax seeds, which may be labeled "flaxseed meal," or grind whole flax seeds in a spice or coffee grinder to a very fine meal. The meal adds a warm, nutty flavor to a wide range of muffins throughout the collection, and is also used as an egg substitute for many of the vegan muffin recipes in Chapter 9. Store ground flax seeds in an airtight bag in the refrigerator for 4 to 5 months, or in the freezer for up to 8 months.

Nuts

I've used a wide variety of nuts in this collection, including walnuts, pecans, almonds, pine nuts and pistachios. Many of the recipes call for the nuts to be toasted before they are added to the muffin batter. Toasting nuts deepens their flavor and makes them crisp. To toast nuts, spread the amount needed for the recipe on a rimmed baking sheet. Bake in a preheated 350°F (180°C) oven for 8 to 10 minutes or until golden and fragrant. Alternatively, toast the nuts in a dry skillet over low heat, stirring constantly, for 2 to 4 minutes or until golden and fragrant.

Sweeteners

Granulated Sugar

Granulated sugar (also called white sugar) is refined cane or beet sugar, and is the most common sweetener used in this book. Once opened, store granulated sugar in an airtight container in a cool, dry place.

Brown Sugar

Brown sugar is granulated sugar with some molasses added to it. The molasses gives the brown sugar a soft texture. Light brown sugar (also known as golden yellow sugar) has less molasses and a more delicate flavor than dark brown sugar. Once opened, store brown sugar in an airtight container or a sealable plastic food bag, to prevent clumping.

Confectioners' (Icing) Sugar

Confectioners' (icing) sugar (also called powdered sugar) is granulated sugar that has been ground to a fine powder. Cornstarch is added to prevent the sugar from clumping together. It is used in recipes where regular sugar would be too grainy.

Turbinado Sugar

Turbinado sugar is raw sugar that has been steam-cleaned. The coarse crystals are blond in color and have a delicate molasses flavor. They are typically used for decoration and texture atop baked goods.

Honey

Honey is plant nectar that has been gathered and concentrated by honey bees. Any variety of honey may be used in the recipes in this collection. Unopened containers of honey may be stored at room temperature. After opening, store honey in the refrigerator to protect against mold. Honey will keep indefinitely when stored properly.

Maple Syrup

Maple syrup is a thick liquid sweetener made by boiling the sap from maple trees. It has a strong, pure maple flavor. Maple-flavored pancake syrup is just corn syrup with coloring and artificial maple flavoring added, and it is not recommended as a substitute for pure maple syrup. Unopened containers of maple syrup may be stored at room temperature. After opening, store maple syrup in the refrigerator to protect against mold. Maple syrup will keep indefinitely when stored properly.

Molasses

Molasses is made from the juice of sugar cane or sugar beets, which is boiled until a syrupy mixture remains. The recipes in this collection were tested using dark (cooking) molasses, but you can substitute light (fancy) molasses if you prefer. Blackstrap molasses is thick and very dark, and it has a bitter flavor; it is not recommended for the recipes in this collection. Unopened containers of molasses may be stored at room temperature. After opening, store molasses in the refrigerator to protect against mold.

Molasses will keep indefinitely when stored properly.

Agave Nectar

Agave nectar (or agave syrup) is a plant-based sweetener derived from the agave cactus, native to Mexico. Used for centuries to make tequila, agave juice produces a light golden syrup.

Fats and Oils

Butter

Fresh butter has a delicate cream flavor and a pale yellow color, and adds tremendous flavor to a wide range of recipes. Although margarine is an acceptable substitute for butter in muffin recipes, I don't recommended using it (with the exception of vegan margarine for vegan recipes), as it lacks the nuanced flavor of butter.

Butter quickly picks up off-flavors during storage and when exposed to oxygen; once the carton or wrap is opened, place it in a zipper-top plastic food bag or an airtight container. Store it away from foods with strong odors, especially items such as onions or garlic.

To melt butter, cut the specified amount into small pieces, place in a small saucepan and melt over the lowest heat setting. Once the butter has melted, remove the pan from the heat and let cool. Alternatively, arrange the small pieces of butter in a medium-size, microwave-safe dish (it will splatter if crowded into a small dish). Loosely cover with a paper towel and microwave on High power for 5 to 10 second intervals, until just melted. To speed the cooling, pour the melted butter into a small bowl or liquid measuring cup.

To soften butter, let the specified amount stand for 30 to 45 minutes at room temperature. Cutting the butter into small chunks will reduce the softening time to about 15 minutes. If time is really limited, try grating cold butter on the large holes of a cheese grater. The small bits of butter will be soft in just a few minutes. Avoid softening butter in the microwave: even if you are watching it closely, at least part of the butter will typically melt.

Vegetable Oil

Vegetable oil is a generic term used to describe any neutral, plant-based oil that is liquid at room temperature. You can use a vegetable oil blend, canola oil, light olive oil, grapeseed oil, safflower oil, sunflower oil, peanut oil or corn oil.

Olive Oil

Olive oil is a monounsaturated oil that is prized for a wide range of cooking preparations, including soups. Plain olive oil (the products are simply labeled "olive oil") contains a combination of refined olive oil and virgin or extra virgin oil. It has a mild flavor and is significantly less expensive than extra virgin olive oil. Extra virgin olive oil is the cold-pressed result of the first pressing of the olives and is considered the finest and fruitiest of the olive oils.

Vegan Margarine

Margarine is used for a small number of vegan recipes in this collection. Read the label closely to ensure that the product is 100% vegan, as some margarines include milk solids.

Eggs and Dairy

Eggs

All of the recipes in this book were tested with large eggs. Select clean, fresh eggs that have been handled properly and refrigerated. Do not use dirty, cracked or leaking eggs, or eggs that have a bad odor or unnatural color when cracked open. They may have become contaminated with harmful bacteria, such as salmonella.

Milk

Both lower-fat and whole milk are used in a wide range of recipes in this book. Be sure to note when whole milk is specified — the extra fat is needed in the recipe, so lower-fat milk should not be substituted. If the recipe does not specify the type of milk, then either lower-fat or whole milk may be used. Nonfat (skim) milk is not recommended, as the decreased fat will lead to dry, crumbly muffins.

Cream

Two varieties of cream are used in this collection: half-and-half (10%) cream and whipping (35%) cream. You can substitute table (18%) cream in recipes calling for half-and-half (10%) cream, and heavy (36%) cream or light whipping cream (30% to 35%) in recipes calling for whipping (35%) cream.

Sour Cream

Commercial sour cream contains 14% to 20% fat and has been treated with a lactic acid culture to add its characteristic tang. Refrigerate sour cream in its container for up to a week after the date stamped on the bottom. If any mold forms on the surface of the cream, discard the entire container immediately.

Buttermilk

Commercially prepared buttermilk is made by culturing nonfat (skim) or lower-fat milk with bacteria. It has a distinctive tang and, when added to baked goods, yields a tender, moist result and a slightly buttery flavor.

If you don't have buttermilk, it's easy to make a substitute. Mix 1 tbsp (15 mL) lemon juice or white vinegar into 1 cup (250 mL) whole or lower-fat milk. Let stand for at least 15 minutes before using, to allow the milk to curdle. Any extra can be stored in the refrigerator for the same amount of time as the milk from which it was made.

Yogurt

Yogurt, like buttermilk, is acidic and tenderizes baked goods. It makes an excellent substitution for sour cream in a wide range of recipes. Always use plain (unflavored) yogurt in these recipes. If the recipe does not specify lower-fat or whole-milk yogurt, then either may be used. Nonfat yogurt is not recommended, as the decreased fat will lead to dry, crumbly muffins.

Cream Cheese

All of the recipes in this book use brick-style cream cheese, typically sold in 8 oz (250 g) rectangular packages. To soften cream cheese, unwrap it and cut it into chunks with a sharp knife. Let it stand at room temperature for 30 to 45 minutes, until softened. To speed the softening, place the chunks of cream cheese on a microwave-safe plate or in a microwave-safe bowl and microwave on High for 15 seconds. If necessary, microwave for 5 or 10 seconds longer.

Ricotta Cheese

Ricotta is a rich, fresh cheese with a texture that is slightly grainy but still far smoother than cottage cheese. It is white and moist and has a slightly sweet flavor. The full-fat variety is readily available and adds considerable richness to baked goods and cheesecakes. Light ricotta may be used with equal success. The muffins will not be quite as moist as when made with full-fat ricotta, but will still be rich and wonderful.

Cottage Cheese

Cottage cheese makes a great addition to both sweet and savory muffins, lending richness, moistness and a tender crumb, not to mention significant nutritional value (most notably in protein and calcium.) For best results, use the type of cottage cheese (small-curd, large-curd, etc.) specified in the recipe.

Mascarpone Cheese

Mascarpone is a buttery, ultra-rich Italian-style double- or triple-cream cheese made from cow's milk. It has a velvety texture and a slightly buttery flavor.

Chocolate and Cocoa

With so many chocolates on the market these days, choosing a good one for the perfect batch of Peanut Butter Chocolate Chunk Muffins (page 114) or Chocolate Ricotta Muffins (page 145) may seem daunting. But it's quite simple. Choose a chocolate with 50% to 70% cocoa solids in the ingredient list, and avoid vegetable fat and artificial flavors. Look for cocoa butter instead. A high percentage of sugar is an indicator of lower quality.

Good chocolate should have an even color, but if chocolate develops a white or gray sheen, it is not spoiled; rather, it has "bloomed," meaning that it got warm enough for the cocoa butter's crystalline bonds to break and reform in an irregular pattern (fat bloom) or that water has condensed on the chocolate's surface (sugar bloom). Bloom does not damage the chocolate for cooking purposes but may make it grainy and less palatable for eating plain.

Semisweet and Bittersweet Baking Chocolate

At its most basic, chocolate is made up of cocoa butter and cocoa powder — which together are called cacao liquor and determine cacao content — along with sugar. As cacao content goes up, sugar content goes down. Semisweet chocolate is the most common chocolate used in baking recipes and has a typical cacao content of 35% to 40%. By comparison, bittersweet chocolate has a higher percentage of cacao (anywhere from 35% to 99%), a more assertive chocolate flavor and a lower percentage of sugar.

Milk Chocolate

Milk chocolate has milk powder, liquid milk or condensed milk added, and therefore has a milder flavor than semisweet and bittersweet chocolate.

Unsweetened Baking Chocolate

Unsweetened chocolate should list one ingredient on the package: chocolate. It is composed of more than 50% cocoa butter, the remainder being cocoa solids.

White Chocolate

White chocolate is primarily composed of cocoa butter. The ingredients listed on a package of white chocolate should be sugar, cocoa butter, milk, soy lecithin (an emulsifier) and vanilla extract. Avoid any white chocolate that lists palm kernel oil or any other vegetable fat, as these are used by the manufacturer as cheap substitutes for some of the cocoa butter.

Chocolate Chips

Chocolate chips are small chunks of chocolate that are typically sold in a round, flat-bottomed teardrop shape. They are available in numerous sizes, from large to miniature, but are usually around $\frac{1}{2}$ inch (1 cm) in diameter. Do not use chocolate chips in recipes that require chopped chocolate to be melted.

Cocoa Powder

Select natural cocoa powder rather than Dutch process for the recipes in this collection. Natural cocoa powder has a deep, true chocolate flavor. The packaging should state whether it is Dutch process or not, but you can also tell the difference by sight: if it is dark to almost black, it is Dutch process; natural cocoa powder is much lighter and is typically brownish-red in color.

Flavorings

Spices

All of the recipes in this collection use ground spices (as opposed to whole spices). With ground spices, freshness is everything. To determine whether a ground spice is fresh, open the container and sniff. A strong fragrance means the spice is still acceptable for use.

Salt

Unless otherwise specified, the recipes in this collection were tested with ordinary table salt. Salt connoisseurs often prefer to use kosher salt, which is all-natural and additive-free; you are welcome to substitute it (the fine kosher salt, not the coarse) for the table salt.

Black Pepper

Black pepper is made by grinding black peppercorns, which have been picked when the berry is not quite ripe, then dried until it shrivels and the skin turns dark brown to black. Black pepper has a strong, slightly hot flavor, with a hint of sweetness.

Vanilla Extract

Vanilla extract adds a sweet, fragrant flavor to countless varieties of muffins; it is particularly good for enhancing the flavors of chocolate and fresh fruit. It is produced by combining an extraction from dried vanilla beans with an alcohol and water mixture. It is then aged for several months. The three most common types of vanilla beans used to make vanilla extract are Bourbon-Madagascar, Mexican and Tahitian.

Almond Extract

Almond extract is a flavoring manufactured by combining bitter almond oil with ethyl alcohol. It is used in much the same way as vanilla extract. Almond extract has a highly concentrated, intense flavor, so measure with care.

Citrus Zest

Zest is the name for the colored outer layer of citrus peel. The oils in zest are intense in flavor. Use a zester, a Microplane-style grater or the small holes of a box grater to grate zest. Avoid grating the white layer (pith) just below the zest; it is very bitter.

Instant Espresso Powder

Stronger than regular coffee powder, a small amount of espresso powder can dramatically flavor a wide variety of muffin batters. It is available where coffee is shelved in most supermarkets and at specialty stores.

Equipment

Great muffins require minimal equipment. Here is a short list of what you'll need:

Essential Checklist

- Standard muffin pans: cups typically hold ½ cup (125 mL)
- Mixing bowls
- 1-cup (250 mL) and 2-cup (500 mL) liquid measuring cups (preferably clear glass or plastic)
- Dry measuring cups in graduated sizes: ¼ cup (60 mL), ⅓ cup (75 mL), ½ cup (125 mL) and 1 cup (250 mL)
- Measuring spoons in graduated sizes
- Wire whisk
- Kitchen/chef's knife
- Cutting boards
- Wooden spoons
- Silicone or rubber spatulas
- Electric blender (standard upright or handheld immersion style)
- Kitchen timer
- Box grater/shredder
- Oven mitts or holders
- Zester or Microplane-style grater (for removing zest from citrus fruits)
- Wooden toothpicks (for testing doneness of muffins)

Extras

- Spring-loaded cookie or ice cream scoop, large size (typically 3 tbsp/45 mL)
- Mini muffin pans: cups typically hold ¼ cup (60 mL)
- Jumbo muffin pans: cups typically hold ¾ cup (175 mL)
- Light-colored metal loaf pans:
  Large: 9 by 5 by 3 inches (23 by 12.5 by 7.5 cm), 8-cup (2 L) capacity
  Medium: 8½ by 4½ by 2½ inches (21 by 11 by cm), 6-cup (1.5 L) capacity
  Small: 6 by 3 by 2 inches (15 by 7.5 by 5 cm), 2-cup (500 mL) capacity

Gluten-Free Muffin-Making

To make perfect gluten-free baked goods in general, and outstanding gluten-free muffins in particular, it helps to know a bit of basic food chemistry: freshly milled wheat flour does not actually contain gluten — it contains two proteins, glutenin and gliadin, which turn into gluten when they come in contact with liquid. If gluten is simply eliminated from a baked goods recipe, the results will be disappointing. Gluten is sticky stuff that helps prevent your baked goodies from crumbling. It also traps pockets of air, improving the texture of your muffins.

To replace gluten in my gluten-free recipes, I rely on xanthan gum, a natural product made with the help of *Xanthomonas campestris*. This microorganism is grown in the lab for its cell coat, which is dried and ground to form xanthan gum. Xanthan gum is added as a powder to the dry

Brown Rice Flour Blend

Here's the recipe for the all-purpose blend I use in the majority of the gluten-free recipes in this collection.

Makes 3 cups (750 mL)

2 cups	finely ground brown rice flour	500 mL
⅔ cup	potato starch	150 mL
⅓ cup	tapioca starch	75 mL

1. In a bowl, whisk together brown rice flour, potato starch and tapioca starch. Use as directed in recipes.

Tips

- You can also make the blend in smaller amounts by using the basic proportions: 2 parts finely ground brown rice flour, ⅔ part potato starch and ⅓ part tapioca starch.

- You can double, triple or quadruple the recipe to have it on hand. Store the blend in an airtight container in the refrigerator for up to 4 months, or in the freezer for up to 1 year. Let warm to room temperature before using.

ingredients. You can buy it at well-stocked supermarkets (typically in the health food section, with alternative flours) and at health and natural food stores.

Gluten-Free Flours and Starches

An increasing number of gluten-free flours have arrived on market shelves in the last few years. For clarity, I have divided the list of flours into two categories: primary flours, used in the majority of my GF recipes, and secondary flours, used in a handful of recipes.

Primary Flours
Finely Ground Brown Rice Flour

Brown rice flour is what I use most often in my gluten-free recipes, by way of the Brown Rice Flour Blend recipe (see left). Brown rice flour is milled from unpolished brown rice and has a higher nutrient value than white rice flour. Since it contains bran, it has a short shelf life and should be refrigerated. It is extremely important to choose a brown rice flour with a fine, powdery texture. Rub the flour between your fingers: it should feel powdery, not gritty. If you use a grittier brown rice flour, the results will have a gritty texture; not terrible, but not ideal.

Potato Starch

Potato starch is used in combination with other flours, rarely by itself. Be careful not to buy potato flour (it can be a bit confusing, since potato starch is occasionally labeled "potato starch flour"). Potato flour has a strong potato taste and a heavy texture; it is rarely used in gluten-free baking.

Tapioca Starch

Tapioca starch (also called tapioca flour) is a light, velvety flour milled from the cassava root. It lightens gluten-free baked goods and gives them a texture more like that of wheat flour baked goods.

Secondary Flours
Almond Flour

Almond flour is simply raw blanched whole almonds that have been ground into a fine powder. It has a wonderfully nutty flavor and typically does not require the addition of xanthan gum when used in recipes for baked goods. Store almond flour in a tightly sealed zipper-top plastic bag or airtight container for up to 3 months in the refrigerator or up to 6 months in the freezer. The flavor and aroma of almond flour will become bitter if it is stored improperly or for an excessively long period.

Amaranth Flour

Amaranth is a whole grain that dates back to the Aztecs. It contains more calcium, fiber, magnesium, vitamin A and vitamin C than most grains. Amaranth has a flavor similar to that of graham crackers, without the sweetness. Amaranth seeds are very high in protein, and once ground they make a nutritious flour for baking. Store amaranth flour in a tightly sealed zipper-top plastic bag or airtight container for up to 3 months in the refrigerator or up to 6 months in the freezer.

Buckwheat Flour

Despite its name, buckwheat is related to rhubarb, not wheat. The small seeds of the plant are ground to make a strongly nutty-flavored flour that works well in a wide variety of muffins. Store buckwheat flour in a tightly sealed zipper-top plastic bag or airtight container for up to 6 months in the refrigerator or up to 12 months in the freezer.

Chickpea Flour

Also known as garbanzo bean flour or besan, chickpea flour is ground from chickpeas and has a strong, slightly nutty taste. It is not generally used on its own, but in combination with other gluten-free flours. Store buckwheat flour in a tightly sealed zipper-top plastic bag or airtight container for up to 3 months in the refrigerator or up to 6 months in the freezer.

Quinoa Flour

Quinoa (pronounced *keen-wah*), a relative of spinach and beets, is a complete protein with all eight amino acids and contains a fair amount of calcium and iron. It has been used for over 5,000 years as a cereal, and the Incas called it the "mother seed." The seeds of the quinoa plant are ground to make the flour. Store quinoa flour in a tightly sealed zipper-top plastic bag or airtight container for up to 3 months in the refrigerator or up to 6 months in the freezer.

Sorghum Flour

Sorghum, a tiny, millet-like grain, is one of the oldest known grains and is a major food source in India and Africa. Ground into flour, it adds a superb, slightly sweet flavor to baked goods and is highly nutritious. Store sorghum flour in a tightly sealed zipper-top plastic bag or airtight container for up to 2 months in the refrigerator or up to 4 months in the freezer.

Soy Flour

Soy flour, ground from soy beans, is high in protein and fat and has a nutty flavor. It is best used in small quantities, in combination with other flours. Store soy flour in a tightly sealed zipper-top plastic bag or airtight container for up to 4 months in the refrigerator or up to 8 months in the freezer.

Teff Flour

Teff is an ancient grain from Ethiopia, now grown in North America, Europe and Australia. Teff is always a whole-grain flour, since it is difficult to sift or separate. It gives baked goods a light, springy texture and is high in protein, B vitamins, calcium and iron. Store teff flour in a tightly sealed zipper-top plastic bag or airtight container for up to 3 months in the refrigerator or up to 6 months in the freezer.

The Top 25 Classics

Like a favorite pair of well-worn blue jeans, my picks for the top 25 classic muffins are sensual harbingers of comfort and nostalgia. These renditions have been tweaked to perfection, guaranteeing success and satisfaction time and again. In keeping with the classic mood, I favored straightforward flavors over complicated ones. Rich molasses, tangy buttermilk and sweet bananas are familiar and soothing, while dark chocolate, bright, fresh herbs and nutty browned butter are all the more scrumptious for being a touch unexpected. Any of these muffins would make a perfect start to the day. They might also serve as the main attraction in a lunch bag or as an afternoon snack. No matter which muffin you fancy, you'll discover that it's quite possible to nibble a masterpiece.

Best Basic Muffins

3 cups	all-purpose flour	750 mL
1 tbsp	baking powder	15 mL
1/2 tsp	baking soda	2 mL
1/2 tsp	salt	2 mL
1 cup	granulated sugar	250 mL
2/3 cup	unsalted butter, softened	150 mL
2	eggs	2
2 tsp	vanilla extract	10 mL
1 1/2 cups	buttermilk	375 mL

Many variations on the classic muffin exist, but most are based on a simple combination of flour, sugar, milk and leavening. This is my favorite basic muffin recipe. I've replaced milk with buttermilk for an extra-tender crumb and made them extra-big (the batter will fill the cups to the rims) for a high-rise muffin resembling bakery versions. Vary them in countless ways or keep them plain, served with a dab of jam.

Makes 12 muffins

- Preheat oven to 375°F (190°C)
- 12-cup muffin pan, greased

1. In a medium bowl, whisk together flour, baking powder, baking soda and salt.

2. In a large bowl, using an electric mixer on medium-high speed, beat sugar and butter until light and fluffy. Add eggs, one at a time, beating until fluffy and pale yellow. Beat in vanilla until blended.

3. With the mixer on low speed, beat in flour mixture alternately with buttermilk, making three additions of flour and two of buttermilk, until just blended.

4. Divide batter equally among prepared muffin cups.

5. Bake in preheated oven for 25 to 30 minutes or until tops are golden and a toothpick inserted in the center comes out clean. Let cool in pan on a wire rack for 3 minutes, then transfer to the rack to cool.

Blueberry Muffins

2 cups	all-purpose flour	500 mL
2 1/2 tsp	baking powder	12 mL
1/2 tsp	ground cinnamon	2 mL
1/2 tsp	baking soda	2 mL
1/2 tsp	salt	2 mL
2/3 cup	granulated sugar	150 mL
2	eggs	2
1/2 cup	unsalted butter, melted	125 mL
1 tsp	vanilla extract	5 mL
1 cup	buttermilk	250 mL
1 1/4 cups	blueberries	300 mL

Tip

If using frozen blueberries, opt for wild blueberries. Do not thaw the berries for more than 5 minutes, or they will bleed into the batter.

Makes 12 muffins

- Preheat oven to 400°F (200°C)
- 12-cup muffin pan, greased

1. In a large bowl, whisk together flour, baking powder, cinnamon, baking soda and salt.

2. In a medium bowl, whisk together sugar, eggs, butter and vanilla until well blended. Whisk in buttermilk until blended.

3. Add the egg mixture to the flour mixture and stir just until blended. Gently fold in blueberries.

4. Divide batter equally among prepared muffin cups.

5. Bake in preheated oven for 16 to 21 minutes or until tops are golden brown and a toothpick inserted in the center comes out clean. Let cool in pan on a wire rack for 3 minutes, then transfer to the rack to cool.

Chocolate Chip Muffins

1½ cups	all-purpose flour	375 mL
½ cup	whole wheat flour	125 mL
2 tsp	baking powder	10 mL
½ tsp	baking soda	2 mL
½ tsp	salt	2 mL
1 cup	granulated sugar	250 mL
2	eggs	2
¼ cup	unsalted butter, softened	60 mL
¼ cup	vegetable oil	60 mL
1½ tsp	vanilla extract	7 mL
⅔ cup	buttermilk	150 mL
2 cups	semisweet chocolate chips	500 mL

Get the kids to help with these delectable muffins. They make a delicious change of pace from chocolate chip cookies.

Makes 12 muffins

- Preheat oven to 350°F (180°C)
- 12-cup muffin pan, lined with paper liners

1. In a large bowl, whisk together all-purpose flour, whole wheat flour, baking powder, baking soda and salt.

2. In a medium bowl, whisk together sugar, eggs, butter, oil and vanilla until well blended. Whisk in buttermilk until blended.

3. Add the egg mixture to the flour mixture and stir until just blended. Gently fold in chocolate chips.

4. Divide batter equally among prepared muffin cups.

5. Bake in preheated oven for 22 to 27 minutes or until tops are golden and a toothpick inserted in the center comes out clean. Let cool in pan on a wire rack for 5 minutes, then transfer to the rack to cool.

Berry Jam Muffins

2¼ cups	all-purpose flour	550 mL
1 tbsp	baking powder	15 mL
½ tsp	baking soda	2 mL
½ tsp	salt	2 mL
¾ cup	granulated sugar	175 mL
2	eggs	2
⅓ cup	unsalted butter, melted	75 mL
1⅓ cups	buttermilk	325 mL
½ tsp	almond extract	2 mL
½ cup	seedless berry jam or preserves	125 mL

These old-fashioned muffins offer a surprise when you bite into them: a burst of fruit jam! Use any variety of jam, jelly, preserves or marmalade you like in place of the berry jam.

Makes 12 muffins

- Preheat oven to 400°F (200°C)
- 12-cup muffin pan, greased

1. In a large bowl, whisk together flour, baking powder, baking soda and salt.

2. In a medium bowl, whisk together sugar, eggs and butter until well blended. Whisk in buttermilk and almond extract until blended.

3. Add the egg mixture to the flour mixture and stir until just blended.

4. Divide half the batter equally among prepared muffin cups. Drop 2 tsp (10 mL) of the jam into the center of each cup of batter. Top with the remaining batter.

5. Bake in preheated oven for 21 to 26 minutes or until tops are golden. Let cool in pan on a wire rack for 5 minutes, then transfer to the rack to cool.

Pumpkin Spice Muffins

2³⁄₄ cups	all-purpose flour	675 mL
2 tsp	ground ginger	10 mL
1¹⁄₂ tsp	ground cinnamon	7 mL
1¹⁄₂ tsp	baking soda	7 mL
1 tsp	salt	5 mL
¹⁄₂ tsp	ground allspice	2 mL
¹⁄₄ tsp	ground cloves	1 mL
1 cup	granulated sugar	250 mL
3	eggs	3
¹⁄₂ cup	vegetable oil	125 mL
1³⁄₄ cups	pumpkin purée (not pie filling)	425 mL
¹⁄₂ cup	liquid honey	125 mL
¹⁄₂ cup	buttermilk	125 mL

Moist and tender, with just the right balance of spices, these favorite muffins are even better the day after you bake them.

Makes 18 muffins

- Preheat oven to 350°F (180°C)
- Two 12-cup muffin pans, 18 cups greased

1. In a large bowl, whisk together flour, ginger, cinnamon, baking soda, salt, allspice and cloves.

2. In a medium bowl, whisk together sugar, eggs and oil until well blended. Whisk in pumpkin, honey and buttermilk until blended.

3. Add the egg mixture to the flour mixture and stir until just blended.

4. Divide batter equally among prepared muffin cups.

5. Bake in preheated oven for 25 to 30 minutes or until a toothpick inserted in the center comes out clean. Let cool in pans on a wire rack for 3 minutes, then transfer to the rack to cool.

Cinnamon Sugar Muffins

3 cups	all-purpose flour	750 mL
1¹⁄₂ cups	packed light brown sugar	375 mL
1 tbsp	ground cinnamon, divided	15 mL
³⁄₄ tsp	salt	3 mL
²⁄₃ cup	unsalted butter, softened	150 mL
¹⁄₂ cup	chopped pecans	125 mL
2 tsp	baking powder	10 mL
¹⁄₂ tsp	baking soda	2 mL
2	eggs	2
1 cup	buttermilk	250 mL

These homey muffins are staples at my house (my little boy loves them; so does my husband). A liberal dose of brown sugar — in the muffin batter as well as the topping — makes them extra-special.

Makes 12 muffins

- Preheat oven to 375°F (190°C)
- 12-cup muffin pan, lined with paper liners

1. In a large bowl, whisk together flour, brown sugar, 2 tsp (10 mL) of the cinnamon and the salt. Using your fingers, mix in butter until mixture is crumbly. Transfer ²⁄₃ cup (150 mL) to a small bowl for the topping and mix in pecans and the remaining cinnamon; set aside.

2. Whisk baking powder and baking soda into the remaining flour mixture.

3. In a small bowl, whisk together eggs and buttermilk until well blended.

4. Add the egg mixture to the flour mixture and stir until just blended.

5. Divide batter equally among prepared muffin cups. Top with the reserved cinnamon-pecan mixture.

6. Bake in preheated oven for 16 to 21 minutes or until tops are golden and a toothpick inserted in the center comes out clean. Let cool in pan on a wire rack for 3 minutes, then transfer to the rack to cool.

Best Bran Muffins

1 cup	all-purpose flour	250 mL
3/4 cup	whole wheat flour	175 mL
2 tsp	baking soda	10 mL
3/4 tsp	salt	3 mL
2 1/4 cups	bran cereal, such as All-Bran, divided	550 mL
1/2 cup	raisins, dried cranberries or dried cherries	50 mL
1/2 cup	packed light brown sugar	125 mL
2	eggs	2
1/3 cup	unsalted butter, melted	75 mL
1/4 cup	dark (cooking) molasses	60 mL
2 tsp	vanilla extract	10 mL
1 3/4 cups	buttermilk	425 mL
3 tbsp	turbinado sugar	45 mL

I developed these muffins especially for my mother, Charlotte, who asked me for what she described as a "real bran muffin": dense with whole grains, not too sweet, easy to prepare and, of course, delicious. Mission accomplished!

Makes 18 muffins

- Preheat oven to 375°F (190°C)
- Food processor
- Two 12-cup muffin pans, 18 cups greased

1. In a large bowl, whisk together all-purpose flour, whole wheat flour, baking soda and salt.

2. In a food processor, finely grind half the bran cereal. Add raisins and process until finely chopped. Add to the flour mixture and stir in the remaining cereal.

3. In a medium bowl, whisk together brown sugar, eggs, butter, molasses and vanilla until well blended. Whisk in buttermilk until blended.

4. Add the egg mixture to the flour mixture and stir until just blended.

5. Divide batter equally among prepared muffin cups. Generously sprinkle muffin tops with turbinado sugar.

6. Bake in preheated oven for 21 to 26 minutes or until tops are golden brown and a toothpick inserted in the center comes out clean. Let cool in pans on a wire rack for 3 minutes, then transfer to the rack to cool.

Whole Wheat Morning Muffins

2 cups	whole wheat flour	500 mL
1 tsp	baking soda	5 mL
1 cup	packed light brown sugar	250 mL
1	egg	1
1/3 cup	unsalted butter, melted	75 mL
1/2 tsp	vanilla extract	2 mL
1 1/4 cups	buttermilk	300 mL
1 cup	chopped pecans, toasted	250 mL

Wary of whole grains? Never again, once you try these muffins. Buttermilk keeps them tender and light, and brown sugar, vanilla and toasted pecans provide the great flavor that will keep you coming back for more.

Makes 12 muffins

- Preheat oven to 425°F (220°C)
- 12-cup muffin pan, lined with paper liners

1. In a large bowl, whisk together flour and baking soda.

2. In a medium bowl, whisk together brown sugar, egg, butter and vanilla until well blended. Whisk in buttermilk until blended.

3. Add the egg mixture to the flour mixture and stir until just blended. Gently fold in pecans.

4. Divide batter equally among prepared muffin cups.

5. Bake in preheated oven for 15 to 20 minutes or until tops are golden and a toothpick inserted in the center comes out clean. Let cool in pan on a wire rack for 3 minutes, then transfer to the rack to cool.

Banana Walnut Muffins

³/₄ cup	granulated sugar, divided	175 mL
1¹/₂ tsp	ground cinnamon, divided	7 mL
1¹/₃ cups	all-purpose flour	325 mL
2 tsp	baking powder	10 mL
¹/₂ tsp	salt	2 mL
¹/₂ tsp	ground nutmeg	2 mL
1	egg	1
1 cup	mashed ripe bananas	250 mL
1 cup	plain yogurt	250 mL
¹/₄ cup	unsalted butter, melted	60 mL
¹/₂ cup	golden raisins	125 mL
¹/₂ cup	chopped walnuts	125 mL

Banana muffins are one of the very best ways to use up old bananas; in fact, the browner and mushier they are, the better, for they grow sweeter and easier to mash than their firm, young counterparts. The bananas add moisture to the batter, making these muffins moist and tender.

Makes 12 muffins

- Preheat oven to 375°F (190°C)
- 12-cup muffin pan, lined with paper liners

1. In a small bowl, combine ¹/₄ cup (60 mL) of the sugar and 1 tsp (5 mL) of the cinnamon.

2. In a large bowl, whisk together flour, baking powder, salt, nutmeg and the remaining cinnamon.

3. In a medium bowl, whisk together the remaining sugar, egg, bananas, yogurt and butter until well blended.

4. Add the egg mixture to the flour mixture and stir until just blended. Gently fold in raisins.

5. Divide batter equally among prepared muffin cups. Sprinkle with cinnamon sugar and walnuts.

6. Bake in preheated oven for 23 to 25 minutes or until tops are golden and a toothpick inserted in the center comes out clean. Let cool in pan on a wire rack for 3 minutes, then transfer on the rack to cool.

Favorite Oat Bran Muffins

2 cups	oat bran	500 mL
1 cup	all-purpose flour	250 mL
4 tsp	baking powder	20 mL
1 tsp	ground cinnamon	5 mL
³/₄ tsp	salt	3 mL
¹/₂ cup	packed light brown sugar	125 mL
2	eggs	2
¹/₃ cup	vegetable oil	75 mL
1¹/₄ cups	milk	300 mL
¹/₂ cup	raisins	125 mL

Oat bran is the outer layer of the oat grain. It is normally discarded during the milling process, which is unfortunate, since it contains the bulk of the dietary fiber of the grain, along with a large amount of useful minerals. These muffins have a light texture that both children and adults love.

Makes 15 muffins

- Preheat oven to 425°F (220°C)
- Two 12-cup muffin pans, 15 cups greased

1. In a large bowl, whisk together oat bran, flour, baking powder, cinnamon and salt.

2. In a medium bowl, whisk together brown sugar, eggs and oil until well blended. Whisk in milk until blended.

3. Add the egg mixture to the flour mixture and stir until just blended. Gently fold in raisins.

4. Divide batter equally among prepared muffin cups.

5. Bake in preheated oven for 15 to 19 minutes or until tops are golden and a toothpick inserted in the center comes out clean. Let cool in pans on a wire rack for 5 minutes, then transfer to the rack to cool.

Morning Glory Muffins

1½ cups	all-purpose flour	375 mL
¾ cup	whole wheat flour	175 mL
2 tsp	baking soda	10 mL
1 tsp	ground cinnamon	5 mL
½ tsp	salt	2 mL
1¼ cups	granulated sugar	300 mL
3	eggs	3
½ cup	unsalted butter, melted	125 mL
1 tsp	vanilla extract	5 mL
2 cups	shredded carrots	500 mL
1	can (8 oz/227 mL) crushed pineapple, drained (see tip, below)	1
⅔ cup	sweetened flaked or shredded coconut	150 mL
½ cup	raisins	125 mL
½ cup	chopped walnuts or pecans, toasted	125 mL

Almost every collection of muffins contains at least one recipe for morning glory muffins. With good reason, too, for they are loaded with healthy, delicious ingredients, including pineapple, whole grains, nuts, seeds and raisins.

Tips

These muffins taste best when the carrots are shredded using the large holes of a box grater. That way, the carrots maintain their texture while baking, making these hearty breakfast muffins instead of fine cake.

For the ideal texture, thoroughly drain and pat dry the pineapple with paper towels; otherwise, the muffins will be somewhat gummy.

Makes 12 muffins

- Preheat oven to 375°F (190°C)
- 12-cup muffin pan, greased

1. In a large bowl, whisk together all-purpose flour, whole wheat flour, baking soda, cinnamon and salt.

2. In a medium bowl, whisk together sugar, eggs, butter and vanilla until well blended.

3. Add the egg mixture to the flour mixture and stir until just blended. Gently fold in carrots, pineapple, coconut, raisins and walnuts.

4. Divide batter equally among prepared muffin cups.

5. Bake in preheated oven for 25 to 30 minutes or until tops are golden and a toothpick inserted in the center comes out with just a few crumbs attached. Let cool in pan on a wire rack for 5 minutes, then transfer to the rack to cool.

Sour Cream Coffee Cake Muffins

Topping

1 cup	packed dark brown sugar	250 mL
1 cup	all-purpose flour	250 mL
1 tsp	ground cinnamon	5 mL
1/4 tsp	salt	1 mL
1/2 cup	chilled unsalted butter, cut into small pieces	125 mL

Muffins

1 3/4 cups	all-purpose flour	425 mL
2 tsp	baking powder	10 mL
1 tsp	baking soda	5 mL
1/2 tsp	salt	2 mL
1 cup	granulated sugar	250 mL
1 cup	sour cream	250 mL
1/2 cup	unsalted butter, softened	125 mL
1 tsp	vanilla extract	5 mL
2	eggs	2
2 tbsp	confectioners' (icing) sugar	25 mL

Moist and flavorful, these gorgeous, peaked muffins taste just like full-size, labor-intensive streusel coffee cake, but with minimal effort. Good luck limiting yourself to one!

Makes 12 muffins

- Preheat oven to 350°F (180°C)
- 12-cup muffin pan, greased

1. *Topping:* In a medium bowl, combine brown sugar, flour, cinnamon and salt. Using your fingers or a pastry cutter, rub or cut in butter until mixture resembles coarse crumbs. Refrigerate until ready to use.

2. *Muffins:* In a medium bowl, whisk together flour, baking powder, baking soda and salt.

3. In a large bowl, using an electric mixer on medium speed, beat sugar, sour cream, butter and vanilla until light and fluffy. Beat in eggs, one at a time, until well blended.

4. With the mixer on low speed, beat the flour mixture into the egg mixture until just blended.

5. Divide half the batter equally among prepared muffin cups. Top with half the streusel mixture, then remaining batter and remaining streusel.

6. Bake in preheated oven for 25 to 30 minutes or until a toothpick inserted in the center comes out clean. Let cool in pan on a wire rack for 5 minutes, then transfer to the rack to cool. Dust with confectioners' sugar.

Applesauce Muffins

2 cups	all-purpose flour	500 mL
2 tsp	ground cinnamon	10 mL
1 tsp	baking soda	5 mL
3/4 tsp	salt	3 mL
1/2 tsp	ground nutmeg	2 mL
1/8 tsp	ground cloves	0.5 mL
1 cup	granulated sugar	250 mL
1/2 cup	packed light brown sugar	125 mL
4	eggs	4
1/2 cup	unsalted butter, melted	125 mL
1 1/2 cups	unsweetened applesauce	375 mL
1 cup	chopped pecans, toasted	250 mL

Whether you use store-bought applesauce or make your own, these lovely, moist muffins will be a hit at any occasion.

Makes 18 muffins

- Preheat oven to 350°F (180°C)
- Two 12-cup muffin pans, 18 cups lined with paper liners

1. In a large bowl, whisk together flour, cinnamon, baking soda, salt, nutmeg and cloves.

2. In a medium bowl, whisk together granulated sugar, brown sugar, eggs and butter until well blended. Whisk in applesauce until blended.

3. Add the egg mixture to the flour mixture and stir until just blended. Gently fold in pecans.

4. Divide batter equally among prepared muffin cups.

5. Bake in preheated oven for 18 to 21 minutes or until tops are golden and a toothpick inserted in the center comes out clean. Let cool in pans on a wire rack for 3 minutes, then transfer to the rack to cool.

Gingerbread Muffins

Muffins

2³/₄ cups	all-purpose flour	675 mL
2¹/₂ tsp	baking soda	12 mL
4 tsp	ground ginger	20 mL
1¹/₂ tsp	ground cinnamon	7 mL
¹/₂ tsp	salt	2 mL
¹/₄ tsp	ground cloves	1 mL
¹/₄ tsp	ground nutmeg	1 mL
²/₃ cup	packed dark brown sugar	150 mL
2	eggs	2
³/₄ cup	dark (cooking) molasses	175 mL
¹/₂ cup	unsalted butter, melted	125 mL
1¹/₃ cups	buttermilk	325 mL

Icing

2 cups	confectioners' (icing) sugar	500 mL
¹/₄ cup	freshly squeezed lemon juice	60 mL

Molasses adds richness to these classic muffins. They have a wonderful combination of down-home style and subtle sophistication, and the easy lemon icing offers a fresh counterpoint to the deep, fragrant blend of spices.

Makes 16 muffins

- Preheat oven to 350°F (180°C)
- Two 12-cup muffin pans, 16 cups greased

1. *Muffins:* In a large bowl, whisk together flour, baking soda, ginger, cinnamon, salt, cloves and nutmeg.
2. In a medium bowl, whisk together brown sugar, eggs, molasses and butter until well blended. Whisk in buttermilk until blended.
3. Add the egg mixture to the flour mixture and stir until just blended.
4. Divide batter equally among prepared muffin cups.
5. Bake in preheated oven for 23 to 26 minutes or until a toothpick inserted in the center comes out clean. Let cool in pans on a wire rack for 5 minutes, then transfer to the rack to cool slightly.
6. *Icing:* In a small bowl, whisk together confectioners' sugar and lemon juice until smooth. Spoon over tops of warm muffins and let cool.

Cranberry Orange Nut Muffins

2 cups	all-purpose flour	500 mL
1$\frac{1}{2}$ tsp	baking powder	7 mL
1 tsp	ground nutmeg	5 mL
1 tsp	ground cinnamon	5 mL
$\frac{1}{2}$ tsp	baking soda	2 mL
$\frac{1}{2}$ tsp	ground ginger	2 mL
$\frac{1}{2}$ tsp	salt	2 mL
1 cup	granulated sugar	250 mL
2	eggs	2
2 tsp	finely grated orange zest	10 mL
$\frac{3}{4}$ cup	freshly squeezed orange juice	175 mL
$\frac{1}{2}$ cup	vegetable oil	125 mL
1 tbsp	vanilla extract	15 mL
1$\frac{1}{2}$ cups	coarsely chopped cranberries	375 mL
1$\frac{1}{2}$ cups	chopped pecans, toasted	375 mL

The bracing tartness of fresh cranberries is perfectly balanced here by a generous handful of toasted pecans and enticing hints of orange, vanilla and spices.

Makes 18 muffins

- Preheat oven to 375°F (190°C)
- Two 12-cup muffin pans, 18 cups lined with paper liners

1. In a large bowl, whisk together flour, baking powder, nutmeg, cinnamon, baking soda, ginger and salt.
2. In a medium bowl, whisk together sugar, eggs, orange zest, orange juice, oil and vanilla until well blended.
3. Add the egg mixture to the flour mixture and stir until just blended. Gently fold in cranberries and pecans.
4. Divide batter equally among prepared muffin cups.
5. Bake in preheated oven for 18 to 21 minutes or until tops are golden and a toothpick inserted in the center comes out clean. Let cool in pans on a wire rack for 5 minutes, then transfer to the rack to cool.

Lemon Poppy Seed Muffins

3 cups	all-purpose flour	750 mL
$\frac{1}{4}$ cup	poppy seeds	50 mL
1 tbsp	baking powder	15 mL
$\frac{1}{2}$ tsp	baking soda	2 mL
$\frac{1}{2}$ tsp	salt	2 mL
1$\frac{1}{4}$ cups	granulated sugar, divided	300 mL
2	eggs	2
1$\frac{2}{3}$ cups	plain whole-milk yogurt	400 mL
$\frac{1}{2}$ cup	unsalted butter, melted	125 mL
1 tbsp	finely grated lemon zest	15 mL
$\frac{1}{4}$ cup	freshly squeezed lemon juice	60 mL

The poppy seeds add more than polka-dot appeal in these fresh, bright lemon muffins: they also contribute crunch and delicate notes of sweetness and nuttiness.

Makes 12 muffins

- Preheat oven to 375°F (190°C)
- 12-cup muffin pan, greased

1. In a large bowl, whisk together flour, poppy seeds, baking powder, baking soda and salt.
2. In a medium bowl, whisk together 1 cup (250 mL) of the sugar, eggs, yogurt, butter and lemon zest until well blended.
3. Add the egg mixture to the flour mixture and stir until just blended.
4. Divide batter equally among prepared muffin cups.
5. Bake in preheated oven for 25 to 30 minutes or until tops are golden and a toothpick inserted in the center comes out clean. Let cool in pan on a wire rack for 3 minutes, then transfer to the rack to cool slightly.
6. In a small saucepan, heat the remaining sugar and lemon juice over medium heat, stirring, until sugar is dissolved. Brush over warm muffins.

Browned Butter Raspberry Muffins

1/2 cup	unsalted butter	125 mL
2 cups	all-purpose flour	500 mL
2 1/2 tsp	baking powder	12 mL
1/2 tsp	baking soda	2 mL
1/2 tsp	salt	2 mL
1/2 cup	granulated sugar	125 mL
1	egg	1
1 tsp	vanilla extract	5 mL
1 cup	buttermilk	250 mL
1 1/4 cups	raspberries	300 mL

Brown butter — *beurre noisette* — is made by cooking butter long enough to turn the milk solids brown while evaporating much of the water. It has a more complex flavor than melted or clarified butter and adds a deep, nutty flavor to these muffins. Combined with fresh raspberries, it makes a stellar muffin.

Tip

Be sure to transfer the browned butter to a bowl to cool as soon as it is removed from the heat. If left in the hot skillet, the butter will continue to cook and the milk solids may burn.

Makes 12 muffins

- Preheat oven to 375°F (190°C)
- 12-cup muffin pan, lined with paper liners

1. In a large skillet, heat butter over medium heat until foam subsides and butter is deep golden brown. Immediately transfer to a medium bowl and let cool to room temperature.

2. In a large bowl, whisk together flour, baking powder, baking soda and salt.

3. Add sugar, egg and vanilla to browned butter and whisk until well blended. Whisk in buttermilk until blended.

4. Add the egg mixture to the flour mixture and stir until just blended. Gently fold in raspberries.

5. Divide batter equally among prepared muffin cups.

6. Bake in preheated oven for 18 to 22 minutes or until tops are golden and a toothpick inserted in the center comes out clean. Let cool in pan on a wire rack for 5 minutes, then transfer to the rack to cool.

Homestyle Apple Muffins

Topping

1/4 cup	packed light brown sugar	60 mL
1/4 cup	finely chopped pecans	60 mL
1/4 tsp	ground cinnamon	1 mL

Muffins

2 cups	all-purpose flour	500 mL
2 tsp	baking powder	10 mL
2 tsp	ground cinnamon	10 mL
1/2 tsp	ground nutmeg	2 mL
1/2 tsp	baking soda	2 mL
1/2 tsp	salt	2 mL
2/3 cup	granulated sugar	150 mL
2	eggs	2
3/4 cup	buttermilk	175 mL
1/2 cup	vegetable oil	125 mL
1 tsp	vanilla extract	5 mL
2 cups	coarsely chopped peeled apples	500 mL
1 cup	chopped pecans, toasted	250 mL

These not-too-sweet muffins are best when made with fairly sweet apples, such as Fuji or Braeburn.

Makes 12 large muffins

- Preheat oven to 350°F (180°C)
- 12-cup muffin pan, greased

1. *Topping:* In a small bowl, combine brown sugar, pecans and cinnamon; set aside.

2. *Muffins:* In a large bowl, whisk together flour, baking powder, cinnamon, nutmeg, baking soda and salt.

3. In a medium bowl, whisk together sugar, eggs, buttermilk, oil and vanilla until well blended.

4. Add the egg mixture to the flour mixture and stir until just blended. Gently fold in apples and pecans.

5. Divide batter equally among prepared muffin cups. Sprinkle with topping.

6. Bake in preheated oven for 22 to 27 minutes or until a toothpick inserted in the center comes out clean. Let cool in pans on a wire rack for 5 minutes, then transfer to the rack to cool.

Chocolate Muffins

2²⁄₃ cups	all-purpose flour	650 mL
¹⁄₂ cup	unsweetened cocoa powder (not Dutch process)	125 mL
1¹⁄₂ tsp	baking soda	7 mL
¹⁄₂ tsp	salt	2 mL
1¹⁄₂ cups	granulated sugar	375 mL
3	eggs	3
¹⁄₂ cup	unsalted butter, melted	125 mL
2 tsp	vanilla extract	10 mL
1 cup	sour cream	250 mL
1 cup	milk	250 mL
1 cup	semisweet chocolate chips	250 mL

These wickedly rich muffins are the quintessential morning treat for passionate chocoholics. For the best result and the deepest chocolate flavor, choose a good-quality natural cocoa powder.

Makes 18 muffins

- Preheat oven to 325°F (160°C)
- Two 12-cup muffin pans, 18 cups lined with paper liners

1. In a large bowl, whisk together flour, cocoa powder, baking soda and salt.

2. In a medium bowl, whisk together sugar, eggs, butter and vanilla until well blended. Whisk in sour cream and milk until blended.

3. Add the egg mixture to the flour mixture and stir until just blended. Gently fold in chocolate chips.

4. Divide batter equally among prepared muffin cups.

5. Bake in preheated oven for 20 to 25 minutes or until a toothpick inserted in the center comes out clean. Let cool in pans on a wire rack for 5 minutes, then transfer to the rack to cool.

Mocha Muffins

3 cups	all-purpose flour	750 mL
1 tbsp	baking powder	15 mL
¹⁄₂ tsp	baking soda	2 mL
¹⁄₂ tsp	salt	2 mL
¹⁄₂ tsp	ground cinnamon	2 mL
1 cup	packed light brown sugar	250 mL
2	eggs	2
²⁄₃ cup	unsalted butter, melted	150 mL
3 tbsp	instant espresso powder	45 mL
2 tsp	vanilla extract	10 mL
1¹⁄₂ cups	buttermilk	375 mL
1 cup	miniature semisweet chocolate chips	250 mL

Espresso, dark chocolate chips and a tender crumb add up to one terrific muffin. Enjoy one for breakfast, with the morning paper, or on an afternoon coffee break.

Makes 12 muffins

- Preheat oven to 375°F (190°C)
- 12-cup muffin pan, greased

1. In a large bowl, whisk together flour, baking powder, baking soda, salt and cinnamon.

2. In a medium bowl, whisk together brown sugar, eggs, butter, espresso powder and vanilla until well blended. Whisk in buttermilk until blended.

3. Add the egg mixture to the flour mixture and stir until just blended. Gently fold in chocolate chips.

4. Divide batter equally among prepared muffin cups.

5. Bake in preheated oven for 25 to 30 minutes or until tops are golden and a toothpick inserted in the center comes out clean. Let cool in pan on a wire rack for 5 minutes, then transfer to the rack to cool.

Zucchini Raisin Muffins

1⅓ cups	all-purpose flour	325 mL
⅔ cup	wheat germ	150 mL
2 tsp	baking powder	10 mL
1 tsp	ground cinnamon	5 mL
¾ tsp	salt	3 mL
¼ tsp	ground cloves	1 mL
⅔ cup	granulated sugar	150 mL
2	eggs	2
½ cup	unsalted butter, melted	125 mL
⅓ cup	milk	75 mL
1 tsp	vanilla extract	5 mL
2 cups	shredded zucchini	500 mL
½ cup	raisins	125 mL
½ cup	chopped pecans, toasted	125 mL

These tender, lightly spiced muffins are reminiscent of carrot cake. Grated zucchini keeps them exceptionally moist.

Makes 12 muffins

- Preheat oven to 375°F (190°C)
- 12-cup muffin pan, greased

1. In a large bowl, whisk together flour, wheat germ, baking powder, cinnamon, salt and cloves.
2. In a medium bowl, whisk together sugar, eggs, butter, milk and vanilla until well blended.
3. Add the egg mixture to the flour mixture and stir until just blended. Gently fold in zucchini, raisins and pecans.
4. Divide batter equally among prepared muffin cups.
5. Bake in preheated oven for 25 to 30 minutes or until a toothpick inserted in the center comes out clean. Let cool in pan on a wire rack for 5 minutes, then transfer to the rack to cool.

Bacon Buttermilk Muffins

6	slices thick-cut bacon	6
¼ cup	vegetable oil (approx.)	60 mL
2 cups	all-purpose flour	500 mL
2 tsp	baking powder	10 mL
½ tsp	salt	2 mL
½ tsp	baking soda	2 mL
¼ tsp	freshly cracked black pepper	1 mL
2 tbsp	packed light brown sugar	30 mL
2	eggs	2
1 cup	buttermilk	250 mL
1	medium tart-sweet apple, peeled and shredded	1

Here, I pepped up my fail-safe savory buttermilk muffin recipe with a combination of bacon, buttermilk and a handful of coarsely grated tart-sweet apple. They'll be jumping out of bed for this one.

Makes 12 muffins

- Preheat oven to 400°F (200°C)
- 12-cup muffin pan, greased

1. In a large skillet, fry bacon over medium-high heat until crisp. Transfer to paper towels to drain. Let cool, then crumble; set aside.
2. Pour the bacon fat into a heat-resistant glass measuring cup. Add enough of the vegetable oil to measure ⅓ cup (75 mL) total; set aside.
3. In a large bowl, whisk together flour, baking powder, salt, baking soda and pepper.
4. In a medium bowl, whisk together brown sugar, oil mixture and eggs until well blended. Whisk in buttermilk until blended. Stir in apple.
5. Add the egg mixture to the flour mixture and stir until just blended. Gently fold in crumbled bacon.
6. Divide batter equally among prepared muffin cups.
7. Bake in preheated oven for 18 to 23 minutes or until a toothpick inserted in the center comes out clean. Let cool in pan on a wire rack for 5 minutes, then transfer to the rack to cool.

Stone-Ground Cornmeal Muffins

2¼ cups	all-purpose flour	550 mL
1¼ cups	stone-ground yellow cornmeal	300 mL
1 tbsp	baking powder	15 mL
1¼ tsp	salt	6 mL
1 tsp	baking soda	5 mL
3 tbsp	granulated sugar	45 mL
3	eggs	3
½ cup	unsalted butter, melted	125 mL
⅓ cup	vegetable oil	75 mL
1⅓ cups	buttermilk	325 mL

Many Southerners object to the practice of adding sugar to cornbread, but my husband, who hails from Arkansas, is all for it in these muffins. Although they are terrific with any variety of yellow cornmeal, they have the best texture and flavor when made with stone-ground cornmeal.

Makes 12 muffins

- Preheat oven to 400°F (200°C)
- 12-cup muffin pan, greased

1. In a large bowl, whisk together flour, cornmeal, baking powder, salt and baking soda.

2. In a medium bowl, whisk together sugar, eggs, butter and oil until well blended. Whisk in buttermilk until blended.

3. Add the egg mixture to the flour mixture and stir until just blended.

4. Divide batter equally among prepared muffin cups.

5. Bake in preheated oven for 20 to 25 minutes or until tops are golden brown and a toothpick inserted in the center comes out clean. Let cool in pan on a wire rack for 3 minutes, then transfer to the rack to cool.

Fresh Herb Muffins

2 cups	all-purpose flour	500 mL
1 tbsp	baking powder	15 mL
½ tsp	salt	2 mL
¼ tsp	freshly ground black pepper	1 mL
¾ cup	freshly grated Parmesan cheese	175 mL
¼ cup	chopped assorted fresh herbs (such as chives, chervil, tarragon and dill)	60 mL
1	egg	1
¼ cup	olive oil	60 mL
1 cup	milk	250 mL

Anyone who believes muffins are mere breakfast fare must have one of these fresh herb muffins immediately. Perfect for dinner or tucked into lunch boxes, they are a wonderful way to make homemade, savory bread with little time and effort — and no yeast.

Makes 12 muffins

- Preheat oven to 375°F (190°C)
- 12-cup muffin pan, greased

1. In a large bowl, whisk together flour, baking powder, salt and pepper. Whisk in cheese and herbs.

2. In a medium bowl, whisk together egg and oil until well blended. Whisk in milk until blended.

3. Add the egg mixture to the flour mixture and stir until just blended.

4. Divide batter equally among prepared muffin cups.

5. Bake in preheated oven for 18 to 22 minutes or until tops are golden and a toothpick inserted in the center comes out clean. Let cool in pan on a wire rack for 3 minutes, then transfer to the rack to cool.

Ultimate Cheese Muffins

²/₃ cup	coarsely grated Parmesan cheese	150 mL
3 cups	all-purpose flour	750 mL
1 tbsp	baking powder	15 mL
1 tsp	salt	5 mL
¼ tsp	freshly ground black pepper	1 mL
4 oz	extra-sharp (extra-old) Cheddar cheese, cut into ¼-inch (0.5 cm) cubes	125 g
1	egg	1
½ cup	unsalted butter, melted	125 mL
2 tsp	Dijon mustard	10 mL
1 cup	whole milk	250 mL
²/₃ cup	sour cream	150 mL

Extra-sharp (extra-old) Cheddar and Parmesan cheeses star in these flavorful, easy-to-make muffins.

Tip

Use the large holes of a grater to coarsely grate the Parmesan cheese.

Makes 12 muffins
- Preheat oven to 375°F (190°C)
- 12-cup muffin pan, greased

1. Divide the Parmesan cheese between the prepared muffin cups. Tap and shake pan so that cheese evenly coats sides and bottom of each cup.
2. In a large bowl, whisk together flour, baking powder, salt and pepper. Stir in Cheddar cheese.
3. In a medium bowl, whisk together egg, butter and mustard until well blended. Whisk in milk and sour cream until blended.
4. Add the egg mixture to the flour mixture and stir until just blended.
5. Divide batter equally among prepared muffin cups.
6. Bake in preheated oven for 20 to 25 minutes or until tops are golden brown and a toothpick inserted in the center comes out clean. Let cool in pan on a wire rack for 3 minutes, then transfer to the rack to cool.

Breakfast Muffins

• •

Breakfast too often gets short shrift. Had on the run, in the car or on the train or bus, it's rarely savored as it should be, particularly on weekdays. The delicious recipes in this chapter are quick, easy and healthy options to help you start the day — every day — right. They are anything but boring fare, ranging from sweet to savory and from classic to newfangled. Think Fig and Hazelnut Muffins, Good Morning Graham Muffins and Maple Bacon Muffins. Multigrain muffins may not be unique, but when teamed with dark chocolate and toasted pecans, they are guaranteed to please. None of these muffins is complicated to prepare. The batter for Big-Batch Refrigerator and Freezer Bran Muffins, for example, can be made in advance and refrigerated or frozen until you're ready to bake. It's all here, and it's all fantastic!

continued...

Double Apple Oat Bran Muffins

1½ cups	oat bran	375 mL
1 cup	all-purpose flour	250 mL
2 tsp	baking powder	10 mL
¾ tsp	salt	3 mL
½ tsp	ground cinnamon	2 mL
½ cup	packed light brown sugar	125 mL
2	eggs	2
¼ cup	unsalted butter, melted	60 mL
⅔ cup	milk	150 mL
¼ cup	unsweetened applesauce	60 mL
1 tbsp	dark (cooking) molasses	15 mL
1 tsp	vanilla extract	5 mL
1 cup	coarsely chopped tart apple, such as Granny Smith	250 mL
2 tsp	turbinado sugar	10 mL

Apples add moistness and natural sweetness to these delicious, healthful muffins. A light sprinkling of turbinado sugar over the top adds a beautiful and tasty touch.

Makes 12 muffins

- Preheat oven to 400°F (200°C)
- 12-cup muffin pan, greased

1. In a large bowl, whisk together oat bran, flour, baking powder, salt and cinnamon.
2. In a medium bowl, whisk together brown sugar, eggs, butter, milk, applesauce, molasses and vanilla until well blended.
3. Add the egg mixture to the flour mixture and stir until just blended. Gently fold in apple.
4. Divide batter equally among prepared muffin cups. Sprinkle with turbinado sugar.
5. Bake in preheated oven for 16 to 21 minutes or until tops are light golden brown and a toothpick inserted in the center comes out clean. Let cool in pan on a wire rack for 5 minutes, then transfer to the rack to cool.

Whole Wheat Applesauce Muffins

1 cup	all-purpose flour	250 mL
1 cup	whole wheat flour	250 mL
3 tbsp	ground flax seeds	45 mL
1 tsp	ground cinnamon	5 mL
¾ tsp	ground allspice	3 mL
½ tsp	baking soda	2 mL
½ tsp	salt	2 mL
1 cup	packed light brown sugar	250 mL
1	egg	1
½ cup	vegetable oil	125 mL
1½ tsp	vanilla extract	7 mL
1 cup	unsweetened applesauce	250 mL
2 tbsp	turbinado sugar	30 mL

Cinnamon, allspice and turbinado sugar make this a home-style muffin you'll adore.

Makes 12 muffins

- Preheat oven to 350°F (180°C)
- 12-cup muffin pan, lined with paper liners

1. In a large bowl, whisk together all-purpose flour, whole wheat flour, flax seeds, cinnamon, allspice, baking soda and salt.
2. In a medium bowl, whisk together brown sugar, egg, oil and vanilla until well blended. Stir in applesauce until blended.
3. Add the egg mixture to the flour mixture and stir until just blended.
4. Divide batter equally among prepared muffin cups. Sprinkle with turbinado sugar
5. Bake in preheated oven for 20 to 25 minutes or until tops are golden and a toothpick inserted in the center comes out clean. Let cool in pan on a wire rack for 3 minutes, then transfer to the rack to cool.

Allspice Apple Butter Muffins

2 tbsp	granulated sugar	30 mL
1¼ tsp	ground allspice, divided	6 mL
1½ cups	all-purpose flour	375 mL
1½ tsp	baking powder	7 mL
¾ tsp	salt	3 mL
½ tsp	baking soda	2 mL
¾ cup	packed brown sugar	175 mL
2	eggs	2
1 cup	apple butter	250 mL
¾ cup	unsalted butter, melted	175 mL
1 tsp	vanilla extract	5 mL

These moist, subtly spiced muffins keep beautifully for several days after you make them. Look for apple butter where jams, jellies and preserves are shelved in the supermarket.

Makes 12 muffins

- Preheat oven to 400°F (200°C)
- 12-cup muffin pan, greased

1. In a small bowl, combine granulated sugar and ¼ tsp (1 mL) of the allspice. Set aside.
2. In a large bowl, whisk together flour, baking powder, salt, baking soda and the remaining allspice.
3. In a medium bowl, whisk together brown sugar, eggs, apple butter, butter and vanilla until well blended.
4. Add the egg mixture to the flour mixture and stir until just blended.
5. Divide batter equally among prepared muffin cups. Sprinkle with sugar mixture.
6. Bake in preheated oven for 18 to 22 minutes or until tops are golden and a toothpick inserted in the center comes out clean. Let cool in pan on a wire rack for 3 minutes, then transfer to the rack to cool.

Old-Fashioned Cider Muffins

4 cups	all-purpose flour	1 L
1½ tbsp	baking powder	22 mL
2½ tsp	ground cinnamon, divided	12 mL
1½ tsp	salt	7 mL
1 cup	unsalted butter, softened	250 mL
1½ cups	granulated sugar, divided	375 mL
3	eggs	3
2 cups	unsweetened apple cider or apple juice	500 mL
2 cups	chopped peeled tart-sweet apples, such as Gala, Braeburn or Golden Delicious	500 mL

Gala, Braeburn or Golden Delicious are my apples of choice for these old-time classics.

Makes 18 muffins

- Preheat oven to 375°F (190°C)
- Two 12-cup muffin pans, 18 cups lined with paper liners

1. In a medium bowl, whisk together flour, baking powder, 1½ tsp (7 mL) of the cinnamon and the salt.
2. In a large bowl, using an electric mixer on medium-high speed, beat butter and 1¼ cups (300 mL) of the sugar until light and fluffy. Beat in eggs, one at a time, until well blended.
3. With the mixer on low speed, beat in flour mixture alternately with apple cider, making three additions of flour and two of cider, until just blended. Gently fold in apples.
4. Divide batter equally among prepared muffin cups.
5. In a small bowl, combine the remaining sugar and cinnamon. Sprinkle over muffins.
6. Bake in preheated oven for 32 to 36 minutes or until tops are golden and a toothpick inserted in the center comes out clean. Let cool in pans on a wire rack for 5 minutes, then transfer to the rack to cool.

Pennsylvania Dutch Apple Cheese Muffins

Glaze

1/3 cup	granulated sugar	75 mL
2 tbsp	water	30 mL
2 tbsp	unsalted butter	30 mL
1 tbsp	freshly squeezed lemon juice	15 mL
1/2 tsp	ground cinnamon	2 mL

Muffins

2 cups	all-purpose flour	500 mL
1/2 cup	granulated sugar	125 mL
1 tbsp	baking powder	15 mL
1 tsp	salt	5 mL
1/2 cup	cold unsalted butter, cut into 1/2-inch (1 cm) pieces	125 mL
8 oz	sharp (old) Cheddar cheese, cut into 1/2-inch (1 cm) pieces	250 g
1	egg	1
3/4 cup	whole milk	175 mL
2 cups	chopped peeled crisp-sweet apples, such as Gala, Golden Delicious or Fuji	500 mL

How can you resist? A citrus-cinnamon glaze tops a sharp Cheddar-apple batter; for any occasion, it's an unbeatable combination. The easy glaze — brushed on the muffins mid-bake — deepens the apple flavor and keeps the muffins moist.

Makes 12 muffins

- Preheat oven to 375°F (190°C)
- Large food processor
- 12-cup muffin pan, greased

1. *Glaze:* In a small saucepan, combine sugar, water, butter, lemon juice and cinnamon. Bring to a boil over medium heat. Reduce heat and boil gently, stirring, for 1 to 2 minutes or until sugar is dissolved. Set aside.

2. *Muffins:* In food processor fitted with metal blade, combine flour, sugar, baking powder, salt, butter and cheese. Pulse until mixture resembles coarse meal. Transfer to a large bowl.

3. In a small bowl, whisk together egg and milk until well blended.

4. Add the egg mixture to the flour mixture and stir until just blended. Gently fold in apples.

5. Divide batter equally among prepared muffin cups.

6. Bake in preheated oven for 14 to 17 minutes or until tops are just turning golden. Brush the partially baked muffins with glaze.

7. Return muffins to oven and bake for 9 to 12 minutes or until muffins are golden and a toothpick inserted in the center comes out clean. Let cool in pan on a wire rack for 5 minutes, then transfer to the rack to cool.

Apricot Muffins

Topping

3 tbsp	packed light brown sugar	45 mL
1/3 cup	chopped almonds	75 mL
1/2 tsp	ground cardamom	2 mL
1 tbsp	unsalted butter, melted	15 mL

Muffins

1 1/3 cups	quick-cooking rolled oats	325 mL
1 1/4 cups	all-purpose flour	300 mL
1 tbsp	baking powder	15 mL
1 tsp	ground cardamom	5 mL
1/2 tsp	salt	2 mL
1/2 cup	granulated sugar	125 mL
1	egg	1
1/3 cup	unsalted butter, melted	75 mL
1/2 tsp	almond extract	2 mL
1 cup	half-and-half (10%) cream	250 mL
3/4 cup	finely chopped dried apricots	175 mL

Oats lend a hearty texture to these apricot treats, so they maintain the characteristics of a muffin, rather than an oversized cupcake — perfect to pack in a lunchbox.

Makes 12 muffins

- Preheat oven to 400°F (200°C)
- 12-cup muffin pan, lined with paper liners

1. *Topping:* In a small bowl, combine brown sugar, almonds, cardamom and butter until blended. Refrigerate until ready to use.

2. *Muffins:* In a large bowl, whisk together oats, flour, baking powder, cardamom and salt.

3. In a medium bowl, whisk together sugar, egg, butter and almond extract until well blended. Whisk in cream until blended.

4. Add the egg mixture to the flour mixture and stir until just blended. Gently fold in apricots.

5. Divide batter equally among prepared muffin cups. Sprinkle with topping.

6. Bake in preheated oven for 17 to 21 minutes or until tops are golden and a toothpick inserted in the center comes out clean. Let cool in pan on a wire rack for 3 minutes, then transfer to the rack to cool.

Aloha Muffins with Coconut Topping

Topping

1/4 cup	sweetened flaked or shredded coconut	60 mL
1/4 cup	finely chopped macadamia nuts	60 mL
2 tbsp	granulated sugar	30 mL
2 tbsp	large-flake (old-fashioned) rolled oats	30 mL

Muffins

1 1/3 cups	all-purpose flour	325 mL
1 cup	large-flake (old-fashioned) rolled oats	250 mL
1 tsp	baking powder	5 mL
1/2 tsp	baking soda	2 mL
1/2 tsp	salt	2 mL
1/2 cup	packed light brown sugar	125 mL
1	egg	1
1 cup	mashed ripe bananas	250 mL
1 cup	buttermilk	250 mL
2 tbsp	vegetable oil	30 mL
1 tsp	vanilla extract	5 mL
1/2 cup	drained canned crushed pineapple, patted dry	125 mL
1/2 cup	sweetened flaked or shredded coconut	125 mL
1/3 cup	finely chopped macadamia nuts, toasted	75 mL

Here is a wonderful mid-winter muffin, just the thing when you're longing for brighter flavors and dreaming of a warm-weather escape. The bright and acidic pineapple cuts the sweetness of the coconut and boosts the tropical flair with readily available, inexpensive convenience. Be sure to drain and pat dry the pineapple to keep the muffins from becoming gummy.

Makes 12 muffins

- Preheat oven to 400°F (200°C)
- 12-cup muffin pan, greased

1. *Topping:* In a small bowl, combine coconut, nuts, sugar and oats. Set aside.

2. *Muffins:* In a large bowl, whisk together flour, oats, baking powder, baking soda and salt.

3. In a medium bowl, whisk together brown sugar, egg, bananas, buttermilk, oil and vanilla until well blended. Stir in pineapple until blended.

4. Add the egg mixture to the flour mixture and stir until just blended. Gently fold in coconut and nuts.

5. Divide batter equally among prepared muffin cups. Sprinkle with topping.

6. Bake in preheated oven for 17 to 22 minutes or until a toothpick inserted in the center comes out clean. Let cool in pan on a wire rack for 3 minutes, then transfer to the rack to cool.

Banana Flax Muffins

2 cups	bran cereal, such as All-Bran	500 mL
1/4 cup	ground flax seeds	60 mL
1 cup	buttermilk	250 mL
1 cup	granulated sugar	250 mL
1 1/4 cups	mashed ripe bananas	300 mL
1	egg	1
1/4 cup	vegetable oil	60 mL
1 1/2 cups	all-purpose flour	375 mL
1 tsp	baking powder	5 mL
1/2 tsp	baking soda	2 mL
1/2 tsp	ground cinnamon	2 mL
1/2 tsp	salt	2 mL
1/4 tsp	ground nutmeg	1 mL

By the end of the school or work week, most bananas are past their prime — but they're perfect for these moist flax and bran muffins. Add a handful of dried fruit or chocolate chips to make these healthy treats even more enticing.

Makes 12 muffins

- Food processor
- 12-cup muffin pan, greased

1. In food processor, process cereal, flax seeds and buttermilk until blended. Let stand for 15 to 20 minutes or until cereal is soft.
2. Preheat oven to 350°F (180°C).
3. Add sugar and bananas to the cereal mixture and process until smooth. Add egg and oil; process until smooth.
4. In a large bowl, whisk together flour, baking powder, baking soda, cinnamon, salt and nutmeg.
5. Add the egg mixture to the flour mixture and stir until just blended.
6. Divide batter equally among prepared muffin cups.
7. Bake for 20 to 25 minutes or until tops are golden and a toothpick inserted in the center comes out clean. Let cool in pan on a wire rack for 3 minutes, then transfer to the rack to cool.

Wheat Germ Banana Muffins

1 1/2 cups	all-purpose flour	375 mL
3/4 cup	wheat germ	175 mL
1 tbsp	baking powder	15 mL
3/4 tsp	salt	3 mL
1/2 tsp	ground nutmeg	2 mL
3/4 cup	granulated sugar	175 mL
2	eggs	2
1 1/2 cups	mashed ripe bananas	375 mL
1/2 cup	milk	250 mL
1/3 cup	vegetable oil	75 mL
1 tsp	vanilla extract	5 mL

Banana muffins are a perfect use for bananas that are past their prime. This particular version is a tried and true favorite, made countless times in my tiny kitchen throughout graduate school.

Makes 16 muffins

- Preheat oven to 350°F (180°C)
- Two 12-cup muffin pans, 16 cups lined with paper liners

1. In a large bowl, whisk together flour, wheat germ, baking powder, salt and nutmeg.
2. In a medium bowl, whisk together sugar, eggs, bananas, milk, oil and vanilla until well blended.
3. Add the egg mixture to the flour mixture and stir until just blended.
4. Divide batter equally among prepared muffin cups.
5. Bake for 22 to 25 minutes or until tops are golden brown and a toothpick inserted in the center comes out clean. Let cool in pans on a wire rack for 3 minutes, then transfer to the rack to cool.

Peanut Butter Banana Muffins

1¾ cups	all-purpose flour	425 mL
¼ cup	wheat germ	60 mL
1 tsp	baking soda	5 mL
½ tsp	salt	2 mL
¼ cup	packed dark brown sugar	60 mL
2	eggs	2
1 cup	mashed ripe bananas	250 mL
½ cup	liquid honey	125 mL
½ cup	chunky peanut butter	125 mL
⅓ cup	vegetable oil	75 mL
1 tsp	vanilla extract	5 mL

Elvis loved the combination of peanut butter and banana, and you will too once you try these not-too-sweet muffins.

Makes 12 muffins
- Preheat oven to 400°F (200°C)
- 12-cup muffin pan, lined with paper liners

1. In a medium bowl, whisk together flour, wheat germ, baking soda and salt.
2. In a large bowl, using an electric mixer on medium speed, beat brown sugar, eggs, bananas, honey, peanut butter, oil and vanilla until well blended.
3. Add the flour mixture to the peanut butter mixture and, using a wooden spoon, stir until just blended.
4. Divide batter equally among prepared muffin cups.
5. Bake in preheated oven for 18 to 22 minutes or until tops are golden and a toothpick inserted in the center comes out clean. Let cool in pan on a wire rack for 3 minutes, then transfer to the rack to cool.

Michigan Cherry Muffins

1 cup	all-purpose flour	250 mL
¾ cup	oat bran	175 mL
1 tbsp	baking powder	15 mL
½ tsp	salt	2 mL
⅔ cup	granulated sugar	150 mL
1	egg	1
⅓ cup	unsalted butter, melted	75 mL
2 tsp	grated orange zest	10 mL
1 tsp	almond extract	5 mL
1¼ cups	buttermilk	300 mL
¾ cup	dried sour (tart) cherries, chopped	175 mL
½ cup	sliced almonds, toasted	125 mL

My husband and I have spent several summers camping along the shores of Lake Michigan. One of our favorite stops is Traverse City, Michigan, home of the National Cherry Festival. We always return with several pounds of dried sour (tart) cherries. These simple muffins are a favorite use for our bounty.

Makes 12 muffins
- Preheat oven to 400°F (200°C)
- 12-cup muffin pan, greased

1. In a large bowl, whisk together flour, oat bran, baking powder and salt.
2. In a medium bowl, whisk together sugar, egg, butter, orange zest and almond extract until well blended. Whisk in buttermilk until blended.
3. Add the egg mixture to the flour mixture until just blended. Gently fold in dried cherries and almonds.
4. Divide batter equally among prepared muffin cups.
5. Bake in preheated oven for 20 to 25 minutes or until tops are golden and a toothpick inserted in the center comes out clean. Let cool in pan on a wire rack for 3 minutes, then transfer to the rack to cool.

Maple Cranberry Spelt Muffins

2¼ cups	spelt flour	550 mL
1 tbsp	baking powder	15 mL
½ tsp	salt	2 mL
½ tsp	ground cinnamon	2 mL
3	eggs	3
¼ cup	pure maple syrup	60 mL
1 tbsp	vegetable oil	15 mL
1 tsp	vanilla extract	5 mL
1¼ cups	milk	300 mL
½ cup	dried cranberries	125 mL

It's unlikely you've heard this said before, but I love spelt. Spelt is a cereal grain with a mild, nutty flavor and relatively high protein content; the flour makes incredible baked goods, especially quick breads like these muffins. Use this recipe as a template: vary the dried fruit, add toasted nuts or seeds, or replace the honey with an equal amount of molasses or agave nectar; you can't go wrong.

Tip

Look for spelt flour in most natural foods stores and in well-stocked grocery stores.

Makes 12 muffins

- Preheat oven to 425°F (220°C)
- 12-cup muffin pan, greased

1. In a large bowl, whisk together spelt flour, baking powder, salt and cinnamon
2. In a medium bowl, whisk together eggs, maple syrup, oil and vanilla until well blended. Whisk in milk until blended.
3. Add the egg mixture to the flour mixture and stir until just blended. Gently fold in cranberries.
4. Divide batter equally among prepared muffin cups.
5. Bake in preheated oven for 15 to 18 minutes or until tops are golden and a toothpick inserted in the center comes out clean. Let cool in pan on a wire rack for 3 minutes, then transfer to the rack to cool.

Cranberry Banana Muffins

2 cups	fresh cranberries	500 mL
1 2/3 cups	granulated sugar, divided	400 mL
1 cup	water	250 mL
1 3/4 cups	all-purpose flour	425 mL
2 tsp	baking powder	10 mL
1/2 tsp	salt	2 mL
1/4 tsp	baking soda	1 mL
2	eggs	2
1 cup	mashed ripe bananas	250 mL
1/3 cup	vegetable oil	75 mL
1 tsp	vanilla extract	5 mL

The perennial bakery favorite gets even better with the sweet addition of bananas. These are large muffins (expect the batter to come up to the brims), but you can also make 14 medium-size muffins by using two pans.

Makes 12 muffins

- 12-cup muffin pan, lined with paper liners

1. In a saucepan, combine cranberries, 1 cup (250 mL) of the sugar and the water. Bring to a boil over medium heat; reduce heat and simmer, stirring occasionally, for 5 to 7 minutes or until berries begin to pop. Drain off liquid and let berries cool.
2. Preheat oven to 400°F (200°C).
3. In a large bowl, whisk together flour, baking powder, salt and baking soda.
4. In a medium bowl, whisk together the remaining sugar, eggs, bananas, oil and vanilla until well blended.
5. Add the egg mixture to the flour mixture and stir until just blended. Gently fold in the cooled cranberry mixture.
6. Divide batter equally among prepared muffin cups.
7. Bake for 16 to 21 minutes or until tops are golden and a toothpick inserted in the center comes out clean. Let cool in pan on a wire rack for 5 minutes, then transfer to the rack to cool.

Cranberry Muffins

2 cups	all-purpose flour	500 mL
2 tsp	baking powder	10 mL
1/2 tsp	salt	2 mL
2/3 cup	granulated sugar	150 mL
1	egg	1
2/3 cup	milk	150 mL
1/4 cup	unsalted butter, melted	60 mL
2 tsp	finely grated lemon zest	10 mL
1 tsp	vanilla extract	5 mL
1 cup	coarsely chopped fresh cranberries	250 mL

Cranberries are a classic autumn and mid-winter fruit and are delicious in these moist, lemon-scented muffins.

Makes 12 muffins

- Preheat oven to 400°F (200°C)
- 12-cup muffin pan, greased

1. In a large bowl, whisk together flour, baking powder and salt.
2. In a medium bowl, whisk together sugar, egg, milk, butter, lemon zest and vanilla until well blended.
3. Add the egg mixture to the flour mixture and stir until just blended. Gently fold in cranberries.
4. Divide batter equally among prepared muffin cups.
5. Bake in preheated oven for 17 to 22 minutes or until a toothpick inserted in the center comes out clean. Let cool in pan on a wire rack for 5 minutes, then transfer to the rack to cool.

Strawberry Vanilla Muffins

³/₄ cup	granulated sugar, divided	175 mL
1¹/₂ cups	all-purpose flour	375 mL
1 tsp	baking powder	5 mL
¹/₂ tsp	salt	2 mL
¹/₄ tsp	baking soda	1 mL
1¹/₄ cups	halved strawberries	300 mL
2	eggs	2
3 tbsp	unsalted butter, melted	45 mL
2 tsp	vanilla extract	10 mL

Team the muffins with sausages, and offer tea, coffee and fresh juices for the perfect weekend brunch.

Makes 12 muffins

- Preheat oven to 400°F (200°C)
- 12-cup muffin pan, greased

1. Set 1 tbsp (15 mL) of the sugar aside for topping. In a large bowl, whisk together the remaining sugar, flour, baking powder, salt and baking soda.
2. In a blender or food processor, process strawberries, eggs, butter and vanilla until just blended (it shouldn't be a smooth purée).
3. Add the egg mixture to the flour mixture and stir until just blended.
4. Divide batter equally among prepared muffin cups. Sprinkle with the reserved sugar.
5. Bake in preheated oven for 19 to 24 minutes or until a toothpick inserted in the center comes out clean. Let cool in pan on a wire rack for 5 minutes, then transfer to the rack to cool for 5 minutes. Serve warm.

Strawberry Lime Muffins

2¹/₄ cups	all-purpose flour	550 mL
2 tsp	baking powder	10 mL
1 tsp	ground cinnamon	5 mL
¹/₂ tsp	baking soda	2 mL
¹/₂ tsp	salt	2 mL
¹/₂ cup	granulated sugar	125 mL
¹/₄ cup	packed light brown sugar	60 mL
2	eggs	2
¹/₂ cup	unsalted butter, melted	125 mL
1 tbsp	finely grated lime zest	15 mL
1 cup	buttermilk	250 mL
1¹/₂ cups	thinly sliced strawberries	375 mL

Strawberries and limes are fast friends, as the popularity of strawberry margaritas attests. The combination is exceptionally good in these muffins. And because this recipe is so easy to make, it will become one of your summer breakfast standbys.

Makes 12 muffins

- Preheat oven to 375°F (190°C)
- 12-cup muffin pan, greased

1. In a large bowl, whisk together flour, baking powder, cinnamon, baking soda and salt.
2. In a medium bowl, whisk together granulated sugar, brown sugar, eggs, butter and lime zest until well blended. Whisk in buttermilk.
3. Add the egg mixture to the flour mixture and stir until just blended. Gently fold in strawberries.
4. Divide batter equally among prepared muffin cups.
5. Bake in preheated oven for 23 to 26 minutes or until tops are golden and a toothpick inserted in the center comes out clean. Let cool in pan on a wire rack for 3 minutes, then transfer to the rack to cool.

Raspberry Jam Cinnamon Muffins

1½ cups	all-purpose flour	375 mL
2½ tsp	baking powder	12 mL
1¼ tsp	ground cinnamon, divided	6 mL
½ tsp	salt	2 mL
½ cup	granulated sugar	125 mL
1	egg	1
⅔ cup	buttermilk	150 mL
¼ cup	unsalted butter, melted	60 mL
½ cup	seedless raspberry preserves	125 mL
1 tbsp	granulated sugar	15 mL

These cinnamon-spiced muffins with hidden raspberry centers are always a hit.

Makes 12 muffins

- Preheat oven to 400°F (200°C)
- 12-cup muffin pan, greased

1. In a large bowl, whisk together flour, baking powder, 1 tsp (5 mL) of the cinnamon and the salt.
2. In a medium bowl, whisk together the ½ cup (125 mL) sugar, egg, buttermilk and butter until well blended.
3. Add the egg mixture to the flour mixture and stir until just blended.
4. Divide half the batter equally among prepared muffin cups. Spoon 2 tsp (10 mL) preserves in the center of each cup of batter. Top with the remaining batter.
5. In a small bowl, combine the 1 tbsp (15 mL) sugar and the remaining cinnamon. Sprinkle over muffins.
6. Bake in preheated oven for 17 to 22 minutes or until a toothpick inserted in the center comes out clean. Let cool in pan on a wire rack for 3 minutes, then transfer to the rack to cool.

Double Raspberry Muffins

2½ cups	all-purpose flour	625 mL
2½ tsp	baking powder	12 mL
1 tsp	salt	5 mL
1 cup	granulated sugar	250 mL
2	eggs	2
1 cup	buttermilk	250 mL
¼ cup	unsalted butter, melted	60 mL
¼ cup	vegetable oil	60 mL
1½ tsp	vanilla extract	7 mL
1 cup	raspberries	250 mL
¼ cup	seedless raspberry jam	60 mL

For raspberry-lovers everywhere, these quick muffins are a sublime morning indulgence. Those who love all varieties of berries can use any seasonal berry — and matching jam or preserves — they like.

Makes 12 muffins

- Preheat oven to 375°F (190°C)
- 12-cup muffin pan, greased

1. In a large bowl, whisk together flour, baking powder and salt.
2. In a medium bowl, whisk together sugar and eggs until well blended. Whisk in buttermilk, butter, oil and vanilla until well blended.
3. Add the egg mixture to the flour mixture and stir until just blended. Gently fold in raspberries.
4. Divide batter equally among prepared muffin cups. Spoon 1 tsp (5 mL) raspberry jam in the center of each mound of batter. Using the tip of a knife, swirl the jam into batter.
5. Bake in preheated oven for 17 to 21 minutes or until tops are golden and a toothpick inserted in the center comes out clean. Let cool in pan on a wire rack for 5 minutes, then transfer to the rack to cool.

Raspberry Oat Muffins

2 cups	all-purpose flour	500 mL
1 cup	large-flake (old-fashioned) rolled oats	250 mL
1 cup	packed light brown sugar	250 mL
2 tsp	baking powder	10 mL
1/2 tsp	baking soda	2 mL
1/2 tsp	salt	2 mL
1/2 tsp	ground allspice	2 mL
1	egg	1
1 cup	milk	250 mL
1/4 cup	unsalted butter, melted	60 mL
1 tsp	vanilla extract	5 mL
1 1/2 cups	raspberries	375 mL
1/4 cup	granulated sugar	60 mL

These tempting, raspberry-filled muffins are a nice (and healthy) way to get started in the morning.

Makes 15 muffins

- Preheat oven to 400°F (200°C)
- Two 12-cup muffin pans, 15 cups greased

1. In a large bowl, whisk together flour, oats, brown sugar, baking powder, baking soda, salt and allspice.
2. In a medium bowl, whisk together egg, milk, butter and vanilla until well blended.
3. Add the egg mixture to the flour mixture and stir until just blended. Gently fold in raspberries.
4. Divide batter equally among prepared muffin cups. Sprinkle with granulated sugar.
5. Bake in preheated oven for 16 to 21 minutes or until tops are light golden brown and a toothpick inserted in the center comes out clean. Let cool in pans on a wire rack for 5 minutes, then transfer to the rack to cool.

Sour Cream Berry Muffins

2 cups	all-purpose flour	500 mL
1 cup	granulated sugar	250 mL
1 tsp	baking powder	5 mL
1/2 tsp	baking soda	2 mL
1/2 tsp	salt	2 mL
2	eggs	2
1 cup	sour cream	250 mL
1/2 cup	vegetable oil	125 mL
1 tsp	vanilla extract	5 mL
1 1/2 cups	raspberries, blueberries or blackberries	375 mL

Sour cream and plump, fresh berries are a sublime combination in these pretty little muffins. Their tender texture is offset by the slight tang of sour cream in the batter.

Makes 12 muffins

- Preheat oven to 400°F (200°C)
- 12-cup muffin pan, lined with paper liners

1. In a large bowl, whisk together flour, sugar, baking powder, baking soda and salt.
2. In a medium bowl, whisk together eggs, sour cream, oil and vanilla until well blended.
3. Add the egg mixture to the flour mixture and stir until just blended. Gently fold in berries.
4. Divide batter equally among prepared muffin cups.
5. Bake in preheated oven for 20 to 25 minutes or until a toothpick inserted in the center comes out clean. Let cool in pan on a wire rack for 3 minutes, then transfer to the rack to cool.

Lemon Blackberry Muffins

2 cups	all-purpose flour	500 mL
2 tsp	baking powder	10 mL
1/2 tsp	salt	2 mL
1/4 tsp	baking soda	1 mL
3/4 cup	packed light brown sugar	175 mL
2	eggs	2
3/4 cup	buttermilk	175 mL
1/4 cup	unsalted butter, melted	60 mL
1 tsp	grated lemon zest	5 mL
3 tbsp	freshly squeezed lemon juice, divided	45 mL
1 tsp	vanilla extract	5 mL
1 cup	fresh or frozen (unthawed) blackberries	250 mL
2 tbsp	granulated sugar	30 mL

Sweet and juicy blackberries are fantastic with this tangy lemon-buttermilk batter that crisps along the edges while staying cakey and tender within.

Tip

If you use frozen blackberries, keep them in the freezer right up until the last minute to prevent them from thawing and subsequently bleeding into the batter.

Makes 12 muffins

- Preheat oven to 375°F (190°C)
- 12-cup muffin pan, greased

1. In a large bowl, whisk together flour, baking powder, salt and baking soda.

2. In a medium bowl, whisk together brown sugar and eggs until blended. Whisk in buttermilk, butter, lemon zest, 1 tbsp (15 mL) of the lemon juice and vanilla until well blended.

3. Add the egg mixture to the flour mixture and stir until just blended. Gently fold in blackberries.

4. Divide batter equally among prepared muffin cups.

5. Bake in preheated oven for 25 to 28 minutes or until tops are golden and a toothpick inserted in the center comes out clean. Let cool in pan on a wire rack for 5 minutes, then transfer to the rack to cool while you prepare the glaze.

6. In a small saucepan, heat the remaining lemon juice and the granulated sugar over low heat, stirring occasionally, until sugar is dissolved. Brush warm muffin tops with lemon syrup. Let cool for at least 5 minutes before serving or let cool completely.

Whole Wheat Blueberry Muffins

Topping

1/4 cup	packed light brown sugar	60 mL
1/2 tsp	ground cinnamon	2 mL

Muffins

1 cup	all-purpose flour	250 mL
1 cup	whole wheat flour	250 mL
1 tbsp	baking powder	15 mL
1/2 tsp	salt	2 tsp
1	egg	1
3/4 cup	lower-fat milk	175 mL
1/4 cup	vegetable oil	60 mL
1/4 cup	liquid honey	60 mL
1 tsp	vanilla extract	5 mL
1 cup	frozen (unthawed) blueberries	250 mL

Makes 12 muffins

- Preheat oven to 400°F (200°C)
- 12-cup muffin pan, lined with paper liners

1. *Topping:* In a small bowl, combine brown sugar and cinnamon until blended. Set aside.
2. *Muffins:* In a large bowl, whisk together all-purpose flour, whole wheat flour, baking powder and salt.
3. In a medium bowl, whisk together egg, milk, oil, honey and vanilla until well blended.
4. Add the egg mixture to the flour mixture and stir until just blended. Gently fold in blueberries.
5. Divide batter equally among prepared muffin cups. Sprinkle with topping.
6. Bake in preheated oven for 18 to 22 minutes or until tops are golden and a toothpick inserted in the center comes out clean. Let cool in pan on a wire rack for 5 minutes, then transfer to the rack to cool.

Double Pear Muffins

Topping

1/2 cup	chopped pecans	125 mL
2 tbsp	packed brown sugar	30 mL
1/2 tsp	ground nutmeg	2 mL

Muffins

2 cups	all-purpose flour	500 mL
1 tsp	baking soda	5 mL
1/2 tsp	salt	2 mL
3/4 cup	packed brown sugar	175 mL
2	eggs	2
1/3 cup	unsalted butter, melted	75 mL
2	jars (each 4 oz or 128 mL) pear baby food	2
1 tsp	vanilla extract	5 mL
3/4 cup	buttermilk	175 mL
1 cup	diced pears	250 mL

Pears and pecans combine in these buttery muffins. There's no need to peel the pears; the peel adds fiber and becomes very tender once baked.

Makes 12 muffins

- Preheat oven to 400°F (200°C)
- 12-cup muffin pan, greased

1. *Topping:* In a small bowl, combine pecans, brown sugar and nutmeg. Set aside.
2. *Muffins:* In a medium bowl, whisk together flour, baking soda and salt.
3. In a large bowl, whisk together brown sugar, eggs and butter until well blended. Whisk in pear baby food and vanilla until blended.
4. Stir the flour mixture into the egg mixture alternately with the buttermilk, making two additions of flour and one of buttermilk, until just blended. Gently fold in diced pears.
5. Divide batter equally among prepared muffin cups. Sprinkle with topping.
6. Bake in preheated oven for 19 to 23 minutes or until tops are golden and a toothpick inserted in the center comes out clean. Let cool in pan on a wire rack for 5 minutes, then transfer to the rack to cool.

Pear Berry Muffins

Topping

2 tbsp	granulated sugar	30 mL
1/4 tsp	ground nutmeg	1 mL
1/2 cup	sliced almonds	125 mL

Muffins

1 1/4 cups	all-purpose flour	300 mL
1 1/4 cups	large-flake (old-fashioned) rolled oats	300 mL
2 tsp	baking powder	10 mL
1 tsp	ground cinnamon	5 mL
1/2 tsp	baking soda	2 mL
1/2 tsp	salt	2 mL
3/4 cup	packed light brown sugar	175 mL
2	eggs	2
2/3 cup	milk	150 mL
1/4 cup	vegetable oil	60 mL
2/3 cup	dried cranberries	150 mL
1	firm ripe pear, finely chopped	1

Your morning rush will be much improved with one of these sweet pear and berry muffins to awaken your senses. Or to prove that they're not just for breakfast, pack one in your lunch bag for a late-afternoon coffee break.

Tip

There's no need to peel the pear here; it becomes very soft with baking and adds fiber.

Makes 12 muffins

- Preheat oven to 375°F (190°C)
- 12-cup muffin pan, lined with paper liners

1. *Topping:* In a small bowl, combine sugar and nutmeg. Stir in almonds and set aside.

2. *Muffins:* In a large bowl, whisk together flour, oats, baking powder, cinnamon, baking soda and salt.

3. In a medium bowl, whisk together brown sugar, eggs, milk and oil until well blended.

4. Add the egg mixture to the flour mixture and stir until just blended. Gently fold in cranberries and pear.

5. Divide batter equally among prepared muffin cups. Sprinkle with topping.

6. Bake in preheated oven for 21 to 24 minutes or until a toothpick inserted in the center comes out clean. Let cool in pan on a wire rack for 5 minutes, then transfer to the rack to cool.

Grapefruit Ginger Muffins

Muffins

2 cups	all-purpose flour	500 mL
2½ tsp	baking powder	12 mL
1½ tsp	ground ginger	7 mL
½ tsp	salt	2 mL
1 cup	granulated sugar	250 mL
3	eggs	3
1 cup	plain yogurt	250 mL
½ cup	unsalted butter, melted	125 mL
1 tbsp	finely grated grapefruit zest	15 mL
2 tbsp	freshly squeezed grapefruit juice	30 mL

Glaze

1 cup	sifted confectioners' (icing) sugar	250 mL
1 tsp	finely grated grapefruit zest	5 mL
2 tbsp	freshly squeezed grapefruit juice	30 mL

Grapefruit and ginger is a heaven-made match.

Makes 12 muffins

- Preheat oven to 350°F (180°C)
- 12-cup muffin pan, greased

1. *Muffins:* In a large bowl, whisk together flour, baking powder, ginger and salt.
2. In a medium bowl, whisk together sugar, eggs, yogurt, butter, grapefruit zest and grapefruit juice until well blended.
3. Add the egg mixture to the flour mixture and stir until just blended.
4. Divide batter equally among prepared muffin cups.
5. Bake in preheated oven for 22 to 27 minutes or until tops are light golden brown and a toothpick inserted in the center comes out clean. Let cool in pan on a wire rack for 5 minutes, then transfer to the rack to cool while you prepare the glaze.
6. *Glaze:* In a small bowl, combine confectioners' sugar, grapefruit zest and grapefruit juice until blended. Spoon over tops of warm muffins and let cool.

Orange Juice Muffins

2 cups	all-purpose flour	500 mL
2 tsp	baking powder	10 mL
¾ tsp	salt	3 mL
½ cup	granulated sugar	125 mL
1	egg	1
1 tbsp	finely grated orange zest	15 mL
1 cup	unsweetened orange juice	250 mL
¼ cup	vegetable oil	60 mL
½ cup	finely chopped dried apricots	125 mL
1 tbsp	granulated sugar	15 mL

Moist, light and perfumed with fresh orange juice and zest, these are incomparably refreshing muffins. Dried apricots deepen and enhance the orange flavor.

Makes 12 muffins

- Preheat oven to 400°F (200°C)
- 12-cup muffin pan, greased

1. In a large bowl, whisk together flour, baking powder and salt.
2. In a medium bowl, whisk together the ½ cup (125 mL) sugar, egg, orange zest, orange juice and oil until well blended.
3. Add the egg mixture to the flour mixture and stir until just blended. Gently fold in apricots.
4. Divide batter equally among prepared muffin cups. Sprinkle with the 1 tbsp (15 mL) sugar.
5. Bake in preheated oven for 18 to 22 minutes or until tops are light golden brown and a toothpick inserted in the center comes out clean. Let cool in pan on a wire rack for 5 minutes, then transfer to the rack to cool.

Orange Prune Muffins

Muffins

1 cup	all-purpose flour	250 mL
1 cup	whole wheat flour	250 mL
1 tbsp	baking powder	15 mL
1/2 tsp	baking soda	2 mL
1/2 tsp	salt	2 mL
1/2 cup	granulated sugar	125 mL
1	egg	1
1 cup	plain yogurt	250 mL
1/4 cup	vegetable oil	60 mL
1 tbsp	finely grated orange zest	15 mL
1 tsp	vanilla extract	5 mL
1 1/2 cups	pitted prunes, chopped	375 mL

Icing

3/4 cup	confectioners' (icing) sugar	175 mL
1/2 tsp	finely grated orange zest	2 mL
1 tbsp	freshly squeezed orange juice	15 mL

Because these muffins are packed with such healthful and delicious ingredients, just one really satisfies, all morning long.

Makes 12 muffins

- Preheat oven to 350°F (180°C)
- 12-cup muffin pan, lined with paper liners

1. *Muffins:* In a large bowl, whisk together all-purpose flour, whole wheat flour, baking powder, baking soda and salt.

2. In a medium bowl, whisk together sugar, egg, yogurt, oil, orange zest and vanilla until well blended.

3. Add the egg mixture to the flour mixture and stir until just blended. Gently fold in prunes.

4. Divide batter equally among prepared muffin cups.

5. Bake in preheated oven for 23 to 27 minutes or until tops are golden and a toothpick inserted in the center comes out clean. Let cool in pan on a wire rack for 3 minutes, then transfer to the rack to cool while you prepare the icing.

6. *Icing:* In a small bowl, combine confectioners' sugar, orange zest and orange juice until blended. Drizzle over warm muffins. Let cool.

Honey Orange Oat Muffins

Muffins

1 cup	large-flake (old-fashioned) rolled oats	250 mL
2/3 cup	buttermilk	150 mL
1/2 cup	unsweetened orange juice	125 mL
1/4 cup	liquid honey	60 mL
1/4 cup	vegetable oil	60 mL
2 tsp	finely grated orange zest	10 mL
1 1/4 cups	all-purpose flour	300 mL
1/4 cup	wheat germ	60 mL
2 1/2 tsp	baking powder	12 mL
1/2 tsp	baking soda	2 mL
1/2 tsp	salt	2 mL
1	egg	1

Glaze

1/2 cup	confectioners' (icing) sugar	125 mL
3 tbsp	liquid honey	45 mL
2 tbsp	unsweetened orange juice	30 mL

If you think oat muffins are heavy, think again: these honey-oat muffins have a delicate texture and a toasty flavor that pairs ever so well with jam or marmalade.

Makes 12 muffins

- 12-cup muffin pan, lined with paper liners

1. *Muffins:* In a medium bowl, combine oats, buttermilk, orange juice, honey, oil and orange zest until blended. Let stand for 15 minutes.
2. Preheat oven to 400°F (200°C).
3. In a large bowl, whisk together flour, wheat germ, baking powder, baking soda and salt.
4. Whisk egg into oat mixture until blended. Add the oat mixture to the flour mixture and stir until just blended.
5. Divide batter equally among prepared muffin cups.
6. Bake for 18 to 22 minutes or until tops are golden and a toothpick inserted in the center comes out clean. Let cool in pan on a wire rack for 3 minutes, then transfer to the rack to cool while you prepare the glaze.
7. *Glaze:* In a microwave-safe measuring cup or bowl, combine confectioners' sugar, honey and orange juice. Microwave on High for 10 seconds or until thinned enough to brush. Generously brush mixture over warm muffins. Let cool for at least 10 minutes and serve warm or let cool completely.

Mandarin Orange Muffins

1	can (15 oz/425 mL) mandarin oranges, drained (or 1$\frac{1}{2}$ cans, each 10 oz/287 mL)	1
1$\frac{1}{2}$ cups	all-purpose flour	375 mL
1$\frac{1}{2}$ tsp	baking powder	7 mL
1 tsp	ground ginger	5 mL
$\frac{1}{2}$ tsp	salt	2 mL
$\frac{1}{4}$ tsp	baking soda	1 mL
$\frac{1}{3}$ cup	granulated sugar	75 mL
1	egg	1
1 cup	buttermilk	250 mL
$\frac{1}{2}$ cup	unsalted butter, melted	125 mL
1 tbsp	finely grated orange zest	15 mL

I love canned mandarin oranges. (I have been known to eat them unadorned, straight from the can.) They make a delightful stir-in for these simple, tangy muffins.

Makes 12 muffins
- Preheat oven to 400°F (200°C)
- 12-cup muffin pan, greased

1. Pat the mandarin oranges dry between paper towels. Transfer to a cutting board and coarsely chop.
2. In a large bowl, whisk together flour, baking powder, ginger, salt and baking soda.
3. In a medium bowl, whisk together sugar, egg, buttermilk, butter and orange zest until well blended.
4. Add the egg mixture to the flour mixture and stir until just blended. Gently fold in mandarin oranges.
5. Divide batter equally among prepared muffin cups.
6. Bake in preheated oven for 19 to 21 minutes or until tops are golden and a toothpick inserted in the center comes out clean. Let cool in pan on a wire rack for 5 minutes, then transfer to the rack to cool.

Lemon Cottage Muffins

1$\frac{1}{2}$ cups	all-purpose flour	375 mL
2$\frac{1}{2}$ tsp	baking powder	12 mL
$\frac{1}{2}$ tsp	salt	2 mL
$\frac{1}{3}$ cup	granulated sugar	75 mL
2	eggs	2
$\frac{1}{4}$ cup	unsalted butter, melted	60 mL
1 tbsp	finely grated lemon zest	15 mL
1 tsp	vanilla extract	5 mL
$\frac{2}{3}$ cup	small-curd cottage cheese	150 mL
$\frac{1}{3}$ cup	milk	75 mL

Cottage cheese is the stealth ingredient here, adding tenderness and moisture to these lemon-vanilla muffins. It also packs in some good-for-you protein, meaning just one muffin will help sustain you through a busy morning.

Makes 12 muffins
- Preheat oven to 425°F (220°C)
- 12-cup muffin pan, greased

1. In a large bowl, whisk together flour, baking powder and salt.
2. In a medium bowl, whisk together sugar, eggs, butter, lemon zest and vanilla until well blended. Whisk in cottage cheese and milk until blended.
3. Add the egg mixture to the flour mixture and stir until just blended.
4. Divide batter equally among prepared muffin cups.
5. Bake in preheated oven for 16 to 20 minutes or until tops are golden and a toothpick inserted in the center comes out clean. Let cool in pan on a wire rack for 5 minutes, then transfer to the rack to cool.

Lemon Streusel Muffins

Topping

1/2 cup	all-purpose flour	125 mL
1/2 cup	granulated sugar	125 mL
2 tsp	finely grated lemon zest	10 mL
1/4 cup	unsalted butter, melted	60 mL

Muffins

2 cups	all-purpose flour	500 mL
2 1/2 tsp	baking powder	12 mL
1/2 tsp	baking soda	2 mL
1/2 tsp	salt	2 mL
3/4 cup	granulated sugar	175 mL
2	eggs	2
1/2 cup	vegetable oil	125 mL
2 tsp	vanilla extract	10 mL
3/4 cup + 2 tbsp	milk	205 mL
1 tbsp	finely grated lemon zest	15 mL
2 tbsp	freshly squeezed lemon juice	30 mL

Serve these delicately flavored muffins with tea.

Makes 12 muffins

- Preheat oven to 350°F (180°C)
- 12-cup muffin pan, lined with paper liners

1. *Topping:* In a small bowl, combine flour, sugar and lemon zest. Mix in butter until streusel is crumbly. Refrigerate until ready to use.
2. *Muffins:* In a large bowl, whisk together flour, baking powder, baking soda and salt.
3. In a medium bowl, whisk together sugar, eggs, oil and vanilla until well blended. Whisk in milk, lemon zest and lemon juice until blended.
4. Add the egg mixture to the flour mixture and stir until just blended.
5. Divide batter equally among prepared muffin cups. Sprinkle with topping.
6. Bake in preheated oven for 20 to 25 minutes or until tops are golden and a toothpick inserted in the center comes out clean. Let cool in pan on a wire rack for 3 minutes, then transfer to the rack to cool.

Lemon-Lime Yogurt Muffins

3 cups	all-purpose flour	750 mL
2 1/2 tsp	baking powder	12 mL
1 tsp	salt	5 mL
3/4 tsp	baking soda	3 mL
3/4 cup	granulated sugar	175 mL
2	eggs	2
1 1/3 cups	plain yogurt	325 mL
1/2 cup	unsalted butter, melted	125 mL
1 tbsp	finely grated lemon zest	15 mL
1 tbsp	finely grated lime zest	15 mL
1 tbsp	freshly squeezed lemon juice	15 mL
1 tbsp	freshly squeezed lime juice	15 mL

One of these tasty, tender muffins is a perfect match for a hot cup of green tea.

Makes 12 muffins

- Preheat oven to 400°F (200°C)
- 12-cup muffin pan, lined with paper liners

1. In a large bowl, whisk together flour, baking powder, salt and baking soda.
2. In a medium bowl, whisk together sugar, eggs, yogurt, butter, lemon zest, lime zest, lemon juice and lime juice until well blended.
3. Add the egg mixture to the flour mixture and stir until just blended.
4. Divide batter equally among prepared muffin cups.
5. Bake in preheated oven for 20 to 24 minutes or until tops are golden brown and a toothpick inserted in the center comes out clean. Let cool in pan on a wire rack for 3 minutes, then transfer to the rack to cool.

Fig and Hazelnut Muffins

1 1/2 cups	all-purpose flour	375 mL
1 1/2 tsp	baking powder	7 mL
1 1/2 tsp	ground cinnamon	7 mL
1 tsp	ground ginger	5 mL
1/4 tsp	baking soda	1 mL
1/4 tsp	salt	1 mL
3/4 cup	packed light brown sugar	175 mL
1	egg	1
2/3 cup	milk	150 mL
1/2 cup	unsalted butter, melted	125 mL
1 cup	chopped stemmed dried figs	250 mL
1/2 cup	chopped hazelnuts, toasted	125 mL

Toasted hazelnuts and plump dried figs add sophisticated notes to these homey muffins. For best results, choose dried figs that are vacuum-sealed; they are particularly soft and plump.

Tip

Toast the hazelnuts while the oven is preheating. Spread them on a large baking sheet and place in the oven as soon as you turn it on. The nuts should be toasted after 10 to 12 minutes.

Makes 12 muffins

- Preheat oven to 375°F (190°C)
- 12-cup muffin pan, lined with paper liners

1. In a large bowl, whisk together flour, baking powder, cinnamon, ginger, baking soda and salt.
2. In a medium bowl, whisk together brown sugar, egg, milk and butter until well blended.
3. Add the egg mixture to the flour mixture and stir until just blended. Gently fold in figs and hazelnuts.
4. Divide batter equally among prepared muffin cups.
5. Bake in preheated oven for 20 to 23 minutes or until tops are golden and a toothpick inserted in the center comes out clean. Let cool in pan on a wire rack for 3 minutes, then transfer to the rack to cool.

Whole Wheat Fig Muffins

1 cup	whole wheat flour	250 mL
1/2 cup	all-purpose flour	125 mL
1/2 cup	wheat germ	125 mL
2 tsp	baking powder	10 mL
1/2 tsp	salt	2 mL
1	egg	1
1/2 cup	liquid honey	125 mL
1/4 cup	unsalted butter, melted	60 mL
2 tsp	finely grated lemon zest	10 mL
1/2 cup	milk	125 mL
1 cup	chopped dried figs	250 mL

Look for vacuum-packed dried figs where raisins are shelved in the supermarket; they are particularly soft and flavorful. If your dried figs are hard, soften them in hot water for 15 minutes, then drain before using.

Makes 12 muffins

- Preheat oven to 375°F (190°C)
- 12-cup muffin pan, greased

1. In a large bowl, whisk together whole wheat flour, all-purpose flour, wheat germ, baking powder and salt.

2. In a medium bowl, whisk together egg, honey, butter and lemon zest until well blended. Whisk in milk until blended.

3. Add the egg mixture to the flour mixture and stir until just blended. Gently fold in figs.

4. Divide batter equally among prepared muffin cups.

5. Bake in preheated oven for 19 to 23 minutes or until tops are golden and a toothpick inserted in the center comes out clean. Let cool in pan on a wire rack for 3 minutes, then transfer to the rack to cool.

Mango Morning Muffins

2 cups	all-purpose flour	500 mL
2 tsp	baking powder	10 mL
1/2 tsp	salt	2 mL
1/2 tsp	baking soda	2 mL
1/2 tsp	ground cardamom	2 mL
2/3 cup	granulated sugar	150 mL
1	egg	1
3/4 cup	buttermilk	175 mL
1/4 cup	unsalted butter, melted	60 mL
1 tsp	vanilla extract	5 mL
1 cup	chopped ripe mango	250 mL
2 tbsp	turbinado sugar	30 mL

When you're desperate for a tropical escape but don't have the opportunity, try a batch of these muffins instead. They may not be quite the same as a vacation, but they run a close second. If mangos are not in season, use frozen (thawed) or drained canned mangos in their place.

Makes 12 muffins

- Preheat oven to 400°F (200°C)
- 12-cup muffin pan, greased

1. In a large bowl, whisk together flour, baking powder, salt, baking soda and cardamom.

2. In a medium bowl, whisk together granulated sugar, egg, buttermilk, butter and vanilla until well blended.

3. Add the egg mixture to the flour mixture and stir until just blended. Gently fold in mango.

4. Divide batter equally among prepared muffin cups. Sprinkle with turbinado sugar.

5. Bake in preheated oven for 20 to 25 minutes or until tops are light golden brown and a toothpick inserted in the center comes out clean. Let cool in pan on a wire rack for 5 minutes, then transfer to the rack to cool.

Tropical Fruit Muffins

Muffins

2 cups	all-purpose flour	500 mL
2 tsp	baking powder	10 mL
1 tsp	baking soda	5 mL
1/2 tsp	salt	2 mL
3/4 cup	granulated sugar	175 mL
3	eggs	3
1 cup	plain yogurt	250 mL
1/2 cup	unsalted butter, melted	125 mL
1 tbsp	grated lime zest	15 mL
1 tsp	vanilla extract	5 mL
1 cup	chopped dried tropical fruit	250 mL

Icing

3/4 cup	confectioners' (icing) sugar	175 mL
1 tbsp	freshly squeezed lime juice	15 mL

Assorted chopped tropical fruit bits can be found alongside raisins at the grocer. Teamed with a fresh lime glaze, they make easy, extraordinary muffins.

Makes 12 muffins

- Preheat oven to 350°F (180°C)
- 12-cup muffin pan, lined with paper liners

1. *Muffins:* In a large bowl, whisk together flour, baking powder, baking soda and salt.
2. In a medium bowl, whisk together sugar, eggs, yogurt, butter, lime zest and vanilla until well blended.
3. Add the egg mixture to the flour mixture and stir until just blended. Gently fold in dried fruit.
4. Divide batter equally among prepared muffin cups.
5. Bake in preheated oven for 20 to 25 minutes or until tops are golden and a toothpick inserted in the center comes out clean. Let cool in pan on a wire rack for 3 minutes, then transfer to the rack to cool while you prepare the icing.
6. *Icing:* In a small bowl, combine confectioners' sugar and lime juice until blended. Drizzle over warm muffins and let cool.

Golden Raisin Rosemary Muffins

3/4 cup	milk	175 mL
1/2 cup	golden raisins	125 mL
1 tsp	dried rosemary	5 mL
1/4 cup	unsalted butter, cut into small pieces	60 mL
1 1/2 cups	all-purpose flour	375 mL
2/3 cup	granulated sugar	150 mL
2 tsp	baking powder	10 mL
1/2 tsp	salt	2 mL
1	egg	1
1 tbsp	granulated sugar	15 mL

Rosemary lends an unexpected nuance to these otherwise humble muffins. Elegant in their simplicity, they are especially nice on day two, split and toasted, once the flavors have had more time to develop.

Makes 12 muffins

- 12-cup muffin pan, greased

1. In a 2-cup (500 mL) glass measuring cup, combine milk, raisins and rosemary. Microwave on High for 2 minutes; let stand for 1 minute. Add butter and stir until melted. Let cool to room temperature.
2. Preheat oven to 350°F (180°C).
3. In a large bowl, whisk together flour, the 2/3 cup (150 mL) sugar, baking powder and salt.
4. Whisk egg into cooled milk mixture until well blended.
5. Add the milk mixture to the flour mixture and stir until just blended.
6. Divide batter equally among prepared muffin cups. Sprinkle with the 1 tbsp (15 mL) sugar.
7. Bake for 18 to 23 minutes or until a toothpick inserted in the center comes out clean. Let cool in pan on a wire rack for 3 minutes, then transfer to the rack to cool.

Raisin Rye Muffins

2 cups	rye flour	500 mL
4 tsp	baking powder	20 mL
1 tsp	ground cinnamon	5 mL
1/2 tsp	salt	2 mL
1	egg	1
3/4 cup	milk	175 mL
1/4 cup	liquid honey	60 mL
1/4 cup	vegetable oil	60 mL
1 cup	raisins	250 mL

Akin to colonial brown bread, these easily assembled muffins are dense and fragrant. Look for rye flour at natural foods stores, specialty food stores and many well-stocked supermarkets.

Makes 12 muffins

- Preheat oven to 400°F (200°C)
- 12-cup muffin pan, greased

1. In a large bowl, whisk together flour, baking powder, cinnamon and salt.
2. In a medium bowl, whisk together egg, milk, honey and oil until well blended.
3. Add the egg mixture to the flour mixture and stir until just blended. Gently fold in raisins.
4. Divide batter equally among prepared muffin cups.
5. Bake in preheated oven for 15 to 20 minutes or until tops are golden and a toothpick inserted in the center comes out clean. Let cool in pan on a wire rack for 3 minutes, then transfer to the rack to cool.

Lemon-Glazed Currant Muffins

Muffins

2 1/2 cups	all-purpose flour	625 mL
2 1/2 tsp	baking powder	12 mL
3/4 tsp	salt	3 mL
1 cup	packed light brown sugar	250 mL
2	eggs	2
1 tbsp	finely grated lemon zest	15 mL
1/2 cup	vegetable oil	125 mL
1 cup	buttermilk	250 mL
1 1/2 tsp	vanilla extract	7 mL
3/4 cup	dried currants	175 mL
1/3 cup	finely chopped pistachios	75 mL

Glaze

1 cup	confectioners' (icing) sugar	250 mL
1 1/2 tbsp	freshly squeezed lemon juice	22 mL

These muffins are a quick and easy version of a cake I remember from my childhood, made and served by a family friend at church coffee hour. One taste makes me feel like a kid again.

Makes 12 muffins

- Preheat oven to 425°F (220°C)
- 12-cup muffin pan, greased

1. *Muffins:* In a large bowl, whisk together flour, baking powder and salt.
2. In a medium bowl, whisk together brown sugar and eggs until well blended. Whisk in lemon zest, oil, buttermilk and vanilla until blended.
3. Add the egg mixture to the flour mixture and stir until just blended. Gently fold in currants and pistachios.
4. Divide batter equally among prepared muffin cups.
5. Bake in preheated oven for 17 to 20 minutes or until tops are golden and just firm. Let cool in pan on a wire rack for 5 minutes, then transfer to the rack to cool completely.
6. *Glaze:* In a small bowl, whisk together the confectioners' sugar and lemon juice until smooth. Drizzle each cooled muffin with the glaze.

Four-Grain Fruit Muffins

1 1/4 cups	whole wheat flour	300 mL
3/4 cup	oat bran	175 mL
1/4 cup	yellow cornmeal	60 mL
1 tsp	baking powder	5 mL
1/2 tsp	baking soda	2 mL
1/4 tsp	salt	1 mL
1/2 cup	packed light brown sugar	125 mL
1	egg	1
1 1/4 cups	lower-fat plain yogurt	300 mL
1/4 cup	vegetable oil	60 mL
1/2 cup	chopped mixed dried fruit	125 mL
1/2 cup	cooled cooked brown rice	125 mL

The wholesome combination of multiple whole grains and bits of dried fruit give these muffins a homey, satisfying flavor.

Tips

Look for packages of pre-chopped assorted dried fruit, or chop your favorite combination of dried fruits.

I've chose lower-fat yogurt for this recipe, to keep the muffins super-healthy, but an equal amount of full-fat yogurt may be substituted.

Makes 12 muffins

- Preheat oven to 400°F (200°C)
- 12-cup muffin pan, greased

1. In a large bowl, whisk together flour, oat bran, cornmeal, baking powder, baking soda and salt until blended.

2. In a medium bowl, whisk together brown sugar, egg, yogurt and oil until well blended.

3. Add the egg mixture to the flour mixture and stir until just blended. Gently fold in dried fruit and rice.

4. Divide batter equally among prepared muffin cups.

5. Bake in preheated oven for 20 to 24 minutes or until tops are golden and a toothpick inserted in the center comes out clean. Let cool in pan on a wire rack for 5 minutes, then transfer to the rack to cool.

Maple Bran Muffins

2	eggs	2
3/4 cup	pure maple syrup	175 mL
3 cups	bran flakes cereal, crushed	750 mL
1 cup	all-purpose flour	250 mL
1 tsp	baking soda	5 mL
1/2 tsp	salt	2 mL
1 cup	sour cream	250 mL
3/4 tsp	vanilla extract	3 mL

Maple syrup isn't exclusive to New England; Central and Eastern Canada, as well as northern Minnesota and Wisconsin, produce it too. The sweet syrup teams up here in a new-fangled version of old-fashioned bran muffins, with scrumptious success.

Makes 12 muffins

- Preheat oven to 400°F (200°C)
- 12-cup muffin pan, lined with paper liners

1. In a large bowl, whisk together eggs and syrup until well blended and frothy. Stir in bran flakes. Let stand for 5 minutes.

2. In another large bowl, whisk together flour, baking soda and salt.

3. Stir sour cream and vanilla into cereal mixture until blended. Add to the flour mixture and stir until just blended.

4. Divide batter equally among prepared muffin cups.

5. Bake in preheated oven for 19 to 24 minutes or until tops are golden and a toothpick inserted in the center comes out clean. Let cool in pan on a wire rack for 3 minutes, then transfer to the rack to cool.

Chocolate Bran Muffins

1 cup	bran cereal, such as All-Bran	250 mL
1 1/3 cups	buttermilk	325 mL
1/2 cup	whole wheat flour	125 mL
1/2 cup	all-purpose flour	125 mL
1/2 cup	unsweetened cocoa powder (not Dutch process)	125 mL
1 tsp	baking soda	5 mL
1/2 tsp	salt	2 mL
3/4 cup	packed dark brown sugar	175 mL
1	egg	1
1/4 cup	vegetable oil	60 mL
1 tsp	vanilla extract	5 mL
1/2 cup	miniature semisweet chocolate chips	125 mL

Bran muffins never tasted so incredible! Unsweetened cocoa powder and a smattering of miniature semisweet chocolate chips add both rich flavor and good health: cocoa powder and dark chocolate are very high in antioxidants.

Makes 12 muffins

- Preheat oven to 375°F (190°C)
- 12-cup muffin pan, lined with paper liners

1. Place the cereal in a resealable plastic bag. Seal bag and crush cereal with a rolling pin or meat mallet (or crush in a food processor). Transfer to a large bowl and stir in buttermilk. Let stand for 5 minutes.

2. In a medium bowl, whisk together whole wheat flour, all-purpose flour, cocoa powder, baking soda and salt.

3. Mix brown sugar, egg, oil and vanilla into the cereal mixture until blended.

4. Add the flour mixture to the cereal mixture and stir until just blended. Gently fold in chocolate chips.

5. Divide batter equally among prepared muffin cups.

6. Bake in preheated oven for 15 to 20 minutes or until tops are golden and a toothpick inserted in the center comes out clean. Let cool in pan on a wire rack for 3 minutes, then transfer to the rack to cool.

Fruit and Flax Bran Muffins

1 1/2 cups	all-purpose flour	375 mL
3/4 cup	ground flax seeds	175 mL
3/4 cup	oat bran	175 mL
2 1/2 tsp	ground cinnamon	12 mL
2 tsp	baking powder	10 mL
2 tsp	baking soda	10 mL
1/2 tsp	salt	2 mL
1 1/2 cups	shredded carrots	375 mL
1 1/2 cups	shredded apples	375 mL
1 cup	chopped walnuts or pecans	250 mL
1/2 cup	raisins	125 mL
3/4 cup	packed dark brown sugar	175 mL
2	eggs	2
3/4 cup	milk	175 mL
2 tsp	vanilla extract	10 mL

Makes 12 muffins

- Preheat oven to 350°F (180°C)
- 12-cup muffin pan, lined with paper liners

1. In a large bowl, whisk together flour, flax seeds, oat bran, cinnamon, baking powder, baking soda and salt. Stir in carrots, apples, nuts and raisins.
2. In a medium bowl, whisk together brown sugar, eggs, milk and vanilla until well blended.
3. Add the egg mixture to the flour mixture and stir until just blended.
4. Divide batter equally among prepared muffin cups.
5. Bake in preheated oven for 16 to 21 minutes or until tops are golden and a toothpick inserted in the center comes out clean. Let cool in pan on a wire rack for 3 minutes, then transfer to the rack to cool.

Flax is rich in nutrients that protect against heart disease and cancer. It has a very mild taste and, when used in quick breads, contributes great moisture.

Sour Cream Bran Muffins

1 cup	all-purpose flour	250 mL
1 cup	natural bran	250 mL
1 tsp	baking soda	5 mL
1/4 tsp	salt	1 mL
1/2 cup	unsalted butter, softened	125 mL
1/4 cup	firmly packed light brown sugar	60 mL
1	egg	1
1 cup	sour cream	250 mL
1/4 cup	dark (cooking) molasses	60 mL
1 tsp	vanilla extract	5 mL
2/3 cup	raisins	150 mL

Makes 12 muffins

- Preheat oven to 400°F (200°C)
- 12-cup muffin pan, greased

1. In a medium bowl, whisk together flour, bran, baking soda and salt.
2. In a large bowl, using an electric mixer on medium speed, beat butter and brown sugar until light and fluffy. Beat in egg, sour cream, molasses and vanilla until blended.
3. Add the flour mixture to the egg mixture and stir until just blended. Gently fold in raisins.
4. Divide batter equally among prepared muffin cups.
5. Bake in preheated oven for 15 to 19 minutes or until a toothpick inserted in the center comes out clean. Let cool in pan on a wire rack for 3 minutes, then transfer to the rack to cool.

Can bran muffins be decadent? Absolutely, and here, they are.

Big-Batch Refrigerator and Freezer Bran Muffins

2¹/₂ cups	bran cereal, such as All-Bran, divided	625 mL
1 cup	raisins	250 mL
1 cup	boiling water	250 mL
1¹/₂ cups	all-purpose flour	375 mL
1 cup	whole wheat flour	250 mL
1 tbsp	baking soda	15 mL
1¹/₂ tsp	ground cinnamon	7 mL
1 tsp	salt	5 mL
³/₄ cup	granulated sugar	175 mL
³/₄ cup	light (fancy) molasses, liquid honey or pure maple syrup	175 mL
¹/₂ cup	vegetable oil	125 mL
¹/₂ cup	pasteurized liquid whole eggs	125 mL
2 cups	buttermilk	500 mL

Having two batches of ready-to-be-baked bran muffins in the refrigerator or freezer makes eating a healthy delicious breakfast a breeze. My version makes 24 muffins that will keep for 10 days in the refrigerator or 3 months in the freezer.

Makes 24 muffins

- 12-cup muffin pan, greased (per batch)

1. In a large heatproof bowl, combine 1 cup (250 mL) of the bran cereal, the raisins and boiling water. Let stand for 15 minutes.

2. In a large bowl, whisk together all-purpose flour, whole wheat flour, baking soda, cinnamon and salt.

3. In another large bowl, whisk together sugar, molasses, oil and eggs until well blended. Whisk in buttermilk until blended. Stir in the remaining bran cereal, then the raisin mixture.

4. Add the egg mixture to the flour mixture and stir until just blended.

5. Divide into two airtight containers and refrigerate for up to 10 days.

6. When ready to bake, preheat oven to 400°F (200°C). Divide batter equally among prepared muffin cups.

7. Bake for 15 to 20 minutes or until a toothpick inserted in the center comes out clean. Let cool in pan on a wire rack for 5 minutes, then transfer to the rack to cool.

Freezer Option

1. Follow steps 1 through 4 as directed.

2. Divide batter equally among prepared muffin cups. Place muffin pans in the freezer. When frozen solid, transfer frozen muffins to two large, heavy-duty, zipper-top plastic freezer bags or airtight containers and freeze for up to 3 months.

3. When ready to bake, preheat oven to 400°F (200°C). Transfer the desired number of frozen muffins back into prepared cups of muffin pan.

4. Bake, from frozen, for 23 to 28 minutes or until a toothpick inserted in the center comes out clean. Let cool in pan on a wire rack for 5 minutes, then transfer to the rack to cool.

Bowl of Oatmeal Muffins

1½ cups	all-purpose flour	375 mL
¾ cup	large-flake (old-fashioned) rolled oats	175 mL
1 tbsp	baking powder	15 mL
1 tsp	salt	5 mL
¾ tsp	ground cinnamon	3 mL
1 cup	packed dark brown sugar, divided	250 mL
2	eggs	2
1 cup	plain yogurt	250 mL
⅔ cup	milk	150 mL
½ cup	vegetable oil	125 mL
⅔ cup	raisins	150 mL

I love a warm bowl of oatmeal (preferably with ample amounts of brown sugar), but when I'm on the run, I like to have a batch of these muffins ready for packing into my bag. They require minimal mixing and cleanup, call for ingredients usually stocked in my pantry and are tasty yet healthful.

Tip

Use any variety of dried fruit here, in place of the raisins. Dried cherries and dried blueberries are two of my favorites.

Makes 12 muffins

- Preheat oven to 400°F (200°C)
- 12-cup muffin pan, lined with paper liners

1. In a large bowl, whisk together flour, oats, baking powder, salt and cinnamon.

2. In a medium bowl, whisk together ¾ cup (175 mL) of the brown sugar, eggs, yogurt, milk and oil until well blended.

3. Add the egg mixture to the flour mixture and stir until just blended. Gently fold in raisins.

4. Divide batter equally among prepared muffin cups. Sprinkle with the remaining brown sugar.

5. Bake in preheated oven for 25 to 30 minutes or until tops are golden and a toothpick inserted in the center comes out clean. Let cool in pan on a wire rack for 3 minutes, then transfer to the rack to cool.

Double Oat Muffins

Topping

1/2 cup	large-flake (old-fashioned) rolled oats	125 mL
2 tbsp	packed light brown sugar	30 mL
2 tbsp	unsalted butter, melted	30 mL

Muffins

2 cups	oat bran	500 mL
1/4 cup	all-purpose flour	60 mL
2 tsp	baking powder	10 mL
1/2 tsp	baking soda	2 mL
1/2 tsp	salt	2 mL
1/2 cup	packed light brown sugar	125 mL
1	egg	1
1 cup	buttermilk	250 mL
1/4 cup	vegetable oil	60 mL
1 1/2 tsp	vanilla extract	7 mL

Oats are a great source of dietary fiber, about 55% soluble and 45% insoluble. Happily, both rolled oats and oat bran make sensational quick breads, like these muffins. Brown sugar and vanilla are great flavor complements, and tangy buttermilk renders the muffins light and tender.

Makes 12 muffins

- Preheat oven to 400°F (200°C)
- 12-cup muffin pan, lined with paper liners

1. *Topping:* In a small bowl, combine oats, brown sugar and butter until crumbly. Refrigerate until ready to use.
2. *Muffins:* In a large bowl, whisk together oat bran, flour, baking powder, baking soda and salt.
3. In a medium bowl, whisk together brown sugar, egg, buttermilk, oil and vanilla until well blended.
4. Add the egg mixture to the oat bran mixture and stir until just blended.
5. Divide batter equally among prepared muffin cups. Sprinkle with topping.
6. Bake in preheated oven for 20 to 24 minutes or until tops are golden and a toothpick inserted in the center comes out clean. Let cool in pan on a wire rack for 3 minutes, then transfer to the rack to cool.

Overnight Oatmeal Muffins with Dried Blueberries

2 cups	buttermilk	500 mL
1 cup	large-flake (old-fashioned) rolled oats	250 mL
1²⁄₃ cups	whole wheat flour	400 mL
1 tsp	baking powder	5 mL
1 tsp	baking soda	5 mL
1 tsp	salt	5 mL
³⁄₄ cup	packed dark brown sugar	175 mL
2	eggs	2
3 tbsp	vegetable oil	45 mL
³⁄₄ cup	dried blueberries	175 mL

Prep a batch of this healthy, dried-blueberry muffin batter as you program your coffeemaker; it will take mere minutes. Come morning, breakfast is as simple as whisking in the remaining ingredients, plopping it into pans and sliding it into the oven for a quick bake. By the time you're done your first cup of coffee, breakfast is ready!

Makes 18 muffins

- Two 12-cup muffin pans, 18 cups greased

1. In a large bowl, combine buttermilk and oats. Loosely cover and refrigerate overnight.
2. In a medium bowl, whisk together flour, baking powder, baking soda and salt. Cover and let stand at room temperature overnight.
3. Preheat oven to 350°F (180°C).
4. In a small bowl, whisk together brown sugar, eggs and oil until well blended. Stir into the oat mixture until well blended.
5. Add the flour mixture to the oat mixture and stir until just blended. Gently fold in dried blueberries.
6. Divide batter equally among prepared muffin cups.
7. Bake in preheated oven for 20 to 25 minutes or until tops are light golden brown and a toothpick inserted in the center comes out clean. Let cool in pans on a wire rack for 5 minutes, then transfer to the rack to cool.

Oatmeal and Prune Muffins

1 cup	all-purpose flour	250 mL
1¹⁄₂ tsp	baking powder	7 mL
³⁄₄ tsp	salt	3 mL
¹⁄₂ tsp	baking soda	2 mL
1¹⁄₃ cups	quick-cooking rolled oats	325 mL
¹⁄₄ cup	granulated sugar	60 mL
1	egg	1
1 cup	buttermilk	250 mL
¹⁄₄ cup	unsalted butter, melted	60 mL
¹⁄₄ cup	dark (cooking) molasses	60 mL
1 cup	chopped pitted prunes	250 mL

It almost goes without saying that these muffins are good for you, but they are also absolutely delicious. The prunes remain plump and moist after baking, making these muffins good keepers for a week of breakfasts.

Makes 12 muffins

- Preheat oven to 400°F (200°C)
- 12-cup muffin pan, greased

1. In a large bowl, whisk together flour, baking powder, salt and baking soda. Stir in oats.
2. In a medium bowl, whisk together sugar, egg, buttermilk, butter and molasses until well blended.
3. Add the egg mixture to the flour mixture and stir until just combined. Gently fold in prunes.
4. Divide batter equally among prepared muffin cups.
5. Bake in preheated oven for 20 to 25 minutes or until tops are golden and a toothpick inserted in the center comes out clean. Let cool in pan on a wire rack for 3 minutes, then transfer to the rack to cool.

Morning Multigrain Muffins

1 cup	whole wheat flour	250 mL
1/2 cup	all-purpose flour	125 mL
3/4 cup	oat bran	175 mL
1/4 cup	yellow cornmeal	60 mL
2 tsp	baking powder	10 mL
1 tsp	baking soda	5 mL
1/4 tsp	salt	1 mL
1/2 cup	packed dark brown sugar	125 mL
2	eggs	2
1/4 cup	vegetable oil	60 mL
1 1/4 cups	buttermilk	300 mL
1 cup	chopped mixed dried fruit	250 mL
1/2 cup	chopped walnuts	125 mL

These hearty, home-style multigrain muffins are great for toasting, spreading with marmalade or eating as is.

Makes 12 muffins

- Preheat oven to 375°F (190°C)
- 12-cup muffin pan, lined with paper liners

1. In a large bowl, whisk together whole wheat flour, all-purpose flour, oat bran, cornmeal, baking powder, baking soda and salt.

2. In a medium bowl, whisk together brown sugar, eggs and oil until well blended. Whisk in buttermilk until blended.

3. Add the egg mixture to the flour mixture and stir until just blended. Gently fold in dried fruit and walnuts.

4. Divide batter among prepared muffin cups.

5. Bake in preheated oven for 23 to 26 minutes or until tops are firm to the touch and a toothpick inserted in the center comes out clean. Let cool in pan on a wire rack for 3 minutes, then transfer to the rack to cool.

Granola Muffins

1 cup	whole wheat flour	250 mL
1 cup	all-purpose flour	250 mL
1 tbsp	baking powder	15 mL
1 tsp	ground cinnamon	5 mL
1/2 tsp	salt	2 mL
1 1/2 cups	granola, divided	375 mL
2/3 cup	packed light brown sugar	150 mL
2	eggs	2
2/3 cup	milk	150 mL
1/3 cup	vegetable oil	75 mL
1 tsp	vanilla extract	5 mL
2	large ripe bananas, diced	2
1/2 cup	dried cherries or dried cranberries	125 mL

My family is addicted to these granola muffins, studded with bananas and dried cherries. They are excellent travelers, perfect for packing into lunches (or when you're running out the door, travel mug of coffee in hand).

Makes 12 muffins

- Preheat oven to 350°F (180°C)
- 12-cup muffin pan, greased

1. In a large bowl, whisk together whole wheat flour, all-purpose flour, baking powder, cinnamon and salt. Stir in 3/4 cup (175 mL) of the granola.

2. In a medium bowl, whisk together brown sugar, eggs, milk, oil and vanilla until well blended.

3. Add the egg mixture to the flour mixture and stir until just blended. Gently fold in bananas and dried cherries.

4. Divide batter among prepared muffin cups. Sprinkle with the remaining granola and press lightly into batter.

5. Bake in preheated oven for 18 to 21 minutes or until tops are golden brown and a toothpick inserted in the center comes out clean. Let cool in pan on a wire rack for 3 minutes, then transfer to the rack to cool.

Trail Mix Muffins

1½ cups	whole wheat flour	375 mL
½ cup	natural bran	125 mL
2 tsp	baking powder	10 mL
¼ tsp	salt	1 mL
⅔ cup	packed light brown sugar	150 mL
2	eggs	2
½ cup	milk	125 mL
½ cup	vegetable oil	125 mL
¾ cup	carob chips	175 mL
¾ cup	lightly salted roasted sunflower seeds	175 mL
½ cup	chopped mixed dried fruit	125 mL
1 cup	granola	250 mL

These muffins travel well and sustain travelers well, too.

Makes 12 muffins

- Preheat oven to 425°F (220°C)
- 12-cup muffin pan, greased

1. In a large bowl, whisk together flour, bran, baking powder and salt.
2. In a medium bowl, whisk together brown sugar, eggs, milk and oil until well blended.
3. Add the egg mixture to the flour mixture and stir until just combined. Gently fold in carob chips, sunflower seeds and dried fruit.
4. Divide batter equally among prepared muffin cups. Sprinkle with granola and press lightly into batter.
5. Bake in preheated oven for 20 to 25 minutes or until tops are golden and a toothpick inserted in the center comes out clean. Let cool in pan on a wire rack for 3 minutes, then transfer to the rack to cool.

Apricot Millet Muffins

½ cup	millet	125 mL
1¾ cups	all-purpose flour	425 mL
1 tbsp	baking powder	15 mL
1½ tsp	ground cinnamon	7 mL
½ tsp	salt	2 mL
¾ cup	packed light brown sugar	175 mL
2	eggs	2
⅔ cup	apricot nectar	150 mL
½ cup	unsalted butter, melted	125 mL
¼ tsp	almond extract	1 mL
1	can (14 or 15 oz/398 or 425 mL) apricot halves, drained, diced	1

Toasting the millet enhances its nutty flavor and crunch. Apricot nectar underscores the bright sunny notes of the canned apricots, but in a pinch, orange juice may be used in its place.

Makes 12 muffins

- Preheat oven to 350°F (180°C)
- 12-cup muffin pan, greased

1. In a large, dry skillet over medium heat, toast millet, stirring constantly, for 5 minutes or until it turns golden, smells nutty and begins to pop. Remove from heat and let cool.
2. In a large bowl, whisk together flour, baking powder, cinnamon and salt. Stir in toasted millet.
3. In a medium bowl, whisk together brown sugar, eggs, apricot nectar, butter and almond extract until well blended.
4. Add the egg mixture to the flour mixture and stir until just blended. Gently fold in apricots.
5. Divide batter among prepared muffin cups.
6. Bake in preheated oven for 23 to 25 minutes or until tops are golden and a toothpick inserted in the center comes out clean. Let cool in pan on a wire rack for 3 minutes, then transfer to the rack to cool.

Muesli Muffins

Muesli

1/2 cup	large-flake (old-fashioned) rolled oats	125 mL
1/2 cup	dried blueberries	125 mL
1/4 cup	chopped walnuts	60 mL
1/4 cup	roasted sunflower seeds	60 mL
1/4 cup	wheat germ	60 mL
2 tbsp	ground flax seeds	30 mL

Muffins

1 1/4 cups	all-purpose flour	300 mL
1/2 cup	natural wheat bran	125 mL
1 tsp	baking soda	5 mL
1/2 tsp	salt	2 mL
1/4 tsp	ground cinnamon	1 mL
1/3 cup	unsalted butter, softened	75 mL
1/3 cup	packed light brown sugar	75 mL
2	eggs	2
1 cup	finely chopped ripe bananas	250 mL
2/3 cup	unsweetened applesauce	150 mL
1 tsp	vanilla extract	5 mL

Serve these hearty muffins, based on the traditional Scandinavian cereal, alongside a cup of yogurt or skim latte to start the day off with both good health and great taste. You can substitute any combination of chopped dried fruit for the dried blueberries — raisins, apricots, apples, figs, cherries or cranberries are all delicious. And try almonds, hazelnuts or pepitas in place of the walnuts and sunflower seeds.

Makes 12 muffins

- Preheat oven to 375°F (190°C)
- 12-cup muffin pan, lined with paper liners

1. *Muesli:* In a medium bowl, combine oats, dried blueberries, walnuts, sunflower seeds, wheat germ and flax seeds. Set aside.

2. *Muffins:* In a medium bowl, whisk together flour, bran, baking soda, salt and cinnamon.

3. In a large bowl, using an electric mixer on medium-high speed, beat butter and brown sugar until light and fluffy. Beat in eggs, one at a time, until well combined after each addition. Beat in bananas, applesauce and vanilla until blended.

4. With the mixer on low speed, beat in flour mixture until just combined. Stir in 3/4 cup (175 mL) of the muesli.

5. Divide batter equally among prepared muffin cups. Sprinkle with the remaining muesli and press lightly into batter.

6. Bake in preheated oven for 20 to 23 minutes or until tops are golden and a toothpick inserted in the center comes out clean. Let cool in pan on a wire rack for 5 minutes, then transfer to the rack to cool.

Poppy Seed Power Muffins

1 cup	large-flake (old fashioned) rolled oats	250 mL
1 cup	all-purpose flour	250 mL
1 cup	whole wheat flour	250 mL
3 tbsp	ground flax seeds	45 mL
3 tbsp	poppy seeds	45 mL
2$\frac{1}{2}$ tsp	baking powder	12 mL
$\frac{1}{2}$ tsp	baking soda	2 mL
$\frac{1}{2}$ tsp	salt	2 mL
$\frac{1}{4}$ tsp	ground cloves	1 mL
1	egg	1
$\frac{2}{3}$ cup	liquid honey	150 mL
1$\frac{1}{4}$ cups	buttermilk	300 mL
2 tsp	finely grated orange zest	10 mL

In addition to being utterly delicious, these are also favorite on-the-move muffins because they do not crumble.

Makes 12 muffins

- Preheat oven to 400°F (200°C)
- 12-cup muffin pan, lined with paper liners

1. In a large bowl, whisk together oats, all-purpose flour, whole wheat flour, flax seeds, poppy seeds, baking powder, baking soda, salt and cloves.
2. In a medium bowl, whisk together egg and honey until well blended. Whisk in buttermilk and orange zest until blended.
3. Add the egg mixture to the flour mixture and stir until just blended.
4. Divide batter equally among prepared muffin cups.
5. Bake in preheated oven for 16 to 21 minutes or until tops are golden and a toothpick inserted in the center comes out clean. Let cool in pan on a wire rack for 3 minutes, then transfer to the rack to cool.

Good Morning Graham Muffins

1$\frac{1}{3}$ cups	graham cracker crumbs	325 mL
1$\frac{1}{4}$ cups	all-purpose flour	300 mL
$\frac{1}{2}$ cup	chopped pecans, toasted	125 mL
1 tsp	baking powder	5 mL
$\frac{3}{4}$ tsp	baking soda	3 mL
$\frac{1}{2}$ tsp	salt	2 mL
$\frac{1}{2}$ cup	packed light brown sugar	125 mL
1	egg	1
$\frac{1}{3}$ cup	vegetable oil	75 mL
1 tsp	vanilla extract	5 mL
1 cup	buttermilk	250 mL

Everyone knows how good graham crackers are with chocolate and marshmallows, but few know how incredible they are in muffins. Here, they lend toasty, nutty flavor — enhanced further by toasted pecans and vanilla — to a simple brown sugar–buttermilk muffin.

Makes 12 muffins

- Preheat oven to 375°F (190°C)
- 12-cup muffin pan, greased

1. In a large bowl, whisk together graham cracker crumbs, flour, pecans, baking powder, baking soda and salt.
2. In a medium bowl, whisk together brown sugar, egg, oil and vanilla until well blended. Whisk in buttermilk until blended.
3. Add the egg mixture to the flour mixture and stir until just blended.
4. Divide batter equally among prepared muffin cups.
5. Bake in preheated oven for 15 to 18 minutes or until tops are golden and a toothpick inserted in the center comes out clean. Let cool in pan on a wire rack for 3 minutes, then transfer to the rack to cool.

Cereal Nugget Pecan Muffins

1 cup	wheat and barley nugget cereal, such as Grape-Nuts or Kashi 7 Whole Grain Nuggets	250 mL
1/2 cup	raisins	125 mL
1/2 cup	boiling water	125 mL
1 3/4 cups	all-purpose flour	425 mL
1 tbsp	baking powder	15 mL
1/2 tsp	salt	2 mL
3/4 cup	packed dark brown sugar	175 mL
1	egg	1
1/2 cup	vegetable oil	125 mL
1 tsp	vanilla extract	5 mL
1/2 tsp	almond extract	2 mL
2/3 cup	milk	150 mL
1/2 cup	chopped pecans, toasted	125 mL

The softened cereal in the recipe adds a light, springy texture and a mellow, slightly sweet grain taste from the barley in the cereal.

Makes 12 muffins

- Preheat oven to 375°F (190°C)
- 12-cup muffin pan, lined with paper liners

1. In a small bowl, combine cereal, raisins and boiling water. Let stand for 20 minutes.
2. In a large bowl, whisk together flour, baking powder and salt.
3. In a medium bowl, whisk together brown sugar, egg, oil, vanilla and almond extract until well blended. Stir in milk and the cereal mixture until blended.
4. Add the egg mixture to the flour mixture and stir until just blended. Gently fold in pecans.
5. Divide batter equally among prepared muffin cups.
6. Bake in preheated oven for 20 to 25 minutes or until tops are golden and a toothpick inserted in the center comes out clean. Let cool in pan on a wire rack for 3 minutes, then transfer to the rack to cool.

Honey Muffins

2 cups	all-purpose flour	500 mL
2 1/2 tsp	baking powder	12 mL
1/2 tsp	baking soda	2 mL
1/2 tsp	salt	2 mL
1/2 cup	granulated sugar	125 mL
1	egg	1
1/4 cup	unsalted butter, melted	60 mL
1/4 cup	liquid honey	60 mL
1 cup	buttermilk	250 mL

A light texture and a sweet honey flavor make these old-fashioned muffins irresistible.

Makes 12 muffins

- Preheat oven to 400°F (200°C)
- 12-cup muffin pan, lined with paper liners

1. In a large bowl, whisk together flour, baking powder, baking soda and salt.
2. In a medium bowl, whisk together sugar, egg, butter and honey until well blended. Whisk in buttermilk until blended.
3. Add the egg mixture to the flour mixture and stir until just blended.
4. Divide batter equally among prepared muffin cups.
5. Bake in preheated oven for 15 to 18 minutes or until tops are golden and a toothpick inserted in the center comes out clean. Let cool in pan on a wire rack for 3 minutes, then transfer to the rack to cool.

Molasses Muffins

1 1/2 cups	all-purpose flour	375 mL
3/4 cup	whole wheat flour	175 mL
2 tsp	ground cinnamon	10 mL
1 tsp	baking soda	5 mL
1/4 tsp	ground cloves	1 mL
1/4 tsp	salt	1 mL
1	egg	1
3/4 cup	dark (cooking) molasses	175 mL
1/4 cup	unsalted butter, melted	60 mL
1 cup	buttermilk	250 mL

I like to bake these dark muffins, redolent with rich spices and notes of caramel from the molasses, in early December — perfect for gift-giving.

Makes 12 muffins

- Preheat oven to 350°F (180°C)
- 12-cup muffin pan, lined with paper liners

1. In a large bowl, whisk together all-purpose flour, whole wheat flour, cinnamon, baking soda, cloves and salt.
2. In a medium bowl, whisk together egg, molasses and butter until well blended. Whisk in buttermilk until blended.
3. Add the egg mixture to the flour mixture and stir until just blended.
4. Divide batter equally among prepared muffin cups.
5. Bake in preheated oven for 20 to 25 minutes or until a toothpick inserted in the center comes out clean. Let cool in pan on a wire rack for 3 minutes, then transfer to the rack to cool.

Spice Muffins

2 cups	all-purpose flour	500 mL
1 tbsp	baking powder	15 mL
1 1/2 tsp	ground cinnamon	7 mL
1 1/2 tsp	ground nutmeg	7 mL
1 tsp	ground cardamom	5 mL
1/2 tsp	salt	2 mL
2/3 cup	granulated sugar	150 mL
1	egg	1
1/2 cup	unsalted butter, melted	125 mL
1 cup	whipping (35%) cream	250 mL
1/3 cup	milk	75 mL

These richly spiced, delightful muffins are just the thing for a morning wake-up. Try them split and toasted, with a bit of cream cheese.

Makes 12 muffins

- Preheat oven to 400°F (200°C)
- 12-cup muffin pan, greased

1. In a large bowl, whisk together flour, baking powder, cinnamon, nutmeg, cardamom and salt.
2. In a medium bowl, whisk together sugar, egg, butter, cream and milk until well blended.
3. Add the egg mixture to the flour mixture and stir until just blended.
4. Divide batter equally among prepared muffin cups.
5. Bake in preheated oven for 18 to 22 minutes or until tops are golden and a toothpick inserted in the center comes out clean. Let cool in pan on a wire rack for 3 minutes, then transfer to the rack to cool.

Carrot Apple Muffins

1 cup	all-purpose flour	250 mL
1 cup	whole wheat flour	250 mL
1/4 cup	oat bran	60 mL
2 tsp	baking powder	10 mL
1 1/2 tsp	ground cinnamon, divided	7 mL
1/2 tsp	baking soda	2 mL
1/4 tsp	salt	1 mL
2/3 cup	firmly packed dark brown sugar	150 mL
2	eggs	2
1/4 cup	unsalted butter, melted	60 mL
1 1/2 cups	plain yogurt	375 mL
1 1/4 cups	shredded tart apple	300 mL
1 1/4 cups	finely grated carrots	300 mL
1/2 cup	chopped walnuts or pecans, toasted	60 mL
1/2 cup	golden raisins	60 mL
2 tbsp	granulated sugar	30 mL

This moist, healthy, deeply flavored carrot muffin, studded with juicy golden raisins, tart apple and crunchy nuts, will garner compliments from one and all.

Makes 16 muffins

- Preheat oven to 400°F (200°C)
- Two 12-cup muffin pan, 16 cups lined with paper liners

1. In a large bowl, whisk together all-purpose flour, whole wheat flour, oat bran, baking powder, 1 tsp (5 mL) of the cinnamon, baking soda and salt.
2. In a medium bowl, whisk together brown sugar, eggs and butter until well blended. Whisk in yogurt until blended.
3. Add the egg mixture to the flour mixture and stir until just blended. Gently fold in apple, carrots, nuts and raisins.
4. Divide batter equally among prepared muffin cups.
5. In a small bowl, combine granulated sugar and the remaining cinnamon. Sprinkle over muffins.
6. Bake in preheated oven for 15 to 19 minutes or until a toothpick inserted in the center comes out clean. Let cool in pan on a wire rack for 3 minutes, then transfer to the rack to cool.

Spiced Carrot Muffins

1 3/4 cups	all-purpose flour	425 mL
2 tsp	Chinese five-spice powder	10 mL
1 1/2 tsp	ground ginger	7 mL
2 tsp	baking powder	10 mL
3/4 tsp	baking soda	3 mL
1/2 tsp	salt	2 mL
3/4 cup	granulated sugar	175 mL
1	egg	1
3/4 cup	lower-fat plain yogurt	175 mL
1/4 cup	unsalted butter, melted	60 mL
2 1/2 cups	finely grated carrots	625 mL

Packed with flavorful, wholesome ingredients, these carrot-yogurt muffins make a good snack or breakfast.

Makes 12 muffins

- Preheat oven to 375°F (190°C)
- 12-cup muffin pan, lined with paper liners

1. In a large bowl, whisk together flour, five-spice powder, ginger, baking powder, baking soda and salt.
2. In a medium bowl, whisk together sugar, egg, yogurt and butter until well blended.
3. Add the egg mixture to the flour mixture and stir until just blended. Gently fold in carrots.
4. Divide batter equally among prepared muffin cups.
5. Bake in preheated oven for 19 to 23 minutes or until tops are golden and a toothpick inserted in the center comes out clean. Let cool in pan on a wire rack for 5 minutes, then transfer to the rack to cool.

Sunny Zucchini Muffins

2 cups	all-purpose flour	500 mL
1 tbsp	baking powder	15 mL
3/4 tsp	salt	3 mL
1/2 cup	granulated sugar	125 mL
2	eggs	2
1/2 cup	milk	125 mL
1/3 cup	vegetable oil	75 mL
2 tsp	finely grated lemon zest	10 mL
1 cup	grated zucchini	250 mL
1/2 cup	chopped walnuts, toasted	125 mL
1/2 cup	golden raisins	125 mL

Perfect for anyone looking to add more vegetables to their diet, these tender, moist muffins are delicately scented with lemon and accented with sunny golden raisins.

Makes 12 muffins

- Preheat oven to 400°F (200°C)
- 12-cup muffin pan, greased

1. In a large bowl, whisk together flour, baking powder and salt.
2. In a medium bowl, whisk together sugar and eggs until well blended. Whisk in milk, oil, and lemon zest until blended.
3. Add the egg mixture to the flour mixture and stir until just blended. Gently fold in zucchini, walnuts and raisins.
4. Divide batter equally among prepared muffin cups.
5. Bake in preheated oven for 20 to 25 minutes or until tops are golden and a toothpick inserted in the center comes out clean. Let cool in pan on a wire rack for 5 minutes, then transfer to the rack to cool.

Sweet Potato Marmalade Muffins

Muffins

1 3/4 cups	all-purpose flour	425 mL
1 1/2 tsp	baking powder	7 mL
1 tsp	ground cinnamon	5 mL
1/2 tsp	baking soda	2 mL
1/2 tsp	salt	2 mL
1 cup	drained canned sweet potatoes	250 mL
1/3 cup	packed brown sugar	75 mL
1	egg	1
1/2 cup	buttermilk	125 mL
1/3 cup	orange marmalade	75 mL
1/4 cup	vegetable oil	60 mL

Icing

3/4 cup	confectioners' (icing) sugar	175 mL
1 tbsp	orange marmalade	15 mL
1 tbsp	buttermilk	15 mL
1/2 tsp	vanilla extract	2 mL

These golden muffins are beautiful plain, but if you cannot get enough of a good thing, spread them with more marmalade and a dollop of crème fraîche.

Makes 12 muffins

- Preheat oven to 400°F (200°C)
- 12-cup muffin pan, greased

1. *Muffins:* In a large bowl, whisk together flour, baking powder, cinnamon, baking soda and salt.
2. In a medium bowl, using a potato masher or fork, mash sweet potatoes. Whisk in brown sugar, egg, buttermilk, marmalade and oil until well blended.
3. Add the egg mixture to the flour mixture and stir until just blended.
4. Divide batter equally among prepared muffin cups.
5. Bake in preheated oven for 18 to 22 minutes or until tops are golden and a toothpick inserted in the center comes out clean. Let cool in pan on a wire rack for 3 minutes, then transfer to the rack to cool while you prepare the icing.
6. *Icing:* In a small bowl, whisk together confectioners' sugar, marmalade, buttermilk and vanilla until smooth. Spoon or drizzle over the tops of the warm muffins and let cool.

Pear and Pumpkin Muffins

2½ cups	all-purpose flour	625 mL
2½ tsp	pumpkin pie spice	12 mL
1 tsp	baking soda	5 mL
1 tsp	salt	5 mL
1 cup	granulated sugar	250 mL
2	eggs	2
1 cup	pumpkin purée (not pie filling)	250 mL
½ cup	vegetable oil	125 mL
2 cups	chopped pears	500 mL
⅓ cup	packed light brown sugar	75 mL

This easy-to-make muffin tastes like pumpkin spice cake and pear crisp baked together.

Makes 18 muffins

- Preheat oven to 350°F (180°C)
- Two 12-cup muffin pans, 18 cups greased

1. In a large bowl, whisk together flour, pumpkin pie spice, baking soda and salt.

2. In a medium bowl, whisk together granulated sugar, eggs, pumpkin and oil until well blended. Stir in pears until combined.

3. Add the egg mixture into the flour mixture and stir until just blended.

4. Divide batter equally among prepared muffin cups. Sprinkle with brown sugar.

5. Bake in preheated oven for 30 to 35 minutes or until tops are golden and a toothpick inserted in the center comes out clean. Let cool in pans on a wire rack for 5 minutes, then transfer to the rack to cool.

Sugar Crunch Pumpkin Muffins

2¾ cups	all-purpose flour	675 mL
1 tbsp	baking powder	15 mL
1 tsp	baking soda	5 mL
1 tsp	ground cinnamon	5 mL
½ tsp	salt	2 mL
1 cup	granulated sugar	250 mL
2	eggs	2
1 cup	pumpkin purée (not pie filling)	250 mL
¾ cup	sour cream	175 mL
⅓ cup	milk	75 mL
¼ cup	vegetable oil	60 mL
1 tsp	vanilla extract	5 mL
3 tbsp	turbinado sugar	45 mL

Pumpkin and sour cream are a winning combination in this muffin. It's topped with a generous sprinkle of turbinado sugar, which delivers the eponymous "sugar crunch."

Makes 18 muffins

- Preheat oven to 375°F (190°C)
- Two 12-cup muffin pans, 18 cups greased

1. In a large bowl, whisk together flour, baking powder, baking soda, cinnamon and salt.

2. In a medium bowl, whisk together granulated sugar, eggs, pumpkin, sour cream, milk, oil and vanilla until well blended.

3. Add the egg mixture to the flour mixture and stir until just blended.

4. Divide batter equally among prepared muffin cups. Sprinkle with turbinado sugar.

5. Bake in preheated oven for 24 to 28 minutes or until a toothpick inserted in the center comes out clean. Let cool in pans on a wire rack for 3 minutes, then transfer to the rack to cool.

Date and Walnut Muffins

1 cup	all-purpose flour	250 mL
1 cup	whole wheat flour	250 mL
2 tsp	baking powder	10 mL
1 tsp	ground cinnamon	5 mL
1 tsp	ground ginger	5 mL
1/2 tsp	salt	2 mL
1/4 tsp	baking soda	1 mL
3/4 cup	packed light brown sugar	175 mL
2	eggs	2
3/4 cup	unsweetened applesauce	175 mL
1/2 cup	unsalted butter, melted	125 mL
1/4 cup	buttermilk	60 mL
1/4 cup	liquid honey	60 mL
1 tsp	vanilla	5 mL
3/4 cup	chopped pitted dates	175 mL
3/4 cup	chopped walnuts	175 mL

Makes 12 muffins

- Preheat oven to 400°F (200°C)
- 12-cup muffin pan, greased

1. In a large bowl, whisk together all-purpose flour, whole wheat flour, baking powder, cinnamon, ginger, salt and baking soda.
2. In a medium bowl, whisk together brown sugar, eggs, applesauce, butter, buttermilk, honey and vanilla until well blended.
3. Add the egg mixture to the flour mixture and stir until just blended. Gently fold in dates.
4. Divide batter equally among prepared muffin cups. Sprinkle with walnuts.
5. Bake in preheated oven for 20 to 25 minutes or until puffed and a toothpick inserted in the center comes out clean. Let cool in pan on a wire rack for 5 minutes, then transfer to the rack to cool.

Like many Greek and Middle Eastern desserts, these tender, spiced muffins get both flavor and moisture from the addition of honey.

Pecan and Strawberry Jam Muffins

1 1/2 cups	all-purpose flour	375 mL
1 1/2 tsp	baking powder	7 mL
1/4 tsp	baking soda	1 mL
1/4 tsp	salt	1 mL
1/2 cup	granulated sugar	125 mL
1	egg	1
1 cup	sour cream	250 mL
1/2 cup	unsalted butter, melted	125 mL
1 tsp	vanilla extract	5 mL
1/2 cup	strawberry jam	125 mL
1/2 cup	finely chopped pecans	125 mL

Makes 12 muffins

- Preheat oven to 400°F (200°C)
- 12-cup muffin pan, greased

1. In a large bowl, whisk together flour, baking powder, baking soda and salt.
2. In a medium bowl, whisk together sugar, egg, sour cream, butter and vanilla until well blended.
3. Add the egg mixture to the flour mixture and stir until just blended.
4. Divide half the batter equally among prepared muffin cups. Spoon 2 tsp (10 mL) jam in the center of each cup of batter. Top with the remaining batter and sprinkle with pecans.
5. Bake in preheated oven for 12 to 15 minutes or until tops are golden and pull away from the sides of the pan. Let cool in pan on a wire rack for 3 minutes, then transfer to the rack to cool.

I love the combination of strawberry jam and pecans here, but use your imagination to create different combinations. Some other personal favorites are orange marmalade–walnut, lemon curd–pistachio and grape jelly–peanut.

Chocolate Pecan Multigrain Muffins

1 cup	all-purpose flour	250 mL
1 cup	multigrain hot cereal (see tip, below)	250 mL
1 tsp	salt	5 mL
1 tsp	baking powder	5 mL
1 tsp	baking soda	5 mL
1/2 cup	packed light brown sugar	125 mL
1	egg	1
1/3 cup	unsalted butter, melted	75 mL
1 1/4 cups	buttermilk	300 mL
1/2 cup	miniature semisweet chocolate chips	125 mL
1/2 cup	chopped pecans, toasted	125 mL
3 tbsp	turbinado sugar	45 mL

Tip

There are many multigrain hot cereals available, such as Bob's Red Mill, Hodgson Mill, Quaker Oats or Red River. Just be sure not to use an instant variety.

Makes 12 muffins

- Preheat oven to 400°F (200°C)
- 12-cup muffin pan, lined with paper liners

1. In a large bowl, whisk together flour, multigrain cereal, salt, baking powder and baking soda.

2. In a medium bowl, whisk together brown sugar, egg and butter until well blended. Whisk in buttermilk until blended.

3. Add the egg mixture to the flour mixture and stir until just blended. Gently fold in chocolate chips and pecans.

4. Divide batter equally among prepared muffin cups. Sprinkle with turbinado sugar.

5. Bake in preheated oven for 15 to 18 minutes or until tops are golden and a toothpick inserted in the center comes out clean. Let cool in pan on a wire rack for 5 minutes, then transfer to the rack to cool.

Banana Crumb Cake Muffins

Topping

1/3 cup	packed light brown sugar	75 mL
2 tbsp	all-purpose flour	30 mL
1/4 tsp	ground cinnamon	1 mL
2 tbsp	unsalted butter, melted	30 mL

Muffins

1 1/2 cups	all-purpose flour	375 mL
1 tsp	baking soda	5 mL
1 tsp	baking powder	5 mL
1/2 tsp	salt	2 mL
3/4 cup	granulated sugar	175 mL
1	egg	1
1 1/3 cups	mashed ripe bananas	325 mL
1/2 cup	unsalted butter, melted	125 mL
1 tsp	vanilla extract	5 mL

These muffins are based on a coffee cake I used to make from a flour package. It's boastful of me to say, but my muffins are even better than the original.

Makes 12 muffins

- Preheat oven to 375°F (190°C)
- 12-cup muffin pan, lined with paper liners

1. *Topping:* In a small bowl, combine brown sugar, flour, cinnamon and butter until blended and crumbly. Set aside.

2. *Muffins:* In a large bowl, whisk together flour, baking soda, baking powder and salt.

3. In a medium bowl, whisk together sugar, egg, bananas, butter and vanilla until well blended.

4. Add the egg mixture to the flour mixture until just blended.

5. Divide batter equally among prepared muffin cups. Sprinkle with topping.

6. Bake in preheated oven for 18 to 22 minutes or until tops are golden and a toothpick inserted in the center comes out clean. Let cool in pan on a wire rack for 3 minutes, then transfer to the rack to cool.

Pistachio Citrus Muffins

Topping

$2/3$ cup	all-purpose flour	150 mL
$1/4$ cup	packed light brown sugar	60 mL
1 tsp	finely grated lemon zest	5 mL
$1/2$ cup	chopped pistachios	125 mL
$1/4$ cup	unsalted butter, melted	60 mL

Muffins

1	can (15 oz/425 g) mandarin oranges (or $1 1/2$ cans, each 10 oz/287 mL), drained	1
2 cups	all-purpose flour	500 mL
2 tsp	baking powder	10 mL
$1/2$ tsp	baking soda	2 mL
$1/2$ tsp	salt	2 mL
$3/4$ cup	granulated sugar	175 mL
2	eggs	2
$1/2$ cup	vegetable oil	125 mL
2 tsp	finely grated lemon zest	10 mL
$1/2$ cup	milk	125 mL
1 tbsp	freshly squeezed lemon juice	15 mL

I have always loved the combination of pistachios and citrus; the acidity of the latter partners so well with the richness of the former. As exemplar, I offer these incredible muffins.

Makes 12 muffins

- Preheat oven to 375°F (190°C)
- 12-cup muffin pan, lined with paper liners

1. *Topping:* In a small bowl, combine flour, brown sugar, lemon zest, pistachios and butter until blended. Refrigerate until ready to use.

2. *Muffins:* Pat mandarin oranges dry between paper towels. Transfer to a cutting board and coarsely chop.

3. In a large bowl, whisk together flour, baking powder, baking soda and salt.

4. In a medium bowl, whisk together granulated sugar, eggs, oil and lemon zest until well blended. Whisk in milk and lemon juice until blended.

5. Add the egg mixture to the flour mixture and stir until just blended. Gently fold in mandarin oranges.

6. Divide batter equally among prepared muffin cups. Sprinkle with topping and press lightly into batter.

7. Bake in preheated oven for 25 to 30 minutes or until tops are golden and a toothpick inserted in the center comes out clean. Let cool in pan on a wire rack for 3 minutes, then transfer to the rack to cool.

French Toast Muffins

Topping

3 tbsp	milk	45 mL
1	egg	1
3½ cups	cubed firm white bread	875 mL

Muffins

2 cups	all-purpose flour	500 mL
2 tsp	baking powder	10 mL
2 tsp	ground cinnamon, divided	10 mL
½ tsp	salt	2 mL
¾ cup	packed light brown sugar	175 mL
1	egg	1
½ cup	unsalted butter, melted	125 mL
1 tsp	vanilla extract	5 mL
1 cup	milk	250 mL
¼ cup	pure maple syrup	60 mL
2 tbsp	granulated sugar	30 mL

Here, French toast is as timeless as ever, reinvented in muffin form. You can remove the crust from the bread, but I prefer to leave it on.

Makes 12 muffins

- Preheat oven to 375°F (190°C)
- 12-cup muffin pan, greased

1. *Topping:* In a medium bowl, whisk together milk and egg until blended. Stir in bread, tossing to coat. Set aside.

2. *Muffins:* In a large bowl, whisk together flour, baking powder, 1½ tsp (7 mL) of the cinnamon and the salt.

3. In a medium bowl, whisk together brown sugar, egg, butter and vanilla until well blended. Whisk in milk until blended.

4. Add the egg mixture to the flour mixture and stir until just blended.

5. Divide batter equally among prepared muffin cups. Spoon topping evenly over batter and press lightly into batter.

6. Bake in preheated oven for 21 to 26 minutes or until a toothpick inserted in the center comes out clean.

7. Immediately brush the warm muffins with maple syrup. In a small bowl, combine the remaining cinnamon and granulated sugar and sprinkle over muffins. Let cool in pan on a wire rack for 3 minutes, then transfer to the rack to cool slightly. Serve warm.

"Better Than Danishes" Almond Jam Muffins

1¼ cups	whole wheat flour	300 mL
1 cup	all-purpose flour	250 mL
1½ tsp	baking powder	7 mL
½ tsp	baking soda	2 mL
¼ tsp	salt	1 mL
½ cup	packed light brown sugar	125 mL
2	eggs	2
1 cup	buttermilk	250 mL
¼ cup	unsweetened orange juice	60 mL
¼ cup	vegetable oil	60 mL
1 tsp	vanilla extract	5 mL
½ tsp	almond extract	2 mL
⅓ cup	blackberry, blueberry, raspberry or cherry jam	75 mL
½ cup	sliced almonds	125 mL
1 tbsp	granulated sugar	15 mL

Reminiscent of some of my favorite Swedish and Danish pastries, these almond-flecked muffins are rich with good-for-you ingredients.

Makes 12 muffins

- Preheat oven to 400°F (200°C)
- 12-cup muffin pan, greased

1. In a large bowl, whisk together whole wheat flour, all-purpose flour, baking powder, baking soda and salt.

2. In a medium bowl, whisk together brown sugar and eggs until well blended. Whisk in buttermilk, orange juice, oil, vanilla and almond extract until blended.

3. Add the egg mixture to the flour mixture and stir until just blended.

4. Divide half the batter equally among prepared muffin cups. Spoon a generous teaspoon (5 mL) jam in the center of each cup of batter. Top with the remaining batter and sprinkle with almonds and granulated sugar.

5. Bake in preheated oven for 22 to 25 minutes or until tops are golden and a toothpick inserted in the center comes out clean. Let cool in pan on a wire rack for 3 minutes, then transfer to the rack to cool.

Pineapple Upside-Down Muffins

1/4 cup	packed light brown sugar, divided	60 mL
1	can (10 oz/287 mL) pineapple slices, drained	1

Muffins

3/4 cup	whole wheat flour	175 mL
3/4 cup	all-purpose flour	175 mL
1/2 cup	large-flake (old-fashioned) rolled oats	125 mL
1 tbsp	ground cinnamon	15 mL
2 tsp	baking powder	10 mL
1/2 tsp	baking soda	2 mL
1/2 tsp	salt	2 mL
1/2 cup	packed light brown sugar	125 mL
2	eggs	2
1/4 cup	vegetable oil	60 mL
2 tbsp	unsweetened orange juice	30 mL
1 tsp	vanilla extract	5 mL
1	can (8 oz/227 mL) crushed pineapple with juice	1
1 cup	shredded carrots	250 mL
3/4 cup	raisins	175 mL

Top down is the way to go for these cinnamon-spiced muffins, loaded with carrots and raisins.

Makes 12 muffins

- Preheat oven to 400°F (200°C)
- 12-cup muffin pan, greased

Topping

1. *Topping:* Sprinkle 1 tsp (5 mL) brown sugar into each prepared muffin cup. Stack pineapple slices and cut into 3 wedges. Place 2 wedges in each muffin cup. Set aside.

2. *Muffins:* In a large bowl, whisk together whole wheat flour, all-purpose flour, oats, cinnamon, baking powder, baking soda and salt.

3. In a medium bowl, whisk together brown sugar and eggs until well blended. Whisk in oil, orange juice and vanilla until blended. Stir in crushed pineapple.

4. Add the egg mixture to the flour mixture and stir until just blended. Gently fold in carrots and raisins.

5. Divide batter equally among prepared muffin cups.

6. Bake in preheated oven for 18 to 23 minutes or until tops are golden and a toothpick inserted in the center comes out clean.

7. Immediately run a knife around edges of cups and turn muffins out onto a baking sheet. Reposition any stray pineapple pieces. Let cool for at least 10 minutes. Serve upside down, either warm or at room temperature.

Jelly Doughnut Muffins

1¾ cups	all-purpose flour	425 mL
1½ tsp	baking powder	7 mL
½ tsp	salt	2 mL
½ tsp	ground nutmeg	2 mL
1 cup	granulated sugar, divided	250 mL
1	egg	1
⅓ cup	vegetable oil	75 mL
¾ cup	milk	175 mL
⅓ cup	seedless raspberry preserves	75 mL
1 tsp	ground cinnamon	5 mL
¼ cup	unsalted butter, melted	60 mL

Anyone who's ever enjoyed a fresh jelly doughnut from the local bakery will understand the appeal of these muffins. Brushing the muffins with butter while they are still warm from the oven makes them taste fried rather than baked.

Makes 10 muffins

- Preheat oven to 350°F (180°C)
- 12-cup muffin pan, 10 cups lined with paper liners

1. In a large bowl, whisk together flour, baking powder, salt and nutmeg.
2. In a medium bowl, whisk together ¾ cup (175 mL) of the sugar, egg and oil until well blended. Whisk in milk until blended.
3. Add the egg mixture to the flour mixture and stir until just blended.
4. Divide batter equally among prepared muffin cups. Drop a heaping teaspoon (5 mL) of preserves on top of each muffin (the preserves will sink as the muffins bake).
5. Bake in preheated oven for 20 to 25 minutes or until tops are golden and a toothpick inserted in the center comes out clean. Let cool in pan on a wire rack for 3 minutes, then transfer to the rack to cool while you prepare the topping.
6. In a small bowl, combine the remaining sugar with cinnamon. Generously brush warm muffin tops with butter, then sprinkle with cinnamon mixture. Let cool.

Peanut Butter and Jelly Muffins

2 cups	all-purpose flour	500 mL
1 tbsp	baking powder	15 mL
1 tsp	salt	5 mL
⅔ cup	packed light brown sugar	150 mL
2	eggs	2
1 cup	creamy peanut butter	250 mL
1 tsp	vanilla extract	5 mL
1 cup	milk	250 mL
½ cup	strawberry jam	125 mL

If you love peanut butter, these muffins are for you. I created them for my dad, Daniel, a lifelong, die-hard peanut butter fanatic (his father was the same). They are very peanut-buttery, yet still light, and the bright strawberry jam centers are the perfect complement.

Makes 12 muffins

- Preheat oven to 400°F (200°C)
- 12-cup muffin pan, lined with paper liners

1. In a large bowl, whisk together flour, baking powder and salt.
2. In a medium bowl, whisk together brown sugar, eggs, peanut butter and vanilla until well blended. Whisk in milk until blended.
3. Add the egg mixture to the flour mixture and stir until just blended.
4. Divide half the batter equally among prepared muffin cups. Spoon 2 tsp (10 mL) jam in the center of each cup of batter. Top with the remaining batter.
5. Bake in preheated oven for 18 to 21 minutes or until tops are golden and a toothpick inserted in the center comes out clean. Let cool in pan on a wire rack for 3 minutes, then transfer to the rack to cool.

Mincemeat Muffins

2 cups	all-purpose flour	500 mL
1 tbsp	baking powder	15 mL
1/4 tsp	salt	1 mL
2/3 cup	granulated sugar	150 mL
2	eggs	2
1/2 cup	whole milk	125 mL
1/3 cup	unsalted butter, melted	75 mL
1 tbsp	finely grated orange zest	15 mL
2/3 cup	prepared mincemeat	150 mL

Prepared mincemeat, a compote of apples and raisins, makes fantastic muffins that are the ideal choice for winter holiday mornings.

Tip

Do not used condensed mincemeat, which is dry and crumbly and requires the addition of water before use.

Makes 12 muffins

- Preheat oven to 400°F (200°C)
- 12-cup muffin pan, lined with paper liners

1. In a large bowl, whisk together flour, baking powder and salt.

2. In a medium bowl, whisk together sugar, eggs, milk, butter and orange zest until well blended. Stir in mincemeat until blended.

3. Add the egg mixture to the flour mixture, stirring until just blended.

4. Divide batter equally among prepared muffin cups.

5. Bake in preheated oven for 22 to 25 minutes or until tops are light golden brown and toothpick inserted in the center comes out clean. Let cool in pan on a wire rack for 5 minutes, then transfer to the rack to cool.

Citrus Coffeecake Muffins

Topping

1/4 cup	chopped pecans	60 mL
1/4 cup	packed light brown sugar	60 mL
2 tbsp	all-purpose flour	30 mL
1 tbsp	unsalted butter, melted	15 mL
1 tsp	finely grated lemon zest	5 mL

Muffins

1 1/2 cups	all-purpose flour	375 mL
2 tsp	baking powder	10 mL
1/2 tsp	salt	2 mL
1/2 cup	granulated sugar	125 mL
1	egg	1
1 cup	milk	250 mL
1/2 cup	unsalted butter, melted	125 mL
3 tbsp	thawed frozen orange juice concentrate	45 mL
2 tsp	finely grated lemon zest	10 mL

Nutty and fragrant with citrus, these muffins are equally delicious a day or two after baking.

Makes 12 muffins

- Preheat oven to 400°F (200°C)
- 12-cup muffin pan, greased

1. *Topping:* In a small bowl, combine pecans, brown sugar, flour, butter and lemon zest until blended. Refrigerate until ready to use.

2. *Muffins:* In a large bowl, whisk together flour, baking powder and salt.

3. In a medium bowl, whisk together sugar, egg, milk, butter, orange juice concentrate and lemon zest until well blended

4. Add the egg mixture to the flour mixture and stir until just blended.

5. Divide batter equally among prepared muffin cups. Sprinkle with topping.

6. Bake in preheated oven for 14 to 17 minutes or until tops are golden and a toothpick inserted in the center comes out clean. Let cool in pan on a wire rack for 5 minutes, then transfer to the rack to cool.

Lemon Thyme Corn Muffins

2 cups	all-purpose flour	500 mL
1 cup	yellow cornmeal	250 mL
1½ tsp	baking powder	7 mL
1½ tsp	dried thyme	7 mL
1 tsp	baking soda	5 mL
½ tsp	salt	2 mL
¾ cup	granulated sugar	175 mL
2	eggs	2
1¼ cups	buttermilk	300 mL
½ cup	unsalted butter, melted	125 mL
1 tbsp	finely grated lemon zest	15 mL
½ cup	golden raisins	125 mL
½ cup	toasted pine nuts	125 mL

Don't be thrown by the addition of a savory herb to a sweet muffin; thyme and lemon are a culinary match made in heaven. You'll find these tender muffins so delicious, they'll disappear in no time.

Makes 12 muffins

- Preheat oven to 400°F (200°C)
- 12-cup muffin pan, greased

1. In a large bowl, whisk together flour, cornmeal, baking powder, thyme, baking soda and salt.
2. In a medium bowl, whisk together sugar and eggs until well blended. Whisk in buttermilk, butter and lemon zest until blended.
3. Add the egg mixture to the flour mixture and stir until just blended. Gently fold in raisins and pine nuts.
4. Divide batter equally among prepared muffin cups.
5. Bake in preheated oven for 17 to 20 minutes or until tops are light golden brown and a toothpick inserted in the center comes out clean. Let cool in pan on a wire rack for 5 minutes, then transfer to the rack to cool.

Polenta Peach Muffins

1½ cups	all-purpose flour	375 mL
1 cup	quick-cooking polenta or yellow cornmeal	250 mL
1 tbsp	baking powder	15 mL
¼ tsp	salt	1 mL
1 cup	granulated sugar	250 mL
2	eggs	2
1 cup	whole milk	250 mL
½ cup	unsalted butter, melted	125 mL
1 tbsp	finely grated lemon zest	15 mL
1½ cups	chopped fresh or thawed frozen peaches	375 mL
2 tbsp	granulated sugar	30 mL

These polenta muffins are mildly sweet, with a delicate crunch and rich corn flavor. For a delicious twist, try any other stone fruit — plums, apricots or nectarines — in place of the peaches.

Makes 12 muffins

- Preheat oven to 375°F (190°C)
- 12-cup muffin pan, lined with paper liners

1. In a large bowl, whisk together flour, polenta, baking powder and salt.
2. In a medium bowl, whisk together the 1 cup (250 mL) sugar, eggs, milk, butter and lemon zest until well blended.
3. Add the egg mixture to the polenta mixture and stir until just combined. Gently fold in peaches.
4. Divide batter equally among prepared muffin cups. Sprinkle with the 2 tbsp (30 mL) sugar.
5. Bake in preheated oven for 22 to 27 minutes or until tops are golden and a toothpick inserted in the center comes out clean. Let cool in pan on a wire rack for 5 minutes, then transfer to the rack to cool.

Berry Corn Muffins

1 cup	yellow cornmeal	250 mL
1 cup	all-purpose flour	250 mL
1 tsp	baking powder	5 mL
1 tsp	baking soda	5 mL
1/4 tsp	salt	1 mL
1/2 cup	granulated sugar	125 mL
2	eggs	2
1 1/4 cups	plain yogurt	300 mL
1/4 cup	unsalted butter, melted	60 mL
2 tsp	finely grated orange zest	10 mL
1 1/4 cups	raspberries or blueberries	300 mL

Yellow cornmeal stands in for half the flour in these not-too-sweet berry muffins. I love the textural differences between the crunch of the cornmeal and the lushness of the berries — it sings summer.

Tip

If using frozen berries, do not thaw before adding to batter; if thawed, the berries will bleed into the batter. If using frozen blueberries, opt for wild blueberries.

Makes 12 muffins

- Preheat oven to 375°F (190°C)
- 12-cup muffin pan, greased

1. In a large bowl, whisk together cornmeal, flour, baking powder, baking soda and salt.

2. In a medium bowl, whisk together sugar, eggs, yogurt, butter and orange zest until well blended.

3. Add the egg mixture to the flour mixture and stir until just blended. Gently fold in raspberries.

4. Divide batter equally among prepared muffin cups.

5. Bake in preheated oven for 18 to 22 minutes or until a toothpick inserted in the center comes out clean. Let cool in pan on a wire rack for 5 minutes, then transfer to the rack to cool.

Pecan Cornmeal Muffins

2¼ cups	all-purpose flour	550 mL
¾ cup	yellow cornmeal	175 mL
1 tbsp	baking powder	15 mL
¾ tsp	salt	3 mL
½ tsp	ground cinnamon	2 mL
½ tsp	baking soda	2 mL
¾ cup	packed dark brown sugar	175 mL
2	eggs	2
½ cup	unsalted butter, melted	125 mL
¼ cup	vegetable oil	60 mL
1 tsp	vanilla extract	5 mL
1½ cups	buttermilk	375 mL
1 cup	chopped pecans, toasted	250 mL

I based these flavorful muffins on anadama bread, a traditional New England yeast bread made with cornmeal and molasses. I use dark brown sugar in place of the molasses, but the caramel notes are still prominent and pair deliciously with the toasted pecans.

Makes 16 muffins

- Preheat oven to 400°F (200°C)
- Two 12-cup muffin pans, 16 cups lined with paper liners

1. In a large bowl, whisk together flour, cornmeal, baking powder, salt, cinnamon and baking soda.

2. In a medium bowl, whisk together brown sugar and eggs until well blended. Whisk in butter, oil and vanilla until blended. Whisk in buttermilk.

3. Add the egg mixture to the flour mixture and stir until just blended. Gently fold in pecans.

4. Divide batter equally among prepared muffin cups.

5. Bake in preheated oven for 15 to 18 minutes or until tops are golden and a toothpick inserted in the center comes out clean. Let cool in pans on a wire rack for 5 minutes, then transfer to the rack to cool.

Canadian Bacon Brunch Muffins

2 cups	all-purpose flour	500 mL
1 cup	whole wheat flour	250 mL
1 tbsp	baking powder	15 mL
$\frac{1}{2}$ tsp	baking soda	2 mL
$\frac{1}{2}$ tsp	freshly ground pepper	2 mL
$\frac{1}{4}$ tsp	salt	1 mL
2	eggs	2
$1\frac{1}{3}$ cups	buttermilk	325 mL
$\frac{1}{3}$ cup	vegetable oil	75 mL
1 cup	thinly sliced green onions	250 mL
$\frac{3}{4}$ cup	diced Canadian bacon	175 mL
$\frac{1}{2}$ cup	shredded sharp (old) Cheddar cheese	125 mL
$\frac{1}{2}$ cup	finely diced red bell pepper	125 mL

Even if you're partial to the well-known breakfast sandwich with egg, cheese and Canadian bacon, you'll eschew it once you try this much healthier, and far more delicious, alternative.

Makes 12 muffins

- Preheat oven to 400°F (200°C)
- 12-cup muffin pan, greased

1. In a large bowl, whisk together all-purpose flour, whole wheat flour, baking powder, baking soda, pepper and salt.
2. In a medium bowl, whisk together eggs, buttermilk and oil until well blended. Stir in green onions, bacon, cheese and red pepper.
3. Add the egg mixture to the flour mixture and stir until just blended.
4. Divide batter equally among prepared muffin cups.
5. Bake in preheated oven for 20 to 25 minutes or until tops are golden and a toothpick inserted in the center comes out clean. Let cool in pan on a wire rack for 3 minutes, then transfer to the rack to cool.

Maple Bacon Muffins

2 cups	all-purpose flour	500 mL
$\frac{3}{4}$ cup	crumbled cooked bacon	175 mL
1 tbsp	baking powder	15 mL
$\frac{1}{4}$ tsp	salt	1 mL
1	egg	1
$\frac{2}{3}$ cup	pure maple syrup	150 mL
$\frac{1}{2}$ cup	milk	125 mL
$\frac{1}{2}$ cup	vegetable oil	125 mL

If you're tired of too-sweet breakfast muffins, or just love the combination of salty and sweet, then try these — you'll love the smoky flavor from the bacon and the mellow sweetness of the maple syrup.

Makes 12 muffins

- Preheat oven to 400°F (200°C)
- 12-cup muffin pan, lined with paper liners

1. In a large bowl, whisk together flour, bacon, baking powder and salt.
2. In a medium bowl, whisk together egg, maple syrup, milk and oil until well blended.
3. Add the egg mixture to the flour mixture and stir until just blended.
4. Divide batter equally among prepared muffin cups.
5. Bake in preheated oven for 21 to 25 minutes or until tops are golden and a toothpick inserted in the center comes out clean. Let cool in pan on a wire rack for 3 minutes, then transfer to the rack to cool.

Bacon Apple Muffins

2 cups	all-purpose flour	500 mL
1¼ tsp	baking soda	6 mL
¼ tsp	salt	1 mL
¼ tsp	freshly ground black pepper	1 mL
8	slices bacon, coarsely chopped	8
⅓ cup	unsalted butter	75 mL
2 cups	chopped peeled tart-sweet apples, such as Braeburn, Gala or Pippin	500 mL
3 tbsp	granulated sugar	45 mL
1	egg	1
1¼ cups	buttermilk	300 mL

These not-so-humble muffins pack a range of flavors: tangy, smoky and tart-sweet. They add up to irresistible.

Makes 12 muffins

- Preheat oven to 400°F (200°C)
- 12-cup muffin pan, lined with paper liners

1. In a large bowl, whisk together flour, baking soda, salt and pepper.
2. In a large skillet, cook bacon over medium heat, stirring, until crisp. Using a slotted spoon, transfer bacon to a small bowl.
3. Add butter to the bacon fat in skillet and melt over medium heat. Add apples and cook, stirring frequently, for 4 to 5 minutes or until softened. Remove from heat and return bacon to pan.
4. In a medium bowl, whisk together sugar, egg and buttermilk until well blended.
5. Add the egg mixture and the bacon mixture to the flour mixture and stir until just blended.
6. Divide batter equally among prepared muffin cups.
7. Bake in preheated oven for 19 to 22 minutes or until tops are golden and a toothpick inserted in the center comes out clean. Let cool in pan on a wire rack for 5 minutes, then transfer to the rack to cool.

Toad-in-the-Hole Muffins

2 cups	all-purpose flour	500 mL
½ cup	yellow cornmeal	125 mL
2 tsp	baking powder	10 mL
1 tsp	salt	5 mL
3 tbsp	packed light brown sugar	45 mL
2	eggs	2
½ cup	unsalted butter, melted	125 mL
1 cup	milk	250 mL
1 cup	thawed frozen corn kernels	250 mL
12 oz	kielbasa sausage, cut crosswise into 12 equal pieces	375 g

Savory sausage muffins are ideal for breakfast on the run. This particular version is based on toad-in-the-hole, a traditional English dish made of sausages in Yorkshire pudding.

Makes 12 muffins

- Preheat oven to 375°F (190°C)
- 12-cup muffin pan, greased

1. In a large bowl, whisk together flour, cornmeal, baking powder and salt.
2. In a medium bowl, whisk together brown sugar, eggs and butter until well blended. Whisk in milk until blended.
3. Add the egg mixture to the flour mixture and stir until just blended. Gently fold in corn.
4. Divide batter equally among prepared muffin cups. Press 1 piece of sausage down into the center of each cup of batter until almost covered.
5. Bake in preheated oven for 18 to 22 minutes or until tops are golden and a toothpick inserted in the center comes out clean. Let cool in pan on a wire rack for 5 minutes, then transfer to the rack to cool.

Cheese Grits Muffins

1 cup	all-purpose flour	250 mL
1 cup	quick-cooking hominy grits	250 mL
1 tsp	baking powder	5 mL
3/4 tsp	baking soda	3 mL
1/2 tsp	salt	2 mL
1 tbsp	granulated sugar	15 mL
1	egg	1
1 1/2 cups	buttermilk	375 mL
1/3 cup	unsalted butter, melted	75 mL
1/2 tsp	hot pepper sauce	2 mL
1 1/2 cups	shredded sharp (old) Cheddar cheese, divided	375 mL
2 tbsp	minced fresh chives (optional)	30 mL

Cheese grits are pure comfort food, so it was pure pleasure developing a muffin version. Much like cornmeal, the grits add toothsome crunch; the hot pepper sauce, buttermilk, butter and cheese make these muffins undeniably Southern.

Makes 12 muffins

- Preheat oven to 400°F (200°C)
- 12-cup muffin pan, greased

1. In a large bowl, whisk together flour, grits, baking powder, baking soda and salt.

2. In a medium bowl, whisk together sugar, egg, buttermilk, butter and hot pepper sauce until well blended.

3. Add the egg mixture to the flour mixture and stir until just blended. Gently fold in 1 cup (250 mL) of the cheese and chives (if using).

4. Divide batter equally among prepared muffin cups. Sprinkle with the remaining cheese.

5. Bake in preheated oven for 20 to 25 minutes or until a toothpick inserted in the center comes out clean. Let cool in pan on a wire rack for 3 minutes, then transfer to the rack to cool.

Coffeehouse Muffins

• •

The word "coffeehouse" implies far more than a place to grab a cup of joe. It conveys relaxation, rejuvenation, style and spirit, a space to catch up or slow down, and (topping my list) a place to indulge in a rich confection. The muffins in this chapter are just that: decidedly decadent with a bit of something extra added, something that sets them apart as special and exceptionally fine, but not burdensome to prepare and enjoy. As you peruse the options, you will note that each recipe has its own distinct persona. The Vanilla Rice Pudding Muffins are cozy. You imagine a chilly afternoon, a great book and a broken-in easy chair. Lavender Lemon Muffins, on the other hand, are refined, almost elegant, perfect for a tea party, a bridal shower or an afternoon in the garden. The Salted Caramel Chocolate Muffins pull out all the stops. *You* decide the occasion. Coffee with a friend? A sweet surprise for a spouse? Saturday breakfast in bed? Maybe all three. One thing I am sure of: wonderful treats are in store.

continued...

Apple Pie Muffins

Topping

1/4 cup	packed light brown sugar	60 mL
3 tbsp	all-purpose flour	45 mL
2 tbsp	unsalted butter, melted	30 mL
1/4 tsp	ground cinnamon	1 mL

Muffins

2 cups	all-purpose flour	500 mL
2 1/2 tsp	baking powder	12 mL
1 1/4 tsp	ground cinnamon	6 mL
1/2 tsp	baking soda	2 mL
1/2 tsp	salt	2 mL
1 cup	granulated sugar	250 mL
2	eggs	2
1/4 cup	unsalted butter, melted	60 mL
1 cup	sour cream	250 mL
1 1/2 cups	chopped peeled tart-sweet apples, such as Braeburn, Gala or Pippin	375 mL

These indispensible muffins are perfect any morning, any day of the year.

Makes 16 muffins

- Preheat oven to 400°F (200°C)
- Two 12-cup muffin pans, 16 cups lined with paper liners

1. *Topping:* In a small bowl, using your fingers or a fork, combine brown sugar, flour, butter and cinnamon until blended and crumbly. Refrigerate until ready to use.

2. *Muffins:* In a large bowl, whisk together flour, baking powder, cinnamon, baking soda and salt.

3. In a medium bowl, whisk together sugar, eggs and butter until well blended. Whisk in sour cream until blended.

4. Add the egg mixture to the flour mixture and stir until just blended. Gently fold in apples.

5. Divide batter equally among prepared muffin cups. Sprinkle with topping.

6. Bake in preheated oven for 17 to 20 minutes or until tops are golden and a toothpick inserted in the center comes out clean. Let cool in pans on a wire rack for 5 minutes, then transfer to the rack to cool.

Caramel Apple Muffins

Muffins

1½ lbs	small tart apples, preferably Granny Smith (6 to 7)	750 g
2 to 3 tbsp	butter, divided (approx.)	30 to 45 mL
1½ cups	all-purpose flour	375 mL
1 tsp	baking powder	5 mL
1 tsp	ground cinnamon	5 mL
½ tsp	baking soda	2 mL
½ tsp	salt	2 mL
1 cup	granulated sugar	250 mL
2	eggs	2
⅓ cup	vegetable oil	75 mL
1 tsp	vanilla extract	5 mL
1¼ cups	chopped pecans, toasted, divided	300 mL

Frosting

1	can (14 oz or 300 mL) sweetened condensed milk	1
¼ cup	packed light brown sugar	60 mL
¼ cup	unsalted butter	60 mL
1 tsp	vanilla extract	5 mL

Any baked apple concoction — baked apples, apple pie, apple cake, apple dumpling — you name it, I love it. These muffins are no exception. They require a bit more time than most muffins, but they are worth it.

Makes 12 muffins

- Preheat oven to 350°F (180°C)
- 12-cup muffin pan, greased

1. *Muffins:* Peel, core and cut 2 of the apples into six ¼-inch (0.5 cm) rings each.

2. In a skillet, melt 1 tbsp (15 mL) butter over medium heat. Working in batches, sauté apple rings for 1 to 2 minutes per side or until lightly browned. Transfer 1 ring to the bottom of each prepared muffin cup. Add more butter to the skillet, 1 tbsp (15 mL) at a time, between batches.

3. Peel, core and finely chop enough remaining apples to equal 1½ cups (375 mL).

4. In a medium bowl, whisk together flour, baking powder, cinnamon, baking soda and salt.

5. In a large bowl, whisk together sugar, eggs, oil and vanilla until well blended.

6. Add the egg mixture to the flour mixture and stir until just combined. Gently fold in chopped apples and ½ cup (125 mL) of the pecans.

7. Divide batter equally on top of apple rings in prepared muffin cups.

8. Bake in preheated oven for 23 to 26 minutes or until tops are golden and a toothpick inserted in the center comes out clean. Let cool in pan on a wire rack for 5 minutes, then invert onto the rack.

9. *Frosting:* In a medium saucepan, combine condensed milk, brown sugar and butter; bring to a boil over medium heat. Reduce heat to low and cook, stirring, for 3 to 5 minutes or until thickened to pudding consistency. Remove from heat.

10. Gently press the handle of a wooden spoon straight down into each muffin, at the center of each apple ring, making a 1-inch (2.5 cm) deep indentation. Spoon warm frosting over top, dividing equally and filling indentations. Sprinkle with the remaining pecans. Let cool.

Cranberry Orange Nut Muffins (page 453)
and Lemon Poppy Seed Muffins (page 458)

Raspberry Oat Muffins (page 50)

Pineapple Upside-Down Muffins (page 84)

Mango Morning Muffins (page 60)

Banana, Walnut and Chocolate Chunk Muffins (page 97)

Sparkling Rhubarb Muffins (page 108)

Italian Chocolate Surprise Muffins (page 126)

Antipasto Muffins (page 196)

Banana, Walnut and Chocolate Chunk Muffins

Topping

1/2 cup	all-purpose flour	125 mL
1/2 cup	packed dark brown sugar	125 mL
3 tbsp	unsalted butter, melted	45 mL
1/2 tsp	vanilla extract	2 mL

Muffins

2 cups	all-purpose flour	500 mL
2 tsp	baking powder	10 mL
1/2 tsp	baking soda	2 mL
1/2 tsp	salt	2 mL
3/4 cup	granulated sugar	175 mL
1	egg	1
1 1/3 cups	mashed ripe bananas	325 mL
1/2 cup	vegetable oil	125 mL
1 cup	plain yogurt	250 mL
1 cup	chopped walnuts, toasted	250 mL
1 cup	semisweet chocolate chunks	250 mL

These banana muffins are full of dark chocolate chunks and toasted walnuts, so you get a taste of nuts and chocolate in each bite. The combination of ripe, mashed bananas and yogurt in the batter renders extremely moist and tender results.

Makes 18 muffins

- Preheat oven to 400°F (200°C)
- Two 12-cup muffin pans, 18 cups lined with paper liners

1. *Topping:* In a small bowl, combine flour, brown sugar, butter and vanilla until blended and crumbly. Refrigerate until ready to use.

2. *Muffins:* In a large bowl, whisk together flour, baking powder, baking soda and salt.

3. In a medium bowl, whisk together sugar, egg, bananas and oil until well blended. Whisk in yogurt until blended.

4. Add the egg mixture to the flour mixture and stir until just blended. Gently fold in walnuts and chocolate.

5. Divide batter equally among prepared muffin cups. Sprinkle with topping.

6. Bake in preheated oven for 18 to 21 minutes or until a toothpick inserted in the center comes out clean. Let cool in pans on a wire rack for 5 minutes, then transfer to the rack to cool.

Chunky Double Banana Muffins

1 1/2 cups	all-purpose flour	375 mL
1 tsp	baking powder	5 mL
3/4 tsp	baking soda	3 mL
1/2 tsp	salt	2 mL
1/4 tsp	ground nutmeg	1 mL
1 cup	packed light brown sugar	250 mL
2	eggs	2
1/3 cup	vegetable oil	75 mL
1 tbsp	finely grated lime zest	15 mL
1 tsp	vanilla extract	5 mL
1 cup	mashed ripe banana	250 mL
1	large ripe banana, peeled and cut into 1/4-inch (0.5 cm) pieces	1

A great way to use ripe bananas, these easy-to-make muffins incorporate everything you love about banana bread in a more refined manner that really showcases the bananas.

Makes 12 muffins

- Preheat oven to 325°F (160°C)
- 12-cup muffin pan, lined with paper liners

1. In a large bowl, whisk together flour, baking powder, baking soda, salt and nutmeg.
2. In a medium bowl, whisk together brown sugar, eggs, oil, lime zest and vanilla until blended. Stir in mashed banana.
3. Add the egg mixture to the flour mixture and stir until just blended. Gently fold in banana pieces.
4. Divide batter among prepared muffin cups.
5. Bake in preheated oven for 22 to 25 minutes or until tops are golden and a toothpick inserted in the center comes out clean. Let cool in pan on a wire rack for 3 minutes, then transfer to the rack to cool.

Bananas Foster Muffins

1 1/2 cups	all-purpose flour	375 mL
1 1/2 tsp	baking powder	7 mL
1/4 tsp	salt	1 mL
1/4 tsp	ground nutmeg	1 mL
2/3 cup	packed light brown sugar	150 mL
1	egg	1
1 cup	mashed ripe bananas	250 mL
1/2 cup	unsalted butter, melted	125 mL
2 tbsp	milk	30 mL
2 tbsp	brandy	30 mL
1 cup	diced firm ripe bananas	250 mL

Bananas Foster, a favorite New Orleans dessert, was created at Brennan's restaurant in the French Quarter in the 1950s. It was named for a regular customer, Dick Foster. It never fails to please, whether in the traditional preparation or in my new-fangled muffin interpretation.

Makes 12 muffins

- Preheat oven to 350°F (180°C)
- 12-cup muffin pan, lined with paper liners

1. In a large bowl, whisk together flour, baking powder, salt and nutmeg.
2. In a medium bowl, whisk together brown sugar, egg, mashed bananas, butter, milk and brandy until well blended.
3. Add the egg mixture to the flour mixture and stir until just blended. Gently fold in diced bananas.
4. Divide batter equally among prepared muffin cups.
5. Bake in preheated oven for 25 to 30 minutes or until tops are pale golden and a toothpick inserted in the center comes out clean. Let cool in pan on a wire rack for 5 minutes, then transfer to the rack to cool.

Piña Colada Muffins

2 cups	all-purpose flour	500 mL
3/4 tsp	baking soda	3 mL
3/4 tsp	baking powder	3 mL
1/2 tsp	salt	2 mL
1/2 cup	packed light brown sugar	125 mL
2	eggs	2
1 1/2 cups	mashed ripe bananas	375 mL
1/2 cup	unsalted butter, melted	125 mL
1/4 cup	liquid honey	60 mL
1 tbsp	finely grated lime zest	15 mL
1 tsp	vanilla extract	5 mL
1 cup	chopped dried pineapple	250 mL
1/2 cup	sweetened flaked or shredded coconut	125 mL

I love a good piña colada, and I think the same combination — sunny pineapple and mellow coconut — is smashing in muffin form. You can use either sweetened or unsweetened dried pineapple here; I prefer the texture of the former in these muffins.

Makes 12 muffins

- Preheat oven to 350°F (180°C)
- 12-cup muffin pan, lined with paper liners

1. In a large bowl, whisk together flour, baking soda, baking powder and salt.

2. In a medium bowl, whisk together brown sugar, eggs, bananas, butter, honey, lime zest and vanilla until well blended.

3. Add the egg mixture to the flour mixture and stir until just blended. Gently fold in pineapple.

4. Divide batter equally among prepared muffin cups. Sprinkle with coconut and gently press into batter.

5. Bake in preheated oven for 25 to 28 minutes or until tops are golden and a toothpick inserted in the center comes out clean. Let cool in pan on a wire rack for 5 minutes, then transfer to the rack to cool.

Cocoa Banana Muffins

1 1/2 cups	all-purpose flour	375 mL
1/4 cup	unsweetened cocoa powder (not Dutch process)	60 mL
1 tsp	baking soda	5 mL
1/2 tsp	salt	2 mL
1/4 tsp	baking powder	1 mL
1 cup	granulated sugar	250 mL
1	egg	1
1 1/3 cups	mashed ripe bananas	325 mL
1/3 cup	vegetable oil	75 mL
1 cup	miniature semisweet chocolate chips	250 mL

These muffins have all the great banana flavor of their plain counterparts, with a double fillip of chocolate flavor added to the batter: first from cocoa powder, second from a handful of chocolate chips.

Makes 12 muffins

- Preheat oven to 350°F (180°C)
- 12-cup muffin pan, lined with paper liners

1. In a large bowl, whisk together flour, cocoa powder, baking soda, salt and baking powder.

2. In a medium bowl, whisk together sugar, egg, bananas and oil until well blended.

3. Add the egg mixture to the flour mixture and stir until just blended. Gently fold in chocolate chips.

4. Divide batter equally among prepared muffin cups.

5. Bake in preheated oven for 20 to 24 minutes or until a toothpick inserted in the center comes out clean. Let cool in pan on a wire rack for 3 minutes, then transfer to the rack to cool.

Banana Brickle Muffins

2 cups	all-purpose flour	500 mL
1 tbsp	baking powder	15 mL
1/2 tsp	salt	2 mL
1/2 cup	packed dark brown sugar	125 mL
1	egg	1
1 cup	mashed ripe bananas	250 mL
1/2 cup	milk	125 mL
1/3 cup	vegetable oil	75 mL
1 cup	toffee baking bits	250 mL

Here's a simple way to transform those overripe bananas in the fruit bowl into a coffee-time treat. They are so easy to stir together and stay moist for days.

Makes 12 muffins

- Preheat oven to 350°F (180°C)
- 12-cup muffin pan, lined with paper liners

1. In a large bowl, whisk together flour, baking powder and salt.
2. In a medium bowl, whisk together brown sugar, egg, bananas, milk and oil until well blended.
3. Add the egg mixture to the flour mixture and stir until just blended. Gently fold in toffee bits.
4. Divide batter equally among prepared muffin cups.
5. Bake in preheated oven for 18 to 22 minutes or until tops are golden and a toothpick inserted in the center comes out clean. Let cool in pan on a wire rack for 3 minutes, then transfer to the rack to cool.

Blueberry Streusel Muffins

Streusel

2/3 cup	all-purpose flour	150 mL
1/3 cup	packed dark brown sugar	75 mL
1/2 tsp	ground cinnamon	2 mL
1/8 tsp	salt	0.5 mL
1/4 cup	unsalted butter, melted	60 mL

Muffins

2 cups	all-purpose flour	500 mL
1 tbsp	baking powder	15 mL
1/2 tsp	salt	2 mL
1 cup	granulated sugar	500 mL
1	egg	1
1/2 cup	buttermilk	125 mL
1/3 cup	unsalted butter, melted	75 mL
2 tsp	vanilla extract	10 mL
1 1/2 cups	fresh or frozen (unthawed) blueberries	375 mL

Here is a fantastic blueberry muffin that tastes like blueberry streusel pie. If using frozen berries, don't let them thaw before adding them to the batter and, if available, opt for wild blueberries.

Makes 12 muffins

- Preheat oven to 375°F (190°C)
- 12-cup muffin pan, greased

1. *Streusel:* In a medium bowl, whisk together flour, brown sugar, cinnamon and salt. Mix in butter until mixture is crumbly. Refrigerate until ready to use.
2. *Muffins:* In a large bowl, whisk together flour, baking powder and salt.
3. In a medium bowl, whisk together sugar, egg, buttermilk, butter and vanilla until well blended.
4. Add the egg mixture to the flour mixture and stir until just blended. Gently fold in blueberries.
5. Divide batter equally among prepared muffin cups. Sprinkle with streusel.
6. Bake in preheated oven for 24 to 27 minutes or until golden and a toothpick inserted in the center comes out clean. Let cool in pan on a wire rack for 5 minutes, then transfer to the rack to cool.

Sour Cherry Muffins with Almond Crumble

Topping

1/3 cup	packed light brown sugar	75 mL
3 tbsp	unsalted butter, melted	45 mL
3 tbsp	all-purpose flour	45 mL
1/4 tsp	ground cinnamon	1 mL
1/2 cup	sliced almonds	125 mL

Muffins

1 1/2 cups	all-purpose flour	375 mL
1 tsp	baking powder	5 mL
1/2 tsp	baking soda	2 mL
1/4 tsp	salt	1 mL
1 cup	granulated sugar	250 mL
2	eggs	2
1/2 cup	sour cream	125 mL
1/4 cup	vegetable oil	60 mL
1/2 tsp	almond extract	2 mL
1 1/3 cups	drained canned or jarred sour (tart) cherries	325 mL

Enjoy the perfect blend of tart and sweet flavors, cakey and crispy textures in these delicious muffins, perfect for impressing brunch guests or bake sale buyers.

Makes 12 muffins

- Preheat oven to 375°F (190°C)
- 12-cup muffin pan, greased

1. *Topping:* In a small bowl, combine brown sugar, butter, flour and cinnamon until blended and crumbly. Stir in almonds. Refrigerate until ready to use.

2. *Muffins:* In a large bowl, whisk together flour, baking powder, baking soda and salt.

3. In a medium bowl, whisk together sugar, eggs, sour cream, oil and almond extract until well blended.

4. Add the egg mixture to the flour mixture and stir until just blended. Gently fold in cherries.

5. Divide batter equally among prepared muffin cups. Sprinkle with topping.

6. Bake in preheated oven for 25 to 30 minutes or until tops are golden and a toothpick inserted in the center comes out clean. Let cool in pan on a wire rack for 5 minutes, then transfer to the rack to cool.

Tart Cherry Chocolate Chip Muffins

2 cups	all-purpose flour	500 mL
2 tsp	baking powder	10 mL
1/2 tsp	baking soda	2 mL
1/2 tsp	salt	2 mL
2/3 cup	granulated sugar	150 mL
2	eggs	2
1 cup	sour cream	250 mL
1/2 cup	unsalted butter, melted	125 mL
1/2 tsp	almond extract	2 mL
1 cup	semisweet chocolate chips	250 mL
3/4 cup	dried sour (tart) cherries, coarsely chopped	175 mL
2/3 cup	sliced almonds, toasted	150 mL

As good as they are fresh from the oven, the rich flavor of these chocolate and cherry muffins becomes more pronounced the day after baking.

Makes 12 muffins

- Preheat oven to 375°F (190°C)
- 12-cup muffin pan, greased

1. In a large bowl, whisk together flour, baking powder, baking soda and salt.
2. In a medium bowl, whisk together sugar, eggs, sour cream, butter and almond extract until well blended.
3. Add the egg mixture to the flour mixture and stir until just blended. Gently fold in chocolate chips, cherries and almonds.
4. Divide batter equally among prepared muffin cups.
5. Bake in preheated oven for 21 to 24 minutes or until tops are golden and a toothpick inserted in the center comes out clean. Let cool in pan on a wire rack for 3 minutes, then transfer to the rack to cool.

White Chocolate Raspberry Muffins

2 1/4 cups	all-purpose flour	550 mL
1 tbsp	baking powder	15 mL
1/2 tsp	salt	2 mL
3/4 cup	granulated sugar	175 mL
1	egg	1
1/4 cup	unsalted butter, melted	60 mL
1 tsp	vanilla extract	5 mL
1/2 tsp	almond extract	2 mL
1 cup	half-and-half (10%) cream	250 mL
1 cup	raspberries	250 mL
2/3 cup	white chocolate chips, roughly chopped	150 mL

I love white chocolate, especially paired with berries, as I've done here. A generous amount of baking powder in the batter helps these beauties rise triumphantly high and virtually guarantees a perfect-every-time creation. An excellent black tea, such as Darjeeling or Assam, makes an ideal accompaniment.

Makes 12 muffins

- Preheat oven to 375°F (190°C)
- 12-cup muffin pan, lined with paper liners

1. In a large bowl, whisk together flour, baking powder and salt.
2. In a medium bowl, whisk together sugar, egg, butter, vanilla and almond extract until well blended. Whisk in cream until blended.
3. Add the egg mixture to the flour mixture and stir until just blended. Gently fold in raspberries and white chocolate.
4. Divide batter equally among prepared muffin cups.
5. Bake in preheated oven for 25 to 30 minutes or until tops are golden and a toothpick inserted in the center comes out clean. Let cool in pan on a wire rack for 5 minutes, then transfer to the rack to cool.

Ricotta Raspberry Muffins

2 cups	all-purpose flour	500 mL
2$\frac{1}{4}$ tsp	baking powder	11 mL
$\frac{1}{4}$ tsp	baking soda	1 mL
$\frac{1}{2}$ tsp	salt	2 mL
$\frac{2}{3}$ cup	granulated sugar	150 mL
2	eggs	2
$\frac{3}{4}$ cup	ricotta cheese	175 mL
$\frac{1}{2}$ cup	unsalted butter, melted	125 mL
2 tsp	finely grated lemon zest	10 mL
1 tsp	vanilla extract	5 mL
1$\frac{1}{2}$ cups	raspberries	375 mL

A sweet ricotta base is the perfect counterpoint to the bright, lush flavor of fresh raspberries in these muffins.

Makes 12 muffins

- Preheat oven to 400°F (200°C)
- 12-cup muffin pan, lined with paper liners

1. In a large bowl, whisk together flour, baking powder, baking soda and salt.
2. In a medium bowl, whisk together sugar, eggs, cheese, butter, lemon zest and vanilla until well blended.
3. Add the egg mixture to the flour mixture and stir until just blended. Gently fold in raspberries.
4. Divide batter equally among prepared muffin cups.
5. Bake in preheated oven for 17 to 21 minutes or until tops are golden and a toothpick inserted in the center comes out clean. Let cool in pan on a wire rack for 5 minutes, then transfer to the rack to cool.

Strawberry Marzipan Muffins

1$\frac{1}{2}$ cups	all-purpose flour	375 mL
$\frac{1}{4}$ cup	yellow cornmeal	60 mL
$\frac{1}{2}$ tsp	baking soda	2 mL
$\frac{1}{2}$ tsp	ground mace	2 mL
$\frac{1}{2}$ tsp	salt	2 mL
1 cup	granulated sugar	250 mL
2	eggs	2
$\frac{1}{3}$ cup	vegetable oil	75 mL
$\frac{1}{3}$ cup	milk	75 mL
1 tsp	almond extract	5 mL
1$\frac{1}{2}$ cups	coarsely chopped strawberries	375 mL
$\frac{1}{2}$ cup	crumbled marzipan	125 mL
$\frac{1}{2}$ cup	sliced almonds	125 mL

I have hosted quite a few baby and wedding showers, and these elegant muffins are always present. A crumble of nutty marzipan is a delicious contrast to the sweet-tart strawberries in this muffin recipe.

Tip

Look for marzipan in the baking aisle of the supermarket.

Makes 10 muffins

- Preheat oven to 375°F (190°C)
- 12-cup muffin pan, 10 cups lined with paper liners

1. In a large bowl, whisk together flour, cornmeal, baking soda, mace and salt.
2. In a medium bowl, whisk together sugar, eggs, oil, milk and almond extract until well blended.
3. Add the egg mixture to the flour mixture and stir until just blended. Gently fold in strawberries and marzipan.
4. Divide batter equally among prepared muffin cups. Sprinkle with almonds.
5. Bake in preheated oven for 23 to 28 minutes or until tops are golden and a toothpick inserted in the center comes out clean. Let cool in pan on a wire rack for 5 minutes, then transfer to the rack to cool.

Brandied Pear and Honey Muffins

Topping

1/2 cup	chopped walnuts	125 mL
1/3 cup	packed light brown sugar	75 mL
1/3 cup	all-purpose flour	75 mL
3 tbsp	unsalted butter, melted	45 mL

Muffins

2 cups	all-purpose flour	500 mL
1 tbsp	baking powder	15 mL
1/2 tsp	salt	2 mL
1/4 tsp	ground nutmeg	1 mL
1	egg	1
1/3 cup	liquid honey	75 mL
1/4 cup	unsalted butter, melted	60 mL
3/4 cup	milk	175 mL
1/4 cup	brandy	60 mL
1 1/2 cups	chopped peeled pears	375 mL

This recipe provides a classic combination of flavors. The brandy zeroes in on the flavors of pear and honey, elevating them to new levels of deliciousness.

Makes 12 muffins

- Preheat oven to 375°F (190°C)
- 12-cup muffin pan, greased

1. *Topping:* In a small bowl, combine walnuts, brown sugar and flour. Drizzle with butter, then mix until mixture resembles large crumbs. Refrigerate until ready to use.
2. *Muffins:* In a large bowl, whisk together flour, baking powder, salt and nutmeg.
3. In a medium bowl, whisk together egg, honey and butter until well blended. Whisk in milk and brandy until well blended.
4. Add the egg mixture to the flour mixture and stir until just blended. Gently fold in pears.
5. Divide batter equally among prepared muffin cups.
6. Bake in preheated oven for 24 to 28 minutes or until tops are golden and a toothpick inserted in the center comes out clean. Let cool in pan on a wire rack for 5 minutes, then transfer to the rack to cool.

Gingerbread Pear Muffins

1 1/2 cups	all-purpose flour	375 mL
1 tsp	baking powder	5 mL
1 tsp	ground ginger	5 mL
1 tsp	ground cinnamon	5 mL
1/2 tsp	baking soda	2 mL
1/4 tsp	salt	1 mL
1/4 cup	packed light brown sugar	60 mL
1	egg	1
2/3 cup	dark (cooking) molasses	150 mL
1/4 cup	unsalted butter, melted	60 mL
1/2 cup	boiling water	125 mL
2	small pears, cored and each cut into 6 wedges	2

Tip

For the best flavor, let pears ripen at room temperature for a day or two.

Makes 12 muffins

- Preheat oven to 350°F (180°C)
- 12-cup muffin pan, greased

1. In a large bowl, whisk together flour, baking powder, ginger, cinnamon, baking soda and salt.
2. In a medium bowl, whisk together brown sugar, egg, molasses and butter until well blended.
3. Add the egg mixture to the flour mixture and stir until just blended. Whisk in boiling water until blended.
4. Divide batter equally among prepared muffin cups. Gently press 1 pear wedge into each cup of batter.
5. Bake in preheated oven for 15 to 18 minutes or until tops are golden and a toothpick inserted in the center comes out clean. Let cool in pan on a wire rack for 5 minutes, then transfer to the rack to cool.

Lime and Fresh Ginger Muffins

Muffins

³⁄₄ cup	granulated sugar	175 mL
¹⁄₄ cup	chopped peeled gingerroot	60 mL
2 tbsp	finely grated lime zest	30 mL
2 cups	all-purpose flour	500 mL
2 tsp	baking powder	10 mL
¹⁄₂ tsp	baking soda	2 mL
¹⁄₂ tsp	salt	2 mL
2	eggs	2
³⁄₄ cup	buttermilk	175 mL
¹⁄₃ cup	vegetable oil	75 mL

Icing

1 cup	confectioners' (icing) sugar	250 mL
1 tsp	finely grated lime zest	5 mL
2 tbsp	freshly squeezed lime juice	30 mL

Peppery with fresh ginger and tangy with lime, these golden muffins, with their tart-sweet glaze, rank at the top of my list of muffin favorites. If you share them with friends, be prepared to proffer the recipe, too.

Makes 12 muffins

- Preheat oven to 375°F (190°C)
- Food processor
- 12-cup muffin pan, lined with paper liners

1. *Muffins:* In food processor, process sugar, ginger and lime zest until finely chopped and mixture resembles wet sand.

2. In a large bowl, whisk together flour, baking powder, baking soda and salt.

3. In a medium bowl, whisk together ginger mixture, eggs, buttermilk and oil until well blended.

4. Add the egg mixture to the flour mixture and stir until just blended.

5. Divide batter equally among prepared muffin cups.

6. Bake in preheated oven for 18 to 22 minutes or until tops are light golden brown and a toothpick inserted in the center comes out clean. Let cool in pan on a wire rack for 3 minutes, then transfer to the rack to cool while you prepare the icing.

7. *Icing:* In a small bowl, combine confectioners' sugar, lime zest and lime juice until smooth. Spoon over tops of warm muffins and let cool.

Lime Meltaway Muffins

3 cups	all-purpose flour	750 mL
1 tbsp	baking powder	15 mL
1 tsp	salt	5 mL
1/2 tsp	baking soda	2 mL
1 cup	granulated sugar	250 mL
2/3 cup	unsalted butter, softened	150 mL
2	eggs	2
1/2 cup	milk	125 mL
2 tbsp	finely grated lime zest	30 mL
1/2 cup	freshly squeezed lime juice	125 mL
2 tbsp	confectioners' (icing) sugar	30 mL

Fresh flavor and an appealing look enliven these citrus muffins, based on one of my favorite cookies of the same name. A buttery batter is punctuated with both lime juice and lime zest; a snow shower of confectioners' sugar adds a celebratory note to an otherwise everyday muffin.

Makes 12 muffins

- Preheat oven to 350°F (180°C)
- 12-cup muffin pan, lined with paper liners

1. In a medium bowl, whisk together flour, baking powder, salt and baking soda.

2. In a large bowl, using an electric mixer on medium-high speed, beat granulated sugar and butter until light and fluffy. Beat in eggs, one at a time, until fluffy and pale yellow. Beat in milk and lime zest until blended.

3. With the mixer on low speed, beat in flour mixture alternately with lime juice, making two additions of flour and one of juice, until just blended.

4. Divide batter equally among prepared muffin cups.

5. Bake in preheated oven for 23 to 28 minutes or until tops are golden and a toothpick inserted in the center comes out clean. Let cool in pan on a wire rack for 3 minutes, then transfer to the rack to cool. Sift confectioners' sugar over tops of cooled muffins.

Orange Marmalade Muffins

2 1/2 cups	all-purpose flour	625 mL
2 tsp	baking powder	10 mL
1/2 tsp	salt	2 mL
1 2/3 cups	granulated sugar	400 mL
3	eggs	3
1/3 cup	orange marmalade	75 mL
2 tsp	finely grated orange zest	10 mL
1 tsp	vanilla extract	5 mL
2/3 cup	freshly squeezed orange juice	150 mL
3/4 cup	unsalted butter, melted	175 mL

Orange marmalade is a great — and unexpected — addition to basic muffin batter. Here I've upped the orange flavor further with both orange zest and fresh orange juice.

Makes 18 muffins

- Preheat oven to 350°F (180°C)
- Two 12-cup muffin pans, 18 cups lined with paper liners

1. In a large bowl, whisk together flour, baking powder and salt.

2. In a medium bowl, whisk together sugar, eggs, marmalade, orange zest and vanilla until well blended. Whisk in orange juice and butter until blended.

3. Add the egg mixture to the flour mixture and stir until just blended.

4. Divide batter equally among prepared muffin cups.

5. Bake in preheated oven for 16 to 21 minutes or until tops are golden and a toothpick inserted in the center comes out clean. Let cool in pans on a wire rack for 3 minutes, then transfer to the rack to cool.

Lavender Lemon Muffins

1³/₄ cups	all-purpose flour	425 mL
2 tsp	baking powder	10 mL
¹/₂ tsp	baking soda	2 mL
¹/₄ tsp	salt	1 mL
²/₃ cup	granulated sugar	150 mL
1 tbsp	finely grated lemon zest	15 mL
1¹/₂ tsp	dried lavender	7 mL
1	egg	1
²/₃ cup	buttermilk	150 mL
¹/₃ cup	olive oil	75 mL
2 tbsp	unsalted butter, melted	30 mL

The floral notes of lavender meld with the bright, fresh flavor of lemon in the most heavenly way in these light, golden muffins. The secret to the moistness of the tender muffins is olive oil — a common ingredient in Provençal cakes.

Makes 12 muffins

- Preheat oven to 400°F (200°C)
- Food processor
- 12-cup muffin pan, lined with paper liners

1. In a large bowl, whisk together flour, baking powder, baking soda and salt.
2. In food processor, process sugar, lemon zest and lavender until lavender is finely chopped. Transfer 2 tbsp (30 mL) to a small bowl and set aside.
3. In a medium bowl, whisk together remaining lavender mixture, egg, buttermilk and oil until well blended.
4. Add the egg mixture to the flour mixture and stir until just blended.
5. Divide batter equally among prepared muffin cups.
6. Bake in preheated oven for 17 to 21 minutes or until tops are light golden and a toothpick inserted in the center comes out clean. Let cool in pan on a wire rack for 3 minutes, then transfer to the rack.
7. Brush warm muffin tops with butter and sprinkle with reserved lavender mixture. Let cool.

Lemon Curd Muffins

2 cups	all-purpose flour	500 mL
1 tsp	baking powder	5 mL
1/2 tsp	baking soda	2 mL
1/2 tsp	salt	2 mL
3/4 cup	granulated sugar	175 mL
1/2 cup	unsalted butter, softened	125 mL
1 tbsp	finely grated lemon zest	15 mL
8 oz	cream cheese, softened	250 g
1	egg	1
2 tbsp	freshly squeezed lemon juice	30 mL
1 tsp	vanilla extract	5 mL
1/2 cup	prepared lemon curd	125 mL
2 tbsp	turbinado sugar	30 mL

Diminutive and beautiful, sweet and tart, these muffins have lots of lemon flavor and plenty of style, too. If ever there was the perfect teatime muffin, this is it.

Makes 12 muffins

- Preheat oven to 350°F (180°C)
- 12-cup muffin pan, lined with paper liners

1. In a medium bowl, whisk together flour, baking powder, baking soda and salt.

2. In a large bowl, using an electric mixer on medium-high speed, beat granulated sugar, butter and lemon zest until light and fluffy. Beat in cream cheese until blended. Beat in egg, lemon juice and vanilla until blended.

3. Add the flour mixture to the egg mixture and gently stir with a wooden spoon until just blended.

4. Divide half the batter equally among prepared muffin cups. Spoon 2 tsp (10 mL) of the lemon curd into the center of each cup of batter. Top with the remaining batter and sprinkle with turbinado sugar.

5. Bake in preheated oven for 22 to 24 minutes or until tops are golden brown and spring back when touched. Let cool in pan on a wire rack for 5 minutes, then transfer to the rack to cool.

Sparkling Rhubarb Muffins

2 1/4 cups	all-purpose flour	550 mL
2 tsp	baking powder	10 mL
1 1/2 tsp	ground cinnamon	10 mL
1 tsp	baking soda	5 mL
1/2 tsp	salt	2 mL
3/4 cup	granulated sugar	175 mL
1	egg	1
1/2 cup	milk	125 mL
1/2 cup	sour cream	125 mL
1/3 cup	unsalted butter, melted	75 mL
1 cup	finely chopped fresh or frozen (thawed) rhubarb	250 mL
3 tbsp	turbinado sugar	45 mL

Rhubarb is extremely tart and astringent, but once sugar is added, it is transformed, offering bright, fruity flavor that is lovely on its own or marries beautifully with other fruits.

Makes 12 muffins

- Preheat oven to 400°F (200°C)
- 12-cup muffin pan, greased

1. In a large bowl, whisk together flour, baking powder, cinnamon, baking soda and salt.

2. In a medium bowl, whisk together granulated sugar, egg, milk, sour cream and butter until well blended.

3. Add the egg mixture to the flour mixture and stir until just blended. Gently fold in rhubarb.

4. Divide batter equally among prepared muffin cups. Sprinkle with turbinado sugar.

5. Bake in preheated oven for 15 to 18 minutes or until tops are golden and a toothpick inserted in the center comes out clean. Let cool in pan on a wire rack for 5 minutes, then transfer to the rack to cool.

Chestnut, Apple and Pumpkin Muffins

3 cups	all-purpose flour	750 mL
2 tsp	baking soda	10 mL
2 tsp	ground cinnamon	10 mL
1 tsp	ground ginger	5 mL
1 tsp	ground nutmeg	5 mL
3/4 tsp	salt	3 mL
1/4 tsp	ground cloves	1 mL
2 cups	granulated sugar	500 mL
4	eggs	4
1	can (15 oz/425 mL) pumpkin purée (not pie filling)	1
3/4 cup	vegetable oil	175 mL
2 cups	chopped peeled apples	500 mL
1 cup	chopped jarred chestnuts	250 mL

You can taste the chestnuts in these muffins, but the flavor is not overwhelming — perfect if you are new to chestnuts. These muffins are undeniably festive, ideal for baking from autumn through the winter holidays.

Tips

If you prefer to use homemade pumpkin purée, you'll need 1 3/4 cups (425 mL).

Chestnuts in a jar are available steamed or roasted — both work equally well in this recipe.

Makes 18 muffins

- Preheat oven to 350°F (180°C)
- Two 12-cup muffin pans, 18 cups greased

1. In a large bowl, whisk together flour, baking soda, cinnamon, ginger, nutmeg, salt and cloves.

2. In another large bowl, whisk together sugar, eggs, pumpkin and oil until well blended.

3. Add the egg mixture to the flour mixture and stir until just blended. Gently fold in apples and chestnuts.

4. Divide batter equally among prepared muffin cups.

5. Bake in preheated oven for 18 to 22 minutes or until tops are golden and a toothpick inserted in the center comes out clean. Let cool in pans on a wire rack for 5 minutes, then transfer to the rack to cool.

Pumpkin Chip Muffins

1½ cups	all-purpose flour	375 mL
1½ tsp	baking powder	7 mL
1 tsp	ground cinnamon	5 mL
½ tsp	baking soda	2 mL
½ tsp	salt	2 mL
1 cup	granulated sugar	250 mL
2	eggs	2
1 cup	pumpkin purée (not pie filling)	250 mL
¾ cup	vegetable oil	175 mL
½ tsp	vanilla extract	2 mL
1 cup	miniature semisweet chocolate chips	250 mL

Moist and delicious, these muffins are terrific as a quick snack or a delicious start to the day.

Makes 12 muffins

- Preheat oven to 400°F (200°C)
- 12-cup muffin pan, lined with paper liners

1. In a large bowl, whisk together flour, baking powder, cinnamon, baking soda and salt.
2. In a medium bowl, whisk together sugar, eggs, pumpkin, oil and vanilla until well blended.
3. Add the egg mixture to the flour mixture and stir until just blended. Gently fold in chocolate chips.
4. Divide batter equally among prepared muffin cups.
5. Bake in preheated oven for 15 to 18 minutes or until tops are golden and a toothpick inserted in the center comes out clean. Let cool in pan on a wire rack for 5 minutes, then transfer to the rack to cool.

Cashew Butterscotch Muffins

1½ cups	all-purpose flour	375 mL
¾ tsp	baking powder	3 mL
¾ tsp	baking soda	3 mL
¼ tsp	salt	1 mL
⅔ cup	packed dark brown sugar	150 mL
1	egg	1
⅓ cup	unsalted butter, melted	75 mL
2 tsp	vanilla extract	10 mL
1 cup	sour cream	250 mL
1 cup	lightly salted roasted cashews, coarsely chopped	250 mL
½ cup	toffee baking bits	125 mL

I don't know anyone who dislikes butterscotch; I do know that these muffins are off the charts. The combination of salty (from the cashews) and sweet (toffee and brown sugar) is utterly irresistible.

Makes 12 muffins

- Preheat oven to 350°F (180°C)
- 12-cup muffin pan, lined with paper liners

1. In a large bowl, whisk together flour, baking powder, baking soda and salt.
2. In a medium bowl, whisk together brown sugar, egg, butter and vanilla until well blended. Whisk in sour cream.
3. Add the egg mixture to the flour mixture and stir until just blended. Gently fold in cashews and toffee bits.
4. Divide batter equally among prepared muffin cups.
5. Bake in preheated oven for 18 to 22 minutes or until tops are golden and a toothpick inserted in the center comes out clean. Let cool in pan on a wire rack for 3 minutes, then transfer to the rack to cool.

Almond Poppy Seed Muffins

3 cups	all-purpose flour	750 mL
3 tbsp	poppy seeds	45 mL
1 tbsp	baking powder	15 mL
1/2 tsp	baking soda	2 mL
1/2 tsp	salt	2 mL
1 cup	packed light brown sugar	250 mL
2/3 cup	unsalted butter, softened	150 mL
2	eggs	2
1 1/2 cups	plain whole-milk yogurt	375 mL
2 tsp	almond extract	10 mL

Simple is so very often best. Bite into one of these tender muffins and you'll agree. At times, I wonder why we bother baking with an armload of complicated ingredients when muffins, crafted of little more than butter, sugar, flour and a few accents (poppy seeds and almond seem to please one and all) yield such wondrous results.

Tip

Be sure to get your poppy seeds from a good source. They need to be fresh, as they can become rancid very quickly.

Makes 12 muffins

- Preheat oven to 375°F (190°C)
- 12-cup muffin pan, greased

1. In a medium bowl, whisk together flour, poppy seeds, baking powder, baking soda and salt.

2. In a large bowl, using an electric mixer on medium-high speed, beat brown sugar and butter until light and fluffy. Beat in eggs, one at a time, until fluffy and pale yellow. Beat in yogurt and almond extract until blended.

3. Add the flour mixture to the egg mixture and stir until just blended.

4. Divide batter equally among prepared muffin cups.

5. Bake in preheated oven for 25 to 30 minutes or until tops are golden and a toothpick inserted in the center comes out clean. Let cool in pan on a wire rack for 3 minutes, then transfer to the rack to cool.

Coconut Almond Joyful Muffins

2 cups	all-purpose flour	500 mL
2½ tsp	baking powder	12 mL
½ tsp	salt	2 mL
1 cup	granulated sugar	250 mL
2	eggs	2
¼ cup	unsalted butter, melted	60 mL
¼ cup	vegetable oil	60 mL
¾ tsp	almond extract	3 mL
1 cup	sour cream	250 mL
1 cup	sweetened flaked or shredded coconut	250 mL
¾ cup	miniature semisweet chocolate chips	175 mL
½ cup	sliced almonds	125 mL

Based on one of my favorite candy bars of a similar name, this decadent, coffee-cake-like treat is terrific for a coffee break, afternoon tea or brunch.

Makes 12 muffins

- Preheat oven to 375°F (190°C)
- 12-cup muffin pan, lined with paper liners

1. In a large bowl, whisk together flour, baking powder and salt.

2. In a medium bowl, whisk together sugar, eggs, butter, oil and almond extract until well blended. Whisk in sour cream.

3. Add the egg mixture to the flour mixture and stir until just blended. Gently fold in coconut and chocolate chips.

4. Divide batter equally among prepared muffin cups. Sprinkle with almonds.

5. Bake in preheated oven for 18 to 21 minutes or until tops are golden and a toothpick inserted in the center comes out clean. Let cool in pan on a wire rack for 5 minutes, then transfer to the rack to cool.

Macadamia Muffins

2 cups	all-purpose flour	500 mL
2 tsp	baking powder	10 mL
½ tsp	baking soda	2 mL
½ tsp	salt	2 mL
¾ cup	packed light brown sugar	175 mL
2	eggs	2
½ cup	unsalted butter, melted	125 mL
2 tsp	vanilla extract	10 mL
¾ cup	sour cream	175 mL
1 cup	chopped macadamia nuts, toasted	250 mL

These golden, buttery muffins are deliciously simple, with an understated sophistication. The fragrant taste of the toasted macadamia nuts gives the muffins an elusive hint that is at once familiar and exotic.

Makes 12 muffins

- Preheat oven to 375°F (190°C)
- 12-cup muffin pan, lined with paper liners

1. In a large bowl, whisk together flour, baking powder, baking soda and salt.

2. In a medium bowl, whisk together brown sugar, eggs, butter and vanilla until well blended. Whisk in sour cream until blended.

3. Add the egg mixture to the flour mixture and stir until just blended. Gently fold in nuts.

4. Divide batter equally among prepared muffin cups.

5. Bake in preheated oven for 18 to 22 minutes or until tops are golden and a toothpick inserted in the center comes out clean. Let cool in pan on a wire rack for 3 minutes, then transfer to the rack to cool.

Coconut Crumb Muffins

Topping

2/3 cup	sweetened flaked or shredded coconut	150 mL
1/4 cup	packed light brown sugar	60 mL
3 tbsp	all-purpose flour	45 mL
3 tbsp	unsalted butter, melted	45 mL

Muffins

2 cups	all-purpose flour	500 mL
2 tsp	baking powder	10 mL
1/2 tsp	baking soda	2 mL
1/2 tsp	salt	2 mL
1/2 cup	granulated sugar	125 mL
1	egg	1
2/3 cup	buttermilk	150 mL
1/3 cup	vegetable oil	75 mL
2 tsp	vanilla extract	10 mL
1 cup	sweetened flaked or shredded coconut, toasted	250 mL

Though the presentation of these muffins, with their old-fashioned charm and toasted coconut topping, will tempt one and all at first glance, I promise that it will only get better from there — and the muffins' rich, coconutty flavor belies the minimal effort.

Tip

To toast coconut: Preheat oven to 350°F (180°C). Spread coconut on a rimmed baking sheet and bake for 3 to 5 minutes, stirring after each minute, until coconut is dry and light brown, with some white shreds.

Makes 12 muffins

- Preheat oven to 400°F (200°C)
- 12-cup muffin pan, lined with paper liners

1. *Topping:* In a small bowl, combine coconut, brown sugar, flour and butter until blended. Refrigerate until ready to use.

2. *Muffins:* In a large bowl, whisk together flour, baking powder, baking soda and salt.

3. In a medium bowl, whisk together sugar, egg, buttermilk, oil and vanilla until well blended.

4. Add the egg mixture to the flour mixture and stir until just blended. Gently fold in toasted coconut.

5. Divide batter equally among prepared muffin cups. Sprinkle with topping and gently press into batter.

6. Bake in preheated oven for 16 to 20 minutes or until tops are golden and a toothpick inserted in the center comes out clean. Let cool in pan on a wire rack for 5 minutes, then transfer to the rack to cool.

Peanut Brittle Muffins

2 cups	all-purpose flour	500 mL
2 tsp	baking powder	10 mL
1/2 tsp	baking soda	2 mL
1/2 tsp	salt	2 mL
2/3 cup	packed light brown sugar	150 mL
2	eggs	2
1/2 cup	unsalted butter, melted	125 mL
3/4 cup	buttermilk	175 mL
2 tsp	vanilla extract	10 mL
1 cup	coarsely chopped lightly salted roasted peanuts	250 mL
1 cup	toffee baking bits	250 mL

My husband's maternal grandmother — Mamaw — was renowned for her peanut brittle; here I've reinvented the favorite Southern treat in a scandalously good muffin. If you love salty-sweet, this muffin is for you.

Makes 12 muffins

- Preheat oven to 375°F (190°C)
- 12-cup muffin pan, lined with paper liners

1. In a large bowl, whisk together flour, baking powder, baking soda and salt.
2. In a medium bowl, whisk together brown sugar, eggs, butter, buttermilk and vanilla until well blended.
3. Add the egg mixture to the flour mixture and stir until just blended. Gently fold in peanuts and toffee bits.
4. Divide batter equally among prepared muffin cups.
5. Bake in preheated oven for 18 to 22 minutes or until tops are golden and a toothpick inserted in the center comes out clean. Let cool in pan on a wire rack for 5 minutes, then transfer to the rack to cool.

Peanut Butter Chocolate Chunk Muffins

2 cups	all-purpose flour	500 mL
1 tbsp	baking powder	15 mL
1/2 tsp	salt	2 mL
2/3 cup	packed light brown sugar	150 mL
2	eggs	2
2/3 cup	creamy peanut butter	150 mL
1/3 cup	unsalted butter, melted	75 mL
1 tsp	vanilla extract	5 mL
1 1/4 cups	milk	300 mL
1 cup	semisweet chocolate chunks or chips	250 mL

As good as these muffins are warm from the oven, they are even better — notably more peanut-buttery — a day or two later.

Makes 16 muffins

- Preheat oven to 400°F (200°C)
- Two 12-cup muffin pans, 16 cups greased

1. In a large bowl, whisk together flour, baking powder and salt.
2. In a medium bowl, combine brown sugar, eggs, peanut butter, butter and vanilla until blended and smooth. Whisk in milk until well blended.
3. Add the egg mixture to the flour mixture and stir until just blended. Gently fold in chocolate.
4. Divide batter equally among prepared muffin cups.
5. Bake in preheated oven for 15 to 19 minutes or until tops are golden and a toothpick inserted in the center comes out clean. Let cool in pans on a wire rack for 3 minutes, then transfer to the rack to cool.

Fluffynut Marshmallow Muffins

2 cups	all-purpose flour	500 mL
1 tbsp	baking powder	15 mL
1/2 tsp	salt	2 mL
3/4 cup	creamy peanut butter, divided	175 mL
2 tbsp	unsalted butter, softened	30 mL
2/3 cup	packed light brown sugar	150 mL
2	eggs	2
1 1/2 tsp	vanilla extract	7 mL
1 cup	milk	250 mL
3/4 cup	marshmallow fluff or crème	175 mL

Children of all ages will adore these homemade treats, based on the popular marshmallow fluff–peanut butter sandwiches of the same name.

Makes 12 muffins

- Preheat oven to 400°F (200°C)
- 12-cup muffin pan, lined with paper liners

1. In a large bowl, whisk together flour, baking powder and salt. Using your fingers or a pastry cutter, rub or cut 1/2 cup (125 mL) of the peanut butter and the butter into flour mixture until it resembles coarse crumbs.
2. In a medium bowl, whisk together brown sugar, eggs and vanilla until well blended. Whisk in milk until blended.
3. Add the egg mixture to the flour mixture and stir until just blended.
4. Divide half the batter equally among prepared muffin cups. Spoon 1 tbsp (15 mL) of the marshmallow fluff and 1 tsp (5 mL) of the remaining peanut butter into the center of each cup of batter. Top with the remaining batter (the batter doesn't need to cover the filling perfectly).
5. Bake in preheated oven for 15 to 18 minutes or until tops are golden and spring back when touched. Let cool in pan on a wire rack for 5 minutes, then transfer to the rack to cool.

Pecan Pie Muffins

1/2 cup	all-purpose flour	125 mL
1 cup	chopped pecans	250 mL
1/4 tsp	salt	1 mL
1 cup	packed dark brown sugar	250 mL
2	eggs	2
2/3 cup	unsalted butter, melted	150 mL
1/2 tsp	vanilla extract	2 mL

You have to try these muffins to believe them: they really do taste like little pecan pies. And as scrumptious as they are with pecans, they are equally fabulous when made with cashews, pistachios, walnuts or peanuts.

Makes 12 muffins

- Preheat oven to 350°F (180°C)
- 12-cup muffin pan, greased

1. In a medium bowl, whisk together flour, pecans and salt.
2. In another medium bowl, whisk together brown sugar, eggs, butter and vanilla until well blended.
3. Add the egg mixture to the flour mixture and stir until just blended.
4. Divide batter equally among prepared muffin cups.
5. Bake in preheated oven for 22 to 25 minutes or until tops are golden and a toothpick inserted in the center comes out clean. Let cool in pan on a wire rack for 3 minutes, then transfer to the rack to cool.

Pecan and White Chocolate Chunk Muffins

1⅓ cups	quick-cooking rolled oats	325 mL
1¼ cups	all-purpose flour	300 mL
1 tbsp	baking powder	15 mL
½ tsp	salt	2 mL
⅓ cup	packed light brown sugar	75 mL
¼ cup	granulated sugar	60 mL
1	egg	1
⅓ cup	unsalted butter, melted	75 mL
2 tsp	vanilla extract	10 mL
1 cup	half-and-half (10%) cream	250 mL
1 cup	white chocolate chunks or chips	250 mL
½ cup	chopped pecans, toasted	125 mL

Chunks of white chocolate and buttery toasted pecans dress up oatmeal muffins for everyday coffee break bliss.

Makes 12 muffins

- Preheat oven to 400°F (200°C)
- 12-cup muffin pan, lined with paper liners

1. In a large bowl, whisk together oats, flour, baking powder and salt.

2. In a medium bowl, whisk together brown sugar, granulated sugar, egg, butter and vanilla until well blended. Whisk in cream until blended.

3. Add the egg mixture to the flour mixture and stir until just blended. Gently fold in white chocolate chunks and pecans.

4. Divide batter equally among prepared muffin cups.

5. Bake in preheated oven for 17 to 21 minutes or until tops are golden and a toothpick inserted in the center comes out clean. Let cool in pan on a wire rack for 3 minutes, then transfer to the rack to cool.

Praline Muffins

1½ cups	quick-cooking rolled oats	375 mL
1⅓ cups	all-purpose flour	325 mL
1 tbsp	baking powder	15 mL
½ tsp	baking soda	2 mL
½ tsp	salt	2 mL
1¼ cups	chopped pecans, divided	300 mL
¾ cup	packed dark brown sugar	175 mL
4 oz	cream cheese, softened	125 g
½ cup	unsalted butter, softened	125 mL
2	eggs	2
¾ cup	buttermilk	175 mL
1½ tsp	vanilla extract	7 mL

You don't have to be a pastry chef to master these winning muffins; you just need to be passionate about the blend of brown sugar, butter and pecans.

Makes 12 muffins

- Preheat oven to 400°F (200°C)
- 12-cup muffin pan, lined with paper liners

1. In a medium bowl, whisk together oats, flour, baking powder, baking soda and salt. Stir in ¾ cup (175 mL) of the pecans.

2. In a large bowl, using an electric mixer on medium-high speed, beat brown sugar, cream cheese and butter until light and fluffy. Beat in eggs, one at a time, until well blended. Beat in buttermilk and vanilla until blended.

3. Stir the flour mixture into the egg mixture until just blended.

4. Divide batter equally among prepared muffin cups. Sprinkle with the remaining pecans.

5. Bake in preheated oven for 20 to 24 minutes or until tops are golden and a toothpick inserted in the center comes out clean. Let cool in pan on a wire rack for 5 minutes, then transfer to the rack to cool.

Lemon Pistachio Muffins

Lemon Syrup

1/4 cup	granulated sugar	60 mL
3 tbsp	freshly squeezed lemon juice	45 mL

Muffins

2 cups	all-purpose flour	500 mL
2 tsp	baking powder	10 mL
3/4 tsp	salt	3 mL
1 1/4 cups	granulated sugar	300 mL
3/4 cup	unsalted butter, softened	175 mL
3	eggs	3
3/4 cup	milk	175 mL
2 tbsp	finely grated lemon zest	30 mL
3/4 cup	unsalted pistachios, chopped	175 mL

Bright citrus perfectly tempers the richness of pistachios in these pretty muffins. I sometimes have trouble locating unsalted shelled pistachios. Rather than shelling unsalted pistachios, I opt for the more readily available salted shelled pistachios. I give them a very quick rinse with warm water in a colander (to remove most of the salt), then immediately dry them with a tea towel.

Makes 12 muffins

- Preheat oven to 350°F (180°C)
- 12-cup muffin pan, greased

1. *Lemon syrup:* In a small saucepan, combine sugar and lemon juice over low heat; cook, stirring, until sugar has dissolved. Set aside to cool while you prepare the muffins.

2. *Muffins:* In a medium bowl, whisk together flour, baking powder and salt.

3. In a large bowl, using an electric mixer on medium-high speed, beat sugar and butter until light and fluffy. Beat in eggs, one at a time, until fluffy and pale yellow. Beat in milk and lemon zest until blended.

4. Add the flour mixture to the egg mixture and stir until just blended. Gently fold in pistachios.

5. Divide batter among prepared muffin cups.

6. Bake in preheated oven for 23 to 26 minutes or until tops are golden and a toothpick inserted in the center comes out clean. Let cool in pan on a wire rack for 3 minutes, then transfer to the rack.

7. Using a fork, gently pierce the top of each muffin three or four times. Brush warm muffins with lemon syrup. Let cool.

Chocolate Pistachio Muffins

1¾ cups	all-purpose flour	425 mL
¼ cup	unsweetened cocoa powder (not Dutch process)	60 mL
1 tsp	baking powder	5 mL
1 tsp	baking soda	5 mL
¼ tsp	salt	1 mL
1 cup	packed dark brown sugar	250 mL
2	eggs	2
¾ cup	buttermilk	175 mL
½ cup	unsalted butter, melted	125 mL
¾ tsp	almond extract	3 mL
1 cup	miniature semisweet chocolate chips	250 mL
¾ cup	lightly salted roasted pistachios, coarsely chopped	175 mL

Makes 12 muffins

- Preheat oven to 375°F (190°C)
- 12-cup muffin pan, lined with paper liners

1. In a large bowl, whisk together flour, cocoa powder, baking powder, baking soda and salt.
2. In a medium bowl, whisk together brown sugar, eggs, buttermilk, butter and almond extract until well blended.
3. Add the egg mixture to the flour mixture and stir until just blended. Gently fold in chocolate chips and pistachios.
4. Divide batter equally among prepared muffin cups.
5. Bake in preheated oven for 22 to 25 minutes or until a toothpick inserted in the center comes out clean. Let cool in pan on a wire rack for 5 minutes, then transfer to the rack to cool.

Chocolate muffins freckled with dark chocolate and green pistachios trump all others as the ideal coffeehouse muffin: lighter than cake, richer than a cookie and utterly indulgent.

Chai Spice Muffins

2 cups	all-purpose flour	500 mL
1½ tsp	ground ginger	7 mL
1 tsp	baking powder	5 mL
1 tsp	ground cinnamon	5 mL
1 tsp	ground cardamom	5 mL
½ tsp	baking soda	2 mL
½ tsp	salt	2 mL
⅔ cup	packed dark brown sugar	150 mL
2	eggs	2
⅓ cup	unsalted butter, melted	75 mL
1 tsp	vanilla extract	5 mL
1 cup	plain whole-milk yogurt	250 mL
2 tbsp	turbinado sugar	30 mL

Makes 12 muffins

- Preheat oven to 375°F (190°C)
- 12-cup muffin pan, lined with paper liners

1. In a large bowl, whisk together flour, ginger, baking powder, cinnamon, cardamom, baking soda and salt.
2. In a medium bowl, whisk together brown sugar, eggs, butter and vanilla until well blended. Whisk in yogurt until blended.
3. Add the egg mixture to the flour mixture and stir until just blended.
4. Divide batter equally among prepared muffin cups. Sprinkle with turbinado sugar.
5. Bake in preheated oven for 17 to 21 minutes or until tops are golden and a toothpick inserted in the center comes out clean. Let cool in pan on a wire rack for 3 minutes, then transfer to the rack to cool.

Chai tea spices — ginger, cinnamon and cardamom — flavor these delicious muffins.

Hermit Muffins

2 cups	all-purpose flour	500 mL
2 tsp	ground ginger	10 mL
1 tsp	baking powder	5 mL
1 tsp	ground cinnamon	5 mL
1/2 tsp	salt	2 mL
1/2 tsp	baking soda	2 mL
1/4 tsp	ground nutmeg	1 mL
1/8 tsp	ground cloves	0.5 mL
1/2 cup	raisins	125 mL
1/4 cup	finely chopped crystallized ginger	60 mL
1/4 cup	packed dark brown sugar	60 mL
1	egg	1
1/2 cup	dark (cooking) molasses	125 mL
1/3 cup	buttermilk	75 mL
1/3 cup	unsalted butter, melted	75 mL

Hermits are simple, drop-style spice cookies loaded with tiny currants and chopped walnuts. My mother made them for me — a recipe from *The Fannie Farmer Baking Book* — when I was a child, so I've always loved them. Here I've adapted the flavors to an equally easy muffin recipe. Together with a cup of tea (and a new mystery book in hand), it is my idea of late-afternoon heaven.

Makes 12 muffins

- Preheat oven to 400°F (200°C)
- 12-cup muffin pan, lined with paper liners

1. In a medium bowl, whisk together flour, ground ginger, baking powder, cinnamon, salt, baking soda, nutmeg and cloves. Stir in raisins and crystallized ginger.

2. In a large bowl, whisk together brown sugar, egg, molasses, buttermilk and butter until well blended.

3. Add the flour mixture to the egg mixture and stir until just blended.

4. Divide batter equally among prepared muffin cups.

5. Bake in preheated oven for 18 to 22 minutes or until tops are golden and spring back when touched. Let cool in pan on a wire rack for 5 minutes, then transfer to the rack to cool.

Cardamom Orange Muffins

Muffins

2 cups	all-purpose flour	500 mL
1 tsp	baking powder	5 mL
1 tsp	ground cardamom	5 mL
1/2 tsp	salt	2 mL
1/2 tsp	baking soda	2 mL
1/4 cup	granulated sugar	60 mL
1	egg	1
1/2 cup	liquid honey	125 mL
1/3 cup	milk	75 mL
1/3 cup	unsalted butter, melted	75 mL
1 tsp	vanilla extract	5 mL

Glaze

3/4 cup	confectioners' (icing) sugar	175 mL
1 tsp	finely grated orange zest	5 mL
2 tbsp	freshly squeezed orange juice	30 mL

Who says plain butter muffins have to be, well, plain? Add a bit of cardamom — exotic and fragrant, with notes of grapefruit zest — and an extra-easy, double-orange glaze and watch as your guests satisfy their muffin cravings with this elegant upgrade.

Makes 12 muffins

- Preheat oven to 400°F (200°C)
- 12-cup muffin pan, lined with paper liners

1. *Muffins:* In a large bowl, whisk together flour, baking powder, cardamom, salt and baking soda.

2. In a medium bowl, whisk together sugar, egg, honey, milk, butter and vanilla until well blended.

3. Add the egg mixture to the flour mixture and stir until just blended.

4. Divide batter equally among prepared muffin cups.

5. Bake in preheated oven for 18 to 22 minutes or until tops are golden and a toothpick inserted in the center comes out clean. Let cool in pan on a wire rack for 3 minutes, then transfer to the rack to cool while you prepare the glaze.

6. *Glaze:* In a small bowl, whisk together confectioners' sugar, orange zest and orange juice until blended. Spoon over tops of warm muffins and let cool.

Cappuccino Muffins

Topping

1/4 cup	all-purpose flour	60 mL
2 tbsp	packed light brown sugar	30 mL
1/4 tsp	ground cinnamon	1 mL
2 tbsp	unsalted butter, melted	30 mL

Muffins

3 cups	all-purpose flour	750 mL
1 tbsp	baking powder	15 mL
1/2 tsp	baking soda	2 mL
1/2 tsp	salt	2 mL
1/4 tsp	ground cinnamon	1 mL
1 cup	granulated sugar	250 mL
2	eggs	2
1/3 cup	unsalted butter, melted	75 mL
2 tbsp	instant espresso powder	30 mL
1 tsp	vanilla extract	5 mL
1 2/3 cups	buttermilk	400 mL

Makes 12 muffins

- Preheat oven to 375°F (190°C)
- 12-cup muffin pan, lined with paper liners

1. *Topping:* In a small bowl, combine flour, brown sugar and cinnamon. Stir in butter until blended and clumpy. Refrigerate until ready to use.

2. *Muffins:* In a large bowl, whisk together flour, baking powder, baking soda, salt and cinnamon.

3. In a medium bowl, whisk together sugar, eggs, butter, espresso powder and vanilla until well blended. Whisk in buttermilk until blended.

4. Add the egg mixture to the flour mixture and stir until just blended.

5. Divide batter equally among prepared muffin cups. Sprinkle with topping.

6. Bake in preheated oven for 23 to 26 minutes or until tops are golden and a toothpick inserted in the center comes out clean. Let cool in pan on a wire rack for 5 minutes, then transfer to the rack to cool.

Candied Ginger Muffins

2 cups	all-purpose flour	500 mL
1 tsp	baking powder	5 mL
2 tsp	ground ginger	10 mL
1/2 tsp	salt	2 mL
1/2 tsp	baking soda	2 mL
1/2 cup	finely chopped crystallized ginger	125 mL
1/4 cup	packed light brown sugar	60 mL
1	egg	1
1/2 cup	liquid honey	125 mL
1/3 cup	milk	75 mL
1/3 cup	unsalted butter, melted	75 mL
2 tsp	finely grated lemon zest	10 mL
2 tbsp	turbinado sugar	30 mL

With their golden color and sparkling sugar tops, these gorgeous muffins have jewels of candied ginger hidden inside.

Makes 12 muffins

- Preheat oven to 400°F (200°C)
- 12-cup muffin pan, lined with paper liners

1. In a large bowl, whisk together flour, baking powder, ground ginger, salt and baking soda. Stir in crystallized ginger.

2. In a medium bowl, whisk together brown sugar, egg, honey, milk, butter and lemon zest until well blended.

3. Add the egg mixture to the flour mixture and stir until just blended.

4. Divide batter equally among prepared muffin cups. Sprinkle with turbinado sugar.

5. Bake in preheated oven for 18 to 22 minutes or until tops are golden and a toothpick inserted in the center comes out clean. Let cool in pan on a wire rack for 5 minutes, then transfer to the rack to cool.

Rich Nutmeg Muffins

2 cups	all-purpose flour	500 mL
1 tbsp	baking powder	15 mL
2¼ tsp	freshly grated nutmeg	11 mL
½ tsp	salt	2 mL
¾ cup	packed light brown sugar	175 mL
1	egg	1
⅓ cup	unsalted butter, melted	75 mL
2 tsp	finely grated orange zest	10 mL
1 tsp	vanilla extract	5 mL
¾ cup	heavy or whipping (35%) cream	175 mL
⅔ cup	milk	150 mL

Spice muffins are often limited to a pinch of nutmeg. Here, nutmeg comes to the fore in a rich, buttery batter that showcases its exotic flavor. Orange zest plays a perfect supporting role to the slightly evergreen notes of the spice.

Tip

Because nutmeg is the star of this recipe, consider freshly grating it to maximize the flavorful oils of the spice, which diminish the longer they sit in a jar. Use a nutmeg grater, Microplane grater or the smallest holes on a box grater to grate the whole nutmeg.

Makes 12 muffins

- Preheat oven to 400°F (200°C)
- 12-cup muffin pan, greased

1. In a large bowl, whisk together flour, baking powder, nutmeg and salt.

2. In a medium bowl, whisk together brown sugar, egg, butter, orange zest and vanilla until well blended. Whisk in cream and milk until blended.

3. Add the egg mixture to the flour mixture and stir until just blended.

4. Divide batter equally among prepared muffin cups.

5. Bake in preheated oven for 18 to 22 minutes or until tops are golden and a toothpick inserted in the center comes out clean. Let cool in pan on a wire rack for 3 minutes, then transfer to the rack to cool.

Vanilla Buttermilk Bran Muffins

2 cups	natural bran	500 mL
1½ cups	all-purpose flour	375 mL
½ cup	whole wheat flour	125 mL
1 tbsp	baking powder	15 mL
1 tsp	salt	5 mL
¼ tsp	baking soda	1 mL
1 cup	packed light brown sugar	250 mL
2	eggs	2
½ cup	unsalted butter, melted	125 mL
1 tbsp	vanilla extract	15 mL
2 cups	buttermilk	500 mL

Vanilla and buttermilk are meant to be together, like Bert and Ernie. Here they transform regular bran muffins into coffeehouse-worthy treats.

Makes 18 muffins

- Preheat oven to 375°F (190°C)
- Two 12-cup muffin pans, 18 cups greased

1. In a large bowl, whisk together bran, all-purpose flour, whole wheat flour, baking powder, salt and baking soda.
2. In a medium bowl, whisk together brown sugar, eggs, butter and vanilla until well blended. Whisk in buttermilk until blended.
3. Add the egg mixture to the flour mixture and stir until just blended.
4. Divide batter equally among prepared muffin cups.
5. Bake in preheated oven for 21 to 26 minutes or until tops are golden brown and a toothpick inserted in the center comes out clean. Let cool in pans on a wire rack for 3 minutes, then transfer to the rack to cool.

Agave Muffins

1¾ cups	all-purpose flour	425 mL
2 tsp	baking powder	10 mL
1 tsp	baking soda	5 mL
½ tsp	salt	2 mL
1	egg	1
½ cup	unsalted butter, melted	125 mL
1 cup	sour cream	250 mL
2 tsp	finely grated lime zest	10 mL
¾ cup	agave nectar	175 mL

If you have yet to try the liquid sweetener agave nectar, produced in Mexico, here's your chance. You can find it in light, amber and dark varieties, any of which can be used in these muffins. Light has a mild, almost neutral flavor; amber has a medium-intensity caramel flavor; and dark has stronger caramel notes. Agave nectar is now readily available in supermarkets, and very reasonably priced. Trust me, you will love it!

Makes 12 muffins

- Preheat oven to 350°F (180°C)
- 12-cup muffin pan, lined with paper liners

1. In a large bowl, whisk together flour, baking powder, baking soda and salt.
2. In a medium bowl, whisk together egg, butter, sour cream and lime zest until well blended. Whisk in agave nectar until blended.
3. Add the egg mixture to the flour mixture and stir until just blended.
4. Divide batter equally among prepared muffin cups.
5. Bake in preheated oven for 20 to 25 minutes or until tops are golden and a toothpick inserted in the center comes out clean. Let cool in pan on a wire rack for 3 minutes, then transfer to the rack to cool.

Salted Caramel Chocolate Muffins

1⅓ cups	all-purpose flour	325 mL
¼ cup	unsweetened cocoa powder (not Dutch process)	60 mL
¾ tsp	baking soda	3 mL
¾ tsp	fine sea salt, divided	3 mL
¾ cup	granulated sugar	175 mL
2	eggs	2
½ cup	sour cream	125 mL
⅓ cup	milk	75 mL
¼ cup	unsalted butter, melted	60 mL
1 tsp	vanilla extract	5 mL
½ cup	miniature semisweet chocolate chips	125 mL
½ cup	canned dulce de leche	125 mL

Chocolate is a perfect flavor in its own right, but it also loves to mingle with countless other flavors. Caramel is a natural partner, made even better with a light sprinkling of sea salt.

Tip

Look for cans of dulce de leche in the international foods aisle of the supermarket or at Hispanic grocery stores.

Makes 12 muffins

- Preheat oven to 325°F (160°C)
- 12-cup muffin pan, lined with paper liners

1. In a large bowl, whisk together flour, cocoa powder, baking soda and ½ tsp (2 mL) of the sea salt.

2. In a medium bowl, whisk together sugar, eggs, sour cream, milk, butter and vanilla until well blended.

3. Add the egg mixture to the flour mixture and stir until just blended. Gently fold in chocolate chips.

4. Divide batter equally among prepared muffin cups.

5. Bake in preheated oven for 20 to 25 minutes or until tops are golden and a toothpick inserted in the center comes out clean. Let cool in pan on a wire rack for 5 minutes, then transfer to the rack.

6. Top each warm muffin with 2 tsp (10 mL) of the dulce de leche. Let stand for 30 seconds, then spread over muffin tops. Sprinkle evenly with the remaining sea salt. Let cool.

Lime White Chocolate Muffins

Topping

$1/2$ cup	chopped macadamia nuts	125 mL
$1/3$ cup	all-purpose flour	75 mL
$1/4$ cup	packed light brown sugar	60 mL
$1/4$ cup	unsalted butter, melted	60 mL

Muffins

2 cups	all-purpose flour	500 mL
$1 1/2$ tsp	baking powder	7 mL
$1/2$ tsp	baking soda	2 mL
$1/2$ tsp	salt	2 mL
1 cup	granulated sugar	250 mL
1	egg	1
$1/2$ cup	unsalted butter, melted	125 mL
1 tbsp	finely grated lime zest	15 mL
1 tsp	vanilla extract	5 mL
1 cup	buttermilk	250 mL
2 tbsp	freshly squeezed lime juice	30 mL
1 cup	white chocolate chips	250 mL

Lime two ways — both the juice and the zest — and a macadamia nut crumble enhance the creamy white chocolate chips in these muffins.

Makes 12 muffins

- Preheat oven to 375°F (190°C)
- 12-cup muffin pan, lined with paper liners

1. *Topping:* In a small bowl, combine nuts, flour, brown sugar and butter until blended and crumbly. Refrigerate until ready to use.
2. *Muffins:* In a large bowl, whisk together flour, baking powder, baking soda and salt.
3. In a medium bowl, whisk together sugar, egg, butter, lime zest and vanilla until well blended. Whisk in buttermilk and lime juice until blended.
4. Add the egg mixture to the flour mixture and stir until just blended. Gently fold in white chocolate chips.
5. Divide batter equally among prepared muffin cups. Sprinkle with topping and gently press into batter.
6. Bake in preheated oven for 24 to 28 minutes or until tops are golden and a toothpick inserted in the center comes out clean. Let cool in pan on a wire rack for 3 minutes, then transfer to the rack to cool.

Italian Chocolate Surprise Muffins

1¼ cups	all-purpose flour	300 mL
½ cup	unsweetened cocoa powder (not Dutch process)	125 mL
1 tsp	baking powder	5 mL
½ tsp	baking soda	2 mL
½ tsp	salt	2 mL
½ cup	granulated sugar	125 mL
2	eggs	2
½ cup	unsalted butter, melted	125 mL
½ cup	sour cream	125 mL
3 tbsp	hazelnut or coffee liqueur	45 mL
½ cup	chocolate-hazelnut spread	125 mL

These decadent muffins are great for dessert or breakfast. Look for the chocolate-hazelnut spread where peanut butter is shelved in the supermarket.

Makes 12 muffins

- Preheat oven to 350°F (180°C)
- 12-cup muffin pan, greased

1. In a large bowl, whisk together flour, cocoa powder, baking powder, baking soda and salt.

2. In a medium bowl, whisk together sugar, eggs, butter, sour cream and liqueur until well blended.

3. Add the egg mixture to the flour mixture and stir until just blended.

4. Divide half the batter equally among prepared muffin cups. Spoon 2 tsp (10 mL) of the chocolate-hazelnut spread in the center of each cup of batter. Top with the remaining batter.

5. Bake in preheated oven for 21 to 25 minutes or until tops are firm and a toothpick inserted in the center comes out clean. Let cool in pan on a wire rack for 5 minutes, then transfer to the rack to cool.

Sealed with a Kiss Muffins

2¼ cups	all-purpose flour	550 mL
1 tbsp	baking powder	15 mL
½ tsp	baking soda	2 mL
½ tsp	salt	2 mL
¾ cup	packed light brown sugar	175 mL
2	eggs	2
⅓ cup	unsalted butter, melted	75 mL
2 tsp	vanilla extract	10 mL
1⅓ cups	plain whole-milk yogurt	325 mL
12	milk chocolate kiss candies, unwrapped	12
2 tbsp	turbinado sugar	30 mL

For their cuteness alone, these hidden-treasure muffins are enticing. The vanilla-laced batter is not too sweet, a fitting foil to the gooey chocolate surprise center.

Makes 12 muffins

- Preheat oven to 400°F (200°C)
- 12-cup muffin pan, greased

1. In a large bowl, whisk together flour, baking powder, baking soda and salt.

2. In a medium bowl, whisk together brown sugar, eggs, butter and vanilla until well blended. Whisk in yogurt until blended.

3. Add the egg mixture to the flour mixture and stir until just blended.

4. Divide batter equally among prepared muffin cups. Gently push a chocolate kiss, tip up, into the center of each cup until covered with batter. Sprinkle with turbinado sugar.

5. Bake in preheated oven for 21 to 26 minutes or until tops are golden and a toothpick inserted in the center comes out clean. Let cool in pan on a wire rack for 5 minutes, then transfer to the rack to cool.

Peppermint Chocolate Chunk Muffins

2 cups	all-purpose flour	500 mL
2 tsp	baking powder	10 mL
1/2 tsp	baking soda	2 mL
1/2 tsp	salt	2 mL
3/4 cup	granulated sugar	175 mL
2	eggs	2
1/2 cup	unsalted butter, melted	125 mL
1 tsp	peppermint extract	5 mL
3/4 cup	sour cream	175 mL
6 oz	bittersweet chocolate, chopped into chunks	175 g
1/3 cup	coarsely crushed red-and-white-striped peppermint candies	75 mL

Makes 12 muffins

- Preheat oven to 375°F (190°C)
- 12-cup muffin pan, lined with paper liners

1. In a large bowl, whisk together flour, baking powder, baking soda and salt.
2. In a medium bowl, whisk together sugar, eggs, butter and peppermint extract until well blended. Whisk in sour cream until blended.
3. Add the egg mixture to the flour mixture and stir until just blended. Gently fold in chocolate.
4. Divide batter equally among prepared muffin cups. Sprinkle with candies.
5. Bake in preheated oven for 18 to 22 minutes or until tops are golden and a toothpick inserted in the center comes out clean. Let cool in pan on a wire rack for 3 minutes, then transfer to the rack to cool.

Chocolate Marble Muffins

3 cups	all-purpose flour	750 mL
1 tbsp	baking powder	15 mL
1/2 tsp	baking soda	2 mL
1/2 tsp	salt	2 mL
1 cup	granulated sugar	250 mL
2/3 cup	unsalted butter, softened	150 mL
2	eggs	2
2 tsp	vanilla extract	10 mL
1 1/2 cups	plain whole-milk yogurt	375 mL
3 tbsp	unsweetened cocoa powder (not Dutch process)	45 mL
1/3 cup	miniature semisweet chocolate chips (optional)	75 mL

Serve these chocolate-vanilla gems mid-morning with coffee, mid-afternoon with a café mocha or in the middle of the night with a glass of warm milk.

Makes 12 muffins

- Preheat oven to 375°F (190°C)
- 12-cup muffin pan, greased

1. In a medium bowl, whisk together flour, baking powder, baking soda and salt.
2. In a large bowl, using an electric mixer on medium-high speed, beat sugar and butter until light and fluffy. Beat in eggs, one at a time, until fluffy and pale yellow. Beat in vanilla until blended.
3. With the mixer on low speed, beat in flour mixture alternately with yogurt, making three additions of flour and two of yogurt, until just blended. Transfer half the batter into another bowl. Whisk cocoa powder into one bowl until blended, then stir in chocolate chips (if using).
4. Divide half the vanilla batter equally among prepared muffin cups, then top with half the chocolate batter. Repeat layers with the remaining vanilla and chocolate batters. Using a wooden skewer, slightly swirl batters.
5. Bake in preheated oven for 25 to 30 minutes or until tops are golden and a toothpick inserted in the center comes out clean. Let cool in pan on a wire rack for 3 minutes, then transfer to the rack to cool.

Chocolate Macaroon Muffins

Filling

1 cup	sweetened flaked or shredded coconut	250 mL
1/4 cup	canned sweetened condensed milk	60 mL
1/4 tsp	almond extract	1 mL

Muffins

2 cups	all-purpose flour	500 mL
1/4 cup	unsweetened cocoa powder (not Dutch process)	60 mL
1 tbsp	baking powder	15 mL
1/2 tsp	salt	2 mL
1/4 tsp	baking soda	1 mL
1/2 cup	granulated sugar	125 mL
1	egg	1
1/3 cup	vegetable oil	75 mL
1 tsp	vanilla extract	5 mL
1 cup	milk	250 mL

Sweet with coconut and rich with chocolate, these muffins skirt the boundary between muffin and cupcake. Regardless, I am more than happy to eat them — unabashedly, I might add — first thing in the morning with my morning coffee.

Makes 12 muffins

- Preheat oven to 400°F (200°C)
- 12-cup muffin pan, greased

1. *Filling:* In a small bowl, combine coconut, condensed milk and almond extract until well blended. Set aside.

2. *Muffins:* In a large bowl, whisk together flour, cocoa powder, baking powder, salt and baking soda.

3. In a medium bowl, whisk together sugar, egg, oil and vanilla until well blended. Whisk in milk until blended.

4. Add the egg mixture to the flour mixture and stir until just blended.

5. Divide half the batter equally among prepared muffin cups. Spoon 2 tsp (10 mL) of the filling into the center of each cup of batter. Top with the remaining batter.

6. Bake in preheated oven for 15 to 19 minutes or until tops are golden and a toothpick inserted in the center comes out clean. Let cool in pan on a wire rack for 3 minutes, then transfer to the rack to cool.

Chocolate Chip Streusel Muffins

Streusel

²/₃ cup	packed light brown sugar	150 mL
¹/₃ cup	all-purpose flour	75 mL
¹/₄ cup	cold unsalted butter, cut into small pieces	60 mL
2 tsp	ground cinnamon	10 mL
¹/₂ cup	miniature semisweet chocolate chips	125 mL

Muffins

1³/₄ cups	all-purpose flour	425 mL
1 tbsp	baking powder	15 mL
¹/₄ tsp	salt	1 mL
¹/₂ cup	granulated sugar	125 mL
2	eggs	2
¹/₃ cup	vegetable oil	75 mL
2 tsp	vanilla extract	10 mL
1 cup	sour cream	250 mL

Here's a variation on everyone's favorite cookie, in streusel muffin form. Kids love them — if they can wrestle one away from the adults!

Makes 12 muffins

- Preheat oven to 375°F (190°C)
- Food processor
- 12-cup muffin pan, lined with paper liners

1. *Streusel:* In a bowl, using your fingers, combine brown sugar, flour, butter and cinnamon until crumbly. Stir in chocolate chips. Refrigerate until ready to use.

2. *Muffins:* In a large bowl, whisk together flour, baking powder and salt.

3. In a medium bowl, whisk together sugar, eggs, oil and vanilla until well blended. Whisk in sour cream until blended.

4. Add the egg mixture to the flour mixture and stir until just blended.

5. Place 1 tbsp (15 mL) of the batter in each prepared muffin cup. Top each with 1 tbsp (15 mL) of the streusel. Divide remaining batter equally on top. Sprinkle with the remaining streusel.

6. Bake in preheated oven for 23 to 25 minutes or until tops are golden and a toothpick inserted in the center comes out with a few dry crumbs attached. Let cool in pan on a wire rack for 10 minutes, then transfer to the rack to cool.

Cacao Nib Muffins

2½ cups	all-purpose flour	625 mL
3½ tsp	baking powder	17 mL
½ tsp	salt	2 mL
1 cup	packed light brown sugar	250 mL
¾ cup	unsalted butter, softened	175 mL
1	vanilla bean	1
2	eggs	2
¾ cup	milk	175 mL
½ cup	cacao nibs	125 mL

Cacao nibs are simply cleaned, roasted and lightly crushed cacao beans. Their taste is nicely bittersweet, and they have the crunchy, toasty flavor of roasted nuts. Fans of dark chocolate will love nibs, which are richer and more intense than the chocolate made from them. You can add them to all sorts of baked goods and desserts, but I am crazy for them in these muffins, where they find perfect contrast in a vanilla bean batter.

Tip
The vanilla bean may be replaced with 1½ tsp (7 mL) vanilla extract.

Makes 12 muffins
- Preheat oven to 350°F (180°C)
- 12-cup muffin pan, lined with paper liners

1. In a medium bowl, whisk together flour, baking powder and salt.

2. In a large bowl, using an electric mixer on medium-high speed, beat brown sugar and butter until light and fluffy. Using a knife, cut vanilla bean in half lengthwise. Scrape seeds into butter mixture (reserve pod for another use, if desired). Beat in eggs, one at a time, until well blended. Beat in milk until blended.

3. Add the flour mixture to the egg mixture and stir until just blended. Gently fold in cacao nibs.

4. Divide batter equally among prepared muffin cups.

5. Bake in preheated oven for 21 to 24 minutes or until tops are golden and a toothpick inserted in the center comes out clean. Let cool in pan on a wire rack for 3 minutes, then transfer to the rack to cool.

Milk Chocolate Sour Cream Muffins

1½ cups	all-purpose flour	375 mL
1½ tsp	baking powder	7 mL
¼ tsp	baking soda	1 mL
¼ tsp	salt	1 mL
½ cup	packed light brown sugar	125 mL
1	egg	1
½ cup	unsalted butter, melted	125 mL
1 cup	sour cream	250 mL
1½ tsp	vanilla extract	7 mL
1¼ cups	milk chocolate chunks	300 mL
2 tbsp	turbinado sugar	30 mL

When I want chocolate that's all comfort — the familiar flavor I remember from childhood — I bake a batch of these muffins. The sour cream imparts a subtle tang and tremendous moistness to the batter, highlighting the hints of luxurious caramel from the milk chocolate.

Makes 12 muffins

- Preheat oven to 400°F (200°C)
- 12-cup muffin pan, greased

1. In a large bowl, whisk together flour, baking powder, baking soda and salt.
2. In a medium bowl, whisk together brown sugar, egg, butter, sour cream and vanilla until blended.
3. Add the egg mixture to the flour mixture and stir until just blended. Gently fold in chocolate chunks.
4. Divide batter equally among prepared muffin cups. Sprinkle with turbinado sugar.
5. Bake in preheated oven for 19 to 21 minutes or until tops are golden and a toothpick inserted in the center comes out clean. Let cool in pan on a wire rack for 3 minutes, then transfer to the rack to cool.

Chocolate–Chocolate Chip Muffins

1¼ cups	all-purpose flour	300 mL
½ cup	unsweetened cocoa powder (not Dutch process)	125 mL
1 tsp	baking powder	5 mL
½ tsp	baking soda	2 mL
½ tsp	salt	2 mL
½ cup	packed dark brown sugar	125 mL
2	eggs	2
⅔ cup	milk	150 mL
¼ cup	unsalted butter, melted	60 mL
¼ cup	vegetable oil	60 mL
2 tsp	vanilla extract	10 mL
1 cup	semisweet, bittersweet or white chocolate chips	250 mL

I love chocolate, and when I'm in need of a quick fix, I turn to these muffins because they are so simple to make and so darn good. They are a perfect treat to warm up from the cold weather.

Makes 12 muffins

- Preheat oven to 350°F (180°C)
- 12-cup muffin pan, greased

1. In a large bowl, whisk together flour, cocoa powder, baking powder, baking soda and salt.
2. In a medium bowl, whisk together brown sugar, eggs, milk, butter, oil and vanilla until well blended.
3. Add the egg mixture to the flour mixture and stir until just blended. Gently fold in chocolate chips.
4. Divide batter equally among prepared muffin cups.
5. Bake in preheated oven for 21 to 25 minutes or until tops are firm and a toothpick inserted in the center comes out clean. Let cool in pan on a wire rack for 3 minutes, then transfer to the rack to cool.

Yogurt Muffins with Almond Cardamom Streusel

Streusel

2/3 cup	sliced almonds, finely chopped	150 mL
1/3 cup	packed light brown sugar	75 mL
2 tbsp	unsalted butter, melted	30 mL
3/4 tsp	ground cardamom	3 mL

Muffins

2 cups	all-purpose flour	500 mL
1 tsp	baking powder	5 mL
1/2 tsp	baking soda	2 mL
1/2 tsp	salt	2 mL
1/2 tsp	ground cinnamon	2 mL
1/4 tsp	ground cardamom	1 mL
2/3 cup	granulated sugar	150 mL
2	eggs	2
1/3 cup	vegetable oil	75 mL
1/2 tsp	almond extract	2 mL
1 cup	plain whole-milk yogurt	250 mL

Topped with a toasty almond streusel and subtly spiced with cardamom and cinnamon, these amazing muffins are a stellar way to begin the day.

Makes 12 muffins

- Preheat oven to 375°F (190°C)
- 12-cup muffin pan, lined with paper liners

1. *Streusel:* In a small bowl, combine almonds, brown sugar, butter and cardamom until blended. Refrigerate until ready to use.

2. *Muffins:* In a large bowl, whisk together flour, baking powder, baking soda, salt, cinnamon and cardamom.

3. In a medium bowl, whisk together sugar, eggs, oil and almond extract until blended. Whisk in yogurt until blended.

4. Add the egg mixture to the flour mixture and stir until just blended.

5. Divide batter equally among prepared muffin cups. Sprinkle with streusel.

6. Bake in preheated oven for 17 to 21 minutes or until tops are golden and a toothpick inserted in the center comes out clean. Let cool in pan on a wire rack for 3 minutes, then transfer to the rack to cool.

Decadent Carrot Cake Muffins

2 cups	all-purpose flour	500 mL
2 tsp	baking soda	10 mL
2 tsp	ground cinnamon	10 mL
1/4 tsp	salt	1 mL
1 1/4 cups	granulated sugar	300 mL
3	eggs	3
1 cup	vegetable oil	250 mL
2 tsp	vanilla extract	10 mL
1	tart apple, such as Granny Smith, peeled and coarsely shredded	1
2 cups	coarsely shredded carrots	500 mL
1/2 cup	raisins	125 mL
1/3 cup	sweetened flaked or shredded coconut	75 mL
1 cup	chopped pecans	250 mL

I regularly make these for coffee hour after church and always have people beg for the recipe. They aren't too sweet and have a moist, dense texture from the carrots, coconut and apple. When I make them to eat at home, I tend to play with what I throw into the batter — for example, a handful of pumpkin seeds or toasted walnuts in place of the pecans, or dried blueberries, cherries or cranberries in place of the raisins. The beauty of this recipe is that you can increase the spices or omit the nuts and it will still taste great.

Makes 18 muffins

- Preheat oven to 350°F (180°C)
- Two 12-cup muffin pans, 18 cups greased

1. In a large bowl, whisk together flour, baking soda, cinnamon and salt.

2. In a medium bowl, whisk together sugar, eggs, oil and vanilla until well blended. Mix in apple.

3. Add the egg mixture to the flour mixture and stir until just blended. Gently fold in carrots, raisins and coconut.

4. Divide batter equally among prepared muffin cups. Sprinkle with pecans.

5. Bake in preheated oven for 18 to 22 minutes or until tops are golden and a toothpick inserted in the center comes out clean. Let cool in pans on a wire rack for 5 minutes, then transfer to the rack to cool.

Malted Milk Muffins

2 cups	all-purpose flour	500 mL
2/3 cup	malted milk powder	150 mL
2 tsp	baking powder	10 mL
1/2 tsp	salt	2 mL
1 cup	granulated sugar	250 mL
1	egg	1
1/3 cup	unsalted butter, melted	75 mL
1 1/2 tsp	vanilla extract	7 mL
1 cup	whole milk	250 mL

These muffins are so easy to make, and whenever I make them, people beg to know the secret ingredient; it adds subtle notes of toasty caramel that are fantastic. Look for the malted milk powder alongside the dry milk products or hot beverage mixes in the supermarket.

Makes 10 muffins

- Preheat oven to 375°F (190°C)
- 12-cup muffin pan, 10 cups lined with paper liners

1. In a large bowl, whisk together flour, malted milk powder, baking powder and salt.

2. In a medium bowl, whisk together sugar, egg, butter and vanilla until well blended. Whisk in milk until blended.

3. Add the egg mixture to the flour mixture and stir until just blended.

4. Divide batter equally among prepared muffin cups.

5. Bake in preheated oven for 16 to 21 minutes or until a toothpick inserted in the center comes out clean. Let cool in pan on a wire rack for 3 minutes, then transfer to the rack to cool.

Ne Plus Ultra Muffins

3/4 cup	unsalted butter, cut into cubes	175 mL
3 cups	all-purpose flour	750 mL
1 tbsp	baking powder	15 mL
3/4 tsp	baking soda	3 mL
3/4 tsp	salt	3 mL
3/4 cup	packed light brown sugar	175 mL
2	eggs	2
2 tsp	vanilla extract	10 mL
1 1/3 cups	buttermilk	325 mL

Brown sugar plus browned butter equals exquisite, hence the eponym, ne plus ultra.

Makes 12 muffins

- 12-cup muffin pan, lined with paper liners

1. In a large skillet, heat butter over medium heat until foam subsides and butter is deep golden brown. Immediately transfer to a bowl and let cool to room temperature.

2. Preheat oven to 375°F (190°C).

3. In a large bowl, whisk together flour, baking powder, baking soda and salt.

4. In a medium bowl, whisk together browned butter, brown sugar, eggs and vanilla until well blended. Whisk in buttermilk until blended.

5. Add the egg mixture to the flour mixture and stir until just blended.

6. Divide batter equally among prepared muffin cups.

7. Bake for 21 to 26 minutes or until tops are golden and a toothpick inserted in the center comes out clean. Let cool in pan on a wire rack for 3 minutes, then transfer to the rack to cool.

Toffee Muffins

2 cups	all-purpose flour	500 mL
2 tsp	baking powder	10 mL
1/2 tsp	baking soda	2 mL
1/2 tsp	salt	2 mL
3/4 cup	packed dark brown sugar	175 mL
1	egg	1
1/2 cup	unsalted butter, melted	125 mL
2 tsp	vanilla extract	10 mL
1 cup	buttermilk	250 mL
1 cup	coarsely chopped milk chocolate-covered toffee bars	250 mL

I was testing a recipe for chocolate chip muffins when I realized I had no chocolate chips! I did, however, have a bag of chocolate-covered toffee bars, so in they went. I loved the final product, as did everyone else who tried them.

Makes 12 muffins

- Preheat oven to 375°F (190°C)
- 12-cup muffin pan, lined with paper liners

1. In a large bowl, whisk together flour, baking powder, baking soda and salt.
2. In a medium bowl, whisk together brown sugar, egg, butter and vanilla until well blended. Whisk in buttermilk until blended.
3. Add the egg mixture to the flour mixture and stir until just blended. Gently fold in toffee.
4. Divide batter equally among prepared muffin cups.
5. Bake in preheated oven for 18 to 21 minutes or until tops are golden and a toothpick inserted in the center comes out clean. Let cool in pan on a wire rack for 3 minutes, then transfer to the rack to cool.

Vanilla Rice Pudding Muffins with Dried Cranberries

2 1/4 cups	all-purpose flour	550 mL
2 1/2 tsp	baking powder	12 mL
3/4 tsp	salt	3 mL
1/2 tsp	baking soda	2 mL
1/2 tsp	ground cinnamon	2 mL
3/4 cup	granulated sugar	175 mL
2	eggs	2
1/3 cup	unsalted butter, melted	75 mL
2 tsp	vanilla extract	10 mL
1 cup	sour cream	250 mL
1/2 cup	whole milk	125 mL
1 cup	cold cooked white rice	250 mL
1/2 cup	dried cranberries	125 mL

Some love rice pudding, others do not, but I have yet to find anyone who can resist these tender rice pudding muffins. You can use any dried fruit in place of the dried cranberries, swap them for miniature semisweet chocolate chips or leave them out altogether.

Makes 12 muffins

- Preheat oven to 400°F (200°C)
- 12-cup muffin pan, greased

1. In a large bowl, whisk together flour, baking powder, salt, baking soda and cinnamon.
2. In a medium bowl, whisk together sugar, eggs, butter and vanilla until well blended. Whisk in sour cream and milk until blended.
3. Add the egg mixture to the flour mixture and stir until just blended. Gently fold in rice and cranberries.
4. Divide batter equally among prepared muffin cups.
5. Bake in preheated oven for 22 to 26 minutes or until tops are golden and a toothpick inserted in the center comes out clean. Let cool in pan on a wire rack for 5 minutes, then transfer to the rack to cool.

Sour Cream Muffins with Poppy Seed Streusel

Streusel

1/4 cup	packed light brown sugar	60 mL
3 tbsp	all-purpose flour	45 mL
2 tbsp	poppy seeds	30 mL
2 tbsp	unsalted butter, melted	30 mL

Muffins

2 cups	all-purpose flour	500 mL
2 tsp	baking powder	10 mL
1 tsp	baking soda	5 mL
1/2 tsp	salt	2 mL
3/4 cup	granulated sugar	175 mL
1	egg	1
1/4 cup	unsalted butter, melted	60 mL
1 tbsp	finely grated orange zest	15 mL
1 tsp	vanilla extract	5 mL
1 cup	sour cream	250 mL
3/4 cup	buttermilk	175 mL

Sweetly scented with orange, these tender, streusel-topped muffins are perfect for winter holiday breakfasts.

Makes 16 muffins

- Preheat oven to 375°F (190°C)
- Two 12-cup muffin pans, 16 cups lined with paper liners

1. *Streusel:* In a small bowl, combine brown sugar, flour, poppy seeds and butter until well blended. Refrigerate until ready to use.

2. *Muffins:* In a large bowl, whisk together flour, baking powder, baking soda and salt.

3. In a medium bowl, whisk together sugar, egg, butter, orange zest and vanilla until well blended. Whisk in sour cream and buttermilk until blended.

4. Add the egg mixture to the flour mixture and stir until just blended.

5. Divide batter equally among prepared muffin cups. Sprinkle with streusel.

6. Bake in preheated oven for 18 to 22 minutes or until tops are light golden brown and a toothpick inserted in the center comes out clean. Let cool in pans on a wire rack for 3 minutes, then transfer to the rack to cool.

Sour Cream Raisin Muffins

Topping

1/2 cup	packed dark brown sugar	125 mL
1/2 cup	chopped pecans	125 mL
1/2 tsp	ground cinnamon	2 mL

Muffins

1 1/2 cups	sour cream	375 mL
1 1/2 tsp	baking soda	7 mL
1 3/4 cups	all-purpose flour	425 mL
2 tsp	baking powder	10 mL
1 tsp	ground cinnamon, divided	5 mL
1/2 tsp	salt	2 mL
1 cup	granulated sugar	250 mL
2	eggs	2
1/2 cup	unsalted butter, melted	125 mL
2/3 cup	raisins	150 mL

I found inspiration for these muffins from one of my favorite old-fashioned pies: sour cream custard pie. Even those who scrunch their noses at the sound of sour cream and raisins swiftly change their minds upon their first bite.

Makes 12 muffins

- Preheat oven to 350°F (180°C)
- 12-cup muffin pan, lined with paper liners

1. *Topping:* In a small bowl, combine brown sugar, pecans and cinnamon. Set aside.
2. *Muffins:* In a medium bowl, whisk together sour cream and baking soda. Let stand for 5 minutes.
3. In a large bowl, whisk together flour, baking powder, cinnamon and salt.
4. Whisk sugar, eggs and butter into the sour cream mixture until well blended.
5. Add the egg mixture to the flour mixture and stir until just blended. Gently fold in raisins.
6. Divide batter equally among prepared muffin cups. Sprinkle with topping.
7. Bake in preheated oven for 24 to 28 minutes or until tops are golden and a toothpick inserted in the center comes out clean. Let cool in pan on a wire rack for 3 minutes, then transfer to the rack to cool.

Eggnog Muffins

Topping

2 tbsp	granulated sugar	30 mL
1/4 tsp	ground cinnamon	1 mL

Muffins

3 cups	all-purpose flour	750 mL
1 tbsp	baking powder	15 mL
1/2 tsp	salt	2 mL
1 tsp	ground nutmeg	5 mL
1/2 tsp	ground cinnamon	2 mL
1/2 cup	granulated sugar	125 mL
1	egg	1
1/2 cup	unsalted butter, melted	125 mL
1 1/2 cups	eggnog	375 mL
1/4 cup	rum, brandy or whiskey	60 mL

You can make these amazing muffins alcohol-free with ease: simply add 1/4 cup (60 mL) more eggnog in place of the rum. If you like, add a splash of rum or brandy extract.

Makes 16 muffins

- Preheat oven to 350°F (180°C)
- Two 12-cup muffin pans, 16 cups lined with paper liners

1. *Topping:* In a small bowl, combine sugar and cinnamon. Set aside.
2. *Muffins:* In a large bowl, whisk together flour, baking powder, salt, nutmeg and cinnamon.
3. In a medium bowl, whisk together sugar, egg and butter until well blended. Whisk in eggnog and rum until blended.
4. Add the egg mixture to the flour mixture and stir until just blended.
5. Divide batter equally among prepared muffin cups. Sprinkle with topping.
6. Bake in preheated oven for 21 to 25 minutes or until tops are golden and a toothpick inserted in the center comes out clean. Let cool in pans on a wire rack for 3 minutes, then transfer to the rack to cool.

Poppy Seed Pound Cake Muffins

2 cups	all-purpose flour	500 mL
3 tbsp	poppy seeds	45 mL
1 tsp	salt	5 mL
1/2 tsp	baking soda	2 mL
1 cup	granulated sugar	250 mL
1 1/2 cups	unsalted butter, softened	375 mL
2	eggs	2
1 cup	plain whole-milk yogurt	250 mL
2 tsp	vanilla extract	10 mL

You know those big, buttery poppy seed muffins in the coffeehouse case? The ones that tempt you every time you order a skim latte? Well, it's a good thing you held out, because my version is the one you really want. These freeze particularly well, so you can savor just a few at a time.

Makes 12 large muffins

- Preheat oven to 400°F (200°C)
- 12-cup muffin pan, lined with paper liners

1. In a medium bowl, whisk together flour, poppy seeds, salt and baking soda.
2. In a large bowl, using an electric mixer on medium-high speed, beat sugar and butter until light and fluffy. Beat in eggs, one at a time, until fluffy and pale yellow. Beat in yogurt and vanilla until blended.
3. Add the flour mixture to the egg mixture and stir with a wooden spoon until just blended.
4. Divide batter equally among prepared muffin cups.
5. Bake in preheated oven for 20 to 25 minutes or until a toothpick inserted in the center comes out clean. Let cool in pan on a wire rack for 3 minutes, then transfer to the rack to cool.

S'more Muffins

1½ cups	all-purpose flour	375 mL
½ cup	graham cracker crumbs	125 mL
1 tsp	baking soda	5 mL
½ tsp	salt	2 mL
¼ cup	packed dark brown sugar	60 mL
1	egg	1
¼ cup	vegetable oil	60 mL
1 tsp	vanilla extract	5 mL
1½ cups	buttermilk	375 mL
¾ cup	semisweet chocolate chips	175 mL
1½ cups	miniature marshmallows, divided	375 mL

Ground graham crackers stirred into the batter give these clever muffin s'mores their characteristic flavor. Leave the marshmallows out on a plate for a day or two to get stale — they'll hold their shape better during baking.

Tip

Ready-made graham cracker crumbs are available in the baking aisle of the supermarket. To make your own, you will need about 8 graham cracker squares to yield ½ cup (125 mL) crumbs.

Makes 12 muffins

- Preheat oven to 375°F (190°C)
- 12-cup muffin pan, lined with paper liners

1. In a large bowl, whisk together flour, graham cracker crumbs, baking soda and salt.

2. In a medium bowl, whisk together brown sugar, egg, oil and vanilla until well blended. Whisk in buttermilk until blended.

3. Add the egg mixture to the flour mixture and stir until just blended. Gently fold in chocolate chips and 1 cup (250 mL) of the marshmallows.

4. Divide batter equally among prepared muffin cups. Sprinkle with the remaining marshmallows and gently press into batter.

5. Bake in preheated oven for 18 to 21 minutes or until tops are golden and a toothpick inserted in the center comes out clean. Let cool in pan on a wire rack for 5 minutes, then transfer to the rack to cool.

Gloreo Muffins

2 1/4 cups	all-purpose flour	550 mL
1 1/2 tsp	baking powder	7 mL
3/4 tsp	baking soda	3 mL
3/4 tsp	salt	3 mL
1/2 cup	granulated sugar	125 mL
2	eggs	2
1/3 cup	unsalted butter, melted	75 mL
1 1/2 tsp	vanilla extract	7 mL
3/4 cup	sour cream	175 mL
2/3 cup	milk	150 mL
1 1/2 cups	chopped cream-filled chocolate sandwich cookies, such as Oreo	375 mL

Sometimes there is nothing better than the taste of a childhood favorite. You'll love the flavor of this classic cookie all over again, crumbled into muffin batter, the happy result of a package being crushed on the trip home from the grocery store.

Makes 12 muffins

- Preheat oven to 400°F (200°C)
- 12-cup muffin pan, greased

1. In a large bowl, whisk together flour, baking powder, baking soda and salt.
2. In a medium bowl, whisk together sugar, eggs, butter and vanilla until well blended. Whisk in sour cream and milk until blended.
3. Add the egg mixture to the flour mixture and stir until just blended. Gently fold in cookies.
4. Divide batter equally among prepared muffin cups.
5. Bake in preheated oven for 22 to 26 minutes or until tops are golden and a toothpick inserted in the center comes out clean. Let cool in pan on a wire rack for 5 minutes, then transfer to the rack to cool.

Cream Cheese Muffins with Raspberries

2 cups	all-purpose flour	500 mL
2 tsp	baking powder	10 mL
1/2 tsp	baking soda	2 mL
1/2 tsp	salt	2 mL
1 1/4 cups	granulated sugar	300 mL
6 oz	cream cheese, softened	175 g
1/4 cup	unsalted butter, softened	60 mL
2	eggs	2
1/2 cup	buttermilk	125 mL
1 1/2 tsp	vanilla extract	7 mL
2 cups	raspberries	500 mL
1/4 cup	finely chopped walnuts	60 mL

Bright red berries and a cream cheese batter make these luscious muffins a late-summer favorite.

Makes 12 muffins

- Preheat oven to 350°F (180°C)
- 12-cup muffin pan, greased

1. In a medium bowl, whisk together flour, baking powder, baking soda and salt.
2. In a large bowl, using an electric mixer on medium-high speed, beat sugar, cream cheese and butter until light and fluffy. Beat in eggs, one at a time, until fluffy and pale yellow. Beat in buttermilk and vanilla until blended.
3. With the mixer on low speed, beat the flour mixture into the egg mixture until just blended. Gently fold in raspberries.
4. Divide batter equally among prepared muffin cups. Sprinkle with walnuts.
5. Bake in preheated oven for 23 to 28 minutes or until tops are golden and a toothpick inserted in the center comes out clean. Let cool in pan on a wire rack for 5 minutes, then transfer to the rack to cool.

Cheesecake Muffins
with Blackberries and Lemon

2 cups	all-purpose flour	500 mL
2 tsp	baking powder	10 mL
1/2 tsp	salt	2 mL
1 1/2 cups	granulated sugar	375 mL
8 oz	cream cheese, softened	250 g
1 cup	unsalted butter, softened	250 mL
4	eggs	4
1 tbsp	finely grated lemon zest	15 mL
1 tsp	vanilla extract	5 mL
2 cups	blackberries	500 mL

Love cheesecake? Then meet your new favorite muffin. You can bang these easy, elegant treats out in under an hour.

Makes 18 muffins

- Preheat oven to 350°F (180°C)
- Two 12-cup muffin pans, 18 cups lined with paper liners

1. In a medium bowl, whisk together flour, baking powder and salt.

2. In a large bowl, using an electric mixer on medium-high speed, beat sugar, cream cheese and butter until light and fluffy. Beat in eggs, one at a time, until fluffy and pale yellow. Beat in lemon zest and vanilla until blended.

3. With the mixer on low speed, beat the flour mixture into the egg mixture until just blended. Gently fold in blackberries.

4. Divide batter equally among prepared muffin cups.

5. Bake in preheated oven for 25 to 30 minutes or until tops are golden and a toothpick inserted in the center comes out clean. Let cool in pans on a wire rack for 5 minutes, then transfer to the rack to cool.

Mascarpone Muffins

2 cups	all-purpose flour	500 mL
1 1/2 tsp	baking powder	7 mL
1/2 tsp	salt	2 mL
1/4 tsp	ground mace or nutmeg	1 mL
1 1/2 cups	granulated sugar	375 mL
8 oz	mascarpone cheese, softened	250 g
1 cup	unsalted butter, softened	250 mL
3	eggs	3
1/4 cup	Marsala wine	60 mL
1 1/2 tsp	vanilla extract	7 mL

Ultra-rich mascarpone in the batter produces an extraordinarily decadent muffin that's almost worthy of dessert. This recipe makes 12 large muffins, but if you prefer a smaller muffin, divide the batter among 14 muffin cups.

Makes 12 large muffins

- Preheat oven to 350°F (180°C)
- 12-cup muffin pan, lined with paper liners

1. In a medium bowl, whisk together flour, baking powder, salt and mace.

2. In a large bowl, using an electric mixer on medium-high speed, beat sugar, cheese and butter until light and fluffy. Beat in eggs, one at a time, until fluffy and pale yellow. Beat in wine and vanilla until blended.

3. With the mixer on low speed, beat the flour mixture into the egg mixture until just blended.

4. Divide batter equally among prepared muffin cups.

5. Bake in preheated oven for 25 to 30 minutes or until tops are golden and a toothpick inserted in the center comes out clean. Let cool in pan on a wire rack for 3 minutes, then transfer to the rack to cool.

Pistachio Mascarpone Muffins with Honey and Orange

2 cups	all-purpose flour	500 mL
1 tbsp	baking powder	15 mL
1/2 tsp	salt	2 mL
1/2 tsp	ground cardamom	2 mL
1/2 cup	granulated sugar	125 mL
8 oz	mascarpone cheese, softened	250 g
1/4 cup	unsalted butter, softened	60 mL
2	eggs	2
1/3 cup	milk	75 mL
1/4 cup	liquid honey	60 mL
1 tbsp	finely grated orange zest	15 mL
1 cup	lightly salted roasted pistachios, chopped	250 mL

These muffins are rich as rubies, yet still light, tender and not too sweet. They are infused with flavor, thanks to a little grated orange zest and cardamom. Pretty pistachios make the muffins company-worthy.

Makes 12 muffins

- Preheat oven to 425°F (220°C)
- 12-cup muffin pan, greased

1. In a medium bowl, whisk together flour, baking powder, salt and cardamom.

2. In a large bowl, using an electric mixer on medium-high speed, beat sugar, cheese and butter until light and fluffy. Beat in eggs, one at a time, until fluffy and pale yellow. Beat in milk, honey and orange zest until blended.

3. With the mixer on low speed, beat the flour mixture into the egg mixture until just blended. Using a rubber spatula, gently fold in pistachios.

4. Divide batter equally among prepared muffin cups.

5. Bake in preheated oven for 16 to 20 minutes or until tops are golden and a toothpick inserted in the center comes out clean. Let cool in pan on a wire rack for 5 minutes, then transfer to the rack to cool.

Cream Cheese Pumpkin Muffins

Filling

8 oz	cream cheese, softened	250 g
2 tbsp	packed light brown sugar	30 mL
1	egg	1

Muffins

2¼ cups	all-purpose flour	550 mL
1 tbsp	pumpkin pie spice	15 mL
1 tsp	baking soda	5 mL
½ tsp	salt	2 mL
2 cups	granulated sugar	500 mL
2	eggs	2
1 cup	pumpkin purée (not pie filling)	250 mL
½ cup	vegetable oil	125 mL

When it comes to favorite flavors, I am a caramel lover first and a lemon lover second, but after several test batches to make these muffins, I might have to move pumpkin into the top ranks. These are such delicious muffins: moist and light, with a brown sugar–cream cheese filling. In addition, they are a snap to make.

Makes 24 muffins

- Preheat oven to 350°F (180°C)
- Two 12-cup muffin pans, lined with paper liners

1. *Filling:* In a small bowl, mix cream cheese, brown sugar and egg until blended. Set aside.
2. *Muffins:* In a large bowl, whisk together flour, pumpkin pie spice, baking soda and salt.
3. In a medium bowl, whisk together sugar, eggs, pumpkin and oil until well blended.
4. Add the egg mixture to the flour mixture and stir until just blended.
5. Divide batter equally among prepared muffin cups. Drop filling by heaping spoonfuls equally over batter (filling will sink as the muffins bake).
6. Bake in preheated oven for 20 to 23 minutes or until tops are golden and a toothpick inserted in the center comes out clean. Let cool in pans on a wire rack for 5 minutes, then transfer to the rack to cool.

Lemon Ricotta Muffins

2 cups	all-purpose flour	500 mL
1/2 tsp	baking powder	2 mL
1/2 tsp	baking soda	2 mL
1/2 tsp	salt	2 mL
3/4 cup	granulated sugar	175 mL
1/2 cup	unsalted butter, softened	125 mL
1 tbsp	finely grated lemon zest	15 mL
1 cup	ricotta cheese	250 mL
1	egg	1
2 tbsp	freshly squeezed lemon juice	30 mL
1/2 tsp	almond extract	2 mL
1/2 cup	sliced almonds	125 mL
2 tbsp	granulated sugar	30 mL

These gently sweet ricotta muffins offer a creamy base to a crispy-crunchy topping of sliced almonds and sugar. They're much lighter than cupcakes and hit all the right spots for a coffee or tea break. I love them warm and at room temperature, and when I chilled a test batch before leaving town for a few days, I discovered on my return that they are also terrific cold.

Makes 12 muffins

- Preheat oven to 350°F (180°C)
- 12-cup muffin pan, lined with paper liners

1. In a medium bowl, whisk together flour, baking powder, baking soda and salt.

2. In a large bowl, using an electric mixer on medium-high speed, beat 3/4 cup (175 mL) sugar, butter and lemon zest until light and fluffy. Beat in cheese. Beat in egg, lemon juice and almond extract until blended.

3. Add the flour mixture to the egg mixture and stir until just blended.

4. Divide batter equally among prepared muffin cups. Sprinkle with almonds and 2 tbsp (30 mL) sugar.

5. Bake in preheated oven for 22 to 24 minutes or until tops are golden and a toothpick inserted in the center comes out clean. Let cool in pan on a wire rack for 5 minutes, then transfer to the rack to cool.

Chocolate Ricotta Muffins

2⅓ cups	all-purpose flour	575 mL
⅓ cup	unsweetened cocoa powder (not Dutch process)	75 mL
2 tsp	baking powder	10 mL
¾ tsp	salt	3 mL
1 cup	granulated sugar	250 mL
2	eggs	2
1 cup	whole-milk ricotta cheese	250 mL
¼ cup	unsalted butter, melted	60 mL
1 tsp	vanilla extract	5 mL
1⅓ cups	milk	325 mL
¾ cup	semisweet chocolate chips	175 mL

This is one of my most requested muffins. Moist and chocolatey, they are absolutely delicious and a snap to make.

Makes 12 muffins

- Preheat oven to 350°F (180°C)
- 12-cup muffin pan, greased

1. In a large bowl, whisk together flour, cocoa powder, baking powder and salt.

2. In a medium bowl, whisk together sugar, eggs, cheese, butter and vanilla until well blended. Whisk in milk until blended.

3. Add the egg mixture to the flour mixture and stir until just blended. Gently fold in chocolate chips.

4. Divide batter equally among prepared muffin cups.

5. Bake in preheated oven for 23 to 27 minutes or until tops are golden and a toothpick inserted in the center comes out clean. Let cool in pan on a wire rack for 5 minutes, then transfer to the rack to cool.

Citrus Olive Oil Muffins

1¾ cups	all-purpose flour	425 mL
⅓ cup	yellow cornmeal	75 mL
2 tsp	baking powder	10 mL
½ tsp	salt	2 mL
¼ tsp	baking soda	1 mL
1 cup	granulated sugar	250 mL
4	eggs	4
1 tbsp	finely grated lemon zest	15 mL
1 tbsp	finely grated orange zest	15 mL
3 tbsp	freshly squeezed lemon juice	45 mL
¾ cup	extra virgin olive oil	175 mL
2 tbsp	confectioners' (icing) sugar	30 mL

Extra virgin olive oil is the secret ingredient in these moist, citrus-scented muffins. They're perfect as an afternoon snack or for breakfast with a café au lait.

Makes 12 muffins

- Preheat oven to 350°F (180°C)
- 12-cup muffin pan, lined with paper liners

1. In a medium bowl, whisk together flour, cornmeal, baking powder, salt and baking soda.

2. In a large bowl, using an electric mixer on medium speed, beat granulated sugar, eggs, lemon zest and orange zest until pale yellow and frothy. Beat in lemon juice and oil until blended.

3. Add the flour mixture to the egg mixture and stir until just blended.

4. Divide batter equally among prepared muffin cups.

5. Bake in preheated oven for 21 to 24 minutes or until tops are golden and a toothpick inserted in the center comes out clean. Let cool in pan on a wire rack for 3 minutes, then transfer to the rack to cool. Sift confectioners' sugar over cooled muffins.

Lemon Olive Oil Polenta Muffins

Muffins

1 cup	whole milk	250 mL
2 tbsp	freshly squeezed lemon juice	30 mL
1¼ cups	yellow cornmeal	300 mL
1 cup	all-purpose flour	250 mL
1 tsp	baking soda	5 mL
½ tsp	salt	2 mL
⅔ cup	granulated sugar	150 mL
1	egg	1
¾ cup	olive oil	175 mL
2 tbsp	finely grated lemon zest	30 mL

Glaze

1½ cups	confectioners' (icing) sugar	375 mL
2 tbsp	freshly squeezed lemon juice	30 mL

These muffins are a variation on a lemon olive oil cake I have been making for years. They're not too sweet, so they're perfect with a cup of tea.

Makes 12 muffins

- Preheat oven to 425°F (220°C)
- 12-cup muffin pan, greased

1. *Muffins:* In a small bowl, whisk together milk and lemon juice. Set aside and let curdle.
2. In a large bowl, whisk together cornmeal, flour, baking soda and salt.
3. In a medium bowl, whisk together sugar, egg, oil and lemon zest until well blended. Whisk in milk mixture until blended.
4. Add the egg mixture to the flour mixture and stir until just blended.
5. Divide batter equally among prepared muffin cups.
6. Bake in preheated oven for 13 to 17 minutes or until tops are golden and a toothpick inserted in the center comes out clean. Let cool in pan on a wire rack for 3 minutes, then transfer to the rack to cool while you prepare the glaze.
7. *Glaze:* In a small bowl, whisk together confectioners' sugar and lemon juice until blended. Spoon over tops of warm muffins and let cool.

Sweet Polenta Muffins

2 cups	all-purpose flour	500 mL
1 cup	stone-ground yellow cornmeal	250 mL
1½ tsp	baking powder	7 mL
1 tsp	baking soda	5 mL
½ tsp	salt	2 mL
¾ cup	granulated sugar	175 mL
2	eggs	2
½ cup	unsalted butter, melted	125 mL
1¼ cups	plain whole-milk yogurt	300 mL

These muffins are delightful with a range of toppings, from butter to jam to marmalade.

Tip

If stone-ground cornmeal is unavailable, substitute an equal amount of plain yellow cornmeal.

Makes 12 muffins

- Preheat oven to 400°F (200°C)
- 12-cup muffin pan, greased

1. In a large bowl, whisk together flour, cornmeal, baking powder, baking soda and salt.
2. In a medium bowl, whisk together sugar, eggs and butter until well blended. Whisk in yogurt until blended.
3. Add the egg mixture to the flour mixture and stir until just blended.
4. Divide batter equally among prepared muffin cups.
5. Bake in preheated oven for 17 to 20 minutes or until tops are light golden brown and a toothpick inserted in the center comes out clean. Let cool in pan on a wire rack for 3 minutes, then transfer to the rack to cool.

Lunch and Supper Muffins

Muffins aren't just for breakfast — it turns out they never have been. Muffins, from the French *moufflet*, or "soft bread," originally referred to English muffins, which were leavened with yeast, shaped into rounds and cooked on griddles. The transformation to sweet breakfast fare came when bakers began making small, round cakes, usually made with baking powder and a small amount of sugar, along with fruits and nuts.

While some muffins straddle the line between savory and sweet, the options in this chapter have no identity crisis. Warm from the oven, meltingly tender and flavored with cheeses, fresh herbs, bacon, ham, peppers and more, they can make a special meal even more so. They're perfect paired with soups, stews or salads, split and made into innovative sandwiches, or simply piled high into a bread basket for almost any lunch or supper menu. Quite a few options — such as Blue Cheese, Bacon and Basil Muffins, Ham and Cheddar Muffins, Italian Sausage Muffins and Reuben Muffins — are handheld meals in themselves. Whichever recipes you choose, you will never think of (or nibble on) muffins the same way again!

continued...

Baking Powder Biscuit Muffins

2 1/2 cups	all-purpose flour	625 mL
4 tsp	baking powder	20 mL
3/4 tsp	salt	3 mL
3/4 cup	cold unsalted butter, cut into 1/4-inch (0.5 cm) cubes	175 mL
3/4 cup	milk	175 mL

These scrumptious, simple-to-make muffins are as variable as the biscuit originals. Add diced or shredded cheese to the batter, top with seeds and/or stir in fresh herbs.

Makes 12 muffins

- Preheat oven to 400°F (200°C)
- 12-cup muffin pan, greased

1. In a large bowl, whisk together flour, baking powder and salt.
2. Using a pastry cutter or fork, cut butter into flour mixture until it resembles coarse crumbs. Stir in milk until just moistened.
3. Divide batter equally among prepared muffin cups.
4. Bake in preheated oven for 16 to 19 minutes or until tops are golden and a toothpick inserted in the center comes out clean. Let cool in pan on a wire rack for 5 minutes, then transfer to the rack. Serve warm or let cool completely.

Basic Corn Muffins

2 cups	all-purpose flour	500 mL
1 cup	yellow cornmeal	250 mL
1 1/2 tsp	baking powder	7 mL
1 tsp	baking soda	5 mL
1/2 tsp	salt	2 mL
1/4 cup	granulated sugar	60 mL
2	eggs	2
1/2 cup	unsalted butter, melted	125 mL
3/4 cup	sour cream	175 mL
1/2 cup	milk	125 mL

Take a bite out of autumn's chill by mixing up a batch of basic corn muffins. The possibilities for variation are endless — spices, fresh herbs, bacon or sausage, cheese — or savor them split, with a simple pat of butter. For the very best flavor, opt for whole-grain cornmeal; it has a fuller flavor than regular (degerminated) cornmeal. Stone-ground cornmeal is most often whole-grain, so check the label closely.

Makes 12 muffins

- Preheat oven to 400°F (200°C)
- 12-cup muffin pan, greased

1. In a large bowl, whisk together flour, cornmeal, baking powder, baking soda and salt.
2. In a medium bowl, whisk together sugar, eggs and butter until well blended. Whisk in sour cream and milk until blended.
3. Add the egg mixture to the flour mixture and stir until just blended.
4. Divide batter equally among prepared muffin cups.
5. Bake in preheated oven for 17 to 20 minutes or until tops are light golden brown and a toothpick inserted in the center comes out clean. Let cool in pan on a wire rack for 5 minutes, then transfer to the rack. Serve warm or let cool completely.

Southern-Style Cornbread Muffins

2 cups	yellow cornmeal, divided (see tip, below)	500 mL
1 tbsp	granulated sugar	15 mL
2 tsp	baking powder	10 mL
1 tsp	salt	5 mL
$\frac{1}{2}$ tsp	baking soda	2 mL
$\frac{3}{4}$ cup	boiling water	175 mL
$1\frac{1}{2}$ cups	buttermilk	375 mL
2	eggs	2

Use a heavy hand to grease the muffin pan for this recipe. Heating the pan in the oven while you mix the batter will make the grease sizzle, yielding a deep brown crust on the muffin bottoms and sides. They have a roasty-toasty flavor and are fantastic with a dollop of almost anything you see on the table.

Tips

You can use bacon fat, vegetable shortening or vegetable oil to grease the muffin cups.

For the best flavor, use stone-ground cornmeal made with whole-grain corn (as opposed to degerminated corn).

Makes 12 muffins

- Preheat oven to 450°F (230°C)
- 12-cup muffin pan, well greased (see tip, at left)

1. Heat muffin pan in preheated oven while you prepare the batter.

2. In a large bowl, whisk together $1\frac{1}{3}$ cups (325 mL) of the cornmeal, sugar, baking powder, salt and baking soda.

3. In a medium bowl, combine the remaining cornmeal and boiling water; stir until blended. Slowly whisk in buttermilk until smooth. Whisk in eggs until blended.

4. Add the egg mixture to the dry mixture and stir until just blended.

5. Divide batter equally among heated prepared muffin cups.

6. Bake in preheated oven for 18 to 22 minutes or until tops are golden brown and a toothpick inserted in the center comes out clean. Immediately remove from pan and transfer to a wire rack. Serve warm or let cool completely.

Honey Cornbread Muffins

1 cup	all-purpose flour	250 mL
1 cup	yellow cornmeal	250 mL
1 tbsp	baking powder	15 mL
1 tsp	salt	5 mL
1/2 cup	granulated sugar	125 mL
2	eggs	2
1/4 cup	butter, melted	60 mL
1/4 cup	liquid honey	60 mL
1 cup	milk	250 mL

Honey adds a hint of floral sweetness to these quick corn muffins. Sliced ham never tasted better than sandwiched between two halves of one of these muffins.

Makes 12 muffins

- Preheat oven to 400°F (200°C)
- 12-cup muffin pan, greased

1. In a large bowl, whisk together flour, cornmeal, baking powder and salt.
2. In a medium bowl, whisk together sugar, eggs, butter and honey until well blended. Whisk in milk until blended.
3. Add the egg mixture to the flour mixture and stir until just blended.
4. Divide batter equally among prepared muffin cups.
5. Bake in preheated oven for 15 to 18 minutes or until tops are golden and a toothpick inserted in the center comes out clean. Let cool in pan on a wire rack for 5 minutes, then transfer to the rack. Serve warm or let cool completely.

Blue Corn Muffins

1 1/2 cups	blue or yellow cornmeal	375 mL
1 cup	all-purpose flour	250 mL
1 tbsp	baking powder	15 mL
2 tsp	ancho chile powder	10 mL
1 tsp	garlic powder	5 mL
1 tsp	salt	5 mL
1/2 tsp	baking soda	2 mL
2 tbsp	granulated sugar	30 mL
4	eggs	4
1/2 cup	vegetable oil	125 mL
1 cup	buttermilk	250 mL
2/3 cup	chopped green onions (scallions)	150 mL
1/3 cup	fresh cilantro leaves, chopped	75 mL

These herb and spice corn muffins are decidedly Southwestern, not Southern. Leftovers are outstanding split and filled with smoked turkey and a dollop of jalapeño jelly.

Makes 12 muffins

- Preheat oven to 400°F (200°C)
- 12-cup muffin pan, greased

1. In a large bowl, whisk together cornmeal, flour, baking powder, ancho powder, garlic powder, salt and baking soda.
2. In a medium bowl, whisk together sugar, eggs and oil until well blended. Whisk in buttermilk until blended. Stir in green onions and cilantro.
3. Add the egg mixture to the cornmeal mixture and stir until just blended.
4. Divide batter among prepared muffin cups.
5. Bake in preheated oven for 16 to 21 minutes or until tops are golden and a toothpick inserted in the center comes out clean. Let cool in pan on a wire rack for 5 minutes, then transfer to the rack. Serve warm or let cool completely.

Rye Supper Muffins

1 cup	rye flour	250 mL
3/4 cup	all-purpose flour	175 mL
2 1/2 tsp	baking powder	12 mL
1/2 tsp	salt	2 mL
1/2 tsp	caraway seeds	2 mL
1/2 tsp	cumin seeds	2 mL
1/4 cup	packed light brown sugar	60 mL
1	egg	1
3/4 cup	milk	175 mL
1/3 cup	vegetable oil	75 mL

You know who you are: you traipse across town for the best whole-grain loaf; you wait in line for fresh bagels; and you leave early for work to ensure a favorite croissant from the French bakery around the corner. Well, here's a petite dinner bread you will find worthy of your efforts. Made with a combination of rye and wheat flours, these are made for easy dinners of all kinds.

Makes 12 muffins

- Preheat oven to 400°F (200°C)
- 12-cup muffin pans, lined with paper liners

1. In a large bowl, whisk together rye flour, all-purpose flour, baking powder, salt, caraway seeds and cumin seeds.
2. In a medium bowl, whisk together brown sugar, egg, milk and oil until well blended.
3. Add the egg mixture to the flour mixture and stir until just blended.
4. Divide batter equally among prepared muffin cups.
5. Bake in preheated oven for 20 to 25 minutes or until tops are golden and a toothpick inserted in the center comes out clean. Let cool in pan on a wire rack for 5 minutes, then transfer to the rack. Serve warm or let cool completely.

Butter Muffins

2 cups	all-purpose flour	500 mL
1 tbsp	baking powder	15 mL
1 tsp	salt	5 mL
1 cup	sour cream	250 mL
1 cup	unsalted butter, melted	250 mL

Five ingredients and 30 minutes are all that stand between you and a perfect supper bread.

Makes 12 muffins

- Preheat oven to 350°F (180°C)
- 12-cup muffin pan, greased

1. In a large bowl, whisk together flour, baking powder and salt.
2. In a medium bowl, whisk together sour cream and butter until well blended.
3. Add the egg mixture to the flour mixture and stir until just blended.
4. Divide batter equally among prepared muffin cups.
5. Bake in preheated oven for 20 to 25 minutes or until tops are golden and a toothpick inserted in the center comes out clean. Let cool in pan on a wire rack for 5 minutes, then transfer to the rack. Serve warm or let cool completely.

Pumpernickel Muffins

1¼ cups	rye flour	300 mL
1¼ cups	all-purpose flour	300 mL
2 tsp	baking powder	10 mL
1 tsp	baking soda	5 mL
1 tsp	salt	5 mL
1	egg	1
1 cup	buttermilk	250 mL
¼ cup	dark (cooking) molasses	60 mL
3 tbsp	unsalted butter, melted	45 mL
1½ tsp	instant espresso powder	7 mL

Despite growing up in California, I grew up eating rye bread. Both my parents love it, so it was not uncommon to have at least two varieties on hand for everyday sandwiches. I particularly liked pumpernickel, a heavy, slightly sweet rye bread traditionally made with coarsely ground rye. I was never tempted by the liverwurst and pickles my parents favored on their pumpernickel, but I loved it with cream cheese (one of my mother's morning favorites). These muffins have all of the flavor I remember and more, with the ease of a muffin. And yes, they are darn good with a schmear of cream cheese.

Makes 12 muffins

- Preheat oven to 375°F (190°C)
- 12-cup muffin pan, greased

1. In a large bowl, whisk together rye flour, all-purpose flour, baking powder, baking soda and salt.

2. In a medium bowl, whisk together egg, buttermilk, molasses, butter and espresso powder until well blended.

3. Add the egg mixture to the flour mixture and stir until just blended.

4. Divide batter equally among prepared muffin cups.

5. Bake in preheated oven for 20 to 25 minutes or until tops spring back when touched and a toothpick inserted in the center comes out clean. Let cool in pan on a wire rack for 5 minutes, then transfer to the rack. Serve warm or let cool completely.

Beer Batter Muffins

3 cups	all-purpose flour	750 mL
1 tbsp	baking powder	15 mL
3 tbsp	granulated sugar	45 mL
1 tsp	salt	5 mL
1	bottle (12 oz/341 mL) beer, at room temperature	1
¼ cup	unsalted butter, melted	60 mL

For a different take on dinner rolls, a few pantry staples are spiked with beer and fortified by rich butter. The beer contributes a maltiness to the muffins that pairs well with a wide range of meats and cheeses.

Makes 12 muffins

- Preheat oven to 375°F (190°C)
- 12-cup muffin pan, greased

1. In a large bowl, whisk together flour, baking powder, sugar and salt.

2. Add beer and butter to the flour mixture all at once and stir as little as possible until just blended.

3. Divide batter equally among prepared muffin cups.

4. Bake in preheated oven for 22 to 25 minutes or until tops are golden and a toothpick inserted in the center comes out clean. Let cool in pan on a wire rack for 5 minutes, then transfer to the rack. Serve warm or let cool completely.

Guinness Muffins

2 cups	all-purpose flour	500 mL
1 cup	rye flour	250 mL
1 tsp	caraway seeds	5 mL
1/2 tsp	baking soda	2 mL
1/2 tsp	salt	2 mL
1/4 cup	packed dark brown sugar	60 mL
1/4 cup	unsalted butter, melted	60 mL
1	bottle (12 oz/341 mL) Guinness or other dark beer	1

The malt flavor of Guinness marries well with the rye, brown sugar and butter in these distinctive muffins, and the faintly bitter aftertaste cuts the sweetness.

Tip
Guinness and other Irish stouts produce a thick head when poured, so chill the can or bottle well to reduce the foam before adding the beer to the batter.

Makes 12 muffins
- Preheat oven to 350°F (180°C)
- 12-cup muffin pan, greased

1. In a large bowl, whisk together all-purpose flour, rye flour, caraway seeds, baking soda and salt.

2. In a medium bowl, whisk together brown sugar and butter until blended.

3. Add the brown sugar mixture and Guinness to the flour mixture and stir until just blended.

4. Divide batter equally among prepared muffin cups.

5. Bake in preheated oven for 24 to 28 minutes or until tops are golden and a toothpick inserted in the center comes out clean. Let cool in pan on a wire rack for 5 minutes, then transfer to the rack. Serve warm or let cool completely.

Boston Brown Bread Muffins

1 cup	whole wheat flour	250 mL
1/2 cup	yellow cornmeal	125 mL
1 1/2 tsp	baking soda	7 mL
3/4 tsp	salt	3 mL
1/3 cup	packed dark brown sugar	75 mL
1	egg	1
1/3 cup	dark (cooking) molasses	75 mL
1/3 cup	vegetable oil	75 mL
1 cup	buttermilk	250 mL
1 cup	raisins	250 mL

The most famous of New England's breads, this wholesome blend of wheat and cornmeal (and, occasionally, rye) is as excellent a whole-grain choice for modern diets as it was those of 300 years ago. Classic recipes involve steaming the bread (often in cans), but I've captured the same flavor and texture here in faster, easier muffin form.

Makes 12 muffins
- Preheat oven to 400°F (200°C)
- 12-cup muffin pans, greased

1. In a large bowl, whisk together flour, cornmeal, baking soda and salt.

2. In a medium bowl, whisk together brown sugar, egg, molasses and oil until well blended. Whisk in buttermilk until blended.

3. Add the egg mixture to the flour mixture and stir until just blended. Gently fold in raisins.

4. Divide batter equally among prepared muffin cups.

5. Bake in preheated oven for 14 to 17 minutes or until a toothpick inserted in the center comes out clean. Let cool in pan on a wire rack for 3 minutes, then transfer to the rack. Serve warm or let cool completely.

Irish Brown Bread Muffins

2 cups	whole wheat flour	500 mL
1/4 cup	wheat germ	60 mL
1 tsp	salt	5 mL
3/4 tsp	baking soda	3 mL
1/2 tsp	cream of tartar	2 mL
3/4 cup	buttermilk	175 mL
1/3 cup	dark (cooking) molasses	75 mL
1/4 cup	unsalted butter, melted	60 mL

These muffins may not be strictly traditional, but whole wheat flour, wheat germ, buttermilk and molasses bring the flavors of true Irish brown bread together in a satisfying — and simple — way.

Makes 12 muffins

- Preheat oven to 350°F (180°C)
- 12-cup muffin pan, greased

1. In a large bowl, whisk together flour, wheat germ, salt, baking soda and cream of tartar.
2. In a medium bowl, whisk together buttermilk, molasses and butter until well blended.
3. Add the buttermilk mixture to the flour mixture and stir until just blended.
4. Divide batter equally among prepared muffin cups. Using the tip of a sharp knife, cut an X across the top of the batter in each cup.
5. Bake in preheated oven for 16 to 20 minutes or until tops are lightly browned and sound hollow when tapped. Let cool in pan on a wire rack for 5 minutes, then transfer to the rack. Serve warm or let cool completely.

Whole Wheat Supper Muffins

1 1/4 cups	whole wheat flour	300 mL
2 tbsp	yellow cornmeal	30 mL
2 tsp	baking powder	10 mL
1/2 tsp	baking soda	2 mL
1/2 tsp	salt	2 mL
3 tbsp	packed dark brown sugar	45 mL
2	eggs, separated	2
1/3 cup	unsalted butter, melted	75 mL
1 cup	buttermilk	250 mL
1 1/2 tbsp	sesame seeds	22 mL

Odds are, whatever else you serve for dinner, everyone will remember these muffins. Fresh and fragrant from the oven, they belie their humble list of ingredients.

Makes 9 muffins

- Preheat oven to 375°F (190°C)
- 12-cup muffin pan, 9 cups greased

1. In a large bowl, whisk together flour, cornmeal, baking powder, baking soda and salt.
2. In a medium bowl, whisk together brown sugar, egg yolks and butter until well blended. Whisk in buttermilk until blended.
3. Add the egg mixture to the flour mixture and stir until just blended.
4. In another medium bowl, using an electric mixer on high speed, beat egg whites until soft peaks form. Gently fold egg whites into batter until blended.
5. Divide batter equally among prepared muffin cups. Sprinkle with sesame seeds.
6. Bake in preheated oven for 22 to 26 minutes or until a toothpick inserted in the center comes out clean. Let cool in pan on a wire rack for 5 minutes, then transfer to the rack. Serve warm or let cool completely.

Scallion, Cranberry and Horseradish Muffins

2 cups	all-purpose flour	500 mL
1 tbsp	baking powder	15 mL
1/4 tsp	salt	1 mL
1/4 tsp	freshly ground black pepper	1 mL
1	egg	1
1/4 cup	unsalted butter, melted	60 mL
1 tbsp	prepared horseradish	15 mL
1 1/4 cups	milk	300 mL
2/3 cup	chopped green onions (scallions)	150 mL
1/2 cup	dried cranberries, chopped	125 mL

Here, the tart quality of dried cranberries is underlined by the distinctive bite of horseradish and fresh flavor of scallions. And if you're wondering what the difference is between green onions and scallions, consider this: grocery stores label long, skinny, green-topped onions with white bottoms as either scallions or green onions, but they are almost always the exact same plant.

Makes 12 muffins

- Preheat oven to 400°F (200°C)
- 12-cup muffin pan, greased

1. In a large bowl, whisk together flour, baking powder, salt and pepper.
2. In a medium bowl, whisk together egg, butter and horseradish until well blended. Whisk in milk until blended.
3. Add the egg mixture to the flour mixture and stir until just blended. Gently fold in green onions and cranberries.
4. Divide batter equally among prepared muffin cups.
5. Bake in preheated oven for 16 to 20 minutes or until tops are golden and a toothpick inserted in the center comes out clean. Let cool in pan on a wire rack for 5 minutes, then transfer to the rack. Serve warm or let cool completely.

Buttermilk Supper Muffins

2 cups	all-purpose flour	500 mL
2 tsp	baking powder	10 mL
1/2 tsp	salt	2 mL
1/2 tsp	baking soda	2 mL
2	eggs	2
1/2 cup	unsalted butter, melted	125 mL
2 tbsp	liquid honey	30 mL
1 cup	buttermilk	250 mL

Homey and deliciously buttery, these golden muffins are an obvious choice for weeknight meals and entertaining alike.

Makes 12 muffins

- Preheat oven to 375°F (190°C)
- 12-cup muffin pan, lined with paper liners

1. In a large bowl, whisk together flour, baking powder, salt and baking soda.
2. In a medium bowl, whisk together eggs, butter and honey until well blended. Whisk in buttermilk until blended.
3. Add the egg mixture to the flour mixture and stir until just blended.
4. Divide batter equally among prepared muffin cups.
5. Bake in preheated oven for 20 to 25 minutes or until tops are golden and a toothpick inserted in the center comes out clean. Let cool in pan on a wire rack for 5 minutes, then transfer to the rack. Serve warm or let cool completely.

Dried Cherry and Sage Corn Muffins

1 cup	dried cherries, roughly chopped	250 mL
1/2 cup	boiling water	125 mL
1 cup	all-purpose flour	250 mL
1 cup	yellow cornmeal	250 mL
1 tbsp	baking powder	15 mL
1 1/2 tsp	dried sage	7 mL
1/2 tsp	salt	2 mL
1/4 cup	granulated sugar	60 mL
1	egg	1
1/2 cup	vegetable oil	125 mL
1 cup	buttermilk	250 mL

If you love dried cherries, you'll love these faintly sweet corn muffins, buoyed here with savory notes of sage. They are a breeze to make and so comforting for any meal: breakfast, brunch, lunch or dinner.

Makes 12 muffins

- Preheat oven to 375°F (190°C)
- 12-cup muffin pan, greased

1. In a small bowl, combine cherries and boiling water. Let stand for 5 minutes, then drain.
2. In a large bowl, whisk together flour, cornmeal, baking powder, sage and salt.
3. In a medium bowl, whisk together sugar, egg and oil until well blended. Whisk in buttermilk until blended.
4. Add the egg mixture to the flour mixture and stir until just blended. Gently fold in cherries.
5. Divide batter equally among prepared muffin cups.
6. Bake in preheated oven for 16 to 19 minutes or until tops are golden and a toothpick inserted in the center comes out clean. Let cool in pan on a wire rack for 5 minutes, then transfer to the rack. Serve warm or let cool completely.

Mango Chutney Muffins

2 1/4 cups	all-purpose flour	550 mL
1 1/2 tsp	baking powder	7 mL
1 tsp	mild curry powder	5 mL
1 tsp	salt	5 mL
1/2 tsp	baking soda	2 mL
2	eggs	2
2/3 cup	plain yogurt	150 mL
1/2 cup	mango chutney	125 mL
1/4 cup	unsalted butter, melted	60 mL
1/4 cup	fresh cilantro leaves, chopped	60 mL

These muffins are a wonderful mix of flavors and textures, despite the short list of ingredients. Serve them with rotisserie chicken, with fresh melon for dessert, for an easy, elegant dinner or picnic lunch.

Makes 12 muffins

- Preheat oven to 375°F (190°C)
- Blender
- 12-cup muffin pan, lined with paper liners

1. In a large bowl, whisk together flour, baking powder, curry powder, salt and baking soda.
2. In blender, process eggs, yogurt, chutney and butter until smooth.
3. Add the egg mixture and cilantro to the flour mixture and stir until just blended.
4. Divide batter equally among prepared muffin cups.
5. Bake in preheated oven for 22 to 26 minutes or until tops are golden and a toothpick inserted in the center comes out clean. Let cool in pan on a wire rack for 3 minutes, then transfer to the rack. Serve warm or let cool completely.

Pear, Walnut and Bacon Muffins

1³/₄ cups	all-purpose flour	425 mL
1 tbsp	baking powder	15 mL
1 tsp	dried thyme	5 mL
¹/₂ tsp	salt	2 mL
¹/₄ cup	packed light brown sugar	60 mL
2	eggs	2
²/₃ cup	unsweetened pear nectar	150 mL
¹/₂ cup	unsalted butter, melted	125 mL
1¹/₂ cups	chopped peeled pears	375 mL
¹/₂ cup	crumbled cooked bacon	125 mL
¹/₂ cup	coarsely chopped walnuts	125 mL

The combination of pears, walnuts and bacon has true synergy. The pears cut the smokiness of the bacon, turning a supper muffin into something extra-special — just what's needed to accompany a simple repast of soup or salad.

Tip

To save time, consider using precooked bacon. Look for pouches of crumbled precooked bacon in the supermarket where salad dressings and croutons are shelved.

Makes 12 muffins

- Preheat oven to 350°F (180°C)
- 12-cup muffin pan, greased

1. In a large bowl, whisk together flour, baking powder, thyme and salt.
2. In a medium bowl, whisk together brown sugar, eggs, pear nectar and butter until well blended.
3. Add the egg mixture to the flour mixture and stir until just blended. Gently fold in pears and bacon.
4. Divide batter equally among prepared muffin cups. Sprinkle with walnuts.
5. Bake in preheated oven for 23 to 25 minutes or until tops are golden and a toothpick inserted in the center comes out clean. Let cool in pan on a wire rack for 3 minutes, then transfer to the rack. Serve warm or let cool completely.

Green Chile Corn Muffins

1¹/₄ cups	yellow cornmeal	300 mL
2 tsp	baking powder	10 mL
¹/₂ tsp	salt	2 mL
1 cup	shredded sharp Cheddar cheese	250 mL
2	eggs	2
1 cup	sour cream	250 mL
¹/₂ cup	vegetable oil	125 mL
1	can (8 oz/227 mL) cream-style corn	1
1	can (4¹/₂ oz/127 mL) diced mild green chiles	1

Cornbread seems like something new in these rich, moist muffins, dolled up with Cheddar cheese, green chiles and sour cream.

Makes 12 muffins

- Preheat oven to 400°F (200°C)
- 12-cup muffin pan, greased

1. In a large bowl, whisk together cornmeal, baking powder and salt. Stir in cheese.
2. In a medium bowl, whisk together eggs, sour cream and oil until well blended. Stir in corn and chiles.
3. Add the egg mixture to the flour mixture and stir until just blended.
4. Divide batter among prepared muffin cups.
5. Bake in preheated oven for 17 to 22 minutes or until tops are light golden brown and a toothpick inserted in the center comes out clean. Let cool in pan on a wire rack for 5 minutes, then transfer to the rack. Serve warm or let cool completely.

Smoky Roasted Red Pepper Muffins

1²/₃ cups	all-purpose flour	400 mL
½ cup	yellow cornmeal	125 mL
1 tbsp	baking powder	15 mL
1 tsp	ground cumin	5 mL
½ tsp	chipotle chile powder	2 mL
½ tsp	salt	2 mL
2 tbsp	granulated sugar	30 mL
1	egg	1
½ cup	milk	125 mL
¼ cup	vegetable oil	60 mL
1 cup	shredded smoked Gouda cheese	250 mL
1 cup	chopped drained roasted red bell peppers, patted dry	250 mL

Makes 12 muffins

- Preheat oven to 375°F (190°C)
- 12-cup muffin pan, lined with paper liners

1. In a large bowl, whisk together flour, cornmeal, baking powder, cumin, chipotle powder and salt.
2. In a medium bowl, whisk together sugar, egg, milk and oil until well blended.
3. Add the egg mixture to the flour mixture and stir until just blended. Gently fold in cheese and roasted peppers.
4. Divide batter equally among prepared muffin cups.
5. Bake in preheated oven for 18 to 22 minutes or until tops are golden and a toothpick inserted in the center comes out clean. Let cool in pan on a wire rack for 3 minutes, then transfer to the rack. Serve warm or let cool completely.

These savory muffins are the perfect accompaniment to tomato soup.

Tip

Look for jars of roasted red bell peppers where pickles and olives are shelved in the grocery store.

Roasted Pepper Feta Muffins

2 cups	all-purpose flour	500 mL
2 tsp	baking powder	10 mL
1 tsp	dried oregano	5 mL
½ tsp	baking soda	2 mL
½ tsp	salt	2 mL
1	egg	1
1 cup	buttermilk	250 mL
¼ cup	olive oil	60 mL
³/₄ cup	crumbled feta cheese	175 mL
½ cup	chopped drained roasted red bell peppers, patted dry	125 mL

Makes 12 muffins

- Preheat oven to 375°F (190°C)
- 12-cup muffin pan, greased

1. In a large bowl, whisk together flour, baking powder, oregano, baking soda and salt.
2. In a medium bowl, whisk together egg, buttermilk and oil until well blended.
3. Add the egg mixture to the flour mixture and stir until just blended. Gently fold in cheese and red peppers.
4. Divide batter equally among prepared muffin cups.
5. Bake in preheated oven for 18 to 22 minutes or until tops are golden and a toothpick inserted in the center comes out clean. Let cool in pan on a wire rack for 5 minutes, then transfer to the rack. Serve warm or let cool completely.

Caution: May require a double batch. Cheesy, herbed, roasted pepper–flecked muffins are sure to please a crowd.

Jalapeño Red Pepper Muffins

1½ cups	all-purpose flour	375 mL
½ cup	yellow cornmeal	125 mL
2½ tsp	baking powder	12 mL
1½ tsp	ground cumin	7 mL
½ tsp	baking soda	2 mL
½ tsp	salt	2 mL
2 tbsp	granulated sugar	30 mL
1	egg	1
¾ cup	buttermilk	175 mL
⅔ cup	chopped drained roasted red bell peppers, patted dry	150 mL
1	jalapeño pepper, seeded and chopped	1
6 oz	Monterey Jack cheese, cut into ¼-inch (0.5 cm) cubes	175 g

Makes 12 muffins

- Preheat oven to 375°F (190°C)
- 12-cup muffin pan, greased

1. In a large bowl, whisk together flour, cornmeal, baking powder, cumin, baking soda and salt.
2. In a medium bowl, whisk together sugar, egg and buttermilk until well blended. Stir in roasted peppers and jalapeño.
3. Add the egg mixture to the flour mixture and stir until just blended. Gently fold in cheese.
4. Divide batter equally among prepared muffin cups.
5. Bake in preheated oven for 18 to 22 minutes or until tops are golden and a toothpick inserted in the center comes out clean. Let cool in pan on a wire rack for 5 minutes, then transfer to the rack. Serve warm or let cool completely.

Sage Brown Butter Muffins

½ cup	unsalted butter, cut into cubes	125 mL
1 tbsp	chopped fresh sage	15 mL
2 cups	all-purpose flour	500 mL
2 tsp	baking powder	10 mL
½ tsp	salt	2 mL
½ tsp	baking soda	2 mL
¼ tsp	freshly cracked black pepper	1 mL
1 tbsp	granulated sugar	15 mL
2	eggs	2
1 cup	buttermilk	250 mL

What's especially nice about these stellar muffins is that, with the exception of the fresh sage, the ingredients are ones you're likely to already have in your refrigerator and pantry. Browning the butter (beurre noisette) adds a subtle nuttiness to the muffins, a flavor that marries harmoniously with the fresh sage.

Makes 12 muffins

- Preheat oven to 375°F (190°C)
- 12-cup muffin pan, greased

1. In a large, heavy skillet, heat butter over medium heat until foam subsides and butter is beginning to brown. Stir in sage and cook, stirring, for 1 to 2 minutes longer or until butter is golden brown. Immediately transfer to a medium bowl and let cool to room temperature.
2. In a large bowl, whisk together flour, baking powder, salt, baking soda and pepper.
3. Add sugar and eggs to browned butter and whisk until well blended. Whisk in buttermilk until blended.
4. Add the egg mixture to the flour mixture and stir until just blended.
5. Divide batter equally among prepared muffin cups.
6. Bake in preheated oven for 20 to 25 minutes or until tops are golden brown and a toothpick inserted in the center comes out clean. Let cool in pan on a wire rack for 5 minutes, then transfer to the rack. Serve warm or let cool completely.

Rosemary Corn Muffins

1 cup	all-purpose flour	250 mL
1 cup	stone-ground yellow cornmeal	250 mL
1½ tsp	baking powder	7 mL
½ tsp	salt	2 mL
¼ tsp	baking soda	1 mL
3 tbsp	granulated sugar	45 mL
2 tsp	finely chopped fresh rosemary	10 mL
1	egg	1
¼ cup	vegetable oil	60 mL
1 cup	buttermilk	250 mL
1¼ cups	fresh or frozen (thawed) corn kernels	300 mL

The delicate sweetness of muffins made with corn and cornmeal is a perfect match for the aromatic intensity of rosemary.

Tip

Plain yellow cornmeal may be substituted for the stone-ground yellow cornmeal.

Makes 12 muffins

- Preheat oven to 375°F (190°C)
- 12-cup muffin pan, greased

1. In a large bowl, whisk together flour, cornmeal, baking powder, salt and baking soda.

2. In a medium bowl, whisk together sugar, rosemary, egg and oil until well blended. Whisk in buttermilk until blended.

3. Add the egg mixture to the flour mixture and stir until just blended. Gently fold in corn.

4. Divide batter equally among prepared muffin cups.

5. Bake in preheated oven for 16 to 19 minutes or until tops are golden and a toothpick inserted in the center comes out clean. Let cool in pan on a wire rack for 5 minutes, then transfer to the rack. Serve warm or let cool completely.

Herb and Pesto Muffins

2 cups	all-purpose flour	500 mL
2 tsp	baking powder	10 mL
1/2 tsp	salt	2 mL
1/2 tsp	baking soda	2 mL
1 tbsp	granulated sugar	15 mL
2	eggs	2
1/2 cup	prepared basil pesto	125 mL
1 cup	buttermilk	250 mL
1/4 cup	fresh parsley leaves, chopped	60 mL
1/4 cup	fresh cilantro leaves, chopped	60 mL
2 tbsp	minced fresh chives	30 mL

Ready-made basil pesto is a harried cook's best friend. Here it stars in a gorgeous, flavor-packed herb muffin that's as lovely to look at as it is to eat.

Makes 12 muffins

- Preheat oven to 375°F (190°C)
- 12-cup muffin pan, lined with paper liners

1. In a large bowl, whisk together flour, baking powder, salt and baking soda.
2. In a medium bowl, whisk together sugar, eggs and pesto until well blended. Whisk in buttermilk until blended. Stir in parsley, cilantro and chives.
3. Add the egg mixture to the flour mixture and stir until just blended.
4. Divide batter equally among prepared muffin cups.
5. Bake in preheated oven for 20 to 25 minutes or until tops are golden and a toothpick inserted in the center comes out clean. Let cool in pan on a wire rack for 5 minutes, then transfer to the rack. Serve warm or let cool completely.

French-Fried Onion Muffins

2 cups	all-purpose flour	500 mL
2 tsp	baking powder	10 mL
2 tsp	fennel seeds	10 mL
3/4 tsp	salt	3 mL
1/2 tsp	baking soda	2 mL
2 tbsp	packed light brown sugar	30 mL
2	eggs	2
1/4 cup	vegetable oil	60 mL
1 cup	sour cream	250 mL
1	can (3 oz/79 g) french-fried onions	1

These crispy-crunchy muffins won't soon be forgotten. Anyone with a penchant for onion rings, in particular, will think (and I quote my friend Susan), "These are the greatest muffins world-over."

Makes 12 muffins

- Preheat oven to 350°F (180°C)
- 12-cup muffin pan, greased

1. In a large bowl, whisk together flour, baking powder, fennel seeds, salt and baking soda.
2. In a medium bowl, whisk together brown sugar, eggs and oil until well blended. Whisk in sour cream until blended.
3. Add the egg mixture to the flour mixture and stir until just blended. Gently fold in onions.
4. Divide batter equally among prepared muffin cups.
5. Bake in preheated oven for 22 to 26 minutes or until tops are golden and a toothpick inserted in the center comes out clean. Let cool in pan on a wire rack for 5 minutes, then transfer to the rack. Serve warm or let cool completely.

NYC Onion Rye Muffins

2 cups	all-purpose flour	500 mL
1 cup	rye flour	250 mL
2 tbsp	caraway seeds	30 mL
1½ tsp	salt	7 mL
1 tsp	baking soda	5 mL
2 tbsp	granulated sugar	30 mL
2	eggs	2
¼ cup	unsalted butter, melted	60 mL
½ cup	minced onion	125 mL
1¼ cups	buttermilk	300 mL
1 tbsp	yellow cornmeal	15 mL

I know I am setting myself up for critique with the name I've chosen for these muffins, but I have had my share of New York City onion rye bread, and these muffins are worthy of their eponym. They are simple to make, but that's not the point here — deliciousness is, and that's where this recipe comes in.

Makes 16 muffins

- Preheat oven to 375°F (190°C)
- Two 12-cup muffin pans, 16 cups greased

1. In a large bowl, whisk together all-purpose flour, rye flour, caraway seeds, salt and baking soda.
2. In a medium bowl, whisk together sugar, eggs, butter and onion until well blended. Whisk in buttermilk until blended.
3. Add the egg mixture to the flour mixture and stir until just blended.
4. Sprinkle cornmeal into prepared muffin cups, shaking to coat bottom and sides, then shake out excess. Divide batter equally among cups.
5. Bake in preheated oven for 20 to 25 minutes or until tops are golden and a toothpick inserted in the center comes out clean. Let cool in pans on a wire rack for 5 minutes, then transfer to the rack. Serve warm or let cool completely.

Sweet Potato Sage Muffins

2¼ cups	all-purpose flour	550 mL
2½ tsp	baking powder	12 mL
1½ tsp	salt	7 mL
1 tsp	dried sage	5 mL
½ tsp	baking soda	2 mL
2 tbsp	granulated sugar	30 mL
1	egg	1
½ cup	buttermilk	125 mL
⅓ cup	vegetable oil	75 mL
1	can (15 oz/425 mL) sweet potatoes, drained and mashed	1
⅓ cup	finely chopped green onions (scallions)	75 mL

Sweet potatoes take beautifully to muffin form. The sage and green onions make an ideal foil for the sweetness of the potatoes.

Makes 12 muffins

- Preheat oven to 350°F (180°C)
- 12-cup muffin pan, greased

1. In a large bowl, whisk together flour, baking powder, salt, sage and baking soda.
2. In a medium bowl, whisk together sugar, egg, buttermilk and oil until well blended. Stir in sweet potatoes until blended.
3. Add the egg mixture to the flour mixture and stir until just blended. Gently fold in green onions.
4. Divide batter equally among prepared muffin cups.
5. Bake in preheated oven for 22 to 27 minutes or until tops are golden and a toothpick inserted in the center comes out clean. Let cool in pan on a wire rack for 5 minutes, then transfer to the rack. Serve warm or let cool completely.

Potato Muffins

1 cup	all-purpose flour	250 mL
1 cup	potato starch	250 mL
1 tbsp	baking powder	15 mL
1/2 tsp	salt	2 mL
1/4 tsp	freshly ground black pepper	1 mL
1 tbsp	granulated sugar	15 mL
1	egg	1
2/3 cup	prepared mashed potatoes, at room temperature	150 mL
1/3 cup	unsalted butter, melted	75 mL
1 cup	milk	250 mL
1/3 cup	freshly grated Parmesan cheese	75 mL
2 tbsp	minced fresh chives	30 mL

I am not dismissing the appeal of mashed potatoes as is, but tender, crusty muffins made from the leftovers are simply terrific. Here, I've kept the embellishments simple: a sprinkling of Parmesan cheese and fresh chives.

Tip

Look for potato starch at health food stores or in the natural foods section of the grocery store, where alternative flours are shelved. Also, make sure the mashed potatoes are not cold when they are added to the batter; warm them up in the microwave for 10 to 15 seconds until room temperature or even slightly warm.

Makes 12 muffins

- Preheat oven to 400°F (200°C)
- 12-cup muffin pan, greased

1. In a large bowl, whisk together flour, potato starch, baking powder, salt and pepper.

2. In a medium bowl, whisk together sugar, egg, mashed potatoes and butter until well blended. Whisk in milk until blended. Stir in cheese and chives.

3. Add the egg mixture to the flour mixture and stir until just blended.

4. Divide batter equally among prepared muffin cups.

5. Bake in preheated oven for 15 to 19 minutes or until tops are golden and a toothpick inserted in the center comes out clean. Let cool in pan on a wire rack for 5 minutes, then transfer to the rack. Serve warm or let cool completely.

Pumpkin Cornmeal Muffins

1½ cups	all-purpose flour	375 mL
1 cup	yellow cornmeal	250 mL
2 tsp	baking powder	10 mL
1 tsp	baking soda	5 mL
1 tsp	dried thyme	5 mL
1 tsp	dried sage	5 mL
½ tsp	salt	2 mL
½ cup	unsalted butter, softened	125 mL
⅓ cup	packed light brown sugar	75 mL
4	eggs	4
½ cup	milk	125 mL
1	can (15 oz/425 mL) pumpkin purée (not pie filling) (or 1¾ cups/425 mL)	1

Canned pumpkin enriches corn muffins for a moist and flavorful dinner bread.

Makes 12 muffins

- Preheat oven to 350°F (180°C)
- 12-cup muffin pan, greased

1. In a large bowl, whisk together flour, cornmeal, baking powder, baking soda, thyme, sage and salt.

2. In a medium bowl, using an electric mixer on medium-high speed, beat butter and brown sugar until light and fluffy. Beat in eggs, one at a time, until blended. Beat in milk and pumpkin until blended.

3. Add the egg mixture to the flour mixture and stir until just blended.

4. Divide batter equally among prepared muffin cups.

5. Bake in preheated oven for 25 to 30 minutes or until tops are golden and a toothpick inserted in the center comes out clean. Let cool in pan on a wire rack for 5 minutes, then transfer to the rack. Serve warm or let cool completely.

Sun-Dried Tomato Muffins

2 cups	all-purpose flour	500 mL
1 tbsp	baking powder	15 mL
1 tsp	dried basil	5 mL
½ tsp	salt	2 mL
¼ tsp	freshly ground black pepper	1 mL
1	egg	1
1 cup	milk	250 mL
¼ cup	olive oil	60 mL
½ cup	freshly grated Parmesan cheese	125 mL
½ cup	chopped drained oil-packed sun-dried tomatoes	125 mL

Savory-sweet sun-dried tomatoes, earthy Parmesan cheese and basil are the stars of this pretty muffin. Pair them with goat cheese and a green salad for a satisfying lunch or light supper.

Makes 12 muffins

- Preheat oven to 375°F (190°C)
- 12-cup muffin pan, greased

1. In a large bowl, whisk together flour, baking powder, basil, salt and pepper.

2. In a medium bowl, whisk together egg, milk and oil until well blended.

3. Add the egg mixture to the flour mixture and stir until just blended. Gently fold in cheese and tomatoes.

4. Divide batter equally among prepared muffin cups.

5. Bake in preheated oven for 18 to 22 minutes or until tops are golden and a toothpick inserted in the center comes out clean. Let cool in pan on a wire rack for 5 minutes, then transfer to the rack. Serve warm or let cool completely.

Tamale Muffins

2 cups	stone-ground yellow cornmeal	500 mL
2 tsp	baking powder	10 mL
1½ tsp	ground cumin	7 mL
1 tsp	salt	5 mL
½ tsp	baking soda	2 mL
¼ tsp	cayenne pepper	1 mL
2 cups	shredded Monterey Jack cheese, divided	500 mL
1	egg	1
⅓ cup	unsalted butter, melted	75 mL
1⅓ cups	buttermilk	325 mL
1	can (4½ oz/127 mL) diced mild green chiles, drained	1
1 cup	fresh or frozen (thawed) corn kernels	250 mL
¼ cup	fresh cilantro leaves, chopped	60 mL

Tamale pie was a standard supper in my mother's weeknight dinner repertoire; it's been years since I've had it, but I still remember it fondly. These muffins hit all the same notes, with ease. Ladle out black bean soup to accompany them and serve a Caesar salad with it. Finish by teaming scoops of mango sorbet and vanilla ice cream.

Makes 12 muffins

- Preheat oven to 425°F (220°C)
- 12-cup muffin pan, greased

1. In a large bowl, whisk together cornmeal, baking powder, cumin, salt, baking soda and cayenne. Stir in 1½ cups (375 mL) of the cheese.
2. In a medium bowl, whisk together egg and butter until well blended. Whisk in buttermilk until blended. Stir in chiles, corn and cilantro.
3. Add the egg mixture to the cornmeal mixture and stir until just blended.
4. Divide batter equally among prepared muffin cups. Sprinkle with the remaining cheese.
5. Bake in preheated oven for 19 to 23 minutes or until tops are puffed and golden brown and a toothpick inserted in the center comes out clean. Let cool in pan on a wire rack for 10 minutes, then transfer to the rack. Serve warm or let cool completely.

Mediterranean Muffins

2 cups	all-purpose flour	500 mL
2 tsp	baking powder	10 mL
1/2 tsp	baking soda	2 mL
3/4 tsp	salt	3 mL
1	egg	1
1 cup	buttermilk	250 mL
1/3 cup	olive oil	75 mL
1/3 cup	chopped drained oil-packed sun-dried tomatoes	75 mL
1/3 cup	crumbled feta cheese	75 mL
1/2 cup	fresh basil, chopped	125 mL
1/4 cup	chopped pitted brine-cured olives	60 mL

Sun-dried tomatoes, olives, feta and herbs turn ordinary muffins into something extraordinary. They are perfect in mid-winter, just as you are dreaming of sun-drenched summer days.

Makes 12 muffins

- Preheat oven to 400°F (200°C)
- 12-cup muffin pan, greased

1. In a large bowl, whisk together flour, baking powder, baking soda and salt.
2. In a medium bowl, whisk together egg, buttermilk and oil until smooth.
3. Add the egg mixture to the flour mixture and stir until just blended. Gently fold in tomatoes, cheese, basil and olives.
4. Divide batter equally among prepared muffin cups.
5. Bake in preheated oven for 20 to 24 minutes or until tops are golden and a toothpick inserted in the center comes out clean. Let cool in pan on a wire rack for 5 minutes, then transfer to the rack. Serve warm or let cool completely.

Caraway Muffins

1 1/2 cups	all-purpose flour	375 mL
1/2 cup	whole wheat flour	125 mL
1 tbsp	caraway seeds, crushed	15 mL
1 1/2 tsp	baking powder	7 mL
1 tsp	salt	5 mL
1/2 tsp	baking soda	2 mL
1/2 tsp	ground mace	2 mL
2	eggs	2
2/3 cup	buttermilk	150 mL
1/4 cup	unsalted butter, melted	60 mL
3 tbsp	liquid honey	45 mL

Crushing the caraway seeds greatly enhances their aromatic flavor. The process is a snap: place the seeds in a small zip-top plastic bag, seal the bag, then pound with a mallet or rolling pin until coarsely crushed.

Makes 12 muffins

- Preheat oven to 375°F (190°C)
- 12-cup muffin pan, lined with paper liners

1. In a large bowl, whisk together all-purpose flour, whole wheat flour, caraway seeds, baking powder, salt, baking soda and mace.
2. In a medium bowl, whisk together eggs, buttermilk, butter and honey until well blended.
3. Add the egg mixture to the flour mixture and stir until just blended.
4. Divide batter equally among prepared muffin cups.
5. Bake in preheated oven for 22 to 26 minutes or until tops are golden and a toothpick inserted in the center comes out clean. Let cool in pan on a wire rack for 3 minutes, then transfer to the rack. Serve warm or let cool completely.

Salsa Muffins

1 cup	all-purpose flour	250 mL
1 cup	yellow cornmeal	250 mL
1 tbsp	baking powder	15 mL
1½ tsp	ground cumin	7 mL
½ tsp	salt	2 mL
3 tbsp	granulated sugar	45 mL
1	egg	1
½ cup	milk	125 mL
⅓ cup	vegetable oil	75 mL
¾ cup	bottled chunky tomato salsa	175 mL

Salsa is great with chips, but it is also a fantastic pantry staple. Think about it: tomatoes, peppers, onions, spice and heat — it's a quick foundation for chili, soup, omelets and casseroles. I love what it does to a basic corn muffin, too. I especially like these made with chipotle salsa, but any thick tomato salsa will do.

Makes 12 muffins

- Preheat oven to 400°F (200°C)
- 12-cup muffin pan, greased

1. In a large bowl, whisk together flour, cornmeal, baking powder, cumin and salt.
2. In a medium bowl, whisk together sugar, egg, milk and oil until well blended. Stir in salsa until blended.
3. Add the egg mixture to the flour mixture and stir until just blended.
4. Divide batter equally among prepared muffin cups.
5. Bake in preheated oven for 23 to 28 minutes or until tops are golden and a toothpick inserted in the center comes out clean. Let cool in pan on a wire rack for 5 minutes, then transfer to the rack. Serve warm or let cool completely.

Spicy Cumin Cheese Muffins

1½ cups	all-purpose flour	375 mL
2 tsp	ground cumin	10 mL
1½ tsp	baking powder	7 mL
1¼ tsp	salt	6 mL
½ tsp	cayenne pepper	2 mL
1¼ cups	shredded sharp Cheddar cheese	300 mL
1	egg	1
⅓ cup	milk	75 mL
¼ cup	vegetable oil	60 mL
1 tbsp	cumin seeds	15 mL

An ancient spice is made modern in these spicy muffins. The aromatic, nutty seeds are even better in conjunction with a generous portion of Cheddar cheese.

Makes 12 muffins

- Preheat oven to 375°F (190°C)
- 12-cup muffin pan, greased

1. In a large bowl, whisk together flour, ground cumin, baking powder, salt and cayenne. Stir in cheese.
2. In a medium bowl, whisk together egg, milk and oil until blended.
3. Add the egg mixture to the flour mixture and stir until just blended.
4. Divide batter equally among prepared muffin cups. Sprinkle with cumin seeds.
5. Bake in preheated oven for 22 to 25 minutes or until tops are golden and a toothpick inserted in the center comes out clean. Let cool in pan on a wire rack for 10 minutes, then transfer to the rack. Serve warm or let cool completely.

Madras Curry Muffins

2½ cups	all-purpose flour	625 mL
1 tbsp	mild curry powder	15 mL
2½ tsp	baking powder	12 mL
1 tsp	ground cumin	5 mL
1 tsp	baking soda	5 mL
1 tsp	salt	5 mL
1 tbsp	granulated sugar	15 mL
2	eggs	2
1 cup	plain whole-milk yogurt	250 mL
⅓ cup	unsalted butter, melted	75 mL
¾ cup	chopped green onions (scallions)	175 mL
⅓ cup	golden raisins, chopped	75 mL

These muffins feature the flavors of India: aromatic curry powder, yogurt and cumin. I love to pair them with cold chicken or chicken salad on steamy Texas summer nights.

Makes 12 muffins

- Preheat oven to 375°F (190°C)
- 12-cup muffin pan, lined with paper liners

1. In a large bowl, whisk together flour, curry powder, baking powder, cumin, baking soda and salt.
2. In a medium bowl, whisk together sugar, eggs, yogurt and butter until well blended.
3. Add the egg mixture to the flour mixture and stir until just blended. Gently fold in green onions and raisins.
4. Divide batter equally among prepared muffin cups.
5. Bake in preheated oven for 22 to 27 minutes or until tops are golden and a toothpick inserted in the center comes out clean. Let cool in pan on a wire rack for 3 minutes, then transfer to the rack. Serve warm or let cool completely.

Onion Walnut Muffins

1½ cups	all-purpose flour	375 mL
1½ tsp	salt	7 mL
1½ tsp	baking powder	7 mL
1 tsp	dried thyme	5 mL
2	onions, quartered	2
⅓ cup	granulated sugar	75 mL
2	eggs	2
½ cup	unsalted butter, melted	125 mL
1½ cups	chopped walnuts, toasted	375 mL

Here, the onions and walnuts offer dual enticements: they are packed with nutrients (vitamin C for the former, omega-3 fatty acids and protein for the latter) and are exceptionally delicious baked into these simple muffins, which will be a great addition to your mid-winter repertoire.

Makes 12 muffins

- Preheat oven to 425°F (220°C)
- Food processor
- 12-cup muffin pan, greased

1. In a large bowl, whisk together flour, salt, baking powder and thyme.
2. In food processor, process onions until puréed. Transfer 1 cup (250 mL) to a medium bowl (reserve any leftover purée for another use). Whisk in sugar, eggs and butter until well blended.
3. Add the egg mixture to the flour mixture and stir until just blended. Gently fold in walnuts.
4. Divide batter equally among prepared muffin cups.
5. Bake in preheated oven for 19 to 22 minutes or until tops are golden and a toothpick inserted in the center comes out clean. Let cool in pan on a wire rack for 5 minutes, then transfer to the rack. Serve warm or let cool completely.

Chipotle Cheddar Muffins

1 cup	all-purpose flour	250 mL
1 cup	stone-ground yellow cornmeal	250 mL
4 tsp	baking powder	20 mL
1 tsp	salt	5 mL
1 tsp	chipotle chile powder	5 mL
1 tsp	ground cumin	5 mL
1½ cups	shredded smoked Cheddar cheese	375 mL
2 tbsp	granulated sugar	30 mL
1	egg	1
½ cup	unsalted butter, melted	125 mL
1 cup	milk	250 mL

The first time I tasted these muffins, I knew I had found an instant comfort food. The smoky elements from the chipotle chile powder, cumin and smoked Cheddar cheese are seductive, and the level of heat from the chiles is spicy but not overwhelming. I often vary the cheese — smoked Gouda, sharp (old) Cheddar or Monterey Jack — and sometimes add a touch of grated lime zest.

Tip

Sharp (old) Cheddar cheese may be substituted for the smoked Cheddar cheese. The muffins will still have a smoky quality from the chipotle chile powder and cumin.

Makes 12 muffins

- Preheat oven to 400°F (200°C)
- 12-cup muffin pan, greased

1. In a large bowl, whisk together flour, cornmeal, baking powder, salt, chipotle powder and cumin. Stir in cheese.

2. In a medium bowl, whisk together sugar, egg and butter until well blended. Whisk in milk until blended.

3. Add the egg mixture to the flour mixture and stir until just blended.

4. Divide batter equally among prepared muffin cups.

5. Bake in preheated oven for 25 to 30 minutes or until tops are golden brown and a toothpick inserted in the center comes out clean. Let cool in pan on a wire rack for 5 minutes, then transfer to the rack. Serve warm or let cool completely.

Seeded Cracked Wheat Muffins

$1/2$ cup	cracked wheat (bulgur)	125 mL
$1/2$ cup	boiling water	125 mL
3 cups	all-purpose flour	750 mL
$1^1/_2$ tbsp	baking powder	22 mL
$3/_4$ tsp	salt	3 mL
$1/4$ cup	packed light brown sugar	60 mL
2	eggs	2
2	jars (each 4 oz or 128 mL) squash or carrot purée baby food	2
$3/_4$ cup	milk	175 mL
$1/2$ cup	vegetable oil	125 mL
2 tbsp	poppy seeds	30 mL
2 tbsp	sesame seeds	30 mL

Who knew that cracked wheat (also known as bulgur) could be so delicious? Okay, I knew; I think bulgur is scrumptious in almost any form. You will be convinced of its excellence, too, once you sample these muffins. They have great substance and fantastic flavor, with a satisfying mix of seeds throughout.

Tip

You can use any type of cracked wheat, from fine to coarse grinds, for this recipe — they all work well.

Makes 18 muffins

- Two 12-cup muffin pans, 18 cups greased

1. In a small bowl, combine cracked wheat and boiling water. Let stand, uncovered, for about 30 minutes or until water is absorbed.
2. Preheat oven to 400°F (200°C).
3. In a large bowl, whisk together flour, baking powder and salt.
4. In a medium bowl, whisk together brown sugar, eggs, squash, milk, oil and poppy seeds until well blended. Stir in cracked wheat.
5. Add the egg mixture to the flour mixture and stir until just blended.
6. Sprinkle sesame seeds in the bottoms of prepared cups and gently shake so some adhere to the sides. Divide batter equally among prepared cups.
7. Bake for 23 to 28 minutes or until tops are golden brown and a toothpick inserted in the center comes out clean. Let cool in pans on a wire rack for 5 minutes, then transfer to the rack. Serve warm or let cool completely.

Three-Seed Muffins

1½ cups	all-purpose flour	375 mL
½ cup	whole wheat flour	125 mL
2 tbsp	sesame seeds, divided	30 mL
1 tbsp	baking powder	15 mL
1 tbsp	poppy seeds	15 mL
1 tbsp	caraway seeds	15 mL
1 tsp	salt	5 mL
2 tbsp	packed dark brown sugar	30 mL
2	eggs	2
¼ cup	unsalted butter	60 mL
1 cup	milk	250 mL

Poppy, caraway and sesame seeds provide just the right amount of flavor and texture in these slightly sweet, down-home muffins.

Makes 12 muffins

- Preheat oven to 400°F (200°C)
- 12-cup muffin pan, greased

1. In a large bowl, whisk together all-purpose flour, whole wheat flour, 1 tbsp (15 mL) of the sesame seeds, baking powder, poppy seeds, caraway seeds and salt.

2. In a medium bowl, whisk together brown sugar, eggs and butter until well blended. Whisk in milk until blended.

3. Add the egg mixture to the flour mixture and stir until just blended.

4. Divide batter equally among prepared muffin cups. Sprinkle with the remaining sesame seeds.

5. Bake in preheated oven for 18 to 22 minutes or until tops are golden and a toothpick inserted in the center comes out clean. Let cool in pan on a wire rack for 5 minutes, then transfer to the rack. Serve warm or let cool completely.

Whole-Meal Pecan Muffins

1½ cups	whole wheat flour	375 mL
1 cup	all-purpose flour	250 mL
1½ tsp	baking powder	7 mL
1 tsp	baking soda	5 mL
½ tsp	salt	2 mL
1½ cups	buttermilk	375 mL
⅓ cup	vegetable oil	75 mL
⅓ cup	dark (cooking) molasses	75 mL
1 cup	chopped pecans, toasted	250 mL

Sweet, salty and nutty elements turn buttermilk muffins into little bites of comfort food, ideal with hearty soups come lunch or dinnertime.

Makes 12 muffins

- Preheat oven to 350°F (180°C)
- 12-cup muffin pan, greased

1. In a large bowl, whisk together whole wheat flour, all-purpose flour, baking powder, baking soda and salt.

2. In a medium bowl, whisk together buttermilk, oil and molasses until well blended.

3. Add the buttermilk mixture to the flour mixture and stir until just blended. Gently fold in pecans.

4. Divide batter equally among prepared muffin cups.

5. Bake in preheated oven for 24 to 28 minutes or until tops spring back when touched and a toothpick inserted in the center comes out clean. Let cool in pan on a wire rack for 5 minutes, then transfer to the rack. Serve warm or let cool completely.

Spiced Pistachio Muffins

2 cups	all-purpose flour	500 mL
1 tbsp	baking powder	15 mL
2 tsp	mild curry powder	10 mL
1 tsp	ground coriander	5 mL
1/2 tsp	salt	2 mL
1/2 tsp	ground ginger	2 mL
1/2 tsp	ground cumin	2 mL
1/4 tsp	cayenne pepper	1 mL
1/8 tsp	ground cinnamon	0.5 mL
1	egg	1
1 cup	milk	250 mL
1/4 cup	olive oil	60 mL
3/4 cup	salted roasted pistachios, coarsely chopped	175 mL

Pistachios make an unusual but addictive muffin. Try making them in miniature muffin pans for the perfect cocktail snack.

Makes 12 muffins

- Preheat oven to 375°F (190°C)
- 12-cup muffin pan, greased

1. In a large bowl, whisk together flour, baking powder, curry powder, coriander, salt, ginger, cumin, cayenne and cinnamon.
2. In a medium bowl, whisk together egg, milk and oil until well blended.
3. Add the egg mixture to the flour mixture and stir until just blended. Gently fold in pistachios.
4. Divide batter equally among prepared muffin cups.
5. Bake in preheated oven for 18 to 22 minutes or until tops are golden and a toothpick inserted in the center comes out clean. Let cool in pan on a wire rack for 5 minutes, then transfer to the rack. Serve warm or let cool completely.

Toasted Walnut Muffins

1 1/2 cups	all-purpose flour	375 mL
1/2 cup	whole wheat flour	125 mL
2 tsp	baking powder	10 mL
1/2 tsp	salt	2 mL
1/2 tsp	baking soda	2 mL
2 tbsp	packed light brown sugar	30 mL
2	eggs	2
1/2 cup	walnut oil or olive oil	125 mL
1 cup	buttermilk	250 mL
1 1/3 cups	chopped walnuts, toasted	325 mL

Toasted walnuts are rich and flavorful unadorned, but they get added personality when stirred into a faintly sweet buttermilk batter.

Makes 12 muffins

- Preheat oven to 375°F (190°C)
- 12-cup muffin pan, lined with paper liners

1. In a large bowl, whisk together all-purpose flour, whole wheat flour, baking powder, salt and baking soda.
2. In a medium bowl, whisk together brown sugar, eggs and oil until well blended. Whisk in buttermilk until blended.
3. Add the egg mixture to the flour mixture and stir until just blended. Gently fold in walnuts.
4. Divide batter equally among prepared muffin cups.
5. Bake in preheated oven for 20 to 25 minutes or until tops are golden and a toothpick inserted in the center comes out clean. Let cool in pan on a wire rack for 5 minutes, then transfer to the rack. Serve warm or let cool completely.

Wild Rice Hazelnut Muffins

³/₄ cup	wild rice	175 mL
1 cup	all-purpose flour	250 mL
1¹/₂ tsp	baking powder	7 mL
1 tsp	salt	5 mL
3 tbsp	granulated sugar	45 mL
2	eggs	2
¹/₂ cup	unsalted butter, melted	125 mL
1¹/₄ cups	finely chopped onion	300 mL
¹/₂ cup	chopped hazelnuts, toasted	125 mL

These hearty, nutty muffins are very easy to prepare, but the addition of cooked wild rice adds an unusual and marvelous twist to the simple batter. They are decidedly cold-weather fare; make a fresh batch to accompany holiday turkey, and don't forget the cranberry sauce.

Tip

Chopped hazelnuts are now available in the baking section of most supermarkets.

Makes 12 muffins

- 12-cup muffin pan, greased

1. In a saucepan, combine wild rice and enough water to cover rice by 1 inch (2.5 cm). Bring to a boil over high heat. Reduce heat to medium-low, cover and simmer for about 45 minutes or until tender. Drain and let cool.
2. Preheat oven to 425°F (220°C).
3. In a large bowl, whisk together flour, baking powder and salt.
4. In a medium bowl, whisk together sugar, eggs and butter until well blended. Stir in rice, onion and hazelnuts.
5. Add the egg mixture to the flour mixture and stir until just blended.
6. Divide batter equally among prepared muffin cups.
7. Bake for 19 to 22 minutes or until tops are golden and a toothpick inserted in the center comes out clean. Let cool in pan on a wire rack for 5 minutes, then transfer to the rack. Serve warm or let cool completely.

Chestnut Muffins

1¾ cups	all-purpose flour	425 mL
¾ cup	yellow cornmeal	175 mL
2½ tsp	baking powder	12 mL
1 tsp	salt	5 mL
1 tsp	dried thyme	5 mL
½ tsp	baking soda	2 mL
3 tbsp	packed light brown sugar	45 mL
2	eggs	2
¼ cup	vegetable oil	60 mL
1½ cups	buttermilk	375 mL
1 cup	grated tart-sweet apple, such as Braeburn, Golden Delicious or Gala (unpeeled)	250 mL
1 cup	jarred chestnuts, chopped	250 mL

For an almost instant holiday bread that will dazzle guests, make these muffins. Chopped chestnuts mixed with tart-sweet apples add texture and layers of complexity with minimal fuss.

Tip

Look for jars of chestnuts in well-stocked grocery stores and gourmet food stores. They're available steamed or roasted — both work equally well in this recipe.

Makes 12 muffins

- Preheat oven to 400°F (200°C)
- 12-cup muffin pan, greased

1. In a large bowl, whisk together flour, cornmeal, baking powder, salt, thyme and baking soda.

2. In a medium bowl, whisk together brown sugar, eggs and oil until well blended. Whisk in buttermilk until blended.

3. Add the egg mixture to the flour mixture and stir until just blended. Gently fold in apple and chestnuts.

4. Divide batter equally among prepared muffin cups.

5. Bake in preheated oven for 23 to 26 minutes or until tops are golden and a toothpick inserted in the center comes out clean. Let cool in pan on a wire rack for 5 minutes, then transfer to the rack. Serve warm or let cool completely.

Blue Cheese Muffins

2 cups	all-purpose flour	500 mL
2 tsp	baking powder	10 mL
3/4 tsp	salt	3 mL
1/2 tsp	baking soda	2 mL
1/4 tsp	ground nutmeg	1 mL
1/8 tsp	freshly ground black pepper	0.5 mL
2	eggs	2
2/3 cup	buttermilk	150 mL
1/3 cup	unsalted butter, melted	75 mL
2 tbsp	liquid honey	30 mL
4 oz	blue cheese, crumbled	125 g

A crumble of blue cheese takes these muffins from good to great in one quick move. Honey, nutmeg and pepper both accentuate and temper the tang of the cheese.

Makes 12 muffins

- Preheat oven to 375°F (190°C)
- 12-cup muffin pan, lined with paper liners

1. In a large bowl, whisk together flour, baking powder, salt, baking soda, nutmeg and pepper.
2. In a medium bowl, whisk together eggs, buttermilk, butter and honey until well blended.
3. Add the egg mixture to the flour mixture and stir until just blended. Gently fold in cheese.
4. Divide batter equally among prepared muffin cups.
5. Bake in preheated oven for 22 to 26 minutes or until tops are golden and a toothpick inserted in the center comes out clean. Let cool in pan on a wire rack for 3 minutes, then transfer to the rack. Serve warm or let cool completely.

Swiss Cheese Muffins

2 cups	all-purpose flour	500 mL
1 tbsp	baking powder	15 mL
1 tsp	dried tarragon	5 mL
1/2 tsp	baking soda	2 mL
1/2 tsp	salt	2 mL
1/4 tsp	freshly ground black pepper	1 mL
1	egg	1
1 cup	sour cream	250 mL
1/4 cup	unsalted butter, melted	60 mL
1 tbsp	Dijon mustard	15 mL
1 1/2 cups	shredded Swiss cheese	375 mL
1/2 cup	chopped green onions (scallions)	60 mL

Swiss cheese can do far more than accompany turkey in a boring sandwich. It is mild, sweet and nutty in flavor, with the added pluses of affordability and lower fat content compared to other semi-firm cheeses.

Makes 12 muffins

- Preheat oven to 425°F (220°C)
- 12-cup muffin pan, greased

1. In a large bowl, whisk together flour, baking powder, tarragon, baking soda, salt and pepper.
2. In a medium bowl, whisk together egg, sour cream, butter and mustard until well blended. Stir in cheese and green onions.
3. Add the egg mixture to the flour mixture and stir until just blended.
4. Divide batter equally among prepared muffin cups.
5. Bake in preheated oven for 15 to 18 minutes or until tops are golden and a toothpick inserted in the center comes out clean. Let cool in pan on a wire rack for 5 minutes, then transfer to the rack. Serve warm or let cool completely.

Boursin Muffins

2 cups	all-purpose flour	500 mL
2 tsp	baking powder	10 mL
1/4 tsp	salt	1 mL
1/8 tsp	freshly ground black pepper	0.5 mL
1	egg	1
1	package (5 oz/150 g) Boursin garlic-herb cheese, softened	1
2 tbsp	unsalted butter, melted	30 mL
1 cup	milk	250 mL
1/2 cup	finely chopped walnuts, toasted	125 mL
1/4 cup	minced green onions (scallions)	60 mL

Boursin is a trademarked brand of Gournay cheese, first made in Normandy in the mid-1950s. I can still remember my first bite, brought to me courtesy of a college friend on a late night of studying: soft and creamy, akin to cream cheese, with a distinctive tang accented by garlic and herbs. It is so good on and in so many things, and these simple muffins are no exception.

Tip

If Boursin is unavailable, use any spreadable garlic-herb cheese in its place.

Makes 12 muffins

- Preheat oven to 400°F (200°C)
- 12-cup muffin pan, greased

1. In a large bowl, whisk together flour, baking powder, salt and pepper.
2. In a medium bowl, whisk together egg, cheese and butter until well blended. Whisk in milk until blended.
3. Add the egg mixture to the flour mixture and stir until just blended. Gently fold in walnuts and green onions.
4. Divide batter equally among prepared muffin cups.
5. Bake in preheated oven for 20 to 25 minutes or until tops are golden and a toothpick inserted in the center comes out clean. Let cool in pan on a wire rack for 3 minutes, then transfer to the rack. Serve warm or let cool completely.

Camembert Muffins
with Hazelnuts and Apple

2 cups	all-purpose flour	500 mL
2 tsp	baking powder	10 mL
3/4 tsp	salt	3 mL
1/2 tsp	baking soda	2 mL
1/4 tsp	freshly cracked black pepper	1 mL
2	eggs	2
2/3 cup	buttermilk	150 mL
1/3 cup	unsalted butter, melted	75 mL
2 tbsp	liquid honey	30 mL
1	small tart-sweet apple, such as Braeburn, Golden Delicious or Gala, peeled and shredded	1
4 oz	Camembert cheese, diced	125 g
1/2 cup	chopped hazelnuts, toasted	125 mL

Elegant and deliciously buttery, these golden muffins are an obvious choice for entertaining. Apples and hazelnuts create perfect harmony with melted Camembert, and despite being swoon-worthy, the muffins are surprisingly easy to put together.

Tip

Chopped hazelnuts are now available in the baking aisle of most supermarkets.

Makes 12 muffins

- Preheat oven to 375°F (190°C)
- 12-cup muffin pan, lined with paper liners

1. In a large bowl, whisk together flour, baking powder, salt, baking soda and pepper.

2. In a medium bowl, whisk together eggs, buttermilk, butter and honey until well blended. Stir in apple.

3. Add the egg mixture to the flour mixture and stir until just blended. Gently fold in cheese and hazelnuts.

4. Divide batter equally among prepared muffin cups.

5. Bake in preheated oven for 22 to 26 minutes or until tops are golden and a toothpick inserted in the center comes out clean. Let cool in pan on a wire rack for 5 minutes, then transfer to the rack. Serve warm or let cool completely.

Smoked Gouda Muffins

2 cups	all-purpose flour	500 mL
2 tbsp	poppy seeds	30 mL
2 tbsp	yellow cornmeal	30 mL
2 tsp	baking powder	10 mL
3/4 tsp	salt	3 mL
1/2 tsp	baking soda	2 mL
2 tbsp	packed light brown sugar	30 mL
1	egg	1
1/3 cup	unsalted butter, melted	75 mL
1 cup	buttermilk	250 mL
6 oz	smoked Gouda cheese, cut into 1/4-inch (0.5 cm) cubes	175 g

Smoked slowly in ancient brick ovens over smoldering hickory chip embers, smoked Gouda gives these muffins instant punch. Try them with your favorite soup (I love them with yellow split pea soup) or a hearty chopped salad. For a sensational appetizer, bake them in mini muffin pans — they're terrific with cold beer.

Makes 12 muffins
- Preheat oven to 400°F (200°C)
- 12-cup muffin pan, greased

1. In a large bowl, whisk together flour, poppy seeds, cornmeal, baking powder, salt and baking soda.

2. In a medium bowl, whisk together brown sugar, egg and butter until well blended. Whisk in buttermilk until blended.

3. Add the egg mixture to the flour mixture and stir until just blended. Gently fold in cheese.

4. Divide batter equally among prepared muffin cups.

5. Bake in preheated oven for 20 to 24 minutes or until tops are golden and a toothpick inserted in the center comes out clean. Let cool in pan on a wire rack for 5 minutes, then transfer to the rack. Serve warm or let cool completely.

Cottage Cheese Muffins

2 cups	all-purpose flour	500 mL
2 1/2 tsp	baking powder	12 mL
1/2 tsp	salt	2 mL
1 tbsp	granulated sugar	15 mL
1	egg	1
3/4 cup	small-curd cottage cheese	175 mL
1/4 cup	unsalted butter, melted	60 mL
1 cup	milk	250 mL

Cottage cheese may sound like an unusual ingredient for bread, but it has transformative properties: it makes quick breads of all kinds (think loaves, pancakes and muffins, such as these) almost soufflé-like in texture, imparting both lightness and a tender crumb. You can add any combination of herbs and aromatics you like, but I prefer them just as they are (with, perhaps, some extra butter).

Makes 12 muffins
- Preheat oven to 375°F (190°C)
- 12-cup muffin pan, greased

1. In a large bowl, whisk together flour, baking powder and salt.

2. In a medium bowl, whisk together sugar, egg, cottage cheese and butter until well blended. Whisk in milk until blended.

3. Add the egg mixture to the flour mixture and stir until just blended.

4. Divide batter equally among prepared muffin cups.

5. Bake in preheated oven for 18 to 23 minutes or until tops are golden and a toothpick inserted in the center comes out clean. Let cool in pan on a wire rack for 5 minutes, then transfer to the rack. Serve warm or let cool completely.

Scallion Dill Cottage Cheese Muffins

2 cups	all-purpose flour	500 mL
2¹/₂ tsp	baking powder	12 mL
1 tbsp	dried dillweed	15 mL
¹/₂ tsp	salt	2 mL
¹/₂ tsp	freshly ground black pepper	2 mL
2 tsp	granulated sugar	10 mL
1	egg	1
1 cup	small-curd cottage cheese	250 mL
¹/₂ cup	milk	125 mL
¹/₄ cup	unsalted butter, melted	60 mL
¹/₂ cup	finely chopped green onions (scallions)	125 mL

Scallions, also called green onions, are commonly paired with dill, but something really great happens when you team them up with a tangy cottage cheese muffin. A basket of these is especially tasty alongside chicken salad.

Makes 12 muffins

- Preheat oven to 400°F (200°C)
- 12-cup muffin pan, greased

1. In a large bowl, whisk together flour, baking powder, dill, salt and pepper.
2. In a medium bowl, whisk together sugar, egg, cottage cheese, milk and butter until well blended. Stir in green onions.
3. Add the egg mixture to the flour mixture and stir until just blended.
4. Divide batter equally among prepared muffin cups.
5. Bake in preheated oven for 16 to 21 minutes or until tops are golden and a toothpick inserted in the center comes out clean. Let cool in pan on a wire rack for 5 minutes, then transfer to the rack. Serve warm or let cool completely.

Walnut Blue Cheese Muffins

2 cups	all-purpose flour	500 mL
2 tsp	baking powder	10 mL
¹/₄ tsp	salt	1 mL
1 tbsp	granulated sugar	15 mL
1	egg	1
³/₄ cup	milk	175 mL
¹/₃ cup	unsalted butter, melted	75 mL
¹/₄ tsp	hot pepper sauce	1 mL
1 cup	coarsely crumbled blue cheese	250 mL
³/₄ cup	finely chopped walnuts, toasted	175 mL

Walnuts and blue cheese have a natural affinity for one another. A splash of hot pepper sauce contributes a bold counterpoint.

Makes 12 muffins

- Preheat oven to 400°F (200°C)
- 12-cup muffin pan, greased

1. In a large bowl, whisk together flour, baking powder and salt.
2. In a medium bowl, whisk together sugar, egg, milk, butter and hot pepper sauce until well blended.
3. Add the egg mixture to the flour mixture and stir until just blended. Gently fold in blue cheese and walnuts.
4. Divide batter equally among prepared muffin cups.
5. Bake in preheated oven for 15 to 20 minutes or until tops are golden and a toothpick inserted in the center comes out clean. Let cool in pan on a wire rack for 5 minutes, then transfer to the rack. Serve warm or let cool completely.

White Cheddar Herb Muffins

1½ cups	all-purpose flour	375 mL
1½ tsp	baking powder	7 mL
1¼ tsp	salt	6 mL
¼ tsp	freshly ground black pepper	1 mL
1¼ cups	shredded extra-sharp white Cheddar cheese	300 mL
1	clove garlic, minced	1
2 tsp	minced fresh marjoram	10 mL
2 tsp	minced fresh thyme	10 mL
2 tsp	minced fresh sage	10 mL
1	egg	1
⅓ cup	milk	75 mL
¼ cup	olive oil	60 mL

Use this muffin recipe as a utility infielder in your culinary repertoire, popping a batch in the oven for dinners, lunch bags, savory breakfasts and easy entertaining. Make a double batch, giving you plenty for several days as well as provender for the freezer (and future meals).

Makes 12 muffins

- Preheat oven to 375°F (190°C)
- 12-cup muffin pan, greased

1. In a medium bowl, whisk together flour, baking powder, salt and pepper. Stir in cheese.
2. In a small bowl, whisk together garlic, marjoram, thyme, sage, egg, milk and oil until blended.
3. Add the egg mixture to the flour mixture and stir until just blended.
4. Divide batter equally among prepared muffin cups.
5. Bake in preheated oven for 22 to 25 minutes or until tops are golden and a toothpick inserted in the center comes out clean. Let cool in pan on a wire rack for 5 minutes, then transfer to the rack. Serve warm or let cool completely.

Havarti Dill Muffins

1¼ cups	milk	300 mL
¾ cup	dry mashed potato flakes	175 mL
1⅔ cups	all-purpose flour	400 mL
2 tsp	dried dillweed	10 mL
2 tsp	baking powder	10 mL
1 tsp	salt	5 mL
1 tbsp	granulated sugar	15 mL
1	egg	1
⅓ cup	vegetable oil	75 mL
1¼ cups	shredded Havarti cheese	300 mL

Havarti is a Danish cheese with a smooth, buttery flavor, and it melts beautifully. But it also boasts a subtle intensity that makes it one of my favorites — especially in these muffins.

Makes 12 muffins

- Preheat oven to 400°F (200°C)
- 12-cup muffin pan, greased

1. In a small saucepan, bring milk to a simmer over medium-high heat. Remove from heat and stir in potato flakes. Let stand for 2 minutes, then transfer to a medium bowl. Let cool slightly.
2. In a large bowl, whisk together flour, dill, baking powder and salt.
3. Whisk sugar, egg and oil into milk mixture until well blended. Stir in cheese.
4. Add the egg mixture to the flour mixture and stir until just blended.
5. Divide batter equally among prepared muffin cups.
6. Bake in preheated oven for 20 to 25 minutes or until tops are golden and a toothpick inserted in the center comes out clean. Let cool in pan on a wire rack for 5 minutes, then transfer to the rack. Serve warm or let cool completely.

Polenta, Goat Cheese and Mushroom Muffins

1/4 cup	unsalted butter, divided	60 mL
8 oz	white mushrooms, coarsely chopped	250 g
1 cup	all-purpose flour	250 mL
1 cup	instant polenta or yellow cornmeal	250 mL
2 tsp	baking powder	10 mL
1 tsp	dried thyme	5 mL
1 tsp	salt	5 mL
1/2 tsp	baking soda	2 mL
1 tbsp	granulated sugar	15 mL
2	eggs	2
1 1/2 cups	buttermilk	375 mL
4 oz	mild goat cheese, crumbled	125 g

Regarded as peasant food for centuries, polenta has achieved culinary stardom in the past few years, thanks to widespread exploration of all aspects of Italian gastronomy. Here, I've reimagined it in muffin form, accented with tangy goat cheese and earthy mushrooms.

Makes 12 muffins

- 12-cup muffin pan, greased

1. In a large skillet, melt 2 tbsp (30 mL) of the butter over medium-high heat. Sauté mushrooms for about 8 minutes or until golden and liquid has evaporated. Add the remaining butter and stir until melted. Remove from heat and let cool.

2. Preheat oven to 425°F (220°C).

3. In a large bowl, whisk together flour, polenta, baking powder, thyme, salt and baking soda.

4. In a medium bowl, whisk together sugar and eggs until well blended. Whisk in buttermilk until blended. Stir in mushroom mixture.

5. Add the egg mixture to the flour mixture and stir just until blended. Gently fold in cheese.

6. Divide batter equally among prepared muffin cups.

7. Bake for 19 to 23 minutes or until tops are puffed and golden and a toothpick inserted in the center comes out clean. Let cool in pan on a wire rack for 5 minutes, then transfer to the rack. Serve warm or let cool completely.

Parmesan Muffins

1 1/2 cups	all-purpose flour	375 mL
2 tsp	baking powder	10 mL
3/4 tsp	salt	3 mL
1/2 tsp	freshly ground black pepper	2 mL
1/4 tsp	baking soda	1 mL
1 1/4 cups	coarsely grated Parmesan cheese, divided	300 mL
2	cloves garlic, minced	2
1 tsp	minced fresh rosemary	5 mL
1 tbsp	granulated sugar	15 mL
2	eggs	2
3/4 cup	milk	175 mL
1/2 cup	olive oil	125 mL

As much as I like an adventurous muffin, the classics always have a strong draw. Case in point: these Parmesan muffins. They're so salty, cheesy and irresistible, I rarely limit myself to one. They have the added advantage of elevating the most basic meals to something special.

Makes 12 muffins

- Preheat oven to 350°F (180°C)
- 12-cup muffin pan, lined with paper liners

1. In a large bowl, whisk together flour, baking powder, salt, pepper and baking soda. Whisk in 1 cup (250 mL) of the cheese.
2. In a medium bowl, whisk together garlic, rosemary, sugar, eggs, milk and oil until blended.
3. Add the egg mixture to the flour mixture and stir until just blended.
4. Divide batter equally among prepared muffin cups. Sprinkle with the remaining cheese.
5. Bake in preheated oven for 18 to 22 minutes or until tops are golden and a toothpick inserted in the center comes out clean. Let cool in pan on a wire rack for 5 minutes, then transfer to the rack. Serve warm or let cool completely.

Feta, Mint and Chive Muffins

1 1/2 cups	all-purpose flour	375 mL
1 tbsp	baking powder	15 mL
1/4 tsp	salt	1 mL
2	eggs	2
1 cup	milk	250 mL
2 tbsp	unsalted butter, melted	30 mL
2/3 cup	crumbled feta cheese	150 mL
2 tbsp	minced fresh mint	30 mL
2 tbsp	minced fresh chives	30 mL

I have yet to visit Greece, but I am certain when I do I will eat myself silly with feta. I love to crumble it into salads, sandwiches, soups and especially my mouth. Here, I've blended it into an easy muffin. The fresh mint and chives give a nod to the Greeks' love of fresh herbs, but both ingredients truly play up the flavors of the feta.

Makes 12 muffins

- Preheat oven to 400°F (200°C)
- 12-cup muffin pan, lined with paper liners

1. In a large bowl, whisk together flour, baking powder and salt.
2. In a medium bowl, whisk together eggs, milk and butter until well blended.
3. Add the egg mixture to the flour mixture and stir until just blended. Gently fold in cheese, mint and chives.
4. Divide batter equally among prepared muffin cups.
5. Bake in preheated oven for 18 to 22 minutes or until tops are golden and a toothpick inserted in the center comes out clean. Let cool in pan on a wire rack for 5 minutes, then transfer to the rack. Serve warm or let cool completely.

Rosemary, Honey and Blue Cheese Muffins

2 cups	all-purpose flour	500 mL
2¹⁄₂ tsp	baking powder	12 mL
¹⁄₂ tsp	freshly cracked black pepper	2 mL
¹⁄₂ tsp	baking soda	2 mL
¹⁄₂ tsp	salt	2 mL
2 tsp	minced fresh rosemary	10 mL
1	egg	1
¹⁄₄ cup	unsalted butter, melted	60 mL
¹⁄₄ cup	liquid honey	60 mL
1 cup	buttermilk	250 mL
4 oz	blue cheese, crumbled	125 g
¹⁄₄ cup	minced fresh chives	60 mL

These addictive muffins can be thrown together at the last minute. If the blue cheese is too soft to crumble, place it in the freezer for 15 to 30 minutes; this simple trick will allow you to crumble it with ease.

Tip

Minced green onions — the green part only — may be used in place of the chives.

Makes 12 muffins

- Preheat oven to 400°F (200°C)
- 12-cup muffin pan, greased

1. In a large bowl, whisk together flour, baking powder, pepper, baking soda and salt.

2. In a medium bowl, whisk together rosemary, egg, butter and honey until well blended. Whisk in buttermilk until blended.

3. Add the egg mixture to the flour mixture and stir until just blended. Gently fold in blue cheese and chives.

4. Divide batter equally among prepared muffin cups.

5. Bake in preheated oven for 15 to 18 minutes or until tops are golden and a toothpick inserted in the center comes out clean. Let cool in pan on a wire rack for 5 minutes, then transfer to the rack. Serve warm or let cool completely.

Welsh Rarebit Muffins

2½ cups	all-purpose flour	625 mL
1 tbsp	baking powder	15 mL
½ tsp	baking soda	2 mL
½ tsp	salt	2 mL
¼ tsp	freshly ground black pepper	1 mL
1	egg	1
¾ cup	beer	175 mL
½ cup	sour cream	125 mL
¼ cup	unsalted butter, melted	60 mL
1 tbsp	Worcestershire sauce	15 mL
6 oz	extra-sharp (extra-old) Cheddar cheese, cut into ¼-inch (0.5 cm) cubes	175 g

My maternal grandmother ("Gran") was an excellent cook and was infuriated by slanders of British cooking. She proved all the critics wrong with her outstanding roasts, pickles, chutneys, Yorkshire pudding, fruit crumbles and custards. I have particularly fond memories of her Welsh rarebit — essentially melted cheese sauce on toast — a nursery treat she would make for me alone. Gran made my Welsh rarebit with milk, but traditional varieties use beer, so that's what I've done here in my muffin interpretation. Make sure the beer is fresh: it plays a role in the leavening process.

Makes 12 muffins

- Preheat oven to 375°F (190°C)
- 12-cup muffin pan, greased

1. In a large bowl, whisk together flour, baking powder, baking soda, salt and pepper.
2. In a medium bowl, whisk together egg, beer, sour cream, butter and Worcestershire sauce until blended.
3. Add the egg mixture to the flour mixture and stir until just blended. Gently fold in cheese.
4. Divide batter equally among prepared muffin cups.
5. Bake in preheated oven for 20 to 25 minutes or until tops are golden and a toothpick inserted in the center comes out clean. Let cool in pan on a wire rack for 5 minutes, then transfer to the rack. Serve warm or let cool completely.

Ricotta Dill Zucchini Muffins

2¼ cups	all-purpose flour	550 mL
1 tbsp	baking powder	15 mL
¾ tsp	salt	3 mL
1 tbsp	dried dillweed	15 mL
3 tbsp	granulated sugar	45 mL
3	eggs	3
⅔ cup	unsalted butter, melted	150 mL
⅔ cup	milk	150 mL
1 cup	ricotta cheese	250 mL
1 cup	shredded zucchini	250 mL

Zucchini and dill have a real affinity. Here they come together in a tender ricotta muffin, which highlights their delicate flavors.

Makes 12 muffins

- Preheat oven to 400°F (200°C)
- 12-cup muffin pan, greased

1. In a large bowl, whisk together flour, baking powder, salt and dill.

2. In a medium bowl, whisk together sugar, eggs, butter and milk until well blended. Stir in cheese and zucchini.

3. Add the egg mixture to the flour mixture and stir until just blended.

4. Divide batter equally among prepared muffin cups.

5. Bake in preheated oven for 20 to 25 minutes or until tops are golden and a toothpick inserted in the center comes out clean. Let cool in pan on a wire rack for 5 minutes, then transfer to the rack. Serve warm or let cool completely.

Savory Cream Cheese Muffins

2 cups	all-purpose flour	500 mL
2½ tsp	baking powder	12 mL
½ tsp	salt	2 mL
8 oz	cream cheese, softened	250 g
1	egg	1
¼ cup	unsalted butter, melted	60 mL
¾ cup	milk	175 mL

I tend to make these muffins in the fall and early winter, not because they are exclusively cold-weather fare, per se (they are wonderful for spring suppers and summer picnics), but because blocks of cream cheese go on sale during that time (am I revealing my inner cheapskate)? With the cream cheese on hand, these muffins are a snap to make. And a bonus: children adore them as much as adults do.

Makes 12 muffins

- Preheat oven to 400°F (200°C)
- 12-cup muffin pan, greased

1. In a medium bowl, whisk together flour, baking powder and salt.

2. In a large bowl, using an electric mixer on medium speed, beat cream cheese and egg until blended and smooth. Beat in butter until blended and smooth.

3. Add the flour mixture to the egg mixture alternately with the milk, making three additions of flour and two of milk, stirring with a wooden spoon until just blended.

4. Divide batter equally among prepared muffin cups.

5. Bake in preheated oven for 18 to 22 minutes or until tops are golden and a toothpick inserted in the center comes out clean. Let cool in pan on a wire rack for 5 minutes, then transfer to the rack. Serve warm or let cool completely.

Brown Rice and Cheese Muffins

1²/₃ cups	all-purpose flour	400 mL
1 tbsp	baking powder	15 mL
³/₄ tsp	salt	3 mL
1 cup	shredded sharp (old) Cheddar cheese	250 mL
2	eggs	2
³/₄ cup	milk	175 mL
¹/₄ cup	unsalted butter, melted	60 mL
1¹/₂ cups	cooled cooked short-grain brown rice	375 mL
¹/₂ cup	chopped green onions	125 mL

I get many requests on my food blog for easy, healthy ideas for lunch. This is one I developed a while back, with lots of good feedback from readers. The key is to make the brown rice ahead of time. Once it's cooled, you can refrigerate it until you're ready to make the muffins or freeze it in 1¹/₂-cup (375 mL) amounts. Dense, flavorful and slightly chewy, the muffins are a meal in themselves or a great partner to soup or salad.

Makes 12 muffins

- Preheat oven to 425°F (220°C)
- 12-cup muffin pan, greased

1. In a large bowl, whisk together flour, baking powder and salt. Stir in cheese.
2. In a medium bowl, whisk together eggs, milk and butter until well blended.
3. Add the egg mixture to the flour mixture and stir until just blended. Gently fold in rice and green onions.
4. Divide batter equally among prepared muffin cups.
5. Bake in preheated oven for 15 to 18 minutes or until tops are golden and a toothpick inserted in the center comes out clean. Let cool in pan on a wire rack for 5 minutes, then transfer to the rack. Serve warm or let cool completely.

Blue Cheese, Bacon and Basil Muffins

2 cups	all-purpose flour	500 mL
1 tbsp	baking powder	15 mL
¹/₂ tsp	salt	2 mL
2 tbsp	granulated sugar	30 mL
1	egg	1
²/₃ cup	milk	150 mL
¹/₃ cup	vegetable oil	75 mL
1 cup	crumbled blue cheese	250 mL
¹/₂ cup	cooked crumbled bacon	125 mL
¹/₄ cup	sliced fresh basil	60 mL

Sometimes it's wonderful to take life a little slower, but that doesn't mean a minimum amount of effort in the kitchen can't yield maximum effect. Welcome blue cheese, bacon and basil muffins. They are nothing short of perfection.

Makes 12 muffins

- Preheat oven to 350°F (180°C)
- 12-cup muffin pan, lined with paper liners

1. In a large bowl, whisk together flour, baking powder and salt.
2. In a medium bowl, whisk together sugar, egg, milk and oil until well blended.
3. Add the egg mixture to the flour mixture and stir until just blended. Gently fold in cheese, bacon and basil.
4. Divide batter equally among prepared muffin cups.
5. Bake in preheated oven for 21 to 25 minutes or until tops are golden and a toothpick inserted in the center comes out clean. Let cool in pan on a wire rack for 5 minutes, then transfer to the rack. Serve warm or let cool completely.

Southwest Muffins with Cheddar Streusel

Streusel

1/2 cup	finely shredded sharp (old) Cheddar cheese	125 mL
3 tbsp	all-purpose flour	45 mL
1 tbsp	packed light brown sugar	15 mL
1/8 tsp	cayenne pepper	0.5 mL
2 tbsp	unsalted butter, melted	30 mL
1/3 cup	roasted salted green pumpkin seeds (pepitas)	75 mL

Muffins

1 cup	all-purpose flour	250 mL
3/4 cup	yellow cornmeal	175 mL
2 1/2 tsp	baking powder	12 mL
1 1/2 tsp	ground cumin	7 mL
1/2 tsp	baking soda	2 mL
1/2 tsp	salt	2 mL
1/4 cup	packed light brown sugar	60 mL
1	egg	1
2/3 cup	buttermilk	150 mL
2/3 cup	pumpkin purée (not pie filling)	150 mL
3 tbsp	vegetable oil	45 mL
1	can (4 1/2 oz/127 mL) diced mild green chiles, drained	1

Plain corn muffins have their place, but when prepared with a sharp Cheddar–pepita streusel and a green chile and pumpkin–enriched batter, they are irresistibly good, with heightened Southwestern flavor.

Makes 12 muffins

- Preheat oven to 400°F (200°C)
- 12-cup muffin pan, greased

1. *Streusel:* In a small bowl, combine cheese, flour, brown sugar and cayenne. Using a fork, toss in butter until crumbly. Stir in pepitas. Refrigerate until ready to use.

2. *Muffins:* In a large bowl, whisk together flour, cornmeal, baking powder, cumin, baking soda and salt.

3. In a medium bowl, whisk together brown sugar, egg, buttermilk, pumpkin and oil until well blended. Stir in chiles.

4. Add the egg mixture to the flour mixture and stir until just blended.

5. Divide batter equally among prepared muffin cups. Sprinkle with streusel.

6. Bake in preheated oven for 15 to 20 minutes or until tops are golden and a toothpick inserted in the center comes out clean. Let cool in pan on a wire rack for 3 minutes, then transfer to the rack. Serve warm or let cool completely.

Bacon, Onion and Swiss Muffins

6	slices bacon, cut into $\frac{1}{2}$-inch (1 cm) pieces	6
$\frac{1}{2}$ cup	minced onion	125 mL
3 cups	all-purpose flour	750 mL
1 tbsp	baking powder	15 mL
1 tsp	salt	5 mL
$\frac{1}{4}$ tsp	freshly cracked black pepper	1 mL
6 oz	Swiss cheese, cut into $\frac{1}{4}$-inch (0.5 cm) cubes	175 g
1	egg	1
$\frac{2}{3}$ cup	sour cream	150 mL
$1\frac{1}{4}$ cups	whole milk	300 mL

Sizzling with the familiar ingredients of quiche Lorraine, these lively muffins keep prep time to a minimum without sacrificing flavor.

Makes 12 muffins

- 12-cup muffin pan, greased

1. In a large skillet, cook bacon over medium-high heat, stirring, for 5 minutes or until crisp and golden brown. Using a slotted spoon, transfer to a plate lined with paper towels to drain.
2. Pour off all but $\frac{1}{4}$ cup (60 mL) of the bacon fat from skillet. Add onion and cook, stirring, for 3 to 4 minutes or until softened. Remove from heat and let cool (do not drain).
3. Preheat oven to 375°F (190°C).
4. In a large bowl, whisk together flour, baking powder, salt and pepper. Stir in cheese.
5. In a medium bowl, whisk together egg and sour cream until well blended. Whisk in milk until blended. Stir in bacon and onion mixture.
6. Add the egg mixture to the flour mixture and stir until just blended.
7. Divide batter equally among prepared muffin cups.
8. Bake for 20 to 25 minutes or until tops are deep golden brown and a toothpick inserted in the center comes out clean. Let cool in pan on a wire rack for 5 minutes, then transfer to the rack. Serve warm or let cool completely.

Bacon Cheddar Cornmeal Muffins

4	slices bacon, chopped	4
1 cup	thinly sliced green onions (scallions)	250 mL
2 cups	all-purpose flour	500 mL
1 cup	yellow cornmeal	250 mL
1½ tsp	baking powder	7 mL
1 tsp	baking soda	5 mL
¾ tsp	salt	3 mL
¼ tsp	freshly ground black pepper	1 mL
⅓ cup	granulated sugar	75 mL
2	eggs	2
½ cup	unsalted butter, melted	125 mL
¾ cup	sour cream	175 mL
½ cup	milk	125 mL
2 cups	coarsely shredded sharp (old) Cheddar cheese, divided	500 mL

Yellow cornmeal, a workhorse of the baking world, takes on depth when combined with two favorite flavors: bacon and Cheddar cheese. These muffins are memorable, so anticipate requests for more from all who partake.

Makes 12 muffins

• 12-cup muffin pan, greased

1. In a large skillet, cook bacon over medium-high heat, stirring, for 5 minutes or until crisp and golden brown. Add green onions and cook, stirring, for 1 minute. Using a slotted spoon, transfer to a plate lined with paper towels to drain. Let cool to room temperature.

2. Preheat oven to 400°F (200°C).

3. In a large bowl, whisk together flour, cornmeal, baking powder, baking soda, salt and pepper.

4. In a medium bowl, whisk together sugar, eggs and butter until well blended. Whisk in sour cream and milk until blended. Stir in bacon mixture and 1½ cups (375 mL) of the cheese.

5. Add the egg mixture to the flour mixture and stir until just blended.

6. Divide batter equally among prepared muffin cups. Sprinkle with the remaining cheese.

7. Bake for 17 to 19 minutes or until tops are light golden brown and a toothpick inserted in the center comes out clean. Let cool in pan on a wire rack for 5 minutes, then transfer to the rack. Serve warm or let cool completely.

Bacon Maple Corn Muffins

5	slices bacon, chopped	5
1/2 cup	finely chopped onion	125 mL
1 cup	all-purpose flour	250 mL
1 cup	yellow cornmeal	250 mL
2 tsp	baking powder	10 mL
1/2 tsp	baking soda	2 mL
1/2 tsp	salt	2 mL
1/4 tsp	freshly cracked black pepper	1 mL
1	egg	1
1 cup	buttermilk	250 mL
1/3 cup	pure maple syrup	75 mL

I'm hot-rodding traditional bacon muffins here, making them extra-special with a fragrant hit of black pepper and a generous dose of maple syrup. The results? Spectacular.

Makes 12 muffins

- 12-cup muffin pan, greased

1. In a large skillet, cook bacon over medium-high heat, stirring, for 5 minutes or until crisp and golden brown. Using a slotted spoon, transfer to a plate lined with paper towels to drain.

2. Add onion to bacon fat in skillet and cook, stirring, for 3 to 4 minutes or until softened. Remove from heat and let cool (do not drain).

3. Preheat oven to 425°F (220°C).

4. In a large bowl, whisk together flour, cornmeal, baking powder, baking soda, salt and pepper.

5. In a medium bowl, whisk together egg, buttermilk and maple syrup until well blended. Stir in onion mixture.

6. Add the egg mixture to the flour mixture and stir until just blended. Gently fold in bacon.

7. Divide batter equally among prepared muffin cups.

8. Bake for 14 to 18 minutes or until tops are golden and a toothpick inserted in the center comes out clean. Let cool in pan on a wire rack for 5 minutes, then transfer to the rack. Serve warm or let cool completely.

Bacon, Corn and Scallion Muffins

1 cup	all-purpose flour	250 mL
1 cup	yellow cornmeal	250 mL
2 tsp	baking powder	10 mL
1½ tsp	salt	7 mL
½ tsp	baking soda	2 mL
⅛ tsp	cayenne pepper	0.5 mL
¼ cup	granulated sugar	60 mL
2	eggs	2
1 cup	sour cream	250 mL
¼ cup	unsalted butter, melted	60 mL
1½ cups	frozen (thawed) corn kernels	375 mL
⅔ cup	chopped green onions (scallions)	150 mL
½ cup	crumbled cooked bacon	125 mL

In an uncertain world, everyone needs a truly excellent bacon muffin recipe, one that will never fail you. This is it. And in case you're wondering, supermarkets use the names "scallions" and "green onions" interchangeably for the same vegetable, so use either.

Tip

Save time by buying crumbled precooked bacon. You can find it in pouches in the section of the supermarket where salad dressings and croutons are shelved.

Makes 12 muffins

- Preheat oven to 425°F (220°C)
- 12-cup muffin pan, lined with paper liners

1. In a large bowl, whisk together flour, cornmeal, baking powder, salt, baking soda and cayenne.
2. In a medium bowl, whisk together sugar, eggs, sour cream and butter until well blended.
3. Add the egg mixture to the flour mixture and stir until just blended. Gently fold in corn, green onions and bacon.
4. Divide batter equally among prepared muffin cups.
5. Bake in preheated oven for 18 to 22 minutes or until tops are golden and a toothpick inserted in the center comes out with only a few crumbs attached. Let cool in pan on a wire rack for 5 minutes, then transfer to the rack. Serve warm or let cool completely.

BLT Muffins

2 cups	all-purpose flour	500 mL
1 tbsp	baking powder	15 mL
1/2 tsp	salt	2 mL
1 tbsp	granulated sugar	15 mL
2	eggs	2
3/4 cup	milk	175 mL
1/4 cup	vegetable oil	60 mL
2 tsp	Dijon mustard	10 mL
3/4 cup	crumbled cooked bacon	175 mL
2/3 cup	chopped seeded plum (Roma) tomatoes	150 mL
1/4 cup	fresh parsley leaves, chopped	60 mL

Everything old is new again: the sweet and savory flavors coaxed from the bacon, tomatoes, Dijon mustard and fresh parsley in these muffins complement the tender crumb of the muffins without overpowering it.

Tip

It's very important to seed the tomatoes here; otherwise, the batter will be too wet.

Makes 12 muffins

- Preheat oven to 400°F (200°C)
- 12-cup muffin pan, lined with paper liners

1. In a large bowl, whisk together flour, baking powder and salt.

2. In a medium bowl, whisk together sugar, eggs, milk, oil and mustard until well blended.

3. Add the egg mixture to the flour mixture and stir until just blended. Gently fold in bacon, tomatoes and parsley.

4. Divide batter equally among prepared muffin cups.

5. Bake in preheated oven for 21 to 25 minutes or until tops are golden and a toothpick inserted in the center comes out clean. Let cool in pan on a wire rack for 5 minutes, then transfer to the rack. Serve warm or let cool completely.

Loaded Baked Potato Muffins

2 cups	all-purpose flour	500 mL
4 tsp	baking powder	20 mL
1 tsp	salt	5 mL
1/4 tsp	freshly ground black pepper	1 mL
2	eggs	2
1/2 cup	prepared mashed potatoes, at room temperature	125 mL
1/3 cup	unsalted butter, melted	75 mL
1 1/2 cups	milk	375 mL
1 1/2 cups	shredded sharp Cheddar cheese, divided	375 mL
1/2 cup	crumbled cooked bacon	125 mL
1/2 cup	chopped green onions (scallions)	125 mL

These muffins have a lot in common with their namesake: both have a potato base and are loaded with all sorts of good things, including bacon, cheese, green onions and butter. However, these are much easier to make and have the added advantage of being portable. Make them for the next big game day; I guarantee they'll fly out of the basket.

Makes 12 muffins

- Preheat oven to 400°F (200°C)
- 12-cup muffin pan, greased

1. In a large bowl, whisk together flour, baking powder, salt and pepper.
2. In a medium bowl, whisk together eggs, mashed potatoes and butter until well blended. Whisk in milk until blended.
3. Add the egg mixture to the flour mixture and stir until just blended. Gently fold in 1 cup (250 mL) of the cheese, bacon and green onions.
4. Divide batter among prepared muffin cups.
5. Bake in preheated oven for 20 minutes. Remove from oven and sprinkle with the remaining cheese. Bake for 4 to 6 minutes or until a toothpick inserted in the center comes out clean. Let cool in pan on a wire rack for 5 minutes, then transfer to the rack. Serve warm or let cool completely.

Pepperoni Asiago Muffins

2 cups	all-purpose flour	500 mL
1 tbsp	baking powder	15 mL
3/4 tsp	dried thyme	3 mL
3/4 tsp	dried oregano	3 mL
1/2 tsp	salt	2 mL
1/4 tsp	freshly ground black pepper	1 mL
2 tbsp	granulated sugar	30 mL
1	egg	1
2/3 cup	milk	150 mL
1/3 cup	vegetable oil	75 mL
2 oz	pepperoni (about 24 small slices), chopped	60 g
1 cup	coarsely shredded Asiago cheese	250 mL

Makes 12 muffins

- Preheat oven to 350°F (180°C)
- 12-cup muffin pan, lined with paper liners

1. In a large bowl, whisk together flour, baking powder, thyme, oregano, salt and pepper.
2. In a medium bowl, whisk together sugar, egg, milk and oil until well blended.
3. Add the egg mixture to the flour mixture and stir until just blended. Gently fold in pepperoni and cheese.
4. Divide batter equally among prepared muffin cups.
5. Bake in preheated oven for 21 to 25 minutes or until tops are golden and a toothpick inserted in the center comes out clean. Let cool in pan on a wire rack for 5 minutes, then transfer to the rack. Serve warm or let cool completely.

Asiago adds a buttery, savory richness to these muffins, while pepperoni adds bold, spicy flavor. Be sure to choose a young Asiago — not aged — for the best results here.

Pepperoni Pizza Muffins

2 cups	all-purpose flour	500 mL
4 tsp	baking powder	20 mL
1 tsp	dried oregano	5 mL
1/4 tsp	salt	1 mL
2 tsp	granulated sugar	10 mL
1	egg	1
1 cup	milk	250 mL
1/2 cup	unsalted butter, melted	125 mL
6 oz	provolone cheese, cut into 1/4-inch (0.5 cm) cubes	175 g
2 oz	pepperoni (about 24 thin slices), chopped	60 g
1/3 cup	chopped drained oil-packed sun-dried tomatoes	75 mL

Makes 12 muffins

- Preheat oven to 375°F (190°C)
- 12-cup muffin pan, greased

1. In a large bowl, whisk together flour, baking powder, oregano and salt.
2. In a medium bowl, whisk together sugar, egg, milk and butter until well blended.
3. Add the egg mixture to the flour mixture and stir until just blended. Gently fold in cheese, pepperoni and tomatoes.
4. Divide batter equally among prepared muffin cups.
5. Bake in preheated oven for 22 to 27 minutes or until tops are golden and a toothpick inserted in the center comes out clean. Let cool in pan on a wire rack for 5 minutes, then transfer to the rack. Serve warm or let cool completely.

A riff on an American classic, these muffins include sun-dried tomatoes to jazz up the flavor. They make an easy, portable addition to your lunch bag.

Antipasto Muffins

2 cups	all-purpose flour	500 mL
2 tsp	baking powder	10 mL
$\frac{1}{2}$ tsp	salt	2 mL
$\frac{1}{2}$ tsp	baking soda	2 mL
2	eggs	2
1 cup	buttermilk	250 mL
$\frac{1}{2}$ cup	olive oil	125 mL
1	jar (6 oz/175 mL) marinated artichoke hearts, drained, chopped	1
$\frac{1}{2}$ cup	chopped drained oil-packed sun-dried tomatoes	125 mL
$\frac{1}{3}$ cup	fresh basil leaves, chopped	75 mL
3 oz	thinly sliced salami, chopped	90 g
$\frac{1}{2}$ cup	freshly grated Parmesan cheese	125 mL

Salami, artichoke hearts, sun-dried tomatoes and cheese go well together on more than a platter. These muffins are staggeringly simple to make, belying their complex taste.

Makes 12 muffins

- Preheat oven to 375°F (190°C)
- 12-cup muffin pan, lined with paper liners

1. In a large bowl, whisk together flour, baking powder, salt and baking soda.
2. In a medium bowl, whisk together eggs, buttermilk and oil until well blended.
3. Add the egg mixture to the flour mixture and stir until just blended. Gently fold in artichokes, tomatoes, basil and salami.
4. Divide batter equally among prepared muffin cups. Sprinkle with cheese.
5. Bake in preheated oven for 20 to 25 minutes or until tops are golden and a toothpick inserted in the center comes out clean. Let cool in pan on a wire rack for 3 minutes, then transfer to the rack. Serve warm or let cool completely.

Italian Sausage Muffins

8 oz	sweet Italian sausage (bulk or removed from casings)	250 g
1¾ cups	all-purpose flour	425 mL
2 tsp	baking powder	10 mL
1 tsp	dried oregano	5 mL
1 tsp	dried basil	5 mL
½ tsp	salt	2 mL
1	egg	1
⅓ cup	milk	75 mL
3 tbsp	olive oil	45 mL
½ cup	shredded provolone or mozzarella cheese	125 mL
½ cup	freshly grated Parmesan cheese	125 mL

Resistance is futile: no one can possibly eat just one of these sausage- and cheese-stuffed muffins. A meal in themselves, they are best stored in the refrigerator.

Makes 9 muffins

- 12-cup muffin pan, 9 cups greased

1. In a large nonstick skillet, cook sausage over medium heat, breaking up with a spoon, for 5 to 6 minutes or until no longer pink. Transfer to a plate lined with paper towels to drain and let cool.
2. Preheat oven to 375°F (190°C).
3. In a large bowl, whisk together flour, baking powder, oregano, basil and salt.
4. In a medium bowl, whisk together egg, milk and oil until well blended.
5. Add the egg mixture to the flour mixture and stir until just blended. Gently fold in sausage, provolone and Parmesan.
6. Divide batter equally among prepared muffin cups.
7. Bake for 15 to 18 minutes or until tops are golden and a toothpick inserted in the center comes out clean. Let cool in pan on a wire rack for 5 minutes, then transfer to the rack. Serve warm or let cool completely.

Country Sausage and Cheese Muffins

8 oz	pork sausage (bulk or removed from casings)	250 g
2 cups	all-purpose flour	500 mL
2 tsp	baking powder	10 mL
1 tsp	baking soda	5 mL
1 tsp	salt	5 mL
1 tsp	dried sage	5 mL
8 oz	sharp (old) Cheddar cheese, cut into ¼-inch (0.5 cm) cubes	250 g
1 cup	chopped onion	250 mL
⅓ cup	cold unsalted butter, cut into ½-inch (1 cm) cubes	75 mL
3 tbsp	granulated sugar	45 mL
1	egg	1
¼ cup	buttermilk	60 mL

There are lots of sausage and cheese recipes in the world, but this one — perfectly compact in a handy, built-in muffin case — has both home-style and modern flair, and is pantry-friendly to boot.

Makes 12 muffins

- Food processor
- 12-cup muffin pan, greased

1. In a large nonstick skillet, cook sausage over medium heat, breaking up with a spoon, for 5 to 6 minutes or until no longer pink. Transfer to a plate lined with paper towels to drain and let cool.
2. Preheat oven to 375°F (190°C).
3. In food processor, pulse flour, baking powder, baking soda, salt, sage, cheese, onion, butter and sausage until mixture resembles coarse meal. Transfer to a large bowl.
4. In a small bowl, whisk together sugar, egg and buttermilk until well blended.
5. Add the egg mixture to the flour mixture and stir until just blended.
6. Divide batter equally among prepared muffin cups.
7. Bake for 22 to 25 minutes or until tops are golden and a toothpick inserted in the center comes out clean. Let cool in pan on a wire rack for 5 minutes, then transfer to the rack. Serve warm or let cool completely.

Smoked Ham Muffins

2 cups	all-purpose flour	500 mL
2$\frac{1}{2}$ tsp	baking powder	12 mL
$\frac{3}{4}$ tsp	salt	3 mL
$\frac{1}{2}$ tsp	baking soda	2 mL
2 tsp	granulated sugar	10 mL
1	egg	1
$\frac{1}{4}$ cup	unsalted butter, melted	60 mL
1 tbsp	coarse-grained mustard	15 mL
1 cup	buttermilk	250 mL
6 oz	Gruyère or Swiss cheese, cut into $\frac{1}{4}$-inch (0.5 cm) cubes	175 g
1 cup	chopped smoked ham	250 mL

Muffins are the name of the game for a handheld lunch on the go, packed with meaty smoked ham, melted Gruyère and a butter-rich buttermilk batter. Have I convinced you? Either way, you must make these muffins — tasting is believing.

Tip

You can use leftover ham in these muffins or head to the deli counter for the exact amount you need. Ask for 4 oz (125 g) smoked ham, thickly cut, then chop it in your kitchen.

Makes 12 muffins

- Preheat oven to 350°F (180°C)
- 12-cup muffin pan, greased

1. In a large bowl, whisk together flour, baking powder, salt and baking soda.
2. In a medium bowl, whisk together sugar, egg, butter and mustard until well blended. Whisk in buttermilk.
3. Add the egg mixture to the flour mixture and stir until just blended. Gently fold in cheese and ham.
4. Divide batter equally among prepared cups.
5. Bake in preheated oven for 25 to 28 minutes or until tops are golden and a toothpick inserted in the center comes out clean. Let cool in pan on a wire rack for 3 minutes, then transfer to the rack. Serve warm or let cool completely.

Ham and Cheddar Muffins

1³/₄ cups	all-purpose flour	425 mL
2 tsp	baking powder	10 mL
1 tsp	ground cumin	5 mL
¹/₂ tsp	baking soda	2 mL
¹/₄ tsp	salt	1 mL
2 cups	shredded sharp (old) Cheddar cheese, divided	500 mL
2	eggs	2
1 tbsp	Dijon mustard	15 mL
1 cup	buttermilk	250 mL
2 cups	diced cooked ham	500 mL

Makes 18 muffins

- Preheat oven to 375°F (190°C)
- Two 12-cup muffin pans, 18 cups greased

1. In a large bowl, whisk together flour, baking powder, cumin, baking soda and salt. Stir in 1¹/₂ cups (375 mL) of the cheese.
2. In a medium bowl, whisk together eggs and mustard until well blended. Whisk in buttermilk until blended.
3. Add the egg mixture to the flour mixture and stir until just blended. Gently fold in ham.
4. Divide batter equally among prepared muffin cups. Sprinkle with the remaining cheese.
5. Bake in preheated oven for 20 to 25 minutes or until tops are golden and a toothpick inserted in the center comes out clean. Let cool in pans on a wire rack for 5 minutes, then transfer to the rack. Serve warm or let cool completely.

Looking for an easy upgrade for your lunchtime routine? Here's a smart and versatile variation on the familiar ham and cheese sandwich. I've also been known to eat one for breakfast, split, with a poached egg in between.

Ham on Rye Muffins

2 cups	rye flour	500 mL
³/₄ cup	all-purpose flour	175 mL
1 tbsp	caraway seeds	15 mL
2¹/₂ tsp	baking powder	12 mL
1 tsp	salt	5 mL
¹/₂ tsp	baking soda	2 mL
2	eggs	2
¹/₂ cup	unsalted butter, melted	125 mL
1¹/₄ cups	buttermilk	300 mL
1 cup	diced smoked ham	250 mL
2 cups	shredded Swiss cheese, divided	500 mL

Makes 12 muffins

- Preheat oven to 375°F (190°C)
- 12-cup muffin pan, greased

1. In a large bowl, whisk together rye flour, all-purpose flour, caraway seeds, baking powder, salt and baking soda.
2. In a medium bowl, whisk together eggs and butter until well blended. Whisk in buttermilk until blended.
3. Add the egg mixture to the flour mixture and stir until just blended. Gently fold in ham and 1¹/₂ cups (375 mL) of the cheese.
4. Divide batter equally among prepared muffin cups. Sprinkle with the remaining cheese.
5. Bake in preheated oven for 24 to 28 minutes or until tops are golden and a toothpick inserted in the center comes out clean. Let cool in pan on a wire rack for 5 minutes, then transfer to the rack. Serve warm or let cool completely.

This play on the deli classic ham on rye forgoes sliced bread for a dark rye, caraway-flecked muffin batter. Buttermilk lightens the batter, offsetting the richness of the meat and cheese.

Reuben Muffins

1½ cups	rye flour	375 mL
1¼ cups	all-purpose flour	300 mL
2½ tsp	baking powder	12 mL
1 tsp	salt	5 mL
½ tsp	baking soda	2 mL
2	eggs	2
½ cup	unsalted butter, melted	125 mL
1 tbsp	coarse-grained mustard	15 mL
1¼ cups	buttermilk	300 mL
8 oz	sliced deli corned beef, roughly chopped	250 g
4 oz	Gruyère or Swiss cheese, diced	125 g
¾ cup	squeezed dry drained sauerkraut	175 mL

I am crazy for an oversized, Jewish deli–style Reuben sandwich, piled high with corned beef and sauerkraut and dripping with melted cheese. By contrast, these muffins are compact and tailored, yet they capture the magic of the sandwich in a half-dozen delicious bites.

Makes 12 muffins

- Preheat oven to 375°F (190°C)
- 12-cup muffin pan, greased

1. In a large bowl, whisk together rye flour, all-purpose flour, baking powder, salt and baking soda.

2. In a medium bowl, whisk together eggs, butter and mustard until well blended. Whisk in buttermilk until blended.

3. Add the egg mixture to the flour mixture and stir until just blended. Gently fold in corned beef, cheese and sauerkraut.

4. Divide batter equally among prepared muffin cups.

5. Bake in preheated oven for 24 to 28 minutes or until tops are golden and a toothpick inserted in the center comes out clean. Let cool in pan on a wire rack for 5 minutes, then transfer to the rack. Serve warm or let cool completely.

Farmers' Market Muffins

• •

I'm a firm believer in making the most of fresh, seasonal, locally grown produce from the farmers' market, and the recipes in this chapter take full advantage of the available bounty. Choose what's in season and what strikes your fancy at the market. What could be more suitable for spring than Fresh Strawberry Muffins or Ricotta Muffins with Spring Herbs? Come summer, make the living easy with Lavender and Honey Blueberry Muffins in the morning and Cherry Tomato and Goat Cheese Muffins at the dinner table. In autumn and winter, choose from a wide range of imaginative pleasures, such as Golden Acorn Squash Muffins, Quince Muffins and Heirloom Apple and Rosemary Muffins. Most of the ingredients called for are available in well-stocked supermarkets, too, so you can easily create these muffins with fresh options from the produce department. But if you do make your way to the market stalls, chances are you'll find a muffin recipe here that will highlight your locally grown discovery.

continued...

Apple Cranberry Harvest Muffins

1¼ cups	whole wheat flour	300 mL
1¼ cups	all-purpose flour	300 mL
1 tbsp	baking powder	15 mL
2 tsp	ground cinnamon	10 mL
2 tsp	baking soda	10 mL
½ tsp	salt	2 mL
¾ cup	granulated sugar	175 mL
2	eggs	2
½ cup	vegetable oil	125 mL
2 cups	shredded tart apples, such as Granny Smith	500 mL
1 cup	fresh cranberries, coarsely chopped	250 mL
1 cup	shredded carrots	250 mL
¾ cup	chopped pecans, toasted	175 mL

Offering a simple but ever-popular pairing, these quick muffins are full of seasonal flavors. I can never make enough of them during the autumn months.

Makes 18 muffins

- Preheat oven to 375°F (190°C)
- Two 12-cup muffin pans, 18 cups greased

1. In a large bowl, whisk together whole wheat flour, all-purpose flour, baking powder, cinnamon, baking soda and salt.

2. In a medium bowl, whisk together sugar, eggs and oil until well blended. Stir in apples, cranberries and carrots.

3. Add the egg mixture to the flour mixture and stir until just blended. Gently fold in pecans.

4. Divide batter equally among prepared muffin cups.

5. Bake in preheated oven for 20 to 25 minutes or until tops are golden and a toothpick inserted in the center comes out clean. Let cool in pans on a wire rack for 5 minutes, then transfer to the rack to cool.

Heirloom Apple and Rosemary Muffins

1 cup	all-purpose flour	250 mL
½ cup	whole wheat pastry flour	125 mL
2 tsp	baking powder	10 mL
¾ tsp	salt	3 mL
¼ tsp	baking soda	1 mL
¾ cup	granulated sugar	175 mL
2	eggs	2
⅓ cup	olive oil	75 mL
3 tbsp	milk	45 mL
2 tsp	minced fresh rosemary	10 mL
2 cups	diced peeled heirloom apples, such as Winesap or Lady (Roman)	500 mL
½ cup	finely chopped walnuts, toasted	125 mL

Rosemary adds sophisticated notes to these old-fashioned muffins. They are great in autumn, when heirloom apples are at their peak.

Makes 16 muffins

- Preheat oven to 350°F (180°C)
- Two 12-cup muffin pans, 16 cups greased

1. In a large bowl, whisk together all-purpose flour, whole wheat pastry flour, baking powder, salt and baking soda.

2. In a medium bowl, whisk together sugar, eggs, oil, milk and rosemary until well blended.

3. Add the egg mixture to the flour mixture and stir until just blended. Gently fold in apples and walnuts.

4. Divide batter equally among prepared muffin cups.

5. Bake in preheated oven for 20 to 25 minutes or until tops are golden and a toothpick inserted in the center comes out clean. Let cool in pans on a wire rack for 5 minutes, then transfer to the rack to cool.

Roasted Apricot Muffins

1¼ lbs	firm ripe apricots (about 7 large)	625 g
2 cups	all-purpose flour	500 mL
1 tsp	baking powder	5 mL
1 tsp	baking soda	5 mL
½ tsp	salt	2 mL
½ cup	granulated sugar	125 mL
2	eggs	2
¼ cup	unsalted butter, melted	60 mL
½ tsp	almond extract	2 mL
1 cup	sour cream	250 mL
2 tbsp	turbinado sugar	30 mL

Apricot season is short, but my love for the fruit endures. Roasting the apricots may sound fussy, but it is worth the extra effort. Once roasted, apricots become even more intense in flavor and color. If you have any left over, serve them with Greek yogurt and a drizzle of honey.

Makes 12 muffins

- Preheat oven to 400°F (200°C)
- 8- or 9-inch (20 or 23 cm) square glass baking dish
- 12-cup muffin pan, lined with paper liners

1. Place apricots in baking dish and bake in preheated oven for 45 minutes or until softened. Let cool in dish for at least 30 minutes or until cool enough to handle.

2. When apricots are cool, preheat oven to 400°F (200°C). Push out apricot pits and discard. Coarsely chop apricots. Set aside.

2. In a large bowl, whisk together flour, baking powder, baking soda and salt.

3. In a medium bowl, whisk together granulated sugar, eggs, butter and almond extract until well blended. Whisk in sour cream until blended.

4. Add the egg mixture to the flour mixture and stir until just blended. Gently fold in apricots.

5. Divide batter equally among prepared muffin cups. Sprinkle with turbinado sugar.

6. Bake for 18 to 21 minutes or until tops are golden and a toothpick inserted in the center comes out clean. Let cool in pan on a wire rack for 3 minutes, then transfer to the rack to cool.

Blueberry Goat Cheese Muffins

2 cups	all-purpose flour	500 mL
2½ tsp	baking powder	12 mL
½ tsp	salt	2 mL
¼ tsp	baking soda	1 mL
⅔ cup	granulated sugar	150 mL
2	eggs	2
1 cup	whole milk	250 mL
½ cup	unsalted butter, melted	125 mL
1 tsp	vanilla extract	5 mL
1 cup	blueberries	250 mL
4 oz	mild creamy goat cheese, crumbled	125 g

I love the classic, but by adding a bit of creamy goat cheese to the batter, I've concocted a fabulous newfangled muffin you will go crazy for.

Makes 16 muffins

- Preheat oven to 400°F (200°C)
- Two 12-cup muffin pans, 16 cups greased

1. In a large bowl, whisk together flour, baking powder, salt and baking soda.

2. In a medium bowl, whisk together sugar, eggs, milk, butter and vanilla until well blended.

3. Add the egg mixture to the flour mixture and stir until just blended. Gently fold in blueberries and cheese.

4. Divide batter equally among prepared muffin cups.

5. Bake in preheated oven for 15 to 20 minutes or until tops are golden and a toothpick inserted in the center comes out clean. Let cool in pans on a wire rack for 5 minutes, then transfer to the rack to cool.

Blackberry Sage Muffins

2 cups	all-purpose flour	500 mL
3 tbsp	yellow cornmeal	45 mL
2 tsp	baking powder	10 mL
1/2 tsp	baking soda	2 mL
1/2 tsp	salt	2 mL
1 1/4 cups	granulated sugar	300 mL
2	eggs	2
1/2 cup	buttermilk	125 mL
1/4 cup	unsalted butter, melted	60 mL
1/4 cup	vegetable oil	60 mL
1 tbsp	minced fresh sage	15 mL
1 tbsp	finely grated lemon zest	15 mL
2 cups	blackberries	500 mL

Blackberries and sage may sound like an unusual combination, but the flavors work in perfect harmony. Fresh blackberries add a lush fruitiness and tame the sweetness of the muffin with their slightly tart flavor.

Makes 18 muffins

- Preheat oven to 375°F (190°C)
- Two 12-cup muffin pans, 18 cups lined with paper liners

1. In a large bowl, whisk together flour, cornmeal, baking powder, baking soda and salt.
2. In a medium bowl, whisk together sugar, eggs, buttermilk, butter, oil, sage and lemon zest until well blended.
3. Add the egg mixture to the flour mixture and stir until just blended. Gently fold in blackberries.
4. Divide batter equally among prepared muffin cups.
5. Bake in preheated oven for 20 to 25 minutes or until tops are golden and a toothpick inserted in the center comes out clean. Let cool in pans on a wire rack for 5 minutes, then transfer to the rack to cool.

Fall Fruit Muffins

1 cup	all-purpose flour	250 mL
1 cup	quick-cooking rolled oats	250 mL
1 tsp	baking powder	5 mL
1/2 tsp	salt	2 mL
1/4 tsp	baking soda	1 mL
3/4 cup	packed light brown sugar	175 mL
1	egg	1
1/2 cup	unsalted butter, melted	125 mL
3/4 cup	unsweetened applesauce	175 mL
2 tsp	finely grated orange zest	10 mL
1 cup	diced firm ripe pears	250 mL
1 cup	cranberries, coarsely chopped	250 mL

Cranberries, pears and applesauce form a sweetly irresistible autumn trinity beneath a tender brown sugar–butter batter.

Makes 12 muffins

- Preheat oven to 350°F (180°C)
- 12-cup muffin pan, lined with paper liners

1. In a large bowl, whisk together flour, oats, baking powder, salt and baking soda.
2. In a medium bowl, whisk together brown sugar, egg and butter until well blended. Whisk in applesauce and orange zest until blended.
3. Add the egg mixture to the flour mixture and stir until just blended. Gently fold in pears and cranberries.
4. Divide batter equally among prepared muffin cups.
5. Bake in preheated oven for 22 to 25 minutes or until tops are golden and a toothpick inserted in the center comes out clean. Let cool in pan on a wire rack for 3 minutes, then transfer to the rack to cool.

Lavender and Honey Blueberry Muffins

2 tbsp	fresh lavender flowers (see tip, below)	30 mL
3/4 cup	milk, divided	175 mL
2 1/4 cups	all-purpose flour	550 mL
2 1/2 tsp	baking powder	12 mL
3/4 tsp	salt	3 mL
1/2 tsp	baking soda	2 mL
2	eggs	2
3/4 cup	liquid honey	175 mL
1/3 cup	vegetable oil	75 mL
1 1/2 cups	blueberries	375 mL

Here, lush summer blueberries are framed by a gently sweet honey muffin with a golden, tender crumb that underlines their tart juiciness. An infusion of fresh lavender draws out a luxurious floral sweetness from the berries. Put out extra honey in a crock so everyone can drizzle more on the warm muffins as they like.

Tip

Be sure your lavender is for culinary use and hasn't been sprayed or preserved in any way. You can use 4 tsp (20 ml) dried lavender flowers in place of the fresh lavender.

Makes 16 muffins

- Two 12-cup muffin pans, 16 cups lined with paper liners

1. In a glass measure, combine lavender and 1/4 cup (60 mL) of the milk. Microwave on Medium-High (70%) for about 1 1/2 minutes or until very hot but not boiling. Remove and let steep for 10 minutes. Strain through a fine-mesh sieve into a medium bowl, discarding flowers. Let cool.

2. Preheat oven to 375°F (190°C).

3. In a large bowl, whisk together flour, baking powder, salt and baking soda.

4. Whisk the remaining milk into the lavender-infused milk. Whisk in eggs, honey and oil until well blended.

5. Add the egg mixture to the flour mixture and stir until just blended. Gently fold in blueberries.

6. Divide batter equally among prepared muffin cups.

7. Bake for 18 to 22 minutes or until tops are golden and a toothpick inserted in the center comes out clean. Let cool in pans on a wire rack for 3 minutes, then transfer to the rack to cool.

Cranberry Muffins
with Walnut Crumble

Crumble

1/2 cup	all-purpose flour	125 mL
1/4 cup	packed light brown sugar	60 mL
1/8 tsp	salt	0.5 mL
3 tbsp	unsalted butter, melted	45 mL
1/2 cup	chopped walnuts	125 mL

Muffins

2 cups	all-purpose flour	500 mL
2 tsp	baking powder	10 mL
1/2 tsp	baking soda	2 mL
1/2 tsp	salt	2 mL
2/3 cup	granulated sugar	150 mL
1	egg	1
1 cup	sour cream	250 mL
1/2 cup	unsalted butter, melted	125 mL
1 1/2 cups	cranberries, coarsely chopped	375 mL

Icing

1 cup	confectioners' (icing) sugar	250 mL

A basket of cranberry-dotted muffins on the kitchen counter always gets attention. And the oohs and aahs will only increase when the toasty walnut crumble and drizzle of icing are revealed.

Makes 12 muffins

- Preheat oven to 425°F (220°C)
- 12-cup muffin pan, greased

1. *Crumble:* In a small bowl, combine flour, brown sugar and salt. Using a fork, stir in butter, tossing until crumbly. Stir in walnuts. Refrigerate until ready to use.

2. *Muffins:* In a large bowl, whisk together flour, baking powder, baking soda and salt.

3. In a medium bowl, whisk together sugar, egg, sour cream and butter until well blended.

4. Add the egg mixture to the flour mixture and stir until just blended. Gently fold in cranberries.

5. Divide batter equally among prepared muffin cups. Sprinkle with crumble and press lightly into batter.

6. Bake in preheated oven for 20 to 22 minutes or until tops are golden and a toothpick inserted in the center comes out clean. Let cool in pan on a wire rack for 5 minutes, then transfer to the rack while you prepare the icing.

7. *Icing:* In a small bowl, whisk together confectioners' sugar and 1 1/2 tbsp (22 mL) water until smooth. Drizzle over warm muffin tops. Let cool.

Fresh Gooseberry Muffins

1 cup	fresh gooseberries, ends and tops trimmed	250 mL
2 tbsp	freshly squeezed lemon juice	30 mL
2 tbsp	liquid honey	30 mL
2 cups	all-purpose flour	500 mL
2 tsp	baking powder	10 mL
3/4 tsp	salt	3 mL
1/2 tsp	baking soda	2 mL
2/3 cup	granulated sugar	150 mL
1	egg	1
3/4 cup	buttermilk	175 mL
1/3 cup	unsalted butter, melted	75 mL

Gooseberries are only around for a short time in the summer, so when you find them at the farmers' market, snap them up! Once they're trimmed, rinse the berries well under running water to remove dust and bits of leaf, and you're ready to cook.

Makes 12 muffins

• 12-cup muffin pan, lined with paper liners

1. In a small saucepan, combine gooseberries, lemon juice and honey. Bring to a simmer over medium-high heat. Reduce heat to low, cover and simmer for 15 minutes. Remove from heat and let cool.
2. Preheat oven to 400°F (200°C).
3. In a large bowl, whisk together flour, baking powder, salt and baking soda.
4. In a medium bowl, whisk together sugar, egg, buttermilk and butter until well blended.
5. Add the egg mixture to the flour mixture and stir until just blended. Gently fold in gooseberry mixture.
6. Divide batter equally among prepared muffin cups.
7. Bake for 20 to 25 minutes or until tops are golden and a toothpick inserted in the center comes out clean. Let cool in pan on a wire rack for 5 minutes, then transfer to the rack to cool.

Olallieberry Herb Muffins

1 cup + 2 tbsp	granulated sugar	275 mL
2 tbsp	minced fresh basil	30 mL
2 tbsp	minced fresh mint	30 mL
1 1/2 cups	all-purpose flour	375 mL
2 tsp	baking powder	10 mL
1/2 tsp	salt	2 mL
1	egg	1
1/2 cup	milk	125 mL
1/3 cup	unsalted butter, melted	75 mL
1 1/2 cups	olallieberries	375 mL

This recipe alone is reason enough to grab your tote bag and head to the farmers' market. An olallieberry is a cross between a youngberry and a loganberry and has a distinctive, sweet flavor. They resemble an elongated blackberry. You can use blackberries (or any other berry that looks great at the market) in their place with equally blissful results.

Makes 12 muffins

• Preheat oven to 400°F (200°C)
• 12-cup muffin pan, lined with paper liners

1. In a small bowl, combine sugar, basil and mint until well blended. Set aside.
2. In a large bowl, whisk together flour, baking powder and salt.
3. In a medium bowl, whisk together 1 cup (250 mL) of the sugar mixture, egg, milk and butter until well blended.
4. Add the egg mixture to the flour mixture and stir until just combined. Gently fold in olallieberries.
5. Divide batter equally among prepared muffin cups. Sprinkle with the remaining sugar mixture.
6. Bake in preheated oven for 22 to 27 minutes or until tops are golden brown and a toothpick inserted in the center comes out clean. Let cool in pan on a wire rack for 5 minutes, then transfer to the rack to cool.

Huckleberry Muffins with Mace Sugar Tops

1²/₃ cups	all-purpose flour	400 mL
¹/₂ cup	yellow cornmeal	125 mL
2 tsp	baking powder	10 mL
¹/₂ tsp	baking soda	2 mL
¹/₂ tsp	ground mace	2 mL
¹/₄ tsp	salt	1 mL
²/₃ cup	packed light brown sugar	150 mL
2	eggs	2
1 cup	milk	250 mL
¹/₃ cup	unsalted butter, melted	75 mL
1 cup	fresh huckleberries	250 mL

Topping

2 tbsp	granulated sugar	30 mL
¹/₄ tsp	ground mace	1 mL

Huckleberries are a wonderful stand-in for blueberries in a host of home-baked muffins. Bright with flavor, they are smaller and slightly less sweet than their cultivated cousins. Feel free to substitute wild blueberries, if that's what's on offer at the market; the' muffins will still be wildly delicious.

Makes 12 muffins

- Preheat oven to 400°F (200°C)
- 12-cup muffin pan, lined with paper liners

1. In a large bowl, whisk together flour, cornmeal, baking powder, baking soda, mace and salt.

2. In a medium bowl, whisk together brown sugar, eggs, milk and butter until well blended.

3. Add the egg mixture to the flour mixture and stir until just blended. Gently fold in huckleberries.

4. Divide batter equally among prepared muffin cups.

5. *Topping:* In a small bowl, combine sugar and mace. Sprinkle over muffins.

6. Bake in preheated oven for 15 to 19 minutes or until tops are golden and a toothpick inserted in the center comes out clean. Let cool in pan on a wire rack for 3 minutes, then transfer to the rack to cool.

Berry Brown Betty Muffins

Topping

1/3 cup	packed light brown sugar	75 mL
1/3 cup	all-purpose flour	75 mL
1/4 cup	unsalted butter, melted	60 mL
1/3 cup	finely chopped pecans	75 mL

Muffins

2 cups	all-purpose flour	500 mL
2 tsp	baking powder	10 mL
1/2 tsp	baking soda	2 mL
1/2 tsp	ground cinnamon	2 mL
1/4 tsp	salt	1 mL
3/4 cup	granulated sugar	175 mL
1	egg	1
1 cup	buttermilk	250 mL
1/3 cup	unsalted butter, melted	75 mL
1 cup	blackberries	250 mL
1 cup	raspberries	250 mL

Brown Betty recipes started showing up in the late 1800s, although the identity of "Betty" remains a mystery. Traditionally, a brown Betty is made with apples, bread crumbs and spices. In this muffin version, fresh blackberries and raspberries stand in for the apples and the bread crumbs are replaced with a brown sugar–pecan topping.

Makes 12 muffins

- Preheat oven to 375°F (190°C)
- 12-cup muffin pan, greased

1. *Topping:* In a small bowl, combine brown sugar and flour. Stir in butter until crumbly. Stir in pecans. Refrigerate until ready to use.

2. *Muffins:* In a large bowl, whisk together flour, baking powder, baking soda, cinnamon and salt.

3. In a medium bowl, whisk together sugar, egg, buttermilk and butter until well blended.

4. Add the egg mixture to the flour mixture and stir until just blended. Gently fold in blackberries and raspberries.

5. Divide batter equally among prepared muffin cups. Sprinkle with topping.

6. Bake in preheated oven for 23 to 28 minutes or until tops are golden and a toothpick inserted in the center comes out clean. Let cool in pan on a wire rack for 3 minutes, then transfer to the rack to cool.

Berry-Banana Smoothie Muffins

1 cup	chopped strawberries	250 mL
2 tbsp	granulated sugar	30 mL
1½ cups	all-purpose flour	375 mL
1½ tsp	baking powder	7 mL
1 tsp	salt	5 mL
½ tsp	baking soda	2 mL
1 cup	granulated sugar	250 mL
2	eggs	2
½ cup	mashed ripe banana	125 mL
¼ cup	vegetable oil	60 mL
1 tsp	vanilla extract	5 mL
1 cup	blueberries	250 mL

Here you have my favorite smoothie ingredients, made over into a muffin. Macerating the strawberries for a few minutes releases their juices, knocking these muffins right out of the park.

Makes 12 muffins

- Preheat oven to 350°F (180°C)
- 12-cup muffin pan, greased

1. In a small bowl, combine strawberries and 2 tbsp (30 mL) sugar. Let stand for 15 minutes to let strawberries release their juice.

2. In a large bowl, whisk together flour, baking powder, salt and baking soda.

3. In a medium bowl, whisk together 1 cup (250 mL) sugar, eggs, banana, oil and vanilla until well blended. Stir in strawberries with juice until blended.

4. Add the egg mixture to the flour mixture and stir until just blended. Gently fold in blueberries.

5. Divide batter equally among prepared muffin cups.

6. Bake in preheated oven for 25 to 28 minutes or until tops are golden and a toothpick inserted in the center comes out with a few moist crumbs attached. Let cool in pan on a wire rack for 5 minutes, then transfer to the rack to cool.

Raspberry Lemon Corn Muffins

1 cup	all-purpose flour	250 mL
1 cup	yellow cornmeal	250 mL
1 tbsp	baking powder	15 mL
½ tsp	salt	2 mL
¾ cup	granulated sugar	175 mL
2	eggs	2
½ cup	unsalted butter, melted	125 mL
¾ cup	milk	175 mL
2 tbsp	finely grated lemon zest	30 mL
1½ cups	raspberries	375 mL
3 tbsp	turbinado sugar	45 mL

Minimal preparation, plus a short bake in the oven, yields a dozen gorgeous yellow and red muffins that showcase summer raspberries in an understated but still glorious way. The cornmeal in the muffins adds great crunch and contrast to the lushness of the fruit.

Makes 12 muffins

- Preheat oven to 400°F (200°C)
- 12-cup muffin pan, lined with paper liners

1. In a large bowl, whisk together flour, cornmeal, baking powder and salt.

2. In a medium bowl, whisk together granulated sugar, eggs, milk, butter and lemon zest until well blended.

3. Add the egg mixture to the flour mixture and stir until just blended. Gently fold in raspberries.

4. Divide batter equally among prepared muffin cups. Sprinkle with turbinado sugar.

5. Bake in preheated oven for 16 to 17 minutes or until tops are golden and a toothpick inserted in the center comes out clean. Let cool in pan on a wire rack for 3 minutes, then transfer to the rack to cool.

Red Currant Muffins

2¼ cups	all-purpose flour	550 mL
2½ tsp	baking powder	12 mL
¾ tsp	salt	3 mL
½ tsp	baking soda	2 mL
¾ cup	granulated sugar	175 mL
2	eggs	2
1 cup	plain whole-milk yogurt	250 mL
⅓ cup	unsalted butter, melted	75 mL
2 tsp	finely grated orange zest	10 mL
⅓ cup	freshly squeezed orange juice	75 mL
1½ cups	red currants	375 mL

The currant is a tiny berry, available in red, black and white, related to the gooseberry. The red and white berries are best for eating out of hand or stirring into delicate cakes — or my luscious little muffins. Tart-sweet and pretty as can be, they are well worth seeking out at the market.

Tip

Fresh currants are in season from June through August. Choose plump currants without hulls. They can be tightly covered and refrigerated for up to 4 days.

Makes 12 muffins

- Preheat oven to 400°F (200°C)
- 12-cup muffin pan, greased

1. In a large bowl, whisk together flour, baking powder, salt and baking soda.

2. In a medium bowl, whisk together sugar, eggs, yogurt, butter, orange zest and orange juice until well blended.

3. Add the egg mixture to the flour mixture and stir until just blended. Gently fold in red currants.

4. Divide batter equally among prepared muffin cups.

5. Bake in preheated oven for 22 to 26 minutes or until tops are golden and a toothpick inserted in the center comes out clean. Let cool in pan on a wire rack for 5 minutes, then transfer to the rack to cool.

Fresh Strawberry Muffins

1½ cups	sliced strawberries	375 mL
⅓ cup	granulated sugar, divided	75 mL
1¾ cups	all-purpose flour	425 mL
2 tsp	baking powder	10 mL
½ tsp	baking soda	2 mL
½ tsp	salt	2 mL
½ tsp	ground cinnamon	2 mL
1	egg	1
1 cup	buttermilk	250 mL
¼ cup	vegetable oil	60 mL
1 tsp	vanilla extract	5 mL
1 tbsp	granulated sugar	15 mL

In my mother's kitchen, fresh summer berries were best served with two ingredients: cream and sugar. These colorful muffins capture the warm-weather synergy and simplicity.

Makes 12 muffins

- Preheat oven to 400°F (200°C)
- 12-cup muffin pan, greased

1. In a small bowl, using a potato masher, mash strawberries and ⅓ cup (75 mL) sugar. Let stand for 15 minutes to let strawberries release their juice.
2. In a large bowl, whisk together flour, baking powder, baking soda, salt and cinnamon.
3. In a medium bowl, whisk together egg, buttermilk, oil and vanilla until well blended. Stir in strawberries with juice until blended.
4. Add the egg mixture to the flour mixture and stir until just blended.
5. Divide batter equally among prepared muffin cups. Sprinkle with 1 tbsp (15 mL) sugar.
6. Bake in preheated oven for 17 to 22 minutes or until tops are golden and a toothpick inserted in the center comes out clean. Let cool in pan on a wire rack for 3 minutes, then transfer to the rack to cool.

Strawberry Rhubarb Muffins

2½ cups	all-purpose flour	625 mL
1 tsp	salt	5 mL
1 tsp	baking soda	5 mL
1½ cups	packed light brown sugar	375 mL
1	egg	1
1 cup	buttermilk	250 mL
⅔ cup	unsalted butter, melted	150 mL
2 tsp	vanilla extract	10 mL
1 cup	finely chopped rhubarb	250 mL
1 cup	coarsely chopped strawberries	250 mL

Strawberries and rhubarb usually meet in late-spring and summer pies. Here, they make friends just as easily in golden buttermilk muffins.

Makes 18 muffins

- Preheat oven to 375°F (190°C)
- Two 12-cup muffin pans, 18 cups greased

1. In a large bowl, whisk together flour, salt and baking soda.
2. In a medium bowl, whisk together brown sugar, egg, buttermilk, butter and vanilla until well blended.
3. Add the egg mixture to the flour mixture and stir until just blended. Gently fold in rhubarb and strawberries.
4. Divide batter equally among prepared muffin cups.
5. Bake in preheated oven for 18 to 23 minutes or until tops are golden and a toothpick inserted in the center comes out clean. Let cool in pans on a wire rack for 3 minutes, then transfer to the rack to cool.

Bing Cherry Bay Leaf Muffins

5	fresh bay leaves	5
1 cup	granulated sugar	250 mL
2 cups	all-purpose flour	500 mL
2½ tsp	baking powder	12 mL
½ tsp	baking soda	2 mL
½ tsp	salt	2 mL
1	egg	1
¾ cup	sour cream	175 mL
½ cup	unsalted butter, melted	125 mL
½ tsp	vanilla extract	2 mL
1 cup	chopped Bing cherries	250 mL

This unbelievably good fruit muffin is contemporary, yet made with familiar ingredients. If fresh bay leaves are unavailable, use dried bay leaves in their place.

Makes 12 muffins

- Preheat oven to 400°F (200°C)
- 12-cup muffin pan, greased

1. In a small saucepan, combine bay leaves, sugar and 2 tbsp (30 mL) water. Bring to a boil over high heat. Reduce heat to low and simmer, stirring, until sugar is dissolved. Remove from heat, cover and let stand for 15 minutes. Discard bay leaves and let syrup cool to room temperature.

2. In a large bowl, whisk together flour, baking powder, baking soda and salt.

3. In a medium bowl, whisk together ⅔ cup (150 mL) of the syrup, egg, sour cream, butter and vanilla until well blended.

4. Add the egg mixture to the flour mixture and stir until just blended. Gently fold in cherries.

5. Divide batter equally among prepared muffin cups.

6. Bake in preheated oven for 15 to 20 minutes or until tops are golden and a toothpick inserted in the center comes out clean. Let cool in pan on a wire rack for 5 minutes, then transfer to the rack. Brush warm muffins with the remaining syrup. Let cool.

Kiwifruit Muffins

1½ cups	all-purpose flour	375 mL
¾ tsp	baking soda	3 mL
½ tsp	ground allspice	2 mL
¼ tsp	salt	1 mL
¾ cup	granulated sugar	175 mL
2	eggs	2
⅔ cup	buttermilk	150 mL
¼ cup	unsalted butter, melted	60 mL
1 cup	chopped peeled kiwifruit	250 mL
⅓ cup	golden raisins, chopped	75 mL

As the main ingredient in these muffins, kiwifruit becomes the belle of the ball.

Makes 12 muffins

- Preheat oven to 425°F (220°C)
- 12-cup muffin pan, greased

1. In a large bowl, whisk together flour, baking soda, allspice and salt.

2. In a medium bowl, whisk together sugar, eggs, buttermilk and butter until well blended.

3. Add the egg mixture to the flour mixture and stir until just blended. Gently fold in kiwifruit and raisins.

4. Divide batter equally among prepared muffin cups.

5. Bake in preheated oven for 15 to 18 minutes or until tops are golden and a toothpick inserted in the center comes out clean. Let cool in pan on a wire rack for 3 minutes, then transfer to the rack to cool.

Cherry Muffins with Almond Crunch Topping

Topping

³⁄₄ cup	slivered almonds, chopped	175 mL
2 tbsp	turbinado sugar	30 mL

Muffins

2¹⁄₂ cups	all-purpose flour	625 mL
2¹⁄₂ tsp	baking powder	12 mL
1 tsp	salt	5 mL
1 cup	packed light brown sugar	250 mL
2	eggs	2
1 cup	buttermilk	250 mL
¹⁄₂ cup	vegetable oil	125 mL
1¹⁄₂ tsp	vanilla extract	7 mL
1 tsp	almond extract	5 mL
1 cup	coarsely chopped cherries	250 mL

These sublime muffins get added sophistication from a sparkling topping and a hint of almond flavor in the batter.

Makes 12 muffins

- Preheat oven to 425°F (220°C)
- 12-cup muffin pan, greased

1. *Topping:* In a small bowl, combine almonds and turbinado sugar. Set aside.
2. *Muffins:* In a large bowl, whisk together flour, baking powder and salt.
3. In a medium bowl, whisk together brown sugar, eggs, buttermilk, oil, vanilla and almond extract until well blended.
4. Add the egg mixture to the flour mixture and stir until just blended. Gently fold in cherries.
5. Divide batter equally among prepared muffin cups. Sprinkle with topping.
6. Bake in preheated oven for 16 to 21 minutes or until tops are golden and a toothpick inserted in the center comes out clean. Let cool in pan on a wire rack for 5 minutes, then transfer to the rack to cool.

Wine Country Grape Muffins

1¹⁄₂ cups	all-purpose flour	375 mL
1¹⁄₂ tsp	baking powder	7 mL
¹⁄₂ tsp	baking soda	2 mL
¹⁄₄ tsp	salt	1 mL
²⁄₃ cup	granulated sugar	150 mL
¹⁄₄ cup	unsalted butter, softened	60 mL
¹⁄₄ cup	olive oil	60 mL
2	eggs	2
1 tbsp	finely grated orange zest	15 mL
²⁄₃ cup	sweet white wine, such as Riesling	150 mL
1¹⁄₄ cups	seedless red grapes, halved if large	300 mL
2 tbsp	confectioners' (icing) sugar	30 mL

I grew up a short distance from Napa, so these muffins remind me of home. Grapes may sound like an unusual addition to a muffin, but they are tart-sweet perfection.

Makes 12 muffins

- Preheat oven to 375°F (190°C)
- 12-cup muffin pan, greased and floured

1. In a medium bowl, whisk together flour, baking powder, baking soda and salt.
2. In a large bowl, using an electric mixer on medium speed, beat granulated sugar, butter, and oil until light and fluffy. Beat in eggs, one at a time, until blended. Beat in orange zest.
3. With the mixer on low speed, beat in flour mixture alternately with wine, making two additions of flour and one of wine, until just blended. Using a rubber spatula, gently fold in grapes.
4. Divide batter equally among prepared muffin cups.
5. Bake in preheated oven for 15 to 19 minutes or until tops are golden and a toothpick inserted in the center comes out clean. Let cool in pan on a wire rack for 3 minutes, then transfer to the rack to cool. Sprinkle with confectioners' sugar before serving.

Fresh Fig Muffins with Honey and Black Pepper

2 cups	all-purpose flour	500 mL
2¹/₂ tsp	baking powder	12 mL
¹/₂ tsp	freshly ground black pepper	2 mL
¹/₂ tsp	baking soda	2 mL
¹/₂ tsp	salt	2 mL
¹/₃ cup	granulated sugar	75 mL
1	egg	1
³/₄ cup	buttermilk	175 mL
¹/₂ cup	unsalted butter, melted	125 mL
¹/₃ cup	liquid honey	75 mL
1¹/₂ cups	diced firm ripe figs	375 mL

These muffins showcase the exquisite flavor of fresh figs through and through.

Makes 12 muffins

- Preheat oven to 400°F (200°C)
- 12-cup muffin pan, greased

1. In a large bowl, whisk together flour, baking powder, pepper, baking soda and salt.
2. In a medium bowl, whisk together sugar, egg, buttermilk, butter and honey until well blended.
3. Add the egg mixture to the flour mixture and stir until just blended. Gently fold in figs.
4. Divide batter equally among prepared muffin cups.
5. Bake in preheated oven for 15 to 20 minutes or until tops are golden and a toothpick inserted in the center comes out clean. Let cool in pan on a wire rack for 3 minutes, then transfer to the rack to cool.

Kumquat Muffins

16	kumquats	16
2 cups	all-purpose flour	500 mL
1 tsp	baking powder	5 mL
1 tsp	baking soda	5 mL
¹/₂ tsp	salt	2 mL
1¹/₃ cups	granulated sugar	325 mL
2	eggs	2
1 cup	sour cream	250 mL
¹/₂ cup	unsalted butter, melted	125 mL
1 tsp	vanilla extract	5 mL
¹/₃ cup	minced crystallized ginger	75 mL
2 tbsp	turbinado sugar	30 mL

Kumquats were one of my maternal grandfather's favorite treats; as soon as they were in season, he would buy a basket, then pop them into his mouth — whole — while soaking up the Southern California sun. I share his affection, but I must admit, I prefer these golden beauties with a little bit more preparation.

Makes 16 muffins

- Preheat oven to 375°F (190°C)
- Two 12-cup muffin pans, 16 cups lined with paper liners

1. Rinse kumquats and pat dry. Trim off any stems. Cut in half, seed and finely chop.
2. In a large bowl, whisk together flour, baking powder, baking soda and salt.
3. In a medium bowl, whisk together granulated sugar, eggs, sour cream, butter and vanilla until well blended.
4. Add the egg mixture to the flour mixture and stir until just blended. Gently fold in kumquats and crystallized ginger.
5. Divide batter equally among prepared muffin cups. Sprinkle with turbinado sugar.
6. Bake in preheated oven for 18 to 22 minutes or until tops are golden and a toothpick inserted in the center comes out clean. Let cool in pans on a wire rack for 5 minutes, then transfer to the rack to cool.

Ruby Red Grapefruit Muffins

Muffins

½ cup	granulated sugar, divided	125 mL
¼ cup	finely grated ruby red grapefruit zest	60 mL
2 tbsp	freshly squeezed ruby red grapefruit juice	30 mL
⅓ cup	unsalted butter	75 mL
2 cups	all-purpose flour	500 mL
1¼ tsp	baking powder	6 mL
1 tsp	baking soda	5 mL
½ tsp	salt	2 mL
½ tsp	ground cardamom	2 mL
2	eggs	2
¾ cup	plain yogurt	175 mL
¾ cup	milk	175 mL

Glaze

1 cup	confectioners' (icing) sugar	250 mL
1 tsp	finely grated ruby red grapefruit zest	5 mL
2 tbsp	freshly squeezed ruby red grapefruit juice	30 mL
Pinch	salt	Pinch

Texas is known for many things, from cowboys to cattle, but few know that it is also prime grapefruit country — specifically, ruby red grapefruits. Jumbo in size, they are incredibly sweet, with gorgeous, hot pink interiors. As soon as they are in season, I make multiple batches of these muffins to celebrate my new home state.

Tip

You'll need about 2 large grapefruits to yield the zest and juice needed for these incredibly delicious citrus muffins.

Makes 16 muffins

- Two 12-cup muffin pans, 16 cups greased

1. *Muffins:* In a small saucepan, combine ¼ cup (60 mL) of the sugar, grapefruit zest and grapefruit juice. Bring to a boil over high heat. Reduce heat to low and simmer, stirring, for 1 to 2 minutes or until sugar has dissolved. Remove from heat and stir in butter until melted. Let cool to room temperature.

2. Preheat oven to 375°F (190°C).

3. In a large bowl, whisk together flour, baking powder, baking soda, salt and cardamom.

4. In a medium bowl, whisk together the remaining sugar, the grapefruit mixture and eggs until well blended. Whisk in yogurt and milk until blended.

5. Add the egg mixture to the flour mixture and stir until just blended.

6. Divide batter equally among prepared muffin cups.

7. Bake for 16 to 21 minutes or until tops are golden and a toothpick inserted in the center comes out clean. Let cool in pans on a wire rack for 5 minutes, then transfer to the rack to cool while you prepare the glaze.

8. *Glaze:* In a small bowl, combine confectioners' sugar, grapefruit zest, grapefruit juice and salt until blended. Spoon over warm muffin tops. Let cool.

Tangerine Muffins

1¼ cups	granulated sugar	300 mL
2 tbsp	finely grated tangerine zest	30 mL
3 cups	all-purpose flour	750 mL
1 tbsp	baking powder	15 mL
½ tsp	baking soda	2 mL
½ tsp	salt	2 mL
⅔ cup	unsalted butter, softened	150 mL
2	eggs	2
1 cup	plain whole-milk yogurt	250 mL
½ cup	freshly squeezed tangerine juice	125 mL

These muffins are as bright as a ray of sun. Tangerines (named after the city of Tangier, Morocco) have a slightly tangier juice than their orange cousins, but in a pinch, oranges can also be used here.

Makes 12 muffins

- Preheat oven to 375°F (190°C)
- 12-cup muffin pan, greased

1. In a small bowl, using the back of a spoon, mash together sugar and tangerine zest. Set aside.
2. In a medium bowl, whisk together flour, baking powder, baking soda and salt.
3. In a large bowl, using an electric mixer on medium-high speed, beat 1 cup (250 mL) of the sugar mixture and butter until light and fluffy. Beat in eggs, one at a time, until fluffy and pale yellow. Beat in yogurt and tangerine juice until blended.
4. With the mixer on low speed, beat the flour mixture into the yogurt mixture until just blended.
5. Divide batter equally among prepared muffin cups. Sprinkle with the remaining sugar mixture.
6. Bake in preheated oven for 25 to 30 minutes or until tops are golden and a toothpick inserted in the center comes out clean. Let cool in pan on a wire rack for 5 minutes, then transfer to the rack to cool.

Lime-Glazed Mango Muffins

Muffins

3 cups	all-purpose flour	750 mL
1 tbsp	baking powder	15 mL
½ tsp	baking soda	2 mL
½ tsp	salt	2 mL
1 cup	granulated sugar	250 mL
2	eggs	2
½ cup	unsalted butter, melted	125 mL
1 tbsp	finely grated lime zest	15 mL
1⅔ cups	buttermilk	400 mL
1½ cups	diced firm ripe mangos	375 mL

Glaze

¼ cup	granulated sugar	60 mL
3 tbsp	freshly squeezed lime juice	45 mL

A tender crumb studded with golden mango and brushed with a fresh lime glaze stacks up to one impressive muffin.

Makes 18 muffins

- Preheat oven to 375°F (190°C)
- Two 12-cup muffin pans, 18 cups greased

1. *Muffins:* In a large bowl, whisk together flour, baking powder, baking soda and salt.
2. In a medium bowl, whisk together sugar, eggs, butter and lime zest until well blended. Whisk in buttermilk until blended.
3. Add the egg mixture to the flour mixture and stir until just blended. Gently fold in mangos.
4. Divide batter equally among prepared muffin cups.
5. Bake in preheated oven for 23 to 28 minutes or until tops are golden and a toothpick inserted in the center comes out clean. Let cool in pan on a wire rack for 3 minutes, then transfer to the rack while you prepare the glaze.
6. *Glaze:* In a small saucepan, combine sugar and lime juice and cook over medium heat, stirring, until sugar is dissolved. Brush over tops of warm muffins. Let cool.

Blood Orange Muffins

4	blood oranges	4
1 cup	granulated sugar	250 mL
1/2 cup	buttermilk (approx.)	125 mL
3	eggs	3
2/3 cup	olive oil	150 mL
1 3/4 cups	all-purpose flour	425 mL
1 1/2 tsp	baking powder	7 mL
1/4 tsp	baking soda	1 mL
1/4 tsp	salt	1 mL

Blood oranges are small, sweet, nearly seedless oranges with vivid, bright red flesh. They have a slightly floral flavor with berry undertones and are in season from December to June.

Makes 10 muffins

- Preheat oven to 375°F (190°C)
- 12-cup muffin pan, 10 cups greased

1. Finely grate 2 tbsp (30 mL) zest from oranges. In a medium bowl, combine zest and sugar. Set aside.

2. Cut off bottoms and tops from 3 of the oranges. Set each upright on a cutting board and, using a sharp knife, cut away peel and pith, following the curve of the fruit. Holding fruit over a bowl to catch the juices, cut segments from membranes and place in another small bowl. Break segments into 1/4-inch (0.5 cm) pieces.

3. Cut the remaining orange in half and squeeze juice into a glass measuring cup. Add any accumulated juices from segments. Add enough of the buttermilk to equal 2/3 cup (150 mL). Whisk into zest mixture until blended. Whisk in eggs and oil until well blended.

4. In a large bowl, whisk together flour, baking powder, baking soda and salt.

5. Add the egg mixture to the flour mixture and stir until just blended. Gently fold in orange segments.

6. Divide batter equally among prepared muffin cups.

7. Bake in preheated oven for 20 to 25 minutes or until tops are golden and a toothpick inserted in the center comes out clean. Let cool in pan on a wire rack for 5 minutes, then transfer to the rack to cool.

Meyer Lemon Crumb Muffins

Topping

1/4 cup	granulated sugar	60 mL
3 tbsp	all-purpose flour	45 mL
2 tbsp	unsalted butter, melted	30 mL
1 tsp	finely grated Meyer lemon zest	5 mL

Muffins

2 cups	all-purpose flour	500 mL
2 1/2 tsp	baking powder	12 mL
1/2 tsp	baking soda	2 mL
1/2 tsp	salt	2 mL
1 cup	granulated sugar	250 mL
2	eggs	2
3/4 cup	sour cream	175 mL
1/3 cup	unsalted butter, melted	75 mL
1 1/2 tbsp	finely grated Meyer lemon zest	22 mL
3 tbsp	freshly squeezed Meyer lemon juice	45 mL

Glaze

1/2 cup	confectioners' (icing) sugar	125 mL
2 tbsp	freshly squeezed Meyer lemon juice	30 mL

These stellar muffins get their bright lemon flavor in three ways: the juice and zest in the batter and a tart-sweet lemon glaze finish.

Makes 12 muffins

- Preheat oven to 400°F (200°C)
- 12-cup muffin pan, lined with paper liners

1. *Topping:* In a small bowl, using your fingers or a fork, mix sugar, flour, butter and lemon zest until blended and crumbly. Refrigerate until ready to use.

2. *Muffins:* In a large bowl, whisk together flour, baking powder, baking soda and salt.

3. In a medium bowl, whisk together sugar, eggs, sour cream, butter, lemon zest and lemon juice until well blended.

4. Add the egg mixture to the flour mixture and stir until just blended.

5. Divide batter equally among prepared muffin cups. Sprinkle with topping.

6. Bake in preheated oven for 17 to 20 minutes or until tops are golden and a toothpick inserted in the center comes out clean. Let cool in pan on a wire rack for 3 minutes, then transfer to the rack while you prepare the glaze.

7. *Glaze:* In a small bowl, whisk together confectioners' sugar and lemon juice until blended. Drizzle over tops of warm muffins. Let cool.

Papaya Ginger Muffins

1½ cups	all-purpose flour	375 mL
1½ tsp	ground ginger	7 mL
1 tsp	baking soda	5 mL
½ tsp	baking powder	2 mL
½ tsp	salt	2 mL
½ tsp	ground cinnamon	2 mL
½ tsp	ground allspice	2 mL
1 cup	granulated sugar	250 mL
2	eggs	2
1 cup	mashed ripe papaya	250 mL
½ cup	unsalted butter, melted	125 mL
½ cup	golden raisins	125 mL
⅓ cup	finely chopped crystallized ginger	75 mL

The juicy, bright flavor of papayas is a nice contrast to the tender crumb of muffins.

Makes 12 muffins

- Preheat oven to 350°F (180°C)
- 12-cup muffin pan, greased

1. In a large bowl, whisk together flour, ground ginger, baking soda, baking powder, salt, cinnamon and allspice.
2. In a medium bowl, whisk together sugar, eggs, papaya and butter until well blended.
3. Add the egg mixture to the flour mixture and stir until just blended. Gently fold in raisins and crystallized ginger.
4. Divide batter equally among prepared muffin cups.
5. Bake in preheated oven for 20 to 25 minutes or until tops are firm at the center and a toothpick inserted in the center comes out clean. Let cool in pan on a wire rack for 5 minutes, then transfer to the rack to cool.

Passion Fruit Muffins

Muffins

2 cups	all-purpose flour	500 mL
1 tbsp	baking powder	15 mL
½ tsp	salt	2 mL
½ cup	granulated sugar	125 mL
2	eggs	2
3 oz	white chocolate, melted	90 g
⅓ cup	unsalted butter, melted	75 mL
⅓ cup	milk	75 mL
¼ cup	passion fruit pulp	60 mL
1 tsp	vanilla extract	5 mL
1 tsp	finely grated lime zest	5 mL

Icing

1¼ cups	confectioners' (icing) sugar	300 mL
1½ tbsp	passion fruit pulp	22 mL
2 tsp	freshly squeezed lime juice	10 mL

Passion fruit's tart-sweet pulp takes these white chocolate muffins in a fantastic direction.

Makes 12 muffins

- Preheat oven to 400°F (200°C)
- 12-cup muffin pan, greased

1. *Muffins:* In a large bowl, whisk together flour, baking powder and salt.
2. In a medium bowl, whisk together sugar, eggs, white chocolate and butter until well blended. Whisk in milk, passion fruit pulp, vanilla and lime zest until blended.
3. Add the egg mixture to the flour mixture and stir until just blended.
4. Divide batter equally among prepared muffin cups.
5. Bake in preheated oven for 15 to 20 minutes or until tops are golden and a toothpick inserted in the center comes out clean. Let cool in pan on a wire rack for 5 minutes, then transfer to the rack while you prepare the icing.
6. *Icing:* In a small bowl, whisk together confectioners' sugar, passion fruit pulp and lime juice until blended. Drizzle over tops of warm muffins. Let cool.

Peach Melba Muffins

2 cups	all-purpose flour	500 mL
2 tsp	baking powder	10 mL
1/2 tsp	baking soda	2 mL
1/2 tsp	salt	2 mL
1/2 cup	granulated sugar	125 mL
2	eggs	2
1/3 cup	unsalted butter, melted	75 mL
1/2 tsp	almond extract	2 mL
1 1/4 cups	sour cream	300 mL
1 cup	raspberries	250 mL
1 cup	coarsely chopped peeled peaches	250 mL
1/3 cup	sliced almonds	75 mL

Midsummer marks high season at the farmers' market, so why not celebrate with these peach and raspberry muffins? Based on the classic dessert invented by the French chef Auguste Escoffier to honor the Australian soprano Dame Nellie Melba, these muffins make the most of the bounty.

Makes 12 muffins

- Preheat oven to 375°F (190°C)
- 12-cup muffin pan, greased

1. In a large bowl, whisk together flour, baking powder, baking soda and salt.
2. In a medium bowl, whisk together sugar, eggs, butter and almond extract until well blended. Whisk in sour cream until blended.
3. Add the egg mixture to the flour mixture and stir until just blended. Gently fold in raspberries and peaches.
4. Divide batter equally among prepared muffins cups. Sprinkle with almonds.
5. Bake in preheated oven for 25 to 30 minutes or until golden brown and a toothpick inserted in the center comes out clean. Let cool in pan on a wire rack for 3 minutes, then transfer to the rack to cool.

Peaches and Cream Muffins

2 cups	all-purpose flour	500 mL
1 1/2 tsp	baking powder	7 mL
1/2 tsp	salt	2 mL
1 1/2 cups	granulated sugar	375 mL
1 cup	unsalted butter, softened	250 mL
8 oz	cream cheese, softened	250 g
1 tsp	finely grated orange zest	5 mL
1 tsp	vanilla extract	5 mL
3	eggs	3
1/4 cup	freshly squeezed orange juice	60 mL
1 1/2 cups	diced peeled ripe peaches	375 mL

These understated muffins capture the heady flavor of ripe summer peaches at their peak.

Makes 16 muffins

- Preheat oven to 350°F (180°C)
- Two 12-cup muffin pans, 16 cups lined with paper liners

1. In a medium bowl, whisk together flour, baking powder and salt.
2. In a large bowl, using an electric mixer on medium-high speed, beat sugar, butter, cream cheese, orange zest and vanilla until light and fluffy. Beat in eggs, one at a time, until well blended. Beat in orange juice until blended.
3. With the mixer on low speed, beat the flour mixture into the egg mixture until just blended. Using a rubber spatula, gently fold in peaches.
4. Divide batter equally among prepared muffin cups.
5. Bake in preheated oven for 25 to 30 minutes or until tops are golden and a toothpick inserted in the center comes out clean. Let cool in pans on a wire rack for 3 minutes, then transfer to the rack to cool.

Nectarine Crumb Muffins

Topping

1 cup	all-purpose flour	250 mL
1/3 cup	packed light brown sugar	75 mL
1 tsp	baking powder	5 mL
1/8 tsp	salt	0.5 mL
1/3 cup	unsalted butter, melted	75 mL

Muffins

1 3/4 cups	all-purpose flour	425 mL
2 1/4 tsp	baking powder	11 mL
1/2 tsp	salt	2 mL
1 cup	granulated sugar	250 mL
2	eggs	2
3/4 cup	whole milk	175 mL
1/2 cup	vegetable oil	125 mL
2 tsp	finely grated orange zest	10 mL
1 tsp	vanilla extract	5 mL
1 1/2 cups	chopped nectarines	375 mL

The nectarine, a subspecies of peach, generally has a sharper, more intense taste than plain peaches. The homey muffins here are studded with them, their summery, sunshiny essence set off by a trace of orange zest. They are buttery and flavorful, yet not too rich; a simple crumb topping gives them an understated flourish.

Makes 18 muffins

- Preheat oven to 375°F (190°C)
- Two 12-cup muffin pans, 18 cups greased

1. *Topping:* In a medium bowl, combine flour, brown sugar, baking powder and salt. Using a fork, stir in butter, tossing until crumbly. Refrigerate until ready to use.

2. *Muffins:* In a large bowl, whisk together flour, baking powder and salt until blended.

3. In a medium bowl, whisk together sugar, eggs, milk, oil, orange zest and vanilla until well blended.

4. Add the egg mixture to the flour mixture and stir until just blended. Gently fold in nectarines.

5. Divide batter equally among prepared muffin cups. Sprinkle with topping.

6. Bake in preheated oven for 25 to 30 minutes or until tops are golden and a toothpick inserted in the center comes out clean. Let cool in pans on a wire rack for 5 minutes, then transfer to the rack to cool.

Persimmon Muffins

1³/₄ cups	all-purpose flour	425 mL
1 tsp	baking soda	5 mL
³/₄ tsp	salt	3 mL
³/₄ tsp	ground cardamom	3 mL
1 cup	granulated sugar	250 mL
2	eggs	2
¹/₂ cup	unsalted butter, melted	125 mL
¹/₃ cup	bourbon or whiskey	75 mL
1 cup	persimmon purée	250 mL
³/₄ cup	chopped walnuts	175 mL
¹/₂ cup	raisins	125 mL
¹/₂ cup	dried cranberries	125 mL

Bright, tender persimmons mellow the intensity of cranberries while lending the muffins a beautiful orange hue. Though there is only a small amount of cardamom in this recipe, the spice plays a big role in bringing out the subtle flavor and fragrance of the persimmon.

Tips

Unsweetened apple juice may be used in place of the bourbon.

Two to 3 very ripe, squishy-soft persimmons yield the 1 cup (250 mL) purée needed for this recipe.

Makes 12 muffins

- Preheat oven to 350°F (180°C)
- 12-cup muffin pan, lined with paper liners

1. In a large bowl, whisk together flour, baking soda, salt and cardamom.

2. In a medium bowl, whisk together sugar, eggs, butter and bourbon until well blended. Whisk in persimmon purée until blended.

3. Add the egg mixture to the flour mixture and stir until just blended. Gently fold in walnuts, raisins and cranberries.

4. Divide batter equally among prepared muffin cups.

5. Bake in preheated oven for 25 to 28 minutes or until tops are golden and a toothpick inserted in the center comes out clean. Let cool in pan on a wire rack for 5 minutes, then transfer to the rack to cool.

Fresh Pineapple Anise Muffins

1 tbsp	anise seeds	15 mL
1¼ cups	granulated sugar, divided	300 mL
2 tbsp	finely grated lemon zest	30 mL
2 cups	all-purpose flour	500 mL
2½ tsp	baking powder	12 mL
¾ tsp	salt	3 mL
½ tsp	baking soda	2 mL
½ cup	unsalted butter, softened	125 mL
1	egg	1
1 cup	buttermilk	250 mL
1½ cups	chopped pineapple	375 mL
2 tbsp	unsalted butter, melted	30 mL

Fragrant pineapple, anise and fresh lemon create a delicious trio of flavors in these easy muffins.

Makes 12 muffins

- Preheat oven to 375°F (190°C)
- 12-cup muffin pan, lined with paper liners

1. In a small bowl, using the back of a wooden spoon, crush anise seeds. Stir in ¼ cup (60 mL) of the sugar and lemon zest. Set aside.

2. In a medium bowl, whisk together flour, baking powder, salt and baking soda.

3. In a large bowl, using an electric mixer on medium speed, beat the remaining sugar and softened butter until light and fluffy. Beat in egg until blended. Beat in buttermilk and 2 tbsp (30 mL) of the anise seed mixture.

4. With the mixer on low speed, beat the flour mixture into the egg mixture until just blended. Gently fold in pineapple.

5. Divide batter equally among prepared muffin cups.

6. Bake in preheated oven for 25 to 30 minutes or until tops are lightly browned and a toothpick inserted in the center comes out clean. Let cool in pan on a wire rack for 5 minutes, then transfer to the rack.

7. Lightly brush warm muffin tops with melted butter and sprinkle with the remaining anise seed mixture. Let cool.

Parsnip Pear Muffins

2 cups	all-purpose flour	500 mL
2 tsp	ground ginger	10 mL
1½ tsp	baking powder	7 mL
¾ tsp	baking soda	3 mL
½ tsp	salt	2 mL
½ tsp	ground nutmeg	2 mL
1 cup	granulated sugar	250 mL
2	eggs	2
¾ cup	vegetable oil	175 mL
½ cup	milk	125 mL
1½ tsp	vanilla extract	7 mL
2 cups	shredded parsnips	500 mL
1 cup	shredded firm ripe pears	250 mL
½ cup	golden raisins	125 mL

Move over, carrot cake — parsnips have come to town. The creamy-white parsnip (it looks like a white carrot) has never become an American favorite, despite its wonderful flavor. The first frost of the year converts the parsnip's starch to sugar and gives it a pleasantly sweet taste. When combined with fall pears in a spiced muffin, parsnips taste delightfully new.

Tips

Although fresh parsnips are available year-round, their peak period is during fall and winter.

There's no need to peel the pear or parsnips.

Makes 18 muffins

- Preheat oven to 350°F (180°C)
- Two 12-cup muffin pans, 18 cups greased

1. In a large bowl, whisk together flour, ginger, baking powder, baking soda, salt and nutmeg.
2. In a medium bowl, whisk together sugar, eggs, oil, milk and vanilla until well blended.
3. Add the egg mixture to the flour mixture and stir until just blended. Gently fold in parsnips, pears and raisins.
4. Divide batter equally among prepared muffin cups.
5. Bake in preheated oven for 25 to 30 minutes or until tops are golden and a toothpick inserted in the center comes out clean. Let cool in pans on a wire rack for 3 minutes, then transfer to the rack to cool.

Cardamom Pear Muffins

2 cups	all-purpose flour	500 mL
2 tsp	baking powder	10 mL
1 tsp	ground cardamom	5 mL
1/2 tsp	salt	2 mL
1/4 tsp	baking soda	1 mL
2/3 cup	granulated sugar	150 mL
2	eggs	2
3/4 cup	ricotta cheese	175 mL
1/2 cup	unsalted butter, melted	125 mL
1 1/2 tsp	vanilla extract	7 mL
1 1/2 cups	chopped firm ripe pears	375 mL
3 tbsp	turbinado sugar	45 mL

Whether you use Anjou, Bosc, or Comice, these simple muffins are all about the pears. For the best results, be sure to use the best, ripest ones you can find.

Makes 12 muffins

- Preheat oven to 400°F (200°C)
- 12-cup muffin pan, greased

1. In a large bowl, whisk together flour, baking powder, cardamom, salt and baking soda.

2. In a medium bowl, whisk together granulated sugar, eggs, cheese, butter and vanilla until well blended.

3. Add the egg mixture to the flour mixture and stir just until blended. Gently fold in pears.

4. Divide batter equally among prepared muffin cups. Sprinkle with turbinado sugar.

5. Bake in preheated oven for 20 to 25 minutes or until tops are golden and a toothpick inserted in the center comes out clean. Let cool in pan on a wire rack for 3 minutes, then transfer to the rack to cool.

Garam Masala–Scented Asian Pear Muffins

2 1/4 cups	all-purpose flour	550 mL
2 1/2 tsp	baking powder	12 mL
1 1/2 tsp	garam masala	7 mL
3/4 tsp	salt	3 mL
1/2 tsp	baking soda	2 mL
3/4 cup	granulated sugar	175 mL
2	eggs	2
1/3 cup	unsalted butter, melted	75 mL
2 tsp	finely grated lime zest	10 mL
1 cup	plain whole-milk yogurt	250 mL
1/3 cup	milk	75 mL
1 1/2 cups	chopped peeled Asian pears	375 mL

Light, refreshing and very sophisticated, Asian pears have a crisp texture, a round shape and a sweet, floral aroma that's quite unlike that of the more familiar buttery "pear-shaped" pear.

Makes 12 muffins

- Preheat oven to 400°F (200°C)
- 12-cup muffin pan, greased

1. In a large bowl, whisk together flour, baking powder, garam masala, salt and baking soda.

2. In a medium bowl, whisk together sugar, eggs, butter and lime zest until well blended. Whisk in yogurt and milk until blended.

3. Add the egg mixture to the flour mixture and stir until just blended. Gently fold in pears.

4. Divide batter equally among prepared muffin cups.

5. Bake in preheated oven for 22 to 26 minutes or until tops are golden and a toothpick inserted in the center comes out clean. Let cool in pan on a wire rack for 5 minutes, then transfer to the rack to cool.

Plum Muffins with Hazelnut Crumble

Topping

3 tbsp	packed light brown sugar	45 mL
2 tbsp	all-purpose flour	30 mL
2 tbsp	unsalted butter, melted	30 mL
1/4 tsp	ground cardamom	1 mL
1/2 cup	chopped hazelnuts	125 mL

Muffins

2 cups	all-purpose flour	500 mL
2 tsp	baking powder	10 mL
1/2 tsp	salt	2 mL
1/2 tsp	ground cardamom	2 mL
1 cup	granulated sugar	250 mL
2	eggs	2
1/2 cup	heavy or whipping (35%) cream	125 mL
1/4 cup	unsalted butter, melted	60 mL
1 tsp	vanilla extract	5 mL
1 1/2 cups	chopped plums	375 mL

Makes 15 muffins

- Preheat oven to 350°F (180°C)
- Two 12-cup muffin pans, 15 cups lined with paper liners

1. *Topping:* In a small bowl, combine brown sugar, flour, butter and cardamom until crumbly. Stir in hazelnuts. Refrigerate until ready to use.

2. *Muffins:* In a large bowl, whisk together flour, baking powder, salt and cardamom.

3. In a medium bowl, whisk together sugar, eggs, cream, butter and vanilla until well blended.

4. Add the egg mixture to the flour mixture and stir until just blended. Gently fold in plums.

5. Divide batter equally among prepared muffin cups. Sprinkle with topping.

6. Bake in preheated oven for 21 to 25 minutes or until tops are golden and a toothpick inserted in the center comes out clean. Let cool in pans on a wire rack for 3 minutes, then transfer to the rack to cool.

Pomegranate Muffins

2 cups	all-purpose flour	500 mL
1 tbsp	baking powder	15 mL
1/2 tsp	salt	2 mL
2/3 cup	granulated sugar	150 mL
1	egg	1
1 cup	milk	250 mL
1/4 cup	unsalted butter, melted	60 mL
1 tbsp	finely grated lime zest	15 mL
1 1/4 cups	pomegranate seeds	300 mL
1/3 cup	minced crystallized ginger	75 mL

Removing the seeds needed for this recipe is no chore. Cut the ends off the pomegranates, then score the skin from end to end with several evenly spaced cuts. Immerse the fruit in a bowl of water, then pull it apart and rub the seeds free. The skin and most of the membrane float; skim these off and discard, then drain the seeds. Done!

Makes 12 muffins

- Preheat oven to 425°F (220°C)
- 12-cup muffin pan, lined with paper liners

1. In a large bowl, whisk together flour, baking powder and salt.

2. In a medium bowl, whisk together sugar, egg, milk, butter and lime zest until well blended.

3. Add the egg mixture to the flour mixture and stir until just blended. Gently fold in pomegranate seeds and crystallized ginger.

4. Divide batter equally among prepared muffin cups.

5. Bake in preheated oven for 16 to 20 minutes or until tops are golden and a toothpick inserted in the center comes out clean. Let cool in pan on a wire rack for 3 minutes, then transfer to the rack to cool.

Rhubarb Fresh Ginger Muffins

1 cup	granulated sugar	250 mL
1/4 cup	chopped peeled gingerroot	60 mL
2 tsp	finely grated orange zest	10 mL
2 cups	all-purpose flour	500 mL
2 1/2 tsp	baking powder	12 mL
1/2 tsp	baking soda	2 mL
1/2 tsp	salt	2 mL
2	eggs	2
1 cup	sour cream	250 mL
1/2 cup	unsalted butter, melted	125 mL
1 1/2 cups	chopped fresh rhubarb	375 mL

There are many good reasons to get up on a late-summer morning, and among the best of them for me is the anticipation of eating these muffins. Although rhubarb and fresh ginger are a luxurious combination, these beautiful muffins are simultaneously familiar and comforting.

Makes 12 muffins

- Preheat oven to 400°F (200°C)
- Food processor
- 12-cup muffin pan, greased

1. In food processor, process sugar, ginger and orange zest until ginger is finely chopped. Transfer to a cup. Set aside.

2. In a large bowl, whisk together flour, baking powder, baking soda and salt.

3. In a medium bowl, whisk together 3/4 cup (175 mL) of the sugar mixture, eggs, sour cream and butter until well blended.

4. Add the egg mixture to the flour mixture and stir until just blended. Gently fold in rhubarb.

5. Divide batter equally among prepared muffin cups. Sprinkle with the remaining sugar mixture.

6. Bake in preheated oven for 17 to 22 minutes or until tops are golden and a toothpick inserted in the center comes out clean. Let cool in pan on a wire rack for 3 minutes, then transfer to the rack to cool.

Sweet Potato Cranberry Muffins

Muffins

1 1/2 cups	all-purpose flour	375 mL
2 tsp	baking powder	10 mL
1 tsp	ground cinnamon	5 mL
3/4 tsp	salt	3 mL
1/2 tsp	ground nutmeg	2 mL
1/2 cup	granulated sugar	125 mL
1	egg	1
1/2 cup	milk	125 mL
1/2 cup	cold mashed sweet potatoes	125 mL
1/4 cup	unsalted butter, melted	60 mL
1 cup	fresh cranberries, coarsely chopped	250 mL

Topping

2 tbsp	granulated sugar	30 mL
1/2 tsp	ground cinnamon	2 mL

Makes 12 muffins

- Preheat oven to 375°F (180°C)
- 12-cup muffin pan, greased

1. *Muffins:* In a large bowl, whisk together flour, baking powder, cinnamon, salt and nutmeg.

2. In a medium bowl, whisk together sugar, egg, milk, sweet potatoes and butter until well blended.

3. Add the egg mixture to the flour mixture and stir until just blended. Gently fold in cranberries.

4. Divide batter equally among prepared muffin cups.

5. *Topping:* In a small bowl, combine sugar and cinnamon. Sprinkle over muffins.

6. Bake in preheated oven for 18 to 22 minutes or until tops are golden and a toothpick inserted in the center comes out clean. Let cool in pan on a wire rack for 5 minutes, then transfer to the rack to cool.

Sweet Potato Muffins

1 lb	sweet potatoes (about 2)	500 g
1³/₄ cups	all-purpose flour	425 mL
2 tsp	baking powder	10 mL
½ tsp	ground cinnamon, divided	2 mL
½ tsp	salt	2 mL
½ cup	packed light brown sugar	125 mL
2	eggs	2
²/₃ cup	milk	150 mL
½ cup	vegetable oil	125 mL
1 tsp	finely grated orange zest	5 mL
1 cup	chopped pecans, toasted	250 mL

Topping

3 tbsp	granulated sugar	45 mL
1 tsp	ground cinnamon	5 mL

Here, the rich, mellow flavor of sweet potatoes escapes the marshmallow-topped cliché to find new expression in a cinnamon-spiced, not-too-sweet muffin.

Makes 12 muffins

- Preheat oven to 400°F (200°C)
- 12-cup muffin pan, greased

1. Using a fork, prick sweet potatoes all over. Place on a large plate and microwave on High, turning every 5 minutes, for 15 to 20 minutes or until very soft. Immediately slice in half to release steam. When cool enough to handle, scoop flesh into a bowl and mash until smooth. Measure 1 cup (250 mL), reserving any extra for another use.

2. In a large bowl, whisk together flour, baking powder, cinnamon and salt.

3. In a medium bowl, whisk together brown sugar, eggs, milk, oil and orange zest until well blended. Whisk in sweet potatoes until blended.

4. Add the egg mixture to the flour mixture and stir until just blended. Gently fold in pecans.

5. Divide batter equally among prepared muffin cups.

6. *Topping:* In a small bowl, combine sugar and cinnamon. Sprinkle over muffins.

7. Bake in preheated oven for 20 to 25 minutes or until tops are golden brown and a toothpick inserted in the center comes out clean. Let cool in pan on a wire rack for 3 minutes, then transfer to the rack to cool.

Sweet Butternut Squash Muffins

1 lb	butternut squash, peeled, seeded and cut into chunks	500 g
2 cups	all-purpose flour	500 mL
1/2 cup	whole wheat flour	125 mL
2 1/2 tsp	baking powder	12 mL
1 tsp	salt	5 mL
1 tsp	ground cinnamon	5 mL
1 1/4 cups	granulated sugar	300 mL
4	eggs	4
1/2 cup	unsalted butter, melted	125 mL
1/4 cup	vegetable oil	60 mL
1 tbsp	finely grated orange zest	15 mL

Taking a cue from carrot cake, in this recipe butternut squash is finely chopped, then folded into a buttery, sweet, cinnamon batter.

Makes 12 muffins

- Preheat oven to 350°F (180°C)
- Food processor
- 12-cup muffin pan, lined with paper liners

1. In food processor, process squash until finely chopped. Measure 2 cups (500 mL), reserving any extra for another use.
2. In a large bowl, whisk together all-purpose flour, whole wheat flour, baking powder, salt and cinnamon.
3. In a medium bowl, whisk together sugar, eggs, butter, oil and orange zest until well blended. Stir in squash.
4. Add the egg mixture to the flour mixture and stir until just blended.
5. Divide batter equally among prepared muffin cups.
6. Bake in preheated oven for 22 to 25 minutes or until tops are golden and a toothpick inserted in the center comes out clean. Let cool in pan on a wire rack for 3 minutes, then transfer to the rack to cool.

Golden Acorn Squash Muffins

1 3/4 cups	all-purpose flour	425 mL
2 tsp	baking powder	10 mL
3/4 tsp	salt	3 mL
1/2 tsp	baking soda	2 mL
1/2 tsp	ground ginger	2 mL
1/4 tsp	ground coriander	1 mL
3/4 cup	granulated sugar	175 mL
1/2 cup	unsalted butter, softened	125 mL
1	egg	1
1 cup	mashed cooked acorn squash	250 mL
1/4 cup	liquid honey	60 mL
1/2 cup	golden raisins, coarsely chopped	125 mL

Moist and cakelike, these muffins make a beautiful addition to any fall baking repertoire.

Makes 12 muffins

- Preheat oven to 375°F (190°C)
- 12-cup muffin pan, greased

1. In a medium bowl, whisk together flour, baking powder, salt, baking soda, ginger and coriander.
2. In a large bowl, using an electric mixer on medium-high speed, beat sugar and butter until light and fluffy. Beat in egg, squash and honey until blended.
3. Add the flour mixture to the squash mixture and, using a wooden spoon, stir until just blended. Gently fold in raisins.
4. Divide batter equally among prepared muffin cups.
5. Bake in preheated oven for 22 to 27 minutes or until tops spring back when touched and a toothpick inserted in the center comes out clean. Let cool in pan on a wire rack for 3 minutes, then transfer to the rack to cool.

Quince Muffins

Quince

1½ cups	chopped peeled quince	375 mL
¾ cup	granulated sugar	175 mL
1 tsp	freshly squeezed lemon juice	5 mL

Topping

½ cup	all-purpose flour	125 mL
¼ cup	packed light brown sugar	60 mL
3 tbsp	unsalted butter, melted	45 mL

Muffins

1½ cups	all-purpose flour	375 mL
2 tsp	baking powder	10 mL
¾ tsp	ground cardamom	3 mL
¾ tsp	salt	3 mL
⅔ cup	granulated sugar	150 mL
2	eggs	2
⅓ cup	unsalted butter, melted	75 mL
⅓ cup	milk	75 mL
1 tsp	vanilla extract	5 mL

Should you find yourself lucky enough to have a bounty of quince, then you must make these muffins. I've highlighted the sweet and floral notes of the quince with subtle notes of vanilla and spice. These muffins take a bit more effort — quinces are extremely hard and bitter when raw, so they need to be cooked before they're added to the batter — but are well worth it. I typically cook the quince a day ahead, streamlining the muffin-making process.

Makes 12 muffins

- 12-cup muffin pan, greased

1. *Quince:* In a small saucepan, combine quince, sugar, lemon juice and 2½ cups (625 mL) water. Bring to a boil over high heat. Reduce heat to low, cover and simmer for 30 to 35 minutes or until tender. Drain and let cool.

2. Preheat oven to 375°F (190°C).

3. *Topping:* In a small bowl, combine flour, brown sugar and butter until crumbly. Refrigerate until ready to use.

4. *Muffins:* In a large bowl, whisk together flour, baking powder, cardamom and salt.

5. In a medium bowl, whisk together sugar, eggs, butter, milk and vanilla until well blended.

6. Add the egg mixture to the flour mixture and stir until just blended. Gently fold in quince.

7. Divide batter equally among prepared muffin cups. Sprinkle with topping.

8. Bake for 18 to 20 minutes or until tops are golden and a toothpick inserted in the center comes out clean. Let cool in pan on a wire rack for 3 minutes, then transfer to the rack to cool.

Chocolate Zucchini Muffins

2 cups	all-purpose flour	500 mL
1 cup	unsweetened cocoa powder (not Dutch process)	250 mL
2 tsp	baking soda	10 mL
1½ tsp	ground cinnamon	7 mL
1 tsp	salt	5 mL
1 cup	packed dark brown sugar	250 mL
3	eggs	3
¾ cup	vegetable oil	175 mL
½ cup	buttermilk	125 mL
¼ cup	unsalted butter, melted	60 mL
1 tsp	vanilla extract	5 mL
2 cups	shredded zucchini	500 mL
1 cup	semisweet chocolate chips	250 mL

These intensely chocolate, oh-so-moist muffins will make you hope for an abundance of zucchini at the farmers' market — or perhaps in your own garden — this year.

Makes 18 muffins

- Preheat oven to 400°F (200°C)
- Two 12-cup muffin pans, 18 cups greased

1. In a large bowl, whisk together flour, cocoa powder, baking soda, cinnamon and salt.
2. In another large bowl, whisk together brown sugar, eggs, oil, buttermilk, butter and vanilla until well blended. Stir in zucchini.
3. Add the egg mixture to the flour mixture and stir until just blended. Gently fold in chocolate chips.
4. Divide batter equally among prepared muffin cups.
5. Bake in preheated oven for 22 to 27 minutes or until tops spring back when touched and a toothpick inserted in the center comes out clean. Let cool in pans on a wire rack for 3 minutes, then transfer to the rack to cool.

Ricotta Muffins with Spring Herbs

2 cups	all-purpose flour	500 mL
2½ tsp	baking powder	12 mL
½ tsp	salt	2 mL
½ tsp	freshly ground black pepper	2 mL
1 tbsp	granulated sugar	15 mL
1	egg	1
1 cup	whole-milk ricotta cheese	250 mL
⅔ cup	milk	150 mL
¼ cup	olive oil	60 mL
¼ cup	chopped fresh chervil	60 mL
2 tbsp	chopped fresh basil	30 mL
2 tbsp	minced fresh chives	30 mL

Ricotta cheese makes a lovely base for fresh herbs, carrying their flavor and punctuating their brightness with its gentle tang. Since ricotta has a relatively high water content, these muffins are best eaten within a day or two.

Makes 12 muffins

- Preheat oven to 400°F (200°C)
- 12-cup muffin pan, greased

1. In a large bowl, whisk together flour, baking powder, salt and pepper.
2. In a medium bowl, whisk together sugar, egg, cheese, milk and oil until well blended. Stir in chervil, basil and chives.
3. Add the egg mixture to the flour mixture and stir until just blended.
4. Divide batter equally among prepared muffin cups.
5. Bake in preheated oven for 15 to 20 minutes or until tops are golden and a toothpick inserted in the center comes out clean. Let cool in pan on a wire rack for 5 minutes, then transfer to the rack to cool.

Fresh Mint Muffins

³/₄ cup	granulated sugar	175 mL
¹/₂ cup	packed fresh mint leaves	125 mL
1 tbsp	finely grated lemon zest	15 mL
2¹/₄ cups	all-purpose flour	550 mL
1 tbsp	baking powder	15 mL
¹/₂ tsp	baking soda	2 mL
¹/₂ tsp	salt	2 mL
2	eggs	2
¹/₃ cup	unsalted butter, melted	75 mL
1¹/₄ cups	buttermilk	300 mL

Fresh mint flourished year-round in the backyard of my childhood home (my parents still live there, and it still does), so I grew up thinking fresh mint was a right, not a privilege. Here I cloak it in a lemon-scented buttermilk batter, which underscores its delicate yet distinctive perfume.

Makes 12 muffins

- Preheat oven to 400°F (200°C)
- Food processor
- 12-cup muffin pan, greased

1. In food processor, process sugar, mint and lemon zest until finely chopped and mixture resembles moist sand. Set aside.
2. In a large bowl, whisk together flour, baking powder, baking soda and salt.
3. In a medium bowl, whisk together sugar mixture, eggs and butter until well blended. Whisk in buttermilk until blended.
4. Add the egg mixture to the flour mixture and stir until just blended.
5. Divide batter equally among prepared muffin cups.
6. Bake in preheated oven for 21 to 26 minutes or until tops are golden and a toothpick inserted in the center comes out clean. Let cool in pan on a wire rack for 5 minutes, then transfer to the rack to cool.

Lemon Verbena Muffins

Muffins

1³/₄ cups	all-purpose flour	425 mL
1 tsp	baking powder	5 mL
³/₄ tsp	baking soda	3 mL
¹/₄ tsp	salt	1 mL
³/₄ cup	granulated sugar	175 mL
1	egg	1
1 cup	plain whole-milk yogurt	250 mL
¹/₃ cup	unsalted butter, melted	75 mL
3 tbsp	minced fresh lemon verbena	45 mL
1 tbsp	freshly squeezed lemon juice	15 mL

Glaze

1 cup	confectioners' (icing) sugar	250 mL
2 tsp	finely grated lemon zest	10 mL
2 tbsp	freshly squeezed lemon juice	30 mL

When life gives you lemon verbena, make muffins. The clean, citrusy spark it adds to the batter is brightened further with an easy lemon glaze.

Makes 12 muffins

- Preheat oven to 400°F (200°C)
- 12-cup muffin pan, greased

1. *Muffins:* In a large bowl, whisk together flour, baking powder, baking soda and salt.
2. In a medium bowl, whisk together sugar, egg, yogurt, butter, lemon verbena and lemon juice until well blended.
3. Add the egg mixture to the flour mixture and stir until just blended.
4. Divide batter equally among prepared muffin cups.
5. Bake in preheated oven for 20 to 24 minutes or until tops are golden and a toothpick inserted in the center comes out clean. Let cool in pan on a wire rack for 3 minutes, then transfer to the rack to cool while you prepare the glaze.
6. *Glaze:* In a small bowl, whisk together confectioners' sugar, lemon zest and lemon juice until smooth and blended. Spoon over warm muffins. Let cool.

Chocolate Basil Muffins

²/₃ cup	packed fresh basil leaves	150 mL
½ cup	granulated sugar	125 mL
1¼ cups	all-purpose flour	300 mL
½ cup	unsweetened cocoa powder (not Dutch process)	125 mL
1 tsp	baking powder	5 mL
½ tsp	baking soda	2 mL
½ tsp	salt	2 mL
2	eggs	2
²/₃ cup	milk	150 mL
½ cup	unsalted butter, melted	125 mL
2 tsp	vanilla extract	10 mL
1 cup	miniature semisweet chocolate chips	250 mL

The warm, sunny sweetness of basil infuses these chocolate muffins with modern, sophisticated flair.

Makes 12 muffins

- Preheat oven to 350°F (180°C)
- Food processor
- 12-cup muffin pan, greased

1. In food processor, process basil and sugar until basil is finely chopped and sugar appears moist and green. Set aside.
2. In a large bowl, whisk together flour, cocoa powder, baking powder, baking soda and salt.
3. In a medium bowl, whisk together basil mixture, eggs, milk, butter and vanilla until well blended.
4. Add the egg mixture to the flour mixture and stir until just blended. Gently fold in chocolate chips.
5. Divide batter equally among prepared muffin cups.
6. Bake in preheated oven for 21 to 25 minutes or until tops spring back when touched and a toothpick inserted in the center comes out clean. Let cool in pan on a wire rack for 5 minutes, then transfer to the rack to cool.

Fresh Ginger Muffins

1 cup	granulated sugar, divided	250 mL
⅓ cup	coarsely chopped peeled gingerroot	75 mL
1 tbsp	finely grated lemon zest	15 mL
¼ cup	freshly squeezed lemon juice	60 mL
¾ cup	buttermilk	175 mL
2 cups	all-purpose flour	500 mL
¾ tsp	baking soda	3 mL
½ tsp	salt	2 mL
2	eggs	2
½ cup	unsalted butter, melted	125 mL

Here comes the sun: golden and graced with ample amounts of my two favorite ingredients — ginger and lemon — a batch of these muffins is always a cheery sight. This is one of my most requested recipes; one taste and you'll understand why.

Makes 15 muffins

- Two 12-cup muffin pans, 15 cups greased

1. In a small saucepan, combine ½ cup (125 mL) of the granulated sugar, ginger, lemon zest and lemon juice. Cook over medium-high heat, stirring, for 4 to 5 minutes or until sugar is dissolved. Scrape into a medium bowl and whisk in buttermilk. Let cool.
2. Preheat oven to 375°F (190°C).
3. In a large bowl, whisk together flour, baking soda and salt.
4. Whisk the remaining sugar, eggs and butter into buttermilk mixture until well blended.
5. Add the egg mixture to the flour mixture and stir until just blended.
6. Divide batter equally among prepared muffin cups.
7. Bake for 16 to 21 minutes or until tops are golden brown and a toothpick inserted in the center comes out clean. Let cool in pans on a wire rack for 5 minutes, then transfer to the rack to cool.

Lemongrass Mint Muffins

2	stalks fresh lemongrass, root ends trimmed, thinly sliced	2
1 cup	granulated sugar	250 mL
2 tbsp	freshly squeezed lemon juice	30 mL
2 tbsp	chopped fresh mint	30 mL
2 cups	all-purpose flour	500 mL
2$\frac{1}{2}$ tsp	baking powder	12 mL
$\frac{1}{2}$ tsp	baking soda	2 mL
$\frac{1}{2}$ tsp	salt	2 mL
1	egg	1
$\frac{3}{4}$ cup	plain whole-milk yogurt	175 mL
$\frac{1}{2}$ cup	unsalted butter, melted	125 mL

Also known as sereh, citronelle root and takrai, lemongrass has long, woody stalks and white root ends. It is inedible unless peeled. To do so, cut off about 1 inch (2.5 cm) from the root end and pull back three to four leaf layers until the tender white portion is exposed.

Makes 12 muffins

• 12-cup muffin pan, greased

1. In a small saucepan, combine lemongrass, sugar and lemon juice. Bring to a boil over high heat. Reduce heat to low and simmer, stirring, until sugar is dissolved. Remove syrup from heat and stir in mint. Cover and let stand for 15 minutes. Strain through a fine-mesh sieve, discarding solids. Let syrup cool to room temperature.

2. Preheat oven to 400°F (200°C).

3. In a large bowl, whisk together flour, baking powder, baking soda and salt.

4. In a medium bowl, whisk together $\frac{2}{3}$ cup (150 mL) of the syrup, egg, yogurt and butter until well blended.

5. Add the egg mixture to the flour mixture and stir until just blended.

6. Divide batter equally among prepared muffin cups.

7. Bake for 15 to 20 minutes or until tops are golden and a toothpick inserted in the center comes out clean. Let cool in pan on a wire rack for 3 minutes, then transfer to the rack. Brush warm muffin tops with the remaining syrup. Let cool.

Parsley Lemon Muffins

1 cup	whole milk	250 mL
2 tsp	grated lemon zest	10 mL
2 tbsp	freshly squeezed lemon juice	30 mL
1$\frac{3}{4}$ cups	all-purpose flour	425 mL
$\frac{1}{2}$ cup	freshly grated Parmesan cheese	125 mL
2 tsp	baking powder	10 mL
$\frac{1}{2}$ tsp	baking soda	2 mL
$\frac{1}{4}$ tsp	salt	1 mL
$\frac{1}{8}$ tsp	freshly ground black pepper	0.5 mL
1	egg	1
$\frac{1}{3}$ cup	unsalted butter, melted	75 mL
$\frac{1}{2}$ cup	fresh parsley leaves, chopped	125 mL

One of the things I love about both parsley and lemon is their versatility. Here, they shine in shades of white, green and gold.

Makes 10 muffins

• Preheat oven to 400°F (200°C)
• 12-cup muffin pan, 10 cups greased

1. In a small bowl, whisk together milk, lemon zest and lemon juice. Let stand for 2 minutes.

2. In a large bowl, whisk together flour, cheese, baking powder, baking soda, salt and pepper.

3. Whisk egg and butter into milk mixture until well blended. Stir in parsley.

4. Add the egg mixture to the flour mixture and stir until just blended.

5. Divide batter equally among prepared muffin cups.

6. Bake in preheated oven for 20 to 22 minutes or until tops are golden and a toothpick inserted in the center comes out clean. Let cool in pan on a wire rack for 5 minutes, then transfer to the rack to cool.

Bell Pepper Basil Muffins

6 tbsp	olive oil, divided	90 mL
2	large red bell peppers, chopped	2
1/2 cup	fresh basil leaves, chopped	125 mL
1 1/2 cups	all-purpose flour	375 mL
1/2 cup	yellow cornmeal	125 mL
2 tsp	baking powder	10 mL
1 tsp	salt	5 mL
1/2 tsp	baking soda	2 mL
2 tbsp	granulated sugar	30 mL
2	eggs	2
1 cup	sour cream	250 mL

So often, bell peppers play a supporting role to other ingredients; here, they take center stage and fresh basil becomes the supporting player. The reviews are in: brilliant.

Makes 12 muffins

- 12-cup muffin pan, greased

1. In a large skillet, heat 1 tbsp (15 mL) of the oil over medium-high heat. Sauté red peppers for 4 to 5 minutes or until softened. Remove from heat and stir in basil. Let cool.
2. Preheat oven to 425°F (220°C).
3. In a large bowl, whisk together flour, cornmeal, baking powder, salt and baking soda.
4. In a medium bowl, whisk together sugar, eggs, sour cream and the remaining oil until well blended.
5. Add the egg mixture to the flour mixture and stir until just blended. Gently fold in red pepper mixture.
6. Divide batter equally among prepared muffin cups.
7. Bake for 14 to18 minutes or until a toothpick inserted in the center comes out clean. Let cool in pan on a wire rack for 3 minutes, then transfer to the rack to cool.

Brie, Papaya and Scallion Muffins

1 2/3 cups	all-purpose flour	400 mL
1/3 cup	yellow cornmeal	75 mL
2 tsp	baking powder	10 mL
1 tsp	salt	5 mL
1/2 tsp	baking soda	2 mL
1/2 tsp	chipotle chile powder	2 mL
2 tbsp	granulated sugar	30 mL
2	eggs	2
1 cup	buttermilk	250 mL
1/3 cup	unsalted butter, melted	75 mL
1/3 cup	finely chopped green onions (scallions)	75 mL
1/4 cup	fresh cilantro leaves, chopped	60 mL
1 cup	diced papaya	250 mL
4 oz	Brie cheese, diced	125 g

Fresh papaya has an unmatched intensity of flavor. I love it here in combination with the mellow creaminess of Brie and the fresh bite of green onions (aka scallions) from the farmers' market.

Makes 12 muffins

- Preheat oven to 425°F (220°C)
- 12-cup muffin pan, greased

1. In a large bowl, whisk together flour, cornmeal, baking powder, salt, baking soda and chipotle powder.
2. In a medium bowl, whisk together sugar, eggs, buttermilk and butter until well blended. Stir in green onions and cilantro.
3. Add the egg mixture to the flour mixture and stir until just blended. Gently fold in papaya and cheese.
4. Divide batter equally among prepared muffin cups.
5. Bake in preheated oven for 14 to 18 minutes or until a toothpick inserted in the center comes out clean. Let cool in pan on a wire rack for 3 minutes, then transfer to the rack to cool.

Fresh Corn and Thyme Muffins

8	slices bacon, coarsely chopped	8
1/3 cup	unsalted butter	75 mL
1/3 cup	finely chopped onion	75 mL
2 cups	all-purpose flour	500 mL
1 1/4 tsp	baking soda	6 mL
1/4 tsp	salt	1 mL
1/4 tsp	freshly ground black pepper	1 mL
1 tbsp	granulated sugar	15 mL
1	egg	1
1 1/4 cups	buttermilk	300 mL
1 1/2 cups	fresh corn kernels	375 mL
1 tbsp	minced fresh thyme	15 mL

When you've had your fill of fresh corn on the cob, shuck the rest and cut off the kernels for these excellent muffins. Serve them warm, with a pat of fresh butter, at your next barbecue. And who could say no to a leftover muffin, toasted and topped with mild, creamy goat cheese?

Makes 12 muffins

- 12-cup muffin pan, greased

1. In a large skillet, cook bacon over medium-high heat, stirring, for 5 minutes or until crisp and golden brown. Using a slotted spoon, transfer to a plate lined with paper towels to drain.
2. Add butter to bacon fat in skillet and melt over medium heat. Add onion and sauté for 4 to 5 minutes or until softened. Remove from heat and return bacon to pan. Let cool.
3. Preheat oven to 400°F (200°C).
4. In a large bowl, whisk together flour, baking soda, salt and pepper.
5. In a medium bowl, whisk together sugar and egg until well blended. Whisk in buttermilk until blended. Stir in bacon mixture, corn and thyme.
6. Add the egg mixture to the flour mixture and stir until just blended.
7. Divide batter equally among prepared muffin cups.
8. Bake for 19 to 22 minutes or until tops are golden and a toothpick inserted in the center comes out clean. Let cool in pan on a wire rack for 3 minutes, then transfer to the rack. Serve warm or let cool.

Wild Mushroom Muffins

1 tbsp	olive oil	15 mL
8 oz	wild or exotic mushrooms, trimmed and coarsely chopped	250 g
	Salt and freshly ground black pepper	
1 tbsp	chopped fresh thyme	15 mL
2 cups	all-purpose flour	500 mL
2 tsp	baking powder	10 mL
1/2 tsp	baking soda	2 mL
1/2 tsp	salt	2 mL
2	eggs	2
1 cup	buttermilk	250 mL
1/2 cup	unsalted butter, melted	125 mL

Wild mushrooms have a rich earthiness that is best accentuated in straightforward preparations, such as these mouthwatering muffins.

Makes 12 muffins

- 12-cup muffin pan, lined with paper liners

1. In a large nonstick skillet, heat oil over medium heat. Sauté mushrooms until tender and liquid has evaporated. Season to taste with salt and pepper. Remove from heat, stir in thyme and let cool.
2. Preheat oven to 375°F (190°C).
3. In a large bowl, whisk together flour, baking powder, baking soda and salt.
4. In a medium bowl, whisk together eggs, buttermilk and butter until well blended.
5. Add the egg mixture to the flour mixture and stir until just blended. Gently fold in mushroom mixture.
6. Divide batter equally among prepared muffin cups.
7. Bake for 20 to 25 minutes or until a toothpick inserted in the center comes out clean. Let cool in pan on a wire rack for 5 minutes, then transfer to the rack to cool.

Vidalia Onion Muffins

1 cup	all-purpose flour	250 mL
1 cup	quick-cooking rolled oats	250 mL
1½ tsp	baking powder	7 mL
½ tsp	salt	2 mL
¼ cup	granulated sugar	60 mL
1	egg	1
¾ cup	milk	175 mL
⅓ cup	unsalted butter, melted	75 mL
2 tsp	chopped fresh rosemary	10 mL
⅔ cup	chopped Vidalia onion	150 mL
½ cup	freshly grated Parmesan cheese	125 mL
½ cup	chopped pecans, toasted	125 mL

The Vidalia onion — the official vegetable of Georgia since 1990 — is renowned for its sweet, mild flavor. Although other sweet onions would make a fine substitute, the Vidalia's signature sweetness is particularly gorgeous with the saltiness of Parmesan cheese and the toasted nuttiness of pecans in these muffins. Serve with a salad and you've got a perfect summertime supper.

Tip

Look for Georgia-grown Vidalias at farmers' markets around the Southeast, from early spring through the summer.

Makes 12 muffins

- Preheat oven to 400°F (200°C)
- 12-cup muffin pan, greased

1. In a large bowl, whisk together flour, oats, baking powder and salt.
2. In a medium bowl, whisk together sugar, egg, milk, butter and rosemary until well blended. Stir in onion, cheese and pecans.
3. Add the egg mixture to the flour mixture and stir until just blended.
4. Divide batter equally among prepared muffin cups.
5. Bake in preheated oven for 16 to 20 minutes or until tops are golden and a toothpick inserted in the center comes out clean. Let cool in pan on a wire rack for 5 minutes, then transfer to the rack to cool.

Kale and Toasted Walnut Muffins

1 cup	whole wheat flour	250 mL
1 cup	all-purpose flour	250 mL
1 tbsp	baking powder	15 mL
1 tsp	salt	5 mL
1/4 tsp	baking soda	1 mL
1	egg	1
1 cup	milk	250 mL
1/4 cup	olive oil	60 mL
2 tbsp	liquid honey	30 mL
2/3 cup	chopped drained cooked kale	150 mL
2/3 cup	chopped walnuts, toasted	150 mL
1/2 cup	freshly grated Parmesan cheese	125 mL

Makes 12 muffins

- Preheat oven to 375°F (190°C)
- 12-cup muffin pan, greased

1. In a large bowl, whisk together whole wheat flour, all-purpose flour, baking powder, salt and baking soda.

2. In a medium bowl, whisk together egg, milk, oil and honey until well blended. Stir in kale, walnuts and cheese.

3. Add the milk mixture to the flour mixture and stir until just blended.

4. Divide batter equally among prepared muffin cups.

5. Bake in preheated oven for 21 to 26 minutes or until tops are golden and a toothpick inserted in the center comes out clean. Let cool in pan on a wire rack for 3 minutes, then transfer to the rack to cool.

When my husband and I were in graduate school, Saturday morning trips to the farmers' market in Bloomington, Indiana, were a regular feature of our weekends. During the early-summer months, though, he would argue that it wasn't worth the trip when kale and turnips were the predominant offerings. His perspective was somewhat skewed — he overlooked the honey and flowers — but there really was a plethora of kale and turnips. Somewhere along the way, I developed these muffins to use up some of the kale bounty. The cooked kale is fantastic with the nutty whole wheat batter and toasted walnuts.

Tip

About 3 cups (750 mL) packed kale leaves produce 2/3 cup (150 mL) chopped drained cooked kale. I just chop it and sauté it in a little olive oil until it's completely wilted.

Zucchini Cornbread Muffins

1 1/4 cups	yellow cornmeal	300 mL
1 1/4 cups	all-purpose flour	300 mL
2 1/2 tsp	baking powder	12 mL
1 tsp	salt	5 mL
1 tsp	ground cumin	5 mL
1/2 tsp	baking soda	2 mL
1/8 tsp	cayenne pepper	1 mL
3 tbsp	granulated sugar	45 mL
2	eggs	2
1/4 cup	vegetable oil	60 mL
1 1/2 cups	buttermilk	375 mL
1 cup	shredded zucchini	250 mL
1/4 cup	freshly grated Parmesan cheese	60 mL

A generous helping of fresh zucchini gives cornbread muffins seasonal flair.

Makes 12 muffins

- Preheat oven to 400°F (200°C)
- 12-cup muffin pan, greased

1. In a large bowl, whisk together cornmeal, flour, baking powder, salt, cumin, baking soda and cayenne.
2. In a medium bowl, whisk together sugar, eggs and oil until well blended. Whisk in buttermilk until blended. Stir in zucchini.
3. Add the egg mixture to the flour mixture and stir until just blended.
4. Divide batter equally among prepared muffin cups. Sprinkle with cheese.
5. Bake in preheated oven for 23 to 26 minutes or until tops are golden and a toothpick inserted in the center comes out clean. Let cool in pan on a wire rack for 3 minutes, then transfer to the rack to cool. Serve warm or let cool.

Summer Squash Muffins with Parsley and Hazelnuts

2 1/2 cups	all-purpose flour	625 mL
2 tsp	baking powder	10 mL
1 1/4 tsp	salt	6 mL
1 tsp	baking soda	5 mL
1/2 tsp	freshly ground black pepper	2 mL
1 tbsp	granulated sugar	15 mL
2	eggs	2
1/2 cup	buttermilk	125 mL
1/4 cup	olive oil	60 mL
2 cups	coarsely shredded yellow summer squash or zucchini or a mixture	500 mL
1/4 cup	fresh parsley leaves, chopped	60 mL
2 tsp	finely grated lemon zest	10 mL
2/3 cup	chopped hazelnuts, toasted	150 mL

Packed with summertime squash and parsley, these muffins evoke the season.

Makes 18 muffins

- Preheat oven to 400°F (200°C)
- Two 12-cup muffin pans, 18 cups greased

1. In a large bowl, whisk together flour, baking powder, salt, baking soda and pepper.
2. In a medium bowl, whisk together sugar, eggs, buttermilk and oil until well blended. Stir in squash, parsley and lemon zest.
3. Add the egg mixture to the flour mixture and stir until just blended. Gently fold in hazelnuts.
4. Divide batter equally among prepared muffin cups.
5. Bake in preheated oven for 18 to 22 minutes or until tops are golden and a toothpick inserted in the center comes out clean. Let cool in pans on a wire rack for 5 minutes, then transfer to the rack to cool.

Fresh Broccoli Parmesan Muffins

1 cup	finely chopped broccoli	250 mL
1¾ cups	all-purpose flour	425 mL
1 cup	quick-cooking rolled oats	250 mL
2 tsp	baking powder	10 mL
½ tsp	salt	2 mL
1 tbsp	granulated sugar	15 mL
2	eggs	2
¾ cup	milk	175 mL
⅓ cup	olive oil	75 mL
2 tsp	Dijon mustard	10 mL
½ cup	chopped green onions (scallions)	125 mL
1 cup	coarsely grated Parmesan cheese, divided	250 mL

While developing these muffins, I had the kind of trouble all recipe developers wish for: it was impossible to mess up. We usually have an assortment of cheeses in our cheese drawer, so I tried sharp Cheddar, Swiss, Gruyère, blue cheese, goat cheese, even manchego. Regardless of which I chose, the resulting muffins tasted great. So use what's on hand — you cannot go wrong.

Makes 12 muffins

- 12-cup muffin pan, lined with paper liners

1. In a small microwave-safe bowl, combine broccoli and 1 tbsp (15 mL) water. Microwave on High for 2 minutes. Drain and refrigerate until cooled to room temperature.
2. Preheat oven to 400°F (200°C).
3. In a large bowl, whisk together flour, oats, baking powder and salt.
4. In a medium bowl, whisk together sugar, eggs, milk, oil and mustard until well blended. Stir in broccoli, green onions and ½ cup (125 mL) of the cheese.
5. Add the egg mixture to the flour mixture and stir until just blended.
6. Divide batter equally among prepared muffin cups. Sprinkle with the remaining cheese.
7. Bake for 18 to 22 minutes or until a toothpick inserted in the center comes out clean. Let cool in pan on a wire rack for 5 minutes, then transfer to the rack. Serve warm or let cool.

Green Onion Goat Cheese Muffins

1½ cups	all-purpose flour	375 mL
1 tbsp	baking powder	15 mL
½ tsp	salt	2 mL
2 tsp	granulated sugar	10 mL
1	egg	1
1 cup	milk	250 mL
⅓ cup	unsalted butter, melted	75 mL
1 cup	chopped green onions (scallions)	250 mL
4 oz	mild creamy goat cheese, crumbled	125 g

These muffins are a pretty and scrumptious way to showcase locally made goat cheese and farm-fresh green onions.

Makes 12 muffins

- Preheat oven to 400°F (200°C)
- 12-cup muffin pan, lined with paper liners

1. In a large bowl, whisk together flour, baking powder and salt.
2. In a medium bowl, whisk together sugar, egg, milk and butter until well blended. Stir in green onions.
3. Add the egg mixture to the flour mixture and stir until just combined.
4. Divide half the batter equally among prepared muffin cups. Sprinkle evenly with cheese. Top with the remaining batter.
5. Bake in preheated oven for 18 to 22 minutes or until tops are golden and a toothpick inserted in the center comes out clean. Let cool in pan on a wire rack for 5 minutes, then transfer to the rack to cool.

Fresh Corn Jalapeño Muffins

½ cup	vegetable oil, divided	125 mL
1⅓ cups	fresh corn kernels	325 mL
2	small jalapeños, seeded and finely chopped	2
1 cup	yellow cornmeal	250 mL
1 cup	all-purpose flour	250 mL
1 tbsp	baking powder	15 mL
¾ tsp	salt	3 mL
3 tbsp	granulated sugar	45 mL
1	egg	1
1 cup	buttermilk	250 mL

Corn may grow on tall stalks and jalapeños on petite plants, but they taste like they were destined to be together.

Tip

About 2 large cobs of corn yield the 1⅓ cups (325 mL) kernels needed for this recipe.

Makes 12 muffins

- 12-cup muffin pan, greased

1. In a medium skillet, heat 1 tbsp (15 mL) of the oil over medium-high heat. Sauté corn and jalapeños for 2 to 3 minutes or until tender-crisp. Remove from heat and let cool.
2. Preheat oven to 375°F (190°C).
3. In a large bowl, whisk together cornmeal, flour, baking powder and salt.
4. In a medium bowl, whisk together sugar, egg, buttermilk and the remaining oil until well blended.
5. Add the egg mixture to the flour mixture and stir until just blended. Gently fold in corn mixture.
6. Divide batter equally among prepared muffin cups.
7. Bake for 16 to 19 minutes or until tops are golden and a toothpick inserted in the center comes out clean. Let cool in pan on a wire rack for 5 minutes, then transfer to the rack to cool.

Leek and Gorgonzola Muffins

4 tbsp	olive oil, divided	60 mL
2	medium-large leeks (white and light green parts only), split lengthwise, sliced crosswise	2
2 cups	all-purpose flour	500 mL
1 tbsp	baking powder	15 mL
1 tsp	dried tarragon	5 mL
½ tsp	salt	2 mL
1 tbsp	granulated sugar	15 mL
2	eggs	2
1 cup	milk	250 mL
4 oz	Gorgonzola cheese, crumbled	125 g

These tender muffins feature creamy Gorgonzola and the sweet succulence of leeks.

Tip

After cutting leeks lengthwise, be sure to rinse them well under running water and rub out any sand and grit before slicing.

Makes 12 muffins

- Preheat oven to 400°F (200°C)
- 12-cup muffin pan, lined with paper liners

1. In a large nonstick skillet, heat 1 tbsp (15 mL) of the oil over medium heat. Sauté leeks for 7 to 10 minutes or until softened. Remove from heat and let cool.
2. In a large bowl, whisk together flour, baking powder, tarragon and salt.
3. In a medium bowl, whisk together sugar, eggs, milk and the remaining oil until well blended.
4. Add the egg mixture to the flour mixture and stir until just blended. Gently fold in leeks and cheese.
5. Divide batter equally among prepared muffin cups.
6. Bake in preheated oven for 21 to 25 minutes or until tops are golden and a toothpick inserted in the center comes out clean. Let cool in pan on a wire rack for 5 minutes, then transfer to the rack to cool.

Cheese and Chard Muffins

6 tbsp	olive oil, divided	90 mL
1	bunch red Swiss chard, thick stems and middle vein removed	1
1¼ cups	all-purpose flour	300 mL
¾ cup	whole wheat flour	175 mL
2 tsp	baking powder	10 mL
¾ tsp	salt	3 mL
½ tsp	freshly ground black pepper	2 mL
2 tbsp	granulated sugar	30 mL
1	egg	1
1 cup	buttermilk	250 mL
1½ cups	shredded white Cheddar cheese	375 mL

The pile of raw chard may look daunting, but don't worry: one bunch cooks down to about 1 cup (250 mL).

Tip

Be sure to wash chard leaves under running water to remove any sand and grit, and drain well before using.

Makes 12 muffins

- 12-cup muffin pan, greased

1. In a large skillet, heat 1 tbsp (15 mL) of the oil over medium-high heat. Sauté chard for 3 to 5 minutes or until wilted and softened. Transfer to a plate lined with paper towels, blot and let drain and cool. Chop and set aside.
2. Preheat oven to 375°F (190°C).
3. In a large bowl, whisk together all-purpose flour, whole wheat flour, baking powder, salt and pepper.
4. In a medium bowl, whisk together sugar, egg, buttermilk and the remaining oil until well blended.
5. Add the egg mixture to the flour mixture and stir until just blended. Gently fold in chard and cheese.
6. Divide batter equally among prepared muffin cups.
7. Bake for 22 to 25 minutes or until tops are golden and a toothpick inserted in the center comes out clean. Let cool in pan on a wire rack for 5 minutes, then transfer to the rack to cool.

Eggplant Feta Muffins

2 cups	all-purpose flour	500 mL
1 tbsp	baking powder	15 mL
1½ tsp	baking soda	7 mL
½ tsp	salt	2 mL
⅛ tsp	freshly ground black pepper	0.5 mL
1 tbsp	granulated sugar	15 mL
2	eggs	2
¾ cup	buttermilk	175 mL
⅓ cup	olive oil	75 mL
2 tsp	minced fresh marjoram	10 mL
2 cups	coarsely shredded peeled eggplant	500 mL
¼ cup	chopped green onions (scallions)	60 mL
1 cup	crumbled feta cheese	250 mL

Makes 12 muffins

- Preheat oven to 400°F (200°C)
- 12-cup muffin pan, greased

1. In a medium bowl, whisk together flour, baking powder, baking soda, salt and pepper.
2. In a large bowl, whisk together sugar, eggs, buttermilk, oil and marjoram until well blended. Stir in eggplant and green onions.
3. Add the egg mixture to the flour mixture and stir until just blended. Gently fold in cheese.
4. Divide batter equally among prepared muffin cups.
5. Bake in preheated oven for 22 to 25 minutes or until tops are golden and a toothpick inserted in the center comes out clean. Let cool in pan on a wire rack for 5 minutes, then transfer to the rack to cool.

Rhubarb, Blue Cheese, and Walnut Muffins

2¹/₂ cups	all-purpose flour	625 mL
1 tsp	baking soda	5 mL
1 tsp	baking powder	5 mL
¹/₂ tsp	salt	2 mL
¹/₄ tsp	freshly ground black pepper	1 mL
³/₄ cup	packed light brown sugar	175 mL
1	egg	1
1 cup	buttermilk	250 mL
¹/₂ cup	vegetable oil	125 mL
1 tsp	vanilla extract	5 mL
3 oz	blue cheese, crumbled	90 g
1¹/₂ cups	chopped rhubarb	375 mL
²/₃ cup	chopped walnuts	150 mL

Rich blue cheese pairs with the sweet, toasty flavor of walnuts to create a tangy environment for showcasing the tangy freshness of summer rhubarb.

Makes 12 muffins

- Preheat oven to 375°F (190°C)
- 12-cup muffin pan, greased

1. In a large bowl, whisk together flour, baking soda, baking powder, salt and pepper.
2. In a medium bowl, whisk together brown sugar, egg, buttermilk, oil and vanilla until well blended.
3. Add the egg mixture to the flour mixture and stir until just blended. Gently fold in cheese and rhubarb.
4. Divide batter equally among prepared muffin cups. Sprinkle with walnuts.
5. Bake in preheated oven for 20 to 25 minutes or until a toothpick inserted in the center comes out clean. Let cool in pan on a wire rack for 5 minutes, then transfer to the rack to cool.

Fresh Fennel Parmesan Muffins

¹/₂ cup	unsalted butter	125 mL
1¹/₂ cups	chopped fennel bulb	375 mL
2 tbsp	chopped fennel fronds	30 mL
2 tsp	finely grated lemon zest	10 mL
2 cups	all-purpose flour	500 mL
1 cup	freshly grated Parmesan cheese	250 mL
2 tsp	baking powder	10 mL
³/₄ tsp	salt	3 mL
¹/₂ tsp	baking soda	2 mL
¹/₄ tsp	freshly ground black pepper	1 mL
2	eggs, beaten	2
1 cup	buttermilk	250 mL
2 tbsp	liquid honey	30 mL

Fresh fennel and Parmesan cheese make one of the most delectable combinations of food around. Need proof? Make these muffins, pronto.

Makes 12 muffins

- 12-cup muffin pan, greased

1. In a large nonstick skillet, melt butter over medium heat. Sauté fennel bulb for 5 minutes or until softened. Scrape into a medium bowl and stir in fennel fronds and lemon zest. Let cool.
2. Preheat oven to 375°F (190°C).
3. In a large bowl, whisk together flour, cheese, baking powder, salt, baking soda and pepper.
4. Stir eggs, buttermilk and honey into fennel mixture until well blended.
5. Add the egg mixture to the flour mixture and stir until just blended.
6. Divide batter equally among prepared muffin cups.
7. Bake for 20 to 25 minutes or until a toothpick inserted in the center comes out clean. Let cool in pan on a wire rack for 5 minutes, then transfer to the rack to cool.

Arugula Muffins with Bacon

6	slices bacon, chopped	6
1	large shallot, finely chopped	1
3	cloves garlic, chopped	3
4 cups	baby arugula, coarsely chopped	1 L
2 cups	all-purpose flour	500 mL
2 tsp	baking powder	10 mL
1/2 tsp	baking soda	2 mL
1/2 tsp	salt	2 mL
1/4 tsp	freshly ground black pepper	1 mL
2	eggs	2
1 cup	buttermilk	250 mL
3 tbsp	olive oil	45 mL

Also called rocket, roquette, rugula and rucola, arugula is a peppery, aromatic salad green with a distinctive mustard flavor. Here, it finds new life with a light buttermilk batter and a smoky pairing of bacon.

Tip

Arugula is very perishable and should be tightly wrapped in a plastic bag and refrigerated for no more than 2 days.

Makes 12 muffins

• 12-cup muffin pan, greased

1. In a large skillet, cook bacon over medium-high heat, stirring, for 5 minutes or until crisp and golden brown. Using a slotted spoon, transfer to a plate lined with paper towels to drain.

2. Add shallot to bacon fat in skillet and sauté over medium heat for 2 minutes. Add garlic and arugula; sauté until arugula is wilted. Remove from heat and let cool.

3. Preheat oven to 400°F (200°C).

4. In a large bowl, whisk together flour, baking powder, baking soda, salt and pepper.

5. In a medium bowl, whisk together eggs, buttermilk and oil until well blended.

6. Add the egg mixture to the flour mixture and stir until just blended. Gently fold in bacon and arugula mixture.

7. Divide batter equally among prepared muffin cups.

8. Bake for 18 to 23 minutes or until a toothpick inserted in the center comes out clean. Let cool in pan on a wire rack for 5 minutes, then transfer to the rack to cool.

Peach, Basil and Prosciutto Muffins

²⁄₃ cup	coarsely grated Parmesan cheese	150 mL
3 cups	all-purpose flour	750 mL
1 tbsp	baking powder	15 mL
1 tsp	salt	5 mL
¼ tsp	freshly ground black pepper	1 mL
1	egg	1
¾ cup	sour cream	175 mL
3 tbsp	olive oil	45 mL
1¼ cups	milk	300 mL
1½ cups	diced peeled peaches	375 mL
¼ cup	packed fresh basil leaves, chopped	60 mL
3 oz	sliced prosciutto, chopped	90 g

These sophisticated muffins make the most of contrasting flavors and textures. The prosciutto becomes crispy as the muffins bake, and the subtle flavor of fresh basil connects all of the components.

Makes 16 muffins

- Preheat oven to 375°F (190°C)
- Two 12-cup muffin pans, 16 cups greased

1. Divide cheese equally among prepared muffin cups, tapping and shaking pans to evenly coat bottom and sides of each cup with cheese.

2. In a large bowl, whisk together flour, baking powder, salt and pepper.

3. In a medium bowl, whisk together egg, sour cream and oil until well blended. Whisk in milk until blended.

4. Add the egg mixture to the flour mixture and stir until just blended. Gently fold in peaches and basil.

5. Divide batter equally among prepared muffin cups. Sprinkle with prosciutto.

6. Bake in preheated oven for 20 to 25 minutes or until a toothpick inserted in the center comes out clean and prosciutto is crisp. Let cool in pans on a wire rack for 5 minutes, then transfer to the rack to cool.

Cherry Tomato and Goat Cheese Muffins

2½ cups	all-purpose flour	625 mL
3½ tsp	baking powder	17 mL
½ tsp	salt	2 mL
2	eggs	2
⅓ cup	unsalted butter, melted	75 mL
1¼ cups	milk	300 mL
½ cup	minced green onions (scallions)	125 mL
¼ cup	packed fresh basil leaves, chopped	60 mL
4 oz	mild creamy goat cheese, crumbled	125 g
1½ cups	cherry tomatoes, quartered	375 mL

Nothing can beat the tiny cherry tomatoes from the farmers' market — they're so beautiful, delicate and fresh, you can't help buying some. Together with goat cheese and fresh basil, one of these muffins is summer in your hand.

Makes 12 muffins

- Preheat oven to 400°F (200°C)
- 12-cup muffin pan, greased

1. In a large bowl, whisk together flour, baking powder and salt.

2. In a medium bowl, whisk together eggs and butter until well blended. Whisk in milk until blended. Stir in green onions and basil.

3. Add the egg mixture to the flour mixture and stir until just blended. Gently fold in cheese.

4. Divide batter equally among prepared muffin cups. Divide tomatoes equally among cups and press lightly into batter.

5. Bake in preheated oven for 18 to 22 minutes or until tops are light golden brown and a toothpick inserted in the center comes out clean. Let cool in pan on a wire rack for 5 minutes, then transfer to the rack to cool.

Tarragon, Tomato and Bacon Muffins

6	slices bacon, chopped	6
1/2 cup	minced onion	125 mL
2 cups	all-purpose flour	500 mL
2 1/2 tsp	baking powder	12 mL
1/2 tsp	baking soda	2 mL
1/2 tsp	salt	2 mL
2 tbsp	granulated sugar	30 mL
2	eggs	2
1 cup	buttermilk	250 mL
2 tbsp	chopped fresh tarragon	30 mL
1 cup	seeded chopped tomatoes	250 mL

If there is anything better than summer tomatoes, I don't know about it — especially when they're cast with tarragon and bacon in a command performance of seasonal flavor.

Makes 12 muffins

- 12-cup muffin pan, greased

1. In a large skillet, cook bacon over medium-high heat, stirring, for 5 minutes or until crisp and golden brown. Using a slotted spoon, transfer to a plate lined with paper towels to drain.

2. Pour off all but 1/4 cup (60 mL) of the bacon fat from skillet. Add onion and sauté for 3 to 4 minutes or until softened. Remove from heat and let cool (do not drain).

3. Preheat oven to 375°F (190°C).

4. In a large bowl, whisk together flour, baking powder, baking soda and salt.

5. In a medium bowl, whisk together sugar, eggs, buttermilk and tarragon until well blended. Stir in onion mixture and bacon.

6. Add the egg mixture to the flour mixture and stir until just blended. Gently fold in tomatoes.

7. Divide batter equally among prepared muffin cups.

8. Bake for 20 to 25 minutes or until tops are deep golden brown and a toothpick inserted in the center comes out clean. Let cool in pan on a wire rack for 5 minutes, then transfer to the rack to cool.

Global Muffins

This chapter boasts a tempting collection of muffins from around the world. Recasting international dishes and ingredients into familiar muffin form is the perfect way to try and savor new tastes. With once-exotic ingredients now readily available, eating your way around the globe has never been so quick and easy. Dried Papaya Muffins with Cashew Crumble (Costa Rica), Couscous Date Muffins (Morocco) and Star Anise Pineapple Muffins (Malaysia) are at the top of my list of favorites, but all of the muffins in this chapter are easily prepared, delicious and fun to eat. So whether you want to recreate a culinary experience from your travels or simply be inspired by something new, this collection of global recipes has you covered.

continued...

Butter Tart Muffins (Canada)

Topping

1¼ cups	cake flour	300 mL
⅔ cup	packed dark brown sugar	150 mL
½ cup	chopped walnuts	125 mL
⅛ tsp	salt	0.5 mL
½ cup	unsalted butter, melted	125 mL

Muffins

1½ cups	cake flour	375 mL
¼ tsp	baking soda	1 mL
¼ tsp	salt	1 mL
½ cup	granulated sugar	125 mL
⅓ cup	unsalted butter, softened	75 mL
2	eggs	2
¼ cup	buttermilk	60 mL
1 tsp	vanilla extract	5 mL
½ cup	dried currants	125 mL

Though my mother moved to Southern California in her teens, she never forgot her Manitoba roots. She remains nostalgic over the butter tarts she would have on special shopping trips to downtown Winnipeg, and with good reason — they are a brown sugar lover's dream come true. It was a labor of love recreating the tarts in muffin form; I think both you and Mom will be pleased.

Tip

This may seem like a lot of topping for a muffin. It is, but it is by design, to capture the butterscotch flavor of butter tarts.

Makes 12 muffins

- Preheat oven to 350°F (180°C)
- 12-cup muffin pan, lined with paper liners

1. *Topping:* In a medium bowl, combine flour, brown sugar, walnuts and salt. Mix in butter until combined and crumbly. Refrigerate until ready to use.

2. *Muffins:* In another medium bowl, whisk together flour, baking soda and salt.

3. In a large bowl, using an electric mixer on medium-high speed, beat sugar and butter until light and fluffy. Beat in eggs, one at a time, until well blended. Beat in buttermilk and vanilla until blended.

4. Add the flour mixture to the egg mixture and, using a wooden spoon, stir until just blended. Gently fold in currants.

5. Divide batter equally among prepared muffin cups. Crumble topping into pea-size pieces and sprinkle over batter in cups.

6. Bake in preheated oven for 21 to 24 minutes or until tops are golden and a toothpick inserted in the center comes out clean. Let cool in pan on a wire rack for 5 minutes, then transfer to the rack to cool.

Maple Sugar Muffins (Canada)

1¾ cups	all-purpose flour	425 mL
2 tsp	baking powder	10 mL
1 tsp	baking soda	5 mL
½ tsp	salt	2 mL
1	egg	1
1 cup	pure maple syrup, divided	250 mL
1 cup	sour cream	250 mL
½ cup	unsalted butter, melted	125 mL
¾ cup	chopped walnuts, toasted	175 mL
¼ cup	confectioners' (icing) sugar	60 mL

For a gentle boost of sweetness, these buttery muffins feature maple in both the batter and the topping.

Makes 12 muffins

- Preheat oven to 400°F (200°C)
- 12-cup muffin pan, greased

1. In a medium bowl, whisk together flour, baking powder, baking soda and salt.
2. In a large bowl, whisk together egg, ¾ cup (175 mL) of the maple syrup, sour cream and butter until well blended.
3. Add the egg mixture to the flour mixture and stir until just blended. Gently fold in walnuts.
4. Divide batter equally among prepared muffin cups.
5. Bake in preheated oven for 14 to 18 minutes or until tops are golden and a toothpick inserted in the center comes out clean. Let cool in pan on a wire rack for 3 minutes, then transfer to the rack.
6. In a shallow microwave-safe dish, microwave the remaining maple syrup on High for 15 seconds or until heated. Dip warm muffin tops in warm syrup, then dust with confectioners' sugar. Return to rack and let cool.

Rum and Coconut Muffins (Jamaica)

2 cups	all-purpose flour	500 mL
2 tsp	baking powder	10 mL
½ tsp	salt	2 mL
½ cup	packed dark brown sugar	125 mL
¼ cup	unsalted butter, softened	60 mL
2	eggs	2
1 cup	coconut milk, well-stirred	250 mL
2 tbsp	dark rum	30 mL
1 tsp	coconut flavoring	5 mL
1½ cups	sweetened flaked or shredded coconut, divided	375 mL

You could buy a ticket to the tropics — or you could simply make these muffins. Heady with rum and sweet flaked coconut, these incredibly easy, super-delicious muffins will transport you straight to a table in the sand, under the swaying palms. If only every recipe could be this straightforward and rewarding.

Makes 12 muffins

- Preheat oven to 350°F (180°C)
- 12-cup muffin pan, greased

1. In a medium bowl, whisk together flour, baking powder and salt.
2. In a large bowl, using an electric mixer on medium-high speed, beat brown sugar and butter until blended. Beat in eggs, one at a time, until well blended. Beat in coconut milk, rum and coconut flavoring until blended.
3. Add the flour mixture to the egg mixture and, using a wooden spoon, stir until just blended. Gently fold in 1 cup (250 mL) of the coconut.
4. Divide batter equally among prepared muffin cups. Sprinkle with the remaining coconut.
5. Bake in preheated oven for 23 to 27 minutes or until tops are golden and a toothpick inserted in the center comes out clean. Let cool in pan on a wire rack for 5 minutes, then transfer to the rack to cool.

Mayan Chocolate Muffins (Mexico)

1/3 cup	unsalted butter	75 mL
4 oz	bittersweet chocolate, chopped, divided	125 g
2 cups	all-purpose flour	500 mL
1/3 cup	unsweetened cocoa powder (not Dutch process)	75 mL
1 tbsp	baking powder	15 mL
1 tsp	ground cinnamon	5 mL
1/2 tsp	baking soda	2 mL
1/2 tsp	salt	2 mL
1/4 tsp	cayenne pepper	1 mL
2/3 cup	granulated sugar	150 mL
1	egg	1
1 tsp	vanilla extract	5 mL
1/2 tsp	almond extract	2 mL
1 1/4 cups	buttermilk	300 mL

Looking for a showstopper muffin? Look no further. Chocolate and spice may be a fashionable combination, but it is a trend backed up with centuries of history and appeal. Don't chop the chocolate too fine; you want big, melty chunks when you bite into the muffins.

Makes 12 muffins

- 12-cup muffin pan, lined with paper liners

1. In a heatproof bowl set over a saucepan of simmering water, melt butter and half the chocolate, stirring until smooth. Remove from heat and let cool.
2. Preheat oven to 375°F (190°C).
3. In a large bowl, whisk together flour, cocoa powder, baking powder, cinnamon, baking soda, salt and cayenne.
4. In a small bowl, whisk together chocolate mixture, sugar, egg, vanilla and almond extract until well blended. Whisk in buttermilk until blended.
5. Add the egg mixture to the flour mixture and stir until just blended. Gently fold in the remaining chocolate.
6. Divide batter equally among prepared muffin cups.
7. Bake for 19 to 22 minutes or until a toothpick inserted in the center comes out clean. Let cool in pan on a wire rack for 5 minutes, then transfer to the rack to cool.

Roast Banana Coconut Muffins (Honduras)

2	large ripe bananas (unpeeled)	2
2 cups	all-purpose flour	500 mL
2 tsp	baking powder	10 mL
³/₄ tsp	salt	3 mL
¹/₂ tsp	baking soda	2 mL
²/₃ cup	packed light brown sugar	150 mL
2	eggs	2
¹/₂ cup	coconut milk, well-stirred	125 mL
¹/₃ cup	unsalted butter, melted	75 mL
1 tsp	vanilla extract	5 mL
1 cup	sweetened flaked or shredded coconut	250 mL

Bananas and coconut are ubiquitous ingredients in Honduras, and these easy muffins showcase the two in a delicious new way. Roasting bananas in the peel is one of my favorite techniques for deepening their flavor and imparting notes of caramel to whatever I am using them in.

Makes 12 muffins

- Preheat oven to 350°F (180°C)
- Rimmed baking sheet
- 12-cup muffin pan, greased

1. Place bananas on baking sheet. Bake in preheated oven for 10 to 14 minutes or until skins are black and starting to seep. Remove from oven, leaving oven on, and let cool.

2. In a large bowl, whisk together flour, baking powder, salt and baking soda.

3. In a medium bowl, whisk together brown sugar, eggs, coconut milk, butter and vanilla until well blended. Squeeze banana flesh out of skins and into bowl and whisk until blended.

4. Add the egg mixture to the flour mixture and stir until just blended.

5. Divide batter equally among prepared muffin cups. Sprinkle with coconut and gently press into batter.

6. Bake for 22 to 27 minutes or until tops are golden brown and a toothpick inserted in the center comes out clean. Let cool in pan on a wire rack for 3 minutes, then transfer to the rack to cool.

Sweetened Condensed Milk Muffins (Brazil)

²/₃ cup	all-purpose flour	150 mL
1¹/₂ tsp	baking powder	7 mL
¹/₄ tsp	salt	1 mL
4	eggs	4
1	can (12 oz or 300 mL) sweetened condensed milk	1
¹/₄ cup	unsalted butter, melted	60 mL

Sweetened condensed milk is a key component of countless Brazilian desserts. Here, it stars in a streamlined muffin recipe.

Tip

Run a butter knife around the edge of these muffins before removing them from the pan. It will seem as if they are sticking at first, but they will quickly and easily come free with a bit of gentle nudging with the knife.

Makes 9 muffins

- Preheat oven to 350°F (180°C)
- 12-cup muffin pan, 9 cups greased

1. In a large bowl, whisk together flour, baking powder and salt.

2. In a medium bowl, whisk together eggs, sweetened condensed milk and butter until well blended.

3. Add the egg mixture to the flour mixture and stir until just blended.

4. Divide batter equally among prepared muffin cups.

5. Bake in preheated oven for 18 to 22 minutes or until tops are golden and a toothpick inserted in the center comes out clean. Let cool in pan on a wire rack for 5 minutes, then transfer to the rack to cool.

Dried Papaya Muffins
with Cashew Crumble (Costa Rica)

Crumble

¼ cup	all-purpose flour	60 mL
¼ cup	packed light brown sugar	60 mL
½ cup	chopped roasted lightly salted cashews	125 mL
3 tbsp	unsalted butter, melted	45 mL

Muffins

1¾ cups	all-purpose flour	425 mL
1 tsp	baking powder	5 mL
½ tsp	ground allspice	2 mL
¼ tsp	baking soda	1 mL
⅛ tsp	salt	0.5 mL
½ cup	packed light brown sugar	125 mL
2	eggs	2
⅔ cup	buttermilk	150 mL
⅓ cup	unsalted butter, melted	75 mL
1 tsp	vanilla extract	5 mL
1 cup	chopped dried papaya	250 mL

The sweetness of dried papaya brings Costa Rican flair to allspice-scented, brown sugar and butter–based muffins. The crowning touch? A delectable crumble made of rain forest cashews.

Makes 12 muffins

- Preheat oven to 400°F (200°C)
- 12-cup muffin pan, greased

1. *Crumble:* In a small bowl, combine flour, brown sugar and cashews. Drizzle with butter, tossing with a fork until crumbly. Refrigerate until ready to use.

2. *Muffins:* In a large bowl, whisk together flour, baking powder, allspice, baking soda and salt.

3. In a medium bowl, whisk together brown sugar, eggs, buttermilk, butter and vanilla until well blended.

4. Add the egg mixture to the flour mixture and stir until just blended. Gently fold in papaya.

5. Divide batter equally among prepared muffin cups. Sprinkle with crumble and gently press into batter.

6. Bake in preheated oven for 18 to 22 minutes or until tops are golden and a toothpick inserted in the center comes out clean. Let cool in pan on a wire rack for 5 minutes, then transfer to the rack to cool.

Andean Quinoa Muffins (Bolivia, Peru, Ecuador)

²/₃ cup	quinoa, rinsed	150 mL
2 cups	all-purpose flour	500 mL
2¹/₂ tsp	baking powder	12 mL
1 tsp	ground cinnamon	5 mL
¹/₂ tsp	baking soda	2 mL
¹/₂ tsp	salt	2 mL
¹/₄ cup	packed light brown sugar	60 mL
1	egg	1
1 cup	buttermilk	250 mL
¹/₂ cup	liquid honey	125 mL
¹/₄ cup	unsalted butter, melted	60 mL
1¹/₂ tsp	vanilla extract	7 mL

Quinoa was highly significant to the Incas and other peoples of the Andes. It works beautifully as a fold-in for both muffins and breads, adding moisture, texture and tremendous nutrition (particularly protein). I love it here, with accents of other distinctive Andean flavors: vanilla, cinnamon and honey.

Makes 12 muffins

- 12-cup muffin pan, lined with paper liners

1. In a small saucepan, bring 1¹/₃ cups (325 mL) water to a boil over medium-high heat. Add quinoa, reduce heat to low, cover and cook for about 15 minutes or until all of the liquid is absorbed. Fluff with a fork and let cool.
2. Preheat oven to 400°F (200°C).
3. In a large bowl, whisk together flour, baking powder, cinnamon, baking soda and salt.
4. In a medium bowl, whisk together brown sugar, egg, buttermilk, honey, butter and vanilla until well blended.
5. Add the egg mixture to the flour mixture and stir until just blended. Gently fold in quinoa.
6. Divide batter equally among prepared muffin cups.
7. Bake for 15 to 18 minutes or until tops are golden and a toothpick inserted in the center comes out clean. Let cool in pan on a wire rack for 5 minutes, then transfer to the rack to cool.

Alfajores Muffins (Latin America and Spain)

2¹/₄ cups	all-purpose flour	550 mL
2¹/₂ tsp	baking powder	12 mL
¹/₂ tsp	baking soda	2 mL
¹/₂ tsp	salt	2 mL
³/₄ cup	granulated sugar	175 mL
1	egg	1
¹/₄ cup	unsalted butter, melted	60 mL
1 tsp	vanilla extract	5 mL
1 cup	sour cream	250 mL
¹/₂ cup	canned dulce de leche	125 mL
3 tbsp	confectioners' (icing) sugar	45 mL

An *alfajor* is a traditional confection found in select regions of Spain and in Latin America. Its basic form consists of two round, sweet biscuits joined together with dulce de leche or jam and covered with powdered sugar. I've captured the same sensation with these muffins.

Makes 12 muffins

- Preheat oven to 375°F (190°C)
- 12-cup muffin pan, lined with paper liners

1. In a large bowl, whisk together flour, baking powder, baking soda and salt.
2. In a medium bowl, whisk together granulated sugar, egg, butter and vanilla until well blended. Whisk in sour cream until blended.
3. Add the egg mixture to the flour mixture and stir until just blended.
4. Divide half the batter equally among prepared muffin cups. Spoon 2 tsp (10 mL) dulce de leche into the center of each cup. Top with the remaining batter.
5. Bake in preheated oven for 25 to 30 minutes or until tops are golden and firm to the touch. Let cool in pan on a wire rack for 3 minutes, then transfer to the rack to cool. Sprinkle cooled muffin tops with confectioners' sugar just before serving.

Pear, Walnut and Bacon Muffins (page 158)

Peach Melba Muffins (page 222)

Blueberry Goat Cheese Muffins (page 204) and
Heirloom Apple and Rosemary Muffins (page 203)

Leek and Gorgonzola Muffins
(page 243)

Gajar Halva Carrot Muffins
(page 302)

Rum and Coconut Muffins (page 252)
and Orange Muffins (page 280)

Rugalach Muffins (page 287)

Papaya Oat Muffins (page 326)

Almond Tres Leches Muffins
(Ecuador and Mexico)

2 cups	all-purpose flour	500 mL
2 tsp	baking powder	10 mL
1/2 tsp	salt	2 mL
2/3 cup	granulated sugar	150 mL
1/2 cup	unsalted butter, softened	125 mL
2	eggs	2
1/3 cup	sweetened condensed milk	75 mL
1/3 cup	heavy or whipping (35%) cream	75 mL
1/3 cup	whole milk	75 mL
1/2 tsp	almond extract	2 mL
1/2 cup	sliced almonds	125 mL
1/4 cup	sweetened condensed milk	60 mL

The origins of tres leches — a rich and creamy confection served with cafecito throughout Latin America — are disputed, but most culinary historians agree that its roots lie in Ecuador and Mexico. It makes a seamless transition from cake to muffin: tender, not too sweet and utterly irresistible. You can make two batches with one can of sweetened condensed milk, and I strongly advise doing so!

Makes 12 muffins

- Preheat oven to 400°F (200°C)
- 12-cup muffin pan, greased

1. In a medium bowl, whisk together flour, baking powder and salt.

2. In a large bowl, using an electric mixer on medium-high speed, beat sugar and butter until light and fluffy. Beat in eggs, one at a time, until well blended. Beat in 1/3 cup (75 mL) sweetened condensed milk, cream, milk and almond extract until blended.

3. Add the flour mixture to the milk mixture and, using a wooden spoon, gently stir until just blended.

4. Divide batter equally among prepared muffin cups. Sprinkle with almonds.

5. Bake in preheated oven for 17 to 22 minutes or until tops are golden and a toothpick inserted in the center comes out clean. Let cool in pan on a wire rack for 5 minutes, then transfer to the rack.

6. Drizzle each warm muffin top with 1 tsp (5 mL) sweetened condensed milk. Let cool.

Raspberry Trifle Muffins (England)

Filling

3 oz	cream cheese, softened	90 g
2 tbsp	confectioners' (icing) sugar	30 mL
½ tsp	vanilla extract	2 mL

Muffins

2 cups	all-purpose flour	500 mL
2½ tsp	baking powder	12 mL
½ tsp	salt	2 mL
⅔ cup	granulated sugar	150 mL
2	eggs	2
¾ cup	milk	175 mL
½ cup	unsalted butter, melted	125 mL
2 tbsp	cream sherry	30 mL
1½ cups	raspberries, divided	375 mL
¼ cup	seedless raspberry jam	60 mL

Trifle is not only one of the most elegant desserts around, but it's also one of the most exuberant — which is why I had to recreate it as a muffin. The nontraditional muffin version here has many of the hallmarks, including a buttery crumb, dollops of raspberry jam, a hint of sherry and a vanilla cream cheese filling in place of the custard.

Makes 12 muffins

- Preheat oven to 400°F (200°C)
- 12-cup muffin pan, lined with paper liners

1. *Filling:* In a small bowl, mix cream cheese, confectioners' (icing) sugar and vanilla until smooth.

2. *Muffins:* In a large bowl, whisk together flour, baking powder and salt.

3. In a medium bowl, whisk together sugar, eggs, milk, butter and sherry until well blended.

4. Add the egg mixture to the flour mixture and stir until just blended. Gently stir in ¾ cup (175 mL) of the raspberries.

5. Divide half the batter equally among prepared muffin cups. Spoon 1 tsp (5 mL) jam and 2 tsp (10 mL) filling into the center of each cup. Top with the remaining batter. Gently press the remaining berries into batter.

6. Bake in preheated oven for 19 to 23 minutes or until tops are golden and firm to the touch. Let cool in pan on a wire rack for 5 minutes, then transfer to the rack to cool.

Banoffee Muffins (England)

1½ cups	all-purpose flour	375 mL
1½ tsp	baking powder	7 mL
½ tsp	baking soda	2 mL
¼ tsp	salt	1 mL
1 cup	packed light brown sugar	250 mL
2	eggs	2
⅔ cup	unsalted butter, melted	150 mL
1 cup	mashed ripe bananas	250 mL
1	large firm-ripe banana, peeled and diced	1
¾ cup	canned dulce de leche, divided	150 mL

Banoffee pie, from which these muffins take their cue, is an easy take on toffee with bananas (hence the name). It made its debut at the Hungry Monk, a pub in England, in 1972 and has been a hit ever since. Traditional recipes involve boiling unopened cans of condensed milk, but since that sometimes results in explosions, I suggest using ready-made dulce de leche.

Tip

Look for cans of dulce de leche where Mexican foods are shelved in the supermarket or at Hispanic grocery stores.

Makes 12 muffins

- Preheat oven to 400°F (200°C)
- 12-cup muffin pan, greased

1. In a large bowl, whisk together flour, baking powder, baking soda and salt.

2. In a medium bowl, whisk together brown sugar and eggs until well blended. Gradually whisk in butter until mixture is creamy. Stir in mashed bananas until blended.

3. Add the egg mixture to the flour mixture and stir until just blended. Gently fold in diced banana.

4. Divide half the batter equally among prepared muffin cups. Spoon 2 tsp (10 mL) dulce de leche into the center of each cup. Top with the remaining batter.

5. Bake in preheated oven for 17 to 20 minutes or until tops are puffed, golden and firm to the touch. Let cool in pan on a wire rack for 3 minutes, then transfer to the rack to cool.

6. In a small microwave-safe bowl, microwave the remaining dulce de leche on High for 5 seconds or until warm. Drizzle over cooled muffins.

Hot Cross Bun Muffins (England)

Muffins

2 cups	all-purpose flour	500 mL
1 tsp	baking powder	5 mL
1 tsp	baking soda	5 mL
1/2 tsp	salt	2 mL
1/2 tsp	ground cinnamon	2 mL
1/4 tsp	ground allspice	1 mL
1/4 tsp	ground nutmeg	1 mL
1/2 cup	granulated sugar	125 mL
2	eggs	2
1 cup	sour cream	250 mL
1/4 cup	unsalted butter, melted	60 mL
2 tsp	finely grated orange zest	10 mL
1 tsp	vanilla extract	5 mL
1 cup	dried currants	250 mL

Icing

1 1/4 cups	confectioners' (icing) sugar	300 mL
2 tbsp	unsalted butter, softened	30 mL
1 tbsp	milk	15 mL
1 tsp	vanilla extract	5 mL

Despite a teeny tiny kitchen and a short list of modern appliances, my mother was (and is) a fantastic baker. She baked throughout the year, but it is her holiday creations I remember best. She turned out hot cross buns (special sweet buns marked with a symbolic cross) every Good Friday before Easter. My muffin version tastes much like Mom's, but it's much simpler — ideal for all who fear baking with yeast.

Makes 12 muffins

- Preheat oven to 400°F (200°C)
- 12-cup muffin pan, lined with paper liners

1. *Muffins:* In a large bowl, whisk together flour, baking powder, baking soda, salt, cinnamon, allspice and nutmeg.

2. In a medium bowl, whisk together sugar, eggs, sour cream, butter, orange zest and vanilla until well blended.

3. Add the egg mixture to the flour mixture and stir until just blended. Gently fold in currants.

4. Divide batter equally among prepared muffin cups.

5. Bake in preheated oven for 18 to 21 minutes or until tops are golden and a toothpick inserted in the center comes out clean. Let cool in pan on a wire rack for 5 minutes, then transfer to the rack to cool completely.

6. *Icing:* In a small bowl, stir together confectioners' sugar, butter, milk and vanilla until smooth and thick. Spoon into one corner of a sturdy plastic bag. Snip off the corner tip, gather the bag above the icing and squeeze a cross of icing onto each cooled muffin top.

Simnel Muffins (England)

2 tsp	finely grated orange zest	10 mL
1/3 cup	freshly squeezed orange juice	75 mL
1/2 cup	dried sour (tart) cherries	125 mL
1/2 cup	chopped dried apricots	125 mL
1 cup + 2 tbsp	all-purpose flour	280 mL
1/2 cup	granulated sugar	125 mL
1 1/2 tsp	baking powder	7 mL
1 tsp	pumpkin pie spice	5 mL
1/2 tsp	ground nutmeg	2 mL
1/4 tsp	salt	1 mL
1/3 cup	unsalted butter	75 mL
1	package (7 oz/210 g) almond paste, crumbled	1
3	eggs	3

Simnel cakes — so called because of the fine flour (Latin *simila*) used to make them — are traditional Lenten fruit cakes covered in marzipan. Here, I've simplified all by incorporating the almond paste directly into the batter and using dried cherries and apricots in place of candied cherries and apricot jam.

Makes 10 muffins

- Preheat oven to 375°F (190°C)
- 12-cup muffin pan, 10 cups greased

1. In a small saucepan, bring orange juice, cherries and apricots to a simmer over medium-high heat. Remove from heat and let stand for 10 minutes.

2. In a large bowl, whisk together flour, sugar, baking powder, pumpkin pie spice, nutmeg and salt.

3. In a microwave-safe bowl, microwave butter on Medium (50%) until melted (or melt in a saucepan over medium heat).

4. In another large bowl, using an electric mixer on medium speed, beat hot butter and almond paste until well blended, with some small pieces of paste remaining. Beat in eggs, one at a time, until well blended. Stir in orange juice mixture and orange zest until blended.

5. Add the egg mixture to the flour mixture and, using a wooden spoon, stir until just blended.

6. Divide batter equally among prepared muffin cups.

7. Bake in preheated oven for 18 to 22 minutes or until tops are golden and a toothpick inserted in the center comes out clean. Let cool in pan on a wire rack for 5 minutes, then transfer to the rack to cool.

Plum Pudding Muffins (England)

Muffins

2 cups	all-purpose flour	500 mL
1 tbsp	baking powder	15 mL
2 tsp	pumpkin pie spice	10 mL
1/4 tsp	salt	1 mL
1/8 tsp	freshly ground black pepper	0.5 mL
1/3 cup	packed dark brown sugar	75 mL
1	egg	1
1/2 cup	milk	125 mL
1/3 cup	unsalted butter, melted	75 mL
1/4 cup	brandy	60 mL
1 1/3 cups	prepared mincemeat	325 mL
1/2 cup	dried currants	125 mL
2 tsp	finely grated orange zest	10 mL

Icing

1 cup	confectioners' (icing) sugar	250 mL
1 tbsp	brandy	15 mL

Some of the very best plum puddings are considered at their best when made a year in advance and allowed to mellow. It was customary to make plum pudding early in Advent (the religious season before Christmas) and use it the following year. Everyone in the family was supposed to stir the pudding once for good luck. If you do not have a year of prep time, try these fantastic muffins instead. They are fabulous, if I do say so myself.

Tip

Do not used condensed mincemeat, which is dry and crumbly and requires the addition of water before use.

Makes 12 muffins

- Preheat oven to 400°F (200°C)
- 12-cup muffin pan, greased

1. *Muffins:* In a large bowl, whisk together flour, baking powder, pumpkin pie spice, salt and pepper.
2. In a medium bowl, whisk together brown sugar, egg, milk, butter and brandy until well blended. Stir in mincemeat, currants and orange zest until blended.
3. Add the egg mixture to the flour mixture and stir until just blended.
4. Divide batter equally among prepared muffin cups.
5. Bake in preheated oven for 19 to 22 minutes or until a toothpick inserted in the center comes out clean. Let cool in pan on a wire rack for 3 minutes, then transfer to the rack while you prepare the icing.
6. *Icing:* In a small bowl, whisk together confectioners' sugar and brandy until smooth. Spread over warm muffin tops. Let cool.

Sticky Toffee Muffins (England)

1¼ cups	all-purpose flour	300 mL
1½ tsp	baking powder	7 mL
¼ tsp	baking soda	1 mL
¼ tsp	salt	1 mL
⅓ cup	packed dark brown sugar	75 mL
1	egg	1
¾ cup	unsalted butter, melted	175 mL
⅓ cup	golden syrup or liquid honey	75 mL
1¾ cups	pitted dates, chopped	425 mL

Sticky toffee pudding — the scrumptious, moist cake made with fresh dates and brown sugar in a buttery toffee-caramel sauce — is my idea of dessert nirvana. Here, I've converted it into an equally amazing muffin that I can more easily justify eating first thing in the morning.

Makes 12 muffins

- Preheat oven to 400°F (200°C)
- 12-cup muffin pan, greased

1. In a large bowl, whisk together flour, baking powder, baking soda and salt.
2. In a medium bowl, whisk together brown sugar, egg, butter and syrup until well blended.
3. Add the egg mixture to the flour mixture and stir until just blended. Gently fold in dates.
4. Divide batter equally among prepared muffin cups.
5. Bake in preheated oven for 15 to 18 minutes or until tops are golden and a toothpick inserted in the center comes out clean. Let cool in pan on a wire rack for 3 minutes, then transfer to the rack to cool.

Bara Brith Muffins (Wales)

2	black tea bags	2
½ cup	finely chopped dried apricots	125 mL
½ cup	finely chopped prunes	125 mL
½ cup	dried cherries	125 mL
1¾ cups	all-purpose flour	425 mL
1 tbsp	baking powder	15 mL
1½ tsp	pumpkin pie spice	7 mL
½ tsp	salt	2 mL
½ cup	packed dark brown sugar	125 mL
2	eggs	2
½ cup	unsalted butter, melted	125 mL
1 tsp	finely grated lemon zest	5 mL

Bara Brith is Wales' traditional rich fruit bread. It can be made with baking powder (South Wales) or yeast (North Wales) as the leavener, so I feel perfectly comfortable with my baking powder muffin interpretation. Tea is a key flavor in the bread: the dried fruits are soaked in it and the cooled tea is stirred into the batter. Need I suggest the perfect drink accompaniment?

Makes 12 muffins

- 12-cup muffin pan, lined with paper liners

1. In a medium saucepan, bring 1 cup (250 mL) water to a simmer over medium heat, then add tea bags. Remove from heat, transfer to a bowl and let steep for 5 minutes. Add apricots, prunes and cherries to bowl. Let stand for 30 minutes. Discard tea bags, pressing out liquid, but do not drain fruit.
2. Preheat oven to 350°F (180°C).
3. In a large bowl, whisk together flour, baking powder, pumpkin pie spice and salt.
4. In a medium bowl, whisk together brown sugar, eggs, butter and lemon zest until well blended. Stir in fruit mixture.
5. Add the egg mixture to the flour mixture and stir until just blended.
6. Divide batter equally among prepared muffin cups.
7. Bake in preheated oven for 20 to 25 minutes or until tops are golden and a toothpick inserted in the center comes out clean. Let cool in pan on a wire rack for 3 minutes, then transfer to the rack to cool.

Scottish Oat Muffins (Scotland)

Topping

1/3 cup	packed dark brown sugar	75 mL
1/3 cup	large-flake (old-fashioned) rolled oats	75 mL
1/3 cup	unsalted butter, melted	75 mL
2 tbsp	all-purpose flour	30 mL

Muffins

1 cup	large-flake (old-fashioned) rolled oats	250 mL
1 cup	buttermilk	250 mL
1/4 cup	unsalted butter, melted	60 mL
1 cup	all-purpose flour	250 mL
2 tsp	baking powder	10 mL
1/2 tsp	baking soda	2 mL
1/2 tsp	salt	2 mL
1/2 cup	packed dark brown sugar	125 mL
1	egg	1

Makes 12 muffins

- Preheat oven to 400°F (200°C)
- 12-cup muffin pan, lined with paper liners

1. *Topping:* In a small bowl, mix brown sugar, oats, butter and flour until crumbly. Refrigerate until ready to use.
2. In a large bowl, stir together oats, buttermilk and butter until blended. Let stand for 5 minutes.
3. In a medium bowl, whisk together flour, baking powder, baking soda and salt.
4. Whisk brown sugar and egg into the buttermilk mixture and stir until well blended. Stir in flour mixture until just blended.
5. Divide batter equally among prepared muffin cups. Sprinkle with topping.
6. Bake in preheated oven for 18 to 22 minutes or until tops are golden and a toothpick inserted in the center comes out clean. Let cool in pan on a wire rack for 5 minutes, then transfer to the rack to cool.

Tea Brack Muffins (Ireland)

1 cup	milk	250 mL
2	black tea bags	2
2 cups	all-purpose flour	500 mL
2 1/2 tsp	baking powder	12 mL
1 tsp	ground cinnamon	5 mL
1/2 tsp	ground allspice	2 mL
1/2 tsp	salt	2 mL
1/4 tsp	ground cloves	1 mL
1/4 tsp	baking soda	1 mL
2/3 cup	granulated sugar	150 mL
2	eggs	2
1/2 cup	unsalted butter, melted	125 mL
1 tbsp	finely grated orange zest	15 mL
1/2 cup	golden raisins	125 mL
1/2 cup	dried currants	125 mL

Barm brack (Irish: *Báirín Breac*) is a dark and fruity yeast-raised cake (*barm* means "yeast"; *brack* means "speckled"). Tea brack is the much more common baking powder version.

Makes 16 muffins

- Two 12-cup muffin pans, 16 cups lined with paper liners

1. In a small saucepan, heat milk and tea over medium heat until very hot. Remove from heat, cover and let steep for 10 minutes. Discard tea bags, pressing out liquid. Transfer milk to a small heatproof measuring cup and place in freezer until cool.
2. Preheat oven to 400°F (200°C).
3. In a large bowl, whisk together flour, baking powder, cinnamon, allspice, salt, cloves and baking soda.
4. In a medium bowl, whisk together sugar, eggs, butter and orange zest until well blended. Whisk in milk mixture until blended.
5. Add the egg mixture to the flour mixture and stir until just blended. Gently fold in raisins and currants.
6. Divide batter equally among prepared muffin cups.
7. Bake for 15 to 20 minutes or until tops are golden and a toothpick inserted in the center comes out clean. Let cool in pans on a wire rack for 3 minutes, then transfer to the rack to cool.

Guinness Stout Ginger Muffins (Ireland)

³⁄₄ cup	Guinness or other dark beer	175 mL
³⁄₄ cup	dark (cooking) molasses	175 mL
³⁄₄ tsp	baking soda	3 mL
1³⁄₄ cups	all-purpose flour	425 mL
1 tbsp	ground ginger	15 mL
2 tsp	baking powder	10 mL
1 tsp	ground cinnamon	5 mL
¹⁄₂ tsp	salt	2 mL
¹⁄₂ tsp	ground cardamom	2 mL
¹⁄₄ tsp	ground nutmeg	1 mL
¹⁄₄ tsp	ground cloves	1 mL
1 cup	packed dark brown sugar	250 mL
2	eggs	2
¹⁄₃ cup	vegetable oil	75 mL

I made a Guinness ginger cake as the groom's cake for our wedding, so my husband and I feel some sentimental attachment to these muffins. The Guinness and molasses add rich depth of flavor, unlike any other ginger muffin you've ever tried.

Makes 12 muffins

- 12-cup muffin pan, lined with paper liners

1. In a medium saucepan, bring beer and molasses to a boil over medium-high heat. Remove from heat and stir in baking soda. Transfer to a bowl and let cool to room temperature.
2. Preheat oven to 350°F (180°C).
3. In a large bowl, whisk together flour, ginger, baking powder, cinnamon, salt, cardamom, nutmeg and cloves.
4. Whisk brown sugar, eggs and oil into beer mixture until well blended.
5. Add the egg mixture to the flour mixture and stir until just blended.
6. Divide batter equally among prepared muffin cups.
7. Bake for 20 to 25 minutes or until tops spring back when touched and a toothpick inserted in the center comes out clean. Let cool in pan on a wire rack for 5 minutes, then transfer to the rack to cool.

Omenakakku Muffins (Finland)

1¹⁄₂ cups	sour cream	375 mL
1¹⁄₂ tsp	baking soda	7 mL
1³⁄₄ cups	all-purpose flour	425 mL
2 tsp	baking powder	10 mL
¹⁄₂ tsp	salt	2 mL
1 cup	granulated sugar	250 mL
2	eggs	2
¹⁄₂ cup	unsalted butter, melted	125 mL
2 cups	diced peeled sweet-tart apples, such as Braeburn, Jonathan or Winesap	500 mL
2 tbsp	granulated sugar	30 mL

Not too sweet, these sour cream–rich muffins elevate everyday apples to new heights.

Makes 12 muffins

- Preheat oven to 350°F (180°C)
- 12-cup muffin pan, lined with paper liners

1. In a medium bowl, whisk together sour cream and baking soda. Let stand for 5 minutes.
2. In a large bowl, whisk together flour, baking powder and salt.
3. Whisk 1 cup (250 mL) sugar, eggs and butter into sour cream mixture until well blended.
4. Add the egg mixture to the flour mixture and stir until just blended. Gently fold in apples.
5. Divide batter equally among prepared muffin cups. Sprinkle with 2 tbsp (30 mL) sugar.
6. Bake in preheated oven for 24 to 28 minutes or until tops are golden and a toothpick inserted in the center comes out clean. Let cool in pan on a wire rack for 5 minutes, then transfer to the rack to cool.

Limpa Muffins (Sweden)

1½ cups	all-purpose flour	375 mL
½ cup	rye flour	125 mL
2½ tsp	baking powder	12 mL
¾ tsp	fennel seeds, crushed	3 mL
½ tsp	caraway seeds, crushed	2 mL
½ tsp	cumin seeds, crushed	2 mL
½ tsp	baking soda	2 mL
½ tsp	salt	2 mL
1	egg	1
¾ cup	buttermilk	175 mL
⅓ cup	unsalted butter, melted	75 mL
¼ cup	dark (cooking) molasses	60 mL
1½ tsp	finely grated orange zest	7 mL

Based on Swedish rye bread, these quick and easy limpa muffins have a clean-tasting combination of spice and sweetness that is characteristic of so much of Scandinavian cooking.

Makes 12 muffins

- Preheat oven to 400°F (200°C)
- 12-cup muffin pan, greased

1. In a large bowl, whisk together all-purpose flour, rye flour, baking powder, fennel seeds, caraway seeds, cumin seeds, baking soda and salt.
2. In a medium bowl, whisk together egg, buttermilk, butter, molasses and orange zest until well blended.
3. Add the egg mixture to the flour mixture and stir until just blended.
4. Divide batter equally among prepared muffin cups.
5. Bake in preheated oven for 18 to 22 minutes or until a toothpick inserted in the center comes out clean. Let cool in pan on a wire rack for 5 minutes, then transfer to the rack to cool.

Julekage Muffins (Norway, Denmark, Sweden)

2 cups	all-purpose flour	500 mL
1 tbsp	baking powder	15 mL
¾ tsp	ground cardamom	3 mL
½ tsp	salt	2 mL
¼ tsp	ground nutmeg	1 mL
¼ tsp	ground cinnamon	1 mL
⅔ cup	granulated sugar	150 mL
1	egg	1
1 cup	milk	250 mL
¼ cup	unsalted butter, melted	60 mL
½ cup	raisins	125 mL
½ cup	chopped citron	125 mL

The rich, spiced Scandinavian bread known as *julekage* makes a seamless transition here into muffin form. The classic is traditionally served at Christmas (*julekage* means "Yule bread"), but these muffins are fitting throughout the year.

Makes 12 muffins

- Preheat oven to 425°F (220°C)
- 12-cup muffin pan, lined with paper liners

1. In a large bowl, whisk together flour, baking powder, cardamom, salt, nutmeg and cinnamon.
2. In a medium bowl, whisk together sugar, egg, milk and butter until well blended.
3. Add the egg mixture to the flour mixture and stir until just blended. Gently fold in raisins and citron.
4. Divide batter equally among prepared muffin cups.
5. Bake in preheated oven for 16 to 20 minutes or until tops are golden and a toothpick inserted in the center comes out clean. Let cool in pan on a wire rack for 3 minutes, then transfer to the rack to cool.

Santa Lucia Muffins (Sweden)

1 tbsp	boiling water	15 mL
Pinch	saffron threads	Pinch
2 cups	all-purpose flour	500 mL
1 tbsp	baking powder	15 mL
1/2 tsp	salt	2 mL
2/3 cup	granulated sugar	150 mL
1/2 cup	unsalted butter, softened	125 mL
2	eggs	2
2/3 cup	milk	150 mL
1/2 cup	raisins	125 mL

Swedish lore has it that on December 13, 1764, a gentleman was awakened in the middle of the night by the singing of a young, winged woman in white. It was Saint Lucia and she arrived bearing light, food and wine as comfort on what was, in the Gregorian calendar, the longest night of the year. Saint Lucia continues to be celebrated on December 13 in Sweden, marked by children walking with lit candles, singing the beautiful Lucia carol and bringing the Lucia bread.

Makes 12 muffins

- Preheat oven to 375°F (190°C)
- 12-cup muffin pan, greased

1. In a small bowl, combine boiling water and saffron. Let stand for 5 minutes.
2. In a medium bowl, whisk together flour, baking powder and salt.
3. In a large bowl, using an electric mixer on medium speed, beat sugar and butter until light and fluffy. Beat in eggs, one at a time, until well blended. Beat in saffron mixture.
4. With the mixer on low speed, beat in flour mixture alternately with milk, making three additions of flour and two of milk, until just blended. Gently fold in raisins.
5. Divide batter equally among prepared muffin cups.
6. Bake in preheated oven for 15 to 20 minutes or until a toothpick inserted in the center comes out clean. Let cool in pan on a wire rack for 5 minutes, then transfer to the rack to cool.

Pom Koek Muffins (Belgium)

3 cups	all-purpose flour	750 mL
1 tsp	baking soda	5 mL
1 tsp	salt	5 mL
1 tsp	ground cinnamon	5 mL
1/4 tsp	ground cloves	1 mL
1/2 cup	granulated sugar	125 mL
1	egg	1
1 cup	liquid honey	250 mL
1/3 cup	vegetable oil	75 mL
1 cup	hot strong coffee	250 mL

Pom Koek is a Belgian coffee cake flavored with strong coffee, honey and spices. In other words, yum! If you choose one for breakfast, you get your meal and coffee fix all in one.

Makes 12 muffins

- Preheat oven to 350°F (180°C)
- 12-cup muffin pan, lined with paper liners

1. In a large bowl, whisk together flour, baking soda, salt, cinnamon and cloves.
2. In a medium bowl, whisk together sugar, egg, honey and oil until well blended.
3. Add the egg mixture and coffee to the flour mixture and stir until just blended.
4. Divide batter equally among prepared muffin cups.
5. Bake in preheated oven for 23 to 28 minutes or until tops are golden and a toothpick inserted in the center comes out clean. Let cool in pan on a wire rack for 5 minutes, then transfer to the rack to cool.

Ontbijtkoek Muffins (Holland)

1½ cups	all-purpose flour	375 mL
½ cup	rye flour	125 mL
1 tbsp	baking powder	15 mL
1 tsp	salt	5 mL
1 tsp	ground cloves	5 mL
1 tsp	ground cinnamon	5 mL
1 tsp	ground ginger	5 mL
½ tsp	ground nutmeg	2 mL
½ cup	packed dark brown sugar	125 mL
1 cup	milk	250 mL
⅓ cup	dark (cooking) molasses	75 mL

Ontbijtkoek is a traditional spice bread typically eaten for breakfast in the Netherlands. Because the recipe is free of eggs and oil, I take particular pleasure in slathering the still-warm muffins with butter and jam.

Makes 12 muffins

- Preheat oven to 350°F (180°C)
- 12-cup muffin pan, greased

1. In a large bowl, whisk together all-purpose flour, rye flour, baking powder, salt, cloves, cinnamon, ginger and nutmeg.
2. In a medium bowl, whisk together brown sugar, milk and molasses until well blended.
3. Add the molasses mixture to the flour mixture and stir until just blended.
4. Divide batter equally among prepared muffin cups.
5. Bake in preheated oven for 24 to 28 minutes or until tops are golden and a toothpick inserted in the center comes out clean. Let cool in pan on a wire rack for 5 minutes, then transfer to the rack to cool.

Dutch Almond Boterkoek Muffins (Holland)

3 cups	all-purpose flour	750 mL
1 tbsp	baking powder	15 mL
½ tsp	baking soda	2 mL
½ tsp	salt	2 mL
⅔ cup	unsalted butter, softened	150 mL
1 cup	packed light brown sugar	250 mL
2	eggs	2
2 tsp	almond extract	10 mL
1½ tsp	vanilla extract	7 mL
1½ cups	buttermilk	375 mL
½ cup	sliced almonds	125 mL

Boterkoek is similar to shortbread and is a favorite in the Netherlands, especially for the feast of St. Nicholas.

Makes 12 muffins

- Preheat oven to 375°F (190°C)
- 12-cup muffin pan, greased

1. In a medium bowl, whisk together flour, baking powder, baking soda and salt.
2. In a large bowl, using an electric mixer on medium-high speed, beat butter and brown sugar until light and fluffy. Beat in eggs, one at a time, until well blended. Beat in almond extract and vanilla until blended.
3. With the mixer on low speed, beat in flour mixture alternately with buttermilk, making three additions of flour and two of buttermilk, until just blended.
4. Divide batter equally among prepared muffin cups. Sprinkle with almonds.
5. Bake in preheated oven for 25 to 30 minutes or until tops are golden and a toothpick inserted in the center comes out clean. Let cool in pan on a wire rack for 5 minutes, then transfer to the rack to cool.

Baba au Rhum Muffins (France)

Muffins

3 cups	all-purpose flour	750 mL
4 tsp	baking powder	20 mL
1½ tsp	salt	7 mL
1 tsp	ground nutmeg	5 mL
½ tsp	baking soda	2 mL
¾ cup	unsalted butter, softened	175 mL
¾ cup	granulated sugar	175 mL
2	eggs	2
1⅔ cups	milk	400 mL
¼ cup	dark rum	60 mL
1 tbsp	finely grated orange zest	15 mL
1 cup	dried currants	250 mL

Glaze

½ cup	apricot preserves	125 mL
1 tbsp	dark rum	15 mL

Baba au rhum is a small yeast cake studded with dried fruit, saturated in rum and finished with a shiny glaze or filled with whipped cream. These muffins bear wickedly close resemblance.

Makes 18 muffins

- Preheat oven to 350°F (180°C)
- Two 12-cup muffin pans, 18 cups greased

1. *Muffins:* In a large bowl, whisk together flour, baking powder, salt, nutmeg and baking soda.

2. In another large bowl, using an electric mixer on medium-high speed, beat butter and sugar until light and fluffy. Beat in eggs, one at a time, until just blended.

3. In a glass measuring cup, whisk together milk, rum and orange zest until blended.

4. Using a wooden spoon, stir the flour mixture into the egg mixture alternately with the milk mixture, making three additions of flour and two of milk, until just blended. Gently fold in currants.

5. Divide batter equally among prepared muffin cups.

6. Bake in preheated oven for 23 to 26 minutes or until tops are golden and a toothpick inserted in the center comes out clean. Let cool in pans on a wire rack for 3 minutes, then transfer to the rack while you prepare the glaze.

7. *Glaze:* In a small saucepan, combine preserves and rum over low heat, stirring until preserves are melted. Spoon and spread over warm muffin tops. Let cool.

Pain d'Épices Muffins (France)

1 cup	milk	250 mL
1 cup	liquid honey	250 mL
1/2 cup	granulated sugar	125 mL
2 cups	all-purpose flour	500 mL
1/2 cup	dark rye flour	125 mL
1 tsp	baking soda	5 mL
1 tsp	salt	5 mL
1 tsp	ground cinnamon	5 mL
1 tsp	ground ginger	5 mL
1/4 tsp	ground nutmeg	1 mL
1/4 tsp	anise seeds, crushed	1 mL
1/8 tsp	freshly ground black pepper	0.5 mL
1	egg	1
1/4 cup	unsalted butter, melted	60 mL
2 tsp	finely grated orange zest	10 mL

Pain d'épices is a dark, aromatic French loaf, part cake, part bread, with a mélange of spices and a generous dose of honey. These gorgeous dark muffins taste just like the real thing; all you need is a cup of tea.

Makes 12 muffins

- 12-cup muffin pan, greased

1. In a medium saucepan, bring milk to a simmer over medium heat. Whisk in honey and sugar, whisking until sugar is dissolved. Transfer to a medium bowl and let cool.
2. Preheat oven to 325°F (160°C).
3. In a large bowl, whisk together all-purpose flour, rye flour, baking soda, salt, cinnamon, ginger, nutmeg, anise seeds and pepper.
4. Whisk egg, butter and orange zest into milk mixture until well blended.
5. Add the egg mixture to the flour mixture and stir until just blended.
6. Divide batter equally among prepared muffin cups.
7. Bake for 25 to 30 minutes or until tops are golden and a toothpick inserted in the center comes out clean. Let cool in pan on a wire rack for 5 minutes, then transfer to the rack to cool.

Gougère Muffin Puffs (France)

1 cup	milk	250 mL
1/2 cup	unsalted butter, cut into cubes	125 mL
2 tsp	Dijon mustard	10 mL
1 cup	all-purpose flour	250 mL
1/4 tsp	salt	1 mL
1/4 tsp	freshly ground black pepper	1 mL
4	eggs	4
1 cup	shredded Gruyère cheese	250 mL

These have the lively, crisp exterior and cloudlike interior you expect from a gougère (a petite cheese puff), including the sharp bite of Dijon mustard and melted cheesiness of Gruyère. I'm hard-pressed to ask for anything more.

Makes 12 muffins

- Preheat oven to 350°F (180°C)
- 12-cup muffin pan, greased

1. In a saucepan, bring milk, butter and mustard to a boil over medium heat. Remove from heat. Using a wooden spoon, vigorously stir in flour, salt and pepper. Let stand for 5 minutes.
2. Whisk eggs into the flour mixture, one at a time, until smooth. Stir in cheese.
3. Divide batter equally among prepared muffin cups.
4. Bake in preheated oven for 45 to 50 minutes or until tops are puffed and golden brown and a toothpick inserted in the center comes out clean. Let cool in pan on a wire rack for 5 minutes, then transfer to the rack to cool slightly. Serve warm.

Madeleine Muffins (France)

3 cups	all-purpose flour	750 mL
1 tbsp	baking powder	15 mL
$1/2$ tsp	salt	2 mL
1 cup	granulated sugar	250 mL
$2/3$ cup	unsalted butter, softened	150 mL
4	eggs	4
2 tsp	orange flower water or vanilla extract	10 mL
1 cup	milk	250 mL
3 tbsp	confectioners' (icing) sugar	45 mL

These buttery muffins, scented with orange flower water, are based on madeleines, petite cakes made with a génoise (sponge) batter and flavored with lemon, orange flower water or vanilla. What makes them particularly enticing is their shape: the batter is poured into special oval, shell-shaped molds, making cookies that are ideal for nibbling and dipping into tea. Madeleines were made famous by Marcel Proust in his novel *Remembrance of Things Past*, but it's their taste that keeps them in high regard.

Makes 12 muffins

- Preheat oven to 375°F (190°C)
- 12-cup muffin pan, greased

1. In a medium bowl, whisk together flour, baking powder and salt.

2. In a large bowl, using an electric mixer on medium-high speed, beat granulated sugar and butter until light and fluffy. Beat in eggs, one at a time, until well blended. Beat in orange flower water until blended.

3. With the mixer on low speed, beat in flour mixture alternately with milk, making three additions of flour and two of milk, until just blended.

4. Divide batter equally among prepared muffin cups.

5. Bake in preheated oven for 25 to 30 minutes or until tops are golden and a toothpick inserted in the center comes out clean. Let cool in pan on a wire rack for 3 minutes, then transfer to the rack to cool. Dust cooled muffin tops with confectioners' sugar.

Pissaladière Muffins (France)

6 tbsp	olive oil, divided	90 mL
1	onion, finely chopped	1
1 cup	chopped red bell pepper	250 mL
1 tsp	dried rosemary	5 mL
3/4 tsp	salt, divided	3 mL
1/4 tsp	freshly ground black pepper	1 mL
1/4 cup	pitted brine-cured black olives, chopped	60 mL
2 cups	all-purpose flour	500 mL
2 tsp	baking powder	10 mL
1/2 tsp	baking soda	2 mL
1	egg	1
1 cup	buttermilk	250 mL

Provence's pissaladière is a savory tart spread with the region's seasonal vegetables and herbs. My muffins are far less labor-intensive and equally fabulous.

Makes 12 muffins

- 12-cup muffin pan, greased

1. In a large skillet, heat 2 tbsp (30 mL) of the oil over medium heat. Sauté onion, red pepper, rosemary, 1/4 tsp (1 mL) of the salt and pepper for 8 minutes or until onion is golden. Transfer to a bowl and stir in olives. Let cool.
2. Preheat oven to 375°F (190°C).
3. In a large bowl, whisk together flour, baking powder, baking soda and the remaining salt.
4. In a medium bowl, whisk together the remaining oil, egg and buttermilk until well blended.
5. Add the buttermilk mixture to the flour mixture and stir until just blended. Gently fold in onion mixture.
6. Divide batter equally among prepared muffin cups.
7. Bake for 18 to 22 minutes or until a toothpick inserted in the center comes out clean. Let cool in pan on a wire rack for 5 minutes, then transfer to the rack to cool slightly. Serve warm.

Kugelhopf Muffins (France and Austria)

2 1/2 cups	all-purpose flour	625 mL
3 1/2 tsp	baking powder	17 mL
1/2 tsp	salt	2 mL
1 cup	granulated sugar	250 mL
3/4 cup	unsalted butter, softened	175 mL
2	eggs	2
3/4 cup	milk	175 mL
1 tsp	finely grated lemon zest	5 mL
1 tsp	finely grated orange zest	5 mL
1 cup	golden raisins	250 mL
1/2 cup	slivered almonds	125 mL

Though it originated in Austria, kugelhopf has become a specialty of the Alsace region of France, where it is often served for breakfast or brunch. It is traditionally baked in a tall, decorative tube pan, which gives the cake its characteristic angled and ridged pattern, but it is equally impressive here in miniature form.

Makes 12 muffins

- Preheat oven to 350°F (180°C)
- 12-cup muffin pan, lined with paper liners

1. In a medium bowl, whisk together flour, baking powder and salt.
2. In a large bowl, using an electric mixer on medium-high speed, beat sugar and butter until light and fluffy. Beat in eggs, one at a time, until well blended. On low speed, beat in milk, lemon zest and orange zest until blended.
3. Add the flour mixture to the egg mixture and, using a wooden spoon, stir until just blended. Gently fold in raisins.
4. Divide batter among prepared muffin cups. Sprinkle with almonds.
5. Bake in preheated oven for 21 to 24 minutes or until tops are golden and a toothpick inserted in the center comes out clean. Let cool in pan on a wire rack for 5 minutes, then transfer to the rack to cool.

Linzer Raspberry Almond Muffins (Austria)

2¼ cups	all-purpose flour	550 mL
1 tbsp	baking powder	15 mL
½ tsp	baking soda	2 mL
½ tsp	salt	2 mL
½ tsp	ground cinnamon	2 mL
¾ cup	granulated sugar	175 mL
2	eggs	2
⅓ cup	unsalted butter, melted	75 mL
1 tsp	almond extract	3 mL
1⅓ cups	plain whole-milk yogurt	325 mL
½ cup	seedless raspberry jam or preserves	125 mL
½ cup	sliced almonds	125 mL
3 tbsp	confectioners' (icing) sugar	45 mL

These muffins find inspiration from Vienna's linzertorte, a traditional treat made with nuts and raspberry jam.

Makes 12 muffins

- Preheat oven to 400°F (200°C)
- 12-cup muffin pan, greased

1. In a large bowl, whisk together flour, baking powder, baking soda, salt and cinnamon.

2. In a medium bowl, whisk together granulated sugar, eggs, butter and almond extract until well blended. Whisk in yogurt until blended.

3. Add the egg mixture to the flour mixture and stir until just blended.

4. Divide half the batter equally among prepared muffin cups. Spoon 2 tsp (10 mL) jam into the center of each cup. Top with the remaining batter. Sprinkle with almonds.

5. Bake in preheated oven for 21 to 26 minutes or until tops are golden and firm to the touch. Let cool in pan on a wire rack for 5 minutes, then transfer to the rack to cool. Dust cooled muffin tops with confectioners' sugar.

Sachertorte Muffins (Austria)

2 cups	all-purpose flour	500 mL
1 cup	unsweetened cocoa powder (not Dutch process)	250 mL
1 tbsp	baking powder	15 mL
½ tsp	baking soda	2 mL
½ tsp	salt	2 mL
1 cup	granulated sugar	250 mL
2	eggs	2
1 cup	sour cream	250 mL
½ cup	unsalted butter, melted	125 mL
1 tsp	almond extract	5 mL
1½ cups	miniature semisweet chocolate chips	375 mL
½ cup	apricot preserves	125 mL

I adore the flavor combination of chocolate and apricots that characterizes Sachertorte. The original is a refined, elegant ensemble, and these muffins follow suit. They are as at ease in a modern coffeehouse as in a 19th-century Viennese *kaffeehaus*.

Makes 12 muffins

- Preheat oven to 400°F (200°C)
- 12-cup muffin pan, greased

1. In a large bowl, whisk together flour, cocoa powder, baking powder, baking soda and salt.

2. In a medium bowl, whisk together sugar, eggs, sour cream, butter and almond extract until well blended.

3. Add the egg mixture to the flour mixture and stir until just blended. Gently fold in chocolate chips.

4. Divide half the batter equally among prepared muffin cups. Spoon 2 tsp (10 mL) preserves into the center of each cup. Top with the remaining batter.

5. Bake in preheated oven for 21 to 25 minutes or until tops are firm to the touch. Let cool in pan on a wire rack for 5 minutes, then transfer to the rack to cool.

Basel Läckerli Muffins (Switzerland)

2 cups	all-purpose flour	500 mL
1 tbsp	baking powder	15 mL
3/4 tsp	ground cinnamon	3 mL
1/2 tsp	salt	2 mL
1/4 tsp	ground nutmeg	1 mL
1/8 tsp	ground cloves	0.5 mL
1	egg	1
3/4 cup	milk	175 mL
1/3 cup	liquid honey	75 mL
1/4 cup	Kirsch (cherry brandy)	60 mL
1/4 cup	vegetable oil	60 mL
1 tsp	finely grated lemon zest	5 mL
1 tsp	finely grated orange zest	5 mL
1 cup	almonds, toasted and chopped	250 mL

If you have never had *Basel Läckerli* (also *Leckerli* or *Läggerli*, *lecker* meaning "delicious" in German), seek them out: they are traditional hard spice biscuits made of honey, almonds, candied peel and Kirsch, a cherry-flavored spirit. In short, scrumptious. According to Swiss lore, they were originally created by local spice merchants in Basel, Switzerland, over 700 years ago. My muffin version is brand new, but equally delicious.

Makes 12 muffins

- Preheat oven to 375°F (190°C)
- 12-cup muffin pan, greased

1. In a large bowl, whisk together flour, baking powder, cinnamon, salt, nutmeg and cloves.

2. In a medium bowl, whisk together egg, milk, honey, Kirsch, oil, lemon zest and orange zest until well blended.

3. Add the egg mixture to the flour mixture and stir until just blended. Gently fold in almonds.

4. Divide batter equally among prepared muffin cups.

5. Bake in preheated oven for 24 to 28 minutes or until a toothpick inserted in the center comes out clean. Let cool in pan on a wire rack for 5 minutes, then transfer to the rack to cool.

Gianduja Muffins (Switzerland)

1 cup	chopped hazelnuts, toasted and cooled	250 mL
1 cup	granulated sugar, divided	250 mL
1½ cups	all-purpose flour	375 mL
⅔ cup	unsweetened cocoa powder (not Dutch process)	150 mL
1 tsp	baking powder	5 mL
1 tsp	baking soda	5 mL
½ tsp	salt	2 mL
½ cup	unsalted butter, softened	125 mL
3	eggs	3
1¼ cups	sour cream	300 mL
1½ tsp	vanilla extract	7 mL
1 cup	miniature semisweet chocolate chips	250 mL

The rich hazelnut-flavored chocolate called *gianduja* (or *gianduia* in Italy) — named for the masked character Gianduia of the centuries-old Italian *commedia dell'arte* — makes for a muffin that is sophisticated and intensely delicious.

Makes 12 muffins

- Preheat oven to 350°F (180°C)
- Food processor
- 12-cup muffin pan, greased

1. In food processor, process hazelnuts with ¼ cup (60 mL) of the sugar until finely chopped.
2. In a medium bowl, whisk together hazelnut mixture, flour, cocoa powder, baking powder, baking soda and salt.
3. In a large bowl, using an electric mixer on medium-high speed, beat the remaining sugar and butter until light and fluffy. Beat in eggs, one at a time, until well blended. Beat in sour cream and vanilla until blended.
4. On low speed, beat the flour mixture into the sour cream mixture until just blended. Using a rubber spatula, gently fold in chocolate chips.
5. Divide batter equally among prepared muffin cups.
6. Bake in preheated oven for 25 to 30 minutes or until tops are golden and a toothpick inserted in the center comes out clean. Let cool in pan on a wire rack for 5 minutes, then transfer to the rack to cool.

Lebkuchen Muffins (Germany)

2½ cups	all-purpose flour	625 mL
2½ tsp	baking powder	12 mL
1 tsp	ground cinnamon	5 mL
¾ tsp	ground allspice	3 mL
½ tsp	ground nutmeg	2 mL
½ tsp	salt	2 mL
¼ tsp	ground cloves	1 mL
2	eggs	2
¾ cup	whole milk	175 mL
½ cup	liquid honey	125 mL
½ cup	dark (cooking) molasses	125 mL
½ cup	unsalted butter, melted	125 mL
½ cup	chopped hazelnuts, toasted	125 mL
⅓ cup	chopped candied fruit	75 mL

These moist muffins take their cue from the flavors in lebkuchen cookies. Honey adds floral sweetness; molasses, notes of caramel.

Makes 12 muffins

- Preheat oven to 350°F (180°C)
- 12-cup muffin pan, greased

1. In a large bowl, whisk together flour, baking powder, cinnamon, allspice, nutmeg, salt and cloves.
2. In a medium bowl, whisk together eggs, milk, honey, molasses and butter until well blended.
3. Add the egg mixture to the flour mixture and stir until just blended. Gently fold in hazelnuts and candied fruit.
4. Divide batter equally among prepared muffin cups.
5. Bake in preheated oven for 23 to 25 minutes or until tops are golden and a toothpick inserted in the center comes out clean. Let cool in pan on a wire rack for 5 minutes, then transfer to the rack to cool.

Stollen Muffins (Germany)

2 cups	all-purpose flour	500 mL
1 tbsp	baking powder	15 mL
1/2 tsp	salt	2 mL
1/4 tsp	ground mace	1 mL
1	egg	1
3/4 cup	milk	175 mL
1/3 cup	liquid honey	75 mL
1/4 cup	unsalted butter, melted	60 mL
1/4 cup	dark rum	60 mL
2 tsp	finely grated lemon zest	10 mL
2/3 cup	mixed candied fruit, chopped	150 mL
1/2 cup	chopped almonds, toasted	125 mL
1/2 cup	confectioners' (icing) sugar	125 mL

Although these muffins bear all of the classic flavors of traditional stollen — the German Christmas bread laden with candied and dried fruit, nuts and spices — they are far lighter and much easier to make (gone is the yeast). Use a heavy hand to sift the confectioners' sugar over the cooled muffin tops.

Makes 12 muffins

- Preheat oven to 375°F (190°C)
- 12-cup muffin pan, greased

1. In a large bowl, whisk together flour, baking powder, salt and mace.
2. In a medium bowl, whisk together egg, milk, honey, butter, rum and lemon zest until well blended.
3. Add the egg mixture to the flour mixture and stir until just blended. Gently fold in candied fruit and almonds.
4. Divide batter equally among prepared muffin cups.
5. Bake in preheated oven for 24 to 28 minutes or until tops are golden and a toothpick inserted in the center comes out clean. Let cool in pan on a wire rack for 5 minutes, then transfer to the rack to cool.
6. Generously sift confectioners' sugar over cooled muffin tops just before serving.

Golden Olive Oil Muffins (Italy)

2 1/2 cups	all-purpose flour	625 mL
2 1/2 tsp	baking powder	12 mL
1/4 tsp	salt	1 mL
1 cup	granulated sugar	250 mL
2	eggs	2
3/4 cup	milk	175 mL
1/2 cup	extra virgin olive oil	125 mL
1 tbsp	finely grated lemon zest	15 mL
1/2 cup	golden raisins	125 mL
1/2 cup	pine nuts	125 mL

Fruity olive oil is the secret to making these moist, dense, lightly sweet muffins perfect. They are ideal with a cup of afternoon tea or with a morning coffee.

Makes 12 muffins

- Preheat oven to 350°F (180°C)
- 12-cup muffin pan, greased

1. In a large bowl, whisk together flour, baking powder and salt.
2. In a medium bowl, whisk together sugar, eggs, milk, oil and lemon zest until well blended.
3. Add the egg mixture to the flour mixture and stir until just blended. Gently fold in raisins.
4. Divide batter equally among prepared muffin cups. Sprinkle with pine nuts.
5. Bake in preheated oven for 23 to 25 minutes or until tops are golden and a toothpick inserted in the center comes out clean. Let cool in pan on a wire rack for 5 minutes, then transfer to the rack to cool.

Piemontese Hazelnut, Chocolate and Orange Muffins (Italy)

1³⁄₄ cups	all-purpose flour	425 mL
1 tsp	baking powder	5 mL
¹⁄₂ tsp	baking soda	2 mL
¹⁄₂ tsp	salt	2 mL
¹⁄₂ cup	granulated sugar	125 mL
1	egg	1
¹⁄₂ cup	sour cream	125 mL
¹⁄₂ cup	orange marmalade	125 mL
1 tsp	vanilla extract	5 mL
1 cup	chopped hazelnuts, toasted	250 mL
1 cup	miniature semisweet chocolate chips	250 mL

This easy muffin draws inspiration from a divine Italian cake: *torta di nocciole*. The recipe for the cake was crafted by the extraordinary Lidia Bastianich, author and expert cook of all things Italian.

Makes 12 muffins

- Preheat oven to 400°F (200°C)
- 12-cup muffin pan, lined with paper liners

1. In a large bowl, whisk together flour, baking powder, baking soda and salt.
2. In a medium bowl, whisk together sugar, egg, sour cream, marmalade and vanilla until well blended.
3. Add the egg mixture to the flour mixture and stir until just blended. Gently fold in hazelnuts and chocolate chips.
4. Divide batter equally among prepared muffin cups.
5. Bake in preheated oven for 18 to 23 minutes or until a toothpick inserted in the center comes out clean. Let cool in pan on a wire rack for 5 minutes, then transfer to the rack to cool.

Cannoli Muffins (Italy)

2 cups	all-purpose flour	500 mL
2 tsp	baking powder	10 mL
¹⁄₂ tsp	salt	2 mL
¹⁄₄ tsp	baking soda	1 mL
²⁄₃ cup	granulated sugar	150 mL
2	eggs	2
³⁄₄ cup	whole-milk ricotta cheese	175 mL
¹⁄₂ cup	unsalted butter, melted	125 mL
1 tsp	vanilla extract	5 mL
³⁄₄ tsp	almond extract	3 mL
³⁄₄ cup	miniature semisweet chocolate chips	175 mL
¹⁄₂ cup	roasted pistachios, coarsely chopped	125 mL

A vanilla- and almond-flavored ricotta batter, with chocolate chips and flecks of pistachio speckled throughout, makes for a perfect marriage of Italian and American.

Makes 12 muffins

- Preheat oven to 400°F (200°C)
- 12-cup muffin pan, greased

1. In a large bowl, whisk together flour, baking powder, salt and baking soda.
2. In a medium bowl, whisk together sugar, eggs, cheese, butter, vanilla and almond extract until well blended.
3. Add the egg mixture to the flour mixture and stir until just blended. Gently fold in chocolate chips and pistachios.
4. Divide batter equally among prepared muffin cups.
5. Bake in preheated oven for 22 to 25 minutes or until tops are golden and a toothpick inserted in the center comes out clean. Let cool in pan on a wire rack for 5 minutes, then transfer to the rack to cool.

Panettone Muffins (Italy)

³⁄₄ cup	golden raisins	175 mL
¹⁄₄ cup	Marsala wine	60 mL
2 cups	all-purpose flour	500 mL
2 tsp	baking powder	10 mL
¹⁄₂ tsp	baking soda	2 mL
¹⁄₂ tsp	salt	2 mL
¹⁄₂ cup	granulated sugar	125 mL
2	eggs	2
³⁄₄ cup	sour cream	175 mL
¹⁄₂ cup	unsalted butter, melted	125 mL
2 tsp	finely grated lemon zest	10 mL
¹⁄₂ cup	finely chopped citron	125 mL

This muffin gets its inspiration from panettone, a Milanese egg bread studded with raisins and candied fruit. Long a Christmastime specialty, panettone is becoming increasingly available throughout the year, not only in Italy, but also in North America.

Makes 12 muffins

- 12-cup muffin pan, greased

1. In a small saucepan, bring raisins and Marsala to a simmer over medium heat, then simmer for 2 minutes. Remove from heat and let cool to room temperature.
2. Preheat oven to 375°F (190°C).
3. In a large bowl, whisk together flour, baking powder, baking soda and salt.
4. In a medium bowl, whisk together sugar, eggs, sour cream, butter and lemon zest until well blended. Stir in raisin mixture until blended.
5. Add the egg mixture to the flour mixture and stir until just blended. Gently fold in citron.
6. Divide batter equally among prepared muffin cups.
7. Bake for 21 to 24 minutes or until tops are golden and a toothpick inserted in the center comes out clean. Let cool in pan on a wire rack for 5 minutes, then transfer to the rack to cool.

Caffè Corretto Muffins (Italy)

2¹⁄₄ cups	all-purpose flour	550 mL
1 tbsp	baking powder	15 mL
¹⁄₂ tsp	baking soda	2 mL
¹⁄₂ tsp	salt	2 mL
3 tbsp	grappa	45 mL
2 tbsp	instant espresso powder	30 mL
²⁄₃ cup	granulated sugar	150 mL
2	eggs	2
1 cup	sour cream	250 mL
¹⁄₂ cup	unsalted butter, melted	125 mL
2 tbsp	turbinado sugar	30 mL

For some, a day without espresso is unthinkable, but that doesn't mean you can't jazz up an old standby. Consider *caffè corretto*, espresso with a splash of liquor (e.g., grappa, sambuca, brandy). It's fantastic and provided ample inspiration for these spiked muffins.

Makes 12 muffins

- Preheat oven to 400°F (200°C)
- 12-cup muffin pan, greased

1. In a large bowl, whisk together flour, baking powder, baking soda and salt.
2. In a medium bowl, whisk together grappa and espresso powder until espresso powder is dissolved. Whisk in granulated sugar, eggs, sour cream and butter until well blended.
3. Add the egg mixture to the flour mixture and stir until just blended.
4. Divide batter equally among prepared muffin cups. Sprinkle with turbinado sugar.
5. Bake in preheated oven for 21 to 26 minutes or until tops are golden and a toothpick inserted in the center comes out clean. Let cool in pan on a wire rack for 5 minutes, then transfer to the rack to cool.

Napolitano Muffins (Italy)

1½ cups	sliced strawberries	375 mL
⅓ cup	granulated sugar	75 mL
1¾ cups	all-purpose flour	425 mL
2 tsp	baking powder	10 mL
½ tsp	baking soda	2 mL
½ tsp	salt	2 mL
1	egg	1
1 cup	sour cream	250 mL
¼ cup	unsalted butter, melted	60 mL
1 tsp	vanilla extract	5 mL
¾ cup	miniature semisweet chocolate chips	175 mL
1 tbsp	granulated sugar	15 mL

The combination of chocolate, strawberry and vanilla — Napolitano or Neapolitan — isn't just for ice cream sandwiches. Turning it into a muffin takes it in a different and delectable direction.

Makes 12 muffins

- Preheat oven to 400°F (200°C)
- 12-cup muffin pan, lined with paper liners

1. In a small bowl, using a potato masher, mash strawberries and ⅓ cup (75 mL) sugar. Let stand for 15 minutes to let strawberries release their juice.

2. In a large bowl, whisk together flour, baking powder, baking soda and salt.

3. In a medium bowl, whisk together egg, sour cream, butter and vanilla until well blended. Stir in strawberries with juice until blended.

4. Add the egg mixture to the flour mixture and stir until just blended. Gently fold in chocolate chips.

5. Divide batter equally among prepared muffin cups. Sprinkle with 1 tbsp (15 mL) sugar.

6. Bake in preheated oven for 17 to 22 minutes or until tops are golden and a toothpick inserted in the center comes out clean. Let cool in pan on a wire rack for 5 minutes, then transfer to the rack to cool.

Green Olive Almond Muffins (Spain)

2 cups	all-purpose flour	500 mL
2 tsp	baking powder	10 mL
1 tsp	dried oregano	5 mL
½ tsp	salt	5 mL
½ tsp	baking soda	5 mL
1 tbsp	granulated sugar	15 mL
2	eggs	2
1 cup	buttermilk	250 mL
½ cup	olive oil	125 mL
¾ cup	chopped pitted green olives	175 mL
½ cup	sliced almonds, toasted	125 mL

Olives and almonds are common offerings in many tapas restaurants across Spain. The combination also works wonders in these tender muffins.

Makes 12 muffins

- Preheat oven to 375°F (190°C)
- 12-cup muffin pan, lined with paper liners

1. In a large bowl, whisk together flour, baking powder, oregano, salt and baking soda.

2. In a medium bowl, whisk together sugar, eggs, buttermilk and oil until well blended.

3. Add the egg mixture to the flour mixture and stir until just blended. Gently fold in olives and almonds.

4. Divide batter equally among prepared muffin cups.

5. Bake in preheated oven for 20 to 25 minutes or until tops are golden and a toothpick inserted in the center comes out clean. Let cool in pan on a wire rack for 5 minutes, then transfer to the rack to cool.

Orange Muffins (Spain)

Muffins

¼ cup	finely grated orange zest (about 4 navel oranges)	60 mL
2 tbsp	freshly squeezed orange juice	30 mL
½ cup	granulated sugar, divided	125 mL
2 cups	all-purpose flour	500 mL
1½ tsp	baking powder	7 mL
1 tsp	baking soda	5 mL
½ tsp	salt	2 mL
2	eggs	2
⅓ cup	olive oil	75 mL
1½ cups	plain whole-milk yogurt	375 mL

Glaze

1 cup	confectioners' (icing) sugar	250 mL
1 tsp	finely grated orange zest	5 mL
2 tbsp	freshly squeezed orange juice	30 mL

My friends Anna and Jim spent a year living in Seville, and my husband and I were lucky enough to visit them during their stay. I'll never forget walking the orange tree–lined streets, nor the scent of orange blossoms that perfumed the air. As an homage, I created this muffin. The refreshing flavor of orange, mingled with subtle olive oil, makes for a guaranteed favorite.

Makes 16 muffins

- Preheat oven to 375°F (190°C)
- Two 12-cup muffin pans, 16 cups greased

1. *Muffins:* In a small saucepan, combine orange zest, orange juice and ¼ cup (60 mL) of the sugar. Bring to a simmer over medium heat. Simmer, stirring, for 2 to 3 minutes or until sugar is dissolved. Remove from heat and let cool slightly.

2. In a large bowl, whisk together flour, baking powder, baking soda and salt.

3. In a medium bowl, whisk together orange mixture, the remaining sugar, eggs and oil until well blended. Whisk in yogurt until blended.

4. Add the egg mixture to the flour mixture and stir until just blended.

5. Divide batter equally among prepared muffin cups.

6. Bake in preheated oven for 18 to 22 minutes or until tops are golden and a toothpick inserted in the center comes out clean. Let cool in pans on a wire rack for 5 minutes, then transfer to the rack while you prepare the glaze.

7. *Glaze:* In a small bowl, whisk together confectioners' sugar, orange zest and orange juice until blended. Spoon over warm muffin tops. Let cool.

Churros Muffins (Spain)

3 cups	cake flour	750 mL
1 tbsp	baking powder	15 mL
1 tsp	salt	5 mL
1/2 tsp	ground nutmeg	2 mL
2/3 cup	vegetable shortening	150 mL
1 3/4 cups	granulated sugar, divided	425 mL
2	eggs	2
1 cup	milk	250 mL
1/2 cup	unsalted butter, melted and still warm	125 mL
1 1/2 tsp	ground cinnamon	7 mL

Based on Spain's deep-fried doughnuts, these simple muffins are outrageously good. Rolling the feather-light muffins in butter and cinnamon sugar while they are still warm gives them the taste of being deep-fried. Once they are made, enjoy them with the ideal Spanish drink: rich hot chocolate.

Tip

Don't be tempted to use all-purpose flour here; cake flour makes these muffins light as a feather.

Makes 18 muffins

- Preheat oven to 325°F (160°C)
- Two 12-cup muffin pans, 18 cups greased

1. In a medium bowl, whisk together flour, baking powder, salt and nutmeg.
2. In large bowl, using an electric mixer on medium speed, beat shortening and 1 cup (250 mL) of the sugar until light and fluffy. Beat in eggs, one at a time, until well blended and pale yellow.
3. With the mixer on low speed, beat in flour mixture alternately with milk, making three additions of flour and two of milk, until just blended.
4. Divide batter equally among prepared muffin cups.
5. Bake in preheated oven for 23 to 26 minutes or until tops are golden and a toothpick inserted in the center comes out clean. Let cool in pans on a wire rack for 5 minutes, then transfer to the rack.
6. Pour butter into a small bowl. In another small bowl, combine cinnamon and the remaining sugar. Roll warm muffins in butter, then in sugar mixture to coat. Return to rack and let cool.

Golden Sherry Muffins (Spain)

2 cups	all-purpose flour	500 mL
2 1/2 tsp	baking powder	12 mL
1/2 tsp	salt	2 mL
2/3 cup	granulated sugar	150 mL
2	eggs	2
1/2 cup	heavy or whipping (35%) cream	125 mL
1/3 cup	sherry	75 mL
1/2 cup	unsalted butter, melted	125 mL
3 tbsp	turbinado sugar	45 mL

The mellow almond flavor of amontillado sherry works especially well in these refined muffins, but truth be told, almost any type of sweet sherry will yield stellar results.

Makes 12 muffins

- Preheat oven to 400°F (200°C)
- 12-cup muffin pan, lined with paper liners

1. In a large bowl, whisk together flour, baking powder and salt.
2. In a medium bowl, whisk together granulated sugar, eggs, cream and sherry until well blended. Whisk in butter until blended.
3. Add the egg mixture to the flour mixture and stir until just blended.
4. Divide batter equally among prepared muffin cups. Sprinkle with turbinado sugar.
5. Bake in preheated oven for 19 to 23 minutes or until tops are golden and firm to the touch and a toothpick inserted in the center comes out clean. Let cool in pan on a wire rack for 5 minutes, then transfer to the rack to cool.

Greek Yogurt Muffins (Greece)

1½ cups	plain whole-milk Greek yogurt	375 mL
1½ tsp	baking soda	7 mL
1¾ cups	all-purpose flour	425 mL
2 tsp	baking powder	10 mL
½ tsp	salt	2 mL
½ tsp	ground cloves	2 mL
¼ cup	granulated sugar	60 mL
2	eggs	2
½ cup	unsalted butter, melted	125 mL
½ cup	liquid honey	125 mL
2 tsp	finely grated lemon zest	10 mL
⅔ cup	golden raisins, chopped	150 mL

Greek yogurt is a gift from the gods, divine in all its thick, rich, creamy glory. I play up those attributes here with other traditional Greek flavors. Lemon zest and cloves bolster the yogurt's pleasing tartness; honey and golden raisins add sweetness and body.

Makes 12 muffins

- Preheat oven to 350°F (180°C)
- 12-cup muffin pan, lined with paper liners

1. In a medium bowl, whisk together yogurt and baking soda. Let stand for 5 minutes.
2. In a large bowl, whisk together flour, baking powder, salt and cloves.
3. Whisk sugar, eggs, butter, honey and lemon zest into yogurt mixture until well blended.
4. Add the egg mixture to the flour mixture and stir until just blended. Gently fold in raisins.
5. Divide batter equally among prepared muffin cups.
6. Bake in preheated oven for 24 to 28 minutes or until tops are golden and a toothpick inserted in the center comes out clean. Let cool in pan on a wire rack for 3 minutes, then transfer to the rack to cool.

Spanakopita Muffins (Greece)

3 cups	all-purpose flour	750 mL
1 tbsp	baking powder	15 mL
1½ tsp	dried dillweed	7 mL
1¼ tsp	salt	6 mL
3	eggs	3
1 cup	milk	250 mL
⅔ cup	vegetable oil	150 mL
½ cup	prepared basil pesto	125 mL
1	package (10 oz/300 g) frozen chopped spinach, thawed and squeezed dry	1
4 oz	feta cheese, crumbled	125 g

Spanakopita is a Greek spinach pie that is one of the most beloved dishes on the menus of Greek-American restaurants. Here, I've abandoned the fussy phyllo dough but kept all of the sensational flavors.

Makes 12 muffins

- Preheat oven to 400°F (200°C)
- 12-cup muffin pan, greased

1. In a large bowl, whisk together flour, baking powder, dill and salt.
2. In a medium bowl, whisk together eggs, milk, oil and pesto until well blended. Stir in spinach until blended.
3. Add the egg mixture to the flour mixture and stir until just blended. Gently fold in cheese.
4. Divide batter equally among prepared muffin cups.
5. Bake in preheated oven for 21 to 25 minutes or until tops are golden and a toothpick inserted in the center comes out clean. Let cool in pan on a wire rack for 5 minutes, then transfer to the rack to cool.

Baklava Muffins (Greece and the Middle East)

1½ cups	walnuts, toasted	375 mL
6 tbsp	packed light brown sugar, divided	90 mL
1½ tsp	ground cinnamon, divided	7 mL
¾ tsp	salt, divided	3 mL
1 tbsp	freshly squeezed lemon juice	15 mL
2 cups	all-purpose flour	500 mL
1 tsp	baking powder	5 mL
½ tsp	baking soda	2 mL
½ tsp	ground cardamom	2 mL
⅛ tsp	ground cloves	0.5 mL
1	egg	1
½ cup	liquid honey	125 mL
⅓ cup	milk	75 mL
⅓ cup	unsalted butter, melted	75 mL

Based on the buttery, nut-layered, spice- and lemon-infused pastry of the same name, these stuffed muffins could become a new coffee-time classic. This is one those muffins that magically improves as it sits. Don't get me wrong, they are scrumptious shortly after they emerge from the oven, but they are even better on the second day, as the flavors continue to mingle and meld.

Makes 12 muffins

- Preheat oven to 350°F (180°C)
- Food processor
- 12-cup muffin pan, greased

1. In food processor, process walnuts, 2 tbsp (30 mL) of the brown sugar, ½ tsp (2 mL) of the cinnamon and ¼ tsp (1 mL) of the salt until walnuts are finely ground. Add lemon juice and process until combined. Transfer ⅓ cup (75 mL) to a small bowl and set aside. Shape the remaining walnut mixture into 12 balls.

2. In a large bowl, whisk together the remaining cinnamon, the remaining salt, flour, baking powder, baking soda, cardamom and cloves.

3. In a medium bowl, whisk together the remaining brown sugar, egg, honey, milk and butter until well blended.

4. Add the egg mixture to the flour mixture and stir until just blended.

5. Divide batter equally among prepared muffin cups. Place a walnut ball in center of each cup, gently pressing into batter until covered. Sprinkle with the reserved walnut mixture.

6. Bake in preheated oven for 18 to 22 minutes or until tops are golden. Let cool in pan on a wire rack for 5 minutes, then transfer to the rack to cool.

Mogyoró Muffins (Hungary)

Muffins

2 cups	all-purpose flour	500 mL
2 tsp	baking powder	10 mL
1 tsp	ground cinnamon	5 mL
3/4 tsp	baking soda	3 mL
1/2 tsp	salt	2 mL
1/8 tsp	ground cloves	1 mL
3/4 cup	granulated sugar	175 mL
1/2 cup	unsalted butter, softened	125 mL
2	eggs	2
2 tsp	finely grated orange zest	10 mL
1 tsp	vanilla extract	5 mL
1/2 cup	freshly squeezed orange juice	125 mL
1 1/2 cups	chopped hazelnuts, toasted	375 mL

Glaze

1 cup	confectioners' (icing) sugar	250 mL
2 tbsp	freshly squeezed orange juice	30 mL

Mogyoró — hazelnuts — are ubiquitous in Hungarian confections, from cookies to cakes to candies. Here, they star in an easily assembled muffin. A tender crumb, crunchy nuts and a tangy-sweet orange glaze add up to a muffin with Old World style.

Makes 12 muffins

- Preheat oven to 400°F (200°C)
- 12-cup muffin pan, lined with paper liners

1. *Muffins:* In a large bowl, whisk together flour, baking powder, cinnamon, baking soda, salt and cloves.

2. In a large bowl, using an electric mixer on medium-high speed, beat sugar and butter until light and fluffy. Beat in eggs, one at a time, until well blended. Beat in orange zest and vanilla until blended. Beat in orange juice until blended.

3. Add the flour mixture to the egg mixture and, using a wooden spoon, stir until just blended. Gently fold in hazelnuts.

4. Divide batter equally among prepared muffin cups.

5. Bake in preheated oven for 18 to 21 minutes or until tops are golden and a toothpick inserted in the center comes out clean. Let cool in pan on a wire rack for 3 minutes, then transfer to the rack to cool.

6. *Glaze:* In a small bowl, whisk together confectioners' sugar and orange juice until blended. Spoon and spread over cooled muffin tops.

Turkish Coffee Muffins (Turkey)

2 cups	all-purpose flour	500 mL
1 1/4 tsp	ground cardamom	6 mL
1 1/4 tsp	baking soda	6 mL
1/4 tsp	salt	1 mL
2/3 cup	hot water	150 mL
3 tbsp	instant espresso powder	45 mL
3/4 cup	granulated sugar	175 mL
2	eggs	2
1/2 cup	dark (cooking) molasses	125 mL
1/3 cup	vegetable oil	75 mL
2 tbsp	confectioners' (icing) sugar	30 mL

Turkish coffee is prepared by boiling finely powdered roasted coffee beans along with sugar and cardamom in a pot called a *cezve*. It is then served in a small cup, where the dregs settle. The same marriage of cardamom and dark coffee is exceptional in these muffins.

Makes 12 muffins

- Preheat oven to 350°F (180°C)
- 12-cup muffin pan, lined with paper liners

1. In a medium bowl, whisk together flour, cardamom, baking soda and salt.

2. In a small bowl or glass measuring cup, whisk together hot water and espresso powder until espresso powder is dissolved.

3. In a large bowl, using an electric mixer on medium speed, beat granulated sugar and eggs until thick and pale yellow. Beat in molasses and oil until smooth.

4. With the mixer on low speed, beat in flour mixture alternately with espresso mixture, making three additions of flour and two of espresso, until just blended.

4. Divide batter equally among prepared muffin cups.

5. Bake in preheated oven for 24 to 27 minutes or until a toothpick inserted in the center comes out clean. Let cool in pan on a wire rack for 3 minutes, then transfer to the rack to cool. Dust cooled muffin tops with confectioners' (icing) sugar.

Simit Muffins (Turkey)

2 cups	all-purpose flour	500 mL
1 tbsp	baking powder	15 mL
1/2 tsp	salt	2 mL
1	egg	1
1 cup	milk	250 mL
2 tbsp	olive oil	30 mL
2 tbsp	unsalted butter, melted	30 mL
2 tbsp	sesame seeds	30 mL

Simit is a circular bread with sesame seeds; it is sometimes called a "Turkish bagel." Simit are often sold by street vendors, who either have a simit trolley or carry the simit in a tray on their head. Here, I recreate the classic simit taste in muffin form and add a deep depression in each muffin to mimic the characteristic circular shape.

Makes 12 muffins

- Preheat oven to 375°F (190°C)
- 12-cup muffin pan, greased

1. In a large bowl, whisk together flour, baking powder and salt.

2. In a medium bowl, whisk together egg, milk, oil and butter until well blended.

3. Add the egg mixture to the flour mixture and stir until just blended.

4. Divide batter equally among prepared muffin cups. Using a spoon, make a deep depression in the center of the batter in each cup. Generously sprinkle with sesame seeds.

5. Bake in preheated oven for 18 to 22 minutes or until tops are golden and a toothpick inserted in the center comes out clean. Let cool in pan on a wire rack for 5 minutes, then transfer to the rack to cool.

Spiced Fig Muffins (Albania)

2½ cups	all-purpose flour	625 mL
2½ tsp	baking powder	12 mL
½ tsp	salt	2 mL
½ tsp	ground cinnamon	2 mL
½ tsp	baking soda	2 mL
¼ tsp	ground cloves	1 mL
⅛ tsp	freshly ground black pepper	0.5 mL
2	eggs	2
1 cup	liquid honey	250 mL
¾ cup	whole-milk yogurt	175 mL
½ cup	olive oil	125 mL
1 tbsp	finely grated lemon zest	15 mL
1 cup	chopped dried figs	300 mL

These muffins were developed for my dear friend Eralda, a beautiful, brilliant woman and fabulous cook, who hails from Albania. We share a strong affection for figs (they are native to her homeland, Albania, and are grown in my home state, California), so I thought it fitting to develop a muffin based on an Albanian honey and spice stewed fig recipe, *hoshaf me fiq të thatë*. In a word, they are heavenly.

Tip
Choose vacuum-packed dried figs for this recipe. They are typically shelved with raisins in the supermarket and are far softer than some of the hard-skinned options found in other sections of the store.

Makes 12 muffins
- Preheat oven to 350°F (180°C)
- 12-cup muffin pan, greased

1. In a large bowl, whisk together flour, baking powder, salt, cinnamon, baking soda, cloves and pepper.
2. In a medium bowl, whisk together eggs, honey, yogurt, oil and lemon zest until well blended.
3. Add the egg mixture to the flour mixture and stir until just blended. Gently fold in figs.
4. Divide batter equally among prepared muffin cups.
5. Bake in preheated oven for 23 to 25 minutes or until tops are golden and a toothpick inserted in the center comes out clean. Let cool in pan on a wire rack for 5 minutes, then transfer to the rack to cool.

Rugalach Muffins (Eastern Europe)

2 cups	all-purpose flour	500 mL
1 1/2 tsp	baking powder	7 mL
1/2 tsp	salt	2 mL
1 1/2 cups	granulated sugar, divided	375 mL
8 oz	cream cheese, softened	250 g
1 cup	unsalted butter, softened	250 mL
1 tsp	vanilla extract	5 mL
4	eggs	4
1/2 cup	golden raisins, chopped	125 mL
1/2 cup	finely chopped walnuts, toasted	125 mL
1 tsp	ground cinnamon	5 mL
1/4 cup	apricot preserves	60 mL

Popular throughout Eastern Europe, rugalach are rolled triangles of tender pastry encasing a not-too-sweet fruit, nut and spice filling. I've captured the same flavors here: each muffin boasts a batter rich in cream cheese and butter, layered with walnuts, raisins and cinnamon, imbued with the floral notes of vanilla and finished with a surprise of apricot preserves.

Makes 18 muffins

- Preheat oven to 350°F (180°C)
- Two 12-cup muffin pans, 18 cups lined with paper liners

1. In a medium bowl, whisk together flour, baking powder and salt.
2. In a large bowl, using an electric mixer on medium-high speed, beat 1 1/4 cups (300 mL) of the sugar, cream cheese, butter and vanilla until light and fluffy. Beat in eggs, one at a time, until well blended.
3. With the mixer on low speed, beat the flour mixture into the egg mixture until just blended.
4. In a small bowl, combine the remaining sugar, raisins, walnuts and cinnamon.
5. Divide half the batter equally among prepared muffin cups. Spoon 1 tsp (5 mL) preserves, then 1 tbsp (15 mL) raisin mixture into the center of each cup. Top with the remaining batter.
6. Bake in preheated oven for 25 to 30 minutes or until tops are golden and firm to the touch. Let cool in pans on a wire rack for 5 minutes, then transfer to the rack to cool.

Khachapuri Muffins (Georgia)

2 1/4 cups	all-purpose flour	550 mL
4 tsp	baking powder	20 mL
2 tsp	granulated sugar	10 mL
2 tsp	sweet paprika, divided	10 mL
3/4 tsp	freshly ground black pepper	3 mL
3/4 tsp	salt	3 mL
3/4 tsp	ground coriander	3 mL
2	eggs	2
1/2 cup	unsalted butter, melted	125 mL
1 1/4 cups	whole milk	300 mL
4 oz	shredded Muenster cheese	125 g
4 oz	mild creamy goat cheese, crumbled	125 g

Georgians make khachapuri into large loaves for special occasions, but it can also be found fashioned into handheld diamond shapes, or "beggars' purses."

Makes 16 muffins

- Preheat oven to 400°F (200°C)
- Two 12-cup muffin pans, 16 cups greased

1. In a large bowl, whisk together flour, baking powder, sugar, 1 tsp (5 mL) of the paprika, pepper, salt and coriander.
2. In a medium bowl, whisk together eggs and butter until well blended. Whisk in milk until blended.
3. Add the egg mixture to the flour mixture and stir until just blended. Gently fold in Muenster and goat cheese.
4. Divide batter equally among prepared muffin cups. Sprinkle with the remaining paprika.
5. Bake in preheated oven for 21 to 26 minutes or until a toothpick inserted in the center comes out clean. Let cool in pans on a wire rack for 5 minutes, then transfer to the rack to cool.

Russian Tea Cake Muffins (Russia)

1¼ cups	chopped hazelnuts, toasted and cooled	300 mL
¾ cup	granulated sugar	175 mL
2 tsp	finely grated lemon zest	10 mL
1⅓ cups	all-purpose flour	325 mL
2 tsp	baking powder	10 mL
½ tsp	salt	2 mL
1	egg	1
1 cup	milk	250 mL
⅓ cup	unsalted butter, melted	75 mL
1 tsp	vanilla extract	5 mL
¼ tsp	almond extract	1 mL
2 tbsp	confectioners' (icing) sugar	30 mL

These melt-in-your mouth muffins are based on a shortbread-like cookie that goes by many names: Russian tea cake, Mexican wedding cake, Italian butter nut, Southern pecan butterball and snowball, to name a few. The secret to making these muffins as good as the cookies is to use the freshest butter and nuts and pure vanilla extract.

Tip

It is very important to let the toasted nuts cool completely before grinding them in the food processor. If they are still warm, they will turn to paste rather than ground meal.

Variation

Mexican Wedding Muffins: Prepare as directed, substituting cooled toasted slivered almonds for the hazelnuts. Increase the almond extract to ½ tsp (2 mL) and replace the lemon zest with ½ tsp (2 mL) ground cinnamon.

Makes 12 muffins

- Preheat oven to 400°F (200°C)
- Food processor
- 12-cup muffin pan, greased

1. In food processor, process hazelnuts, granulated sugar and lemon zest until finely ground.

2. In a large bowl, whisk together hazelnut mixture, flour, baking powder and salt.

3. In a medium bowl, whisk together egg, milk, butter, vanilla and almond extract until well blended.

4. Add the egg mixture to the flour mixture and stir until just blended.

5. Divide batter equally among prepared muffin cups.

6. Bake in preheated oven for 18 to 22 minutes or until tops are golden and a toothpick inserted in the center comes out clean. Let cool in pan on a wire rack for 5 minutes, then transfer to the rack to cool.

7. Sprinkle cooled muffin tops with confectioners' sugar just before serving.

Kulich Muffins (Russia)

Muffins

2 tbsp	dark rum	30 mL
3/4 cup	chopped mixed dried fruit	175 mL
Pinch	saffron threads	Pinch
2 1/3 cups	all-purpose flour	575 mL
1 tbsp	baking powder	15 mL
1/2 tsp	salt	2 mL
3/4 cup	granulated sugar	175 mL
1	egg	1
1 cup	half-and-half (10%) cream	250 mL
1/4 cup	unsalted butter, melted	60 mL
1 tsp	vanilla extract	5 mL
1/2 cup	sliced almonds, toasted	125 mL

Icing

1 cup	confectioners' (icing) sugar	250 mL
1 tsp	finely grated lemon zest	5 mL
1 1/2 tbsp	freshly squeezed lemon juice	22 mL

Kulich is a traditional Russian Easter bread, rich with candied fruit, almonds and raisins and flavored with rum and saffron. It is always baked in a tall, cylindrical pan, and once done, it is decorated with white or lemon frosting drizzled down the sides. On the side, spelled out in pieces of candied fruit, are the letters "XB," representing the Cyrillic letters for *Christos voskres* — "Christ is risen." While classic kulich takes days to prepare, my muffins are ready to savor in an hour.

Makes 12 muffins

- 12-cup muffin pan, lined with paper liners

1. *Muffins:* In a small saucepan, bring rum to a simmer over medium-high heat. Remove from heat and add dried fruit and saffron. Let stand for 15 minutes.
2. Preheat oven to 375°F (190°C).
3. In a large bowl, whisk together flour, baking powder and salt.
4. In a medium bowl, whisk together sugar, egg, cream, butter and vanilla until well blended.
5. Add the egg mixture to the flour mixture and stir until just blended. Gently fold in rum mixture and almonds.
6. Divide batter equally among prepared muffin cups.
7. Bake for 25 to 30 minutes or until tops are golden and a toothpick inserted in the center comes out clean. Let cool in pan on a wire rack for 5 minutes, then transfer to the rack while you prepare the icing.
8. *Icing:* In a small bowl, whisk together confectioners' sugar, lemon zest and lemon juice until blended. Spoon over warm muffin tops. Let cool.

Black Bread Muffins (Russia)

1 cup	rye flour	250 mL
1 cup	all-purpose flour	250 mL
1/3 cup	natural bran	75 mL
2 tbsp	unsweetened cocoa powder (not Dutch process)	30 mL
2 tsp	baking powder	10 mL
1 tsp	baking soda	5 mL
1 tsp	salt	5 mL
3/4 tsp	fennel seeds, crushed	3 mL
1/2 tsp	caraway seeds, crushed	2 mL
2 tsp	instant espresso powder	10 mL
1	egg	1
1/4 cup	dark (cooking) molasses	60 mL
1/4 cup	unsalted butter, melted	60 mL
1 tbsp	cider vinegar	15 mL
1 cup	buttermilk	250 mL

Makes 12 muffins

- Preheat oven to 375°F (190°C)
- 12-cup muffin pan, greased

1. In a large bowl, whisk together rye flour, all-purpose flour, bran, cocoa powder, baking powder, baking soda, salt, fennel seeds and caraway seeds.

2. In a medium bowl, whisk together espresso powder, egg, molasses, butter and vinegar until well blended. Whisk in buttermilk until blended.

3. Add the egg mixture to the flour mixture and stir until just blended.

4. Divide batter equally among prepared muffin cups.

5. Bake in preheated oven for 20 to 25 minutes or until a toothpick inserted in the center comes out clean. Let cool in pan on a wire rack for 5 minutes, then transfer to the rack to cool.

Chocolate Babka Muffins (Poland and Russia)

Topping

2 tbsp	granulated sugar	30 mL
1/4 tsp	ground cinnamon	1 mL

Muffins

2 cups	all-purpose flour	500 mL
1 tsp	salt	5 mL
1 tsp	baking powder	5 mL
1/2 tsp	baking soda	2 mL
1 1/2 cups	unsalted butter, softened	375 mL
1 cup	granulated sugar	250 mL
2	eggs	2
1 cup	sour cream	250 mL
1 tsp	vanilla extract	5 mL
6 oz	bittersweet chocolate, chopped	175 g

Laden with chocolate, butter and Old World charm, these babka-inspired muffins are spectacular served with coffee or espresso drinks.

Makes 14 muffins

- Preheat oven to 400°F (200°C)
- Two 12-cup muffin pans, 14 cups lined with paper liners

1. *Topping:* In a small bowl, combine sugar and cinnamon. Set aside.

2. *Muffins:* In a medium bowl, whisk together flour, salt, baking powder and baking soda.

3. In a large bowl, using an electric mixer on medium-high speed, beat butter and sugar until light and fluffy. Beat in eggs, one at a time, until well blended. Beat in sour cream and vanilla until blended.

4. Add the flour mixture to the egg mixture and, using a wooden spoon, stir until just blended.

5. Divide half the batter equally among prepared muffin cups. Sprinkle chocolate evenly in each cup. Top with the remaining batter. Sprinkle with topping.

6. Bake in preheated oven for 20 to 25 minutes or until a toothpick inserted in the center comes out clean. Let cool in pans on a wire rack for 5 minutes, then transfer to the rack to cool.

Tahini Muffins (Israel)

Muffins

2 cups	quick-cooking rolled oats	500 mL
1 cup	all-purpose flour	250 mL
1/2 cup	whole wheat flour	125 mL
2 tsp	baking powder	10 mL
1/2 tsp	baking soda	2 mL
1/2 tsp	salt	2 mL
1 cup	packed light brown sugar	250 mL
2	eggs	2
1 cup	milk	250 mL
1/2 cup	tahini, well-stirred	125 mL
1/2 cup	unsalted butter, melted	125 mL
1 tsp	vanilla extract	5 mL
1/2 cup	finely chopped walnuts, toasted	125 mL

Glaze

1/3 cup	tahini, well-stirred	75 mL
2 tbsp	milk	30 mL
1 tsp	vanilla extract	5 mL
1 cup	confectioners' (icing) sugar	250 mL

Tahini is just as delicious — I would argue even more so — in sweets as it is in hummus and baba ghanouj.

Makes 18 muffins

- Preheat oven to 350°F (180°C)
- Two 12-cup muffin pans, 18 cups greased

1. *Muffins:* In a large bowl, whisk together oats, all-purpose flour, whole wheat flour, baking powder, baking soda and salt.

2. In a medium bowl, whisk together brown sugar, eggs, milk, tahini, butter and vanilla until well blended.

3. Add the egg mixture to the flour mixture and stir until just blended. Gently fold in walnuts.

4. Divide batter equally among prepared muffin cups.

5. Bake in preheated oven for 22 to 27 minutes or until tops are golden brown and a toothpick inserted in the center comes out clean. Let cool in pans on a wire rack for 5 minutes, then transfer to the rack to cool.

6. *Glaze:* In a small bowl, whisk together tahini, milk and vanilla until blended. Whisk in confectioners' sugar until blended and smooth. Spoon over cooled muffin tops.

Rose Water Muffins (Iraq, Iran, Turkey, India)

Muffins

2¼ cups	all-purpose flour	550 mL
1 tbsp	baking powder	15 mL
½ tsp	baking soda	2 mL
½ tsp	salt	2 mL
½ tsp	ground cardamom	2 mL
¾ cup	granulated sugar	175 mL
2	eggs	2
⅓ cup	unsalted butter, melted	75 mL
1 tsp	rose water	5 mL
1⅓ cups	plain whole-milk yogurt	325 mL

Icing

1 cup	confectioners' (icing) sugar	250 mL
2 tbsp	milk	30 mL
½ tsp	rose water	2 mL

These easily assembled butter and yogurt muffins, with a drizzle of rose-scented icing and a cardamom-infused batter, are inspired by the aromatics found in Persian, Turkish and Indian confections.

Makes 12 muffins

- Preheat oven to 400°F (200°C)
- 12-cup muffin pan, greased

1. *Muffins:* In a large bowl, whisk together flour, baking powder, baking soda, salt and cardamom.

2. In a medium bowl, whisk together sugar, eggs, butter and rose water until well blended. Whisk in yogurt until blended.

3. Add the egg mixture to the flour mixture and stir until just blended.

4. Divide batter equally among prepared muffin cups.

5. Bake in preheated oven for 21 to 26 minutes or until tops are golden and firm to the touch. Let cool in pan on a wire rack for 5 minutes, then transfer to the rack to cool.

6. *Icing:* In a small bowl, whisk together confectioners' sugar, milk and rose water until blended and smooth. Drizzle over cooled muffin tops.

Ma'amoul Muffins (Saudi Arabia)

2 cups	all-purpose flour	500 mL
2 tsp	baking powder	10 mL
¾ tsp	salt	3 mL
1¼ cups	granulated sugar	300 mL
¾ cup	unsalted butter, softened	175 mL
3	eggs	3
¾ cup	milk	175 mL
2 tsp	rose water	10 mL
⅔ cup	finely chopped walnuts or pistachios, toasted	150 mL
⅔ cup	pitted dates, chopped	150 mL

Ma'amoul are traditional cookies served in the Middle East during special holidays. There are three kinds of *ma'amoul* fillings: walnut, pistachio and date. Here, I've combined both dates and nuts into one exceptional muffin.

Makes 12 muffins

- Preheat oven to 350°F (180°C)
- 12-cup muffin pan, greased

1. In a medium bowl, whisk together flour, baking powder and salt.

2. In a large bowl, using an electric mixer on medium-high speed, beat sugar and butter until light and fluffy. Beat in eggs, one at a time, until well blended. Beat in milk and rose water until blended.

3. Add the flour mixture to the egg mixture and, using a wooden spoon, stir until just blended. Gently fold in walnuts and dates.

4. Divide batter equally among prepared muffin cups.

5. Bake in preheated oven for 23 to 26 minutes or until tops are golden and a toothpick inserted in the center comes out clean. Let cool in pan on a wire rack for 5 minutes, then transfer to the rack to cool.

Persian Apricot Muffins (Iran)

2¼ cups	all-purpose flour	550 mL
1 tbsp	baking powder	15 mL
1½ tsp	ground cardamom	7 mL
½ tsp	ground cinnamon	2 mL
½ tsp	ground ginger	2 mL
½ tsp	baking soda	2 mL
½ tsp	salt	2 mL
1 cup	granulated sugar	250 mL
3	jars (each 4 oz or 128 mL) apricot purée baby food	3
2	eggs	2
½ cup	plain whole-milk yogurt	125 mL
½ cup	unsalted butter, melted	125 mL
¾ cup	chopped dried apricots	175 mL

Apricots are a favored fruit in Iranian cuisine. They are typically served very simply, but also make their way into more complex desserts, combined with fragrant herbs and spices, such as cardamom, ginger and cinnamon.

Tips

The secret to these moist muffins comes from the baby food section of the grocery store: puréed apricots.

The batter will come up to the rim of each filled cup.

Makes 12 muffins

- Preheat oven to 350°F (180°C)
- 12-cup muffin pan, greased

1. In a large bowl, whisk together flour, baking powder, cardamom, cinnamon, ginger, baking soda and salt.

2. In a medium bowl, whisk together sugar, apricot purée, eggs, yogurt and butter until well blended.

3. Add the egg mixture to the flour mixture and stir until just blended. Gently fold in apricots.

4. Divide batter equally among prepared muffin cups.

5. Bake in preheated oven for 24 to 28 minutes or until tops are golden and a toothpick inserted in the center comes out clean. Let cool in pan on a wire rack for 5 minutes, then transfer to the rack to cool.

Pistachio Streusel Muffins (Iran)

³/₄ cup	packed light brown sugar	175 mL
³/₄ cup	chopped pistachios	175 mL
1¹/₄ tsp	ground cardamom, divided	6 mL
2 cups	all-purpose flour	500 mL
2¹/₂ tsp	baking powder	12 mL
¹/₂ tsp	baking soda	2 mL
¹/₂ tsp	salt	2 mL
1 cup	granulated sugar	250 mL
2	eggs	2
1 cup	plain whole-milk yogurt	250 mL
¹/₄ cup	unsalted butter, melted	60 mL
³/₄ tsp	almond extract	3 mL

These delicious, exotic, Persian-influenced muffins incorporate a blend of Iranian ingredients — pistachios, cardamom and yogurt — in a golden, buttery muffin.

Makes 12 muffins

- Preheat oven to 400°F (200°C)
- 12-cup muffin pan, lined with paper liners

1. In a small bowl, combine brown sugar, pistachios and ¹/₄ tsp (1 mL) of the cardamom.
2. In a large bowl, whisk together flour, baking powder, baking soda, salt and the remaining cardamom.
3. In a medium bowl, whisk together granulated sugar, eggs, yogurt, butter and almond extract until well blended.
4. Add the egg mixture to the flour mixture and stir until just blended.
5. Divide half the batter equally among prepared muffin cups. Sprinkle with half the pistachio mixture. Top with the remaining batter. Sprinkle with the remaining pistachio mixture and gently press into batter.
6. Bake in preheated oven for 22 to 26 minutes or until tops are golden and a toothpick inserted in the center comes out clean. Let cool in pan on a wire rack for 3 minutes, then transfer to the rack to cool.

Stuffed Date Almond Muffins (Lebanon)

2 cups	pitted dates, chopped	500 mL
1 cup	boiling water	250 mL
1 tsp	baking soda	5 mL
2 cups	all-purpose flour	500 mL
1 tsp	baking powder	5 mL
¹/₂ tsp	salt	2 mL
¹/₄ tsp	ground cloves	1 mL
³/₄ cup	packed dark brown sugar	175 mL
1	egg	1
²/₃ cup	plain whole-milk yogurt	150 mL
¹/₃ cup	unsalted butter, melted	75 mL
1 tbsp	finely grated lemon zest	15 mL
³/₄ cup	slivered almonds, toasted	175 mL

I've captured the essential flavors of *Murabba el balah* — dates, almonds, a pinch of cloves and lemon zest — in these rich muffins.

Makes 12 muffins

- 12-cup muffin pan, greased

1. In a medium bowl, combine dates, boiling water and baking soda. Cover and let stand for 30 minutes. Do not drain.
2. Preheat oven to 350°F (180°C).
3. In a large bowl, whisk together flour, baking powder, salt and cloves.
4. In another medium bowl, whisk together brown sugar, egg, yogurt, butter and lemon zest until well blended. Stir in date mixture until blended.
5. Add the egg mixture to the flour mixture and stir until just blended. Gently fold in almonds.
6. Divide batter equally among muffin cups, smoothing batter with a rubber spatula.
7. Bake in preheated oven for 22 to 25 minutes or until tops are dark golden and a toothpick inserted in the center comes out with a few crumbs attached. Let cool in pan on a wire rack for 5 minutes, then transfer to the rack to cool.

Tabbouleh Muffins (Lebanon, Israel, Syria)

1/2 cup	bulgur	125 mL
1 cup	boiling water	250 mL
1 1/2 cups	all-purpose flour	375 mL
2 1/2 tsp	baking powder	12 mL
1 1/4 tsp	salt	6 mL
3/4 tsp	baking soda	3 mL
1/4 tsp	ground cinnamon	1 mL
2 tbsp	granulated sugar	30 mL
1	egg	1
2/3 cup	milk	150 mL
1/2 cup	olive oil	125 mL
1 tbsp	finely grated lemon zest	15 mL
2 tbsp	freshly squeezed lemon juice	30 mL
1/2 cup	chopped green onions (scallions)	125 mL
1/2 cup	loosely packed fresh mint leaves, chopped	125 mL
1/2 cup	chopped drained oil-packed sun-dried tomatoes	125 mL

Tabbouleh is quintessential Middle Eastern fare, a delectable combination of bulgur (cracked wheat), tomatoes, fresh herbs and lemon. When I was experimenting with bulgur in several other recipes in this collection, it dawned on me that I could reinterpret this favorite salad into a portable muffin. I think you'll love the result as much as I do.

Tip

You can use the oil from the tomatoes to make up some of the oil needed for the muffin batter.

Makes 12 muffins

- 12-cup muffin pan, greased

1. In a small bowl, combine bulgur and boiling water. Let stand for 30 minutes. Drain off any excess water.
2. Preheat oven to 425°F (220°C).
3. In a large bowl, whisk together flour, baking powder, salt, baking soda and cinnamon.
4. In a medium bowl, whisk together sugar, egg, milk, oil, lemon zest and lemon juice until well blended.
5. Add the egg mixture to the flour mixture and stir until just blended. Gently stir in bulgur, green onions, mint and tomatoes.
6. Divide batter equally among prepared muffin cups.
7. Bake in preheated oven for 16 to 20 minutes or until tops are golden brown and a toothpick inserted in the center comes out clean. Let cool in pan on a wire rack for 5 minutes, then transfer to the rack to cool slightly and serve warm or let cool completely.

Muhammara Muffins (Syria)

2 cups	all-purpose flour	500 mL
1 tbsp	baking powder	15 mL
2 tsp	ground cumin	10 mL
1/2 tsp	salt	2 mL
1/4 tsp	cayenne pepper	1 mL
1/4 tsp	baking soda	1 mL
1 cup	walnut halves, toasted, finely chopped	250 mL
1	egg	1
2/3 cup	milk	150 mL
1/3 cup	olive oil	75 mL
1 tsp	finely grated lemon zest	5 mL
1 tbsp	freshly squeezed lemon juice	15 mL
1 tbsp	pomegranate molasses or liquid honey	15 mL
1	jar (7 oz/200 g) roasted red peppers, drained, patted dry and chopped	1

Makes 12 muffins

- Preheat oven to 350°F (180°C)
- 12-cup muffin pan, lined with paper liners

1. In a large bowl, whisk together flour, baking powder, cumin, salt, cayenne and baking soda. Stir in walnuts.

2. In a medium bowl, whisk together egg, milk, oil, lemon zest, lemon juice and pomegranate molasses until well blended.

3. Add the egg mixture to the flour mixture and stir until just blended. Gently fold in roasted peppers.

4. Divide batter equally among prepared muffin cups.

5. Bake in preheated oven for 21 to 25 minutes or until a toothpick inserted in the center comes out clean. Let cool in pan on a wire rack for 5 minutes, then transfer to the rack to cool.

Muhammara is a roasted red pepper purée seasoned with walnuts, pomegranate molasses and hot red pepper. I've captured the same multiplex of flavor in these muffins.

Sesame Pistachio Muffins (Syria)

2 cups	all-purpose flour	500 mL
1 1/2 tsp	baking soda	7 mL
1/2 tsp	salt	2 mL
2	eggs	2
1 cup	plain whole-milk yogurt	250 mL
1/2 cup	liquid honey	125 mL
1/3 cup	unsalted butter, melted	75 mL
1/2 cup	lightly salted pistachios, chopped	125 mL
1/2 cup	sesame seeds, divided	125 mL

Makes 12 muffins

- Preheat oven to 350°F (180°C)
- 12-cup muffin pan, greased

1. In a large bowl, whisk together flour, baking soda and salt.

2. In a medium bowl, whisk together eggs, yogurt, honey and butter until well blended.

3. Add the egg mixture to the flour mixture and stir until just blended. Gently fold in pistachios and all but 1 tbsp (15 mL) of the sesame seeds.

4. Divide batter equally among prepared muffin cups. Sprinkle with the remaining sesame seeds.

5. Bake in preheated oven for 15 to 20 minutes or until tops are golden and a toothpick inserted in the center comes out clean. Let cool in pan on a wire rack for 5 minutes, then transfer to the rack to cool.

You will be captivated by the taste of these muffins, based on barazak cookies, which have been peddled on the streets of Damascus for centuries.

Orange Flower Water Muffins (Algeria)

2½ cups	all-purpose flour	625 mL
2½ tsp	baking powder	12 mL
½ tsp	salt	2 mL
2	eggs	2
1 cup	liquid honey	250 mL
¾ cup	milk	175 mL
½ cup	olive oil	125 mL
1 tbsp	finely grated orange zest	15 mL
1½ tsp	orange flower water	7 mL
¾ cup	golden raisins, chopped	175 mL

A perfumed distillation of bitter orange blossoms, orange flower water is used in many North African sweets. It has a delicate, floral taste and fragrance that works especially well with citrus and honey.

Tip
Look for orange flower water at liquor stores and in the international or specialty foods sections of some supermarkets.

Makes 12 muffins
- Preheat oven to 350°F (180°C)
- 12-cup muffin pan, greased

1. In a large bowl, whisk together flour, baking powder and salt.

2. In a medium bowl, whisk together eggs, honey, milk, oil, orange zest and orange flower water until well blended.

3. Add the egg mixture to the flour mixture and stir until just blended. Gently fold in raisins.

4. Divide batter equally among prepared muffin cups.

5. Bake in preheated oven for 23 to 25 minutes or until tops are golden and a toothpick inserted in the center comes out clean. Let cool in pan on a wire rack for 5 minutes, then transfer to the rack to cool.

Ethiopian Honey Muffins (Ethiopia)

2¾ cups	all-purpose flour	675 mL
1 tbsp	baking powder	15 mL
1½ tsp	ground coriander	7 mL
½ tsp	ground cinnamon	2 mL
½ tsp	baking soda	2 mL
½ tsp	salt	2 mL
¼ tsp	ground cloves	1 mL
½ cup	unsalted butter, softened	125 mL
¾ cup	liquid honey	175 mL
2	eggs	2
1 cup	milk	250 mL

Based on the bread *Yemarina Yewotet Dabo*, these muffins showcase an underutilized spice, coriander.

Makes 12 muffins
- Preheat oven to 400°F (200°C)
- 12-cup muffin pan, greased

1. In a medium bowl, whisk together flour, baking powder, coriander, cinnamon, baking soda, salt and cloves.

2. In a large bowl, using an electric mixer on medium-high speed, beat butter and honey until well blended. Beat in eggs, one at a time, until well blended. Beat in milk until blended.

3. Add the flour mixture to the egg mixture and, using a wooden spoon, stir until just blended.

4. Divide batter equally among prepared muffin cups.

5. Bake in preheated oven for 20 to 25 minutes or until tops are golden and a toothpick inserted in the center comes out clean. Let cool in pan on a wire rack for 5 minutes, then transfer to the rack to cool.

Ras el Hanout Muffins (Morocco and Tunisia)

2 cups	all-purpose flour	500 mL
2 tsp	baking powder	10 mL
3/4 tsp	ground cumin	3 mL
1/2 tsp	ground ginger	2 mL
1/2 tsp	baking soda	2 mL
1/2 tsp	salt	2 mL
1/4 tsp	freshly ground black pepper	1 mL
1/4 tsp	ground cinnamon	1 mL
1/4 tsp	ground coriander	1 mL
1/4 tsp	cayenne pepper	1 mL
1/4 tsp	ground allspice	1 mL
1/8 tsp	ground cloves	0.5 mL
1 tbsp	granulated sugar	15 mL
2	eggs	2
1 cup	plain whole-milk yogurt	250 mL
1/2 cup	olive oil	125 mL

Ras el hanout is a complex blend of many herbs and spices that is used across the Middle East and North Africa. The name means "head of the shop" in Arabic and refers to a mixture of the best spices a seller has to offer. The fragrant blend shines in a simple batter made with two other common North African ingredients: yogurt and olive oil. Serve these muffins with roast chicken or a vegetable stew.

Makes 12 muffins

- Preheat oven to 375°F (190°C)
- 12-cup muffin pan, lined with paper liners

1. In a large bowl, whisk together flour, baking powder, cumin, ginger, baking soda, salt, pepper, cinnamon, coriander, cayenne, allspice and cloves.
2. In a medium bowl, whisk together sugar, eggs, yogurt and oil until well blended.
3. Add the egg mixture to the flour mixture and stir until just blended.
4. Divide batter equally among prepared muffin cups.
5. Bake in preheated oven for 20 to 25 minutes or until tops are golden and a toothpick inserted in the center comes out clean. Let cool in pan on a wire rack for 5 minutes, then transfer to the rack to cool slightly. Serve warm.

Couscous Date Muffins (Morocco)

1 cup	couscous	250 mL
1 cup	boiling water	250 mL
1¾ cups	all-purpose flour	425 mL
1 tsp	baking powder	5 mL
½ tsp	baking soda	2 mL
½ tsp	salt	2 mL
½ cup	granulated sugar	125 mL
1	egg	1
½ cup	plain whole-milk yogurt	125 mL
½ cup	orange marmalade	125 mL
1 cup	pitted dates, chopped	250 mL

Couscous and dates are staples of the Moroccan table. Both are used in savory dishes but also star in a variety of simple desserts. These muffins showcase both ingredients with panache. Orange marmalade adds extra flavor.

Makes 12 muffins

- Preheat oven to 400°F (200°C)
- 12-cup muffin pan, lined with paper liners

1. In a small bowl, combine couscous and boiling water. Cover with a plate and let stand for 5 minutes. Uncover and fluff with a fork. Let cool to room temperature.
2. In a large bowl, whisk together flour, baking powder, baking soda and salt.
3. In a medium bowl, whisk together sugar, egg, yogurt and marmalade until well blended.
4. Add the egg mixture to the flour mixture and stir until just blended. Gently fold in couscous and dates.
5. Divide batter evenly among prepared muffin cups.
6. Bake in preheated oven for 17 to 22 minutes or until a toothpick inserted in the center comes out clean. Let cool in pan on a wire rack for 5 minutes, then transfer to the rack to cool.

Caakiri Muffins (West Africa)

1 cup	millet	250 mL
1½ cups	all-purpose flour	375 mL
2 tsp	baking powder	10 mL
½ tsp	baking soda	2 mL
½ tsp	salt	2 mL
¼ tsp	ground nutmeg	1 mL
1¼ cups	packed light brown sugar	300 mL
2	eggs	2
⅔ cup	unsalted butter, melted	150 mL
1 tsp	vanilla extract	5 mL
1¾ cups	buttermilk	425 mL
1 cup	golden raisins	250 mL

Caakiri is a West African dessert akin to rice pudding, made with millet, fermented milk, sugar, butter and raisins. I've long been a fan of millet muffins, so it was pure pleasure to transform this classic African dessert into muffin form.

Makes 16 muffins

- Preheat oven to 350°F (180°C)
- Two 12-cup muffin pans, 16 cups greased

1. Place millet in a large ziplock bag and seal bag. Using a kitchen mallet, gently hammer until coarsely crushed but not pulverized.
2. In a large bowl, whisk together flour, baking powder, baking soda, salt and nutmeg. Whisk in millet.
3. In a medium bowl, whisk together brown sugar, eggs, butter and vanilla until well blended. Whisk in buttermilk until blended.
4. Add the egg mixture to the flour mixture and stir until just blended. Gently fold in raisins.
5. Divide batter equally among prepared muffin cups.
6. Bake in preheated oven for 20 to 25 minutes or until tops are golden and a toothpick inserted in the center comes out clean. Let cool in pans on a wire rack for 5 minutes, then transfer to the rack to cool.

Sugared Peanut Muffins
(West and Central Africa)

Topping

2/3 cup	lightly salted dry-roasted peanuts	150 mL
1/3 cup	granulated sugar	75 mL
2 tbsp	unsalted butter, melted	30 mL

Muffins

2 cups	all-purpose flour	500 mL
1 tsp	baking powder	5 mL
1/2 tsp	baking soda	2 mL
1/2 tsp	salt	2 mL
1/2 tsp	ground cinnamon	2 mL
2/3 cup	packed light brown sugar	150 mL
2	eggs	2
1 cup	buttermilk	250 mL
1/3 cup	vegetable oil	75 mL
1 tsp	vanilla extract	5 mL

In many countries in West and Central Africa, any town large enough to have bars, cafés and restaurants is also likely to have vendors selling roasted nuts and sugared peanuts. The vendor is often a girl or woman balancing her wares on a tray on her head. The peanuts are sometimes sold in recycled liquor bottles that have been collected, cleaned and packed with sugar.

Makes 12 muffins

- Preheat oven to 375°F (190°C)
- 12-cup muffin pan, lined with paper liners

1. *Topping:* In a small bowl, combine peanuts, sugar and butter until blended. Refrigerate until ready to use.

2. *Muffins:* In a large bowl, whisk together flour, baking powder, baking soda, salt and cinnamon.

3. In a medium bowl, whisk together brown sugar, eggs, buttermilk, oil and vanilla until well blended.

4. Add the egg mixture to the flour mixture and stir until just blended.

5. Divide batter equally among prepared muffin cups. Sprinkle with topping.

6. Bake in preheated oven for 17 to 21 minutes or until tops are golden and a toothpick inserted in the center comes out clean. Let cool in pan on a wire rack for 5 minutes, then transfer to the rack to cool.

Jasmine Rice Muffins with Vanilla and Lime (Thailand)

2¼ cups	all-purpose flour	550 mL
2½ tsp	baking powder	12 mL
½ tsp	salt	2 mL
½ tsp	baking soda	2 mL
¾ cup	granulated sugar	175 mL
2	eggs	2
1 cup	buttermilk	250 mL
½ cup	unsalted butter, melted	125 mL
2 tsp	finely grated lime zest	10 mL
2 tbsp	freshly squeezed lime juice	30 mL
2 tsp	vanilla extract	10 mL
1 cup	cooled cooked jasmine rice	250 mL

Fragrant jasmine rice harmonizes with vanilla and lime in these Thai-inspired muffins. They will surprise and delight you.

Makes 12 muffins

- Preheat oven to 400°F (200°C)
- 12-cup muffin pan, greased

1. In a large bowl, whisk together flour, baking powder, salt and baking soda.
2. In a medium bowl, whisk together sugar, eggs, buttermilk, butter, lime zest, lime juice and vanilla until well blended.
3. Add the egg mixture to the flour mixture and stir until just blended. Gently fold in rice.
4. Divide batter equally among prepared muffin cups.
5. Bake in preheated oven for 22 to 26 minutes or until tops are golden and a toothpick inserted in the center comes out clean. Let cool in pan on a wire rack for 5 minutes, then transfer to the rack to cool.

Thai Coffee Muffins (Thailand)

2 cups	all-purpose flour	500 mL
1 tbsp	baking powder	15 mL
1 tsp	ground coriander	5 mL
¾ tsp	ground cardamom	3 mL
½ tsp	salt	2 mL
¾ cup	packed light brown sugar	175 mL
1½ tbsp	instant espresso powder	22 mL
1	egg	1
⅓ cup	unsalted butter, melted	75 mL
¾ cup	heavy or whipping (35%) cream	175 mL
⅔ cup	milk	150 mL

Fans of Thai coffee will go crazy for these enticing muffins, scented with the distinctive additions of coriander and cardamom. If you will be serving them to caffeine-wary adults, use decaffeinated coffee granules in place of the espresso powder.

Makes 12 muffins

- Preheat oven to 400°F (200°C)
- 12-cup muffin pan, greased

1. In a large bowl, whisk together flour, baking powder, coriander, cardamom and salt.
2. In a medium bowl, whisk together brown sugar, espresso powder, egg and butter until well blended. Whisk in cream and milk until blended.
3. Add the egg mixture to the flour mixture and stir until just blended.
4. Divide batter equally among prepared muffin cups.
5. Bake in preheated oven for 18 to 22 minutes or until tops are golden and a toothpick inserted in the center comes out clean. Let cool in pan on a wire rack for 3 minutes, then transfer to the rack to cool.

Star Anise Pineapple Muffins (Malaysia)

1	can (15 oz/425 mL) pineapple tidbits	1
2¾ cups	all-purpose flour	675 mL
1 tbsp	baking powder	15 mL
½ tsp	baking soda	2 mL
½ tsp	salt	2 mL
½ tsp	ground star anise	2 mL
½ cup	unsalted butter, softened	125 mL
¾ cup	liquid honey	175 mL
2	eggs	2
1 tbsp	finely grated lime zest	15 mL

Licorice-like star anise is a common spice in Malay cooking, used in both sweet and savory dishes. It perfumes these buttery tropical muffins, complementing the bright notes of another Malaysian favorite, pineapple.

Makes 12 muffins

- Preheat oven to 400°F (200°C)
- 12-cup muffin pan, greased

1. Drain juice from pineapple tidbits into a glass measuring cup. Pat tidbits dry and set aside. Add enough water to juice in measuring cup to make 1 cup (250 mL). Set aside.
2. In a medium bowl, whisk together flour, baking powder, baking soda, salt and star anise.
3. In a large bowl, using an electric mixer on medium-high speed, beat butter and honey until blended. Beat in eggs, one at a time, until well blended. Beat in lime zest, then pineapple juice mixture until blended.
3. Add the flour mixture to the egg mixture and, using a wooden spoon, stir until just blended. Gently fold in pineapple tidbits.
4. Divide batter equally among prepared muffin cups.
5. Bake in preheated oven for 20 to 25 minutes or until tops are golden and a toothpick inserted in the center comes out clean. Let cool in pan on a wire rack for 5 minutes, then transfer to the rack to cool.

Gajar Halva Carrot Muffins (India)

1⅔ cups	all-purpose flour	400 mL
1½ tsp	baking powder	7 mL
1 tsp	ground cardamom	5 mL
½ tsp	baking soda	2 mL
½ tsp	salt	2 mL
1 cup	packed light brown sugar	250 mL
3	eggs	3
½ cup	unsalted butter, melted	125 mL
1 tbsp	finely grated orange zest	15 mL
3 cups	finely shredded carrots	750 mL
⅔ cup	golden raisins, chopped	150 mL
½ cup	chopped pistachios	125 mL

Gajar halvah, a luxurious Indian dessert made from carrots slowly cooked down with sweetened milk and spices, is the inspiration for these muffins. This riff is fast enough for any day of the week and makes for an amazing start to the day.

Makes 18 muffins

- Preheat oven to 350°F (180°C)
- Two 12-cup muffin pans, 18 cups greased

1. In a large bowl, whisk together flour, baking powder, cardamom, baking soda and salt.
2. In a medium bowl, whisk together brown sugar, eggs, butter and orange zest until blended.
3. Add the egg mixture to the flour mixture and stir until just blended. Gently fold in carrots and raisins.
4. Divide batter equally among prepared muffin cups. Sprinkle with pistachios.
5. Bake in preheated oven for 20 to 25 minutes or until tops are golden and a toothpick inserted in the center comes out clean. Let cool in pans on a wire rack for 5 minutes, then transfer to the rack to cool.

Mango Lassi Muffins (India)

2 cups	all-purpose flour	500 mL
1 tbsp	baking powder	15 mL
1 tsp	ground cardamom	5 mL
1 tsp	ground ginger	5 mL
1/2 tsp	baking soda	2 mL
1/2 tsp	salt	2 mL
1 cup	granulated sugar	250 mL
2	eggs	2
1/4 cup	unsalted butter, melted	60 mL
2 tsp	grated lime zest	10 mL
2 tbsp	freshly squeezed lime juice	30 mL
1 1/2 cups	plain whole-milk yogurt	375 mL
1 1/2 cups	chopped fresh mangos	375 mL

East meets West in my muffin version of a mango lassi. Look for the smaller yellow-skinned mangos, which have a more pronounced flavor than the larger red and green ones.

Tip

If mangos are out of season, use thawed frozen or drained canned or jarred mangos instead.

Makes 18 muffins

- Preheat oven to 375°F (190°C)
- Two 12-cup muffin pans, 18 cups greased

1. In a large bowl, whisk together flour, baking powder, cardamom, ginger, baking soda and salt.

2. In a medium bowl, whisk together sugar, eggs, butter, lime zest and lime juice until well blended. Whisk in yogurt until blended.

3. Add the egg mixture to the flour mixture and stir until just blended. Gently fold in mangos.

4. Divide batter equally among prepared muffin cups.

5. Bake in preheated oven for 18 to 21 minutes or until tops are golden and a toothpick inserted in the center comes out clean. Let cool in pans on a wire rack for 5 minutes, then transfer to the rack to cool.

Coconut Cardamom Burfi Muffins (India)

2 cups	sweetened flaked or shredded coconut	500 mL
1 1/2 cups	all-purpose flour	375 mL
2 tsp	baking powder	10 mL
1 1/4 tsp	ground cardamom	6 mL
1/2 tsp	baking soda	2 mL
1/2 tsp	salt	2 mL
1/2 cup	granulated sugar	125 mL
2	eggs	2
1/4 cup	unsalted butter, melted	60 mL
1 1/4 cups	coconut milk, well-stirred	300 mL

Burfi are square or diamond-shaped, bite-size Indian confections. Somewhat fudge-like in consistency, burfi are mostly festive or celebratory fare and come in a mind-boggling variety of flavors and colors, depending on the region of India. The traditional coconut burfi, however, comprises little more than coconut, water, ghee (clarified butter), cardamom and sugar. I've captured all of the essential flavors here.

Makes 12 muffins

- Preheat oven to 400°F (200°C)
- Large rimmed baking sheet
- 12-cup muffin pan, greased

1. Spread coconut on baking sheet. Bake in preheated oven, stirring occasionally, for 6 to 7 minutes or until golden brown. Remove from oven, leaving oven on, and transfer to a large bowl. Let cool slightly, then whisk in flour, baking powder, cardamom, baking soda and salt.

2. In a medium bowl, whisk together sugar, eggs and butter until well blended. Whisk in coconut milk until blended.

3. Add the egg mixture to the flour mixture and stir until just blended.

4. Divide batter equally among prepared muffin cups.

5. Bake for 15 to 18 minutes or until a toothpick inserted in the center comes out clean. Let cool in pan on a wire rack for 5 minutes, then transfer to the rack to cool.

Papaya Banana Muffins (Philippines)

1½ cups	all-purpose flour	375 mL
1 tsp	baking powder	5 mL
1 tsp	ground ginger	5 mL
¾ tsp	baking soda	3 mL
½ tsp	salt	2 mL
⅛ tsp	cayenne pepper	0.5 mL
1 cup	granulated sugar	250 mL
½ cup	unsalted butter, softened	125 mL
2	eggs	2
½ cup	mashed ripe banana	125 mL
½ cup	mashed ripe papaya	125 mL
1¼ cups	sweetened shredded or flaked coconut, divided	300 mL

Here is a wonderful summer muffin that showcases three of the most beloved fruits from the Philippines: banana, papaya and coconut. The touch of heat from the ginger and cayenne gives the muffins extra tropical flair.

Makes 12 muffins

- Preheat oven to 325°F (160°C)
- 12-cup muffin pan, lined with paper liners

1. In a medium bowl, whisk together flour, baking powder, ginger, baking soda, salt and cayenne.

2. In a large bowl, using an electric mixer on medium-high speed, beat sugar and butter until light and fluffy. Beat in eggs, one at a time, until well blended. Beat in banana, papaya and ¾ cup (175 mL) of the coconut until blended.

3. Add the flour mixture to the egg mixture and, using a wooden spoon, stir until just blended.

4. Divide batter equally among prepared muffin cups. Sprinkle with the remaining coconut and gently press into batter.

5. Bake in preheated oven for 23 to 26 minutes or until tops are firm to the touch and a toothpick inserted in the center comes out clean. Let cool in pan on a wire rack for 5 minutes, then transfer to the rack to cool.

Sesame Ginger Muffins (China)

3 cups	all-purpose flour	750 mL
1½ cups	packed light brown sugar	375 mL
2½ tsp	ground ginger, divided	12 mL
1 tsp	Chinese five-spice powder	5 mL
¾ tsp	salt	3 mL
½ cup	vegetable shortening	125 mL
2 tbsp	toasted sesame oil	30 mL
⅓ cup	sesame seeds	75 mL
2 tsp	baking powder	10 mL
½ tsp	baking soda	2 mL
2	eggs	2
1 cup	buttermilk	250 mL

In China, dessert often means a simple piece of fruit. These muffins, though more complex, ring so clearly of popular Chinese flavors — ginger and sesame — that I think an exception may be made. (Moreover, these muffins are better suited to breakfast or teatime than dessert.) Sesame seeds thread their way through the muffins in two ways: via toasted sesame oil in the batter and a ginger-spiced crumble on top.

Makes 12 muffins

- Preheat oven to 375°F (190°C)
- 12-cup muffin pan, lined with paper liners

1. In a large bowl, whisk together flour, brown sugar, 1½ tsp (7 mL) of the ginger, five-spice powder and salt. Using your fingers, rub in shortening and sesame oil until mixture is crumbly. Transfer ⅔ cup (150 mL) to a small bowl for topping and set aside.

2. Whisk the remaining ginger, sesame seeds, baking powder and baking soda into the large bowl of flour mixture.

3. In a medium bowl, whisk together eggs and buttermilk until well blended.

4. Add the egg mixture to the flour mixture and stir until just blended.

5. Divide batter equally among prepared muffin cups. Sprinkle with topping.

6. Bake in preheated oven for 16 to 21 minutes or until tops are golden and a toothpick inserted in the center comes out clean. Let cool in pan on a wire rack for 5 minutes, then transfer to the rack to cool.

Lamington Muffins (Australia)

Muffins

2 cups	all-purpose flour	500 mL
2 tsp	baking powder	10 mL
1/2 tsp	baking soda	2 mL
1/2 tsp	salt	2 mL
3/4 cup	granulated sugar	175 mL
1	egg	1
1 cup	buttermilk	250 mL
1/2 cup	unsalted butter, melted	125 mL
1 tsp	vanilla extract	5 mL
1/2 cup	red currant jelly	125 mL

Icing

1/4 cup	milk	60 mL
2 tbsp	unsalted butter	30 mL
2 cups	confectioners' (icing) sugar	500 mL
1/3 cup	unsweetened cocoa powder	75 mL
2/3 cup	sweetened flaked or shredded coconut, chopped	150 mL

An homage to one of Australia's favorite sweet treats, these tender muffins provide nice hits of mellow vanilla and piquant fruit to complement the rich chocolate-coconut topping. They make a lovely nibble on their own or with a cup of tea.

Makes 12 muffins

- Preheat oven to 375°F (190°C)
- 12-cup muffin pan, lined with paper liners

1. *Muffins:* In a large bowl, whisk together flour, baking powder, baking soda and salt.

2. In a medium bowl, whisk together sugar, egg, buttermilk, butter and vanilla until well blended.

3. Add the egg mixture to the flour mixture and stir until just blended.

4. Divide batter equally among prepared muffin cups. Spoon 2 tsp (10 mL) of the jelly into the center of each cup of batter (jelly will sink as muffin bakes).

5. Bake in preheated oven for 18 to 21 minutes or until tops are golden and firm to the touch. Let cool in pan on a wire rack for 5 minutes, then transfer to the rack to cool.

6. *Icing:* In a small saucepan, heat milk and butter over medium heat until butter is melted. Remove from heat. Whisk in confectioners' sugar and cocoa powder until blended and smooth. Spoon and spread over cooled muffin tops. Sprinkle with coconut.

Anzac Muffins (Australia and New Zealand)

1 cup	large-flake (old-fashioned) rolled oats	250 mL
1 cup	buttermilk	250 mL
1 cup	all-purpose flour	250 mL
2 tsp	baking powder	10 mL
1/2 tsp	baking soda	2 mL
1/2 tsp	salt	2 mL
1/2 cup	granulated sugar	125 mL
1	egg	1
1/2 cup	unsalted butter, melted	125 mL
2 tbsp	golden syrup or liquid honey	30 mL
3/4 cup	sweetened flaked or shredded coconut	175 mL

Anzac cookies were popularized by World War I care packages to soldiers of the Australian and New Zealand Army Corps (ANZAC), since they kept well on the overseas voyage to Europe. Here, I've refashioned the cookies into equally delectable muffins — they, too, are excellent travelers!

Makes 12 muffins

- Preheat oven to 400°F (200°C)
- 12-cup muffin pan, greased

1. In a medium bowl, combine oats and buttermilk. Let stand for 30 minutes.
2. Preheat oven to 400°F (200°C).
3. In a large bowl, whisk together flour, baking powder, baking soda and salt.
4. Whisk sugar, egg, butter and syrup into oat mixture until well blended.
5. Add the egg mixture to the flour mixture and stir until just blended. Gently fold in coconut.
6. Divide batter equally among prepared muffin cups.
7. Bake in preheated oven for 19 to 24 minutes or until a toothpick inserted in the center comes out clean. Let cool in pan on a wire rack for 5 minutes, then transfer to the rack to cool.

Superfood Muffins

• •

Nature has provided us with an abundance of natural energy-boosting foods that have recently been categorized as "superfoods." These multitasking options provide an abundance of disease-fighting nutrients, they fill you up so you can enjoy plenty of food without excess calories, and they are easy to include in everyday meals — or, in the case of this chapter, everyday muffins. Think berries, orange vegetables (such as sweet potatoes and pumpkin), citrus, eggs, green foods, green leafy vegetables, nuts, oats, yogurt and whole grains. And that's but a few. So go on, get healthy; these innovative muffins will fuel you in the most delicious way.

continued…

McIntosh Apple Oat Muffins

1½ cups	whole wheat pastry flour	375 mL
1 cup	quick-cooking rolled oats	250 mL
1½ tsp	baking powder	7 mL
1½ tsp	ground cinnamon	7 mL
½ tsp	baking soda	2 mL
½ tsp	salt	2 mL
⅔ cup	packed light brown sugar	150 mL
1	egg	1
3 tbsp	vegetable oil	45 mL
1 tsp	vanilla extract	5 mL
1 cup	low-fat (1%) plain yogurt	250 mL
¼ cup	low-fat (1%) milk	60 mL
2 cups	shredded McIntosh apples (unpeeled)	500 mL

There's no doubt that these are seriously delicious muffins, but a touch of brown sugar and vanilla add doses of down-home comfort, making them the muffin you'll want to eat on cool autumn mornings. Apples and oats are both excellent sources of soluble fiber. Oats further contribute good amounts of protein and whole-grain carbohydrates.

Tip

It takes about 12 oz (375 g) of apples (2 to 3 medium) to produce 2 cups (500 mL) shredded apples.

Makes 12 muffins

- Preheat oven to 400°F (200°C)
- 12-cup muffin pan, greased

1. In a large bowl, whisk together flour, oats, baking powder, cinnamon, baking soda and salt.
2. In a medium bowl, whisk together brown sugar, egg, oil and vanilla until well blended. Whisk in yogurt and milk until blended.
3. Add the egg mixture to the flour mixture and stir until just blended. Gently fold in apples.
4. Divide batter equally among prepared muffin cups.
5. Bake in preheated oven for 20 to 25 minutes or until a toothpick inserted in the center comes out clean. Let cool in pan on a wire rack for 3 minutes, then transfer to the rack to cool.

Fuss-Free Apple Muffins

2½ cups	whole wheat pastry flour	625 mL
1 tbsp	baking powder	15 mL
2 tsp	ground cinnamon	10 mL
1 tsp	salt	5 mL
½ cup	packed dark brown sugar	125 mL
2	eggs	2
1 cup	buttermilk	250 mL
¼ cup	vegetable oil	60 mL
2 tsp	vanilla extract	10 mL
2 cups	chopped red apples (unpeeled)	500 mL
3 tbsp	turbinado sugar	45 mL

Humble, old-fashioned apples are rich in a flavonoid called quercetin, which has been shown to reduce allergic reactions and inflammation. Keeping the skin on boosts their already high fiber content, and the bits of red peel become very tender once baked and offer pretty peaks of color in the finished muffins.

Makes 12 muffins

- Preheat oven to 400°F (200°C)
- 12-cup muffin pan, greased

1. In a large bowl, whisk together flour, baking powder, cinnamon and salt.

2. In a medium bowl, whisk together brown sugar, eggs, buttermilk, oil and vanilla until well blended.

3. Add the egg mixture to the flour mixture and stir until just blended. Gently fold in apples.

4. Divide batter equally among prepared muffin cups. Sprinkle with turbinado sugar.

5. Bake in preheated oven for 21 to 25 minutes or until tops are golden brown and a toothpick inserted in the center comes out clean. Let cool in pan on a wire rack for 5 minutes, then transfer to the rack to cool.

Yogurt, Bran and Dried Apricot Muffins

2	eggs	2
1¼ cups	low-fat (1%) plain yogurt	300 mL
1¼ cups	unsweetened applesauce	300 mL
½ cup	liquid honey	125 mL
⅓ cup	vegetable oil	75 mL
½ tsp	almond extract	2 mL
2 cups	bran cereal, such as All-Bran	500 mL
1½ cups	whole wheat flour	375 mL
2½ tsp	baking powder	12 mL
½ tsp	salt	2 mL
½ tsp	baking soda	2 mL
1 cup	chopped dried apricots	250 mL

Based on the title alone, these muffins sound like they are in the running for world's healthiest muffins — and they may well be. Dried apricots are studded throughout, adding golden sweetness, as well as beta carotene and fiber.

Makes 12 muffins

- Preheat oven to 400°F (200°C)
- 12-cup muffin pan, greased

1. In a large bowl, whisk together eggs, yogurt, applesauce, honey, oil and almond extract until well blended. Stir in cereal. Let stand for 10 minutes to soften cereal.

2. In another large bowl, whisk together flour, baking powder, salt and baking soda.

3. Add the flour mixture to the cereal mixture and stir until just blended. Gently fold in apricots.

4. Divide batter equally among prepared muffin cups.

5. Bake in preheated oven for 23 to 26 minutes or until tops are golden and a toothpick inserted in the center comes out clean. Let cool in pan on a wire rack for 5 minutes, then transfer to the rack to cool.

Apple Dried Blueberry Muffins

Streusel

¹/₄ cup	finely chopped walnuts	60 mL
2 tbsp	packed light brown sugar	30 mL
1 tbsp	unsalted butter, melted	15 mL

Muffins

1³/₄ cups	whole wheat pastry flour	425 mL
³/₄ cup	ground flax seeds	175 mL
2 tsp	baking powder	10 mL
1 tsp	baking soda	5 mL
¹/₂ tsp	salt	2 mL
³/₄ cup	packed light brown sugar	175 mL
2	eggs	2
¹/₂ cup	low-fat (1%) plain yogurt	125 mL
¹/₂ cup	unsweetened apple juice	125 mL
2 tbsp	vegetable oil	30 mL
1 tsp	vanilla extract	5 mL
2 cups	chopped Granny Smith apples (unpeeled)	500 mL
¹/₂ cup	dried blueberries	125 mL

Apples are a ubiquitous fruit at every supermarket, so it's easy to overlook their health benefits. For starters, they contain a long list of phytonutrients — including quercetin, catechin, phlorizin and chlorogenic acid — that function as antioxidants and support heart health. They are also a good source of dietary fiber and vitamin C.

Makes 12 muffins

- Preheat oven to 350°F (180°C)
- 12-cup muffin pan, greased

1. *Streusel:* In a small bowl, mix walnuts, brown sugar and butter until blended. Refrigerate until ready to use.

2. *Muffins:* In a large bowl, whisk together flour, flax seeds, baking powder, baking soda and salt.

3. In a medium bowl, whisk together brown sugar, eggs, yogurt, apple juice, oil and vanilla until well blended.

4. Add the egg mixture to the flour mixture and stir until just blended. Gently fold in apples and blueberries.

5. Divide batter equally among prepared muffin cups. Sprinkle with streusel.

6. Bake in preheated oven for 20 to 25 minutes or until tops are golden and a toothpick inserted in the center comes out clean. Let cool in pan on a wire rack for 5 minutes, then transfer to the rack to cool.

Bran, Banana and Chocolate Muffins

1¼ cups	natural bran	300 mL
1¼ cups	whole wheat flour	300 mL
1½ tsp	baking soda	7 mL
1 tsp	baking powder	5 mL
½ tsp	salt	2 mL
½ tsp	ground nutmeg	2 mL
⅓ cup	packed light brown sugar	75 mL
1	egg	1
¾ cup	mashed ripe bananas	175 mL
¾ cup	low-fat (1%) plain yogurt	175 mL
¼ cup	vegetable oil	60 mL
½ cup	miniature semisweet chocolate chips	125 mL

Bran for high fiber, bananas for potassium and vitamin A, and chocolate for antioxidants — eating well never tasted so good. My three-year-old can hardly believe it when I say he is welcome to have more than one!

Makes 12 muffins

- Preheat oven to 400°F (200°C)
- Blender
- 12-cup muffin pan, greased

1. In a large bowl, whisk together bran, flour, baking soda, baking powder, salt and nutmeg.
2. In blender, process brown sugar, egg, bananas, yogurt and oil until blended and smooth.
3. Add the egg mixture to the flour mixture and stir until just blended. Gently fold in chocolate chips.
4. Divide batter equally among prepared muffin cups.
5. Bake in preheated oven for 18 to 22 minutes or until tops are golden brown and a toothpick inserted in the center comes out clean. Let cool in pan on a wire rack for 3 minutes, then transfer to the rack to cool.

Vanilla Banana Whole-Grain Muffins

1¼ cups	whole wheat pastry flour	300 mL
1¼ cups	oat bran	300 mL
⅔ cup	packed light brown sugar	150 mL
1 tbsp	baking powder	15 mL
1 tsp	baking soda	5 mL
1 tsp	ground cinnamon	5 mL
½ tsp	salt	2 mL
⅔ cup	low-fat (1%) cottage cheese	150 mL
⅔ cup	buttermilk	150 mL
2	eggs	2
2 tbsp	walnut oil or vegetable oil	30 mL
1 tbsp	vanilla extract	15 mL
1 cup	mashed ripe bananas	250 mL

Humble bananas are packed with high amounts of vitamin B_6, potassium, vitamin C and fiber — and are available for pocket change, to boot!

Makes 12 muffins

- Preheat oven to 400°F (200°C)
- Blender
- 12-cup muffin pan, greased

1. In a large bowl, whisk together flour, oat bran, brown sugar, baking powder, baking soda, cinnamon and salt.
2. In blender, process cheese and buttermilk until blended and smooth. Add eggs, oil and vanilla; pulse until smooth. Add bananas and pulse until just blended.
3. Add the banana mixture to the flour mixture and stir until just blended.
4. Divide batter equally among prepared muffin cups.
5. Bake in preheated oven for 17 to 20 minutes or until a toothpick inserted in the center comes out clean. Let cool in pan on a wire rack for 3 minutes, then transfer to the rack to cool.

Whole Wheat Banana Muffins

2 cups	whole wheat pastry flour	500 mL
1/4 cup	ground flax seeds	60 mL
1 tbsp	ground cinnamon	15 mL
1 tsp	baking soda	5 mL
1 tsp	salt	5 mL
2	eggs	2
1 1/2 cups	mashed ripe bananas	375 mL
2/3 cup	low-fat (1%) plain yogurt	150 mL
1/2 cup	agave nectar	125 mL
3 tbsp	vegetable oil	45 mL
2 tsp	vanilla extract	10 mL
2 tbsp	turbinado sugar	30 mL

Even though I offer a wide range of recipes on my blog, I am always interested in the requests I get from my readers. Hands down, the number-one request is for a healthy, delicious banana bread/muffin. I have developed several over the years, but this one, made with whole wheat pastry flour, remains my favorite.

Makes 12 muffins

- Preheat oven to 350°F (180°C)
- 12-cup muffin pan, greased

1. In a large bowl, whisk together flour, flax seeds, cinnamon, baking soda and salt.

2. In a medium bowl, whisk together eggs, bananas, yogurt, agave nectar, oil and vanilla until well blended.

3. Add the egg mixture to the flour mixture and stir until just blended.

4. Divide batter equally among prepared muffin cups. Sprinkle with turbinado sugar.

5. Bake in preheated oven for 23 to 28 minutes or until tops are golden and a toothpick inserted in the center comes out clean. Let cool in pan on a wire rack for 3 minutes, then transfer to the rack to cool.

Banana Ricotta Muffins

2 1/2 cups	whole wheat pastry flour	625 mL
1 tbsp	baking powder	15 mL
1 tsp	baking soda	5 mL
1 tsp	ground allspice	5 mL
1 tsp	ground ginger	5 mL
3/4 tsp	salt	3 mL
2	eggs	2
1 cup	mashed ripe bananas	250 mL
2/3 cup	buttermilk	150 mL
2/3 cup	low-fat ricotta cheese	150 mL
2/3 cup	agave nectar or liquid honey	150 mL
2 tbsp	vegetable oil	30 mL
2 tsp	vanilla extract	10 mL

Low-fat ricotta cheese is an excellent option for baked goods such as these muffins, imparting richness while offering high levels of calcium and protein.

Makes 16 muffins

- Preheat oven to 400°F (200°C)
- Two 12-cup muffin pans, 16 cups greased

1. In a large bowl, whisk together flour, baking powder, baking soda, allspice, ginger and salt.

2. In a medium bowl, whisk together eggs, bananas, buttermilk, cheese, agave nectar, oil and vanilla until well blended.

3. Add the egg mixture to the flour mixture and stir until just blended.

4. Divide batter equally among prepared muffin cups.

5. Bake in preheated oven for 16 to 21 minutes or until tops are golden and a toothpick inserted in the center comes out clean. Let cool in pans on a wire rack for 3 minutes, then transfer to the rack to cool.

Blackberry Oat Muffins

1 1/3 cups	quick-cooking rolled oats	325 mL
1 cup	whole wheat pastry flour	250 mL
1 1/2 tsp	baking powder	7 mL
1 tsp	ground cardamom	5 mL
3/4 tsp	salt	3 mL
1/2 tsp	baking soda	2 mL
1	egg	1
1 cup	buttermilk	250 mL
1/2 cup	liquid honey, agave nectar or pure maple syrup	125 mL
1/4 cup	vegetable oil	60 mL
1 tsp	vanilla extract	5 mL
1 1/2 cups	blackberries	375 mL

Don't get me wrong, I am an equal-opportunity berry lover, but blackberries, with their lush flavor and inky color, top my list. Good thing, too, because they are high in antioxidants, fiber, vitamins C and K, phytoestrogens and manganese. If that weren't enough, one cup (144 g) of blackberries also contains 135 mg of omega-3 fatty acids.

Makes 12 muffins

- Preheat oven to 400°F (200°C)
- 12-cup muffin pan, greased

1. In a large bowl, whisk together oats, flour, baking powder, cardamom, salt and baking soda.
2. In a medium bowl, whisk together egg, buttermilk, honey, oil and vanilla until well blended.
3. Add the egg mixture to the flour mixture and stir until just blended. Gently fold in blackberries.
4. Divide batter equally among prepared muffin cups.
5. Bake in preheated oven for 20 to 25 minutes or until tops are golden and a toothpick inserted in the center comes out clean. Let cool in pan on a wire rack for 3 minutes, then transfer to the rack to cool.

Blueberry Almond Muffins

1 cup	whole wheat pastry flour	250 mL
3/4 cup	all-purpose flour	175 mL
1/4 cup	wheat germ	60 mL
2 tsp	baking powder	10 mL
1/2 tsp	salt	2 mL
3/4 cup	packed light brown sugar	175 mL
2	eggs	2
3/4 cup	low-fat (1%) plain yogurt	175 mL
1/4 cup	low-fat (1%) milk	60 mL
2 tbsp	vegetable oil	30 mL
1 tsp	almond extract	5 mL
1 cup	blueberries	250 mL
1/2 cup	chopped almonds, toasted	125 mL

This is a grown-up blueberry muffin — rich in nutrition, low in sugar and loaded with good-for-you ingredients — but kids are crazy for them too.

Makes 12 muffins

- Preheat oven to 350°F (180°C)
- 12-cup muffin pan, greased

1. In a large bowl, whisk together whole wheat pastry flour, all-purpose flour, wheat germ, baking powder and salt.
2. In a medium bowl, whisk together brown sugar, eggs, yogurt, milk, oil and almond extract until well blended.
3. Add the egg mixture to the flour mixture and stir until just blended. Gently fold in blueberries and almonds.
4. Divide batter equally among prepared muffin cups.
5. Bake in preheated oven for 22 to 26 minutes or until tops are golden and a toothpick inserted in the center comes out clean. Let cool in pan on a wire rack for 5 minutes, then transfer to the rack to cool.

Blueberry Oat Muffins

1¾ cups	quick-cooking rolled oats	425 mL
1 cup	whole wheat pastry flour	250 mL
2 tsp	ground cinnamon	10 mL
1 tsp	baking powder	5 mL
1 tsp	baking soda	5 mL
¾ tsp	salt	3 mL
¾ cup	packed light brown sugar	175 mL
2	eggs	2
¼ cup	vegetable oil	60 mL
2 tsp	finely grated lemon zest	10 mL
2 tsp	vanilla extract	10 mL
1½ cups	buttermilk	375 mL
1½ cups	blueberries	375 mL

Most people do not need any incentive to eat up a heaping handful of fresh blueberries. But it's nice to know that something so delicious is also so good for you. Multiple studies have found that blueberries are high in antioxidants, help fight cancer, boost brain cells and promote strong bones.

Makes 12 muffins

- Preheat oven to 400°F (200°C)
- Food processor
- 12-cup muffin pan, greased

1. In food processor, pulse oats five or six times or until oats resemble coarse meal.
2. In a large bowl, whisk together oats, flour, cinnamon, baking powder, baking soda and salt.
3. In a medium bowl, whisk together brown sugar, eggs, oil, lemon zest and vanilla until well blended. Whisk in buttermilk until blended.
4. Add the egg mixture to the flour mixture and stir until just blended. Gently fold in blueberries.
5. Divide batter equally among prepared muffin cups.
6. Bake in preheated oven for 18 to 23 minutes or until tops are golden and a toothpick inserted in the center comes out clean. Let cool in pan on a wire rack for 5 minutes, then transfer to the rack to cool.

Blueberry, Cranberry and Orange Muffins

2 cups	whole wheat pastry flour	500 mL
2 tsp	baking powder	10 mL
½ tsp	baking soda	2 mL
½ tsp	salt	2 mL
1	egg	1
½ cup	liquid honey	125 mL
¼ cup	olive oil	60 mL
1 tbsp	finely grated orange zest	15 mL
1 tsp	vanilla extract	5 mL
1¼ cups	low-fat (1%) plain yogurt	300 mL
½ cup	dried blueberries	125 mL
½ cup	dried cranberries	125 mL
2 tbsp	turbinado sugar	30 mL

With blueberries, cranberries and orange, these muffins have a fabulous bright, lush flavor, but are also packed with antioxidants and fiber.

Makes 12 muffins

- Preheat oven to 400°F (200°C)
- 12-cup muffin pan, greased

1. In a large bowl, whisk together flour, baking powder, baking soda and salt.
2. In a medium bowl, whisk together egg, honey, oil, orange zest and vanilla until well blended. Whisk in yogurt until blended.
3. Add the egg mixture to the flour mixture and stir until just blended. Gently fold in blueberries and cranberries.
4. Divide batter equally among prepared muffin cups. Sprinkle with turbinado sugar.
5. Bake in preheated oven for 18 to 22 minutes or until tops are golden and a toothpick inserted in the center comes out clean. Let cool in pan on a wire rack for 5 minutes, then transfer to the rack to cool.

Blueberry Power Muffins

1 cup	unsweetened apple juice	250 mL
1/2 cup	dried blueberries	125 mL
1/4 cup	quinoa, rinsed	60 mL
1 1/2 cups	soy flour	375 mL
2 tsp	baking powder	10 mL
1 tsp	ground cinnamon	5 mL
1/2 tsp	baking soda	2 mL
1/2 tsp	salt	2 mL
2	eggs	2
1/4 cup	liquid honey	60 mL
3 tbsp	vegetable oil	45 mL
1 tsp	vanilla extract	5 mL
1 cup	low-fat (1%) milk	250 mL
1/2 cup	mashed ripe banana	125 mL
1/2 cup	chopped walnuts	125 mL

Quinoa, soy flour, blueberries, bananas and walnuts — oh my! These muffins are off the charts in nutrition. But you will make them again and again because of their great taste and texture.

Tip

Dried blueberries are a particularly nutritious dried fruit choice here, but any other dried fruit may be substituted.

Makes 12 muffins

- 12-cup muffin pan, greased

1. In a small saucepan, bring apple juice to a boil over high heat. Stir in blueberries and quinoa. Remove from heat and let stand for 20 minutes.

2. Preheat oven to 350°F (180°C).

3. In a large bowl, whisk together flour, baking powder, cinnamon, baking soda and salt.

4. In a medium bowl, whisk together eggs, honey, oil and vanilla until well blended. Whisk in milk and banana until blended.

5. Add the egg mixture to the flour mixture and stir until just blended. Gently fold in the blueberry mixture until blended.

6. Divide batter equally among prepared muffin cups. Sprinkle with walnuts.

7. Bake for 24 to 28 minutes or until tops are golden brown and a toothpick inserted in the center comes out clean. Let cool in pan on a wire rack for 3 minutes, then transfer to the rack to cool.

Peanut Butter Berry Muffins

1 cup	all-purpose flour	250 mL
3/4 cup	whole wheat flour	175 mL
1 tbsp	baking powder	15 mL
1/2 tsp	salt	2 mL
1	egg	1
1/4 cup	liquid honey	60 mL
1/2 cup	natural peanut butter, well-stirred	125 mL
3 tbsp	vegetable oil	45 mL
1 tsp	vanilla extract	5 mL
1 1/4 cups	low-fat (1%) milk	300 mL
1/2 cup	dried cranberries, chopped	125 mL
1/2 cup	strawberry all-fruit preserves	125 mL

Peanut butter is energy food to the max, high in protein, niacin, manganese, copper and tryptophan.

Makes 12 muffins

- Preheat oven to 400°F (200°C)
- 12-cup muffin pan, greased

1. In a large bowl, whisk together all-purpose flour, whole wheat flour, baking powder and salt.
2. In a medium bowl, whisk together egg, honey, peanut butter, oil and vanilla until well blended. Whisk in milk until blended.
3. Add the egg mixture to the flour mixture and stir until just blended. Gently fold in cranberries.
4. Divide half the batter equally among prepared muffin cups. Spoon 2 tsp (10 mL) preserves into the center of each cup. Top with the remaining batter.
5. Bake in preheated oven for 18 to 22 minutes or until tops are golden and firm to the touch. Let cool in pan on a wire rack for 5 minutes, then transfer to the rack to cool.

Cranberry Walnut Muffins

1 1/4 cups	whole wheat pastry flour	300 mL
1/4 cup	wheat germ	60 mL
1 1/2 tsp	baking powder	7 mL
1 tsp	ground cinnamon	5 mL
1/2 tsp	salt	2 mL
1/4 tsp	baking soda	1 mL
2	eggs	2
1/4 cup	ground flax seeds	60 mL
1/2 cup	agave nectar	125 mL
1/3 cup	low-fat (1%) plain yogurt	75 mL
1/4 cup	vegetable oil	60 mL
1 tsp	vanilla extract	5 mL
1 cup	fresh cranberries, coarsely chopped	250 mL
1 cup	chopped walnuts, toasted	250 mL

The cranberry is praised for its sauce capabilities at the Thanksgiving table, but the ruby fruit is underappreciated as a health food. Cranberries are loaded with disease-fighting antioxidants and are a good source of vitamin C, fiber, manganese and potassium.

Makes 12 muffins

- Preheat oven to 350°F (180°C)
- 12-cup muffin pan, greased

1. In a large bowl, whisk together flour, wheat germ, baking powder, cinnamon, salt and baking soda.
2. In a medium bowl, whisk together eggs, flax seeds, agave nectar, yogurt, oil and vanilla until well blended.
3. Add the egg mixture to the flour mixture and stir until just blended. Gently fold in cranberries and walnuts.
4. Divide batter equally among prepared muffin cups.
5. Bake in preheated oven for 20 to 25 minutes or until tops are golden and a toothpick inserted in the center comes out clean. Let cool in pan on a wire rack for 5 minutes, then transfer to the rack to cool.

Cranberry Multigrain Muffins

1 1/2 cups	whole wheat pastry flour	375 mL
3/4 cup	quick-cooking rolled oats	175 mL
1/4 cup	ground flax seeds	60 mL
2 tsp	baking powder	10 mL
1/2 tsp	baking soda	2 mL
1/2 tsp	salt	2 mL
2/3 cup	granulated sugar	150 mL
2	eggs	2
3/4 cup	buttermilk	175 mL
1/3 cup	vegetable oil	75 mL
1 tbsp	finely grated lemon zest	15 mL
1 cup	fresh cranberries, coarsely chopped	250 mL
1/2 cup	chopped pecans or walnuts, toasted	125 mL

Makes 12 muffins

- Preheat oven to 350°F (180°C)
- 12-cup muffin pan, greased

1. In a large bowl, whisk together flour, oats, flax seeds, baking powder, baking soda and salt.
2. In a medium bowl, whisk together sugar, eggs, buttermilk, oil and lemon zest until well blended.
3. Add the egg mixture to the flour mixture and stir until just blended. Gently fold in cranberries and pecans.
4. Divide batter among prepared muffin cups.
5. Bake in preheated oven for 18 to 22 minutes or until tops are golden and a toothpick inserted in the center comes out clean. Let cool in pan on a wire rack for 3 minutes, then transfer to the rack to cool.

In study after study, cranberries come out at or near the top of the antioxidant heap. They are particularly rich in polyphenols and have many other helpful phytochemicals as well.

Avocado Cranberry Muffins

1 1/2 cups	whole wheat pastry flour	375 mL
3/4 cup	wheat germ	175 mL
3/4 cup	granulated sugar	175 mL
1 tbsp	baking powder	15 mL
3/4 tsp	salt	3 mL
1/2 tsp	ground allspice	2 mL
2	eggs	2
1 cup	mashed ripe avocado	250 mL
1 cup	low-fat (1%) milk	250 mL
1/3 cup	vegetable oil	75 mL
1 tsp	vanilla extract	5 mL
1 cup	fresh cranberries, coarsely chopped	250 mL

Makes 16 muffins

- Preheat oven to 350°F (180°C)
- Two 12-cup muffin pans, 16 cups lined with paper liners

1. In a large bowl, whisk together flour, wheat germ, sugar, baking powder, salt and allspice.
2. In a food processor or blender, process eggs, avocado, milk, oil and vanilla until blended and smooth.
3. Add the egg mixture to the flour mixture and stir until just blended. Gently fold in cranberries.
4. Divide batter equally among prepared muffin cups.
5. Bake in preheated oven for 22 to 25 minutes or until tops are golden brown and a toothpick inserted in the center comes out clean. Let cool in pans on a wire rack for 5 minutes, then transfer to the rack to cool.

Avocado adds buttery richness to these tender muffins, a fine foil to tart cranberries. The nutritional profile of avocados is phenomenal: they offer 20 vitamins, minerals and beneficial plant compounds.

Goji Berry Orange Muffins

½ cup	dried goji berries	125 mL
	Hot water	
1¾ cups	whole wheat pastry flour	425 mL
2 tsp	baking powder	10 mL
1 tsp	ground ginger	5 mL
½ tsp	salt	2 mL
⅓ cup	packed light brown sugar	75 mL
1	egg	1
1 cup	low-fat (1%) milk	250 mL
⅓ cup	vegetable oil	75 mL
2 tsp	finely grated orange zest	10 mL
¼ cup	freshly squeezed orange juice	60 mL
½ cup	sliced almonds, toasted	125 mL

Goji berries are bright orange-red berries that come from a shrub native to China. They have a delicious tart flavor, akin to that of cranberries. Research indicates that eating goji berries (much like eating other dark-colored berries, such as blueberries, cranberries and strawberries) offers definite health benefits. They are packed with powerful antioxidants and other compounds that may help prevent cancer and heart disease. In addition, eating foods high in antioxidants may slow the aging process.

Makes 12 muffins

- Preheat oven to 375°F (190°C)
- 12-cup muffin pan, greased

1. In a small bowl, combine goji berries and enough hot water to cover. Let stand for 10 minutes, then drain.
2. In a large bowl, whisk together flour, baking powder, ginger and salt.
3. In a medium bowl, whisk together brown sugar, egg, milk, oil, orange zest and orange juice until well blended.
4. Add the egg mixture to the flour mixture and stir until just blended. Gently fold in berries and almonds.
5. Divide batter equally among prepared muffin cups.
6. Bake in preheated oven for 17 to 22 minutes or until a toothpick inserted in the center comes out clean. Let cool in pan on a wire rack for 3 minutes, then transfer to the rack to cool.

Multigrain Raspberry Muffins

1 cup	quick-cooking rolled oats	250 mL
1 cup	whole wheat pastry flour	250 mL
1/3 cup	multigrain hot cereal (see tip, at left)	75 mL
2 1/2 tsp	baking powder	12 mL
1 tsp	ground cinnamon	5 mL
1/2 tsp	salt	2 mL
1/2 tsp	baking soda	2 mL
1	egg	1
3/4 cup	low-fat (1%) plain yogurt	175 mL
1/2 cup	liquid honey	125 mL
1/4 cup	vegetable oil	60 mL
3/4 tsp	almond extract	3 mL
1 1/2 cups	raspberries	375 mL

Plump, juicy raspberries are a perennial summer favorite. But the sweet flavor is only one reason to indulge in the delicate fruit. Rich in vitamin C, folate, iron and potassium, raspberries also provide high amounts of insoluble fiber (thanks to all those little seeds), as well as good amounts of the soluble fiber pectin, which helps control cholesterol levels. Finally, raspberries are a good source of ellagic acid and other cancer-fighting antioxidants.

Tip

There are many multigrain hot cereals available, such as Bob's Red Mill, Hodgson Mill, Quaker or Red River. Just be sure not to use an instant variety.

Makes 12 muffins

- Preheat oven to 400°F (200°C)
- 12-cup muffin pan, lined with paper liners

1. In a large bowl, whisk together oats, flour, cereal, baking powder, cinnamon, salt and baking soda.
2. In a medium bowl, whisk together egg, yogurt, honey, oil and almond extract until well blended.
3. Add the egg mixture to the flour mixture and stir until just blended. Gently fold in raspberries.
4. Divide batter equally among prepared muffin cups.
5. Bake in preheated oven for 18 to 23 minutes or until tops are light golden brown and a toothpick inserted in the center comes out clean. Let cool in pan on a wire rack for 3 minutes, then transfer to the rack to cool.

Raspberry Bran Muffins

1½ cups	whole wheat pastry flour	375 mL
1 cup	natural bran	250 mL
3 tbsp	ground flax seeds	45 mL
1¼ tsp	baking soda	6 mL
½ tsp	salt	2 mL
2	eggs	2
½ cup	liquid honey	125 mL
¼ cup	vegetable oil	60 mL
1 tsp	vanilla extract	5 mL
1¼ cups	low-fat (1%) plain yogurt	300 mL
1½ cups	raspberries	375 mL

Sweet-tart, lush raspberries? Bran never had it so good. But bran is no slouch — 1 cup (250 mL) of wheat bran contains 99% of the US Dietary Reference Intake (DRI) of fiber, 9 grams of protein and 34% of the DRI for iron. Wheat bran is also high in magnesium, manganese, niacin, phosphorus, zinc and vitamin B_6, is low in fat and has no cholesterol, sugar or sodium.

Makes 12 muffins

- Preheat oven to 400°F (200°C)
- 12-cup muffin pan, greased

1. In a large bowl, whisk together flour, bran, flax seeds, baking soda and salt.
2. In a medium bowl, whisk together eggs, honey, oil and vanilla until well blended. Whisk in yogurt until blended.
3. Add the egg mixture to the flour mixture and stir until just blended. Gently fold in raspberries.
4. Divide batter equally among prepared muffin cups.
5. Bake in preheated oven for 18 to 23 minutes or until tops are light golden brown and a toothpick inserted in the center comes out clean. Let cool in pan on a wire rack for 3 minutes, then transfer to the rack to cool.

Strawberry Kiwi Muffins

1½ cups	whole wheat pastry flour	375 mL
½ cup	wheat germ	125 mL
2 tsp	baking powder	10 mL
½ tsp	salt	2 mL
½ tsp	baking soda	2 mL
1	egg	1
½ cup	liquid honey	125 mL
½ cup	low-fat (1%) plain yogurt	125 mL
¼ cup	vegetable oil	60 mL
¾ cup	diced strawberries	175 mL
¾ cup	diced peeled kiwifruit	175 mL

These muffins are unequivocally fantastic, bright with the flavors of summer. Both strawberries and kiwifruit are high in vitamin C and have high levels of fiber.

Makes 12 muffins

- Preheat oven to 375°F (190°C)
- 12-cup muffin pan, greased

1. In a large bowl, whisk together flour, wheat germ, baking powder, salt and baking soda.
2. In a medium bowl, whisk together egg, honey, yogurt and oil until well blended.
3. Add the egg mixture to the flour mixture and stir until just blended. Gently fold in strawberries and kiwifruit.
4. Divide batter equally among prepared muffin cups.
5. Bake in preheated oven for 19 to 23 minutes or until tops are golden and a toothpick inserted in the center comes out clean. Let cool in pan on a wire rack for 3 minutes, then transfer to the rack to cool.

Dark Cherry Muffins

²/₃ cup	low-fat (1%) plain yogurt	150 mL
¹/₂ cup	old-fashioned rolled oats	125 mL
1¹/₄ cups	all-purpose flour	300 mL
1 cup	whole wheat flour	250 mL
2 tsp	baking powder	10 mL
¹/₂ tsp	salt	2 mL
¹/₂ tsp	baking soda	2 mL
2	eggs	2
¹/₂ cup	agave nectar	125 mL
¹/₃ cup	vegetable oil	75 mL
1 tsp	vanilla extract	5 mL
¹/₄ tsp	almond extract	1 mL
1 cup	chopped fresh or frozen (thawed) dark cherries	250 mL
¹/₂ cup	slivered almonds	125 mL

Fresh dark cherries are one of nature's finest treats. They are also high in antioxidants and are a good source of calcium, iron and vitamins A and C.

Makes 12 muffins

- Preheat oven to 400°F (200°C)
- 12-cup muffin pan, greased

1. In a small bowl, combine yogurt and oats. Let stand for 5 minutes.
2. In a large bowl, whisk together all-purpose flour, whole wheat flour, baking powder, salt and baking soda.
3. Whisk eggs, agave nectar, oil, vanilla and almond extract into yogurt mixture until well blended.
4. Add the egg mixture to the flour mixture and stir until just blended. Gently fold in cherries.
5. Divide batter equally among prepared muffin cups. Sprinkle with almonds.
5. Bake in preheated oven for 15 to 18 minutes or until tops are golden and a toothpick inserted in the center comes out clean. Let cool in pan on a wire rack for 5 minutes, then transfer to the rack to cool.

Tart Cherry Applesauce Muffins

1¹/₄ cups	whole wheat pastry flour	300 mL
1 cup	quick-cooking rolled oats	250 mL
³/₄ cup	natural bran	175 mL
1 tsp	baking powder	5 mL
1 tsp	ground cinnamon	5 mL
³/₄ tsp	baking soda	3 mL
¹/₂ tsp	salt	2 mL
¹/₂ cup	packed light brown sugar	125 mL
1	egg	1
1 cup	unsweetened applesauce	250 mL
¹/₃ cup	low-fat (1%) milk	75 mL
¹/₄ cup	vegetable oil	60 mL
¹/₂ cup	sour (tart) dried cherries, coarsely chopped	125 mL

Although these muffins boast multiple superfoods, tart cherries star. They are high in vitamin C and fiber, as well as melatonin.

Makes 12 muffins

- Preheat oven to 375°F (190°C)
- 12-cup muffin pan, greased

1. In a large bowl, whisk together flour, oats, bran, baking powder, cinnamon, baking soda and salt.
2. In a medium bowl, whisk together brown sugar, egg, applesauce, milk and oil until well blended.
3. Add the egg mixture to the flour mixture and stir until just blended. Gently fold in cherries.
4. Divide batter equally among prepared muffin cups.
5. Bake in preheated oven for 17 to 22 minutes or until a toothpick inserted in the center comes out clean. Let cool in pan on a wire rack for 3 minutes, then transfer to the rack to cool.

Red Grape Muffins

1 cup	all-purpose flour	250 mL
1 cup	whole wheat flour	250 mL
1 tbsp	baking powder	15 mL
1/2 tsp	salt	2 mL
1/2 tsp	baking soda	2 mL
1	egg	1
1 cup	low-fat (1%) plain yogurt	250 mL
1/2 cup	liquid honey	125 mL
1/4 cup	olive oil	60 mL
1 tsp	vanilla extract	5 mL
2 cups	halved seedless red grapes	500 mL

Makes 12 muffins

- Preheat oven to 350°F (180°C)
- 12-cup muffin pan, greased

1. In a large bowl, whisk together all-purpose flour, whole wheat flour, baking powder, salt and baking soda.
2. In a medium bowl, whisk together egg, yogurt, honey, oil and vanilla until well blended.
3. Add the egg mixture to the flour mixture and stir until just blended. Gently fold in grapes.
4. Divide batter equally among prepared muffin cups.
5. Bake in preheated oven for 24 to 28 minutes or until tops are golden and a toothpick inserted in the center comes out clean. Let cool in pan on a wire rack for 3 minutes, then transfer to the rack to cool.

The flavonoids that give red grapes their gorgeous color also deliver health benefits. Red grapes are particularly high in the flavonoid resveratrol, which promotes heart health, and in quercetin, which is not only an antioxidant but also has antihistamine-type effects, which may help in the treatment of allergies.

Raisin Spice Muffins

1 cup	whole wheat pastry flour	250 mL
1 cup	oat flour	250 mL
2 tsp	baking powder	10 mL
1 1/2 tsp	ground allspice	7 mL
1/2 tsp	salt	2 mL
1/2 tsp	ground cinnamon	2 mL
1/4 cup	packed light brown sugar	60 mL
1	egg	1
1 cup	low-fat (1%) milk	250 mL
2 tbsp	vegetable oil	30 mL
1 tsp	vanilla extract	5 mL
2/3 cup	raisins	150 mL

Makes 12 muffins

- Preheat oven to 350°F (180°C)
- 12-cup muffin pan, greased

1. In a large bowl, whisk together whole wheat pastry flour, oat flour, baking powder, allspice, salt and cinnamon.
2. In a medium bowl, whisk together brown sugar, egg, milk, oil and vanilla until well blended.
3. Add the egg mixture to the flour mixture and stir until just blended. Gently fold in raisins.
4. Divide batter equally among prepared muffin cups.
5. Bake in preheated oven for 22 to 25 minutes or until tops are golden and a toothpick inserted in the center comes out clean. Let cool in pan on a wire rack for 3 minutes, then transfer to the rack to cool.

Cholesterol-free, low in sodium, high in fiber and fat-free, raisins boast an array of vitamins and minerals. They are also an excellent source of quick energy, especially post-workout: they contain 70% pure fructose, which gets digested by the body easily and gives instant energy.

Pear Walnut Muffins

1¼ cups	all-purpose flour	300 mL
¾ cup	whole wheat flour	175 mL
1 tbsp	baking powder	15 mL
½ tsp	salt	2 mL
½ tsp	ground cinnamon	2 mL
⅔ cup	packed light brown sugar	150 mL
1	egg	1
¾ cup	buttermilk	175 mL
¼ cup	toasted walnut oil or vegetable oil	60 mL
1¼ cups	finely chopped firm-ripe pears	300 mL
½ cup	chopped walnuts, toasted	125 mL

These sophisticated muffins marry the simplicity of fresh pears with the flavor and depth of toasty walnuts. The pears are a good source of vitamin C and fiber, and the walnuts an excellent source of protein and omega-3 fatty acids.

Makes 12 muffins

- Preheat oven to 400°F (200°C)
- 12-cup muffin pan, greased

1. In a large bowl, whisk together all-purpose flour, whole wheat flour, baking powder, salt and cinnamon.
2. In a medium bowl, whisk together brown sugar, egg, buttermilk and oil until well blended.
3. Add the egg mixture to the flour mixture and stir until just blended. Gently fold in pears and walnuts.
4. Divide batter equally among prepared muffin cups.
5. Bake in preheated oven for 18 to 23 minutes or until tops are golden and a toothpick inserted in the center comes out clean. Let cool in pan on a wire rack for 3 minutes, then transfer to the rack to cool.

Papaya Oat Muffins

1½ cups	all-purpose flour	375 mL
1 cup	quick-cooking rolled oats	250 mL
1½ tsp	baking powder	7 mL
1½ tsp	ground ginger	7 mL
½ tsp	baking soda	2 mL
½ tsp	salt	2 mL
⅔ cup	packed light brown sugar	150 mL
1	egg	1
2 tbsp	vegetable oil	30 mL
1 tsp	vanilla extract	5 mL
1 cup	low-fat (1%) plain yogurt	250 mL
¼ cup	low-fat (1%) milk	60 mL
2 cups	chopped ripe papaya	500 mL

Papayas pack a nutritional wallop. Long trumpeted for their benefits to digestion, they also are rich in vitamin C, folate and potassium and are a good source of fiber, vitamin A, vitamin C and lutein.

Makes 12 muffins

- Preheat oven to 400°F (200°C)
- 12-cup muffin pan, greased

1. In a large bowl, whisk together flour, oats, baking powder, ginger, baking soda and salt.
2. In a medium bowl, whisk together brown sugar, egg, oil and vanilla until well blended. Whisk in yogurt and milk until blended.
3. Add the egg mixture to the flour mixture and stir until just blended. Gently fold in papaya.
4. Divide batter equally among prepared muffin cups.
5. Bake in preheated oven for 18 to 23 minutes or until tops are golden and a toothpick inserted in the center comes out clean. Let cool in pan on a wire rack for 3 minutes, then transfer to the rack to cool.

Fresh Plum Ricotta Muffins

2½ cups	whole wheat pastry flour	625 mL
1 cup	quick-cooking rolled oats, divided	250 mL
1 tbsp	baking powder	15 mL
1 tsp	baking soda	5 mL
½ tsp	salt	2 mL
½ tsp	ground cardamom	2 mL
½ tsp	ground allspice	2 mL
2	eggs	2
¾ cup	low-fat ricotta cheese	175 mL
⅔ cup	buttermilk	150 mL
½ cup	liquid honey	125 mL
¼ cup	vegetable oil	60 mL
1 tbsp	vanilla extract	15 mL
1½ cups	diced firm-ripe plums	375 mL

The plum season extends from May to October: eat up while you can. Tart-sweet plums are fantastic eaten out of hand or baked into these delectable muffins. Plums are high in fiber, potassium and vitamins C and A.

Makes 18 muffins

- Preheat oven to 400°F (200°C)
- Two 12-cup muffin pans, 18 cups lined with paper liners

1. In a large bowl, whisk together flour, ½ cup (125 mL) of the oats, baking powder, baking soda, salt, cardamom and allspice.
2. In a medium bowl, whisk together eggs, cheese, buttermilk, honey, oil and vanilla until well blended.
3. Add the egg mixture to the flour mixture and stir until just blended. Gently fold in plums.
4. Divide batter equally among prepared muffin cups. Sprinkle with the remaining oats.
5. Bake in preheated oven for 16 to 21 minutes or until tops are golden and a toothpick inserted in the center comes out clean. Let cool in pans on a wire rack for 5 minutes, then transfer to the rack to cool.

Prune and Yogurt Muffins

2 cups	whole wheat flour	500 mL
1½ cups	natural bran	375 mL
1¼ tsp	baking soda	11 mL
1 tsp	salt	5 mL
2 tbsp	packed dark brown sugar	30 mL
1	egg	1
½ cup	liquid honey	125 mL
2 tbsp	vegetable oil	30 mL
1 tbsp	vanilla extract	15 mL
2 cups	low-fat (1%) plain yogurt	500 mL
1 cup	pitted prunes, chopped	250 mL

Prunes have an impressive bio, as well as an intensely rich, moist and delicious flavor. Packed with antioxidants, they are also high in vitamin A, fiber and potassium.

Makes 18 muffins

- Preheat oven to 425°F (220°C)
- Two 12-cup muffin pans, 18 cups greased

1. In a large bowl, whisk together flour, bran, baking soda and salt.
2. In a medium bowl, whisk together brown sugar, egg, honey, oil and vanilla until well blended. Whisk in yogurt until blended.
3. Add the egg mixture to the flour mixture and stir until just blended. Gently fold in prunes.
4. Divide batter equally among prepared muffin cups.
5. Bake in preheated oven for 16 to 22 minutes or until tops are golden brown and a toothpick inserted in the center comes out clean. Let cool in pans on a wire rack for 3 minutes, then transfer to the rack to cool.

Kiwifruit Orange Muffins

2 cups	whole wheat pastry flour	500 mL
1 1/2 tsp	baking powder	7 mL
1 tsp	salt	5 mL
1/2 tsp	baking soda	2 mL
2	eggs	2
1/2 cup	liquid honey	125 mL
1 tbsp	grated orange zest	15 mL
1/3 cup	orange juice	75 mL
1/4 cup	vegetable oil	60 mL
1 1/2 cups	diced peeled kiwifruit	375 mL
1/2 cup	golden raisins	125 mL

Oranges and kiwis are among the fruits highest in calcium. Both are also bursting with vitamin C. In addition, kiwis are rich in dietary fiber and are a good source of potassium, magnesium, copper, vitamin E and manganese.

Makes 12 muffins

- Preheat oven to 350°F (180°C)
- 12-cup muffin pan, lined with paper liners

1. In a large bowl, whisk together flour, baking powder, salt and baking soda.
2. In a medium bowl, whisk together eggs, honey, orange zest, orange juice and oil until well blended.
3. Add the egg mixture to the flour mixture and stir until just blended. Gently fold in kiwifruit and raisins.
4. Divide batter equally among prepared muffin cups.
5. Bake in preheated oven for 23 to 28 minutes or until tops are golden and a toothpick inserted in the center comes out clean. Let cool in pan on a wire rack for 5 minutes, then transfer to the rack to cool.

Olive Oil Citrus Muffins

2 cups	whole wheat pastry flour	500 mL
1/4 cup	ground flax seeds	60 mL
2 tsp	baking powder	10 mL
1/2 tsp	baking soda	2 mL
1/2 tsp	salt	2 mL
2	eggs	2
1/2 cup	agave nectar	125 mL
3/4 cup	buttermilk	175 mL
1/4 cup	olive oil	60 mL
1 tbsp	finely grated lemon zest	15 mL
1 tbsp	finely grated orange zest	15 mL
1/4 cup	freshly squeezed orange juice	60 mL

Olive oil is renowned for its extensive health benefits thanks to its high content of both monounsaturated fatty acids and antioxidants. Studies have shown that olive oil offers protection against heart disease by controlling LDL ("bad") cholesterol levels while raising HDL ("good") cholesterol levels.

Makes 12 muffins

- Preheat oven to 350°F (180°C)
- 12-cup muffin pan, greased

1. In a large bowl, whisk together flour, flax seeds, baking powder, baking soda and salt.
2. In a medium bowl, whisk together eggs, agave nectar, buttermilk, oil, lemon zest, orange zest and orange juice until well blended.
3. Add the egg mixture to the flour mixture and stir until just blended.
4. Divide batter equally among prepared muffin cups.
5. Bake in preheated oven for 18 to 23 minutes or until tops are golden and a toothpick inserted in the center comes out clean. Let cool in pan on a wire rack for 3 minutes, then transfer to the rack to cool.

Lemony Dried Fig Muffins

3 tbsp	finely grated lemon zest	45 mL
2 tbsp	freshly squeezed lemon juice	30 mL
1/2 cup	liquid honey	125 mL
1 cup	chopped dried figs	250 mL
2 cups	whole wheat pastry flour	500 mL
1 1/2 tsp	baking powder	7 mL
1 tsp	baking soda	5 mL
1/2 tsp	salt	2 mL
2	eggs	2
1/3 cup	olive oil	75 mL
1 1/3 cups	low-fat (1%) plain yogurt	325 mL

Figs? A superfood? You bet. They are high in fiber, potassium and manganese, and the dried ones are available year-round at a reasonable cost.

Makes 16 muffins

- Preheat oven to 375°F (190°C)
- Two 12-cup muffin pans, 16 cups greased

1. In a small saucepan, bring lemon zest, lemon juice and honey to a simmer over medium heat. Transfer to a medium bowl, stir in figs and let cool slightly.
2. In a large bowl, whisk together flour, baking powder, baking soda and salt.
3. Whisk eggs and oil into lemon mixture until well blended. Whisk in yogurt until blended.
4. Add the egg mixture to the flour mixture and stir until just blended.
5. Divide batter equally among prepared muffin cups.
6. Bake in preheated oven for 18 to 22 minutes or until tops are golden and a toothpick inserted in the center comes out clean. Let cool in pans on a wire rack for 5 minutes, then transfer to the rack to cool.

Sweet Potato Molasses Muffins

2 1/2 cups	whole wheat pastry flour	625 mL
1 1/2 tsp	baking powder	7 mL
1/2 tsp	baking soda	2 mL
1/2 tsp	salt	2 mL
1/4 tsp	ground cinnamon	1 mL
1/4 tsp	ground nutmeg	1 mL
3	eggs	3
3/4 cup	mashed cooked sweet potato (see tip, page 330)	175 mL
3/4 cup	dark (cooking) molasses	175 mL
1/3 cup	low-fat (1%) milk	75 mL
1/4 cup	vegetable oil	60 mL

I would like to suggest a new adage: "A sweet potato a day keeps the doctor away." At the very least, they promote great health. Their levels of vitamin A (in the form of beta carotene) are off the charts: 1 cooked sweet potato has 262.2% of your daily supply.

Makes 16 muffins

- Preheat oven to 350°F (180°C)
- Two 12-cup muffin pans, 16 cups greased

1. In a large bowl, whisk together flour, baking powder, baking soda, salt, cinnamon and nutmeg.
2. In a medium bowl, whisk together eggs, sweet potato, molasses, milk and oil until well blended.
3. Add the egg mixture to the flour mixture and stir until just blended.
4. Divide batter equally among prepared muffin cups.
5. Bake in preheated oven for 22 to 27 minutes or until tops are golden and a toothpick inserted in the center comes out clean. Let cool in pans on a wire rack for 5 minutes, then transfer to the rack to cool.

Fresh Ginger Sweet Potato Muffins

¾ cup	whole wheat pastry flour	175 mL
¾ cup	all-purpose flour	175 mL
1 tbsp	baking powder	15 mL
1 tsp	ground cinnamon	5 mL
1 tsp	baking soda	5 mL
¾ tsp	salt	3 mL
1 cup	packed light brown sugar	250 mL
2	eggs	2
3 tbsp	vegetable oil	45 mL
2 tbsp	finely grated gingerroot	30 mL
1 tbsp	finely grated orange zest	15 mL
1 cup	cold mashed cooked sweet potatoes (see tip, at left)	250 mL

I am of the mindset that almost anything made with sweet potatoes is delicious, but these muffins, enhanced with fresh ginger, are particularly so. Sweet potatoes are even more easy to love based on their nutrition: they are an excellent source of vitamin A (in the form of beta carotene), a very good source of vitamin C and manganese and a good source of copper, dietary fiber, vitamin B_6, potassium and iron.

Tip

Prepare the mashed sweet potato without milk and butter. Here's how to easily cook it in the microwave: scrub sweet potatoes (about 2 medium for this recipe) and pierce each a few times with a fork. Place on a microwave-safe plate lined with a paper towel. Microwave on High, turning halfway through, for 4 to 5 minutes for the first potato plus 2 to 3 minutes for each additional potato. Let cool. Cut in half, scoop the flesh into a bowl and mash with a fork.

Makes 12 muffins

- Preheat oven to 400°F (200°C)
- 12-cup muffin pan, greased

1. In a large bowl, whisk together whole wheat pastry flour, all-purpose flour, baking powder, cinnamon, baking soda and salt.

2. In a medium bowl, whisk together brown sugar, eggs, oil, ginger and orange zest until blended. Stir in sweet potatoes until blended.

3. Add the egg mixture to the flour mixture and stir until just blended.

4. Divide batter equally among prepared muffin cups.

5. Bake in preheated oven for 18 to 22 minutes or until tops are golden and a toothpick inserted in the center comes out clean. Let cool in pan on a wire rack for 5 minutes, then transfer to the rack to cool.

Maple Squash Muffins

1 cup	whole wheat flour	250 mL
1 cup	all-purpose flour	250 mL
1/4 cup	ground flax seeds	60 mL
2 tsp	baking powder	10 mL
2 tsp	pumpkin pie spice	10 mL
1/2 tsp	baking soda	5 mL
1/2 tsp	salt	5 mL
2	eggs	2
1	package (12 oz/375 g) frozen winter squash purée, thawed	1
1/2 cup	pure maple syrup	125 mL
1/3 cup	buttermilk	75 mL
1/4 cup	vegetable oil	60 mL
1 tsp	vanilla extract	5 mL

Can't find frozen winter squash purée? Not a problem; simply take a stroll to the baby food section of the supermarket. Three 4-ounce (128 mL) jars of baby food squash purée yield the quantity needed here.

Makes 12 muffins

- Preheat oven to 400°F (200°C)
- 12-cup muffin pan, lined with paper liners

1. In a large bowl, whisk together whole wheat flour, all-purpose flour, flax seeds, baking powder, pumpkin pie spice, baking soda and salt.

2. In a medium bowl, whisk together eggs, squash, maple syrup, buttermilk, oil and vanilla until well blended.

3. Add the egg mixture to the flour mixture and stir until just blended.

4. Divide batter equally among prepared muffin cups.

5. Bake in preheated oven for 16 to 20 minutes or until tops are golden and a toothpick inserted in the center comes out clean. Let cool in pan on a wire rack for 5 minutes, then transfer to the rack to cool.

Pepita Pumpkin Muffins

2 cups	whole wheat pastry flour	500 mL
2 1/2 tsp	pumpkin pie spice	12 mL
1 tsp	baking soda	5 mL
1 tsp	salt	5 mL
3/4 cup	packed dark brown sugar	175 mL
2	eggs	2
1/4 cup	dark (cooking) molasses	60 mL
1/4 cup	vegetable oil	60 mL
1 tsp	vanilla extract	5 mL
1 cup	pumpkin purée (not pie filling)	250 mL
3/4 cup	buttermilk	175 mL
1/2 cup	raw green pumpkin seeds (pepitas)	250 mL

Pumpkin is chock full of powerful antioxidants known as carotenoids. Pepitas add great crunch and nutty flavor, as well as protein.

Makes 12 muffins

- Preheat oven to 400°F (200°C)
- 12-cup muffin pan, greased

1. In a large bowl, whisk together flour, pumpkin pie spice, baking soda and salt.

2. In a medium bowl, whisk together brown sugar, eggs, molasses, oil and vanilla until well blended. Whisk in pumpkin and buttermilk until blended.

3. Add the egg mixture to the flour mixture and stir until just blended.

4. Divide batter equally among prepared muffin cups. Sprinkle with pumpkin seeds.

5. Bake in preheated oven for 18 to 22 minutes or until tops are golden and a toothpick inserted in the center comes out clean. Let cool in pan on a wire rack for 5 minutes, then transfer to the rack to cool.

Whole-Meal Pumpkin Chocolate Chip Muffins

1 cup	all-purpose flour	250 mL
1 cup	whole wheat flour	250 mL
2 tsp	baking powder	10 mL
2 tsp	pumpkin pie spice	10 mL
1/2 tsp	salt	2 mL
1/4 tsp	baking soda	1 mL
2/3 cup	packed light brown sugar	150 mL
2	eggs	2
1/2 cup	vegetable oil	125 mL
1 tsp	vanilla extract	5 mL
3/4 cup	pumpkin purée (not pie filling)	175 mL
1/3 cup	buttermilk	75 mL
1 cup	miniature semisweet chocolate chips	250 mL

Besides its unmistakable flavor, dark chocolate is packed with antioxidants called flavonols, which benefit heart health and cholesterol levels.

Makes 12 muffins

- Preheat oven to 400°F (200°C)
- 12-cup muffin pan, greased

1. In a large bowl, whisk together all-purpose flour, whole wheat flour, baking powder, pumpkin pie spice, salt and baking soda.
2. In a medium bowl, whisk together brown sugar, eggs, oil and vanilla until well blended. Whisk in pumpkin and buttermilk until blended.
3. Add the egg mixture to the flour mixture and stir until just blended. Gently fold in chocolate.
4. Divide batter equally among prepared muffin cups.
5. Bake in preheated oven for 17 to 21 minutes or until a toothpick inserted in the center comes out clean. Let cool in pan on a wire rack for 5 minutes, then transfer to the rack to cool.

Pumpkin Oat Bran Muffins

1 1/2 cups	oat bran	375 mL
1/2 cup	whole wheat pastry flour	125 mL
2 tsp	baking powder	10 mL
1 tsp	pumpkin pie spice	5 mL
1/2 tsp	salt	2 mL
1	egg	1
1/2 cup	liquid honey	125 mL
1/2 cup	low-fat (1%) milk	125 mL
1/4 cup	vegetable oil	60 mL
1 tsp	vanilla extract	5 mL
1 cup	pumpkin purée (not pie filling)	250 mL

These pumpkin muffins are moist and full of flavor. Oat bran contains B-complex vitamins, protein, minerals and heart-healthy soluble fiber.

Makes 12 muffins

- Preheat oven to 425°F (220°C)
- 12-cup muffin pan, greased

1. In a large bowl, whisk together oat bran, flour, baking powder, pumpkin pie spice and salt.
2. In a medium bowl, whisk together egg, honey, milk, oil and vanilla until well blended. Whisk in pumpkin until blended.
3. Add the egg mixture to the oat bran mixture and stir until just blended.
4. Divide batter equally among prepared muffin cups.
5. Bake in preheated oven for 18 to 22 minutes or until tops are golden and a toothpick inserted in the center comes out clean. Let cool in pan on a wire rack for 3 minutes, then transfer to the rack to cool.

Multigrain Pumpkin Spice Muffins

1½ cups	whole wheat pastry flour	375 mL
1 cup	yellow cornmeal	250 mL
¼ cup	ground flax seeds	60 mL
1 tbsp	pumpkin pie spice	15 mL
2 tsp	baking powder	10 mL
1 tsp	baking soda	5 mL
½ tsp	salt	2 mL
¾ cup	packed light brown sugar	175 mL
3	eggs	3
¾ cup	buttermilk	175 mL
½ cup	vegetable oil	125 mL
1	can (15 oz/425 mL) pumpkin purée (not pie filling) (or 1¾ cups/425 mL)	1

Makes 18 muffins

- Preheat oven to 350°F (180°C)
- Two 12-cup muffin pans, 18 cups greased

1. In a large bowl, whisk together flour, cornmeal, flax seeds, pumpkin pie spice, baking powder, baking soda and salt.

2. In a medium bowl, whisk together brown sugar, eggs, buttermilk and oil until well blended. Whisk in pumpkin until blended.

3. Add the egg mixture to the flour mixture and stir until just blended.

4. Divide batter equally among prepared muffin cups.

5. Bake in preheated oven for 24 to 28 minutes or until tops are golden and a toothpick inserted in the center comes out clean. Let cool in pans on a wire rack for 5 minutes, then transfer to the rack to cool.

I have loved pumpkin — in breads, muffins and soups — since I was a child, but I adore it now that I'm an adult and know all of the nutritional benefits that accompany its wonderful flavor and texture. It is considered one of the most nutritionally valuable foods around, packing an abundance of disease-fighting nutrients. Moreover, it is inexpensive, available year-round in canned form, incredibly easy to incorporate into recipes, high in fiber and low in calories. Need I add more? Perhaps just that it is scrumptious in these spiced multigrain muffins.

Pumpkin Dried Cherry Muffins

1¼ cups	whole wheat pastry flour	300 mL
1 cup	all-purpose flour	250 mL
1 tbsp	pumpkin pie spice	15 mL
1½ tsp	baking soda	7 mL
¼ tsp	salt	1 mL
1 cup	packed light brown sugar	250 mL
2	eggs	2
⅓ cup	buttermilk	75 mL
⅓ cup	vegetable oil	75 mL
¼ cup	liquid honey	60 mL
1 tsp	vanilla extract	5 mL
1 cup	pumpkin purée (not pie filling)	250 mL
1 cup	dried sour (tart) cherries	250 mL

Cherry season may be brief, but you can always opt for the intense, tart-sweet flavor and year-round availability of dried cherries. Dried cherries are high in certain minerals and vitamins, such as potassium, vitamin C and B-complex vitamins.

Makes 18 muffins

- Preheat oven to 400°F (200°C)
- Two 12-cup muffin pans, 18 cups greased

1. In a large bowl, whisk together whole wheat pastry flour, all-purpose flour, pumpkin pie spice, baking soda and salt.

2. In a medium bowl, whisk together brown sugar, eggs, buttermilk, oil, honey and vanilla until well blended. Whisk in pumpkin until blended.

3. Add the egg mixture to the flour mixture and stir until just blended. Gently fold in cherries.

4. Divide batter equally among prepared muffin cups.

5. Bake in preheated oven for 18 to 23 minutes or until tops are golden and a toothpick inserted in the center comes out clean. Let cool in pans on a wire rack for 3 minutes, then transfer to the rack to cool.

Zucchini Oat Muffins

1¼ cups	whole wheat flour	300 mL
1¼ cups	all-purpose flour	300 mL
½ cup	quick-cooking rolled oats	125 mL
1 tbsp	baking powder	15 mL
1 tsp	salt	5 mL
1 tsp	ground cinnamon	5 mL
1 cup	packed light brown sugar	250 mL
4	eggs	4
¾ cup	vegetable oil	175 mL
1½ cups	shredded zucchini	375 mL
½ cup	raisins	125 mL
½ cup	chopped walnuts, toasted	125 mL

How could something so humble — and so nutritious — be so scrumptious? These muffins steer clear of being overly sweet. Toasty walnuts add great crunch and flavor, as well as protein and omega-3s.

Makes 18 muffins

- Preheat oven to 400°F (200°C)
- Two 12-cup muffin pans, 18 cups lined with paper liners

1. In a large bowl, whisk together whole wheat flour, all-purpose flour, oats, baking powder, salt and cinnamon.

2. In a medium bowl, whisk together brown sugar, eggs and oil until well blended. Stir in zucchini.

3. Add the egg mixture to the flour mixture and stir until just blended. Gently fold in raisins and walnuts.

4. Divide batter equally among prepared muffin cups.

5. Bake in preheated oven for 20 to 25 minutes or until tops are golden and a toothpick inserted in the center comes out clean. Let cool in pans on a wire rack for 5 minutes, then transfer to the rack to cool.

Zucchini Pecan Muffins

1 1/3 cups	whole wheat flour	325 mL
2/3 cup	natural bran	150 mL
2 tsp	baking powder	10 mL
1 tsp	ground cinnamon	5 mL
3/4 tsp	salt	3 mL
1/4 tsp	ground cloves	1 mL
2/3 cup	granulated sugar	150 mL
2	eggs	2
1/3 cup	vegetable oil	75 mL
1/4 cup	low-fat (1%) milk	60 mL
1 tsp	vanilla extract	5 mL
2 cups	coarsely shredded zucchini	500 mL
1/2 cup	chopped pecans	125 mL

For maximum health benefits, leave your zucchini unpeeled. Zucchini provides large amounts of folate and potassium, and the dark green peel contains beta carotene. It also adds pretty specks of emerald throughout the muffins.

Makes 12 muffins

- Preheat oven to 375°F (180°C)
- 12-cup muffin pan, greased

1. In a large bowl, whisk together flour, bran, baking powder, cinnamon, salt and cloves.
2. In a medium bowl, whisk together sugar, eggs, oil, milk and vanilla until well blended. Stir in zucchini.
3. Add the egg mixture to the flour mixture and stir until just blended. Gently fold in pecans.
4. Divide batter equally among prepared muffin cups.
5. Bake in preheated oven for 25 to 30 minutes or until a toothpick inserted in the center comes out clean. Let cool in pan on a wire rack for 5 minutes, then transfer to the rack to cool.

Brown Sugar Buttermilk Spelt Muffins

2 1/3 cups	spelt flour	575 mL
1/4 cup	ground flax seeds	60 mL
2 tsp	ground cinnamon	10 mL
1 tsp	baking powder	5 mL
1/2 tsp	salt	2 mL
1/4 tsp	baking soda	1 mL
1/4 tsp	ground nutmeg	1 mL
1/2 cup	packed dark brown sugar	125 mL
2	eggs	2
1 cup	buttermilk	250 mL
2/3 cup	mashed ripe bananas	150 mL
1 tsp	vanilla extract	5 mL

Spelt is a very nutritious ancient grain with a nutty flavor. When ground into flour, it yields incredibly delicious baked goods. It is an excellent source of vitamin B_2, a very good source of manganese and a good source of niacin, thiamin and copper.

Makes 12 muffins

- Preheat oven to 375°F (190°C)
- 12-cup muffin pan, greased

1. In a large bowl, whisk together flour, flax seeds, cinnamon, baking powder, salt, baking soda and nutmeg.
2. In a medium bowl, whisk together brown sugar, eggs, buttermilk, bananas and vanilla until well blended.
3. Add the egg mixture to the flour mixture and stir until just blended.
4. Divide batter equally among prepared muffin cups.
5. Bake in preheated oven for 22 to 25 minutes or until tops are golden and a toothpick inserted in the center comes out clean. Let cool in pan on a wire rack for 3 minutes, then transfer to the rack to cool.

Almond Butter Bran Muffins

1½ cups	bran cereal, such as All-Bran	375 mL
1½ cups	low-fat (1%) milk	375 mL
½ cup	almond butter, well stirred	125 mL
¾ cup	all-purpose flour	175 mL
½ cup	whole wheat flour	125 mL
1 tbsp	baking powder	15 mL
1 tsp	salt	5 mL
½ cup	packed light brown sugar	125 mL
1	egg	1
¼ cup	vegetable oil	60 mL
1 tsp	almond extract	5 mL
½ cup	slivered almonds	125 mL

Here, almond butter enriches bran cereal, creating a dense and delicious muffin that will sustain you through the most rigorous morning without a thought of lunch.

Tip
Any natural nut butter may be used in place of the almond butter.

Makes 18 muffins

- Preheat oven to 400°F (200°C)
- Two 12-cup muffin pans, 18 cups lined with paper liners

1. In a medium bowl, combine cereal and milk. Let stand for 5 minutes. Stir in almond butter until blended.
2. In a large bowl, whisk together all-purpose flour, whole wheat flour, baking powder and salt.
3. Whisk brown sugar, egg, oil and almond extract into cereal mixture until well blended.
4. Add the egg mixture to the flour mixture and stir until just blended.
5. Divide batter equally among prepared muffin cups. Sprinkle with almonds.
6. Bake in preheated oven for 20 to 25 minutes or until tops are golden and a toothpick inserted in the center comes out clean. Let cool in pans on a wire rack for 3 minutes, then transfer to the rack to cool.

Eight-Grain Muffins

1 cup	8-grain or other multigrain hot cereal (see tip, page 322)	250 mL
1¼ cups	buttermilk	300 mL
1 cup	whole wheat flour	250 mL
1 tsp	salt	5 mL
1 tsp	baking powder	5 mL
1 tsp	baking soda	5 mL
½ cup	packed light brown sugar	125 mL
1	egg	1
⅓ cup	vegetable oil	75 mL
1 tsp	vanilla extract	5 mL

Looking to incorporate more whole grains into your diet? Here's my quick, easy, portable and delicious solution.

Makes 12 muffins

- 12-cup muffin pan, greased

1. In a large bowl, combine cereal and buttermilk. Let stand for 20 minutes.
2. Preheat oven to 400°F (200°C).
3. In another large bowl, whisk together flour, salt, baking powder and baking soda.
4. Whisk brown sugar, egg, oil and vanilla into cereal mixture until well blended.
5. Add the egg mixture to the flour mixture and stir until just blended.
6. Divide batter equally among prepared muffin cups.
7. Bake for 15 to 18 minutes or until tops are golden and a toothpick inserted in the center comes out clean. Let cool in pan on a wire rack for 3 minutes, then transfer to the rack to cool.

Whole-Grain Amaranth Muffins with Dried Cranberries

1 cup	boiling water	250 mL
1 cup	dried cranberries	250 mL
1/2 cup	whole-grain amaranth	125 mL
2 cups	whole wheat pastry flour	500 mL
2 tsp	baking powder	10 mL
1 tsp	ground cinnamon	5 mL
1/2 tsp	salt	2 mL
2	eggs, beaten	2
1/2 cup	liquid honey	125 mL
1/4 cup	vegetable oil	60 mL
1 tsp	vanilla extract	5 mL
1 cup	chopped pecans, toasted	250 mL

Amaranth, grown for centuries by the Aztecs, has twice as much iron as wheat and is higher in protein and fiber. The tiny seeds are mild, sweet, nutty and subtly malt-like in flavor. Do use caution in cooking it though: amaranth has a "sticky" texture that contrasts with the fluffier texture of most grains, and if overcooked, it can become somewhat gummy.

Makes 12 muffins

- 12-cup muffin pan, greased

1. In a medium bowl, combine boiling water, cranberries and amaranth. Let stand for 20 minutes.
2. Preheat oven to 350°F (180°C).
3. In a large bowl, whisk together flour, baking powder, cinnamon and salt.
4. Stir eggs, honey, oil and vanilla into cranberry mixture until well blended.
5. Add the egg mixture to the flour mixture and stir until just blended. Gently fold in pecans.
6. Divide batter equally among prepared muffin cups.
7. Bake for 20 to 25 minutes or until tops are golden and a toothpick inserted in the center comes out clean. Let cool in pan on a wire rack for 3 minutes, then transfer to the rack to cool.

Amaranth and Hazelnut Muffins

1 cup	amaranth flour	250 mL
1/2 cup	whole wheat pastry flour	125 mL
2 tsp	baking powder	10 mL
1/4 tsp	salt	1 mL
1	egg	1
1/2 cup	low-fat (1%) milk	125 mL
1/4 cup	vegetable oil	60 mL
1/4 cup	liquid honey	60 mL
1 tsp	vanilla extract	5 mL
3/4 cup	chopped hazelnuts, toasted	175 mL

In addition to being very high in protein and iron, amaranth contains tocotrienols (a form of vitamin E), which studies indicate have a cholesterol-lowering function in humans.

Makes 12 muffins

- Preheat oven to 350°F (180°C)
- 12-cup muffin pan, greased

1. In a large bowl, whisk together amaranth flour, whole wheat pastry flour, baking powder and salt.
2. In a medium bowl, whisk together egg, milk, oil, honey and vanilla until well blended.
3. Add the egg mixture to the flour mixture and stir until just blended. Gently fold in hazelnuts.
4. Divide batter equally among prepared muffin cups.
5. Bake in preheated oven for 18 to 23 minutes or until tops are golden and a toothpick inserted in the center comes out clean. Let cool in pan on a wire rack for 3 minutes, then transfer to the rack to cool.

Flax Seed Morning Glory Muffins

1 cup	bran cereal, such as All-Bran	250 mL
2/3 cup	low-fat (1%) milk	150 mL
1 1/4 cups	all-purpose flour	300 mL
1/2 cup	ground flax seeds	125 mL
1 tbsp	baking powder	15 mL
2 tsp	ground cinnamon	10 mL
1/2 tsp	salt	2 mL
1/2 cup	packed light brown sugar	125 mL
2	eggs	2
2 tbsp	vegetable oil	30 mL
1 tsp	vanilla extract	5 mL
3/4 cup	chopped apple	175 mL
1/2 cup	finely shredded carrot	125 mL
1/2 cup	chopped dried cherries or dried blueberries	125 mL
1/4 cup	unsweetened flaked or shredded coconut	60 mL

These morning glory muffins are chock full of goodness and great taste. Flax seeds — which are high in omega-3 fatty acids — replace a significant amount of fat in the recipe, and shredded carrots and chopped apples keep the muffins moist.

Makes 12 muffins

- Preheat oven to 375°F (190°C)
- 12-cup muffin pan, greased

1. Place cereal in a ziplock bag and seal bag. Using a rolling pin or kitchen mallet, hammer gently until pulverized, resembling bread crumbs. (Or crush cereal in a food processor.)

2. In a large bowl, combine cereal and milk. Let stand for 5 minutes.

3. In a medium bowl, whisk together flour, flax seeds, baking powder, cinnamon and salt.

4. Whisk brown sugar, eggs, oil and vanilla into cereal mixture until well blended.

5. Add the flour mixture to the cereal mixture and stir until just blended. Gently fold in apple, carrot, cherries and coconut.

6. Divide batter equally among prepared muffin cups.

7. Bake in preheated oven for 22 to 25 minutes or until tops are golden and a toothpick inserted in the center comes out clean. Let cool in pan on a wire rack for 3 minutes, then transfer to the rack to cool.

Orange Bran Flax Muffins

1 1/2 cups	oat bran	375 mL
1 cup	natural bran	250 mL
1 cup	all-purpose flour	250 mL
1/2 cup	ground flax seeds	125 mL
1 tbsp	baking powder	15 mL
1 tsp	baking soda	5 mL
1/2 tsp	salt	2 mL
1 cup	granulated sugar	250 mL
2	navel oranges, peeled and quartered	2
2	eggs	2
1 cup	buttermilk	250 mL
1/2 cup	vegetable oil	125 mL
1 cup	golden raisins	250 mL

Oranges are an excellent source of vitamin C and flavonoids. In addition, oranges are a good source of vitamin A, B vitamins, amino acids, beta carotene, pectin, potassium, folate, calcium, iodine, phosphorus, sodium, zinc, manganese, chlorine and iron.

Makes 12 muffins

- Preheat oven to 375°F (190°C)
- 12-cup muffin pan, greased

1. In a large bowl, whisk together oat bran, natural bran, flour, flax seeds, baking powder, baking soda and salt.
2. In a blender or food processor, process sugar, oranges, eggs, buttermilk and oil until blended and smooth.
3. Add the egg mixture to the flour mixture and stir until just blended. Gently fold in raisins.
4. Divide batter equally among prepared muffin cups.
5. Bake in preheated oven for 18 to 22 minutes or until tops are light golden brown and a toothpick inserted in the center comes out clean. Let cool in pan on a wire rack for 3 minutes, then transfer to the rack to cool.

Flax and Date Whole Wheat Muffins

1 1/2 cups	whole wheat pastry flour	375 mL
3/4 cup	ground flax seeds	175 mL
1 tsp	ground cinnamon	5 mL
1 tsp	baking soda	5 mL
1/2 tsp	salt	2 mL
1	egg	1
1 cup	low-fat (1%) plain yogurt	250 mL
1/3 cup	dark (cooking) molasses	75 mL
1 tsp	vanilla extract	5 mL
1 cup	pitted dates, chopped	250 mL

Beyond sheer deliciousness, dates are a great source of dietary fiber, are one of the best natural sources of potassium and contain a variety of B-complex vitamins: thiamin, riboflavin, niacin, vitamin B_6 and pantothenic acid.

Makes 12 muffins

- Preheat oven to 350°F (180°C)
- 12-cup muffin pan, greased

1. In a large bowl, whisk together flour, flax seeds, cinnamon, baking soda and salt.
2. In a medium bowl, whisk together egg, yogurt, molasses and vanilla until well blended.
3. Add the egg mixture to the flour mixture and stir until just blended. Gently fold in dates.
4. Divide batter equally among prepared muffin cups.
5. Bake in preheated oven for 22 to 27 minutes or until tops are light golden brown and a toothpick inserted in the center comes out clean. Let cool in pan on a wire rack for 3 minutes, then transfer to the rack to cool.

Golden Apricot Quinoa Muffins

1 cup	yellow cornmeal	250 mL
3/4 cup	chopped dried apricots	175 mL
1/3 cup	quinoa, rinsed	75 mL
1 tbsp	finely grated orange zest	15 mL
1 1/4 cups	orange juice	300 mL
1 1/4 cups	whole wheat pastry flour	300 mL
2 tsp	baking powder	10 mL
1/2 tsp	salt	2 mL
1/4 tsp	baking soda	1 mL
1	egg, beaten	1
1/4 cup	liquid honey	60 mL
1/4 cup	vegetable oil	60 mL

Sweet and nutty in flavor, quinoa is a superfood if ever there was one. More than 100 varieties are grown in the Andes (most of the supply in natural food stores is from Ecuador and Bolivia), and they come in various colors of ivory-tan, black or red. Use any variety here — you cannot go wrong, in flavor or nutrition.

Makes 12 muffins

- 12-cup muffin pan, greased

1. In a large heatproof bowl, combine cornmeal, apricots and quinoa.
2. In a small saucepan, bring orange juice to a boil over high heat. Pour over cornmeal mixture and stir to combine. Let stand for at least 1 hour or for up to 12 hours.
3. Preheat oven to 375°F (190°C).
4. In another large bowl, whisk together flour, baking powder, salt and baking soda.
5. Stir orange zest, egg, honey and oil into quinoa mixture until well blended.
6. Add the egg mixture to the flour mixture and stir until just blended.
7. Divide batter equally among prepared muffin cups.
8. Bake for 24 to 28 minutes or until tops are golden and a toothpick inserted in the center comes out clean. Let cool in pan on a wire rack for 3 minutes, then transfer to the rack to cool.

Whole Wheat and Rye Muffins

1 cup	whole wheat pastry flour	250 mL
1 cup	dark rye flour	250 mL
1 1/2 tsp	baking powder	7 mL
1 tsp	salt	5 mL
1/2 tsp	baking soda	2 mL
1/3 cup	packed dark brown sugar	75 mL
1	egg	1
1 cup	low-fat (1%) milk	250 mL
1/2 cup	vegetable oil	125 mL

A cinch to prepare, these muffins are built on a foundation of two superfood flours. The first is whole wheat pastry flour, which has all of the nutrition of regular whole wheat flour but delivers a much lighter crumb and texture. The second, dark rye flour, adds a rich nuttiness to the muffins, as well as high levels of whole-grain fiber and manganese.

Makes 12 muffins

- Preheat oven to 400°F (200°C)
- 12-cup muffin pan, greased

1. In a large bowl, whisk together whole wheat pastry flour, rye flour, baking powder, salt and baking soda.
2. In a medium bowl, whisk together brown sugar, egg, milk and oil until well blended.
3. Add the egg mixture to the flour mixture and stir until just blended.
4. Divide batter equally among prepared muffin cups.
5. Bake in preheated oven for 20 to 25 minutes or until tops are golden and a toothpick inserted in the center comes out clean. Let cool in pan on a wire rack for 3 minutes, then transfer to the rack to cool.

Power-Packed Health Nut Muffins

1 cup	whole wheat flour	250 mL
3/4 cup	wheat germ	175 mL
1/2 cup	instant skim milk powder	125 mL
1/2 cup	brewer's yeast	125 mL
1/2 cup	sesame seeds	125 mL
1/2 cup	unsalted roasted sunflower seeds	125 mL
1/4 cup	ground flax seeds	60 mL
1/4 cup	large-flake (old-fashioned) rolled oats	60 mL
2 1/2 tsp	baking powder	12 mL
1 tsp	salt	5 mL
1/2 tsp	baking soda	2 mL
3/4 cup	packed dark brown sugar	175 mL
2	eggs	2
1/2 cup	vegetable oil	125 mL
2 tbsp	blackstrap or dark (cooking) molasses	30 mL
1 1/2 cups	low-fat (1%) plain yogurt	375 mL
1 cup	raisins	250 mL
1 cup	chopped walnuts, toasted	250 mL

Forget power bars: these delectable muffins are the mother lode of superfoods when it comes to healthy handheld food to go. In addition to providing healthy carbohydrates from the whole wheat flour, wheat germ, raisins and oats, they are also protein-rich thanks to the skim milk powder, sesame seeds, sunflower seeds, yogurt and walnuts.

Tip

If you cannot find unsalted roasted sunflower seeds, use salted roasted seeds and decrease the salt in the recipe by 1/4 tsp (1 mL).

Makes 16 muffins

- Preheat oven to 375°F (190°C)
- Two 12-cup muffin pans, 16 cups greased

1. In a large bowl, whisk together flour, wheat germ, milk powder, brewer's yeast, sesame seeds, sunflower seeds, flax seeds, oats, baking powder, salt and baking soda.

2. In a medium bowl, whisk together brown sugar, eggs, oil and molasses until well blended. Whisk in yogurt until blended.

3. Add the egg mixture to the flour mixture and stir until just blended. Gently fold in raisins and walnuts.

4. Divide batter equally among prepared muffin cups.

5. Bake in preheated oven for 18 to 22 minutes or until tops are golden and a toothpick inserted in the center comes out clean. Let cool in pans on a wire rack for 3 minutes, then transfer to the rack to cool.

Maple Millet Muffins

½ cup	millet	125 mL
2¼ cups	whole wheat pastry flour	550 mL
1½ tsp	baking powder	7 mL
1 tsp	baking soda	5 mL
1 tsp	salt	5 mL
2	eggs	2
1 cup	buttermilk	250 mL
½ cup	vegetable oil	125 mL
½ cup	pure maple syrup	125 mL

Millet may look familiar if you have ever filled a bird feeder: it is a primary ingredient in most bird seed mixes. But it is extremely nutritious and delicious for humans, too, and is a staple food across Africa and the Far East. Easily digested because it is alkaline (most grains are acidic), millet adds great crunch and nutty flavor to all sorts of baked goods and is a wonderful — and inexpensive — substitute for nuts.

Tip

Liquid honey, agave nectar or brown rice syrup may be used in place of the maple syrup.

Makes 12 muffins

- 12-cup muffin pan, greased

1. Heat a large skillet over medium-high heat. Toast millet, stirring occasionally, for 3 to 4 minutes or until golden brown and just beginning to pop. Transfer to a plate and let cool.
2. Preheat oven to 400°F (200°C).
3. In a large bowl, whisk together millet, flour, baking powder, baking soda and salt.
4. In a medium bowl, whisk together eggs, buttermilk, oil and maple syrup until well blended.
5. Add the egg mixture to the flour mixture and stir until just blended.
6. Divide batter equally among prepared muffin cups.
7. Bake for 15 to 20 minutes or until tops are golden and a toothpick inserted in the center comes out clean. Let cool in pan on a wire rack for 3 minutes, then transfer to the rack to cool.

Quinoa Raisin Muffins

1 cup	quinoa, rinsed	250 mL
1 cup	whole wheat pastry flour	250 mL
1 cup	all-purpose flour	250 mL
1½ tsp	baking powder	7 mL
1 tsp	salt	5 mL
½ tsp	baking soda	2 mL
1	egg	1
¾ cup	low-fat (1%) plain yogurt	175 mL
½ cup	liquid honey	125 mL
¼ cup	vegetable oil	60 mL
1 tsp	vanilla extract	5 mL
½ cup	raisins	125 mL

Botanically speaking, quinoa is an herb used as a grain — and we should all be eating it by the heaping bowlful. It is loaded with all of the essential amino acids, as well as vitamins and minerals. It's also delicious and makes a tender raisin muffin that you will likely make one of your new standards.

Makes 12 muffins

- 12-cup muffin pan, greased

1. In a small saucepan, combine quinoa and 1 cup (250 mL) water. Bring to a boil over medium-high heat. Reduce heat to low, cover and simmer for 15 minutes or until water is absorbed. Fluff with a fork and let cool.
2. Preheat oven to 350°F (180°C).
3. In a large bowl, whisk together whole wheat pastry flour, all-purpose flour, baking powder, salt and baking soda.
4. In a medium bowl, whisk together egg, yogurt, honey, oil and vanilla until well blended.
5. Add the egg mixture to the flour mixture and stir until just blended. Gently fold in quinoa and raisins.
6. Divide batter equally among prepared muffin cups.
7. Bake for 25 to 30 minutes or until a toothpick inserted in the center comes out clean. Let cool in pan on a wire rack for 5 minutes, then transfer to the rack to cool.

Honey Spelt Spice Muffins

2⅓ cups	spelt flour	575 mL
¼ cup	ground flax seeds	60 mL
2 tsp	ground cinnamon	10 mL
1 tsp	ground nutmeg	5 mL
1 tsp	baking powder	5 mL
½ tsp	salt	2 mL
¼ tsp	ground cloves	1 mL
2	eggs	2
1 cup	buttermilk	250 mL
½ cup	mashed ripe banana	125 mL
½ cup	liquid honey	125 mL
1 tsp	vanilla extract	5 mL

The glucose in honey is absorbed by the body quickly and gives an immediate energy boost, while the fructose is absorbed more slowly, providing sustained energy.

Makes 12 muffins

- Preheat oven to 375°F (190°C)
- 12-cup muffin pan, greased

1. In a large bowl, whisk together flour, flax seeds, cinnamon, nutmeg, baking powder, salt and cloves.
2. In a medium bowl, whisk together eggs, buttermilk, banana, honey and vanilla until well blended.
3. Add the egg mixture to the flour mixture and stir until just blended.
4. Divide batter equally among prepared muffin cups.
5. Bake in preheated oven for 18 to 22 minutes or until tops are golden and a toothpick inserted in the center comes out clean. Let cool in pan on a wire rack for 3 minutes, then transfer to the rack to cool.

Honey, Whole Wheat and Wheat Germ Muffins

2 cups	whole wheat flour	500 mL
2¹/₂ tbsp	baking powder	32 mL
1 tsp	salt	5 mL
2	eggs	2
³/₄ cup	liquid honey	175 mL
¹/₃ cup	olive oil	75 mL
1¹/₂ tsp	vanilla extract	7 mL
1³/₄ cups	low-fat (1%) milk	425 mL
2 cups	toasted wheat germ (see tip, page 346)	500 mL

Wheat germ, especially the toasted variety, should be a staple in everyone's refrigerator. It adds a great toasty flavor to a wealth of baked goods, can be used in place of bread crumbs in both sweet and savory dishes and is delicious sprinkled atop yogurt and fruit. If the flavor alone isn't convincing enough, consider the nutrition it offers (hold onto your hat): B vitamins (such as folate, niacin, thiamin and vitamin B_6), calcium, complex carbohydrates, fiber, iron, magnesium, manganese, omega-3 fatty acids, phosphorous, potassium, protein, selenium, vitamin E and zinc.

Makes 18 muffins

- Preheat oven to 350°F (180°C)
- Two 12-cup muffin pans, 18 cups lined with paper liners

1. In a large bowl, whisk together flour, baking powder and salt.

2. In another large bowl, whisk together eggs, honey, oil and vanilla until well blended. Whisk in milk until blended. Stir in wheat germ.

3. Add the egg mixture to the flour mixture and stir until just blended.

4. Divide batter equally among prepared muffin cups.

5. Bake in preheated oven for 18 to 22 minutes or until tops are golden and a toothpick inserted in the center comes out clean. Let cool in pans on a wire rack for 3 minutes, then transfer to the rack to cool.

Honey, Corn and Quinoa Muffins

1 cup	yellow cornmeal	250 mL
1/3 cup	quinoa, rinsed	75 mL
1 1/4 cups	boiling water	300 mL
1 1/4 cups	whole wheat pastry flour	300 mL
2 tsp	baking powder	10 mL
1/2 tsp	baking soda	2 mL
1/2 tsp	salt	2 mL
1	egg	1
1/3 cup	liquid honey	75 mL
1 cup	buttermilk	250 mL

For this recipe, choose stone-ground cornmeal, which retains the hull and germ of the corn kernel and usually has a more noticeable corn flavor. It is more perishable, so it should be stored in the refrigerator or freezer to keep it from getting rancid.

Makes 12 muffins

- 12-cup muffin pan, greased

1. In a large heatproof bowl, combine cornmeal and quinoa. Stir in boiling water until blended. Let stand for at least 1 hour or for up to 12 hours.
2. Preheat oven to 375°F (190°C).
3. In another large bowl, whisk together flour, baking powder, baking soda and salt.
4. Stir egg, honey and buttermilk into quinoa mixture until well blended.
5. Add the egg mixture to the flour mixture and stir until just blended.
6. Divide batter equally among prepared muffin cups.
7. Bake for 23 to 26 minutes or until tops are golden and a toothpick inserted in the center comes out clean. Let cool in pan on a wire rack for 5 minutes, then transfer to the rack to cool.

Tropical Whole-Meal Muffins

1 1/2 cups	bran cereal, such as All-Bran	375 mL
1 cup	buttermilk	250 mL
1 1/2 cups	whole wheat flour	375 mL
1 tbsp	baking powder	15 mL
2 tsp	ground allspice	10 mL
1/2 tsp	salt	2 mL
1/2 tsp	baking soda	2 mL
1	egg, beaten	1
3/4 cup	unsweetened applesauce	175 mL
3/4 cup	dark (cooking) molasses	175 mL
1/3 cup	vegetable oil	75 mL
1 cup	dried tropical fruit bits	250 mL
1/2 cup	unsweetened flaked or shredded coconut	125 mL

The daily recommendations for fruit and fiber may sound daunting, but they are easily — and deliciously — met with whole-grain foods and dried fruit.

Makes 12 muffins

- Preheat oven to 400°F (200°C)
- 12-cup muffin pan, greased

1. In a large bowl, combine cereal and buttermilk. Let stand for 10 minutes.
2. In another large bowl, whisk together flour, baking powder, allspice, salt and baking soda.
3. Stir egg, applesauce, molasses and oil into cereal mixture until well blended.
4. Add the egg mixture to the flour mixture and stir until just blended. Gently fold in fruit bits.
5. Divide batter equally among prepared muffin cups. Sprinkle with coconut.
6. Bake in preheated oven for 18 to 22 minutes or until tops are firm to the touch and a toothpick inserted in the center comes out clean. Let cool in pan on a wire rack for 3 minutes, then transfer to the rack to cool.

Toasted Wheat Germ Muffins

2 cups	toasted wheat germ (see tip, below)	500 mL
1 cup	instant skim milk powder	250 mL
2 tsp	baking powder	10 mL
1/2 tsp	salt	2 mL
4	eggs	4
2/3 cup	unsalted butter, melted	150 mL
2/3 cup	liquid honey	150 mL
2 tsp	vanilla extract	10 mL
1/2 tsp	almond extract	2 mL
1 cup	sliced almonds, toasted	250 mL
1 cup	dried cranberries	250 mL

It's not a mistake: these incredibly delicious muffins have no flour. Toasted wheat germ is not only nutritious — high in folate, fiber, B vitamins, potassium and more — it also has a delectable, nutty flavor.

Tip

You can either use pre-toasted wheat germ in this recipe or toast raw wheat germ yourself: Spread wheat germ on a large rimmed baking sheet and bake in a 350°F (180°C) oven for 5 to 8 minutes, stirring once, until golden and fragrant. Let cool completely before using.

Makes 16 muffins

- Preheat oven to 350°F (180°C)
- Two 12-cup muffin pans, 16 cups lined with paper liners

1. In a large bowl, whisk together wheat germ, milk powder, baking powder and salt.

2. In another large bowl, whisk together eggs, butter, honey, vanilla and almond extract until well blended.

3. Add the egg mixture to the wheat germ mixture and stir until just blended. Gently fold in almonds and cranberries.

4. Divide batter equally among prepared muffin cups.

5. Bake in preheated oven for 15 to 20 minutes or until tops are golden brown and a toothpick inserted in the center comes out clean. Let cool in pans on a wire rack for 3 minutes, then transfer to the rack to cool.

Kasha Muffins

1½ cups	whole wheat pastry flour	375 mL
½ cup	wheat germ	125 mL
2 tsp	baking powder	10 mL
½ tsp	baking soda	2 mL
½ tsp	salt	2 mL
1	egg	1
⅔ cup	low-fat (1%) plain yogurt	150 mL
½ cup	dark (cooking) molasses	125 mL
¼ cup	vegetable oil	60 mL
1 cup	cooked cooled kasha (roasted buckwheat groats)	250 mL

Buckwheat contains all of the essential amino acids, so it is close to being a complete protein. Further, it is composed of 75% complex carbohydrates. Finally, it is wheat- and gluten-free and is high in B vitamins, phosphorus, potassium, iron and calcium.

Makes 12 muffins

- Preheat oven to 375°F (190°C)
- 12-cup muffin pan, greased

1. In a large bowl, whisk together flour, wheat germ, baking powder, baking soda and salt.
2. In a medium bowl, whisk together egg, yogurt, molasses and oil until well blended.
3. Add the egg mixture to the flour mixture and stir until just blended. Gently fold in kasha.
4. Divide batter equally among prepared muffin cups.
5. Bake in preheated oven for 19 to 23 minutes or until tops are golden and a toothpick inserted in the center comes out clean. Let cool in pan on a wire rack for 3 minutes, then transfer to the rack to cool.

Honey Almond Oat Muffins

1½ cups	whole wheat pastry flour	375 mL
¾ cup	quick-cooking rolled oats	175 mL
¼ cup	ground flax seeds	60 mL
1½ tsp	baking powder	7 mL
½ tsp	baking soda	2 mL
½ tsp	salt	2 mL
1	egg	1
⅔ cup	liquid honey	150 mL
3 tbsp	vegetable oil	45 mL
1 tsp	almond extract	5 mL
1 cup	low-fat (1%) plain yogurt	250 mL
¼ cup	low-fat (1%) milk	60 mL
1 cup	almonds, toasted and chopped	250 mL

The delicate, unmistakable flavor of almonds can't be beat — except, perhaps, by their nutrition profile. Almonds are rich in manganese, vitamin E and magnesium and are an excellent source of protein.

Makes 12 muffins

- Preheat oven to 400°F (200°C)
- 12-cup muffin pan, greased

1. In a large bowl, whisk together flour, oats, flax seeds, baking powder, baking soda and salt.
2. In a medium bowl, whisk together egg, honey, oil and almond extract until well blended. Whisk in yogurt and milk until blended.
3. Add the egg mixture to the flour mixture and stir until just blended. Gently fold in almonds.
4. Divide batter equally among prepared muffin cups.
5. Bake in preheated oven for 20 to 25 minutes or until a toothpick inserted in the center comes out clean. Let cool in pan on a wire rack for 3 minutes, then transfer to the rack to cool.

Cracked Wheat Muffins with Cardamom and Dried Fruit

½ cup	bulgur (cracked wheat)	125 mL
1 cup	boiling water	250 mL
1½ cups	whole wheat pastry flour	375 mL
1 tbsp	baking powder	15 mL
1 tsp	salt	5 mL
1 tsp	ground cardamom	5 mL
½ tsp	baking soda	2 mL
1	egg	1
1 cup	low-fat (1%) plain yogurt	250 mL
⅓ cup	liquid honey	75 mL
¼ cup	vegetable oil	60 mL
1 tsp	vanilla extract	5 mL
⅓ cup	chopped dried apricots	75 mL
⅓ cup	dried cranberries	75 mL

Cracked wheat (bulgur) is a Middle East staple with a tender, chewy texture. It is high in protein and minerals and has more fiber than oats, buckwheat or corn.

Makes 12 muffins

- 12-cup muffin pan, greased

1. In a small heatproof bowl, combine bulgur and boiling water. Let stand for 30 minutes. Drain off any water.
2. Preheat oven to 425°F (220°C).
3. In a large bowl, whisk together flour, baking powder, salt, cardamom and baking soda.
4. In a medium bowl, whisk together egg, yogurt, honey, oil and vanilla until well blended.
5. Add the egg mixture to the flour mixture and stir until just blended. Gently fold in bulgur, apricots and cranberries.
6. Divide batter equally among prepared muffin cups.
7. Bake for 16 to 20 minutes or until tops are golden brown and a toothpick inserted in the center comes out clean. Let cool in pan on a wire rack for 3 minutes, then transfer to the rack to cool.

Agave Oat Muffins

1 cup	all-purpose flour	250 mL
1 cup	whole wheat flour	250 mL
1 cup	quick-cooking rolled oats	250 mL
2¼ tsp	baking powder	11 mL
2 tsp	ground cinnamon	10 mL
½ tsp	baking soda	2 mL
½ tsp	salt	2 mL
1	egg	1
1 cup	buttermilk	250 mL
¾ cup	unsweetened applesauce	175 mL
½ cup	agave nectar	125 mL
¼ cup	vegetable oil	60 mL
2 tsp	vanilla extract	10 mL

These muffins are high on the health charts — whole grains, high fiber, natural sugar, low fat — but their greatest asset is superb taste.

Makes 12 muffins

- Preheat oven to 400°F (200°C)
- 12-cup muffin pan, lined with paper liners

1. In a large bowl, whisk together all-purpose flour, whole wheat flour, oats, baking powder, cinnamon, baking soda and salt.
2. In a medium bowl, whisk together egg, buttermilk, applesauce, agave nectar, oil and vanilla until well blended.
3. Add the egg mixture to the flour mixture and stir until just blended.
4. Divide batter equally among prepared muffin cups.
5. Bake in preheated oven for 25 to 28 minutes or until tops are golden brown and a toothpick inserted in the center comes out clean. Let cool in pan on a wire rack for 3 minutes, then transfer to the rack to cool.

Agave Almond Muffins

Topping

1 cup	sliced almonds	250 mL
1/2 tsp	ground cinnamon	2 mL
2 tbsp	agave nectar	30 mL

Muffins

1 1/2 cups	whole wheat pastry flour	375 mL
2 tsp	baking powder	10 mL
1/2 tsp	salt	2 mL
2	eggs	2
3/4 cup	mashed ripe bananas	175 mL
1/2 cup	coconut oil or vegetable oil	125 mL
1/2 cup	agave nectar	125 mL
1/3 cup	low-fat (1%) milk	75 mL
3/4 tsp	almond extract	3 mL

Agave nectar has been in use for centuries, and its popularity is now growing in Western countries. A major part of its appeal lies in its favorable glycemic profile. Its sweetness comes primarily from a complex form of fructose called inulin. (Fructose is the sugar that occurs naturally in fruits and vegetables.) The carbohydrate in agave nectar has a low glycemic index, which provides sweetness without the unpleasant "sugar rush" and blood sugar spike caused by many other sugars. It can be used almost interchangeably with honey in most recipes (though it is not quite as viscous) and makes an especially fragrant contribution to baked goods such as these almond muffins.

Makes 12 muffins

- Preheat oven to 350°F (180°C)
- 12-cup muffin pan, greased

1. *Topping:* In a small bowl, stir together almonds, cinnamon and agave nectar until almonds are evenly coated.

2. *Muffins:* In a large bowl, whisk together flour, baking powder and salt.

3. In a medium bowl, whisk together eggs, bananas, oil, agave nectar, milk and almond extract until well blended.

4. Add the egg mixture to the flour mixture and stir until just blended.

5. Divide batter equally among prepared muffin cups. Sprinkle with topping.

6. Bake in preheated oven for 27 to 30 minutes or until tops are golden and a toothpick inserted in the center comes out clean. Let cool in pan on a wire rack for 5 minutes, then transfer to the rack to cool.

Pistachio Honey Muffins

1 cup	whole wheat flour	250 mL
1 cup	all-purpose flour	250 mL
1/4 cup	ground flax seeds	60 mL
1 1/4 tsp	baking soda	6 mL
1/2 tsp	salt	2 mL
1/2 tsp	ground nutmeg	2 mL
1/2 tsp	ground allspice	2 mL
2	eggs	2
1 cup	buttermilk	250 mL
1/2 cup	liquid honey	125 mL
2 tbsp	vegetable oil	30 mL
1/2 cup	golden raisins	125 mL
1/2 cup	finely chopped pistachios	125 mL

Little bites of pistachio add wonderful texture and color to these muffins; honey contributes a subtle floral sweetness. Like all other nuts, pistachios (which are members of the cashew family) are an excellent source of protein. They are also an excellent source of vitamin B_6, thiamin and fiber.

Makes 12 muffins

- Preheat oven to 350°F (180°C)
- 12-cup muffin pan, greased

1. In a large bowl, whisk together whole wheat flour, all-purpose flour, flax seeds, baking soda, salt, nutmeg and allspice.
2. In a medium bowl, whisk together eggs, buttermilk, honey and oil until well blended.
3. Add the egg mixture to the flour mixture and stir until just blended. Gently fold in raisins and pistachios.
4. Divide batter equally among prepared muffin cups.
5. Bake in preheated oven for 14 to 18 minutes or until a toothpick inserted in the center comes out clean. Let cool in pan on a wire rack for 3 minutes, then transfer to the rack to cool.

Backpacker Carob Muffins

1 1/3 cups	quick-cooking rolled oats	325 mL
1 cup	whole wheat pastry flour	250 mL
1 1/2 tsp	baking powder	7 mL
1 tsp	salt	5 mL
1/2 tsp	baking soda	2 mL
1	egg	1
1 cup	buttermilk	250 mL
1/2 cup	liquid honey	125 mL
1/3 cup	vegetable oil	75 mL
1 cup	chopped mixed dried fruit	250 mL
2/3 cup	carob chips	150 mL

My mother routinely purchased a carob trail mix from the local co-op for snacking and camping trips. It's good stuff, too. Among its many benefits, it is non-dairy, low in fat, a good source of calcium, protein and potassium and, unlike chocolate, does not contain caffeine or theobromine.

Makes 12 muffins

- Preheat oven to 400°F (200°C)
- 12-cup muffin pan, greased

1. In a large bowl, whisk together oats, flour, baking powder, salt and baking soda.
2. In a medium bowl, whisk together egg, buttermilk, honey and oil until well blended.
3. Add the egg mixture to the flour mixture and stir until just blended. Gently fold in dried fruit and carob chips.
4. Divide batter equally among prepared muffin cups.
5. Bake in preheated oven for 21 to 24 minutes or until tops are golden and a toothpick inserted in the center comes out clean. Let cool in pan on a wire rack for 3 minutes, then transfer to the rack to cool.

Dark Chocolate Walnut Muffins

1⅔ cups	whole wheat pastry flour	400 mL
⅔ cup	quick-cooking rolled oats	150 mL
¼ cup	ground flax seeds	60 mL
2 tsp	baking powder	10 mL
½ tsp	baking soda	2 mL
½ tsp	salt	2 mL
½ cup	packed light brown sugar	125 mL
2	eggs	2
¾ cup	low-fat (1%) plain yogurt	175 mL
⅓ cup	olive oil	75 mL
1 tsp	vanilla extract	5 mL
3 oz	bittersweet chocolate, chopped	90 g
½ cup	chopped walnuts, toasted	125 mL

You're not dreaming: dark chocolate really is a superfood. In addition to being chock full of heart-healthy antioxidants, it also stimulates endorphin production and contains serotonin, which acts as an antidepressant (i.e., chocolate = happiness).

Makes 12 muffins

- Preheat oven to 350°F (180°C)
- 12-cup muffin pan, greased

1. In a large bowl, whisk together flour, oats, flax seeds, baking powder, baking soda and salt.
2. In a medium bowl, whisk together brown sugar, eggs, yogurt, oil and vanilla until well blended.
3. Add the egg mixture to the flour mixture and stir until just blended. Gently fold in chocolate and walnuts.
4. Divide batter equally among prepared muffin cups.
5. Bake in preheated oven for 18 to 22 minutes or until tops are golden and a toothpick inserted in the center comes out clean. Let cool in pan on a wire rack for 3 minutes, then transfer to the rack to cool.

Maple Walnut Muffins

1⅓ cups	all-purpose flour	325 mL
1 cup	whole wheat pastry flour	250 mL
1 tsp	baking powder	5 mL
1 tsp	baking soda	5 mL
¾ tsp	salt	3 mL
¼ cup	packed light brown sugar	60 mL
2	eggs	2
⅓ cup	pure maple syrup	75 mL
⅓ cup	vegetable oil	75 mL
1⅓ cups	low-fat (1%) plain yogurt	325 mL
½ cup	chopped walnuts, toasted	125 mL

Walnuts have a superiority complex: they are one of the world's healthiest foods, rich in omega-3 fatty acids, high in protein and high in manganese, copper and tryptophan.

Makes 12 muffins

- Preheat oven to 400°F (200°C)
- 12-cup muffin pan, greased

1. In a large bowl, whisk together all-purpose flour, whole wheat pastry flour, baking powder, baking soda and salt.
2. In a medium bowl, whisk together brown sugar, eggs, maple syrup and oil until well blended. Whisk in yogurt until blended.
3. Add the egg mixture to the flour mixture and stir until just blended. Gently fold in walnuts.
4. Divide batter equally among prepared muffin cups.
5. Bake in preheated oven for 15 to 20 minutes or until tops are golden and a toothpick inserted in the center comes out clean. Let cool in pan on a wire rack for 3 minutes, then transfer to the rack to cool.

Granola Power Muffins

1	can (12 oz/340 mL) frozen unsweetened apple juice concentrate	1
2¼ cups	natural bran	550 mL
1 cup	whole wheat pastry flour	250 mL
4 tsp	baking powder	20 mL
1½ tsp	salt	7 mL
1 tsp	baking soda	5 mL
4	eggs	4
1 cup	vegetable oil	250 mL
2¼ cups	buttermilk	550 mL
1½ cups	raisins or other dried fruit	375 mL
1½ cups	low-fat granola	375 mL
½ cup	sesame seeds	125 mL
½ cup	raw green pumpkin seeds (pepitas)	125 mL
½ cup	ground flax seeds	125 mL
½ cup	unsweetened flaked or shredded coconut	125 mL

Check the box to make sure the granola you choose is made from 100% natural — and preferably organic — ingredients.

Makes 20 muffins

• Two 12-cup muffin pans, 20 cups greased

1. In a saucepan, bring apple juice concentrate to a boil over high heat. Boil for about 10 minutes or until reduced to about 1 cup (250 mL). Remove from heat and let cool to room temperature.
2. Preheat oven to 350°F (180°C)
3. In a large bowl, whisk together bran, flour, baking powder, salt and baking soda.
4. In a medium bowl, whisk together apple juice, eggs and oil until well blended. Whisk in buttermilk until blended.
5. Add the egg mixture to the flour mixture and stir until just blended. Gently fold in raisins, granola, sesame seeds, pumpkin seeds, flax seeds and coconut.
6. Divide batter equally among prepared muffin cups.
7. Bake for 22 to 27 minutes or until tops are golden and a toothpick inserted in the center comes out clean. Let cool in pans on a wire rack for 3 minutes, then transfer to the rack to cool.

Whole Wheat Walnut Muffins

1½ cups	whole wheat pastry flour	375 mL
1½ tsp	baking powder	7 mL
¾ tsp	salt	3 mL
¾ tsp	ground cinnamon	3 mL
¼ tsp	baking soda	1 mL
½ cup	packed light brown sugar	125 mL
2	eggs	2
¾ cup	low-fat (1%) plain yogurt	175 mL
⅓ cup	toasted walnut oil or olive oil	75 mL
1 tsp	vanilla extract	5 mL
1 cup	chopped walnuts, toasted	250 mL

The fat in walnuts is 72.4% heart-healthy polyunsaturated fat, which studies have shown to lower cholesterol. Polyunsaturated fats are the source of vital essential fatty acids (EFAs) — including omega-3s — which we can only get from food.

Makes 9 muffins

• Preheat oven to 350°F (180°C)
• 12-cup muffin pan, 9 cups greased

1. In a large bowl, whisk together flour, baking powder, salt, cinnamon and baking soda.
2. In a medium bowl, whisk together brown sugar, eggs, yogurt, oil and vanilla until well blended.
3. Add the egg mixture to the flour mixture and stir until just blended. Gently fold in walnuts.
4. Divide batter equally among prepared muffin cups.
5. Bake in preheated oven for 20 to 25 minutes or until tops are golden brown and a toothpick inserted in the center comes out clean. Let cool in pan on a wire rack for 3 minutes, then transfer to the rack to cool.

Ricotta Muffins with Honey and Cinnamon

2 cups	whole wheat pastry flour	500 mL
2¹/₂ tsp	baking powder	12 mL
1 tsp	ground cinnamon	5 mL
¹/₂ tsp	salt	2 mL
¹/₄ tsp	baking soda	1 mL
1	egg	1
1 cup	low-fat ricotta cheese	250 mL
¹/₂ cup	low-fat (1%) plain yogurt	125 mL
¹/₃ cup	liquid honey	75 mL
¹/₄ cup	olive oil	60 mL
1 tbsp	finely grated lemon zest	15mL

I love the creamy, velvety texture of ricotta. When stirred into muffin batter, it makes for a rich, moist treat that works especially well with whole-grain flour. Low-fat ricotta packs a significant amount of protein and calcium, too.

Makes 12 muffins

- Preheat oven to 400°F (200°C)
- 12-cup muffin pan, greased

1. In a large bowl, whisk together flour, baking powder, cinnamon, salt and baking soda.
2. In a medium bowl, whisk together egg, cheese, yogurt, honey, oil and lemon zest until well blended.
3. Add the egg mixture to the flour mixture and stir until just blended.
4. Divide batter equally among prepared muffin cups.
5. Bake in preheated oven for 15 to 20 minutes or until tops are golden and a toothpick inserted in the center comes out clean. Let cool in pan on a wire rack for 3 minutes, then transfer to the rack to cool.

Oat, Wheat and Spelt Supper Muffins

1 cup	large-flake (old-fashioned) rolled oats	250 mL
¹/₂ cup	spelt flour	125 mL
¹/₂ cup	whole wheat flour	125 mL
1 tsp	baking soda	5 mL
¹/₄ tsp	salt	1 mL
¹/₄ tsp	freshly ground black pepper	1 mL
¹/₄ cup	packed dark brown sugar	60 mL
1	egg	1
3 tbsp	olive oil	45 mL
1¹/₂ cups	buttermilk	375 mL

The humble list of ingredients here belies the great flavor of these muffins. Rich in whole grains, and heart-healthy thanks to the olive oil and oatmeal, they are one of my favorite go-to supper muffins. Use leftovers to make a quick sandwich with deli turkey or roast beef.

Makes 12 muffins

- Preheat oven to 350°F (180°C)
- 12-cup muffin pan, greased

1. In a large bowl, whisk together oats, spelt flour, whole wheat flour, baking soda, salt and pepper.
2. In a medium bowl, whisk together brown sugar, egg and oil until well blended. Whisk in buttermilk until blended.
3. Add the egg mixture to the flour mixture and stir until just blended.
4. Divide batter equally among prepared muffin cups.
5. Bake in preheated oven for 20 to 25 minutes or until tops are golden and a toothpick inserted in the center comes out clean. Let cool in pan on a wire rack for 3 minutes, then transfer to the rack to cool.

Spiced Yogurt Muffins

Topping

2 tbsp	ground flax seeds	30 mL
1 tbsp	granulated sugar	15 mL
1/2 tsp	ground cinnamon	2 mL

Muffins

1 cup	all-purpose flour	250 mL
1 cup	whole wheat pastry flour	250 mL
1 tbsp	baking powder	15 mL
1 tsp	ground cinnamon	5 mL
1 tsp	ground ginger	5 mL
1/2 tsp	ground nutmeg	2 mL
1/2 tsp	baking soda	2 mL
1/2 tsp	salt	2 mL
1/2 cup	packed light brown sugar	125 mL
2	eggs	2
1/4 cup	vegetable oil	60 mL
1/4 cup	unsweetened applesauce	60 mL
1 tsp	vanilla extract	5 mL
1 1/4 cups	low-fat (1%) plain yogurt	300 mL

Confession: I am a yogurt fiend. I eat it every day, throughout the day, straight up and incorporated into many of our family meals. Thank goodness my favorite food is also so good for my health: it's a very good source of calcium, phosphorus, riboflavin and iodine. It's also a good source of vitamin B_{12}, vitamin B_5, zinc, potassium and protein. This muffin recipe is one of my favorite ways to get my yogurt on the go. You can vary the spices to suit your taste or add dried fruits, nuts or seeds — you cannot go wrong!

Makes 18 muffins

- Preheat oven to 375°F (190°C)
- Two 12-cup muffin pans, 18 cups greased

1. *Topping:* In a small bowl, combine flax seeds, sugar and cinnamon.

2. *Muffins:* In a large bowl, whisk together all-purpose flour, whole wheat pastry flour, baking powder, cinnamon, ginger, nutmeg, baking soda and salt.

3. In a medium bowl, whisk together brown sugar, eggs, oil, applesauce and vanilla until well blended. Whisk in yogurt until blended.

4. Add the egg mixture to the flour mixture and stir until just blended.

5. Divide batter equally among prepared muffin cups. Sprinkle with topping.

6. Bake in preheated oven for 17 to 20 minutes or until tops are golden and a toothpick inserted in the center comes out clean. Let cool in pans on a wire rack for 3 minutes, then transfer to the rack to cool.

Whole Wheat Cottage Cheese Muffins with Sun-Dried Tomatoes

2 cups	whole wheat pastry flour	500 mL
2½ tsp	baking powder	12 mL
1½ tsp	dried oregano	7 mL
½ tsp	salt	2 mL
2	cloves garlic, minced	2
1	egg	1
¼ cup	vegetable oil	60 mL
1 cup	low-fat (1%) milk	250 mL
1 cup	low-fat (1%) cottage cheese	250 mL
½ cup	chopped drained oil-packed sun-dried tomatoes	125 mL

Makes 12 muffins

- Preheat oven to 375°F (190°C)
- 12-cup muffin pan, greased

1. In a large bowl, whisk together flour, baking powder, oregano and salt.
2. In a medium bowl, whisk together garlic, egg and oil until well blended. Whisk in milk and cheese until blended.
3. Add the egg mixture to the flour mixture and stir until just blended. Gently fold in tomatoes.
4. Divide batter equally among prepared muffin cups.
5. Bake in preheated oven for 20 to 25 minutes or until a toothpick inserted in the center comes out clean. Let cool in pan on a wire rack for 5 minutes, then transfer to the rack to cool.

Cottage cheese is the health food of the cheese world. High in protein, phosphorus, iron and magnesium and low in fat, it is delicious on its own, but it also works magic in baked goods such as these muffins, producing tender, moist results every time.

Ancho Chile Cherry Tomato Muffins

1½ cups	whole wheat pastry flour	375 mL
1 cup	all-purpose flour	250 mL
1 tbsp	baking powder	15 mL
1 tsp	ancho chile powder	5 mL
¾ tsp	ground cumin	3 mL
½ tsp	baking soda	2 mL
½ tsp	salt	2 mL
2	eggs	2
1¼ cups	buttermilk	300 mL
⅓ cup	vegetable oil	75 mL
1½ cups	cherry tomatoes, quartered	375 mL
½ cup	chopped green onions (scallions)	125 mL

Makes 12 muffins

- Preheat oven to 400°F (200°C)
- 12-cup muffin pan, greased

1. In a large bowl, whisk together whole wheat pastry flour, all-purpose flour, baking powder, ancho powder, cumin, baking soda and salt.
2. In a medium bowl, whisk together eggs, buttermilk and oil until blended.
3. Add the egg mixture to the flour mixture and stir until just blended. Gently fold in tomatoes and green onions.
4. Divide batter equally among prepared muffin cups.
5. Bake in preheated oven for 20 to 25 minutes or until tops are light golden brown and a toothpick inserted in the center comes out clean. Let cool in pan on a wire rack for 3 minutes, then transfer to the rack to cool slightly. Serve warm.

Tomatoes of all varieties are high in vitamin C and lycopene. Green onions also have high levels of vitamin C, as well as vitamin A.

Mirepoix Muffins

¼ cup	olive oil, divided	60 mL
1 cup	chopped onions	250 mL
½ cup	finely chopped carrot	125 mL
½ cup	finely chopped celery	125 mL
2	cloves garlic, minced	2
1 cup	all-purpose flour	250 mL
1 cup	whole wheat pastry flour	250 mL
2 tsp	baking powder	10 mL
1 tsp	dried thyme	5 mL
¾ tsp	salt	3 mL
½ tsp	baking soda	2 mL
¼ tsp	freshly ground black pepper	1 mL
1	egg	1
1 cup	buttermilk	250 mL

"Mirepoix" is the French name for a combination of onions, carrots and celery, used raw, roasted or sautéed with butter, as the flavor base for a wide number of dishes, such as stocks, soups, stews and sauces. Here, the background trio takes center stage to outstanding reviews. All three vegetables are excellent sources of fiber. Onions and celery are also high in vitamin C, and carrots are rich in vitamin A (in the form of beta carotene).

Makes 12 muffins

- 12-cup muffin pan, greased

1. In a large skillet, heat 2 tbsp (30 mL) of the oil over medium-high heat. Sauté onions for 2 minutes. Add carrot and celery; sauté for 4 to 5 minutes or until softened. Stir in garlic. Remove from heat and let cool.

2. Preheat oven to 375°F (190°C).

3. In a large bowl, whisk together all-purpose flour, whole wheat pastry flour, baking powder, thyme, salt, baking soda and pepper.

4. In a medium bowl, whisk together the remaining oil, egg and buttermilk until well blended.

5. Add the egg mixture to the flour mixture and stir until just blended. Gently fold in onion mixture.

6. Divide batter equally among prepared muffin cups.

7. Bake for 18 to 22 minutes or until a toothpick inserted in the center comes out clean. Let cool in pan on a wire rack for 3 minutes, then transfer to the rack to cool.

Sun-Dried Tomato Spinach Muffins

2 cups	whole wheat pastry flour	500 mL
1 cup	all-purpose flour	250 mL
2 1/2 tsp	baking powder	12 mL
1 tsp	dried basil	5 mL
1/2 tsp	salt	2 mL
1 tbsp	granulated sugar	15 mL
1	egg	1
1/4 cup	olive oil	60 mL
1 cup	low-fat (1%) milk	250 mL
3/4 cup	low-fat ricotta cheese	175 mL
1	package (10 oz/300 g) frozen chopped spinach, thawed and squeezed dry	1
1/3 cup	chopped drained oil-packed sun-dried tomatoes	75 mL

I love the umami flavor of sun-dried tomatoes; they impart a concentrated tomato flavor to everything they are added to. In addition, sun-dried tomatoes are a natural source of vitamin C and a good source of iron.

Makes 16 muffins

- Preheat oven to 375°F (190°C)
- Two 12-cup muffin pans, 16 cups greased

1. In a large bowl, whisk together whole wheat pastry flour, all-purpose flour, baking powder, basil and salt.

2. In a medium bowl, whisk together sugar, egg and oil until well blended. Whisk in milk and cheese until blended. Stir in spinach and tomatoes.

3. Add the egg mixture to the flour mixture and stir until just blended.

4. Divide batter equally among prepared muffin cups.

5. Bake in preheated oven for 18 to 23 minutes or until a toothpick inserted in the center comes out clean. Let cool in pans on a wire rack for 3 minutes, then transfer to the rack to cool.

Whole Wheat Mushroom Muffins

1/3 cup	olive oil, divided	75 mL
8 oz	fresh cremini or button mushrooms, chopped	250 g
	Salt and freshly ground black pepper	
2 cups	whole wheat pastry flour	500 mL
2 1/4 tsp	baking powder	11 mL
1 tsp	dried thyme	5 mL
1/2 tsp	baking soda	2 mL
2	eggs	2
1 1/4 cups	buttermilk	300 mL
1/2 cup	chopped walnuts, toasted	125 mL

I like to serve these earthy muffins with roast chicken or chicken soup for a light, quick, nutritious meal. Mushrooms are particularly high in selenium, which is thought to fight against several forms of cancer. They are also an excellent source of potassium and a good source of three essential B vitamins: niacin, riboflavin and pantothenic acid.

Makes 12 muffins

• 12-cup muffin pan, greased

1. In a large nonstick skillet, heat 1 tbsp (15 mL) of the oil over medium heat. Sauté mushrooms for about 10 minutes or until tender and liquid has evaporated. Season to taste with salt and pepper. Remove from heat and let cool.

2. Preheat oven to 375°F (190°C).

3. In a large bowl, whisk together flour, baking powder, thyme, baking soda, 1/2 tsp (2 mL) salt and 1/8 tsp (0.5 mL) pepper.

4. In a medium bowl, whisk together the remaining oil, eggs and buttermilk until well blended.

5. Add the egg mixture to the flour mixture and stir until just blended. Gently fold in mushroom mixture and walnuts.

6. Divide batter equally among prepared muffin cups.

7. Bake for 20 to 25 minutes or until a toothpick inserted in the center comes out clean. Let cool in pan on a wire rack for 3 minutes, then transfer to the rack to cool slightly. Serve warm.

Gluten-Free Muffins

● ●

You needn't have an intolerance to gluten or a wheat allergy to love gluten-free muffins. A rapidly growing number of people eschew gluten, the protein in wheat, rye and barley, because of an allergy or sensitivity, but others avoid it simply because they believe its absence promotes better health in general, and digestive health in particular. Still others are curious about experimenting with gluten-free flours because of the unique textures and flavors they impart to a range of baked goods. Whatever your reason for thumbing to this chapter, rest assured: these muffins are hands-down delicious and, like all of the muffins in this collection, are easy to prepare. The gluten-free flours used to prepare these recipes have become readily available in the past few years at health and whole foods stores, via mail order and in the health food sections of most well-stocked supermarkets.

continued...

Honey Applesauce Almond Flour Muffins

3 cups	almond flour	750 mL
1½ tsp	ground cinnamon	7 mL
¾ tsp	baking soda	3 mL
¼ tsp	ground nutmeg	1 mL
¼ tsp	salt	1 mL
¼ cup	granulated sugar	60 mL
2	eggs	2
¾ cup	unsweetened applesauce	175 mL
¼ cup	liquid honey	60 mL
3 tbsp	unsalted butter, melted	45 mL
1 tsp	vanilla extract	5 mL
1 cup	chopped walnuts or pecans, toasted	250 mL

Homemade, delicious applesauce muffins add something special to weekday breakfasts. Honey, nuts and spices make these muffins you will adore.

Makes 12 muffins

- Preheat oven to 325°F (160°C)
- 12-cup muffin pan, lined with paper liners

1. In a large bowl, whisk together flour, cinnamon, baking soda, nutmeg and salt.
2. In a medium bowl, whisk together sugar, eggs, applesauce, honey, butter and vanilla until well blended.
3. Add the egg mixture to the flour mixture and stir until just blended. Gently fold in walnuts.
4. Divide batter equally among prepared muffin cups.
5. Bake in preheated oven for 25 to 30 minutes or until tops are set and a toothpick inserted in the center comes out clean. Let cool in pan on a wire rack for 5 minutes, then transfer to the rack to cool.

Dried Apple Maple Muffins

3 cups	almond flour	750 mL
1 tsp	ground cinnamon	5 mL
¾ tsp	baking soda	3 mL
½ tsp	salt	2 mL
2	eggs	2
¼ cup	pure maple syrup	60 mL
¼ cup	unsalted butter, melted	60 mL
1 tsp	vanilla extract	5 mL
⅔ cup	unsweetened applesauce	150 mL
1 cup	chopped dried apple rings	250 mL

If food marriages are made in heaven, then surely apple-maple is one of the select matches. Given how the two flavors bring out the best in each other, you will be hard-pressed to find someone who will turn down an offer of one or more of these muffins.

Makes 12 muffins

- Preheat oven to 325°F (160°C)
- 12-cup muffin pan, lined with paper liners

1. In a large bowl, whisk together flour, cinnamon, baking soda and salt.
2. In a medium bowl, vigorously whisk eggs. Whisk in syrup, butter and vanilla until well blended. Stir in applesauce.
3. Add the egg mixture to the flour mixture and stir until just blended. Gently fold in apples.
4. Divide batter equally among prepared muffin cups.
5. Bake in preheated oven for 25 to 30 minutes or until a toothpick inserted in the center comes out clean. Let cool in pan on a wire rack for 5 minutes, then transfer to the rack to cool.

Apple Cheddar Muffins

1³/₄ + 2 tbsp	Brown Rice Flour Blend (page 19)	455 mL
2¹/₄ tsp	gluten-free baking powder	11 mL
1 tsp	ground cinnamon	5 mL
¹/₂ tsp	xanthan gum	2 mL
¹/₂ tsp	baking soda	2 mL
¹/₂ tsp	salt	2 mL
¹/₄ cup	cold unsalted butter, cut into small pieces	60 mL
4 oz	sharp (old) Cheddar cheese, shredded	125 g
1	egg	1
³/₄ cup	buttermilk	175 mL
1 cup	shredded tart-sweet apple, such as Gala or Braeburn	250 mL

A crumbly slab of Cheddar is a centuries-old accompaniment to apple desserts; it imparts character in a way that a dollop of whipped cream cannot match. Adding cheese directly to the muffin batter here tweaks the tradition, thus bringing an iconic treat full circle.

Makes 12 muffins

- Preheat oven to 375°F (190°C)
- Food processor
- 12-cup muffin pan, greased

1. In food processor, pulse flour blend, baking powder, cinnamon, xanthan gum, baking soda and salt until combined. Add butter and pulse until mixture resembles bread crumbs. Add cheese and pulse until combined. Transfer to a large bowl.
2. In a small bowl, whisk together egg and buttermilk until well blended.
3. Add the egg mixture to the flour mixture and stir until just blended. Gently fold in apple.
4. Divide batter equally among prepared muffin cups.
5. Bake in preheated oven for 22 to 27 minutes or until a toothpick inserted in the center comes out clean. Let cool in pan on a wire rack for 5 minutes, then transfer to the rack to cool.

Applesauce Muffins

2 cups	Brown Rice Flour Blend (page 19)	500 mL
1¹/₂ tsp	ground cinnamon	7 mL
1 tsp	gluten-free baking powder	5 mL
1 tsp	baking soda	5 mL
1 tsp	salt	5 mL
¹/₂ tsp	ground nutmeg	2 mL
¹/₂ tsp	xanthan gum	2 mL
1 cup	packed dark brown sugar	250 mL
¹/₂ cup	unsalted butter, softened	125 mL
2	eggs	2
1¹/₂ cups	unsweetened applesauce	375 mL

Is there a child in this world that doesn't love applesauce? I doubt it. The same holds true for applesauce muffins. My version isn't too sweet and yields muffins with a moist-tender texture.

Makes 18 muffins

- Preheat oven to 350°F (180°C)
- Two 12-cup muffin pans, 18 cups greased

1. In a medium bowl, whisk together flour blend, cinnamon, baking powder, baking soda, salt, nutmeg and xanthan gum.
2. In a large bowl, using an electric mixer on medium speed, beat brown sugar and butter until light and fluffy. Beat in eggs, one at a time, until well blended.
3. With the mixer on low speed, beat in flour mixture alternately with applesauce, making two additions of flour and one of applesauce, until just blended.
4. Divide batter equally among prepared muffin cups.
5. Bake in preheated oven for 25 to 30 minutes or until tops are golden and a toothpick inserted in the center comes out clean. Let cool in pans on a wire rack for 3 minutes, then transfer to the rack to cool.

Fresh Apple Muffins

2 cups	Brown Rice Flour Blend (page 19)	500 mL
1 tbsp	gluten-free baking powder	15 mL
2 tsp	ground cinnamon	10 mL
1 tsp	baking soda	5 mL
³⁄₄ tsp	xanthan gum	3 mL
¹⁄₂ tsp	salt	2 mL
¹⁄₄ tsp	ground nutmeg	1 mL
²⁄₃ cup	packed light brown sugar	150 mL
2	eggs	2
¹⁄₂ cup	buttermilk	125 mL
¹⁄₂ cup	vegetable oil	125 mL
1 tsp	vanilla extract	5 mL
1 cup	chopped peeled tart apple, such as Granny Smith	250 mL
¹⁄₂ cup	chopped pecans, toasted	125 mL

These apple muffins are best served slightly warm, but they are also great served split and toasted for breakfast the next morning, topped with a bit of butter or whipped cream cheese.

Makes 12 muffins

- Preheat oven to 375°F (190°C)
- 12-cup muffin pan, greased

1. In a large bowl, whisk together flour blend, baking powder, cinnamon, baking soda, xanthan gum, salt and nutmeg.
2. In a medium bowl, vigorously whisk together brown sugar, eggs, buttermilk, oil and vanilla until well blended and slightly frothy.
3. Add the egg mixture to the flour mixture and stir until just blended. Gently fold in apple and pecans.
4. Divide batter equally among prepared muffin cups.
5. Bake in preheated oven for 20 to 25 minutes or until a toothpick inserted in the center comes out clean. Let cool in pan on a wire rack for 5 minutes, then transfer to the rack to cool.

Apple Cider Muffins

2 cups	Brown Rice Flour Blend (page 19)	500 mL
2 tsp	gluten-free baking powder	10 mL
1¹⁄₂ tsp	ground cinnamon	7 mL
³⁄₄ tsp	salt	3 mL
¹⁄₂ tsp	xanthan gum	2 mL
¹⁄₄ tsp	ground nutmeg	1 mL
³⁄₄ cup	packed dark brown sugar	175 mL
¹⁄₂ cup	unsalted butter, softened	125 mL
2	eggs	2
1 cup	unsweetened apple cider or apple juice	250 mL

Anyone who swears by blueberry muffins alone is likely to sidle over to the apple cider muffin camp after a taste of this recipe.

Makes 15 muffins

- Preheat oven to 350°F (180°C)
- Two 12-cup muffin pans, 15 cups greased

1. In a medium bowl, whisk together flour blend, baking powder, cinnamon, salt, xanthan gum and nutmeg.
2. In a large bowl, using an electric mixer on medium speed, beat brown sugar and butter until light and fluffy. Beat in eggs, one at a time, until well blended.
3. With the mixer on low speed, beat in flour mixture alternately with cider, making two additions of flour and one of cider, until just blended.
4. Divide batter equally among prepared muffin cups.
5. Bake in preheated oven for 24 to 28 minutes or until tops are golden and a toothpick inserted in the center comes out clean. Let cool in pans on a wire rack for 5 minutes, then transfer to the rack to cool.

Double Banana Brown Sugar Muffins

1 cup	buckwheat flour	250 mL
1 cup	sorghum flour	250 mL
1/2 cup	potato starch	125 mL
1 1/2 tsp	gluten-free baking powder	7 mL
1 tsp	baking soda	5 mL
1 tsp	salt	5 mL
1 tsp	xanthan gum	5 mL
1 tsp	ground cinnamon	5 mL
1/2 tsp	ground nutmeg	2 mL
3	eggs	3
1 cup	mashed ripe bananas	250 mL
2/3 cup	packed light brown sugar	150 mL
1/2 cup	vegetable oil	125 mL
2 tbsp	liquid honey	30 mL
1 tbsp	freshly squeezed lemon juice	15 mL
1 tsp	vanilla extract	5 mL
1 cup	diced firm-ripe banana	250 mL

Bananas, a workhorse of the fruit world, take on sweet depth of flavor when combined with brown sugar, honey and spice in a sorghum-buckwheat batter. These moist muffins will keep beautifully for a day or two after you make them.

Makes 12 muffins

- Preheat oven to 350°F (180°C)
- 12-cup muffin pan, greased

1. In a large bowl, whisk together buckwheat flour, sorghum flour, potato starch, baking powder, baking soda, salt, xanthan gum, cinnamon and nutmeg.

2. In a medium bowl, whisk eggs until well blended and frothy. Whisk in mashed bananas, brown sugar, oil, honey, lemon juice and vanilla until well blended.

3. Add the egg mixture to the flour mixture and stir until just blended. Gently fold in diced banana.

4. Divide batter equally among prepared muffin cups.

5. Bake in preheated oven for 24 to 28 minutes or until a toothpick inserted in the center comes out clean. Let cool in pan on a wire rack for 5 minutes, then transfer to the rack to cool.

Banana Pecan Sorghum Muffins

2 cups	sorghum flour	500 mL
1 1/2 tsp	gluten-free baking powder	7 mL
1 tsp	xanthan gum	5 mL
1/2 tsp	salt	2 mL
1/4 tsp	ground nutmeg	1 mL
1 cup	packed dark brown sugar	250 mL
1	egg	1
1 1/3 cups	mashed ripe bananas	325 mL
1/4 cup	vegetable oil	60 mL
1 tsp	vanilla extract	5 mL
3/4 cup	chopped pecans, toasted	175 mL
2 tbsp	turbinado sugar (optional)	30 mL

Whether at home or on vacation, muffins are a family affair at my house on weekday mornings, and banana muffins are my son's (and husband's) favorite kind. Toasting the pecans gives these muffins a decidedly adult flavor.

Makes 12 muffins

- Preheat oven to 400°F (200°C)
- 12-cup muffin pan, lined with paper liners

1. In a large bowl, whisk together flour, baking powder, xanthan gum, salt and nutmeg.
2. In a medium bowl, whisk together brown sugar, egg, bananas, oil and vanilla until well blended.
3. Add the egg mixture to the flour mixture and stir until just blended. Gently fold in pecans.
4. Divide batter equally among prepared muffin cups. Sprinkle with turbinado sugar (if using).
5. Bake in preheated oven for 22 to 27 minutes or until a toothpick inserted in the center comes out clean. Let cool in pan on a wire rack for 5 minutes, then transfer to the rack to cool.

Banana Sorghum Jumble Muffins

1 cup	sorghum flour	250 mL
1/2 cup	potato starch	125 mL
2 tsp	gluten-free baking powder	10 mL
1 1/2 tsp	xanthan gum	7 mL
1 tsp	ground cinnamon	5 mL
1 tsp	baking soda	5 mL
1/2 tsp	salt	2 mL
1/2 cup	packed light brown sugar	125 mL
2	eggs	2
1 cup	mashed ripe bananas	250 mL
1/4 cup	vegetable oil	60 mL
2 tsp	vanilla extract	10 mL
1/2 cup	gluten-free semisweet chocolate chips, chopped	125 mL
1/2 cup	chopped pecans, toasted	125 mL
1/2 cup	dried cherries, cranberries or blueberries	125 mL

There are lots of banana muffins out there, but these are destined to top your list of all-time favorites.

Makes 12 muffins

- Preheat oven to 375°F (190°C)
- 12-cup muffin pan, greased

1. In a large bowl, whisk together flour, potato starch, baking powder, xanthan gum, cinnamon, baking soda and salt.
2. In a medium bowl, whisk together brown sugar, eggs, bananas, oil and vanilla until well blended.
3. Add the egg mixture to the flour mixture and stir until just blended. Gently fold in chocolate chips, pecans and cherries.
4. Divide batter equally among prepared muffin cups.
5. Bake in preheated oven for 20 to 25 minutes or until tops are puffed and a toothpick inserted in the center comes out clean. Let cool in pan on a wire rack for 5 minutes, then transfer to the rack to cool.

Banana Chocolate Chip Sorghum Teff Muffins

1½ cups	sorghum flour	375 mL
1 cup	teff flour	250 mL
½ cup	tapioca flour	125 mL
2 tsp	gluten-free baking powder	10 mL
1½ tsp	xanthan gum	7 mL
1 tsp	ground cinnamon	5 mL
1 tsp	baking soda	5 mL
1 tsp	salt	5 mL
⅔ cup	packed light brown sugar	150 mL
2	eggs	2
¼ cup	unsalted butter, melted	60 mL
2 tsp	vanilla extract	10 mL
1½ cups	mashed ripe bananas	375 mL
1 cup	milk	250 mL
1 cup	gluten-free semisweet chocolate chips, chopped	250 mL

Satisfy a chocolate craving the healthy way: serve the sweet stuff in a tender muffin made with sweet sorghum flour and teff and loaded with nutrient-rich bananas.

Makes 16 muffins

- Preheat oven to 375°F (190°C)
- Two 12-cup muffin pans, 16 cups greased

1. In a large bowl, whisk together sorghum flour, teff flour, tapioca flour, baking powder, xanthan gum, cinnamon, baking soda and salt.

2. In a medium bowl, whisk together brown sugar, eggs, butter and vanilla until well blended. Whisk in bananas and milk until blended.

3. Add the egg mixture to the flour mixture and stir until just blended. Gently fold in chocolate chips.

4. Divide batter equally among prepared muffin cups.

5. Bake in preheated oven for 20 to 25 minutes or until a toothpick inserted in the center comes out clean. Let cool in pans on a wire rack for 5 minutes, then transfer to the rack to cool.

Blueberry Muffins

2 cups	Brown Rice Flour Blend (page 19)	500 mL
1 tbsp	gluten-free baking powder	15 mL
1 tsp	baking soda	5 mL
¾ tsp	xanthan gum	3 mL
½ tsp	salt	2 mL
¼ tsp	ground nutmeg	1 mL
⅓ cup	granulated sugar	75 mL
⅓ cup	packed light brown sugar	75 mL
2	eggs	2
½ cup	vegetable oil	125 mL
⅓ cup	milk	75 mL
2 tsp	vanilla extract	10 mL
1½ cups	blueberries	375 mL
2 tbsp	turbinado sugar	30 mL

Makes 12 muffins

- Preheat oven to 375°F (190°C)
- 12-cup muffin pan, greased

1. In a large bowl, whisk together flour blend, baking powder, baking soda, xanthan gum, salt and nutmeg.

2. In a medium bowl, whisk together granulated sugar, brown sugar, eggs, oil, milk and vanilla until well blended.

3. Add the egg mixture to the flour mixture and stir until just blended. Gently fold in blueberries.

4. Divide batter equally among prepared muffin cups. Sprinkle with turbinado sugar.

5. Bake in preheated oven for 20 to 25 minutes or until a toothpick inserted in the center comes out clean. Let cool in pan on a wire rack for 5 minutes, then transfer to the rack to cool.

Blueberry Raspberry Muffins

Topping

3 tbsp	packed light brown sugar	45 mL
1/4 tsp	ground nutmeg	1 mL

Muffins

1 1/2 cups	Brown Rice Flour Blend (page 19)	375 mL
2 1/2 tsp	gluten-free baking powder	12 mL
1 tsp	ground cinnamon	5 mL
1/4 tsp	salt	1 mL
1/4 tsp	xanthan gum	1 mL
1/2 cup	granulated sugar	125 mL
1	egg	1
2/3 cup	buttermilk	150 mL
1/4 cup	unsalted butter, melted	60 mL
1 cup	blueberries	250 mL
1/4 cup	seedless raspberry preserves or jam	60 mL

Blueberries, meet your match: raspberry jam. Together with a simple brown sugar and spice sprinkle on top, these muffins verge on swoon-worthy.

Makes 12 muffins

- Preheat oven to 350°F (180°C)
- 12-cup muffin pan, lined with paper liners

1. *Topping:* In a small bowl, combine brown sugar and nutmeg. Set aside.
2. *Muffins:* In a large bowl, whisk together flour blend, baking powder, cinnamon, salt and xanthan gum.
3. In a medium bowl, whisk together sugar, egg, buttermilk and butter until well blended.
4. Add the egg mixture to the flour mixture and stir until just blended. Gently fold in blueberries.
5. Divide half the batter equally among prepared muffin cups. Spoon 1 tsp (5 mL) preserves into the center of each cup. Top with the remaining batter. Sprinkle with topping.
6. Bake in preheated oven for 20 to 25 minutes or until tops spring back when touched. Let cool in pan on a wire rack for 5 minutes, then transfer to the rack to cool.

Maple Blueberry Muffins

1 cup	blueberries	250 mL
2 tbsp	pure maple syrup	30 mL
1 3/4 cups	Brown Rice Flour Blend (page 19)	425 mL
2 tsp	gluten-free baking powder	10 mL
1 tsp	salt	5 mL
1/2 tsp	xanthan gum	2 mL
1/2 tsp	cinnamon	2 mL
1/2 tsp	baking soda	2 mL
1/2 cup	packed light brown sugar	125 mL
2	eggs	2
1/2 cup	vegetable oil	125 mL
1 cup	buttermilk	250 mL

Blueberry muffins are a tried and true favorite, but for something new, try these maple-sweetened treats. You won't be sorry.

Makes 12 muffins

- Preheat oven to 350°F (180°C)
- 12-cup muffin pan, greased

1. In a small bowl, coarsely mash blueberries and syrup.
2. In a large bowl, whisk together flour blend, baking powder, salt, xanthan gum, cinnamon and baking soda.
3. In a medium bowl, whisk together brown sugar, eggs and oil until well blended. Whisk in buttermilk until blended.
4. Add the blueberry mixture and the egg mixture to the flour mixture and stir until just blended.
5. Divide batter equally among prepared muffin cups.
6. Bake in preheated oven for 25 to 30 minutes or until a toothpick inserted in the center comes out clean. Let cool in pan on a wire rack for 5 minutes, then transfer to the rack to cool.

Fresh Cherry and Almond Muffins

1 1/2 cups	Brown Rice Flour Blend (page 19)	375 mL
1/2 cup	almond flour	125 mL
1 tbsp	gluten-free baking powder	15 mL
1 tsp	ground cinnamon	5 mL
1/2 tsp	salt	2 mL
1/2 tsp	xanthan gum	2 mL
1/2 cup	granulated sugar	125 mL
1	egg	1
1/4 cup	vegetable oil	60 mL
3/4 tsp	almond extract	3 mL
1 cup	plain yogurt	250 mL
1/4 cup	milk	60 mL
1 cup	coarsely chopped pitted Bing cherries	250 mL

Tart-sweet bites of fresh cherry punctuate these almond-flavored muffins.

Makes 12 muffins

- Preheat oven to 350°F (180°C)
- 12-cup muffin pan, greased

1. In a large bowl, whisk together flour blend, almond flour, baking powder, cinnamon, salt and xanthan gum.
2. In a medium bowl, whisk together sugar, egg, oil and almond extract until well blended. Whisk in yogurt and milk until blended.
3. Add the egg mixture to the flour mixture and stir until just blended. Gently fold in cherries.
4. Divide batter equally among prepared muffin cups.
5. Bake in preheated oven for 20 to 25 minutes or until tops are golden and a toothpick inserted in the center comes out clean. Let cool in pan on a wire rack for 5 minutes, then transfer to the rack to cool.

Raspberry Lemon Sorghum Muffins

2 cups	Brown Rice Flour Blend (page 19)	500 mL
1 cup	sorghum flour	250 mL
1 1/2 tsp	gluten-free baking powder	7 mL
1/2 tsp	baking soda	2 mL
1/2 tsp	salt	2 mL
1/2 tsp	xanthan gum	2 mL
1 cup	granulated sugar	250 mL
2/3 cup	unsalted butter, softened	150 mL
2	eggs	2
1 tbsp	finely grated lemon zest	15 mL
1 1/2 cups	low-fat (1%) plain yogurt	375 mL
1 1/2 cups	raspberries	375 mL
3 tbsp	turbinado sugar	45 mL

These muffins are an appealing combination of raspberries, lemon and yogurt. The end result is just the right mix of sweet, bright and tangy ingredients — perfect for your next brunch.

Makes 18 muffins

- Preheat oven to 375°F (190°C)
- Two 12-cup muffin pans, 18 cups greased

1. In a medium bowl, whisk together flour blend, sorghum flour, baking powder, baking soda, salt and xanthan gum.
2. In a large bowl, using an electric mixer on medium speed, beat granulated sugar and butter until just blended (do not overbeat or muffins will not rise). Beat in eggs, one at a time, until just blended, then beat in lemon zest until blended.
3. With the mixer on low speed, beat in flour mixture alternately with yogurt, making two additions of flour and one of yogurt, until just blended. Gently fold in raspberries.
4. Divide batter equally among prepared muffin cups. Sprinkle with turbinado sugar.
5. Bake in preheated oven for 30 to 35 minutes or until a toothpick inserted in the center comes out clean. Let cool in pans on a wire rack for 5 minutes, then transfer to the rack to cool.

Strawberry Muffins

Muffins

2 cups	Brown Rice Flour Blend (page 19)	500 mL
1 1/2 tsp	gluten-free baking powder	7 mL
3/4 tsp	xanthan gum	3 mL
1/2 tsp	baking soda	2 mL
2/3 cup	granulated sugar	150 mL
1	egg	1
1/4 cup	unsalted butter, melted	60 mL
3/4 cup	milk	175 mL
1 tsp	vanilla extract	5 mL
1 cup	diced strawberries	250 mL

Glaze

1/2 cup	confectioners' (icing) sugar	125 mL
1 tbsp	milk	15 mL
1/8 tsp	vanilla extract	1 mL

These muffins taste like summer: really fruity and fresh. You can make them with just about any ripe berry that suits your fancy, including blueberries, blackberries and boysenberries.

Makes 12 muffins

- Preheat oven to 350°F (180°C)
- 12-cup muffin pan, lined with paper liners

1. *Muffins:* In a large bowl, whisk together flour blend, baking powder, xanthan gum and baking soda.

2. In a medium bowl, whisk together sugar, egg, butter, milk and vanilla until well blended.

3. Add the egg mixture to the flour mixture and stir until just blended. Gently fold in strawberries.

4. Divide batter equally among prepared muffin cups.

5. Bake in preheated oven for 18 to 22 minutes or until a toothpick inserted in the center comes out clean. Let cool in pan on a wire rack for 5 minutes, then transfer to the rack to cool while you prepare the glaze.

6. *Glaze:* In a small bowl, combine confectioners' sugar, milk and vanilla until blended and smooth. Drizzle over warm muffin tops. Let cool.

Berry Corn Muffins

1 cup	Brown Rice Flour Blend (page 19)	250 mL
1 cup	stone-ground yellow cornmeal	250 mL
2 tsp	gluten-free baking powder	10 mL
3/4 tsp	xanthan gum	3 mL
1/2 tsp	baking soda	2 mL
1/2 tsp	salt	2 mL
1	egg	1
1/2 cup	granulated sugar	125 mL
1 cup	buttermilk	250 mL
1/4 cup	unsalted butter, melted	60 mL
2 tsp	finely grated lemon zest	10 mL
1 cup	raspberries, blackberries or blueberries	250 mL
3 tbsp	turbinado sugar	45 mL

Makes 12 muffins

- Preheat oven to 400°F (200°C)
- 12-cup muffin pan, greased

1. In a large bowl, whisk together flour blend, cornmeal, baking powder, xanthan gum, baking soda and salt.
2. In a medium bowl, vigorously whisk egg. Whisk in granulated sugar, buttermilk, butter and lemon zest until well blended.
3. Add the egg mixture to the flour mixture and stir until just blended. Gently fold in raspberries.
4. Divide batter equally among prepared muffin cups. Sprinkle with turbinado sugar.
5. Bake in preheated oven for 20 to 25 minutes or until a toothpick inserted in the center comes out clean. Let cool in pan on a wire rack for 5 minutes, then transfer to the rack to cool.

These tender, not-too-sweet muffins, which echo the clean corn flavor of polenta, are delicious alongside a steamed latte or a cup of Darjeeling — or all on their own.

Almond Flour Blackberry Muffins

2 cups	fresh or frozen (thawed) blackberries	500 mL
2 1/2 cups	almond flour	625 mL
1 tsp	ground cinnamon	5 mL
1/2 tsp	baking soda	2 mL
1/2 tsp	salt	2 mL
3	eggs	3
1/2 cup	liquid honey	125 mL
1 tsp	vanilla extract	5 mL

Makes 12 muffins

- 12-cup muffin pan, lined with paper liners

1. In a small saucepan, bring blackberries and 1/2 cup (125 mL) water to a boil over medium-high heat. Reduce heat to low and simmer, stirring often, until thickened slightly and blackberries have released their juice. Let cool.
2. Preheat oven to 325°F (160°C).
3. In a medium bowl, whisk together flour, cinnamon, baking soda and salt.
4. In another medium bowl, whisk together eggs, honey and vanilla until well blended.
5. Add the berry mixture and the egg mixture to the flour mixture and stir until just blended.
6. Divide batter equally among prepared muffin cups.
7. Bake for 25 to 30 minutes or until a toothpick inserted in the center comes out clean. Let cool in pan on a wire rack for 5 minutes, then transfer to the rack to cool.

Here I pepped up fail-safe almond flour muffins with the combination of honey and fresh blackberries. They'll be jumping out of bed for these.

Fresh Cranberry Orange Muffins

2 cups	Brown Rice Flour Blend (page 19)	500 mL
1 cup	granulated sugar	250 mL
1 tbsp	finely grated orange zest	15 mL
2 tsp	gluten-free baking powder	10 mL
3/4 tsp	xanthan gum	3 mL
3/4 tsp	salt	3 mL
1/2 tsp	baking soda	2 mL
1/2 tsp	ground cinnamon	2 mL
1/4 cup	cold unsalted butter, cut into small pieces	60 mL
1	egg	1
3/4 cup	freshly squeezed orange juice	175 mL
2 cups	fresh cranberries, coarsely chopped	500 mL
1/2 cup	chopped pecans, toasted	125 mL

A quick spell in the kitchen produces a muffin everyone will fawn over. The tartness of the cranberries is delicious with the sweetness of the orange-cinnamon batter and the nuttiness of the toasted pecans.

Tip

If you do not have a food processor, you can use a pastry cutter or your fingers to cut the butter into the flour mixture.

Makes 12 muffins

- Preheat oven to 350°F (180°C)
- Food processor
- 12-cup muffin pan, greased

1. In food processor, pulse flour blend, sugar, orange zest, baking powder, xanthan gum, salt, baking soda and cinnamon until combined. Add butter and pulse until mixture resembles bread crumbs. Transfer to a large bowl.

2. In a small bowl, whisk together egg and orange juice until well blended.

3. Add the egg mixture to the flour mixture and stir until just blended. Gently fold in cranberries and pecans.

4. Divide batter equally among prepared muffin cups.

5. Bake in preheated oven for 20 to 25 minutes or until a toothpick inserted in the center comes out clean. Let cool in pan on a wire rack for 5 minutes, then transfer to the rack to cool.

Lemon Poppy Seed Muffins

Muffins

2 cups	Brown Rice Flour Blend (page 19)	500 mL
1/4 cup	poppy seeds	60 mL
2 tsp	gluten-free baking powder	10 mL
3/4 tsp	xanthan gum	3 mL
1/2 tsp	baking soda	2 mL
1/2 tsp	salt	2 mL
1 cup	granulated sugar	250 mL
3	eggs	3
1/2 cup	vegetable oil	125 mL
2 tbsp	finely grated lemon zest	30 mL
3/4 cup	buttermilk	175 mL

Glaze

1/2 cup	confectioners' (icing) sugar	125 mL
1 1/2 tsp	freshly squeezed lemon juice	7 mL

These portable treats combine my love of lemon desserts with my affection for poppy seeds. They hold together very well and are fun to eat. Poppy seeds have a tendency to go rancid quickly, so be sure to use a fresh package (and refrigerate or freeze extras afterwards).

Makes 12 muffins

- Preheat oven to 350°F (180°C)
- 12-cup muffin pan, greased

1. *Muffins:* In a medium bowl, whisk together flour blend, poppy seeds, baking powder, xanthan gum, baking soda and salt.

2. In a large bowl, using an electric mixer on medium-high speed, beat sugar, eggs, oil and lemon zest for 1 minute. With the mixer on low speed, beat in buttermilk until well blended.

3. Add the flour mixture to the egg mixture and, using a wooden spoon, stir until just blended.

4. Divide batter equally among prepared muffin cups.

5. Bake in preheated oven for 20 to 25 minutes or until a toothpick inserted in the center comes out clean. Let cool in pan on a wire rack for 5 minutes, then transfer to the rack to cool while you prepare the glaze.

6. *Glaze:* In a small bowl, whisk together confectioners' sugar and lemon juice until blended and smooth. Drizzle or spoon over warm muffin tops. Let cool.

Lemon Ricotta Muffins with Berries

Muffins

2 cups	Brown Rice Flour Blend (page 19)	500 mL
2 tsp	xanthan gum	10 mL
1/2 tsp	gluten-free baking powder	2 mL
1/2 tsp	baking soda	2 mL
1/2 tsp	salt	2 mL
1 cup	granulated sugar	250 mL
1/2 cup	unsalted butter, softened	125 mL
1	egg	1
1 cup	ricotta cheese	250 mL
1/2 tsp	vanilla extract	2 mL
1 tbsp	finely grated lemon zest	15 mL
1 tbsp	freshly squeezed lemon juice	15 mL
1 cup	raspberries, blueberries or blackberries	250 mL

Glaze

1/2 cup	confectioners' (icing) sugar	125 mL
1 1/2 tsp	freshly squeezed lemon juice	7 mL

Berry lovers will be very happy with these moist, lemony muffins.

Makes 12 muffins

- Preheat oven to 350°F (180°C)
- 12-cup muffin pan, greased

1. *Muffins:* In a medium bowl, whisk together flour blend, xanthan gum, baking powder, baking soda and salt.

2. In a large bowl, using an electric mixer on medium-high speed, beat sugar and butter until light and fluffy. Beat in egg until well blended. Beat in cheese, vanilla, lemon zest and lemon juice until blended.

3. Add the flour mixture to the egg mixture and, using a wooden spoon, stir until just blended. Gently fold in raspberries.

4. Divide batter equally among prepared muffin cups.

5. Bake in preheated oven for 18 to 23 minutes or until a toothpick inserted in the center comes out clean. Let cool in pan on a wire rack for 5 minutes, then transfer to the rack to cool while you prepare the glaze.

6. *Glaze:* In a small bowl, whisk together confectioners' sugar and lemon juice until blended and smooth. Drizzle over warm muffin tops. Let cool.

Lemon Thyme Muffins

1 1/2 cups	Brown Rice Flour Blend (page 19)	375 mL
1/2 cup	stone-ground yellow cornmeal	125 mL
2 tsp	gluten-free baking powder	10 mL
3/4 tsp	xanthan gum	3 mL
1/2 tsp	baking soda	2 mL
1/2 tsp	salt	2 mL
1	egg	1
1/2 cup	granulated sugar	125 mL
1 cup	buttermilk	250 mL
1/4 cup	unsalted butter, melted	60 mL
2 tbsp	finely grated lemon zest	30 mL
2 tsp	minced fresh thyme	10 mL

These grown-up muffins are easy to prepare, versatile and delicious.

Makes 12 muffins

- Preheat oven to 400°F (200°C)
- 12-cup muffin pan, greased

1. In a large bowl, whisk together flour blend, cornmeal, baking powder, xanthan gum, baking soda and salt.

2. In a medium bowl, vigorously whisk egg. Whisk in sugar, buttermilk, butter, lemon zest and thyme until well blended.

3. Add the egg mixture to the flour mixture and stir until just blended.

4. Divide batter equally among prepared muffin cups.

5. Bake in preheated oven for 20 to 25 minutes or until a toothpick inserted in the center comes out clean. Let cool in pan on a wire rack for 5 minutes, then transfer to the rack to cool.

Lemon Curd Muffins

2/3 cup	milk	150 mL
2 tsp	finely grated lemon zest	10 mL
1 tbsp	freshly squeezed lemon juice	15 mL
1 1/2 cups	Brown Rice Flour Blend (page 19)	375 mL
1 tbsp	gluten-free baking powder	15 mL
1/2 tsp	salt	2 mL
1/2 tsp	xanthan gum	2 mL
1/3 cup	granulated sugar	75 mL
2	eggs	2
1/2 cup	whole-milk ricotta cheese	125 mL
3 tbsp	unsalted butter, melted	45 mL
1/2 cup	lemon curd	125 mL

Here, the clean, citrus flavor of lemon curd shines in a tender ricotta muffin.

Makes 12 muffins

- Preheat oven to 350°F (180°C)
- 12-cup muffin pan, greased

1. In a glass measuring cup, combine milk, lemon zest and lemon juice. Let stand for 1 to 2 minutes to let milk curdle.
2. In a large bowl, whisk together flour blend, baking powder, salt and xanthan gum.
3. In a medium bowl, whisk together sugar, eggs, cheese, butter and milk mixture until well blended.
4. Add the egg mixture to the flour mixture and stir until just blended.
5. Divide half the batter equally among prepared muffin cups. Spoon 2 tsp (10 mL) lemon curd into the center of each cup. Top with the remaining batter.
6. Bake in preheated oven for 24 to 28 minutes or until tops spring back when touched. Let cool in pan on a wire rack for 5 minutes, then transfer to the rack to cool.

Lemon-Scented Raspberry Muffins

2 cups	Brown Rice Flour Blend (page 19)	500 mL
2 tsp	gluten-free baking powder	10 mL
3/4 tsp	xanthan gum	3 mL
1/4 tsp	salt	1 mL
1 cup	granulated sugar	250 mL
1/4 cup	unsalted butter, softened	60 mL
2	eggs	2
1 tbsp	finely grated lemon zest	15 mL
3/4 cup	milk	175 mL
1 1/2 cups	raspberries	375 mL

Simple, tender butter muffins topped with a fragrant lemon accent: I like them just as they are, full of raspberries, but you could easily substitute any sweet, juicy berries you pick up at the farmers' market.

Makes 12 muffins

- Preheat oven to 350°F (180°C)
- 12-cup muffin pan, lined with paper liners

1. In a medium bowl, whisk together flour blend, baking powder, xanthan gum and salt.
2. In a large bowl, using an electric mixer on medium speed, beat sugar and butter until light and fluffy. Beat in eggs, one at a time, until well blended. Beat in lemon zest and milk until blended.
3. Add the flour mixture to the egg mixture and, using a wooden spoon, stir until just blended. Gently fold in raspberries.
4. Divide batter equally among prepared muffin cups.
5. Bake in preheated oven for 18 to 22 minutes or until tops are golden and a toothpick inserted in the center comes out clean. Let cool in pan on a wire rack for 5 minutes, then transfer to the rack to cool.

Sour Cream Lemon Apricot Muffins

2 cups	Brown Rice Flour Blend (page 19)	500 mL
2 tsp	gluten-free baking powder	10 mL
3/4 tsp	salt	3 mL
1/2 tsp	baking soda	2 mL
1/2 tsp	xanthan gum	2 mL
3/4 cup	granulated sugar	175 mL
1/4 cup	unsalted butter, softened	60 mL
2	eggs	2
1 cup	sour cream	240 mL
1 tbsp	finely grated lemon zest	15 mL
1/4 cup	freshly squeezed lemon juice	60 mL
3/4 cup	finely chopped dried apricots	175 mL

The appealing pairing of lemon and apricot sings in these tender sour cream muffins.

Makes 12 muffins

- Preheat oven to 350°F (180°C)
- 12-cup muffin pan, lined with paper liners

1. In a medium bowl, whisk together flour blend, baking powder, salt, baking soda and xanthan gum.
2. In a large bowl, using an electric mixer on medium-high speed, beat sugar and butter until light and fluffy. Beat in eggs, one at a time, until well blended. Beat in sour cream, lemon zest and lemon juice until blended.
3. Add the flour mixture to the egg mixture and, using a wooden spoon, stir until just blended. Gently fold in apricots.
4. Divide batter equally among prepared muffin cups.
5. Bake in preheated oven for 20 to 25 minutes or until a toothpick inserted in the center comes out clean. Let cool in pan on a wire rack for 5 minutes, then transfer to the rack to cool.

Very Lemon Muffins

Muffins

2 1/2 cups	Brown Rice Flour Blend (page 19)	625 mL
1 tbsp	gluten-free baking powder	15 mL
1 tsp	salt	5 mL
1/2 tsp	xanthan gum	2 mL
1 cup	granulated sugar	250 mL
2	eggs	2
3/4 cup	buttermilk	175 mL
1/2 cup	vegetable oil	125 mL
3 tbsp	finely grated lemon zest	45 mL
1/4 cup	freshly squeezed lemon juice	60 mL

Glaze

1 cup	confectioners' (icing) sugar	250 mL
2 tsp	finely grated lemon zest	10 mL
1 tbsp	freshly squeezed lemon juice	15 mL

These light, double lemon muffins are as good as they sound.

Makes 18 muffins

- Preheat oven to 350°F (180°C)
- Two 12-cup muffin pans, 18 cups greased

1. *Muffins:* In a large bowl, whisk together flour blend, baking powder, salt and xanthan gum.
2. In a medium bowl, whisk together sugar, eggs, buttermilk, oil, lemon zest and lemon juice until well blended.
3. Add the egg mixture to the flour mixture and stir until just blended.
4. Divide batter equally among prepared muffin cups.
5. Bake in preheated oven for 30 to 35 minutes or until tops are golden and a toothpick inserted in the center comes out clean. Let cool in pans on a wire rack for 5 minutes, then transfer to the rack to cool while you prepare the glaze.
6. *Glaze:* In a small bowl, whisk together confectioners' sugar, lemon zest and lemon juice until blended and smooth. Spoon over warm muffin tops. Let cool.

Ginger Lime Muffins

Muffins

2½ cups	Brown Rice Flour Blend (page 19)	625 mL
1 tbsp	gluten-free baking powder	15 mL
2 tsp	ground ginger	10 mL
1 tsp	salt	5 mL
½ tsp	xanthan gum	2 mL
1 cup	granulated sugar	250 mL
2	eggs	2
¾ cup	plain yogurt	175 mL
½ cup	vegetable oil	125 mL
3 tbsp	finely grated lime zest	45 mL
¼ cup	freshly squeezed lime juice	60 mL
2 tsp	vanilla extract	10 mL

Glaze

1 cup	confectioners' (icing) sugar	250 mL
1 tsp	finely grated lime zest	5 mL
1 tbsp	freshly squeezed lime juice	15 mL

These muffins have a marvelous flavor with a bright citrus edge that's just tart enough to offset the sweetness of the muffins. Ginger adds a subtle note of spice.

Makes 18 muffins

- Preheat oven to 350°F (180°C)
- Two 12-cup muffin pans, 18 cups greased

1. *Muffins:* In a large bowl, whisk together flour blend, baking powder, ginger, salt and xanthan gum.
2. In a medium bowl, whisk together sugar, eggs, yogurt, oil, lime zest, lime juice and vanilla until well blended.
3. Add the egg mixture to the flour mixture and stir until just blended.
4. Divide batter equally among prepared muffin cups.
5. Bake in preheated oven for 30 to 35 minutes or until tops are golden and a toothpick inserted in the center comes out clean. Let cool in pans on a wire rack for 5 minutes, then transfer to the rack to cool while you prepare the glaze.
6. *Glaze:* In a small bowl, whisk together confectioners' sugar, lime zest and lime juice until blended. Spoon over warm muffin tops. Let cool.

Marmalade Muffins

2½ cups	Brown Rice Flour Blend (see page 19)	625 mL
2 tsp	gluten-free baking powder	10 mL
1 tsp	baking soda	5 mL
1 tsp	xanthan gum	5 mL
½ tsp	salt	2 mL
2	eggs	2
⅔ cup	plain whole-milk yogurt	150 mL
½ cup	orange marmalade	125 mL
½ cup	vegetable oil	125 mL
1 tsp	vanilla extract	5 mL

These citrusy muffins — which, by the way, are stellar accompaniments to afternoon tea — get their zest from an ample dose of orange marmalade.

Makes 12 muffins

- Preheat oven to 350°F (180°C)
- 12-cup muffin pan, greased

1. In a large bowl, whisk together flour blend, baking powder, baking soda, xanthan gum and salt.
2. In a medium bowl, whisk together eggs, yogurt, marmalade, oil and vanilla until well blended.
3. Add the egg mixture to the flour mixture and stir until just blended.
4. Divide batter equally among prepared muffin cups.
5. Bake in preheated oven for 22 to 27 minutes or until a toothpick inserted in the center comes out clean. Let cool in pan on a wire rack for 5 minutes, then transfer to the rack to cool.

Cinnamon Orange Muffins

Topping

2 tbsp	granulated sugar	30 mL
1/2 tsp	ground cinnamon	7 mL

Muffins

1 1/2 cups	Brown Rice Flour Blend (see page 19)	375 mL
2 tsp	gluten-free baking powder	10 mL
2 tsp	ground cinnamon	10 mL
3/4 tsp	salt	3 mL
1/2 tsp	xanthan gum	2 mL
1 cup	granulated sugar	250 mL
3	eggs	3
1/2 cup	sour cream	125 mL
1/4 cup	vegetable oil	60 mL
2 tbsp	finely grated orange zest	15 mL

Here, a lively dose of cinnamon and orange zest lends a delectable sour cream muffin a subtly spicy citrus edge.

Makes 12 muffins

- Preheat oven to 350°F (180°C)
- 12-cup muffin pan, greased

1. *Topping:* In a small bowl, combine sugar and cinnamon. Set aside.
2. *Muffins:* In a large bowl, whisk together flour blend, baking powder, cinnamon, salt and xanthan gum.
3. In a medium bowl, whisk together sugar, eggs, sour cream, oil and orange zest until well blended.
4. Add the egg mixture to the flour mixture and stir until just blended.
5. Divide batter equally among prepared muffin cups. Sprinkle with topping.
6. Bake in preheated oven for 15 to 20 minutes or until a toothpick inserted in the center comes out clean. Let cool in pan on a wire rack for 3 minutes, then transfer to the rack to cool.

Mango Muffins

Muffins

2 cups	Brown Rice Flour Blend (see page 19)	500 mL
1 1/2 tsp	gluten-free baking powder	7 mL
1 tsp	ground ginger	5 mL
3/4 tsp	xanthan gum	3 mL
1/2 tsp	baking soda	2 mL
2/3 cup	granulated sugar	150 mL
1	egg	1
3/4 cup	orange juice	175 mL
1/4 cup	unsalted butter, melted	60 mL
2 tsp	finely grated lime zest	10 mL
1 cup	diced firm-ripe mango	250 mL
1/3 cup	golden raisins, chopped	75 mL

Glaze

1/2 cup	confectioners' (icing) sugar	125 mL
1 1/2 tsp	freshly squeezed lime juice	7 mL

Mango and golden raisins are enhanced with lime zest and ginger for a tangy yellow and green muffin.

Makes 12 muffins

- Preheat oven to 350°F (180°C)
- 12-cup muffin pan, lined with paper liners

1. *Muffins:* In a large bowl, whisk together flour blend, baking powder, ginger, xanthan gum and baking soda.
2. In a medium bowl, whisk together sugar, egg, orange juice, butter and lime zest until well blended.
3. Add the egg mixture to the flour mixture and stir until just blended. Gently fold in mango and raisins.
4. Divide batter equally among prepared muffin cups.
5. Bake in preheated oven for 18 to 22 minutes or until a toothpick inserted in the center comes out clean. Let cool in pan on a wire rack for 5 minutes, then transfer to the rack to cool while you prepare the glaze.
6. *Glaze:* In a small bowl, whisk together confectioners' sugar and lime juice until blended and smooth. Drizzle over warm muffin tops. Let cool.

Tangerine Muffins with Dried Blueberries

1 1/2 cups	Brown Rice Flour Blend (see page 19)	375 mL
1 1/2 tsp	gluten-free baking powder	7 mL
1/2 tsp	salt	2 mL
1/2 tsp	xanthan gum	2 mL
1 cup	granulated sugar	250 mL
1/2 cup	unsalted butter, softened	125 mL
2	eggs	2
1 tbsp	finely grated tangerine zest	15 mL
1/2 cup	freshly squeezed tangerine juice	125 mL
2/3 cup	dried blueberries	150 mL
2 tbsp	turbinado sugar	30 mL

Of all the citrus fruits, tangerine has perhaps the most complexity: It's floral and gently sweet, with an underlying tartness — like three fruits in one. And these easily assembled muffins, dotted with intensely fruity dried blueberries, allow the tangerine flavor to sparkle (along with the sugar topping).

Makes 10 muffins

- Preheat oven to 350°F (180°C)
- 12-cup muffin pan, 10 cups greased

1. In a medium bowl, whisk together flour blend, baking powder, salt and xanthan gum.

2. In a large bowl, using an electric mixer on medium-high speed, beat granulated sugar and butter until light and fluffy. Beat in eggs, one at a time, until well blended. Beat in tangerine zest and tangerine juice until blended.

3. Add the flour mixture to the egg mixture and, using a wooden spoon, stir until just blended. Gently fold in blueberries.

4. Divide batter equally among prepared muffin cups. Sprinkle with turbinado sugar.

5. Bake in preheated oven for 20 to 25 minutes or until a toothpick inserted in the center comes out clean. Let cool in pan on a wire rack for 5 minutes, then transfer to the rack to cool.

Papaya Almond Muffins

3 cups	almond flour	750 mL
3/4 tsp	baking soda	3 mL
3/4 tsp	ground allspice	3 mL
1/2 tsp	salt	2 mL
2	eggs	2
1/4 cup	liquid honey	60 mL
3 tbsp	unsalted butter, melted	45 mL
1 tbsp	finely grated lime zest	15 mL
1 tsp	vanilla extract	5 mL
3/4 cup	mashed ripe bananas	175 mL
1 cup	diced fresh papaya	175 mL

Papaya brings a fresh twist to everyday muffins. Lime zest, vanilla and allspice up the tropical ante.

Makes 12 muffins

- Preheat oven to 325°F (160°C)
- 12-cup muffin pan, lined with paper liners

1. In a large bowl, whisk together flour, baking soda, allspice and salt.

2. In a medium bowl, vigorously whisk eggs. Whisk in honey, butter, lime zest and vanilla until well blended. Stir in bananas.

3. Add the egg mixture to the flour mixture and stir until just blended. Gently fold in papaya.

4. Divide batter equally among prepared muffin cups.

5. Bake in preheated oven for 25 to 30 minutes or until a toothpick inserted in the center comes out clean. Let cool in pan on a wire rack for 5 minutes, then transfer to the rack to cool.

Kiwifruit Sorghum Muffins

2 cups	sorghum flour	500 mL
1 1/2 tsp	gluten-free baking powder	7 mL
1 tsp	xanthan gum	5 mL
1/2 tsp	salt	2 mL
1/4 tsp	ground allspice	1 mL
1 cup	packed light brown sugar	250 mL
1	egg	1
1 1/3 cups	unsweetened applesauce	325 mL
1/4 cup	unsalted butter, melted	60 mL
1 tsp	vanilla extract	5 mL
1 cup	diced peeled kiwifruit	250 mL
1/2 cup	golden raisins, chopped	125 mL
2 tbsp	turbinado sugar	30 mL

Good taste, in every sense, does not come any easier than with these charming green and gold muffins. They are equally modern and old-fashioned in flavor.

Makes 12 muffins

- Preheat oven to 400°F (200°C)
- 12-cup muffin pan, lined with paper liners

1. In a large bowl, whisk together flour, baking powder, xanthan gum, salt and allspice.

2. In a medium bowl, whisk together brown sugar, egg, applesauce, butter and vanilla until well blended.

3. Add the egg mixture to the flour mixture and stir until just blended. Gently fold in kiwifruit and raisins.

4. Divide batter equally among prepared muffin cups. Sprinkle with turbinado sugar.

5. Bake in preheated oven for 22 to 27 minutes or until a toothpick inserted in the center comes out clean. Let cool in pan on a wire rack for 5 minutes, then transfer to the rack to cool.

Pear Buckwheat Muffins

2 1/2 cups	buckwheat flour	625 mL
1/2 cup	tapioca flour	125 mL
2 tsp	gluten-free baking powder	10 mL
1 tsp	baking soda	5 mL
1 tsp	ground nutmeg	5 mL
1/2 tsp	salt	2 mL
1/2 cup	packed light brown sugar	125 mL
2	eggs	2
1 1/2 cups	unsweetened applesauce	375 mL
1/4 cup	vegetable oil	60 mL
2 tsp	vanilla extract	10 mL
1 1/3 cups	shredded firm-ripe pears	325 mL
1/4 cup	minced crystallized ginger	60 mL
2 tbsp	turbinado sugar	30 mL

Here, pears and applesauce are transformed into scrumptious muffins with nutmeg and gems of crystallized ginger stirred into the batter. And the topping? A sparkling sugar-crunch coating made with turbinado sugar and great ease.

Makes 12 muffins

- Preheat oven to 375°F (190°C)
- 12-cup muffin pan, greased

1. In a large bowl, whisk together buckwheat flour, tapioca flour, baking powder, baking soda, nutmeg and salt.

2. In a medium bowl, whisk together brown sugar, eggs, applesauce, oil and vanilla until well blended.

3. Add the egg mixture to the flour mixture and stir until just blended. Gently fold in pears and crystallized ginger.

4. Divide batter equally among prepared muffin cups. Sprinkle with turbinado sugar.

5. Bake in preheated oven for 24 to 28 minutes or until a toothpick inserted in the center comes out clean. Let cool in pan on a wire rack for 5 minutes, then transfer to the rack to cool.

Fresh Pear Muffins with Chinese Five-Spice

2¹⁄₂ cups	Brown Rice Flour Blend (see page 19)	625 mL
2¹⁄₂ tsp	gluten-free baking powder	12 mL
1¹⁄₂ tsp	Chinese five-spice powder	7 mL
1 tsp	xanthan gum	5 mL
³⁄₄ tsp	baking soda	3 mL
¹⁄₂ tsp	salt	2 mL
2	eggs	2
³⁄₄ cup	milk	175 mL
¹⁄₂ cup	liquid honey	125 mL
¹⁄₂ cup	vegetable oil	125 mL
1 tsp	finely grated orange zest	5 mL
1¹⁄₂ cups	chopped fresh pears	375 mL
3 tbsp	turbinado sugar	45 mL

These wonderful muffins combine fresh pears, floral honey and fragrant Chinese five-spice powder in sophisticated harmony.

Makes 12 muffins

- Preheat oven to 350°F (180°C)
- 12-cup muffin pan, greased

1. In a large bowl, whisk together flour blend, baking powder, five-spice powder, xanthan gum, baking soda and salt.

2. In a medium bowl, whisk together eggs, milk, honey, oil and orange zest until well blended.

3. Add the egg mixture to the flour mixture and stir until just blended. Gently fold in pears.

4. Divide batter equally among prepared muffin cups. Sprinkle with turbinado sugar.

5. Bake in preheated oven for 22 to 27 minutes or until a toothpick inserted in the center comes out clean. Let cool in pan on a wire rack for 5 minutes, then transfer to the rack to cool.

Sorghum Peach Honey Muffins

1¹⁄₂ cups	sorghum flour	375 mL
1 cup	almond flour	250 mL
¹⁄₂ cup	tapioca flour	125 mL
2 tsp	gluten-free baking powder	10 mL
1 tsp	xanthan gum	5 mL
¹⁄₂ tsp	baking soda	2 mL
¹⁄₂ tsp	salt	2 mL
¹⁄₂ tsp	ground nutmeg	2 mL
2	eggs	2
¹⁄₂ cup	liquid honey	125 mL
¹⁄₂ cup	milk	125 mL
¹⁄₃ cup	unsalted butter, melted	75 mL
¹⁄₄ cup	unsweetened applesauce	60 mL
2 tsp	vanilla extract	10 mL
1 tsp	almond extract	5 mL
2 cups	fresh or frozen (thawed) diced peeled peaches	500 mL

Peaches are already ambrosial at the peak of summer, but become even more so in these honey-infused muffins.

Makes 12 muffins

- Preheat oven to 350°F (180°C)
- 12-cup muffin pan, greased

1. In a large bowl, whisk together sorghum flour, almond flour, tapioca flour, baking powder, xanthan gum, baking soda, salt and nutmeg.

2. In a medium bowl, whisk together eggs, honey, milk, butter, applesauce, vanilla and almond extract until well blended.

3. Add the egg mixture to the flour mixture and stir until just blended. Gently fold in peaches.

4. Divide batter equally among prepared muffin cups.

5. Bake in preheated oven for 22 to 27 minutes or until a toothpick inserted in the center comes out clean. Let cool in pan on a wire rack for 5 minutes, then transfer to the rack to cool.

Sour Cream Peach Muffins

1½ cups	Brown Rice Flour Blend (see page 19)	375 mL
½ cup	almond flour	125 mL
1 tbsp	gluten-free baking powder	15 mL
½ tsp	salt	2 mL
½ tsp	xanthan gum	2 mL
¼ tsp	ground cinnamon	1 mL
½ cup	granulated sugar	125 mL
1	egg	1
¼ cup	vegetable oil	60 mL
¾ tsp	almond extract	3 mL
1 cup	sour cream	250 mL
¼ cup	milk	60 mL
1 cup	diced fresh or frozen (thawed) peaches	250 mL

Sour cream and peaches in tender muffin form? Oh, yes. You can make these year-round using frozen peaches.

Makes 12 muffins

- Preheat oven to 350°F (180°C)
- 12-cup muffin pan, greased

1. In a large bowl, whisk together flour blend, almond flour, baking powder, salt, xanthan gum and cinnamon.

2. In a medium bowl, whisk together sugar, egg, oil and almond extract until well blended. Whisk in sour cream and milk until blended.

3. Add the egg mixture to the flour mixture and stir until just blended. Gently fold in peaches.

4. Divide batter equally among prepared muffin cups.

5. Bake in preheated oven for 20 to 25 minutes or until tops are golden and a toothpick inserted in the center comes out clean. Let cool in pan on a wire rack for 5 minutes, then transfer to the rack to cool.

Pumpkin Pie Muffins

1¾ cups	Brown Rice Flour Blend (see page 19)	425 mL
2¼ tsp	pumpkin pie spice	11 mL
1 tsp	baking soda	5 mL
¾ tsp	xanthan gum	3 mL
¾ tsp	gluten-free baking powder	3 mL
¾ tsp	salt	3 mL
1 cup	packed light brown sugar	250 mL
2	eggs	2
1 cup	pumpkin purée (not pie filling)	250 mL
½ cup	vegetable oil	125 mL
¼ cup	milk	60 mL
2 tbsp	liquid honey	30 mL
1 tsp	vanilla extract	5 mL

Consider these "beauty" bites: thanks to the pumpkin, these muffins offer up 26% of your daily dose of vitamin A, which keeps skin and hair healthy. It's far less expensive — and more delicious — than heading to the spa.

Makes 12 muffins

- Preheat oven to 350°F (180°C)
- 12-cup muffin pan, greased

1. In a large bowl, whisk together flour blend, pumpkin pie spice, baking soda, xanthan gum, baking powder and salt.

2. In a medium bowl, whisk together brown sugar, eggs, pumpkin, oil, milk, honey and vanilla until well blended.

3. Add the egg mixture to the flour mixture and stir until just blended.

4. Divide batter equally among prepared muffin cups.

5. Bake in preheated oven for 20 to 25 minutes or until a toothpick inserted in the center comes out clean. Let cool in pan on a wire rack for 5 minutes, then transfer to the rack to cool.

Pecan Streusel Pumpkin Muffins

Streusel

¹/₂ cup	finely chopped pecans, toasted	125 mL
¹/₃ cup	packed light brown sugar	60 mL
2 tbsp	unsalted butter, melted	30 mL
1 tsp	ground cinnamon	5 mL

Muffins

1³/₄ cups	Brown Rice Flour Blend (see page 19)	425 mL
2 tsp	pumpkin pie spice	11 mL
1 tsp	gluten-free baking powder	5 mL
1 tsp	baking soda	5 mL
³/₄ tsp	salt	3 mL
³/₄ tsp	xanthan gum	3 mL
1 cup	granulated sugar	250 mL
2	eggs	2
1 cup	pumpkin purée (not pie filling)	250 mL
¹/₂ cup	vegetable oil	125 mL
¹/₄ cup	milk	60 mL
2 tbsp	pure maple syrup	30 mL
1 tsp	vanilla extract	5 mL

Truth be told, it's hard to reinvent a classic. But this interpretation — a cinnamon-spiced pecan streusel sprinkled in between and atop the batter — is a little kiss of new-fangled heaven. It takes pumpkin muffins to a whole new level.

Makes 12 muffins

- Preheat oven to 350°F (180°C)
- 12-cup muffin pan, greased

1. *Streusel:* In a small bowl, combine pecans, brown sugar, butter and cinnamon until blended. Refrigerate until ready to use.

2. *Muffins:* In a large bowl, whisk together flour blend, pumpkin pie spice, baking powder, baking soda, salt and xanthan gum.

3. In a medium bowl, whisk together sugar, eggs, pumpkin, oil, milk, maple syrup and vanilla until well blended.

4. Add the egg mixture to the flour mixture and stir until just blended.

5. Divide half the batter equally among prepared muffin cups. Sprinkle with half the streusel. Top with the remaining batter. Sprinkle with the remaining streusel.

6. Bake in preheated oven for 20 to 25 minutes or until a toothpick inserted in the center comes out clean. Let cool in pan on a wire rack for 5 minutes, then transfer to the rack to cool.

Pumpkin Almond Flour Muffins

3 cups	almond flour	750 mL
2½ tsp	pumpkin pie spice	12 mL
¾ tsp	baking soda	3 mL
¼ tsp	salt	1 mL
¼ cup	granulated sugar	60 mL
2	eggs	2
¾ cup	pumpkin purée (not pie filling)	175 mL
¼ cup	dark (cooking) molasses	60 mL
¼ cup	unsalted butter, melted	60 mL
1 tsp	vanilla extract	5 mL
1 cup	chopped pecans, toasted	250 mL

Watch out, pumpkin pie! These are downright delectable: a rich and flavorful muffin consisting mostly of almonds (in the form of almond flour), a great source of high-quality protein, with just the right amounts of pumpkin, sugar and spice.

Makes 12 muffins

- Preheat oven to 325°F (160°C)
- 12-cup muffin pan, lined with paper liners

1. In a large bowl, whisk together flour, pumpkin pie spice, baking soda and salt.

2. In a medium bowl, whisk together sugar, eggs, pumpkin, molasses, butter and vanilla until well blended.

3. Add the egg mixture to the flour mixture and stir until just blended. Gently fold in pecans.

4. Divide batter equally among prepared muffin cups.

5. Bake in preheated oven for 25 to 30 minutes or until tops are set and a toothpick inserted in the center comes out clean. Let cool in pan on a wire rack for 5 minutes, then transfer to the rack to cool.

Rhubarb Muffins with Cardamom and Orange

2½ cups	Brown Rice Flour Blend (see page 19)	625 mL
2 tsp	gluten-free baking powder	10 mL
1 tsp	baking soda	5 mL
1 tsp	ground cardamom	5 mL
1 tsp	xanthan gum	5 mL
½ tsp	salt	2 mL
2	eggs	2
2 tsp	finely grated orange zest	10 mL
¾ cup	freshly squeezed orange juice	175 mL
½ cup	liquid honey	125 mL
½ cup	vegetable oil	125 mL
1 tsp	vanilla extract	5 mL
2 cups	chopped fresh rhubarb	500 mL
3 tbsp	turbinado sugar	45 mL

One of my favorite spring ingredients — rhubarb — shines in this muffin recipe.

Makes 12 muffins

- Preheat oven to 350°F (180°C)
- 12-cup muffin pan, greased

1. In a large bowl, whisk together flour blend, baking powder, baking soda, cardamom, xanthan gum and salt.

2. In a medium bowl, whisk together eggs, orange zest, orange juice, honey, oil and vanilla until well blended.

3. Add the egg mixture to the flour mixture and stir until just blended. Gently fold in rhubarb.

4. Divide batter equally among prepared muffin cups. Sprinkle with turbinado sugar.

5. Bake in preheated oven for 22 to 27 minutes or until a toothpick inserted in the center comes out clean. Let cool in pan on a wire rack for 5 minutes, then transfer to the rack to cool.

Italian Fig Muffins

2 cups	Brown Rice Flour Blend (see page 19)	500 mL
2 tsp	gluten-free baking powder	10 mL
3/4 tsp	xanthan gum	3 mL
1/2 tsp	ground cinnamon	2 mL
1/4 tsp	salt	1 mL
1 cup	granulated sugar	250 mL
1/4 cup	unsalted butter, softened	60 mL
2	eggs	2
1 tbsp	finely grated orange zest	15 mL
3/4 cup	milk	175 mL
1/2 cup	dried figs, chopped	125 mL
1/2 cup	pitted dates, chopped	125 mL
1/2 cup	slivered almonds	125 mL

Drawing inspiration from fig crostata, these muffins are studded with figs and dates and imbued with citrusy notes of orange, then topped with an almond crown.

Makes 12 muffins

- Preheat oven to 350°F (180°C)
- 12-cup muffin pan, lined with paper liners

1. In a medium bowl, whisk together flour blend, baking powder, xanthan gum, cinnamon and salt.

2. In a large bowl, using an electric mixer on medium speed, beat sugar and butter until light and fluffy. Beat in eggs, one at a time, until well blended. Beat in orange zest and milk until blended.

3. Add the flour mixture to the egg mixture and, using a wooden spoon, stir until just blended. Gently fold in figs and dates.

4. Divide batter equally among prepared muffin cups. Sprinkle with almonds.

5. Bake in preheated oven for 18 to 22 minutes or until tops are golden and a toothpick inserted in the center comes out clean. Let cool in pan on a wire rack for 5 minutes, then transfer to the rack to cool.

Goat Cheese, Fig and Walnut Muffins

2 cups	Brown Rice Flour Blend (see page 19)	500 mL
1 tbsp	gluten-free baking powder	15 mL
1 tsp	baking soda	5 mL
3/4 tsp	xanthan gum	3 mL
1/2 tsp	salt	2 mL
1/8 tsp	freshly ground black pepper	0.5 mL
2/3 cup	packed light brown sugar	150 mL
2	eggs	2
1/2 cup	vegetable oil	125 mL
1/3 cup	milk	75 mL
1 tsp	vanilla extract	5 mL
3 oz	mild creamy goat cheese, crumbled	90 g
1/2 cup	chopped dried figs	125 mL
1/2 cup	chopped walnuts	125 mL

Everyone will be blown away by how simple, yet fabulous, these muffins are; they will be a runaway hit wherever they are served.

Makes 12 muffins

- Preheat oven to 375°F (190°C)
- 12-cup muffin pan, greased

1. In a large bowl, whisk together flour blend, baking powder, baking soda, xanthan gum, salt and pepper.

2. In a medium bowl, whisk together brown sugar, eggs, oil, milk and vanilla until well blended.

3. Add the egg mixture to the flour mixture and stir until just blended. Gently fold in cheese and figs.

4. Divide batter equally among prepared muffin cups. Sprinkle with walnuts.

5. Bake in preheated oven for 20 to 25 minutes or until a toothpick inserted in the center comes out clean. Let cool in pan on a wire rack for 5 minutes, then transfer to the rack to cool.

Date and Walnut Muffins

³⁄₄ cup	chopped dates	175 mL
²⁄₃ cup	boiling water	150 mL
1¹⁄₂ cups	Brown Rice Flour Blend (see page 19)	375 mL
1 tsp	xanthan gum	5 mL
³⁄₄ tsp	gluten-free baking powder	3 mL
³⁄₄ tsp	baking soda	3 mL
³⁄₄ tsp	ground cinnamon	3 mL
¹⁄₂ tsp	salt	2 mL
³⁄₄ cup	packed dark brown sugar	175 mL
6 tbsp	unsalted butter, softened	90 mL
2	eggs	2
1 tsp	vanilla extract	5 mL
³⁄₄ cup	chopped walnuts, toasted	175 mL

These muffins are inspired by one of my favorite desserts — sticky toffee pudding — but revamped to make them breakfast-appropriate.

Makes 12 muffins

- Preheat oven to 350°F (180°C)
- 12-cup muffin pan, lined with paper liners

1. In a small bowl, combine dates and boiling water. Let stand for 10 minutes (do not drain).

2. In a medium bowl, whisk together flour blend, xanthan gum, baking powder, baking soda, cinnamon and salt.

3. In a large bowl, using an electric mixer on medium speed, beat brown sugar and butter until light and fluffy. Beat in eggs, one at a time, until well blended. Beat in vanilla until blended. Beat in date mixture.

4. Add the flour mixture to the egg mixture and, using a wooden spoon, stir until just blended. Gently fold in walnuts.

5. Divide batter equally among prepared muffin cups.

6. Bake in preheated oven for 16 to 20 minutes or until a toothpick inserted in the center comes out clean. Let cool in pan on a wire rack for 5 minutes, then transfer to the rack to cool.

French Prune Almond Muffins

3 cups	almond flour	750 mL
³⁄₄ tsp	baking soda	3 mL
¹⁄₂ tsp	ground cinnamon	2 mL
¹⁄₂ tsp	salt	2 mL
2	eggs	2
¹⁄₄ cup	liquid honey	60 mL
3 tbsp	unsalted butter, melted	45 mL
1 tsp	almond extract	5 mL
³⁄₄ cup	unsweetened applesauce	175 mL
³⁄₄ cup	chopped pitted prunes	175 mL

Prunes are used in a wide range of French dishes, both sweet and savory, and they are becoming more and more popular in the United States and Canada. They have a velvety texture and deep fruit flavor that is deliciously accented by the fragrance of almond.

Makes 12 muffins

- Preheat oven to 325°F (160°C)
- 12-cup muffin pan, lined with paper liners

1. In a large bowl, whisk together flour, baking soda, cinnamon and salt.

2. In a medium bowl, vigorously whisk eggs. Whisk in honey, butter and almond extract until well blended. Stir in applesauce.

3. Add the egg mixture to the flour mixture and stir until just blended. Gently fold in prunes.

4. Divide batter equally among prepared muffin cups.

5. Bake in preheated oven for 25 to 30 minutes or until a toothpick inserted in the center comes out clean. Let cool in pan on a wire rack for 5 minutes, then transfer to the rack to cool.

Almond Flour Muffins with Dried Cherries and Pecans

3 cups	almond flour	750 mL
3/4 tsp	baking soda	3 mL
1/2 tsp	salt	2 mL
2	eggs	2
1/4 cup	liquid honey	60 mL
3 tbsp	unsalted butter, melted	45 mL
1 tsp	vanilla extract	5 mL
3/4 cup	mashed ripe bananas	175 mL
3/4 cup	chopped pecans, toasted	175 mL
3/4 cup	dried cherries, roughly chopped	175 mL

The best flavors of one of my favorite cakes are converted here into muffins that are a sublime balance of sweet, tart and buttery.

Makes 12 muffins

- Preheat oven to 325°F (160°C)
- 12-cup muffin pan, lined with paper liners

1. In a large bowl, whisk together flour, baking soda and salt.

2. In a medium bowl, vigorously whisk eggs. Whisk in honey, butter and vanilla until well blended. Stir in bananas.

3. Add the egg mixture to the flour mixture and stir until just blended. Gently fold in pecans and cherries.

4. Divide batter equally among prepared muffin cups.

5. Bake in preheated oven for 25 to 30 minutes or until a toothpick inserted in the center comes out clean. Let cool in pan on a wire rack for 5 minutes, then transfer to the rack to cool.

Dried Blueberry Yogurt Muffins

1 1/2 cups	Brown Rice Flour Blend (see page 19)	375 mL
2 tsp	gluten-free baking powder	10 mL
3/4 tsp	salt	3 mL
1/2 tsp	xanthan gum	2 mL
1/4 tsp	ground nutmeg	1 mL
1 cup	granulated sugar	250 mL
3	eggs	3
1/2 cup	plain yogurt	125 mL
1/4 cup	vegetable oil	60 mL
1 tbsp	finely grated orange zest	15 mL
2/3 cup	dried blueberries	150 mL

These scrumptious muffins deliver a sweet and delicate muffin crumb, followed by an intensely fruity burst of blueberries and orange.

Makes 12 muffins

- Preheat oven to 350°F (180°C)
- 12-cup muffin pan, greased

1. In a large bowl, whisk together flour blend, baking powder, salt, xanthan gum and nutmeg.

2. In a medium bowl, whisk together sugar, eggs, yogurt, oil and orange zest until well blended.

3. Add the egg mixture to the flour mixture and stir until just blended. Gently fold in blueberries.

4. Divide batter equally among prepared muffin cups.

5. Bake in preheated oven for 15 to 20 minutes or until a toothpick inserted in the center comes out clean. Let cool in pan on a wire rack for 5 minutes, then transfer to the rack to cool.

Dried Berries and Cherries Muffins

1½ cups	Brown Rice Flour Blend (see page 19)	375 mL
1 tsp	baking soda	5 mL
½ tsp	xanthan gum	2 mL
½ tsp	salt	2 mL
⅔ cup	granulated sugar	150 mL
½ cup	unsalted butter, softened	125 mL
2	eggs	2
½ cup	buttermilk	125 mL
2 tsp	vanilla extract	10 mL
1 cup	dried berries and cherries fruit blend	250 mL
½ cup	finely chopped pecans	125 mL

The flavor and texture of vanilla-buttermilk muffins marries perfectly with the intense flavor of dried cherries and berries. A cup of vanilla yogurt makes an excellent accompaniment.

Makes 12 muffins

- Preheat oven to 350°F (180°C)
- 12-cup muffin pan, greased

1. In a medium bowl, whisk together flour blend, baking soda, xanthan gum and salt.
2. In a large bowl, using an electric mixer on medium speed, beat sugar and butter until light and fluffy. Beat in eggs, one at a time, until well blended. Beat in buttermilk and vanilla until blended.
3. Add the flour mixture to the egg mixture and, using a wooden spoon, stir until just blended. Gently fold in berries and cherries.
4. Divide batter equally among prepared muffin cups. Sprinkle with pecans.
5. Bake in preheated oven for 18 to 22 minutes or until tops are golden and a toothpick inserted in the center comes out clean. Let cool in pan on a wire rack for 5 minutes, then transfer to the rack to cool.

Dried Apricot Muffins

1¾ cups	Brown Rice Flour Blend (see page 19)	425 mL
1 tbsp	gluten-free baking powder	15 mL
½ tsp	salt	2 mL
½ tsp	xanthan gum	2 mL
½ cup	granulated sugar	125 mL
¼ cup	butter, softened	60 mL
1	egg	1
¾ cup	milk	175 mL
1 tsp	vanilla extract	5 mL
½ tsp	almond extract	2 mL
¾ cup	chopped dried apricots	175 mL

These delicious muffins are perfect for weekday baking: they're quick and easy, made with items typically in the pantry. The contrast between the tender vanilla muffin and the sweet apricots will keep guests coming back for more.

Makes 12 muffins

- Preheat oven to 350°F (180°C)
- 12-cup muffin pan, greased

1. In a medium bowl, whisk together flour blend, baking powder, salt and xanthan gum.
2. In a large bowl, using an electric mixer on medium speed, beat sugar and butter until light and fluffy. Beat in egg until well blended. Beat in milk, vanilla and almond extract until blended.
3. Add the flour mixture to the egg mixture and, using a wooden spoon, stir until just blended. Gently fold in apricots.
4. Divide batter equally among prepared muffin cups.
5. Bake in preheated oven for 25 to 28 minutes or until tops are golden and a toothpick inserted in the center comes out clean. Let cool in pan on a wire rack for 5 minutes, then transfer to the rack to cool.

Sour Cream Currant Muffins

1 1/2 cups	Brown Rice Flour Blend (see page 19)	375 mL
2 tsp	gluten-free baking powder	10 mL
3/4 tsp	salt	3 mL
1/2 tsp	xanthan gum	2 mL
1/4 tsp	ground nutmeg	1 mL
1 cup	granulated sugar	250 mL
3	eggs	3
1/2 cup	sour cream	125 mL
1/4 cup	unsalted butter, melted	60 mL
2 tsp	vanilla extract	15 mL
2/3 cup	dried currants	150 mL

The richness of sour cream, together with the subtle mingling of vanilla, nutmeg and dried currants, makes for a guaranteed favorite.

Makes 12 muffins

- Preheat oven to 350°F (180°C)
- 12-cup muffin pan, greased

1. In a large bowl, whisk together flour blend, baking powder, salt, xanthan gum and nutmeg.
2. In a medium bowl, whisk together sugar, eggs, sour cream, butter and vanilla until well blended.
3. Add the egg mixture to the flour mixture and stir until just blended. Gently fold in currants.
4. Divide batter equally among prepared muffin cups.
5. Bake in preheated oven for 15 to 20 minutes or until a toothpick inserted in the center comes out clean. Let cool in pan on a wire rack for 5 minutes, then transfer to the rack to cool.

Golden Raisin Rosemary Muffins

2 1/2 cups	Brown Rice Flour Blend (see page 19)	625 mL
2 tsp	gluten-free baking powder	10 mL
1 tsp	baking soda	5 mL
1 tsp	xanthan gum	5 mL
1/2 tsp	salt	2 mL
2	eggs	2
2/3 cup	buttermilk	150 mL
1/2 cup	liquid honey	125 mL
1/2 cup	olive oil	125 mL
2 tsp	minced fresh rosemary	10 mL
2 tsp	finely grated lemon zest	10 mL
1 tbsp	freshly squeezed lemon juice	15 mL
1 cup	golden raisins	250 mL

While raisins and rosemary may sound like an unusual combination, it is actually a fairly common one — in both sweet and savory preparations — in Italy. The woodsy flavor of the rosemary really complements the sunny fruitiness of the golden raisins.

Makes 12 muffins

- Preheat oven to 350°F (180°C)
- 12-cup muffin pan, greased

1. In a large bowl, whisk together flour blend, baking powder, baking soda, xanthan gum and salt.
2. In a medium bowl, whisk together eggs, buttermilk, honey, oil, rosemary, lemon zest and lemon juice until well blended.
3. Add the egg mixture to the flour mixture and stir until just blended. Gently fold in raisins.
4. Divide batter equally among prepared muffin cups.
5. Bake in preheated oven for 22 to 27 minutes or until a toothpick inserted in the center comes out clean. Let cool in pan on a wire rack for 5 minutes, then transfer to the rack to cool.

Tropical Fruit Muffins

2 1/2 cups	Brown Rice Flour Blend (see page 19)	625 mL
2 tsp	gluten-free baking powder	10 mL
1 tsp	baking soda	5 mL
1 tsp	ground ginger	5 mL
1 tsp	xanthan gum	5 mL
1/2 tsp	salt	2 mL
2	eggs	2
2/3 cup	buttermilk	150 mL
1/2 cup	liquid honey	125 mL
1/2 cup	vegetable oil	125 mL
2 tsp	finely grated lime zest	10 mL
1 tbsp	freshly squeezed lime juice	15 mL
1 cup	dried tropical fruit bits	250 mL
1/2 cup	sweetened flaked or shredded coconut	125 mL

These gorgeously scented fruit- and coconut-rich muffins evoke the tropics.

Makes 12 muffins

- Preheat oven to 350°F (180°C)
- 12-cup muffin pan, greased

1. In a large bowl, whisk together flour blend, baking powder, baking soda, ginger, xanthan gum and salt.

2. In a medium bowl, whisk together eggs, buttermilk, honey, oil, lime zest and lime juice until well blended.

3. Add the egg mixture to the flour mixture and stir until just blended. Gently fold in fruit bits and coconut.

4. Divide batter equally among prepared muffin cups.

5. Bake in preheated oven for 22 to 27 minutes or until a toothpick inserted in the center comes out clean. Let cool in pan on a wire rack for 5 minutes, then transfer to the rack to cool.

Cranberry Banana Oat Muffins

1 cup	certified gluten-free large-flake (old-fashioned) rolled oats	250 mL
1 cup	sorghum flour	250 mL
1 tsp	gluten-free baking powder	5 mL
1 tsp	xanthan gum	5 mL
1 tsp	ground cinnamon	5 mL
1/2 tsp	salt	2 mL
1/4 tsp	baking soda	1 mL
3/4 cup	packed light brown sugar	175 mL
1/2 cup	unsalted butter, softened	125 mL
1	egg	1
1 cup	mashed ripe bananas	250 mL
1/4 cup	milk	60 mL
1 tsp	vanilla extract	5 mL
2/3 cup	dried cranberries	150 mL
1/2 cup	chopped pecans, toasted	125 mL

These old-fashioned muffins combine three of my favorite baking ingredients: oats, cranberries and bananas.

Makes 12 muffins

- Preheat oven to 350°F (180°C)
- Food processor
- 12-cup muffin pan, greased

1. In food processor, pulse oats three or four times, until slightly chopped. Transfer to a medium bowl and whisk in sorghum flour, baking powder, xanthan gum, cinnamon, salt and baking soda.

2. In a large bowl, using an electric mixer on medium speed, beat brown sugar and butter until light and fluffy. Beat in egg until well blended. Beat in bananas, milk and vanilla until blended.

3. Add the flour mixture to the egg mixture and, using a wooden spoon, stir until just blended. Gently fold in cranberries and pecans.

4. Divide batter equally among prepared muffin cups.

5. Bake in preheated oven for 24 to 28 minutes or until a toothpick inserted in the center comes out clean. Let cool in pan on a wire rack for 5 minutes, then transfer to the rack to cool.

Fruit Crumble Muffins

Topping

½ cup	Brown Rice Flour Blend (see page 19)	125 mL
½ cup	light brown sugar	125 mL
½ tsp	ground cinnamon	2 mL
¼ tsp	salt	1 mL
6 tbsp	cold unsalted butter, cut into small pieces	90 mL
2 tbsp	chopped pecans, toasted	30 mL

Muffins

1½ cups	Brown Rice Flour Blend (see page 19)	375 mL
¾ tsp	salt	3 mL
½ tsp	xanthan gum	2 mL
¼ tsp	baking soda	1 mL
1 cup	granulated sugar	250 mL
½ cup	unsalted butter, softened	125 mL
2	eggs	2
½ cup	plain whole-milk yogurt	125 mL
¾ tsp	almond extract	3 mL
⅔ cup	dried cherries and berries fruit blend	150 mL

It's no mystery why crumbles of all varieties are so immensely popular: they pack all the flavor and fragrance of traditional baked fruit desserts beneath a shell of nutty, buttery, cinnamony crumbs. Adding dried cherries and berries to the batter evokes the flavors of summer, even in the depths of winter.

Tip

Be sure to bake the muffins for 10 minutes before adding the topping. Otherwise, the topping will sink straight to the bottom.

Makes 10 muffins

- Preheat oven to 350°F (180°C)
- 12-cup muffin pan, 10 cups greased

1. *Topping:* In a small bowl, whisk together flour blend, brown sugar, cinnamon and salt. Using a pastry cutter or your fingers, cut or rub in butter until mixture is crumbly. Stir in pecans. Refrigerate until ready to use.

2. *Muffins:* In a medium bowl, whisk together flour blend, salt, xanthan gum and baking soda.

3. In a large bowl, using an electric mixer on medium-high speed, beat sugar and butter until light and fluffy. With the mixer on medium-low speed, beat in eggs, one at a time, until well blended. Beat in yogurt and almond extract until blended.

4. Add the flour mixture to the egg mixture and, using a wooden spoon, stir until just blended. Gently fold in cherries and berries.

5. Divide batter equally among prepared muffin cups.

6. Bake in preheated oven for 10 minutes. Remove from oven and sprinkle with topping. Bake for 10 to 15 minutes or until a toothpick inserted in the center comes out clean. Let cool in pan on a wire rack for 5 minutes, then transfer to the rack to cool.

Cranberry, Carrot and Apple Teff Muffins

2 cups	teff flour	500 mL
1/2 cup	tapioca flour	125 mL
2 tsp	gluten-free baking powder	10 mL
1 tsp	pumpkin pie spice	5 mL
1 tsp	xanthan gum	5 mL
1/2 tsp	baking soda	2 mL
1/2 tsp	salt	2 mL
1	egg	1
1/2 cup	unsweetened apple juice	125 mL
1/2 cup	unsweetened applesauce	125 mL
1/2 cup	pure maple syrup	125 mL
1/3 cup	vegetable oil	75 mL
1 cup	finely shredded carrots	250 mL
1 cup	chopped peeled apple	250 mL
1/2 cup	chopped pecans, toasted	125 mL
1/2 cup	dried cranberries	125 mL

Teff, or tef, is a very tiny cereal grain native to northeastern Africa and southwestern Arabia. Although it has been used in Ethiopia, in particular, for centuries — namely as a flour in the flat, pancake-like bread injera — teff was not widely known in other parts of the world until the late 20th century. It packs a serious nutritional punch, delivering an excellent balance of amino acids, as well as protein, calcium and iron. The mild, nutty flour goes with a variety of flavors, so feel free to use this basic recipe as a template for countless variations.

Makes 12 muffins

- Preheat oven to 350°F (180°C)
- 12-cup muffin pan, greased

1. In a large bowl, whisk together teff flour, tapioca flour, baking powder, pumpkin pie spice, xanthan gum, baking soda and salt.
2. In a medium bowl, whisk together egg, apple juice, applesauce, maple syrup and oil until well blended.
3. Add the egg mixture to the flour mixture and stir until just blended. Gently fold in carrots, apple, pecans and cranberries.
4. Divide batter equally among prepared muffin cups.
5. Bake in preheated oven for 25 to 30 minutes or until a toothpick inserted in the center comes out clean. Let cool in pan on a wire rack for 5 minutes, then transfer to the rack to cool.

Oat Muffins with Crumb Topping

Topping

1/4 cup	certified gluten-free large-flake (old-fashioned) rolled oats	60 mL
1/4 cup	packed light brown sugar	60 mL
1/4 cup	unsalted butter, melted	60 mL
1/2 tsp	ground cinnamon	2 mL

Muffins

1 cup	certified gluten-free large-flake (old-fashioned) rolled oats	250 mL
1 1/4 cups	warm milk	300 mL
1 cup	Brown Rice Flour Blend (see page 19)	250 mL
2 tsp	gluten-free baking powder	10 mL
1 tsp	ground cinnamon	5 mL
1/2 tsp	baking soda	2 mL
1/2 tsp	salt	2 mL
1/4 tsp	xanthan gum	1 mL
3/4 cup	packed light brown sugar	175 mL
2	eggs	2
1/4 cup	unsalted butter, melted	60 mL
2 tbsp	liquid honey	30 mL
2 tsp	vanilla extract	10 mL
1 cup	raisins or dried cranberries	250 mL

These are heavenly with your favorite jam, honey or marmalade, or even peanut butter.

Makes 12 muffins

- 12-cup muffin pan, greased

1. *Topping:* In a small bowl, combine oats, brown sugar, butter and cinnamon until blended. Refrigerate until ready to use.

2. *Muffins:* In a small bowl, combine oats and milk. Let stand for 20 minutes.

3. Preheat oven to 400°F (200°C).

4. In a large bowl, whisk together flour blend, baking powder, cinnamon, baking soda, salt and xanthan gum.

5. In a medium bowl, whisk together brown sugar, eggs, butter, honey and vanilla until well blended. Stir in oat mixture until blended.

6. Add the egg mixture to the flour mixture and stir until just blended. Gently fold in raisins.

7. Divide batter equally among prepared muffin cups. Sprinkle with topping.

8. Bake for 18 to 22 minutes or until tops are golden and a toothpick inserted in the center comes out clean. Let cool in pan on a wire rack for 5 minutes, then transfer to the rack to cool.

Blackberry Oat Streusel Muffins

Topping

¼ cup	certified gluten-free large-flake (old-fashioned) rolled oats	60 mL
¼ cup	packed dark brown sugar	60 mL
¼ cup	unsalted butter, melted	60 mL
⅛ tsp	ground cloves	0.5 mL

Muffins

1¼ cups	warm milk	300 mL
1 cup	certified gluten-free large-flake (old-fashioned) rolled oats	250 mL
1 cup	Brown Rice Flour Blend (see page 19)	250 mL
2 tsp	gluten-free baking powder	10 mL
1 tsp	ground cinnamon	5 mL
½ tsp	baking soda	2 mL
½ tsp	salt	2 mL
¼ tsp	xanthan gum	1 mL
¾ cup	granulated sugar	175 mL
2	eggs	2
¼ cup	unsalted butter, melted	60 mL
2 tbsp	pure maple syrup	30 mL
1 tsp	vanilla extract	5 mL
1 cup	blackberries, raspberries or blueberries	250 mL

Cloaked beneath a humble oat streusel topping lies an inky jumble of blackberries — talk about a scrumptious contrast.

Makes 12 muffins

- 12-cup muffin pan, greased

1. *Topping:* In a small bowl, combine oats, brown sugar, butter and cloves until blended. Refrigerate until ready to use.
2. *Muffins:* In a small bowl, combine milk and oats. Let stand for 20 minutes.
3. Preheat oven to 400°F (200°C).
4. In a large bowl, whisk together flour blend, baking powder, cinnamon, baking soda, salt and xanthan gum.
5. In a medium bowl, whisk together sugar, eggs, butter, maple syrup and vanilla until well blended. Stir in oat mixture until blended.
6. Add the egg mixture to the flour mixture and stir until just blended. Gently fold in blackberries.
7. Divide batter equally among prepared muffin cups. Sprinkle with topping.
8. Bake for 18 to 22 minutes or until tops are golden and a toothpick inserted in the center comes out clean. Let cool in pan on a wire rack for 5 minutes, then transfer to the rack to cool.

Scottish Oat Muffins

1¼ cups	buttermilk	300 mL
1¼ cups	certified gluten-free large-flake (old-fashioned) rolled oats, divided	300 mL
1 cup	Brown Rice Flour Blend (see page 19)	250 mL
2 tsp	gluten-free baking powder	10 mL
½ tsp	baking soda	2 mL
½ tsp	salt	2 mL
¼ tsp	xanthan gum	1 mL
¾ cup	packed light brown sugar	175 mL
2	eggs	2
¼ cup	unsalted butter, melted	60 mL
2 tbsp	brown rice syrup, liquid honey or pure maple syrup	30 mL
2 tsp	vanilla extract	10 mL

Makes 12 muffins

- 12-cup muffin pan, greased

1. In a small bowl, combine buttermilk and 1 cup (250 mL) of the oats. Let stand for 20 minutes.
2. Preheat oven to 400°F (200°C).
3. In a large bowl, whisk together flour blend, baking powder, baking soda, salt and xanthan gum.
4. In a medium bowl, whisk together brown sugar, eggs, butter, rice syrup and vanilla until well blended. Stir in oat mixture until blended.
5. Add the egg mixture to the flour mixture and stir until just blended.
6. Divide batter equally among prepared muffin cups. Sprinkle with the remaining oats.
7. Bake for 18 to 22 minutes or until tops are golden and a toothpick inserted in the center comes out clean. Let cool in pan on a wire rack for 5 minutes, then transfer to the rack to cool.

Apple Carrot Bran Muffins

1 cup	Brown Rice Flour Blend (see page 19)	250 mL
½ cup	almond flour	125 mL
¾ cup	ground flax seeds	175 mL
¾ cup	rice bran	175 mL
2 tsp	baking soda	10 mL
2 tsp	ground cinnamon	10 mL
1 tsp	gluten-free baking powder	5 mL
½ tsp	salt	2 mL
½ tsp	xanthan gum	2 mL
1 cup	packed light brown sugar	250 mL
2	eggs	2
¾ cup	milk	175 mL
2 tsp	vanilla extract	10 mL
1½ cups	finely shredded carrots	375 mL
1½ cups	shredded tart-sweet apples, such as Braeburn, Gala or Golden Delicious	375 mL
1 cup	chopped walnuts, toasted	250 mL
1 cup	raisins	250 mL

Makes 18 muffins

- Preheat oven to 350°F (180°C)
- Two 12-cup muffin pans, 18 cups greased

1. In a large bowl, whisk together flour blend, almond flour, flax seeds, rice bran, baking soda, cinnamon, baking powder, salt and xanthan gum.
2. In a medium bowl, whisk together brown sugar, eggs, milk and vanilla until well blended.
3. Add the egg mixture to the flour mixture and stir until just blended. Gently fold in carrots, apples, walnuts and raisins.
4. Divide batter equally among prepared muffin cups.
5. Bake in preheated oven for 20 to 25 minutes or until tops are golden and a toothpick inserted in the center comes out clean. Let cool in pans on a wire rack for 5 minutes, then transfer to the rack to cool.

These moist, deeply flavored bran muffins studded with raisins and crunchy walnuts will garner compliments even for novice bakers. Plus, they keep for days.

Sorghum Applesauce Oatmeal Muffins

Topping

½ cup	sorghum flour	125 mL
½ cup	packed light brown sugar	125 mL
Pinch	salt	Pinch
¼ cup	unsalted butter, melted	60 mL

Muffins

1 cup	certified gluten-free large-flake (old-fashioned) rolled oats	250 mL
1 cup	sorghum flour	250 mL
1 tsp	gluten-free baking powder	5 mL
1 tsp	xanthan gum	5 mL
¾ tsp	ground cinnamon	3 mL
½ tsp	salt	2 mL
¼ tsp	baking soda	1 mL
¾ cup	packed light brown sugar	175 mL
½ cup	unsalted butter, softened	125 mL
1	egg	1
1 cup	unsweetened applesauce	250 mL
¼ cup	milk	60 mL
1 tsp	vanilla extract	5 mL
½ cup	raisins	125 mL

Simple, familiar muffins are often what we crave the most. Case in point, applesauce muffins. Many riffs on applesauce muffins are too sweet, but here I keep things balanced with the addition of hearty oats to the batter.

Makes 12 muffins

- Preheat oven to 350°F (180°C)
- Food processor
- 12-cup muffin pan, greased

1. *Topping:* In a small bowl, combine flour, brown sugar, salt and butter until crumbly. Refrigerate until ready to use.

2. *Muffins:* In food processor, pulse oats three or four times, until slightly chopped. Transfer to a medium bowl and whisk in flour, baking powder, xanthan gum, cinnamon, salt and baking soda.

3. In a large bowl, using an electric mixer on medium speed, beat brown sugar and butter until light and fluffy. Beat in egg until well blended. Beat in applesauce, milk and vanilla.

4. Add the flour mixture to the egg mixture and, using a wooden spoon, stir until just blended. Gently fold in raisins.

5. Divide batter equally among prepared muffin cups. Sprinkle with topping.

6. Bake in preheated oven for 24 to 28 minutes or until a toothpick inserted in the center comes out clean. Let cool in pan on a wire rack for 5 minutes, then transfer to the rack to cool.

Chocolate Banana Teff Muffins

1 cup	Brown Rice Flour Blend (see page 19)	250 mL
1 cup	teff flour	250 mL
1/3 cup	unsweetened cocoa powder (not Dutch process)	75 mL
1 1/2 tsp	ground cinnamon	7 mL
3/4 tsp	baking soda	3 mL
1/2 tsp	salt	2 mL
2	eggs	2
3/4 cup	granulated sugar	175 mL
1 cup	mashed ripe bananas	250 mL
6 tbsp	unsalted butter, melted	90 mL
1/4 cup	plain yogurt	60 mL
1 tsp	vanilla extract	5 mL

Teff is an ancient grain, minute in size and packed with nutrition. It is believed to have originated in Ethiopia between 4000 and 1000 BC. Teff seeds were discovered in a pyramid thought to date back to 3359 BC. As a flour, it produces light, springy baked goods, such as these chocolate banana muffins.

Makes 12 muffins

- Preheat oven to 350°F (180°C)
- 12-cup muffin pan, greased

1. In a medium bowl, whisk together flour blend, teff flour, cocoa powder, cinnamon, baking soda and salt.

2. In a large bowl, using an electric mixer on medium speed, beat eggs until frothy. Beat in sugar, banana, butter, yogurt and vanilla until blended.

3. Add the flour mixture to the egg mixture and, using a wooden spoon, stir until just blended.

4. Divide batter equally among prepared muffin cups.

5. Bake in preheated oven for 20 to 25 minutes or until tops are golden and a toothpick inserted in the center comes out clean. Let cool in pan on a wire rack for 5 minutes, then transfer to the rack to cool.

Not-Bran Muffins

1 cup	Brown Rice Flour Blend (see page 19)	250 mL
1/2 cup	buckwheat flour	125 mL
1/3 cup	ground flax seeds	75 mL
2 tsp	gluten-free baking powder	10 mL
1 tsp	salt	5 mL
1/2 tsp	xanthan gum	2 mL
1/3 cup	packed light brown sugar	75 mL
2	eggs	2
1/2 cup	milk	125 mL
1/4 cup	vegetable oil	60 mL
2 tbsp	dark (cooking) molasses	30 mL
1/2 cup	raisins	125 mL

If you miss the flavor of an old-fashioned bran muffin, look no further. Moist, dark and flavorful, these are both inventive and reassuringly conventional at the same time.

Makes 12 muffins

- Preheat oven to 350°F (180°C)
- 12-cup muffin pan, greased

1. In a large bowl, whisk together flour blend, buckwheat flour, flax seeds, baking powder, salt and xanthan gum.

2. In a medium bowl, whisk together brown sugar, eggs, milk, oil and molasses until well blended.

3. Add the egg mixture to the flour mixture and stir until just blended. Gently fold in raisins.

4. Divide batter equally among prepared muffin cups.

5. Bake in preheated oven for 21 to 25 minutes or until tops are golden and a toothpick inserted in the center comes out clean. Let cool in pan on a wire rack for 5 minutes, then transfer to the rack to cool.

Sesame Ginger Muffins

5 tbsp	sesame seeds, divided	75 mL
1 cup	sorghum flour	250 mL
1 cup	Brown Rice Flour Blend (see page 19)	250 mL
1 tbsp	gluten-free baking powder	15 mL
2½ tsp	ground ginger	12 mL
½ tsp	salt	2 mL
½ tsp	xanthan gum	2 mL
1	egg	1
¼ cup	liquid honey	60 mL
2 tbsp	unsalted butter, melted	30 mL
2 tbsp	toasted sesame oil	30 mL
1¼ cups	milk	300 mL

Sesame and ginger are fairly common flavors, but these muffins are something special — the peppery bite of ginger and the pop of sesame seeds bring out the floral qualities of the honey batter.

Makes 12 muffins

- Preheat oven to 350°F (180°C)
- Rimmed baking sheet
- 12-cup muffin pan, lined with paper liners

1. Spread 4 tbsp (60 mL) of the sesame seeds on baking sheet and bake in preheated oven for 3 to 4 minutes or until toasted and fragrant. Remove from oven, leaving oven on, and let cool.

2. In a large bowl, whisk together sesame seeds, sorghum flour, flour blend, baking powder, ginger, salt and xanthan gum.

3. In a medium bowl, whisk together egg, honey, butter and sesame oil until well blended. Whisk in milk until blended.

4. Add the egg mixture to the flour mixture and stir until just blended.

5. Divide batter equally among prepared muffin cups. Sprinkle with the remaining sesame seeds.

6. Bake for 18 to 22 minutes or until a toothpick inserted in the center comes out clean. Let cool in pan on a wire rack for 5 minutes, then transfer to the rack to cool.

Buckwheat Kasha Muffins

¼ cup	kasha (roasted buckwheat groats)	60 mL
⅓ cup	boiling water	75 mL
1 cup	buckwheat flour	250 mL
1 cup	Brown Rice Flour Blend (see page 19)	250 mL
1 tsp	gluten-free baking powder	5 mL
1 tsp	baking soda	5 mL
½ tsp	salt	5 mL
½ tsp	xanthan gum	5 mL
⅓ cup	firmly packed light brown sugar	75 mL
1	egg	1
1 cup	buttermilk	250 mL
¼ cup	olive oil	60 mL
½ cup	chopped hazelnuts	125 mL

I've turned roasted buckwheat groats into a fantastic muffin studded with toasted hazelnuts.

Makes 12 muffins

- 12-cup muffin pan, greased

1. In a small bowl, stir together kasha and boiling water. Let stand for 15 minutes.

2. Preheat oven to 350°F (180°C).

3. In a large bowl, whisk together buckwheat flour, flour blend, baking powder, baking soda, salt and xanthan gum.

4. In a medium bowl, whisk together brown sugar, egg, buttermilk and oil until well blended.

5. Add the egg mixture to the flour mixture and stir until well blended. Gently fold in kasha mixture and hazelnuts.

6. Divide batter equally among prepared muffin cups.

7. Bake for 23 to 28 minutes or until tops are golden and a toothpick inserted in the center comes out clean. Let cool in pan on a wire rack for 5 minutes, then transfer to the rack to cool.

Toasted Millet Muffins

2/3 cup	millet	150 mL
1 1/2 cups	Brown Rice Flour Blend (see page 19)	375 mL
2 tbsp	ground flax seeds	30 mL
1 1/2 tsp	xanthan gum	7 mL
1 tsp	gluten-free baking powder	5 mL
1/2 tsp	salt	2 mL
1/4 tsp	baking soda	1 mL
1	egg	1
3/4 cup	packed dark brown sugar	175 mL
1 cup	buttermilk	250 mL
1/3 cup	vegetable oil	75 mL
2 tbsp	turbinado sugar	30 mL

Buttermilk gives these muffins a rich, tender texture. Don't be tempted to skip the toasting step for the millet; it takes just a few minutes and makes the millet crisp and toasty.

Makes 12 muffins

- Preheat oven to 375°F (190°C)
- Rimmed baking sheet
- 12-cup muffin pan, greased

1. Spread millet on baking sheet and bake in preheated oven for 3 to 4 minutes or until toasted and fragrant. Remove from oven, leaving oven on, and let cool.
2. In a large bowl, whisk together flour blend, flax seeds, xanthan gum, baking powder, salt and baking soda. Whisk in millet.
3. In a medium bowl, vigorously whisk egg. Whisk in brown sugar, buttermilk and oil until well blended.
4. Add the egg mixture to the flour mixture and stir until just blended.
5. Divide batter equally among prepared muffin cups. Sprinkle with turbinado sugar.
6. Bake for 20 to 25 minutes or until a toothpick inserted in the center comes out clean. Let cool in pan on a wire rack for 5 minutes, then transfer to the rack to cool.

Sugar and Spice Flax Muffins

1 1/2 cups	Brown Rice Flour Blend (see page 19)	375 mL
1/2 cup	ground flax seeds	125 mL
1 tsp	baking soda	5 mL
1 tsp	ground cinnamon	5 mL
1 tsp	ground ginger	5 mL
1/2 tsp	salt	2 mL
1/2 tsp	xanthan gum	2 mL
1/4 tsp	ground nutmeg	1 mL
1/4 tsp	ground cloves	1 mL
2	eggs	2
1/2 cup	packed light brown sugar	125 mL
1 cup	buttermilk	250 mL
1/2 cup	unsweetened applesauce	125 mL
1/4 cup	vegetable oil	60 mL

Consider these your not-too-sweet, always moist go-to muffins.

Makes 12 muffins

- Preheat oven to 375°F (190°C)
- 12-cup muffin pan, greased

1. In a large bowl, whisk together flour blend, flax seeds, baking soda, cinnamon, ginger, salt, xanthan gum, nutmeg and cloves.
2. In a medium bowl, vigorously whisk eggs. Whisk in brown sugar, buttermilk, applesauce and oil until well blended.
3. Add the egg mixture to the flour mixture and stir until just blended.
4. Divide batter equally among prepared muffin cups.
5. Bake in preheated oven for 25 to 30 minutes or until a toothpick inserted in the center comes out clean. Let cool in pan on a wire rack for 5 minutes, then transfer to the rack to cool.

Molasses Flax Muffins

1 cup	sorghum flour	250 mL
1 cup	Brown Rice Flour Blend (see page 19)	250 mL
1/4 cup	ground flax seeds	60 mL
1 tbsp	gluten-free baking powder	15 mL
1/2 tsp	ground cinnamon	2 mL
1/2 tsp	salt	2 mL
1/2 tsp	xanthan gum	2 mL
1/4 tsp	ground cloves	1 mL
1	egg	1
1/4 cup	vegetable oil	60 mL
1/4 cup	dark (cooking) molasses	60 mL
1 1/4 cups	milk	300 mL

Sorghum flour has a natural sweetness that makes any morning muffin extra-delicious. Ground flax seeds make these muffins extra-moist and extremely healthy: flax seeds are rich in nutrients that have been shown to protect against heart disease and cancer.

Makes 12 muffins

- Preheat oven to 350°F (180°C)
- 12-cup muffin pan, lined with paper liners

1. In a large bowl, whisk together sorghum flour, flour blend, flax seeds, baking powder, cinnamon, salt, xanthan gum and cloves.
2. In a medium bowl, whisk together egg, oil and molasses until well blended. Whisk in milk until blended.
3. Add the egg mixture to the flour mixture and stir until just blended.
4. Divide batter equally among prepared muffin cups.
5. Bake in preheated oven for 18 to 22 minutes or until a toothpick inserted in the center comes out clean. Let cool in pan on a wire rack for 5 minutes, then transfer to the rack to cool.

Quinoa Corn Honey Muffins

1 cup	quinoa, rinsed	250 mL
1 cup	yellow cornmeal	250 mL
1 1/4 cups	boiling water	300 mL
1 1/4 cups	Brown Rice Flour Blend (see page 19)	300 mL
2 tsp	gluten-free baking powder	10 mL
1/2 tsp	xanthan gum	2 mL
1/2 tsp	salt	2 mL
1	egg	1
1 cup	milk	250 mL
1/3 cup	liquid honey	75 mL
1 tbsp	finely grated lemon zest	15 mL

These honey-sweetened corn muffins, pumped up with the superfood quinoa, have the good taste to fit in anywhere, from the supper table to the lunch bag to breakfast on the run.

Makes 12 muffins

- 12-cup muffin pan, greased

1. In a medium bowl, combine quinoa and cornmeal. Stir in boiling water. Let stand for 30 minutes.
2. Preheat oven to 375°F (190°C).
3. In a medium bowl, whisk together flour blend, baking powder, xanthan gum and salt.
4. In a large bowl, whisk together egg, milk, honey and lemon zest until well blended. Stir in quinoa mixture until blended.
5. Add the egg mixture to the flour mixture and stir until just blended.
6. Divide batter equally among prepared muffin cups.
7. Bake for 22 to 25 minutes or until tops are golden and a toothpick inserted in the center comes out clean. Let cool in pan on a wire rack for 5 minutes, then transfer to the rack to cool.

Quinoa Muffins with Pecans and Chocolate

1½ cups	Brown Rice Flour Blend (see page 19)	375 mL
1 cup	quinoa flakes	250 mL
1¼ tsp	xanthan gum	6 mL
1 tsp	ground cinnamon	5 mL
1 tsp	gluten-free baking powder	5 mL
1 tsp	baking soda	5 mL
½ tsp	salt	2 mL
¾ cup	packed light brown sugar	175 mL
2	eggs	2
½ cup	milk	125 mL
⅓ cup	vegetable oil	75 mL
1½ tsp	vanilla extract	7 mL
⅔ cup	gluten-free semisweet chocolate chips, chopped	150 mL
½ cup	chopped pecans, toasted	125 mL

This incredibly delicious and super-nutritious recipe includes quinoa flakes, a cereal form of quinoa that looks like quick-cooking rolled oats. The flakes retain all of the nutrition of regular quinoa, yet require minimal or no cooking. Look for them in natural foods stores — typically near dry cereal products — or in the health foods section of the supermarket.

Makes 12 muffins

- Preheat oven to 350°F (180°C)
- 12-cup muffin pan, lined with paper liners

1. In a large bowl, whisk together flour blend, quinoa flakes, xanthan gum, cinnamon, baking powder, baking soda and salt.
2. In a medium bowl, whisk together brown sugar, eggs, milk, oil and vanilla until well blended.
3. Add the egg mixture to the flour mixture and stir until just blended. Gently fold in chocolate chips and pecans.
4. Divide batter equally among prepared muffin cups.
5. Bake in preheated oven for 16 to 20 minutes or until a toothpick inserted in the center comes out clean. Let cool in pan on a wire rack for 5 minutes, then transfer to the rack to cool.

Sweet Breakfast Risotto Muffins

Topping

1/2 cup	chopped walnuts	125 mL
1/4 cup	firmly packed light brown sugar	60 mL
1/4 tsp	ground cinnamon	1 mL

Muffins

1 1/4 cups	Brown Rice Flour Blend (see page 19)	300 mL
2 tsp	gluten-free baking powder	10 mL
1 tsp	ground cinnamon	5 mL
1/2 tsp	salt	2 mL
1/4 tsp	xanthan gum	1 mL
1/4 tsp	ground nutmeg	1 mL
1/4 cup	firmly packed light brown sugar	60 mL
2	eggs	2
1 cup + 1 tbsp	milk	265 mL
1/4 cup	unsalted butter, melted	60 mL
1 cup	cold cooked short grain brown rice	250 mL
1/2 cup	golden raisins, chopped	125 mL

Makes 12 muffins

- Preheat oven to 400°F (200°C)
- 12-cup muffin pan, greased

1. *Topping:* In a small bowl, combine walnuts, brown sugar and cinnamon.
2. *Muffins:* In a large bowl, whisk together flour blend, baking powder, cinnamon, salt, xanthan gum and nutmeg.
3. In a medium bowl, whisk together brown sugar, eggs, milk and butter until well blended.
4. Add the egg mixture to the flour mixture and stir until just blended. Gently fold in rice and raisins.
5. Divide batter among prepared muffin cups.
6. Bake in preheated oven for 10 minutes. Remove from oven and sprinkle with topping. Bake for 10 to 15 minutes or until a toothpick inserted in the center comes out clean. Let cool in pan on a wire rack for 5 minutes, then transfer to the rack to cool.

Carrot Zucchini Muffins

2 1/4 cups	Brown Rice Flour Blend (see page 19)	550 mL
2 1/2 tsp	ground cinnamon	12 mL
2 tsp	baking soda	10 mL
1/2 tsp	ground nutmeg	2 mL
1/2 tsp	salt	2 mL
1/2 tsp	xanthan gum	2 mL
1 cup	packed light brown sugar	250 mL
2	eggs	2
1/2 cup	vegetable oil	125 mL
2 tsp	vanilla extract	10 mL
1 1/2 cups	buttermilk	375 mL
1 cup	finely shredded carrots	250 mL
1 cup	shredded zucchini	250 mL

These muffins are perfect in summer, when zucchini is bountiful — they're full of sugar and spice and everything nice.

Makes 12 muffins

- Preheat oven to 350°F (180°C)
- 12-cup muffin pan, greased

1. In a large bowl, whisk together flour blend, cinnamon, baking soda, nutmeg, salt and xanthan gum.
2. In a medium bowl, whisk together brown sugar, eggs, oil and vanilla until well blended. Whisk in buttermilk until blended.
3. Add the egg mixture to the flour mixture and stir until just blended. Gently fold in carrots and zucchini.
4. Divide batter equally among prepared muffin cups.
5. Bake in preheated oven for 20 to 25 minutes or until a toothpick inserted in the center comes out clean. Let cool in pan on a wire rack for 3 minutes, then transfer to the rack to cool.

Carrot Raisin Buckwheat Muffins

2½ cups	buckwheat flour	625 mL
½ cup	tapioca flour	125 mL
2½ tsp	pumpkin pie spice	12 mL
2 tsp	gluten-free baking powder	10 mL
1 tsp	baking soda	5 mL
½ tsp	salt	2 mL
½ cup	packed light brown sugar	125 mL
2	eggs	2
1½ cups	unsweetened applesauce	375 mL
¼ cup	unsalted butter, melted	60 mL
2 tsp	vanilla extract	10 mL
1 cup	shredded carrots	250 mL
1 cup	raisins	250 mL

Butter and brown sugar enrich these tender buckwheat muffins, which make delicious use of two pantry standbys: carrots and raisins.

Makes 12 muffins

- Preheat oven to 375°F (190°C)
- 12-cup muffin pan, greased

1. In a large bowl, whisk together buckwheat flour, tapioca flour, pumpkin pie spice, baking powder, baking soda and salt.
2. In a medium bowl, whisk together brown sugar, eggs, applesauce, butter and vanilla until well blended.
3. Add the egg mixture to the flour mixture and stir until just blended. Gently fold in carrots and raisins.
4. Divide batter equally among prepared muffin cups.
5. Bake in preheated oven for 24 to 28 minutes or until a toothpick inserted in the center comes out clean. Let cool in pan on a wire rack for 5 minutes, then transfer to the rack to cool.

Carrot Cake Muffins

2 cups	Brown Rice Flour Blend (see page 19)	500 mL
1 tbsp	gluten-free baking powder	15 mL
2 tsp	ground cinnamon	10 mL
1 tsp	baking soda	5 mL
1 tsp	ground ginger	5 mL
¾ tsp	xanthan gum	3 mL
½ tsp	ground nutmeg	2 mL
½ tsp	salt	2 mL
⅔ cup	granulated sugar	150 mL
2	eggs	2
½ cup	vegetable oil	125 mL
⅓ cup	milk	75 mL
1 tsp	vanilla extract	5 mL
1 cup	finely shredded carrots	250 mL
½ cup	chopped pecans, toasted	125 mL
½ cup	sweetened flaked or shredded coconut	125 mL
½ cup	dried currants	125 mL

I'm taking the highway to nostalgia with these moist, spicy muffins. The recipe, by the way, is a breeze to make.

Makes 12 muffins

- Preheat oven to 350°F (180°C)
- 12-cup muffin pan, greased

1. In a large bowl, whisk together flour blend, baking powder, cinnamon, baking soda, ginger, xanthan gum, nutmeg and salt.
2. In a medium bowl, vigorously whisk together sugar, eggs, oil, milk and vanilla until well blended.
3. Add the egg mixture to the flour mixture and stir until just blended. Gently fold in carrots, pecans, coconut and currants.
4. Divide batter equally among prepared muffin cups.
5. Bake in preheated oven for 20 to 25 minutes or until a toothpick inserted in the center comes out clean. Let cool in pan on a wire rack for 5 minutes, then transfer to the rack to cool.

Morning Glory Muffins

2¼ cups	Brown Rice Flour Blend (see page 19)	550 mL
1 tbsp	ground cinnamon	15 mL
2 tsp	baking soda	10 mL
½ tsp	salt	2 mL
½ tsp	xanthan gum	2 mL
1¼ cups	granulated sugar	300 mL
3	eggs	3
¾ cup	unsweetened applesauce	175 mL
½ cup	vegetable oil	125 mL
1 tsp	vanilla extract	5 mL
1	can (8 oz/227 mL) crushed pineapple, drained and patted dry	1
2 cups	shredded carrots	500 mL
1 cup	shredded peeled tart-sweet apple, such as Braeburn, Gala or Cortland	250 mL
½ cup	sweetened flaked coconut	125 mL
½ cup	raisins	125 mL
½ cup	chopped pecans, toasted	125 mL

These delightful muffins are American classics. They're great as soon as they've cooled, but their carrot-cake moistness and hint of spice really come through the day after they're baked.

Makes 18 muffins

- Preheat oven to 350°F (180°C)
- Two 12-cup muffin pans, 18 cups greased

1. In a large bowl, whisk together flour blend, cinnamon, baking soda, salt and xanthan gum.
2. In a medium bowl, whisk together sugar, eggs, applesauce, oil and vanilla until well blended.
3. Add the egg mixture to the flour mixture and stir until just blended. Gently fold in pineapple, carrots, apple, coconut, raisins and pecans.
4. Divide batter equally among prepared muffin cups.
5. Bake in preheated oven for 30 to 35 minutes or until tops are golden and a toothpick inserted in the center comes out clean. Let cool in pans on a wire rack for 5 minutes, then transfer to the rack to cool.

Quinoa Morning Glory Muffins

1 cup	quinoa flour	250 mL
1/2 cup	potato starch	125 mL
1/2 cup	tapioca starch	125 mL
2 1/2 tsp	pumpkin pie spice	12 mL
2 tsp	baking soda	10 mL
2 tsp	xanthan gum	10 mL
1/2 tsp	salt	2 mL
3/4 cup	packed light brown sugar	175 mL
3	eggs	3
2/3 cup	vegetable oil	150 mL
1 tsp	vanilla extract	5 mL
1	sweet-tart apple, such as Braeburn, Gala or Cortland, peeled and finely chopped	1
2 cups	finely shredded carrots	500 mL
1/2 cup	chopped walnuts or pecans, toasted	125 mL
1/2 cup	raisins	125 mL
1/4 cup	sweetened flaked or shredded coconut	60 mL

Morning glory muffins get a new spin here, made with quinoa flour, carrots, coconut and apple. One bite and you'll be off to a glorious morning, indeed.

Makes 12 muffins

- Preheat oven to 350°F (180°C)
- 12-cup muffin pan, lined with paper liners

1. In a large bowl, whisk together flour, potato starch, tapioca starch, pumpkin pie spice, baking soda, xanthan gum and salt.
2. In a medium bowl, using an electric mixer on medium-high speed, beat brown sugar, eggs, oil and vanilla for 1 minute.
3. Add the egg mixture to the flour mixture and, using a wooden spoon, stir until just blended. Gently fold in apple, carrots, walnuts, raisins and coconut.
4. Divide batter equally among prepared muffin cups.
5. Bake in preheated oven for 24 to 28 minutes or until a toothpick inserted in the center comes out clean. Let cool in pan on a wire rack for 5 minutes, then transfer to the rack to cool.

Zucchini Pecan Agave Muffins

2 cups	almond flour	500 mL
1 tsp	ground cinnamon	5 mL
1 tsp	gluten-free baking powder	5 mL
1/2 tsp	baking soda	2 mL
1/2 tsp	salt	2 mL
2	eggs	2
1/2 cup	agave nectar or liquid honey	125 mL
1/4 cup	unsalted butter, melted	60 mL
1 cup	shredded zucchini	250 mL
1 cup	chopped pecans, toasted	250 mL

With little more than a box grater and a mixing bowl, it's easy to transform zucchini into a morning treat that will delight muffin lovers of all ages.

Makes 12 muffins

- Preheat oven to 350°F (180°C)
- 12-cup muffin pan, greased

1. In a large bowl, whisk together flour, cinnamon, baking powder, baking soda and salt.
2. In a medium bowl, whisk together eggs, agave nectar and butter until well blended.
3. Add the egg mixture to the flour mixture and stir until just blended. Gently fold in zucchini and pecans.
4. Divide batter equally among prepared muffin cups.
5. Bake in preheated oven for 25 to 30 minutes or until a toothpick inserted in the center comes out clean. Let cool in pan on a wire rack for 5 minutes, then transfer to the rack to cool.

Winter Squash Thyme Muffins

3 cups	almond flour	750 mL
3/4 tsp	baking soda	3 mL
1/4 tsp	salt	1 mL
1/8 tsp	freshly ground black pepper	0.5 mL
2	eggs	2
3/4 cup	frozen (thawed) winter squash purée	175 mL
1/4 cup	liquid honey	60 mL
1/4 cup	unsalted butter, melted	60 mL
1 1/2 tsp	minced fresh thyme	7 mL

Frozen winter squash purée — widely available in well-stocked supermarkets — adds moisture, flavor and great nutrition to muffins infused with the flavor of fresh thyme.

Makes 12 muffins

- Preheat oven to 325°F (160°C)
- 12-cup muffin pan, lined with paper liners

1. In a large bowl, whisk together flour, baking soda, salt and pepper.

2. In a medium bowl, whisk together eggs, squash, honey, butter and thyme until well blended.

3. Add the egg mixture to the flour mixture and stir until just blended.

4. Divide batter equally among prepared muffin cups.

5. Bake in preheated oven for 25 to 30 minutes or until tops are set and a toothpick inserted in the center comes out clean. Let cool in pan on a wire rack for 5 minutes, then transfer to the rack to cool.

Pignoli Muffins

1 cup	pine nuts, divided	250 mL
1 3/4 cups	Brown Rice Flour Blend (see page 19)	175 mL
1 1/2 tsp	gluten-free baking powder	7 mL
1/2 tsp	salt	2 mL
1/2 tsp	xanthan gum	2 mL
1/4 tsp	ground mace	1 mL
3/4 cup	granulated sugar	175 mL
3/4 cup	unsalted butter, softened	175 mL
3	eggs	3
1/4 cup	milk	60 mL
2 tsp	vanilla extract	10 mL
1/2 cup	golden raisins, chopped	125 mL

The sweetness of the pine nuts and golden raisins in this recipe is a nice foil for the buttery batter.

Makes 16 muffins

- Preheat oven to 350°F (180°C)
- Rimmed baking sheet
- Two 12-cup muffin pans, 16 cups greased

1. Set aside 2 tbsp (30 mL) of the pine nuts. Spread the remaining pine nuts on baking sheet and bake in preheated oven for 4 to 5 minutes or until lightly toasted and fragrant. Remove from oven, leaving oven on, and let cool.

2. In a medium bowl, whisk together flour blend, baking powder, salt, xanthan gum and mace.

3. In a large bowl, using an electric mixer on medium speed, beat sugar and butter until light and fluffy. Beat in eggs, one at a time, until well blended. Beat in milk and vanilla until blended.

4. Add the flour mixture to the egg mixture and, using a wooden spoon, stir until just blended. Gently fold in toasted pine nuts and raisins.

5. Divide batter equally among prepared muffin cups. Sprinkle with the reserved pine nuts.

6. Bake for 22 to 27 minutes or until tops are golden and a toothpick inserted in the center comes out clean. Let cool in pans on a wire rack for 5 minutes, then transfer to the rack to cool.

Peanut Butter Muffins

1¾ cups	Brown Rice Flour Blend (see page 19)	425 mL
1 tbsp	gluten-free baking powder	15 mL
½ tsp	salt	2 mL
½ tsp	xanthan gum	2 mL
½ cup	granulated sugar	125 mL
½ cup	creamy peanut butter	125 mL
1 tsp	vanilla extract	5 mL
2	eggs	2
1 cup	milk	250 mL

Nuts and nut butters enhance the flavor of baked goods — such as these not-too-sweet muffins — like nothing else. The perfect topping? Jelly, of course.

Makes 12 muffins

- Preheat oven to 350°F (180°C)
- 12-cup muffin pan, greased

1. In a medium bowl, whisk together flour blend, baking powder, salt and xanthan gum.
2. In a large bowl, using an electric mixer on medium-high speed, beat sugar, peanut butter and vanilla until light and fluffy. With the mixer on medium speed, beat in eggs, one at a time, until well blended.
3. Add half the flour mixture to the egg mixture. With the mixer on low speed, beat for 30 seconds. Add half the milk and beat for 30 seconds. Add the remaining flour mixture and milk. With the mixer on medium-high speed, beat for 1 minute.
4. Divide batter equally among prepared muffin cups.
5. Bake in preheated oven for 15 to 20 minutes or until a toothpick inserted in the center comes out clean. Let cool in pan on a wire rack for 5 minutes, then transfer to the rack to cool.

Persian Pistachio Muffins

2 cups	Brown Rice Flour Blend (see page 19)	500 mL
2 tsp	gluten-free baking powder	10 mL
1½ tsp	ground cardamom	7 mL
½ tsp	salt	2 mL
½ tsp	xanthan gum	2 mL
¾ cup	granulated sugar	175 mL
¼ cup	unsalted butter, softened	60 mL
1	egg	1
1 cup	milk	250 mL
1 tbsp	finely grated lime zest	15 mL
¾ cup	chopped pistachios	175 mL
½ cup	golden raisins, chopped	125 mL

This easily assembled muffin evokes the very best of Persian sweets. The muffin batter is freckled with rich pistachios and sunny golden raisins and generously flavored with lime zest and cardamom.

Makes 12 muffins

- Preheat oven to 350°F (180°C)
- 12-cup muffin pan, greased

1. In a medium bowl, whisk together flour blend, baking powder, cardamom, salt and xanthan gum.
2. In a large bowl, using an electric mixer on medium speed, beat sugar and butter until light and fluffy. Beat in egg until well blended. Beat in milk and lime zest until blended.
3. Add the flour mixture to the egg mixture and, using a wooden spoon, stir until just blended. Gently fold in pistachios and raisins.
4. Divide batter equally among prepared muffin cups.
5. Bake in preheated oven for 20 to 25 minutes or until tops are golden and a toothpick inserted in the center comes out clean. Let cool in pan on a wire rack for 5 minutes, then transfer to the rack to cool.

Indian Spice Coconut Muffins

1¼ cups	sweetened flaked or shredded coconut	300 mL
2 cups	Brown Rice Flour Blend (see page 19)	500 mL
2 tsp	gluten-free baking powder	10 mL
1 tsp	ground cardamom	5 mL
1 tsp	ground ginger	5 mL
¾ tsp	xanthan gum	3 mL
¼ tsp	salt	1 mL
1 cup	packed light brown sugar	250 mL
¼ cup	unsalted butter, softened	60 mL
2	eggs	2
¾ cup	milk	175 mL

These delicious and slightly exotic Indian-influenced muffins incorporate toasted coconut in a golden muffin sweetened with brown sugar and spiced with cardamom and ginger.

Makes 12 muffins

- Preheat oven to 350°F (180°C)
- Rimmed baking sheet
- 12-cup muffin pan, lined with paper liners

1. Spread coconut on baking sheet and bake in preheated oven for 4 to 6 minutes or until golden brown. Remove from oven, leaving oven on, and let cool.
2. In a medium bowl, whisk together flour blend, baking powder, cardamom, ginger, xanthan gum and salt.
3. In a large bowl, using an electric mixer on medium speed, beat brown sugar and butter until light and fluffy. Beat in eggs, one at a time, until well blended. Beat in milk until blended.
4. Add the flour mixture to the egg mixture and, using a wooden spoon, stir until just blended. Gently fold in coconut.
5. Divide batter equally among prepared muffin cups.
6. Bake for 18 to 22 minutes or until tops are golden and a toothpick inserted in the center comes out clean. Let cool in pan on a wire rack for 5 minutes, then transfer to the rack to cool.

Brown Sugar Cashew Muffins

1¾ cups	Brown Rice Flour Blend (see page 19)	425 mL
1½ tsp	gluten-free baking powder	7 mL
½ tsp	salt	2 mL
½ tsp	xanthan gum	2 mL
¾ cup	packed light brown sugar	175 mL
¾ cup	unsalted butter, softened	175 mL
3	eggs	3
¼ cup	milk	60 mL
2 tsp	vanilla extract	10 mL
1 cup	chopped lightly salted roasted cashews	250 mL

Sweet cashew muffins with brown sugar, butter and vanilla? Oh, yes, please.

Makes 16 muffins

- Preheat oven to 350°F (180°C)
- Two 12-cup muffin pans, 16 cups greased

1. In a medium bowl, whisk together flour blend, baking powder, salt and xanthan gum.
2. In a large bowl, using an electric mixer on medium speed, beat brown sugar and butter until light and fluffy. Beat in eggs, one at a time, until well blended. Beat in milk and vanilla until blended.
3. Add the flour mixture to the egg mixture and, using a wooden spoon, stir until just blended. Gently fold in cashews.
4. Divide batter equally among prepared muffin cups.
5. Bake in preheated oven for 22 to 27 minutes or until tops are golden and a toothpick inserted in the center comes out clean. Let cool in pans on a wire rack for 3 minutes, then transfer to the rack to cool.

Macadamia Coconut Muffins

1¹⁄₂ cups	Brown Rice Flour Blend (see page 19)	375 mL
³⁄₄ tsp	salt	3 mL
¹⁄₂ tsp	xanthan gum	2 mL
¹⁄₄ tsp	baking soda	1 mL
1 cup	packed light brown sugar	250 mL
¹⁄₂ cup	unsalted butter, softened	125 mL
2	eggs	2
¹⁄₂ cup	buttermilk	125 mL
1 tbsp	finely grated lime zest	15 mL
2 tsp	vanilla extract	10 mL
1 cup	chopped macadamia nuts, toasted	250 mL
1¹⁄₂ cups	sweetened flaked or shredded coconut, divided	375 mL

There's something inherently festive about these muffins, packed full of sunny lime zest and buttery macadamia nuts and capped with toasted coconut.

Makes 10 muffins

- Preheat oven to 350°F (180°C)
- 12-cup muffin pan, 10 cups greased

1. In a medium bowl, whisk together flour blend, salt, xanthan gum and baking soda.

2. In a large bowl, using an electric mixer on medium-high speed, beat brown sugar and butter until light and fluffy. With the mixer on medium-low speed, beat in eggs, one at a time, until well blended. Beat in buttermilk, lime zest and vanilla until blended.

3. Add the flour mixture to the egg mixture and, using a wooden spoon, stir until just blended. Gently fold in macadamia nuts and ³⁄₄ cup (175 mL) of the coconut.

4. Divide batter equally among prepared muffin cups.

5. Bake in preheated oven for 10 minutes. Remove from oven and sprinkle with the remaining coconut. Bake for 10 to 15 minutes or until a toothpick inserted in the center comes out clean. Let cool in pan on a wire rack for 5 minutes, then transfer to the rack to cool.

Toasted Coconut Muffins

1¹⁄₂ cups	sweetened flaked or shredded coconut	375 mL
3 cups	almond flour	750 mL
³⁄₄ tsp	baking soda	3 mL
¹⁄₂ tsp	salt	2 mL
2	eggs	2
¹⁄₄ cup	liquid honey	60 mL
3 tbsp	unsalted butter, melted	45 mL
1 tsp	vanilla extract	5 mL
¹⁄₂ tsp	almond extract	2 mL
³⁄₄ cup	mashed ripe bananas	175 mL

We often relegate coconut to toppings and garnishes, but these toasted coconut muffins definitely deserve to be offered up solo. Each golden treat holds a flurry of toasted coconut — an island escape at your fingertips.

Makes 12 muffins

- Preheat oven to 350°F (180°C)
- Rimmed baking sheet
- 12-cup muffin pan, lined with paper liners

1. Spread coconut on baking sheet and bake in preheated oven for 4 to 6 minutes or until golden brown. Remove from oven and let cool. Reduce oven temperature to 325°F (160°C).

2. In a large bowl, whisk together flour, baking soda and salt.

3. In a medium bowl, vigorously whisk eggs. Whisk in honey, butter, vanilla and almond extract until well blended. Stir in bananas.

4. Add the egg mixture to the flour mixture and stir until just blended. Gently fold in coconut.

5. Divide batter equally among prepared muffin cups.

6. Bake oven for 25 to 30 minutes or until a toothpick inserted in the center comes out clean. Let cool in pan on a wire rack for 5 minutes, then transfer to the rack to cool.

Coconut Lime Muffins

2 cups	Brown Rice Flour Blend (see page 19)	500 mL
1 tbsp	gluten-free baking powder	15 mL
1 tsp	baking soda	5 mL
3/4 tsp	xanthan gum	3 mL
1/2 tsp	salt	2 mL
2/3 cup	granulated sugar	150 mL
2	eggs	2
1/2 cup	milk	125 mL
1/2 cup	vegetable oil	125 mL
2 tbsp	finely grated lime zest	30 mL
1 tsp	vanilla extract	5 mL
1 1/2 cups	sweetened flaked or shredded coconut, divided	375 mL

This citrusy coconut treat would be terrific for a summer afternoon tea, brunch or shower.

Makes 12 muffins

- Preheat oven to 350°F (180°C)
- 12-cup muffin pan, greased

1. In a large bowl, whisk together flour blend, baking powder, baking soda, xanthan gum and salt.

2. In a medium bowl, vigorously whisk together sugar, eggs, milk, oil, lime zest and vanilla until well blended.

3. Add the egg mixture to the flour mixture and stir until just blended. Gently fold in 1 cup (250 mL) of the coconut.

4. Divide batter equally among prepared muffin cups. Sprinkle with the remaining coconut and gently press into batter.

5. Bake in preheated oven for 20 to 25 minutes or until a toothpick inserted in the center comes out clean. Let cool in pan on a wire rack for 5 minutes, then transfer to the rack to cool.

Almond Poppy Seed Muffins

3 cups	almond flour	750 mL
1/4 cup	poppy seeds	60 mL
3/4 tsp	baking soda	3 mL
1/2 tsp	salt	2 mL
2	eggs	2
1/4 cup	liquid honey	60 mL
1/4 cup	unsalted butter, melted	60 mL
1 tsp	almond extract	5 mL
2/3 cup	unsweetened applesauce	150 mL

Poppy seeds are more than decoration in these muffins: they have a subtle, slightly earthy flavor and a delicate crunch.

Makes 12 muffins

- Preheat oven to 325°F (160°C)
- 12-cup muffin pan, lined with paper liners

1. In a large bowl, whisk together flour, poppy seeds, baking soda and salt.

2. In a medium bowl, vigorously whisk eggs. Whisk in honey, butter and almond extract until well blended. Stir in applesauce.

3. Add the egg mixture to the flour mixture and stir until just blended.

4. Divide batter equally among prepared muffin cups.

5. Bake in preheated oven for 25 to 30 minutes or until a toothpick inserted in the center comes out clean. Let cool in pan on a wire rack for 5 minutes, then transfer to the rack to cool.

Toasted Almond Muffins

1³⁄₄ cups	Brown Rice Flour Blend (see page 19)	425 mL
1 tbsp	gluten-free baking powder	15 mL
¹⁄₂ tsp	salt	2 mL
¹⁄₂ tsp	xanthan gum	2 mL
¹⁄₂ cup	packed light brown sugar	125 mL
¹⁄₄ cup	butter, softened	60 mL
1	egg	1
³⁄₄ cup	milk	175 mL
1 tsp	almond extract	5 mL
¹⁄₂ tsp	vanilla extract	2 mL
¹⁄₂ cup	sliced almonds	125 mL

What better way to rise and shine than with something fabulous? Though these double-almond muffins are easy to make, they are perfection in their simplicity.

Makes 12 muffins

- Preheat oven to 350°F (180°C)
- 12-cup muffin pan, greased

1. In a medium bowl, whisk together flour blend, baking powder, salt and xanthan gum.
2. In a large bowl, using an electric mixer on medium speed, beat brown sugar and butter until light and fluffy. Beat in egg until well blended. Beat in milk, almond extract and vanilla until blended.
3. Add the flour mixture to the egg mixture and, using a wooden spoon, stir until just blended.
4. Divide batter equally among prepared muffin cups. Sprinkle with almonds.
5. Bake in preheated oven for 25 to 28 minutes or until tops are golden and a toothpick inserted in the center comes out clean. Let cool in pan on a wire rack for 5 minutes, then transfer to the rack to cool.

Trail Mix Muffins

1 cup	Brown Rice Flour Blend (see page 19)	250 mL
¹⁄₂ cup	buckwheat flour	125 mL
¹⁄₃ cup	ground flax seeds	75 mL
2 tsp	gluten-free baking powder	10 mL
1 tsp	salt	5 mL
¹⁄₂ tsp	xanthan gum	2 mL
¹⁄₃ cup	packed dark brown sugar	75 mL
2	eggs	2
¹⁄₂ cup	milk	125 mL
¹⁄₄ cup	vegetable oil	60 mL
2 tbsp	liquid honey	30 mL
¹⁄₃ cup	chopped mixed dried fruit	75 mL
¹⁄₃ cup	gluten-free semisweet chocolate chips, chopped	75 mL
¹⁄₃ cup	lightly salted roasted sunflower seeds	75 mL

Great travelers, these muffins filled with flax, fruit, dark chocolate and sunflower seeds will keep your energy going for a hike up the mountain or a stroll across town.

Makes 12 muffins

- Preheat oven to 350°F (180°C)
- 12-cup muffin pan, greased

1. In a large bowl, whisk together flour blend, buckwheat flour, flax seeds, baking powder, salt and xanthan gum.
2. In a medium bowl, whisk together brown sugar, eggs, milk, oil and honey until well blended.
3. Add the egg mixture to the flour mixture and stir until just blended. Gently fold in fruit, chocolate chips and sunflower seeds.
4. Divide batter equally among prepared muffin cups.
5. Bake in preheated oven for 21 to 25 minutes or until tops are golden and a toothpick inserted in the center comes out clean. Let cool in pan on a wire rack for 5 minutes, then transfer to the rack to cool.

Granola Muffins

1 cup + 2 tbsp	Brown Rice Flour Blend (see page 19)	275 mL
1 cup	almond flour	250 mL
1½ tsp	gluten-free baking powder	7 mL
½ tsp	baking soda	2 mL
½ tsp	salt	2 mL
½ tsp	xanthan gum	2 mL
⅔ cup	packed light brown sugar	150 mL
2	eggs	2
⅔ cup	buttermilk	150 mL
¼ cup	vegetable oil	60 mL
1 tsp	vanilla extract	5 mL
1¼ cups	gluten-free granola	300 mL
⅓ cup	dried cranberries	75 mL

There's nothing quite like a bowl of granola to start off the day, but when I'm in a rush, I love the portability of these granola muffins. You can vary the dried fruit as you like; I prefer the tart-sweet addition of dried cranberries.

Makes 12 muffins

- Preheat oven to 350°F (180°C)
- 12-cup muffin pan, greased

1. In a large bowl, whisk together flour blend, almond flour, baking powder, baking soda, salt and xanthan gum.
2. In a medium bowl, whisk together brown sugar, eggs, buttermilk, oil and vanilla until well blended.
3. Add the egg mixture to the flour mixture and stir until just blended. Gently fold in granola and cranberries.
4. Divide batter equally among prepared muffin cups.
5. Bake in preheated oven for 18 to 23 minutes or until a toothpick inserted in the center comes out clean. Let cool in pan on a wire rack for 5 minutes, then transfer to the rack to cool.

Hungarian Hazelnut Muffins

1¾ cups	Brown Rice Flour Blend (see page 19)	425 mL
1½ tsp	gluten-free baking powder	7 mL
½ tsp	salt	2 mL
½ tsp	xanthan gum	2 mL
¾ cup	packed light brown sugar	175 mL
¾ cup	unsalted butter, softened	175 mL
3	eggs	3
¼ cup	milk	60 mL
1 tsp	vanilla extract	5 mL
½ tsp	almond extract	2 mL
1 cup	chopped hazelnuts, toasted	250 mL
½ cup	apricot preserves, melted	125 mL
3 tbsp	confectioners' (icing) sugar	45 mL

These muffins draw inspiration from the hazelnut tortes and confections for which Eastern Europe is renowned.

Makes 16 muffins

- Preheat oven to 350°F (180°C)
- Two 12-cup muffin pans, 16 cups greased

1. In a medium bowl, whisk together flour blend, baking powder, salt and xanthan gum.
2. In a large bowl, using an electric mixer on medium speed, beat brown sugar and butter until light and fluffy. Beat in eggs, one at a time, until well blended. Beat in milk, vanilla and almond extract until blended.
3. Add the flour mixture to the egg mixture and, using a wooden spoon, stir until just blended. Gently fold in hazelnuts.
4. Divide batter equally among prepared muffin cups.
5. Bake in preheated oven for 22 to 27 minutes or until tops are golden and a toothpick inserted in the center comes out clean. Let cool in pans on a wire rack for 5 minutes, then transfer to the rack.
6. Brush preserves over warm muffin tops. Let cool. Dust with confectioners' sugar.

Walnut Cardamom Crumb Muffins

Topping

1/2 cup	Brown Rice Flour Blend (see page 19)	125 mL
1/3 cup	packed light brown sugar	75 mL
1/4 tsp	ground cardamom	1 mL
1/4 tsp	xanthan gum	1 mL
3 tbsp	unsalted butter, melted	45 mL
1/2 cup	chopped walnuts	125 mL

Muffins

2 cups	Brown Rice Flour Blend (see page 19)	500 mL
1 tbsp	gluten-free baking powder	15 mL
1 tsp	baking soda	5 mL
3/4 tsp	ground cardamom	3 mL
3/4 tsp	xanthan gum	3 mL
1/2 tsp	salt	2 mL
2/3 cup	granulated sugar	150 mL
1/2 cup	unsalted butter, softened	125 mL
2	eggs	2
1/2 cup	buttermilk	125 mL
1 tsp	vanilla extract	5 mL
1/2 tsp	almond extract	2 mL

Makes 12 muffins

- Preheat oven to 375°F (190°C)
- 12-cup muffin pan, greased

1. *Topping:* In a small bowl, combine flour blend, brown sugar, cardamom, xanthan gum and butter until blended and crumbly. Stir in walnuts. Refrigerate until ready to use.

2. *Muffins:* In a medium bowl, whisk together flour blend, baking powder, baking soda, cardamom, xanthan gum and salt.

3. In a large bowl, using an electric mixer on medium-high speed, beat sugar and butter until light and fluffy. Beat in eggs, one at a time, until well blended. Beat in buttermilk, vanilla and almond extract until blended.

4. Add the flour mixture to the egg mixture and, using a wooden spoon, stir until just blended.

5. Divide batter equally among prepared muffin cups.

6. Bake in preheated oven for 10 minutes. Remove from oven and sprinkle with topping. Bake for 10 to 15 minutes or until a toothpick inserted in the center comes out clean. Let cool in pan on a wire rack for 5 minutes, then transfer to the rack to cool.

Linzer Muffins

3 cups	almond flour	750 mL
3/4 tsp	baking soda	3 mL
1/2 tsp	salt	2 mL
2	eggs	2
1/4 cup	liquid honey	60 mL
1/4 cup	unsalted butter, melted	60 mL
3/4 tsp	almond extract	3 mL
2/3 cup	unsweetened applesauce	150 mL
1/2 cup	seedless raspberry preserves	125 mL
1/2 cup	slivered almonds	125 mL

The key to a delicious Linzer muffin is striking just the right balance of tart raspberry preserves filling with tender, almond-scented, slightly sweet batter. I think I've hit it with these — and they only get better on day two.

Makes 12 muffins

- Preheat oven to 325°F (160°C)
- 12-cup muffin pan, lined with paper liners

1. In a large bowl, whisk together flour, baking soda and salt.

2. In a medium bowl, vigorously whisk eggs. Whisk in honey, butter and almond extract until well blended. Stir in applesauce.

3. Add the egg mixture to the flour mixture and stir until just blended.

4. Divide half the batter equally among prepared muffin cups. Spoon 2 tsp (10 mL) preserves into the center of each cup. Top with the remaining batter. Sprinkle with almonds.

5. Bake in preheated oven for 25 to 30 minutes or until a toothpick inserted in the center comes out clean. Let cool in pan on a wire rack for 5 minutes, then transfer to the rack to cool.

Dulce de Leche Muffins

2 cups	Brown Rice Flour Blend (see page 19)	500 mL
2 tsp	gluten-free baking powder	10 mL
3/4 tsp	xanthan gum	3 mL
1/4 tsp	salt	1 mL
1 cup	packed dark brown sugar	250 mL
1/4 cup	unsalted butter, softened	60 mL
2	eggs	2
3/4 cup	milk	175 mL
1/2 cup	canned dulce de leche, divided	125 mL

Brown sugar muffins go Latin with a double dose of dulce de leche, a sweet milk caramel.

Makes 12 muffins

- Preheat oven to 350°F (180°C)
- 12-cup muffin pan, lined with paper liners

1. In a medium bowl, whisk together flour blend, baking powder, xanthan gum and salt.

2. In a large bowl, using an electric mixer on medium speed, beat brown sugar and butter until light and fluffy. Beat in eggs, one at a time, until well blended. Beat in milk until blended.

3. Add the flour mixture to the egg mixture and, using a wooden spoon, stir until just blended.

4. Divide batter equally among prepared muffin cups. Spoon 1 tsp (5 mL) dulce de leche into the center of each cup (the dulce de leche will sink as the muffins bake).

5. Bake in preheated oven for 18 to 22 minutes or until tops are firm to the touch. Let cool in pan on a wire rack for 5 minutes, then transfer to the rack to cool.

6. Drizzle the remaining dulce de leche over cooled muffin tops.

Black Forest Muffins

1 1/4 cups	Brown Rice Flour Blend (see page 19)	300 mL
1/3 cup	unsweetened cocoa powder (not Dutch process)	75 mL
2 tsp	gluten-free baking powder	10 mL
1/2 tsp	baking soda	2 mL
1/4 tsp	ground cinnamon	2 mL
1/4 tsp	salt	1 mL
1/4 tsp	xanthan gum	1 mL
1/2 cup	granulated sugar	125 mL
1	egg	1
3/4 cup	milk	150 mL
1/2 cup	ricotta cheese	125 mL
2 tbsp	unsalted butter, melted	30 mL
3/4 tsp	almond extract	3 mL
1/2 cup	gluten-free semisweet chocolate chips, chopped	125 mL
1/2 cup	dried cherries, chopped	125 mL

Makes 10 muffins

- Preheat oven to 350°F (180°C)
- 12-cup muffin pan, 10 cups greased

1. In a large bowl, whisk together flour blend, cocoa powder, baking powder, baking soda, cinnamon, salt and xanthan gum.

2. In a medium bowl, whisk together sugar, egg, milk, cheese, butter and almond extract until well blended.

3. Add the egg mixture to the flour mixture and stir until just blended. Gently fold in chocolate chips and cherries.

4. Divide batter equally among prepared muffin cups.

5. Bake in preheated oven for 18 to 22 minutes or until a toothpick inserted in the center comes out clean. Let cool in pan on a wire rack for 5 minutes, then transfer to the rack to cool.

Cappuccino Chip Muffins

1 tbsp	instant espresso powder	15 mL
1 tbsp	vanilla extract	15 mL
1¾ cups	Brown Rice Flour Blend (see page 19)	425 mL
1½ tsp	gluten-free baking powder	7 mL
½ tsp	salt	2 mL
½ tsp	xanthan gum	2 mL
¾ cup	packed light brown sugar	175 mL
¾ cup	unsalted butter, softened	175 mL
3	eggs	3
¼ cup	milk	60 mL
⅔ cup	gluten-free semisweet chocolate chips, chopped	150 mL

Rich and gutsy and especially delicious when shared with a fellow coffee lover, these muffins will transport you to your favorite coffeehouse in a few nibbles.

Makes 16 muffins

- Preheat oven to 350°F (180°C)
- Two 12-cup muffin pans, 16 cups greased

1. In a small bowl, stir together espresso powder and vanilla until espresso powder is dissolved.
2. In a medium bowl, whisk together flour blend, baking powder, salt and xanthan gum.
3. In a large bowl, using an electric mixer on medium speed, beat brown sugar and butter until light and fluffy. Beat in eggs, one at a time, until well blended. Beat in milk and espresso powder mixture until blended.
4. Add the flour mixture to the egg mixture and, using a wooden spoon, stir until just blended. Gently fold in chocolate chips.
5. Divide batter equally among prepared muffin cups.
6. Bake in preheated oven for 22 to 27 minutes or until tops are golden and a toothpick inserted in the center comes out clean. Let cool in pans on a wire rack for 5 minutes, then transfer to the rack to cool.

Hazelnut and Chocolate Chunk Muffins

1½ cups	Brown Rice Flour Blend (see page 19)	375 mL
¾ tsp	gluten-free baking powder	3 mL
¾ tsp	salt	3 mL
¼ tsp	xanthan gum	1 mL
⅛ tsp	baking soda	0.5 mL
1 cup	packed light brown sugar	250 mL
2	eggs	2
¾ cup	milk	175 mL
¼ cup	vegetable oil	60 mL
⅔ cup	chopped hazelnuts, toasted	150 mL
3 oz	gluten-free bittersweet chocolate, chopped	90 g

These muffins take their cue from *gianduia*, the Italian combination of hazelnuts and chocolate. Take note that the batter for these muffins will be thin as it goes into the muffin pan, but the end result is rich.

Makes 12 muffins

- Preheat oven to 350°F (180°C)
- 12-cup muffin pan, greased

1. In a large bowl, whisk together flour blend, baking powder, salt, xanthan gum and baking soda.
2. In a medium bowl, whisk together brown sugar, eggs, milk and oil until well blended.
3. Add the egg mixture to the flour mixture and stir until just blended. Gently fold in hazelnuts and chocolate.
4. Divide batter equally among prepared muffin cups.
5. Bake in preheated oven for 25 to 30 minutes or until tops are golden and a toothpick inserted in the center comes out clean. Let cool in pan on a wire rack for 5 minutes, then transfer to the rack to cool.

Cannoli Muffins

1½ cups	Brown Rice Flour Blend (see page 19)	375 mL
1 tbsp	gluten-free baking powder	15 mL
½ tsp	salt	2 mL
½ tsp	xanthan gum	2 mL
⅓ cup	granulated sugar	75 mL
2	eggs	2
⅔ cup	buttermilk	150 mL
½ cup	whole-milk ricotta cheese	125 mL
3 tbsp	unsalted butter, melted	45 mL
1 tsp	vanilla extract	5 mL
½ tsp	almond extract	2 mL
½ cup	chopped pistachios	2 mL
½ cup	gluten-free semisweet chocolate chips, chopped	125 mL

Ricotta, chocolate and pistachios — these amazing muffins have all of the feature flavors of traditional cannoli.

Makes 12 muffins

- Preheat oven to 350°F (180°C)
- 12-cup muffin pan, greased

1. In a large bowl, whisk together flour blend, baking powder, salt and xanthan gum.
2. In a medium bowl, whisk together sugar, eggs, buttermilk, cheese, butter, vanilla and almond extract until well blended.
3. Add the egg mixture to the flour mixture and stir until just blended. Gently fold in pistachios and chocolate chips.
4. Divide batter equally among prepared muffin cups.
5. Bake in preheated oven for 24 to 28 minutes or until a toothpick inserted in the center comes out clean. Let cool in pan on a wire rack for 5 minutes, then transfer to the rack to cool.

Mocha Muffins

1¼ cups	Brown Rice Flour Blend (see page 19)	300 mL
¼ cup	unsweetened cocoa powder (not Dutch process)	60 mL
1½ tsp	gluten-free baking powder	7 mL
½ tsp	baking soda	2 mL
½ tsp	ground cinnamon	2 mL
¼ tsp	salt	1 mL
¼ tsp	xanthan gum	1 mL
½ cup	packed light brown sugar	125 mL
1	egg	1
⅔ cup	milk	150 mL
½ cup	ricotta cheese	125 mL
2 tbsp	vegetable oil	30 mL
1 tbsp	instant espresso powder	15 mL
1½ tsp	vanilla extract	7 mL
⅔ cup	gluten-free semisweet chocolate chips, chopped	150 mL

All-American chocolate muffins get a jolt of flavor from espresso powder.

Makes 10 muffins

- Preheat oven to 350°F (180°C)
- 12-cup muffin pan, 10 cups greased

1. In a large bowl, whisk together flour blend, cocoa powder, baking powder, baking soda, cinnamon, salt and xanthan gum.
2. In a medium bowl, whisk together brown sugar, egg, milk, cheese, oil, espresso powder and vanilla until well blended.
3. Add the egg mixture to the flour mixture and stir until just blended. Gently fold in chocolate chips.
4. Divide batter equally among prepared muffin cups.
5. Bake in preheated oven for 18 to 22 minutes or until a toothpick inserted in the center comes out clean. Let cool in pan on a wire rack for 5 minutes, then transfer to the rack to cool.

Whole-Meal Pumpkin Chocolate Chip Muffins (page 332)

Berry Corn Muffins (page 371)

Zucchini Pecan Agave Muffins (page 405)

Fresh Plum Muffins with Walnut Sugar Tops (page 461)

Pineapple Lime Muffins
(page 466)

Jelly Doughnut Muffins (page 486) and Chai Latte Muffins (page 489)

Rocky Road Muffins

2 cups	Brown Rice Flour Blend (see page 19)	500 mL
2 tsp	gluten-free baking powder	10 mL
3/4 tsp	xanthan gum	3 mL
1/2 tsp	baking soda	2 mL
1/2 tsp	salt	2 mL
1 cup	packed light brown sugar	250 mL
3	eggs	3
1/2 cup	vegetable oil	125 mL
1 tsp	vanilla extract	5 mL
3/4 cup	buttermilk	175 mL
2/3 cup	gluten-free semisweet chocolate chips, coarsely chopped	150 mL
3/4 cup	marshmallow fluff or crème	175 mL
1/2 cup	chopped walnuts or pecans	125 mL

These muffins are pure Americana.

Makes 12 muffins

- Preheat oven to 350°F (180°C)
- 12-cup muffin pan, greased

1. In a medium bowl, whisk together flour blend, baking powder, xanthan gum, baking soda and salt.
2. In a large bowl, using an electric mixer on medium-high speed, beat brown sugar, eggs, oil and vanilla for 1 minute. With the mixer on low speed, beat in buttermilk until well blended.
3. Add the flour mixture to the egg mixture and, using a wooden spoon, stir until just blended. Gently fold in chocolate chips.
4. Divide half the batter equally among prepared muffin cups. Spoon 1 tbsp (15 mL) marshmallow fluff into the center of each cup. Top with the remaining batter. Sprinkle with walnuts.
5. Bake in preheated oven for 20 to 25 minutes or until a toothpick inserted in the center comes out clean. Let cool in pan on a wire rack for 5 minutes, then transfer to the rack to cool.

Jelly Doughnut Muffins

Muffins

1 1/2 cups	Brown Rice Flour Blend (see page 19)	375 mL
2 tsp	gluten-free baking powder	10 mL
1/2 tsp	salt	2 mL
1/2 tsp	xanthan gum	2 mL
1	egg	1
1/2 cup	granulated sugar	125 mL
1/2 cup	milk	125 mL
1/4 cup	vegetable oil	60 mL
3/4 tsp	vanilla extract	3 mL
1/2 cup	seedless raspberry preserves	125 mL

Topping

1/4 cup	granulated sugar	60 mL
1 tsp	ground cinnamon	5 mL
2 tbsp	unsalted butter, melted	30 mL

These jelly doughnut–like muffins taste even better than the original and allow you to forgo a trip to the store and stay in your pajamas on Saturday morning.

Makes 12 muffins

- Preheat oven to 375°F (190°C)
- 12-cup muffin pan, greased

1. *Muffins:* In a large bowl, whisk together flour blend, baking powder, salt and xanthan gum.
2. In a medium bowl, vigorously whisk egg. Whisk in sugar, milk, oil and vanilla until well blended.
3. Add the egg mixture to the flour mixture and stir until just blended.
4. Divide half the batter equally among prepared muffin cups. Spoon 2 tsp (10 mL) preserves into the center of each cup. Top with the remaining batter.
5. Bake in preheated oven for 20 to 25 minutes or until tops spring back when touched. Let cool in pan on a wire rack for 5 minutes, then transfer to the rack.
6. *Topping:* In a small bowl, combine sugar and cinnamon. Brush butter over warm muffin tops, then sprinkle with sugar mixture. Let cool.

Chocolate Chip Muffins

2 cups	Brown Rice Flour Blend (see page 19)	500 mL
1 tbsp	gluten-free baking powder	15 mL
1 tsp	baking soda	5 mL
3/4 tsp	xanthan gum	3 mL
1/2 tsp	ground cinnamon	2 mL
1/2 tsp	salt	2 mL
2/3 cup	packed light brown sugar	150 mL
1/2 cup	unsalted butter, softened	125 mL
2	eggs	2
1/2 cup	buttermilk	125 mL
1 tsp	vanilla extract	5 mL
1 cup	gluten-free semisweet chocolate chips	250 mL
1/2 cup	chopped pecans, toasted	125 mL

Ready to shake things up at the breakfast table? Present a basket of these muffins, warm, and enjoy the kudos.

Makes 12 muffins

- Preheat oven to 375°F (190°C)
- 12-cup muffin pan, greased

1. In a medium bowl, whisk together flour blend, baking powder, baking soda, xanthan gum, cinnamon and salt.

2. In a large bowl, using an electric mixer on medium-high speed, beat brown sugar and butter until light and fluffy. Beat in eggs, one at a time, until well blended. Beat in buttermilk and vanilla until blended.

3. Add the flour mixture to the egg mixture and, using a wooden spoon, stir until just blended. Gently fold in chocolate chips and pecans.

4. Divide batter equally among prepared muffin cups.

5. Bake in preheated oven for 20 to 25 minutes or until a toothpick inserted in the center comes out clean. Let cool in pan on a wire rack for 5 minutes, then transfer to the rack to cool.

Double Chocolate Banana Muffins

1 cup	Brown Rice Flour Blend (see page 19)	250 mL
1 cup	teff flour	250 mL
6 tbsp	unsweetened cocoa powder (not Dutch process)	90 mL
1 1/2 tsp	ground cinnamon	7 mL
3/4 tsp	baking soda	3 mL
1/2 tsp	salt	2 mL
3/4 cup	granulated sugar	175 mL
2	eggs	2
6 tbsp	unsalted butter, melted	90 mL
1 tsp	vanilla extract	5 mL
1 1/2 cups	mashed ripe bananas	375 mL
1/4 cup	low-fat (1%) plain yogurt	60 mL
4 oz	gluten-free bittersweet chocolate, chopped	125 g

These easy (double)-chocolate-enhanced muffins are just right for an afternoon coffee break or a delicious surprise in a weekday lunch bag.

Makes 12 muffins

- Preheat oven to 350°F (180°C)
- 12-cup muffin pan, greased

1. In a large bowl, whisk together flour blend, teff flour, cocoa powder, cinnamon, baking soda and salt.

2. In a medium bowl, whisk together sugar, eggs, butter and vanilla until well blended. Whisk in bananas and yogurt until blended.

3. Add the egg mixture to the flour mixture and stir until just blended. Gently fold in chocolate.

4. Divide batter equally among prepared muffin cups.

5. Bake in preheated oven for 20 to 25 minutes or until a toothpick inserted in the center comes out clean. Let cool in pan on a wire rack for 5 minutes, then transfer to the rack to cool.

Aztec Chocolate Muffins

1½ cups	Brown Rice Flour Blend (see page 19)	375 mL
¼ cup	unsweetened cocoa powder (not Dutch process)	60 mL
1½ tsp	gluten-free baking powder	7 mL
1 tsp	baking soda	5 mL
1 tsp	ground cinnamon	5 mL
½ tsp	salt	2 mL
½ tsp	xanthan gum	2 mL
¼ tsp	cayenne pepper	1 mL
½ cup	packed dark brown sugar	125 mL
1	egg	1
¾ cup	milk	175 mL
½ cup	ricotta cheese	125 mL
3 tbsp	vegetable oil	45 mL
¾ tsp	almond extract	3 mL
1 cup	gluten-free semisweet chocolate chips	250 mL

Makes 10 muffins

- Preheat oven to 350°F (180°C)
- 12-cup muffin pan, 10 cups greased

1. In a large bowl, whisk together flour blend, cocoa powder, baking powder, baking soda, cinnamon, salt, xanthan gum and cayenne.
2. In a medium bowl, whisk together brown sugar, egg, milk, cheese, oil and almond extract until well blended.
3. Add the egg mixture to the flour mixture and stir until just blended. Gently fold in chocolate chips.
4. Divide batter equally among prepared muffin cups.
5. Bake in preheated oven for 18 to 22 minutes or until a toothpick inserted in the center comes out clean. Let cool in pan on a wire rack for 5 minutes, then transfer to the rack to cool.

Chocolate Ricotta Muffins

1⅓ cups	Brown Rice Flour Blend (see page 19)	325 mL
1 cup	quinoa flour	250 mL
⅓ cup	unsweetened cocoa powder (not Dutch process)	75 mL
2 tsp	gluten-free baking powder	10 mL
½ tsp	salt	2 mL
½ tsp	xanthan gum	2 mL
¼ tsp	baking soda	1 mL
1 cup	granulated sugar	250 mL
2	eggs	2
1 cup	ricotta cheese	250 mL
¼ cup	vegetable oil	60 mL
1 tsp	vanilla extract	5 mL
1⅓ cups	milk	325 mL
1 cup	gluten-free semisweet chocolate chips	250 mL

Makes 12 muffins

- Preheat oven to 350°F (180°C)
- 12-cup muffin pan, greased

1. In a large bowl, whisk together flour blend, quinoa flour, cocoa powder, baking powder, salt, xanthan gum and baking soda.
2. In a medium bowl, whisk together sugar, eggs, cheese, oil and vanilla until well blended. Whisk in milk until blended.
3. Add the egg mixture to the flour mixture and stir until just blended. Gently fold in chocolate chips.
4. Divide batter equally among prepared muffin cups.
5. Bake in preheated oven for 24 to 28 minutes or until a toothpick inserted in the center comes out clean. Let cool in pan on a wire rack for 5 minutes, then transfer to the rack to cool.

Chocolate elation? It's right here. Homemade and delicious, these muffins trounce all of the glassed-in pastry options at the coffeehouse.

Crumb Cake Muffins

Topping

½ cup	Brown Rice Flour Blend (see page 19)	125 mL
½ cup	dark brown sugar	125 mL
½ tsp	ground cinnamon	2 mL
¼ tsp	salt	1 mL
6 tbsp	cold unsalted butter, cut into small pieces	90 mL

Muffins

1½ cups	Brown Rice Flour Blend (see page 19)	375 mL
¾ tsp	salt	3 mL
½ tsp	xanthan gum	2 mL
¼ tsp	baking soda	1 mL
1 cup	granulated sugar	250 mL
½ cup	unsalted butter, softened	125 mL
2	eggs	2
½ cup	buttermilk	125 mL
2 tsp	vanilla extract	10 mL

Few things are more inviting on a chilly weekend morning than a basket of cinnamon-spiced crumb muffins, an oversized mug of coffee and the added cheer of a pair of fuzzy slippers.

Makes 10 muffins

- Preheat oven to 350°F (180°C)
- 12-cup muffin pan, 10 cups greased

1. *Topping:* In a small bowl, whisk together flour blend, brown sugar, cinnamon and salt. Using a pastry cutter or your fingers, cut or rub in butter until mixture is crumbly. Refrigerate until ready to use.

2. *Muffins:* In a medium bowl, whisk together flour, salt, xanthan gum and baking soda.

3. In a large bowl, using an electric mixer on medium-high speed, beat sugar and butter until light and fluffy. With the mixer on medium-low speed, beat in eggs, one at a time, until well blended. Beat in buttermilk and vanilla until blended

4. Add the flour mixture to the egg mixture and, using a wooden spoon, stir until just blended.

5. Divide batter equally among prepared muffin cups.

6. Bake in preheated oven for 10 minutes. Remove from oven and sprinkle with topping. Bake for 10 to 15 minutes or until a toothpick inserted in the center comes out clean. Let cool in pan on a wire rack for 5 minutes, then transfer to the rack to cool.

Scandinavian Spice Muffins

2¹⁄₂ cups	Brown Rice Flour Blend (see page 19)	625 mL
2 tsp	gluten-free baking powder	10 mL
1 tsp	baking soda	5 mL
1 tsp	ground cardamom	5 mL
1 tsp	ground cinnamon	5 mL
1 tsp	xanthan gum	5 mL
¹⁄₂ tsp	salt	2 mL
¹⁄₄ tsp	ground cloves	1 mL
2	eggs	2
²⁄₃ cup	buttermilk	150 mL
¹⁄₂ cup	liquid honey	125 mL
¹⁄₂ cup	vegetable oil	125 mL
1 tsp	vanilla extract	5 mL

Rich with spices, these muffins are wonderful any time of the year. However, you'll enjoy them most when the temperature dips and the air turns crisp.

Makes 12 muffins

- Preheat oven to 350°F (180°C)
- 12-cup muffin pan, greased

1. In a large bowl, whisk together flour blend, baking powder, baking soda, cardamom, cinnamon, xanthan gum, salt and cloves.
2. In a medium bowl, whisk together eggs, buttermilk, honey, oil and vanilla until well blended.
3. Add the egg mixture to the flour mixture and stir until just blended.
4. Divide batter equally among prepared muffin cups.
5. Bake in preheated oven for 22 to 27 minutes or until a toothpick inserted in the center comes out clean. Let cool in pan on a wire rack for 5 minutes, then transfer to the rack to cool.

Masala Chai Spice Muffins

1³⁄₄ cups	Brown Rice Flour Blend (see page 19)	425 mL
1¹⁄₂ tsp	gluten-free baking powder	7 mL
1¹⁄₂ tsp	ground ginger	7 mL
1 tsp	ground cinnamon	5 mL
¹⁄₂ tsp	ground cardamom	2 mL
¹⁄₂ tsp	salt	2 mL
¹⁄₂ tsp	xanthan gum	2 mL
¹⁄₈ tsp	ground cloves	0.5 mL
³⁄₄ cup	packed light brown sugar	175 mL
³⁄₄ cup	unsalted butter, softened	175 mL
3	eggs	3
¹⁄₄ cup	milk	60 mL
2 tsp	vanilla extract	10 mL

Masala refers to a combination of spices that can include cardamom, cinnamon, ginger, cloves, pepper, fennel and star anise. The easily assembled spices featured here capture the spirit and flavor of masala chai.

Makes 16 muffins

- Preheat oven to 350°F (180°C)
- Two 12-cup muffin pans, 16 cups greased

1. In a medium bowl, whisk together flour blend, baking powder, ginger, cinnamon, cardamom, salt, xanthan gum and cloves.
2. In a large bowl, using an electric mixer on medium speed, beat brown sugar and butter until light and fluffy. Beat in eggs, one at a time, until well blended. Beat in milk and vanilla until blended.
3. Add the flour mixture to the egg mixture and, using a wooden spoon, stir until just blended.
4. Divide batter equally among prepared muffin cups.
5. Bake in preheated oven for 22 to 27 minutes or until tops are golden and a toothpick inserted in the center comes out clean. Let cool in pans on a wire rack for 5 minutes, then transfer to the rack to cool.

Cinnamon Sugar Muffins

Topping

2 tbsp	granulated sugar	30 mL
1/4 tsp	ground cinnamon	1 mL

Muffins

1¾ cups	Brown Rice Flour Blend (see page 19)	425 mL
1 tbsp	gluten-free baking powder	15 mL
2 tsp	ground cinnamon	10 mL
1/2 tsp	salt	2 mL
1/2 tsp	xanthan gum	2 mL
1/2 cup	granulated sugar	125 mL
1/4 cup	unsalted butter, softened	60 mL
1	egg	1
3/4 cup	milk	175 mL
1 tsp	vanilla extract	5 mL

These old-fashioned muffins have just what kids (of all ages) love.

Makes 12 muffins

- Preheat oven to 350°F (180°C)
- 12-cup muffin pan, lined with paper liners

1. *Topping:* In a small bowl, combine sugar and cinnamon.
2. *Muffins:* In a medium bowl, whisk together flour blend, baking powder, cinnamon, salt and xanthan gum.
3. In a large bowl, using an electric mixer on medium speed, beat sugar and butter until light and fluffy. Beat in egg until well blended. Beat in milk and vanilla until blended.
4. Add the flour mixture to the egg mixture and, using a wooden spoon, stir until just blended.
5. Divide batter equally among prepared muffin cups. Sprinkle with topping.
6. Bake in preheated oven for 15 to 20 minutes or until tops are golden and a toothpick inserted in the center comes out clean. Let cool in pan on a wire rack for 5 minutes, then transfer to the rack to cool.

Maple Sour Cream Muffins

2½ cups	Brown Rice Flour Blend (see page 19)	625 mL
2 tsp	gluten-free baking powder	10 mL
1 tsp	baking soda	5 mL
1 tsp	xanthan gum	5 mL
1/2 tsp	salt	2 mL
2	eggs	2
3/4 cup	sour cream	175 mL
1/2 cup	pure maple syrup	125 mL
1/2 cup	vegetable oil	125 mL

With ample doses of maple syrup and sour cream, this easy option will knock blueberry muffins off their pedestal.

Makes 12 muffins

- Preheat oven to 350°F (180°C)
- 12-cup muffin pan, greased

1. In a large bowl, whisk together flour blend, baking powder, baking soda, xanthan gum and salt.
2. In a medium bowl, whisk together eggs, sour cream, maple syrup and oil until well blended.
3. Add the egg mixture to the flour mixture and stir until just blended.
4. Divide batter equally among prepared muffin cups.
5. Bake in preheated oven for 22 to 27 minutes or until a toothpick inserted in the center comes out clean. Let cool in pan on a wire rack for 5 minutes, then transfer to the rack to cool.

Maple Cinnamon Muffins

2 1/2 cups	Brown Rice Flour Blend (see page 19)	625 mL
2 tsp	gluten-free baking powder	10 mL
1 tsp	baking soda	5 mL
1 tsp	ground cinnamon	5 mL
1 tsp	xanthan gum	5 mL
1/2 tsp	salt	2 mL
2	eggs	2
2/3 cup	buttermilk	150 mL
1/2 cup	pure maple syrup	125 mL
1/2 cup	vegetable oil	125 mL
2 tbsp	turbinado sugar	30 mL

At once old-fashioned and innovative, these tender muffins are a big bite of nostalgia.

Makes 12 muffins

- Preheat oven to 350°F (180°C)
- 12-cup muffin pan, greased

1. In a large bowl, whisk together flour blend, baking powder, baking soda, cinnamon, xanthan gum and salt.

2. In a medium bowl, whisk together eggs, buttermilk, maple syrup and oil until well blended.

3. Add the egg mixture to the flour mixture and stir until just blended.

4. Divide batter equally among prepared muffin cups. Sprinkle with turbinado sugar.

5. Bake in preheated oven for 22 to 27 minutes or until a toothpick inserted in the center comes out clean. Let cool in pan on a wire rack for 5 minutes, then transfer to the rack to cool.

Vanilla Yogurt Muffins

1 1/2 cups	Brown Rice Flour Blend (see page 19)	375 mL
1 1/2 tsp	gluten-free baking powder	7 mL
1/2 tsp	salt	2 mL
1/2 tsp	xanthan gum	2 mL
3	eggs	3
1 cup	granulated sugar	250 mL
1 cup	plain whole-milk yogurt	250 mL
1/3 cup	vegetable oil	75 mL
1 1/2 tsp	vanilla extract	7 mL
2 tbsp	turbinado sugar	30 mL

My love of vanilla and yogurt grows exponentially at the sight of these melt-in-your-mouth muffins. Vanilla perfumes the batter, while yogurt tenderizes the baked muffins.

Makes 10 muffins

- Preheat oven to 350°F (180°C)
- 12-cup muffin pan, 10 cups greased

1. In a medium bowl, whisk together flour blend, baking powder, salt and xanthan gum.

2. In a large bowl, using an electric mixer on medium-high speed, beat eggs until frothy. Slowly beat in sugar until mixture has thickened and is pale yellow. With the mixer on medium-low speed, beat in yogurt, oil and vanilla.

3. With the mixer on low speed, beat flour mixture into egg mixture until just blended.

4. Divide batter equally among prepared muffin cups. Sprinkle with turbinado sugar.

5. Bake in preheated oven for 20 to 25 minutes or until a toothpick inserted in the center comes out clean. Let cool in pan on a wire rack for 5 minutes, then transfer to the rack to cool.

Gingerbread Muffins

1²⁄₃ cups	Brown Rice Flour Blend (see page 19)	400 mL
2 tsp	ground ginger	10 mL
1¹⁄₄ tsp	baking soda	6 mL
1 tsp	ground cinnamon	5 mL
³⁄₄ tsp	salt	3 mL
³⁄₄ tsp	xanthan gum	3 mL
¹⁄₂ tsp	ground nutmeg	2 mL
¹⁄₈ tsp	ground cloves	0.5 mL
¹⁄₂ cup	granulated sugar	125 mL
1	egg	1
¹⁄₂ cup	dark (cooking) molasses	125 mL
¹⁄₂ cup	vegetable oil	125 mL
¹⁄₂ cup	boiling water	125 mL
2 tbsp	confectioners' (icing) sugar	30 mL

Holiday spices and molasses give these muffins seasonal charm.

Makes 12 muffins

- Preheat oven to 350°F (180°C)
- 12-cup muffin pan, greased

1. In a large bowl, whisk together flour blend, ginger, baking soda, cinnamon, salt, xanthan gum, nutmeg and cloves.
2. In a medium bowl, whisk together granulated sugar, egg, molasses and oil until well blended.
3. Using an electric mixer on low speed, beat egg mixture and boiling water into flour mixture until well blended.
4. Divide batter equally among prepared muffin cups.
5. Bake in preheated oven for 20 to 25 minutes or until a toothpick inserted in the center comes out clean. Let cool in pan on a wire rack for 5 minutes, then transfer to the rack to cool.
6. Sprinkle cooled muffin tops with confectioners' sugar.

Russian Tea Cake Muffins

1³⁄₄ cups	Brown Rice Flour Blend (see page 19)	425 mL
1¹⁄₂ tsp	gluten-free baking powder	7 mL
¹⁄₂ tsp	salt	2 mL
¹⁄₂ tsp	xanthan gum	2 mL
¹⁄₄ tsp	ground cinnamon	1 mL
³⁄₄ cup	granulated sugar	175 mL
³⁄₄ cup	unsalted butter, softened	175 mL
3	eggs	3
¹⁄₄ cup	milk	60 mL
1 tsp	finely grated lemon zest	5 mL
1 tsp	vanilla extract	5 mL
¹⁄₄ tsp	almond extract	1 mL
1 cup	finely chopped hazelnuts, toasted	250 mL
3 tbsp	confectioners' (icing) sugar	45 mL

Tender butter muffins, enriched with hazelnuts, vanilla, cinnamon and lemon to evoke Russian tea cakes, make simple — and simply wonderful — muffins.

Makes 12 muffins

- Preheat oven to 350°F (180°C)
- 12-cup muffin pans, greased

1. In a medium bowl, whisk together flour blend, baking powder, salt, xanthan gum and cinnamon.
2. In a large bowl, using an electric mixer on medium speed, beat granulated sugar and butter until light and fluffy. Beat in eggs, one at a time, until well blended. Beat in milk, lemon zest, vanilla and almond extract until blended.
3. Add the flour mixture to the egg mixture and, using a wooden spoon, stir until just blended. Gently fold in hazelnuts.
4. Divide batter equally among prepared muffin cups.
5. Bake in preheated oven for 22 to 27 minutes or until tops are golden and a toothpick inserted in the center comes out clean. Let cool in pan on a wire rack for 5 minutes, then transfer to the rack to cool. Sprinkle cooled muffin tops with confectioners' sugar.

Whole Wheatless Honey Muffins

1 cup	sorghum flour	250 mL
1 cup	Brown Rice Flour Blend (see page 19)	250 mL
¼ cup	rice bran	60 mL
1 tbsp	gluten-free baking powder	15 mL
½ tsp	salt	2 mL
½ tsp	xanthan gum	2 mL
½ tsp	ground cinnamon	2 mL
1	egg	1
¼ cup	vegetable oil	60 mL
¼ cup	liquid honey	60 mL
1¼ cups	milk	300 mL

My college cafeteria made very good food, and they baked almost all of their breads, cookies and muffins in-house. One of my favorite muffins was a humble honey and whole wheat treat that seemed to take well to anything I spread on it, from peanut butter to marmalade to more honey. I'm happy to say I've recreated the muffins here, but without any wheat. You're going to love them.

Makes 12 muffins

- Preheat oven to 350°F (180°C)
- 12-cup muffin pan, lined with paper liners

1. In a large bowl, whisk together sorghum flour, flour blend, rice bran, baking powder, salt, xanthan gum and cinnamon.

2. In a medium bowl, whisk together egg, oil and honey until well blended. Whisk in milk until blended.

3. Add the egg mixture to the flour mixture and stir until just blended.

4. Divide batter equally among prepared muffin cups.

5. Bake in preheated oven for 18 to 22 minutes or until a toothpick inserted in the center comes out clean. Let cool in pan on a wire rack for 5 minutes, then transfer to the rack to cool.

Candied Ginger Muffins

3 cups	almond flour	750 mL
1 tsp	ground ginger	5 mL
1 tsp	ground cinnamon	5 mL
¾ tsp	baking soda	3 mL
½ tsp	salt	2 mL
2	eggs	2
¼ cup	dark (cooking) molasses	60 mL
3 tbsp	unsalted butter, melted	45 mL
1 tsp	vanilla extract	5 mL
¾ cup	mashed ripe bananas	175 mL
⅔ cup	finely chopped crystallized ginger	150 mL

These muffins are tender, spicy and totally addictive. Keep a close eye on them — I made them while a ginger-loving friend was visiting, and she sneaked almost half the batch while they were cooling.

Makes 12 muffins

- Preheat oven to 325°F (160°C)
- 12-cup muffin pan, lined with paper liners

1. In a large bowl, whisk together flour, ground ginger, cinnamon, baking soda and salt.

2. In a medium bowl, vigorously whisk eggs. Whisk in molasses, butter and vanilla until well blended. Stir in bananas.

3. Add the egg mixture to the flour mixture and stir until just blended. Gently fold in crystallized ginger.

4. Divide batter equally among prepared muffin cups.

5. Bake in preheated oven for 25 to 30 minutes or until a toothpick inserted in the center comes out clean. Let cool in pan on a wire rack for 5 minutes, then transfer to the rack to cool.

Millet Cornmeal Muffins with Blueberries

1/4 cup	millet	60 mL
1 1/4 cups	Brown Rice Flour Mix (see page 19)	300 mL
3/4 cup	yellow cornmeal	175 mL
2 tsp	gluten-free baking powder	10 mL
1 1/2 tsp	xanthan gum	7 mL
1 tsp	baking soda	5 mL
1/2 tsp	salt	2 mL
1/2 tsp	ground nutmeg	2 mL
3/4 cup	packed light brown sugar	175 mL
2	eggs	2
3/4 cup	milk	175 mL
1/4 cup	vegetable oil	60 mL
1 tbsp	liquid honey	15 mL
2 tsp	vanilla extract	10 mL
1 1/4 cups	blueberries	300 mL

I doubt you'll have any leftovers from these homey blueberry muffins flecked with toasty millet, but if you do, they will make fabulous additions to your lunch bag.

Makes 12 muffins

- Preheat oven to 350°F (180°C)
- Rimmed baking sheet
- 12-cup muffin pan, greased

1. Spread millet on baking sheet and bake in preheated oven for 4 to 5 minutes or until toasted and fragrant. Remove from oven, leaving oven on, and let cool.

2. In a large bowl, whisk together flour blend, cornmeal, baking powder, xanthan gum, baking soda, salt and nutmeg. Stir in millet.

3. In a medium bowl, whisk together brown sugar, eggs, milk, oil, honey and vanilla until well blended.

4. Add the egg mixture to the flour mixture and stir until just blended. Gently fold in blueberries.

5. Divide batter equally among prepared muffin cups.

6. Bake for 20 to 25 minutes or until tops are golden and a toothpick inserted in the center comes out clean. Let cool in pan on a wire rack for 5 minutes, then transfer to the rack to cool.

Cranberry Maple Cornbread Muffins

1 1/4 cups	yellow cornmeal	300 mL
1 cup	Brown Rice Flour Blend (see page 19)	250 mL
2 tsp	gluten-free baking powder	10 mL
1 tsp	baking soda	5 mL
1 tsp	salt	5 mL
3/4 tsp	xanthan gum	3 mL
2 tbsp	packed light brown sugar	30 mL
4	eggs	4
1/2 cup	milk	125 mL
1/2 cup	unsalted butter, melted	125 mL
6 tbsp	pure maple syrup	90 mL
3/4 cup	dried cranberries	175 mL

These fabulous muffins are at once home-style and sophisticated.

Makes 12 muffins

- Preheat oven to 400°F (200°C)
- 12-cup muffin pan, greased

1. In a large bowl, whisk together cornmeal, flour blend, baking powder, baking soda, salt and xanthan gum.

2. In a medium bowl, whisk together brown sugar, eggs, milk, butter and maple syrup until well blended.

3. Add the egg mixture to the flour mixture and stir until just combined. Gently fold in cranberries.

4. Divide batter equally among prepared muffin cups.

5. Bake in preheated oven for 14 to 17 minutes or until tops are puffed and a toothpick inserted in the center comes out clean. Let cool in pan on a wire rack for 5 minutes, then transfer to the rack to cool.

Sweet Potato Polenta Muffins

1 cup	Brown Rice Flour Blend (see page 19)	250 mL
1 cup	stone-ground yellow cornmeal	250 mL
2 tsp	gluten-free baking powder	10 mL
1½ tsp	pumpkin pie spice	7 mL
½ tsp	baking soda	2 mL
½ tsp	salt	2 mL
½ tsp	xanthan gum	2 mL
3	eggs	3
¾ cup	packed light brown sugar	175 mL
¾ cup	puréed cooked sweet potato	175 mL
½ cup	vegetable oil	125 mL
1 tsp	vanilla extract	5 mL

Move over, pumpkin — these sweet potato muffins will have you (and everyone else) coming back for seconds and thirds.

Tip

Prepare the puréed sweet potato without milk and butter. Here's how to easily cook it in the microwave: Scrub sweet potatoes (about 2 medium for this recipe) and pierce each a few times with a fork. Place on a microwave-safe plate lined with a paper towel. Microwave on High, turning halfway through, for 4 to 5 minutes for the first potato plus 2 to 3 minutes for each additional potato. Let cool. Cut in half, scoop the flesh into a blender or food processor and purée until smooth.

Makes 12 muffins

- Preheat oven to 350°F (180°C)
- 12-cup muffin pan, greased

1. In a large bowl, whisk together flour blend, cornmeal, baking powder, pumpkin pie spice, baking soda, salt and xanthan gum.
2. In a medium bowl, vigorously whisk eggs. Whisk in brown sugar, sweet potato, oil and vanilla until blended.
3. Add the egg mixture to the flour mixture and stir until just blended.
4. Divide batter equally among prepared muffin cups.
5. Bake in preheated oven for 24 to 28 minutes or until a toothpick inserted in the center comes out clean. Let cool in pan on a wire rack for 5 minutes, then transfer to the rack to cool.

Parmesan Polenta Muffins

1¼ cups	Brown Rice Flour Blend (see page 19)	300 mL
1 cup	yellow cornmeal, preferably stone-ground	250 mL
1 cup	freshly grated Parmesan cheese, divided	250 mL
1 tbsp	gluten-free baking powder	15 mL
½ tsp	baking soda	2 mL
½ tsp	salt	2 mL
½ tsp	xanthan gum	2 mL
2 tbsp	granulated sugar	30 mL
1	egg	1
¼ cup	olive oil	60 mL
1 tsp	minced fresh rosemary	5 mL
1¼ cups	buttermilk	300 mL

Fresh rosemary, olive oil and a generous helping of Parmesan cheese add a savory edge and distinctive Italian flair to these scrumptious muffins.

Makes 16 muffins

- Preheat oven to 375°F (190°C)
- Two 12-cup muffin pans, 16 cups greased

1. In a large bowl, whisk together flour blend, cornmeal, ¾ cup (175 mL) of the cheese, baking powder, baking soda, salt and xanthan gum.
2. In a medium bowl, whisk together sugar, egg, oil and rosemary until well blended. Whisk in buttermilk until blended.
3. Add the buttermilk mixture to the flour mixture and stir until just blended.
4. Divide batter equally among prepared muffin cups. Sprinkle with the remaining cheese.
5. Bake in preheated oven for 20 to 25 minutes or until tops are golden and a toothpick inserted in the center comes out clean. Let cool in pans on a wire rack for 5 minutes, then transfer to the rack to cool slightly. Serve warm.

Jalapeño Jack Corn Muffins

1¼ cups	Brown Rice Flour Blend (see page 19)	300 mL
1 cup	yellow cornmeal	250 mL
1 tbsp	gluten-free baking powder	15 mL
1 tsp	ground cumin	5 mL
½ tsp	baking soda	2 mL
½ tsp	salt	2 mL
½ tsp	xanthan gum	2 mL
2 tbsp	granulated sugar	30 mL
1	egg	1
¼ cup	vegetable oil	60 mL
1¼ cups	buttermilk	300 mL
6 oz	Monterey Jack cheese, diced	175 g
1 tbsp	minced seeded jalapeño pepper	15 mL

These easy corn muffins will add a Southwestern kick to everything from roast chicken to black bean soup.

Makes 16 muffins

- Preheat oven to 375°F (190°C)
- Two 12-cup muffin pans, 16 cups greased

1. In a large bowl, whisk together flour blend, cornmeal, baking powder, cumin, baking soda, salt and xanthan gum.
2. In a medium bowl, whisk together sugar, egg and oil until well blended. Whisk in buttermilk until blended.
3. Add the egg mixture to the flour mixture and stir until just blended. Gently fold in cheese and jalapeño.
4. Divide batter equally among prepared muffin cups.
5. Bake in preheated oven for 20 to 25 minutes or until tops are golden and a toothpick inserted in the center comes out clean. Let cool in pans on a wire rack for 5 minutes, then transfer to the rack to cool slightly. Serve warm.

Fresh Corn Muffins with Thyme

1¼ cups	Brown Rice Flour Blend (see page 19)	300 mL
⅔ cup	yellow cornmeal	150 mL
½ cup	freshly grated Parmesan cheese	125 mL
2 tbsp	gluten-free baking powder	30 mL
¾ tsp	salt	3 mL
½ tsp	xanthan gum	2 mL
1	egg	1
2 tbsp	granulated sugar	30 mL
1 cup	milk	250 mL
⅓ cup	unsalted butter, melted	75 mL
2 tsp	minced fresh thyme (or 1 tsp/5 mL dried thyme)	10 mL
1 cup	fresh corn kernels	150 mL

These muffins are particularly delicious when made with sweet white corn, but yellow corn still produces delectable results. To remove the kernels from the cobs, hold each ear of corn upright on a flat surface and run a chef's knife along the cob, cutting downward, as close to the cob as possible.

Makes 12 muffins
- Preheat oven to 425°F (220°C)
- 12-cup muffin pan, greased

1. In a large bowl, whisk together flour blend, cornmeal, cheese, baking powder, salt and xanthan gum.
2. In a medium bowl, vigorously whisk egg. Whisk in sugar, milk, butter and thyme until well blended.
3. Add the egg mixture to the flour mixture and stir until just blended. Gently fold in corn.
4. Divide batter equally among prepared muffin cups.
5. Bake in preheated oven for 18 to 22 minutes or until a toothpick inserted in the center comes out clean. Let cool in pan on a wire rack for 5 minutes, then transfer to the rack to cool slightly. Serve warm.

Old-Fashioned Corn Muffins

1 cup	Brown Rice Flour Blend (see page 19)	250 mL
1 cup	yellow cornmeal	250 mL
2 tsp	gluten-free baking powder	10 mL
½ tsp	salt	2 mL
½ tsp	xanthan gum	2 mL
1	egg	1
3 tbsp	granulated sugar	45 mL
1 cup	milk	250 mL
¼ cup	vegetable oil	60 mL

Familiar as a worn-in pair of blue jeans, homemade corn muffins add something special to the dinner table — and lunch bag. Use the split muffins in place of sliced bread for delectable mini sandwiches.

Makes 12 muffins
- Preheat oven to 400°F (200°C)
- 12-cup muffin pan, greased

1. In a large bowl, whisk together flour blend, cornmeal, baking powder, salt and xanthan gum.
2. In a medium bowl, vigorously whisk egg. Whisk in sugar, milk and oil until well blended.
3. Add the egg mixture to the flour mixture and stir until just blended.
4. Divide batter equally among prepared muffin cups.
5. Bake in preheated oven for 20 to 25 minutes or until a toothpick inserted in the center comes out clean. Let cool in pan on a wire rack for 5 minutes, then transfer to the rack to cool slightly. Serve warm.

Calico Cornbread Muffins

1¼ cups	Brown Rice Flour Blend (see page 19)	300 mL
⅔ cup	yellow cornmeal	150 mL
2 tbsp	gluten-free baking powder	30 mL
1½ tsp	ground cumin	7 mL
¾ tsp	salt	3 mL
½ tsp	xanthan gum	2 mL
1	egg	1
3 tbsp	granulated sugar	45 mL
1 cup	milk	250 mL
⅓ cup	unsalted butter, melted	75 mL
¾ cup	grated sharp (old) Cheddar cheese	175 mL
⅔ cup	frozen (thawed) corn kernels	150 mL
⅓ cup	chopped red bell pepper	75 mL
¼ cup	chopped green onions (scallions)	60 mL

Makes 12 muffins

- Preheat oven to 425°F (220°C)
- 12-cup muffin pan, greased

1. In a large bowl, whisk together flour blend, cornmeal, baking powder, cumin, salt and xanthan gum.
2. In a medium bowl, vigorously whisk egg. Whisk in sugar, milk and butter until well blended.
3. Add the egg mixture to the flour mixture and stir until just blended. Gently fold in cheese, corn, red pepper and green onions.
4. Divide batter equally among prepared muffin cups.
5. Bake in preheated oven for 18 to 22 minutes or until a toothpick inserted in the center comes out clean. Let cool in pan on a wire rack for 5 minutes, then transfer to the rack to cool slightly. Serve warm.

Spicy, cheesy and moist, these cornbread muffins are great for dinner on a blustery autumn or winter evening, whether with chili or a big bowl of chicken noodle soup.

Irish Brown Bread Muffins

2 cups	Brown Rice Flour Blend (see page 19)	500 mL
¼ cup	rice bran	60 mL
2 tsp	gluten-free baking powder	10 mL
2 tsp	caraway seeds, crushed	10 mL
½ tsp	baking soda	2 mL
½ tsp	salt	2 mL
½ tsp	xanthan gum	2 mL
1	egg	1
¼ cup	vegetable oil	60 mL
¼ cup	dark (cooking) molasses	60 mL
1¼ cups	buttermilk	300 mL
⅔ cup	dried currants	150 mL

Makes 12 muffins

- Preheat oven to 350°F (180°C)
- 12-cup muffin pan, lined with paper liners

1. In a large bowl, whisk together flour blend, rice bran, baking powder, caraway seeds, baking soda, salt and xanthan gum.
2. In a medium bowl, whisk together egg, oil and molasses until well blended. Whisk in buttermilk until blended.
3. Add the egg mixture to the flour mixture and stir until just blended. Gently fold in currants.
4. Divide batter equally among prepared muffin cups.
5. Bake in preheated oven for 18 to 22 minutes or until a toothpick inserted in the center comes out clean. Let cool in pan on a wire rack for 5 minutes, then transfer to the rack to cool slightly. Serve warm.

Serve these next Saint Patrick's Day; everyone will love them, and because they taste just like the original, no one will guess that they are wheat-free.

Golden Olive Oil Muffins

1¾ cups	Brown Rice Flour Blend (see page 19)	425 mL
2 tsp	gluten-free baking powder	10 mL
1 tsp	salt	5 mL
½ tsp	xanthan gum	2 mL
½ tsp	ground coriander	2 mL
½ tsp	baking soda	2 mL
½ cup	granulated sugar	125 mL
2	eggs	2
1 cup	buttermilk	250 mL
½ cup	extra virgin olive oil	125 mL
2 tbsp	finely grated lemon zest	30 mL

These are sophisticated, not-too-sweet muffins. I prefer extra virgin olive oil here, but you can use either virgin or regular. Extra virgin yields a fruitier, more pronounced olive oil flavor; regular olive oil results in a lighter taste overall.

Makes 12 muffins

- Preheat oven to 350°F (180°C)
- 12-cup muffin pan, greased

1. In a large bowl, whisk together flour blend, baking powder, salt, xanthan gum, coriander and baking soda.
2. In a medium bowl, whisk together sugar, eggs, buttermilk, oil and lemon zest until well blended.
3. Add the egg mixture to the flour mixture and stir until just blended.
4. Divide batter equally among prepared muffin cups.
5. Bake in preheated oven for 25 to 30 minutes or until a toothpick inserted in the center comes out clean. Let cool in pan on a wire rack for 5 minutes, then transfer to the rack to cool slightly or serve warm.

Scallion Curry Muffins

1½ cups	Brown Rice Flour Blend (see page 19)	375 mL
¾ cup	yellow cornmeal	175 mL
1 tbsp	gluten-free baking powder	15 mL
1 tbsp	mild curry powder	15 mL
½ tsp	baking soda	2 mL
½ tsp	salt	2 mL
½ tsp	xanthan gum	2 mL
2 tbsp	granulated sugar	30 mL
1	egg	1
¼ cup	vegetable oil	60 mL
1¼ cups	plain yogurt	300 mL
¾ cup	chopped green onions (scallions)	175 mL

The flavors of India add complexity and exoticism to these muffins.

Makes 16 muffins

- Preheat oven to 375°F (190°C)
- Two 12-cup muffin pans, 16 cups greased

1. In a large bowl, whisk together flour blend, cornmeal, baking powder, curry powder, salt and xanthan gum.
2. In a medium bowl, whisk together sugar, egg and oil until well blended. Whisk in yogurt until blended.
3. Add the egg mixture to the flour mixture and stir until just blended. Gently fold in green onions.
4. Divide batter equally among prepared muffin cups.
5. Bake in preheated oven for 20 to 25 minutes or until tops are golden and a toothpick inserted in the center comes out clean. Let cool in pans on a wire rack for 5 minutes, then transfer to the rack to cool.

Scallion Goat Cheese Muffins

2 cups	Brown Rice Flour Blend (see page 19)	500 mL
4 tsp	gluten-free baking powder	20 mL
1/2 tsp	salt	2 mL
1/2 tsp	xanthan gum	2 mL
1	egg	1
1 tbsp	granulated sugar	15 mL
1 cup	milk	250 mL
1/4 cup	unsalted butter, melted	60 mL
3/4 cup	chopped green onions (scallions)	175 mL
3 oz	mild creamy goat cheese	90 g
2 tbsp	sesame seeds	30 mL

Makes 12 muffins

- Preheat oven to 375°F (190°C)
- 12-cup muffin pan, greased

1. In a large bowl, whisk together flour blend, baking powder, salt and xanthan gum.
2. In a medium bowl, vigorously whisk egg. Whisk in sugar, milk and butter until well blended.
3. Add the egg mixture to the flour mixture and stir until just blended. Gently fold in green onions and cheese.
4. Divide batter equally among prepared muffin cups. Sprinkle with sesame seeds.
5. Bake in preheated oven for 18 to 22 minutes or until a toothpick inserted in the center comes out clean. Let cool in pan on a wire rack for 5 minutes, then transfer to the rack to cool slightly. Serve warm.

The assertive taste of fresh green onions (also known as scallions) is the perfect counterpoint to the tangy flavor of goat cheese.

Bacon Scallion Muffins

2 cups	Brown Rice Flour Blend (see page 19)	500 mL
1 tbsp	gluten-free baking powder	15 mL
1 tsp	baking soda	5 mL
3/4 tsp	xanthan gum	3 mL
1/2 tsp	salt	2 mL
1/4 tsp	freshly ground black pepper	1 mL
2 tbsp	granulated sugar	30 mL
1	egg	1
1 cup	milk	250 mL
1/4 cup	vegetable oil	60 mL
3/4 cup	crumbled cooked bacon	175 mL
1/2 cup	chopped green onions (scallions)	125 mL

Makes 12 muffins

- Preheat oven to 350°F (180°C)
- 12-cup muffin pan, greased

1. In a large bowl, whisk together flour blend, baking powder, baking soda, xanthan gum, salt and pepper.
2. In a medium bowl, whisk together sugar, egg, milk and oil until well blended.
3. Add the egg mixture to the flour mixture and stir until just blended. Gently fold in bacon and green onions.
4. Divide batter equally among prepared muffin cups.
5. Bake in preheated oven for 20 to 25 minutes or until a toothpick inserted in the center comes out clean. Let cool in pan on a wire rack for 5 minutes, then transfer to the rack to cool slightly. Serve warm.

Crumbled bacon and scallions make an irresistible pairing in these faintly sweet muffins.

BLT Muffins

1¾ cups + 2 tbsp	Brown Rice Flour Blend (see page 19)	455 mL
2¼ tsp	gluten-free baking powder	11 mL
½ tsp	baking soda	2 mL
½ tsp	salt	2 mL
½ tsp	xanthan gum	2 mL
¼ cup	cold unsalted butter, cut into small pieces	45 mL
1	egg	1
¾ cup	buttermilk	175 mL
2 tsp	Dijon mustard	10 mL
¾ cup	crumbled cooked bacon	175 mL
½ cup	drained oil-packed sun-dried tomatoes, chopped	125 mL
¼ cup	fresh flat-leaf (Italian) parsley leaves, chopped	60 mL

I'm taking some liberties with the BLT eponym here, swapping fresh parsley for lettuce (I'm all for innovation, but lettuce muffins sound dreadful!). I'm certain you'll forgive me once you try these — the interplay of familiar flavors is quintessentially comforting.

Makes 12 muffins

- Preheat oven to 375°F (190°C)
- Food processor
- 12-cup muffin pan, greased

1. In food processor, pulse flour blend, baking powder, baking soda, salt and xanthan gum until combined. Add butter and pulse until mixture resembles bread crumbs. Transfer to a large bowl.

2. In a small bowl, whisk together egg, buttermilk and mustard until well blended.

3. Add the egg mixture to the flour mixture and stir until just blended. Gently fold in bacon, tomatoes and parsley.

4. Divide batter equally among prepared muffin cups.

5. Bake in preheated oven for 22 to 27 minutes or until a toothpick inserted in the center comes out clean. Let cool in pan on a wire rack for 5 minutes, then transfer to the rack to cool slightly. Serve warm.

Canadian Bacon Muffins with Cheese and Chives

2 cups	Brown Rice Flour Blend (see page 19)	500 mL
4 tsp	gluten-free baking powder	20 mL
1/2 tsp	salt	2 mL
1/2 tsp	xanthan gum	2 mL
1/8 tsp	freshly ground black pepper	0.5 mL
1	egg	1
1 tbsp	granulated sugar	15 mL
1 cup	milk	250 mL
1/4 cup	unsalted butter, melted	60 mL
1 cup	shredded sharp (old) Cheddar cheese	250 mL
3/4 cup	chopped cooked Canadian bacon	175 mL
2 tbsp	minced chives	30 mL

This is one of my favorite savory breakfasts, especially when I am on the run (i.e., most days).

Makes 12 muffins

- Preheat oven to 375°F (190°C)
- 12-cup muffin pan, greased

1. In a large bowl, whisk together flour blend, baking powder, salt, xanthan gum and pepper.
2. In a medium bowl, vigorously whisk egg. Whisk in sugar, milk and butter until well blended.
3. Add the egg mixture to the flour mixture and stir until just blended. Gently fold in cheese, bacon and chives.
4. Divide batter equally among prepared muffin cups.
5. Bake in preheated oven for 18 to 22 minutes or until a toothpick inserted in the center comes out clean. Let cool in pan on a wire rack for 5 minutes, then transfer to the rack to cool slightly. Serve warm.

Roasted Pepper Feta Muffins

2 cups	Brown Rice Flour Blend (see page 19)	500 mL
4 tsp	gluten-free baking powder	20 mL
1 1/2 tsp	dried oregano	7 mL
1/2 tsp	salt	2 mL
1/2 tsp	xanthan gum	2 mL
1/4 tsp	freshly cracked black pepper	1 mL
1	egg	1
1 cup	milk	250 mL
1/4 cup	unsalted butter, melted	60 mL
3/4 cup	chopped drained roasted red bell peppers, patted dry	175 mL
3/4 cup	crumbled feta cheese	175 mL

It's the combination of briny feta and roasted peppers that really sells these addictive muffins. Adding a generous amount of oregano to the batter heightens the vibrancy of the feta.

Makes 12 muffins

- Preheat oven to 375°F (190°C)
- 12-cup muffin pan, greased

1. In a large bowl, whisk together flour blend, baking powder, oregano, salt, xanthan gum and pepper.
2. In a medium bowl, vigorously whisk egg. Whisk in milk and butter until well blended.
3. Add the egg mixture to the flour mixture and stir until just blended. Gently fold in roasted peppers and cheese.
4. Divide batter equally among prepared muffin cups.
5. Bake in preheated oven for 18 to 22 minutes or until a toothpick inserted in the center comes out clean. Let cool in pan on a wire rack for 5 minutes, then transfer to the rack to cool slightly. Serve warm.

Mushroom Feta Muffins

1 tbsp	olive oil	15 mL
8 oz	cremini mushrooms, coarsely chopped	250 g
1 cup	almond flour	250 mL
1 tsp	gluten-free baking powder	5 mL
1/4 tsp	salt	1 mL
1/4 tsp	freshly ground black pepper	1 mL
4	eggs	4
1/3 cup	small-curd cottage cheese	75 mL
1/4 cup	freshly grated Parmesan cheese	60 mL
3 tbsp	milk	45 mL
3/4 cup	crumbled feta cheese	175 mL
1/4 cup	chopped green onions (scallions)	60 mL

These incredible mushroom muffins are a cross between a quick bread and a quiche, in large part because of the addition of cottage cheese to the batter.

Makes 9 muffins

- 12-cup muffin pan, 9 cups greased

1. In a large skillet, heat oil over medium-high heat. Sauté mushrooms for 4 to 5 minutes or until starting to brown and liquid has evaporated. Remove from heat and let cool.
2. Preheat oven to 400°F (200°C).
3. In a large bowl, whisk together flour, baking powder, salt and pepper.
4. In a medium bowl, whisk together eggs, cottage cheese, Parmesan and milk until well blended.
5. Add the egg mixture to the flour mixture and stir until just blended. Fold in sautéed mushrooms, feta and green onions.
6. Divide batter equally among prepared muffin cups.
7. Bake for 23 to 25 minutes or until tops are golden and a toothpick inserted in the center comes out clean. Let cool in pan on a wire rack for 5 minutes, then transfer to the rack to cool slightly. Serve warm.

Fresh Herb Ricotta Muffins

1 1/2 cups	Brown Rice Flour Blend (see page 19)	375 mL
1 tbsp	gluten-free baking powder	15 mL
1/2 tsp	salt	2 mL
1/2 tsp	xanthan gum	2 mL
1/8 tsp	freshly ground black pepper	0.5 mL
1 tbsp	granulated sugar	75 mL
2	eggs	2
2/3 cup	buttermilk	150 mL
1/2 cup	whole-milk ricotta cheese	125 mL
3 tbsp	unsalted butter, melted	45 mL
1/2 cup	chopped walnuts, toasted	125 mL
1/4 cup	chopped assorted fresh herbs, such as chives, mint, basil, parsley, tarragon and cilantro	60 mL

Serve these alongside cold sliced deli chicken, ham or roast beef for an easy summer lunch or supper.

Makes 12 muffins

- Preheat oven to 350°F (180°C)
- 12-cup muffin pan, greased

1. In a large bowl, whisk together flour blend, baking powder, salt, xanthan gum and pepper.
2. In a medium bowl, whisk together sugar, eggs, buttermilk, cheese and butter until well blended.
3. Add the egg mixture to the flour mixture and stir until just blended. Gently fold in walnuts and herbs.
4. Divide batter equally among prepared muffin cups.
5. Bake in preheated oven for 23 to 27 minutes or until a toothpick inserted in the center comes out clean. Let cool in pan on a wire rack for 5 minutes, then transfer to the rack to cool slightly. Serve warm.

Ham and Cheddar Muffins

1³/₄ + 2 tbsp	Brown Rice Flour Blend (see page 19)	455 mL
2¹/₄ tsp	gluten-free baking powder	11 mL
¹/₂ tsp	baking soda	2 mL
¹/₂ tsp	salt	2 mL
¹/₂ tsp	xanthan gum	2 mL
3 tbsp	cold unsalted butter, cut into small pieces	45 mL
4 oz	sharp (old) Cheddar cheese, shredded	125 g
1	egg	1
³/₄ cup	buttermilk	175 mL
2 tsp	coarse-grained mustard	10 mL
³/₄ cup	chopped cooked ham	175 mL

Your lunch bag may never be the same again: these scrumptious muffins are quite simple to put together.

Makes 12 muffins

- Preheat oven to 375°F (190°C)
- Food processor
- 12-cup muffin pan, greased

1. In food processor, pulse flour blend, baking powder, baking soda, salt and xanthan gum until combined. Add butter and pulse until mixture resembles bread crumbs. Add cheese and pulse until combined. Transfer to a large bowl.
2. In a small bowl, whisk together egg, buttermilk and mustard until well blended.
3. Add the egg mixture to the flour mixture and stir until just blended. Gently fold in ham.
4. Divide batter equally among prepared muffin cups.
5. Bake in preheated oven for 22 to 27 minutes or until a toothpick inserted in the center comes out clean. Let cool in pan on a wire rack for 5 minutes, then transfer to the rack to cool slightly. Serve warm.

Parmesan Risotto Muffins

1¹/₄ cups	Brown Rice Flour Blend (see page 19)	300 mL
2 tsp	gluten-free baking powder	10 mL
¹/₂ tsp	salt	2 mL
¹/₂ tsp	garlic powder	2 mL
¹/₄ tsp	xanthan gum	1 mL
2	eggs	2
1 cup	milk	250 mL
¹/₄ cup	unsalted butter, melted	60 mL
1 cup	cold cooked short-grain brown rice	250 mL
1 cup	freshly grated Parmesan cheese	250 mL
¹/₄ cup	minced green onions (scallions)	60 mL

Risotto, the ultimate comfort food of Milan, heads to America in a muffin revamp of a classic. Parmesan brings a delectable umami element.

Makes 12 muffins

- Preheat oven to 400°F (200°C)
- 12-cup muffin pan, greased

1. In a large bowl, whisk together flour blend, baking powder, salt, garlic powder and xanthan gum.
2. In a medium bowl, whisk together eggs, milk and butter until well blended.
3. Add the egg mixture to the flour mixture and stir until just blended. Gently fold in rice, cheese and green onions.
4. Divide batter among prepared muffin cups.
5. Bake in preheated oven for 20 to 25 minutes or until tops are golden and a toothpick inserted in the center comes out clean. Let cool in pan on a wire rack for 5 minutes, then transfer to the rack to cool slightly. Serve warm.

Rosemary Parmesan Muffins

2 cups	Brown Rice Flour Blend (see page 19)	500 mL
1 cup	finely grated Parmesan cheese, divided	250 mL
4 tsp	gluten-free baking powder	20 mL
1/2 tsp	salt	2 mL
1/2 tsp	xanthan gum	2 mL
1	egg	1
2	cloves garlic, minced	2
2 tsp	minced fresh rosemary	10 mL
1 tbsp	granulated sugar	15 mL
1 cup	milk	250 mL
3 tbsp	unsalted butter, melted	45 mL
1 tbsp	olive oil	15 mL

These substantial muffins are scented with fresh rosemary, spiked with garlic and permeated with salty-nutty notes from freshly grated Parmesan cheese. Don't be at all surprised if they steal the show at your next dinner party.

Makes 12 muffins

- Preheat oven to 375°F (190°C)
- 12-cup muffin pan, greased

1. In a large bowl, whisk together flour blend, 2/3 cup (150 mL) of the cheese, baking powder, salt and xanthan gum.
2. In a medium bowl, vigorously whisk egg. Whisk in garlic, rosemary, sugar, milk, butter and oil until well blended.
3. Add the egg mixture to the flour mixture and stir until just blended.
4. Divide batter equally among prepared muffin cups. Sprinkle with the remaining cheese.
5. Bake in preheated oven for 18 to 22 minutes or until a toothpick inserted in the center comes out clean. Let cool in pan on a wire rack for 5 minutes, then transfer to the rack to cool slightly. Serve warm.

Fresh Herb Romano Muffins

2 cups	Brown Rice Flour Blend (see page 19)	500 mL
1 cup	finely grated Romano cheese, divided	250 mL
4 tsp	gluten-free baking powder	20 mL
1/2 tsp	salt	2 mL
1/2 tsp	xanthan gum	2 mL
1	egg	1
1/4 cup	chopped assorted fresh herbs, such as parsley, chives, oregano and tarragon	60 mL
1 tbsp	granulated sugar	15 mL
1 cup	milk	250 mL
1/4 cup	olive oil	60 mL

These muffins take their flavor cues from the herb and Romano focaccia at one of my favorite Italian restaurants.

Makes 12 muffins

- Preheat oven to 375°F (190°C)
- 12-cup muffin pan, greased

1. In a large bowl, whisk together flour, 2/3 cup (150 mL) of the cheese, baking powder, salt and xanthan gum.
2. In a medium bowl, vigorously whisk egg. Whisk in herbs, sugar, milk and oil until well blended.
3. Add the egg mixture to the flour mixture and stir until just blended.
4. Divide batter equally among prepared muffin cups. Sprinkle with the remaining cheese.
5. Bake in preheated oven for 18 to 22 minutes or until a toothpick inserted in the center comes out clean. Let cool in pan on a wire rack for 5 minutes, then transfer to the rack to cool slightly. Serve warm.

Smoked Paprika and Manchego Muffins

2 cups	Brown Rice Flour Blend (see page 19)	500 mL
1 cup	finely shredded manchego cheese, divided	250 mL
4 tsp	gluten-free baking powder	20 mL
2$\frac{1}{2}$ tsp	sweet smoked paprika (pimentón dulce)	12 mL
1 tsp	ground cumin	5 mL
$\frac{1}{2}$ tsp	salt	2 mL
$\frac{1}{2}$ tsp	xanthan gum	2 mL
$\frac{1}{4}$ tsp	garlic powder	1 mL
1	egg	1
1 tbsp	packed light brown sugar	15 mL
1 cup	milk	250 mL
$\frac{1}{4}$ cup	olive oil	60 mL

Here, smoked paprika, cumin and garlic contribute an alluring smoky spiciness, a vibrant foil to richly flavored manchego cheese. In sum, they transform an ordinary savory muffin into a simply spectacular dinner bread.

Tip
Romano, another sheep's milk cheese, may be substituted for the manchego.

Makes 12 muffins

- Preheat oven to 375°F (190°C)
- 12-cup muffin pan, greased

1. In a large bowl, whisk together flour blend, $\frac{2}{3}$ cup (150 mL) of the cheese, baking powder, paprika, cumin, salt, xanthan gum and garlic powder.
2. In a medium bowl, vigorously whisk egg. Whisk in brown sugar, milk and oil until well blended.
3. Add the egg mixture to the flour mixture and stir until just blended.
4. Divide batter equally among prepared muffin cups. Sprinkle with the remaining cheese.
5. Bake in preheated oven for 18 to 22 minutes or until a toothpick inserted in the center comes out clean. Let cool in pan on a wire rack for 5 minutes, then transfer to the rack to cool slightly. Serve warm.

Blue Cheese Toasted Pecan Muffins

2 cups	Brown Rice Flour Blend (see page 19)	500 mL
4 tsp	gluten-free baking powder	20 mL
1/2 tsp	salt	2 mL
1/2 tsp	xanthan gum	2 mL
1/8 tsp	freshly ground black pepper	0.5 mL
1	egg	1
1 tbsp	granulated sugar	15 mL
1 cup	milk	250 mL
1/4 cup	unsalted butter, melted	60 mL
3 oz	blue cheese, crumbled	90 g
2/3 cup	chopped pecans, toasted	150 mL

Blue cheese aficionados will flip for these savory muffins. Crunchy pecans are a deliciously de rigueur accompaniment.

Makes 12 muffins

- Preheat oven to 375°F (190°C)
- 12-cup muffin pan, greased

1. In a large bowl, whisk together flour blend, baking powder, salt, xanthan gum and pepper.
2. In a medium bowl, vigorously whisk egg. Whisk in sugar, milk and butter until well blended.
3. Add the egg mixture to the flour mixture and stir until just blended. Gently fold in blue cheese and pecans.
4. Divide batter equally among prepared muffin cups.
5. Bake in preheated oven for 18 to 22 minutes or until a toothpick inserted in the center comes out clean. Let cool in pan on a wire rack for 5 minutes, then transfer to the rack to cool slightly. Serve warm.

Smoked Gouda Chive Muffins

1 1/2 cups	Brown Rice Flour Blend (see page 19)	375 mL
3/4 cup	yellow cornmeal	175 mL
1 tbsp	gluten-free baking powder	15 mL
1/2 tsp	baking soda	2 mL
1/2 tsp	salt	2 mL
1/2 tsp	xanthan gum	2 mL
1/8 tsp	freshly ground black pepper	0.5 mL
1 tbsp	packed light brown sugar	15 mL
1	egg	1
1/4 cup	vegetable oil	60 mL
1 1/4 cups	buttermilk	300 mL
6 oz	smoked Gouda cheese, diced	175 g
3 tbsp	minced fresh chives	45 mL

In this terrific side for roast pork loin or roast chicken, smoky cheese and vibrant chives are stirred into tender buttermilk muffins.

Makes 16 muffins

- Preheat oven to 375°F (190°C)
- Two 12-cup muffin pans, 16 cups greased

1. In a large bowl, whisk together flour blend, cornmeal, baking powder, baking soda, salt, xanthan gum and pepper.
2. In a medium bowl, whisk together brown sugar, egg and oil until well blended. Whisk in buttermilk until blended.
3. Add the egg mixture to the flour mixture and stir until just blended. Gently fold in cheese and chives.
4. Divide batter equally among prepared muffin cups.
5. Bake in preheated oven for 20 to 25 minutes or until tops are golden and a toothpick inserted in the center comes out clean. Let cool in pan on a wire rack for 5 minutes, then transfer to the rack to cool slightly. Serve warm.

Cheddar Dill Muffins

1³/₄ cup + 2 tbsp	Brown Rice Flour Blend (see page 19)	455 mL
2¹/₄ tsp	gluten-free baking powder	11 mL
1 tsp	dried dillweed	5 mL
¹/₂ tsp	baking soda	2 mL
¹/₂ tsp	salt	2 mL
¹/₂ tsp	xanthan gum	2 mL
3 tbsp	cold unsalted butter, cut into small pieces	45 mL
4 oz	sharp (old) Cheddar cheese, shredded	125 g
1	egg	1
³/₄ cup	buttermilk	175 mL

These tangy Cheddar muffins are always appealing, so they're a fail-safe option for a supper bread.

Makes 12 muffins

- Preheat oven to 375°F (190°C)
- Food processor
- 12-cup muffin pan, greased

1. In food processor, pulse flour blend, baking powder, dill, baking soda, salt and xanthan gum until combined. Add butter and pulse until mixture resembles bread crumbs. Add cheese and pulse until combined. Transfer to a large bowl.
2. In a small bowl, whisk together egg and buttermilk until well blended.
3. Add the egg mixture to the flour mixture and stir until just blended.
4. Divide batter equally among prepared muffin cups.
5. Bake in preheated oven for 22 to 27 minutes or until a toothpick inserted in the center comes out clean. Let cool in pan on a wire rack for 5 minutes, then transfer to the rack to cool slightly. Serve warm.

Goat Cheese, Chive and Walnut Muffins

2 cups	Brown Rice Flour Blend (see page 19)	500 mL
1 tbsp	gluten-free baking powder	15 mL
1 tsp	baking soda	5 mL
³/₄ tsp	xanthan gum	3 mL
¹/₂ tsp	salt	2 mL
2 tbsp	granulated sugar	30 mL
1	egg	1
1 cup	milk	250 mL
¹/₄ cup	vegetable oil	60 mL
1 cup	chopped walnuts, toasted	250 mL
1 cup	crumbled goat cheese	250 mL
3 tbsp	minced fresh chives	45 mL

These savory muffins balance nutty, pungent, sweet and creamy flavors.

Makes 12 muffins

- Preheat oven to 350°F (180°C)
- 12-cup muffin pan, greased

1. In a large bowl, whisk together flour blend, baking powder, baking soda, xanthan gum and salt.
2. In a medium bowl, whisk together sugar, egg, milk and oil until well blended.
3. Add the egg mixture to the flour mixture and stir until blended. Gently fold in walnuts, cheese and chives.
4. Divide batter equally among prepared muffin cups.
5. Bake in preheated oven for 20 to 25 minutes or until a toothpick inserted in the center comes out clean. Let cool in pan on a wire rack for 5 minutes, then transfer to the rack to cool slightly. Serve warm.

Mediterranean Muffins with Olives and Sun-Dried Tomatoes

1 cup	almond flour	250 mL
1 tsp	gluten-free baking powder	5 mL
1/2 tsp	salt	2 mL
4	eggs	4
1 cup	small-curd cottage cheese	250 mL
3/4 cup	finely grated Parmesan cheese	175 mL
1/4 cup	milk	60 mL
1/4 cup	chopped drained oil-packed sun-dried tomatoes	60 mL
1/4 cup	pitted kalamata olives, finely chopped	60 mL
1/4 cup	fresh basil leaves, chopped	60 mL

The ripe, salty flavors of kalamata olives and the sweetness of sun-dried tomatoes combine to make a rare treat for those who appreciate their dispanctive qualities. Miniature meals unto themselves, these piquant muffins will keep well for several days if covered and stored in the refrigerator.

Makes 9 muffins

- Preheat oven to 400°F (200°C)
- 12-cup muffin pan, 9 cups lined with paper liners

1. In a large bowl, whisk together almond flour, baking powder and salt.
2. In a medium bowl, whisk together eggs, cottage cheese, Parmesan and milk until well blended.
3. Add the egg mixture to the flour mixture and stir until just blended. Gently fold in tomatoes, olives and basil.
4. Divide batter equally among prepared muffin cups.
5. Bake in preheated oven for 30 to 35 minutes or until tops are golden brown and a toothpick inserted in the center comes out clean. Let cool in pan on a wire rack for 5 minutes, then transfer to the rack to cool slightly. Serve warm.

Green Olive, Orange and Almond Muffins

2 cups	Brown Rice Flour Blend (see page 19)	500 mL
4 tsp	gluten-free baking powder	20 mL
1/2 tsp	dried oregano	2 mL
1/2 tsp	salt	2 mL
1/2 tsp	xanthan gum	2 mL
1	egg	1
1 cup	milk	250 mL
1/4 cup	olive oil	60 mL
1 tbsp	finely grated orange zest	15 mL
2/3 cup	pitted green olives, chopped	150 mL
1/2 cup	sliced almonds, toasted	125 mL

Here's a great Spanish-inspired accompaniment for roast chicken or the perfect bread to bring to a potluck feast.

Makes 12 muffins

- Preheat oven to 375°F (190°C)
- 12-cup muffin pan, greased

1. In a large bowl, whisk together flour blend, baking powder, oregano, salt and xanthan gum.

2. In a medium bowl, vigorously whisk egg. Whisk in milk, oil and orange zest until well blended.

3. Add the egg mixture to the flour mixture and stir until just blended. Gently fold in olives and almonds.

4. Divide batter equally among prepared muffin cups.

5. Bake in preheated oven for 18 to 22 minutes or until a toothpick inserted in the center comes out clean. Let cool in pan on a wire rack for 5 minutes, then transfer to the rack to cool slightly. Serve warm.

Sun-Dried Tomato Basil Muffins

2 cups	Brown Rice Flour Blend (see page 19)	500 mL
1 cup	finely grated Parmesan cheese, divided	250 mL
4 tsp	gluten-free baking powder	20 mL
2 tsp	dried basil	10 mL
1/2 tsp	salt	2 mL
1/2 tsp	xanthan gum	2 mL
1	egg	1
1 tbsp	granulated sugar	15 mL
1 cup	milk	250 mL
1/4 cup	olive oil	60 mL
1/2 cup	chopped drained oil-packed sun-dried tomatoes	125 mL

Thanks to a few humble additions — sun-dried tomatoes, basil and Parmesan cheese — these supper muffins have real pizzazz. Best of all, they require little more than a quick bit of chopping and mixing.

Makes 12 muffins

- Preheat oven to 375°F (190°C)
- 12-cup muffin pan, greased

1. In a large bowl, whisk together flour blend, 2/3 cup (150 mL) of the cheese, baking powder, basil, salt and xanthan gum.

2. In a medium bowl, vigorously whisk egg. Whisk in sugar, milk and oil until well blended.

3. Add the egg mixture to the flour mixture and stir until just blended. Gently fold in tomatoes.

4. Divide batter equally among prepared muffin cups. Sprinkle with the remaining cheese.

5. Bake in preheated oven for 18 to 22 minutes or until a toothpick inserted in the center comes out clean. Let cool in pan on a wire rack for 5 minutes, then transfer to the rack to cool slightly. Serve warm.

Pizza Muffins

1³/₄ cup + 2 tbsp	Brown Rice Flour Blend (see page 19)	455 mL
2¹/₄ tsp	gluten-free baking powder	11 mL
1 tsp	dried basil	5 mL
¹/₂ tsp	baking soda	2 mL
¹/₂ tsp	salt	2 mL
¹/₂ tsp	xanthan gum	2 mL
¹/₈ tsp	freshly ground black pepper	0.5 mL
3 tbsp	cold unsalted butter, cut into small pieces	45 mL
¹/₂ cup	coarsely grated Parmesan cheese	125 mL
1	egg	1
³/₄ cup	buttermilk	175 mL
2 oz	pepperoni (about 24 small slices), chopped	60 g
¹/₂ cup	marinara sauce	125 mL

The appeal of these muffins — each a pint-size pizza unto itself — requires little to no explanation. Kids of all ages love them.

Makes 12 muffins

- Preheat oven to 375°F (190°C)
- Food processor
- 12-cup muffin pan, greased

1. In food processor, pulse flour blend, baking powder, basil, baking soda, salt, xanthan gum and pepper until combined. Add butter and pulse until mixture resembles bread crumbs. Add cheese and pulse until combined. Transfer to a large bowl.

2. In a small bowl, whisk together egg and buttermilk until well blended.

3. Add the egg mixture to the flour mixture and stir until just blended. Gently fold in pepperoni.

4. Divide half the batter equally among prepared muffin cups. Spoon 2 tsp (10 mL) marinara sauce into the center of each cup. Top with the remaining batter.

5. Bake in preheated oven for 22 to 27 minutes or until tops spring back when touched. Let cool in pan on a wire rack for 5 minutes, then transfer to the rack to cool slightly. Serve warm.

Jerked Ham Corn Muffins

1 cup	Brown Rice Flour Blend (see page 19)	250 mL
1 cup	yellow cornmeal	250 mL
1½ tsp	Jamaican jerk seasoning	7 mL
2 tsp	gluten-free baking powder	10 mL
½ tsp	salt	2 mL
½ tsp	xanthan gum	2 mL
1	egg	1
2 tbsp	packed light brown sugar	45 mL
1 cup	milk	250 mL
¼ cup	vegetable oil	60 mL
1 cup	chopped cooked ham	250 mL

Find a good-quality jerk spice seasoning and it's like Caribbean magic. You can make a range of amazing island-inspired dishes — like these delectable muffins — in a flash.

Makes 12 muffins

- Preheat oven to 400°F (200°C)
- 12-cup muffin pan, greased

1. In a large bowl, whisk together flour blend, cornmeal, jerk seasoning, baking powder, salt and xanthan gum.

2. In a medium bowl, vigorously whisk egg. Whisk in brown sugar, milk and oil until well blended.

3. Add the egg mixture to the flour mixture and stir until just blended. Gently fold in ham.

4. Divide batter equally among prepared muffin cups.

5. Bake in preheated oven for 20 to 25 minutes or until a toothpick inserted in the center comes out clean. Let cool in pan on a wire rack for 5 minutes, then transfer to the rack to cool slightly. Serve warm.

Vegan Muffins

● ●

Like many people, I had my doubts about vegan baking. Toothsome muffins, breads, cookies and cakes without eggs and dairy? It sounded unlikely, if not impossible. But then I put my skepticism to the test by baking a batch of vegan muffins from a favorite vegetarian magazine. I was delighted and amazed by their ease and undeniable deliciousness; I was hooked, and I'm certain you will be too, once you give any of these muffins a try. These are good times to venture into vegan muffin-making. What might have been considered elusive ingredients a few years ago — non-dairy milk, soy yogurt and ground flax seeds — are now readily available. Tasting is believing, so gather a whisk and bowl and get baking.

continued…

Apple Crumb Muffins

Topping

1/4 cup	all-purpose flour	60 mL
1/4 cup	packed light brown sugar	60 mL
1/2 tsp	ground cinnamon	2 mL
3 tbsp	vegetable oil	45 mL

Muffins

1 1/2 cups	all-purpose flour	375 mL
1 1/2 tsp	baking powder	7 mL
1 tsp	ground cinnamon	5 mL
3/4 tsp	baking soda	3 mL
1/2 tsp	salt	2 mL
1/2 tsp	ground allspice	2 mL
1/4 tsp	ground nutmeg	1 mL
1/3 cup	granulated sugar	75 mL
3/4 cup	vanilla-flavored soy yogurt	175 mL
3/4 cup	unsweetened apple juice	175 mL
1/3 cup	vegetable oil	75 mL
1 tsp	vanilla extract	5 mL

Moist and delectable, these homey muffins — reminiscent of apple streusel pie — have a lovely balance of fall flavors. An equal amount of pears can be used in place of the apples.

Makes 12 muffins

- Preheat oven to 400°F (200°C)
- 12-cup muffin pan, greased

1. *Topping:* In a small bowl, combine flour, brown sugar and cinnamon. Drizzle with oil, tossing with a fork until crumbly. Set aside.
2. *Muffins:* In a large bowl, whisk together flour, baking powder, cinnamon, baking soda, salt, allspice and nutmeg.
3. In a medium bowl, whisk together sugar, yogurt, apple juice, oil and vanilla until well blended.
4. Add the yogurt mixture to the flour mixture and stir until just blended.
5. Divide batter equally among prepared muffin cups. Sprinkle with topping.
6. Bake in preheated oven for 18 to 22 minutes or until tops are golden brown and a toothpick inserted in the center comes out clean. Let cool in pan on a wire rack for 5 minutes, then transfer to the rack to cool.

Applesauce Raisin Muffins

2 cups	all-purpose flour	500 mL
2 tsp	baking powder	10 mL
1 tsp	ground cinnamon	5 mL
1/2 tsp	ground allspice	2 mL
1/2 tsp	baking soda	2 mL
1/2 tsp	salt	2 mL
2/3 cup	granulated sugar	150 mL
1 1/3 cups	unsweetened applesauce	325 mL
1/3 cup	vegetable oil	75 mL
1 tsp	vanilla extract	5 mL
1/2 cup	raisins	125 mL

Whether you use store-bought applesauce or make your own, this pure comfort muffin will make it hard to stop after just one.

Makes 12 muffins

- Preheat oven to 400°F (200°C)
- 12-cup muffin pan, greased

1. In a large bowl, whisk together flour, baking powder, cinnamon, allspice, baking soda and salt.
2. In a medium bowl, whisk together sugar, applesauce, oil and vanilla until well blended.
3. Add the applesauce mixture to the flour mixture and stir until just blended. Gently fold in raisins.
4. Divide batter equally among prepared muffin cups.
5. Bake in preheated oven for 25 to 28 minutes or until tops are golden brown and a toothpick inserted in the center comes out clean. Let cool in pan on a wire rack for 5 minutes, then transfer to the rack to cool.

Caramel Apple Muffins

1 cup	shredded apples	250 mL
1 cup	raisins	250 mL
1 cup	packed dark brown sugar	250 mL
1/2 cup	vegan margarine	125 mL
1 tsp	ground cinnamon	5 mL
1 tsp	ground nutmeg	5 mL
1/4 tsp	ground cloves	1 mL
1 3/4 cups	all-purpose flour	425 mL
2 tsp	pumpkin pie spice	10 mL
1 tsp	baking powder	5 mL
1/4 tsp	salt	1 mL
1/2 cup	chopped pecans, toasted	125 mL

Here, caramel apples are all grown up in a fabulous muffin. Dark brown sugar and spices balance the tart sweetness of apples for a harmony of flavor.

Makes 24 muffins

• Two 12-cup muffin pans, greased

1. In a saucepan, combine apples, raisins, brown sugar, margarine, cinnamon, nutmeg, cloves and 1/2 cup (125 mL) water. Bring to a boil over medium-high heat, stirring until sugar is dissolved. Remove from heat and let cool.
2. Preheat oven to 350°F (180°C).
3. In a large bowl, whisk together flour, pumpkin pie spice, baking powder and salt.
4. Add the apple mixture to the flour mixture and stir until just blended. Gently fold in pecans.
5. Divide batter equally among prepared muffin cups.
6. Bake for 20 to 25 minutes or until a toothpick inserted in the center comes out clean. Let cool in pans on a wire rack for 5 minutes, then transfer to the rack to cool.

Chunky Apple Muffins

1 cup	all-purpose flour	250 mL
1/2 cup	whole wheat flour	125 mL
1 tsp	ground cinnamon	5 mL
1 tsp	baking powder	5 mL
1/2 tsp	baking soda	2 mL
1/2 tsp	salt	2 mL
1/4 tsp	ground nutmeg	1 mL
3 tbsp	ground flax seeds	45 mL
1/3 cup	packed light brown sugar	75 mL
1/3 cup	granulated sugar	75 mL
1/2 cup	vegetable oil	125 mL
1 1/2 tsp	vanilla extract	7 mL
1 1/2 cups	chopped peeled apples	375 mL

Apple pie meets everyone's favorite morning bread. In other words, this is like an apple pie in your hand.

Makes 18 muffins

• Preheat oven to 375°F (190°C)
• Blender
• Two 12-cup muffin pans, 18 cups greased

1. In a large bowl, whisk together all-purpose flour, whole wheat flour, cinnamon, baking powder, baking soda, salt and nutmeg.
2. In blender, process flax seeds and 1/2 cup (125 mL) water for 1 minute or until thickened and frothy. Add brown sugar, granulated sugar, oil and vanilla; process for 2 minutes or until well blended and frothy.
3. Add the flax seed mixture to the flour mixture and stir until just blended. Gently fold in apples.
4. Divide batter equally among prepared muffin cups.
5. Bake in preheated oven for 25 to 28 minutes or until tops are golden brown and a toothpick inserted in the center comes out clean. Let cool in pans on a wire rack for 5 minutes, then transfer to the rack to cool.

Apple Berry Muffins

Topping

2 tbsp	packed light brown sugar	30 mL
1/4 tsp	ground cinnamon	1 mL

Muffins

1 1/4 cups	large-flake (old-fashioned) rolled oats	300 mL
3/4 cup	all-purpose flour	175 mL
1/2 cup	whole wheat flour	125 mL
2 tsp	baking powder	10 mL
1 tsp	ground cinnamon	5 mL
1/2 tsp	baking soda	2 mL
1/2 tsp	salt	2 mL
2/3 cup	granulated sugar	150 mL
3/4 cup	vanilla-flavored non-dairy milk (soy, almond, rice, hemp)	175 mL
1/2 cup	soft silken tofu	125 mL
1/4 cup	vegetable oil	60 mL
2 tbsp	ground flax seeds	30 mL
1 cup	finely chopped apple	250 mL
1 cup	blueberries	250 mL
1/3 cup	dried cranberries	75 mL
1/2 cup	sliced almonds	125 mL

These hearty muffins are packed with good-for-you stuff: both fresh and dried fruit, whole wheat flour, old-fashioned oats and flax seeds.

Makes 12 muffins

- Preheat oven to 375°F (190°C)
- Blender
- 12-cup muffin pan, greased

1. *Topping:* In a small bowl, combine brown sugar and cinnamon. Set aside.

2. *Muffins:* In a large bowl, whisk together oats, all-purpose flour, whole wheat flour, baking powder, cinnamon, baking soda and salt.

3. In blender, process sugar, milk, tofu, oil and flax seeds for 1 minute or until thickened and frothy.

4. Add the milk mixture to the flour mixture and stir until just blended. Gently fold in apple, blueberries and cranberries.

5. Divide batter equally among prepared muffin cups. Sprinkle with topping and almonds.

6. Bake in preheated oven for 21 to 24 minutes or until a toothpick inserted in the center comes out clean. Let cool in pan on a wire rack for 3 minutes, then transfer to the rack to cool.

Double Banana Muffins

1½ cups	all-purpose flour	375 mL
1 tsp	baking powder	5 mL
¾ tsp	baking soda	3 mL
½ tsp	salt	2 mL
¼ tsp	ground nutmeg	1 mL
¾ cup	packed light brown sugar	175 mL
½ cup	vanilla-flavored soy yogurt	125 mL
⅓ cup	vegetable oil	75 mL
1 tsp	cider vinegar	5 mL
1 cup	mashed ripe bananas	250 mL
1	large ripe banana, peeled and cut into ¼-inch (0.5 cm) dice	1

Banana two ways — mashed and diced — in a batter spiked with a little nutmeg makes these fast and easy muffins something special.

Makes 12 muffins

- Preheat oven to 325°F (160°C)
- 12-cup muffin pan, lined with paper liners

1. In a large bowl, whisk together flour, baking powder, baking soda, salt and nutmeg.
2. In a medium bowl, whisk together brown sugar, yogurt, oil and vinegar until well blended. Stir in mashed bananas.
3. Add the yogurt mixture to the flour mixture and stir until just blended. Gently fold in diced banana.
4. Divide batter among prepared muffin cups.
5. Bake in preheated oven for 22 to 25 minutes or until tops are golden and a toothpick inserted in the center comes out clean. Let cool in pan on a wire rack for 3 minutes, then transfer to the rack to cool.

Banana Chocolate Chip Whole-Meal Muffins

1¼ cups	whole wheat flour	300 mL
1¼ cups	natural bran	300 mL
1½ tsp	baking soda	7 mL
1 tsp	baking powder	5 mL
½ tsp	salt	2 mL
½ tsp	ground nutmeg	2 mL
⅓ cup	packed light brown sugar	75 mL
1 cup	vanilla-flavored soy yogurt	250 mL
¾ cup	mashed ripe bananas	175 mL
¼ cup	vegetable oil	60 mL
½ cup	vegan miniature semisweet chocolate chips	125 mL

These muffins were almost my obsession. I desperately wanted a whole-grain muffin that was neither too heavy nor too sweet, and for a while I couldn't make one with the right consistency or the right banana flavor. I think this one comes pretty close to perfect. The flavors marry well with the touch of nutmeg in the batter.

Makes 12 muffins

- Preheat oven to 400°F (200°C)
- Blender
- 12-cup muffin pan, greased

1. In a large bowl, whisk together flour, bran, baking soda, baking powder, salt and nutmeg.
2. In blender, process brown sugar, yogurt, bananas and oil until blended and smooth.
3. Add the yogurt mixture to the flour mixture and stir until just blended. Gently fold in chocolate chips.
4. Divide batter equally among prepared muffin cups.
5. Bake in preheated oven for 18 to 22 minutes or until tops are golden brown and a toothpick inserted in the center comes out clean. Let cool in pan on a wire rack for 3 minutes, then transfer to the rack to cool.

Banana Blueberry Muffins

1½ cups	all-purpose flour	375 mL
1 tsp	baking soda	5 mL
1 tsp	baking powder	5 mL
½ tsp	salt	2 mL
¼ tsp	ground nutmeg	2 mL
2 tbsp	ground flax seeds	30 mL
¾ cup	granulated sugar	175 mL
1⅓ cups	mashed ripe bananas	325 mL
⅓ cup	vegetable oil	75 mL
1 tsp	vanilla extract	5 mL
1½ cups	fresh or frozen (not thawed) blueberries	375 mL

Just wonderful for any morning, any season (you can use frozen blueberries in cooler months), these homey muffins fall into the "most requested" category.

Makes 10 muffins

- Preheat oven to 375°F (190°C)
- Blender
- 12-cup muffin pan, 10 cups lined with paper liners

1. In a large bowl, whisk together flour, baking soda, baking powder, salt and nutmeg.
2. In blender, process flax seeds and 3 tbsp (45 mL) water for 1 minute or until thickened and frothy. Add sugar, bananas, oil and vanilla; process for 2 minutes or until well blended and frothy.
3. Add the flax seed mixture to the flour mixture and stir until just blended. Gently fold in blueberries.
4. Divide batter equally among prepared muffin cups.
5. Bake in preheated oven for 19 to 24 minutes or until tops are golden and a toothpick inserted in the center comes out clean. Let cool in pan on a wire rack for 5 minutes, then transfer to the rack to cool.

Banana Chocolate Chip Teff Muffins

1½ cups	whole wheat pastry flour	375 mL
1⅓ cups	teff flour	325 mL
2 tsp	baking powder	10 mL
1 tsp	ground cinnamon	5 mL
1 tsp	baking soda	5 mL
1 tsp	salt	5 mL
⅔ cup	packed light brown sugar	150 mL
2 cups	mashed ripe bananas	500 mL
1 cup	plain non-dairy milk (soy, almond, rice, hemp)	250 mL
¼ cup	vegetable oil	60 mL
1 tsp	vanilla extract	5 mL
1 cup	vegan miniature semisweet chocolate chips	250 mL

Teff flour lends a springy texture to a newfangled take on a favorite flavor combination. A dash of cinnamon adds a spicy-sweet note to these delectable chocolate-flecked muffins.

Makes 16 muffins

- Preheat oven to 375°F (190°C)
- Two 12-cup muffin pans, 16 cups greased

1. In a large bowl, whisk together whole wheat pastry flour, teff flour, baking powder, cinnamon, baking soda and salt.
2. In a medium bowl, whisk together brown sugar, bananas, milk, oil and vanilla until well blended.
3. Add the banana mixture to the flour mixture and stir until just blended. Gently fold in chocolate chips.
4. Divide batter equally among prepared muffin cups.
5. Bake in preheated oven for 20 to 25 minutes or until tops are golden brown and a toothpick inserted in the center comes out clean. Let cool in pans on a wire rack for 5 minutes, then transfer to the rack to cool.

Banana, Cherry and Quinoa Power Muffins

1 cup	unsweetened apple juice	250 mL
1/2 cup	dried cherries	125 mL
1/4 cup	quinoa, rinsed	60 mL
1 1/2 cups	soy flour	375 mL
2 tsp	baking powder	10 mL
1 tsp	ground cinnamon	5 mL
1/2 tsp	baking soda	2 mL
1/2 tsp	salt	2 mL
1 cup	plain soy milk	250 mL
1/2 cup	soft silken tofu	125 mL
1/2 cup	mashed ripe banana	125 mL
1/4 cup	agave nectar	60 mL
3 tbsp	vegetable oil	45 mL
1 tsp	vanilla extract	5 mL

Quinoa is a fast-cooking, protein-packed whole grain (technically a seed). Lightly cooked, it adds a nutty flavor and hearty texture to these super-power muffins.

Makes 12 muffins

- Blender
- 12-cup muffin pan, greased

1. In a small saucepan, bring apple juice to a boil over high heat. Stir in cherries and quinoa. Remove from heat and let stand for 20 minutes.
2. Preheat oven to 350°F (180°C).
3. In a large bowl, whisk together flour, baking powder, cinnamon, baking soda and salt.
4. In blender, process milk, tofu, banana, agave nectar, oil and vanilla until blended and smooth.
5. Add the milk mixture to the flour mixture and stir until just blended. Gently fold in quinoa mixture until blended.
6. Divide batter equally among prepared muffin cups.
7. Bake for 24 to 28 minutes or until tops are golden brown and a toothpick inserted in the center comes out clean. Let cool in pan on a wire rack for 5 minutes, then transfer to the rack to cool.

Favorite Blueberry Muffins

1 1/2 cups	all-purpose flour	375 mL
1/2 cup	whole wheat pastry flour	125 mL
2 1/2 tsp	baking powder	12 mL
1/2 tsp	baking soda	2 mL
1/2 tsp	salt	2 mL
2/3 cup	granulated sugar	150 mL
1/2 cup	unsweetened applesauce	125 mL
1/2 cup	vanilla-flavored soy yogurt	125 mL
1/4 cup	vegetable oil	60 mL
1 tsp	vanilla extract	5 mL
1 1/2 cups	blueberries	375 mL
2 tbsp	turbinado sugar	30 mL

These tender-as-can-be muffins have an easy style, their sapphire, tart-sweet berries harmonizing with a vanilla-scented batter.

Makes 12 muffins

- Preheat oven to 350°F (180°C)
- 12-cup muffin pan, greased

1. In a large bowl, whisk together all-purpose flour, whole wheat pastry flour, baking powder, baking soda and salt.
2. In a medium bowl, whisk together granulated sugar, applesauce, yogurt, oil and vanilla until well blended.
3. Add the applesauce mixture to the flour mixture and stir until just blended. Gently fold in blueberries.
4. Divide batter equally among prepared muffin cups. Sprinkle with turbinado sugar.
5. Bake in preheated oven for 18 to 22 minutes or until tops are golden brown and a toothpick inserted in the center comes out clean. Let cool in pan on a wire rack for 3 minutes, then transfer to the rack to cool.

Blueberry Lemon Muffins

1⅓ cups	plain non-dairy milk (soy, almond, rice, hemp)	325 mL
1 tbsp	finely grated lemon zest	15 mL
2 tbsp	freshly squeezed lemon juice	30 mL
2 cups	all-purpose flour	500 mL
2 tsp	baking powder	10 mL
½ tsp	baking soda	2 mL
½ tsp	salt	2 mL
⅔ cup	granulated sugar	150 mL
⅓ cup	vegan margarine, melted	75 mL
1 tsp	vanilla extract	5 mL
1½ cups	blueberries	375 mL
2 tbsp	granulated sugar	30 mL

Here, golden vanilla muffins meet sunny lemon and juicy ripe berries, to great breakfast acclaim.

Makes 12 muffins
- Preheat oven to 400°F (200°C)
- 12-cup muffin pan, greased

1. In a medium bowl, combine milk, lemon zest and lemon juice. Let stand for 5 minutes or until curdled.
2. In a large bowl, whisk together flour, baking powder, baking soda and salt.
3. Whisk ⅔ cup (150 mL) sugar, margarine and vanilla into milk mixture until well blended.
4. Add the milk mixture to the flour mixture and stir until just blended. Gently fold in blueberries.
5. Divide batter equally among prepared muffin cups. Sprinkle with 2 tbsp (30 mL) sugar.
6. Bake in preheated oven for 19 to 23 minutes or until tops are golden brown and a toothpick inserted in the center comes out clean. Let cool in pan on a wire rack for 5 minutes, then transfer to the rack to cool.

Cranberry Orange Nut Muffins

1½ cups	all-purpose flour	375 mL
1¼ tsp	baking powder	6 mL
1 tsp	baking soda	5 mL
½ tsp	salt	2 mL
½ cup	granulated sugar	125 mL
2 tsp	finely grated orange zest	10 mL
¾ cup	freshly squeezed orange juice	175 mL
⅓ cup	vegetable oil	75 mL
1 tsp	vanilla extract	5 mL
1¼ cups	fresh or frozen cranberries, chopped	300 mL
½ cup	chopped walnuts, toasted	125 mL
2 tbsp	turbinado sugar	30 mL

With their ruby cranberries and glittering sugar tops, these muffins look labor-intensive. But they're actually a breeze to prepare. Stock up the freezer with cranberries when they are in season so you can make these year-round.

Makes 12 muffins
- Preheat oven to 375°F (190°C)
- 12-cup muffin pan, greased

1. In a large bowl, whisk together flour, baking powder, baking soda and salt.
2. In a medium bowl, whisk together granulated sugar, orange zest, orange juice, oil and vanilla until well blended.
3. Add the orange juice mixture to the flour mixture and stir until just blended. Gently fold in cranberries and walnuts.
4. Divide batter equally among prepared muffin cups. Sprinkle with turbinado sugar.
5. Bake in preheated oven for 21 to 26 minutes or until tops are golden brown and a toothpick inserted in the center comes out clean. Let cool in pan on a wire rack for 3 minutes, then transfer to the rack to cool.

Whole Wheat Blackberry Crumb Muffins

Topping

1/4 cup	packed light brown sugar	60 mL
2 tbsp	whole wheat pastry flour	30 mL
1/2 tsp	ground cinnamon	2 mL
2 tbsp	vegan margarine, melted	30 mL

Muffins

1 1/2 cups	whole wheat pastry flour	375 mL
2 tsp	baking powder	10 mL
1/2 tsp	salt	2 mL
3 tbsp	ground flax seeds	45 mL
2/3 cup	plain non-dairy milk (soy, almond, rice, hemp)	150 mL
2/3 cup	granulated sugar	150 mL
1/3 cup	vegetable oil	75 mL
1 cup	blackberries	250 mL

The charm of these muffins is obvious: sweet summer blackberries are cloaked in a simple batter and baked in a hot oven so that everything good about them becomes even better.

Makes 12 muffins

- Preheat oven to 400°F (200°C)
- Blender
- 12-cup muffin pan, greased

1. *Topping:* In a small bowl, combine brown sugar, flour, cinnamon and margarine until crumbly. Refrigerate until ready to use.
2. *Muffins:* In a large bowl, whisk together flour, baking powder and salt.
3. In blender, process flax seeds and milk for 1 minute or until thickened and frothy. Add sugar and oil; process for 2 minutes or until well blended and frothy.
4. Add the flax seed mixture to the flour mixture and stir until just blended. Gently fold in blackberries.
5. Divide batter equally among prepared muffin cups. Sprinkle with topping.
6. Bake in preheated oven for 18 to 22 minutes or until tops are golden brown and a toothpick inserted in the center comes out clean. Let cool in pan on a wire rack for 5 minutes, then transfer to the rack to cool.

Strawberry Soy Yogurt Muffins

2/3 cup	granulated sugar, divided	150 mL
1 cup	all-purpose flour	250 mL
1/2 cup	whole wheat pastry flour	125 mL
1 tsp	baking powder	5 mL
1/2 tsp	salt	2 mL
1/4 tsp	baking soda	1 mL
1 1/4 cups	halved strawberries	300 mL
1/3 cup	vegetable oil	75 mL
1/3 cup	vanilla-flavored soy yogurt	75 mL
1 tsp	vanilla extract	5 mL

At the height of summer, you can't have too many strawberries. Here, they are enveloped in golden muffins. The slightly tangy, not-too-sweet batter is a breeze to mix up.

Makes 12 muffins

- Preheat oven to 400°F (200°C)
- Blender
- 12-cup muffin pan, greased

1. Set aside 1 tbsp (15 mL) of the sugar. In a large bowl, whisk together the remaining sugar, all-purpose flour, whole wheat pastry flour, baking powder, salt and baking soda.
2. In blender, process strawberries, oil, yogurt and vanilla until blended and smooth.
3. Add the strawberry mixture to the flour mixture and stir until just blended.
4. Divide batter equally among prepared muffin cups. Sprinkle with the reserved sugar.
5. Bake in preheated oven for 19 to 24 minutes or until a toothpick inserted in the center comes out clean. Let cool in pan on a wire rack for 5 minutes, then transfer to the rack to cool.

Cherry Hazelnut Muffins

2 cups	all-purpose flour	500 mL
2 tsp	baking powder	10 mL
1/2 tsp	baking soda	2 mL
1/2 tsp	salt	2 mL
1/3 cup	granulated sugar	75 mL
3/4 cup	plain non-dairy milk (soy, almond, rice, hemp)	175 mL
3/4 cup	vanilla-flavored soy yogurt	175 mL
1/3 cup	vegetable oil	75 mL
1 cup	chopped hazelnuts, toasted	250 ml
1 cup	chopped pitted cherries	250 mL

Just a few years ago, I had to make a special trek to gourmet stores to find shelled hazelnuts. But now I can find them — shelled and chopped — in the baking aisle of all my local supermarkets. Here they share center stage with sweet-tart fresh cherries.

Makes 12 muffins

- Preheat oven to 400°F (200°C)
- 12-cup muffin pan, greased

1. In a large bowl, whisk together flour, baking powder, baking soda and salt.

2. In a medium bowl, whisk together sugar, milk, yogurt and oil until well blended.

3. Add the milk mixture to the flour mixture and stir until just blended. Gently fold in hazelnuts and cherries.

4. Divide batter equally among prepared muffin cups.

5. Bake in preheated oven for 18 to 22 minutes or until tops are golden brown and a toothpick inserted in the center comes out clean. Let cool in pan on a wire rack for 3 minutes, then transfer to the rack to cool.

Lemon Berry Corn Muffins

1 cup	all-purpose flour	250 mL
1 cup	yellow cornmeal	250 mL
1 tbsp	baking powder	15 mL
1/2 tsp	salt	2 mL
1/4 tsp	baking soda	1 mL
1/2 cup	granulated sugar	125 mL
3/4 cup	vanilla-flavored soy yogurt	175 mL
1/3 cup	plain non-dairy milk (soy, almond, rice, hemp)	75 mL
1/3 cup	vegetable oil	75 mL
1 tbsp	finely grated lemon zest	15 mL
1 1/4 cups	blueberries, raspberries or blackberries	300 mL

Cornmeal gives these muffins a coarse, toothsome texture, the perfect backdrop for lush summer berries and the zing of fresh lemon.

Makes 12 muffins

- Preheat oven to 400°F (200°C)
- 12-cup muffin pan, greased

1. In a large bowl, whisk together flour, cornmeal, baking powder, salt and baking soda.

2. In a medium bowl, whisk together sugar, yogurt, milk, oil and lemon zest until well blended.

3. Add the yogurt mixture to the flour mixture and stir until just blended. Gently fold in berries.

4. Divide batter equally among prepared muffin cups.

5. Bake in preheated oven for 20 to 25 minutes or until tops are golden brown and a toothpick inserted in the center comes out clean. Let cool in pan on a wire rack for 5 minutes, then transfer to the rack to cool.

Cranberry Rye Muffins

2 cups	rye flour	500 mL
4 tsp	baking powder	20 mL
1 tsp	ground cinnamon	5 mL
1/2 tsp	salt	2 mL
2/3 cup	plain soy milk	150 mL
1/3 cup	vegetable oil	75 mL
1/4 cup	brown rice syrup	60 mL
1 cup	dried cranberries	250 mL

Cranberries and rye are two great things that go great together. That being said, raisins or dried apricots (or just about any other dried fruit) are terrific in these muffins too.

Makes 12 muffins

- Preheat oven to 400°F (200°C)
- 12-cup muffin pan, greased

1. In a large bowl, whisk together flour, baking powder, cinnamon and salt.

2. In a medium bowl, whisk together soy milk, oil and syrup until well blended.

3. Add the milk mixture to the flour mixture and stir until just blended. Gently fold in cranberries.

4. Divide batter equally among prepared muffin cups.

5. Bake in preheated oven for 15 to 20 minutes or until tops are golden and a toothpick inserted in the center comes out clean. Let cool in pan on a wire rack for 5 minutes, then transfer to the rack to cool.

Raspberry Vanilla Muffins

1 3/4 cups	all-purpose flour	425 mL
2 tsp	baking powder	10 mL
1 tsp	baking soda	5 mL
1/2 tsp	salt	2 mL
3 tbsp	ground flax seeds	45 mL
3/4 cup	granulated sugar	175 mL
1 cup	vanilla-flavored soy yogurt	250 mL
1/2 cup	vegetable oil	125 mL
1 tsp	vanilla extract	5 mL
1 1/3 cups	raspberries	325 mL

These muffins taste like late summer. You can make them with just about any ripe berry that suits your fancy, including blueberries, blackberries or boysenberries.

Makes 12 muffins

- Preheat oven to 400°F (200°C)
- Blender
- 12-cup muffin pan, greased

1. In a large bowl, whisk together flour, baking powder, baking soda and salt.

2. In blender, process flax seeds and 1/3 cup (75 mL) water for 1 minute or until thickened and frothy. Add sugar, yogurt, oil and vanilla; process for 2 minutes or until well blended and frothy.

3. Add the flax seed mixture to the flour mixture and stir until just blended. Gently fold in raspberries.

4. Divide batter equally among prepared muffin cups.

5. Bake in preheated oven for 20 to 25 minutes or until tops are golden brown and a toothpick inserted in the center comes out clean. Let cool in pan on a wire rack for 5 minutes, then transfer to the rack to cool.

Lemon Polenta Muffins

Muffins

1 cup	all-purpose flour	250 mL
1 cup	yellow cornmeal, preferably stone-ground	250 mL
1 tbsp	baking powder	15 mL
1/2 tsp	salt	2 mL
1/3 cup	granulated sugar	75 mL
1/2 cup	olive oil	125 mL
1/2 cup	plain non-dairy milk (soy, almond, rice, hemp)	125 mL
1/3 cup	plain soy yogurt	75 mL
2 tbsp	finely grated lemon zest	30 mL
1 tsp	vanilla extract	5 mL

Glaze

3/4 cup	confectioners' (icing) sugar	175 mL
1 tbsp	freshly squeezed lemon juice	15 mL

Cornmeal — preferably stone-ground — gives these muffins a crunchy texture; a sweet-tangy glaze dresses them up for Sunday brunch. Although olive oil adds great flavor, you can certainly use vegetable oil in its place.

Makes 12 muffins

- Preheat oven to 400°F (200°C)
- 12-cup muffin pan, greased

1. *Muffins:* In a large bowl, whisk together flour, cornmeal, baking powder and salt.

2. In a medium bowl, whisk together sugar, oil, milk, yogurt, lemon zest and vanilla until blended.

3. Add the milk mixture to the flour mixture and stir until just blended.

4. Divide batter equally among prepared muffin cups.

5. Bake in preheated oven for 20 to 25 minutes or until tops are golden brown and a toothpick inserted in the center comes out clean. Let cool in pan on a wire rack for 5 minutes, then transfer to the rack to cool while you prepare the glaze.

6. *Glaze:* In a small bowl, whisk together confectioners' sugar and lemon juice until blended and smooth. Spoon over warm muffin tops. Let cool.

Lemon Poppy Seed Muffins

2 cups	all-purpose flour	500 mL
3 tbsp	poppy seeds	45 mL
2 tsp	baking powder	10 mL
1/2 tsp	baking soda	2 mL
1/2 tsp	salt	2 mL
1/2 cup	granulated sugar	125 mL
2/3 cup	plain non-dairy milk (soy, almond, rice, hemp)	150 mL
2/3 cup	plain soy yogurt	150 mL
1/3 cup	vegetable oil	75 mL
2 tbsp	finely grated lemon zest	30 mL
2 tbsp	freshly squeezed lemon juice	30 mL
1 tsp	vanilla extract	5 mL

With polka dots aplenty, these muffins will make you want to rise and shine on the grayest of mornings. A double dose of lemon (juice and zest) in the batter really makes these sing.

Makes 12 muffins

- Preheat oven to 400°F (200°C)
- 12-cup muffin pan, greased

1. In a large bowl, whisk together flour, poppy seeds, baking powder, baking soda and salt.
2. In a medium bowl, whisk together sugar, milk, yogurt, oil, lemon zest, lemon juice and vanilla until blended.
3. Add the yogurt mixture to the flour mixture and stir until just blended.
4. Divide batter equally among prepared muffin cups.
5. Bake in preheated oven for 18 to 22 minutes or until tops are golden brown and a toothpick inserted in the center comes out clean. Let cool in pan on a wire rack for 3 minutes, then transfer to the rack to cool.

Cardamom Orange Muffins

1	can (15 oz/425 g) mandarin oranges, drained (or 1 1/2 cans, each 10 oz/287 mL)	1
2 cups	all-purpose flour	500 mL
1/2 cup	whole wheat flour	125 mL
1 1/2 tsp	baking soda	7 mL
1 1/2 tsp	ground cardamom	7 mL
1/2 tsp	salt	2 mL
3/4 cup	granulated sugar	175 mL
1/2 cup	plain non-dairy milk (soy, almond, rice, hemp)	125 mL
1/2 cup	vegetable oil	125 mL
1/4 cup	soft silken tofu	60 mL
1 tbsp	finely grated orange zest	15 mL
3/4 cup	freshly squeezed orange juice	175 mL
1 tsp	vanilla extract	5 mL

These muffins not only keep well, but their flavor intensifies over the first day or so.

Makes 12 muffins

- Preheat oven to 350°F (180°C)
- Blender
- 12-cup muffin pan, greased

1. Pat mandarin oranges dry between paper towels. Transfer to a cutting board and coarsely chop.
2. In a large bowl, whisk together all-purpose flour, whole wheat flour, baking soda, cardamom and salt.
3. In blender, process sugar, milk, oil, tofu, orange zest, orange juice and vanilla until blended and smooth.
4. Add the milk mixture to the flour mixture and stir until just blended. Gently fold in oranges.
5. Divide batter equally among prepared muffin cups.
6. Bake in preheated oven for 21 to 26 minutes or until tops are golden brown and a toothpick inserted in the center comes out clean. Let cool in pan on a wire rack for 3 minutes, then transfer to the rack to cool.

Tangerine Muffins

Muffins

1 cup	all-purpose flour	250 mL
1 cup	whole wheat pastry flour	250 mL
1 1/2 tsp	baking soda	7 mL
1/2 tsp	ground cardamom	2 mL
1/2 tsp	salt	2 mL
1/2 cup	granulated sugar	125 mL
1 tbsp	finely grated tangerine zest	15 mL
1 cup	freshly squeezed tangerine juice	250 mL
1/2 cup	vegetable oil	125 mL
2 tbsp	cider vinegar	30 mL

Glaze

1 cup	confectioners' (icing) sugar	250 mL
1 tsp	finely grated tangerine zest	5 mL
2 tbsp	freshly squeezed tangerine juice	30 mL

These fresh, sprightly muffins are so easy to make.

Makes 12 muffins

- Preheat oven to 350°F (180°C)
- 12-cup muffin pan, greased

1. *Muffins:* In a large bowl, whisk together all-purpose flour, whole wheat pastry flour, baking soda, cardamom and salt.
2. In a medium bowl, whisk together sugar, tangerine zest, tangerine juice, oil and vinegar until well blended.
3. Add the tangerine juice mixture to the flour mixture and stir until just blended.
4. Divide batter equally among prepared muffin cups.
5. Bake in preheated oven for 24 to 28 minutes or until tops are golden brown and a toothpick inserted in the center comes out clean. Let cool in pan on a wire rack for 3 minutes, then transfer to the rack to cool while you prepare the glaze.
6. *Glaze:* In a small bowl, whisk together confectioners' sugar, tangerine zest and tangerine juice until blended and smooth. Spoon over warm muffin tops. Let cool.

Citrus Olive Oil Muffins

1 1/4 cups	vanilla-flavored soy milk	300 mL
2 tsp	finely grated lemon zest	10 mL
1 tbsp	freshly squeezed lemon juice	15 mL
2 cups	all-purpose flour	500 mL
1/3 cup	ground flax seeds	75 mL
2 tsp	baking powder	10 mL
1/2 tsp	baking soda	2 mL
1/2 tsp	salt	2 mL
1/2 cup	agave nectar	125 mL
1/4 cup	extra virgin olive oil	60 mL
1 tbsp	finely grated orange zest	15 mL
1/4 cup	freshly squeezed orange juice	60 mL

Extra virgin olive oil is a bit pricey, but it's worth the splurge in these muffins. Because they come together quickly and are full of bright flavors, these muffins are sure to become a year-round staple.

Makes 12 muffins

- Preheat oven to 350°F (180°C)
- 12-cup muffin pan, greased

1. In a medium bowl, combine soy milk and lemon juice. Let stand for 5 minutes or until curdled.
2. In a large bowl, whisk together flour, flax seeds, baking powder, baking soda and salt.
3. Whisk lemon zest, agave nectar, oil, orange zest and orange juice into milk mixture until well blended.
4. Add the milk mixture to the flour mixture and stir until just blended.
5. Divide batter equally among prepared muffin cups.
6. Bake in preheated oven for 18 to 23 minutes or until tops are golden and a toothpick inserted in the center comes out clean. Let cool in pan on a wire rack for 5 minutes, then transfer to the rack to cool.

Orange Spelt Muffins

¾ cup	plain soy milk	175 mL
2 tsp	cider vinegar	10 mL
1 tbsp	finely grated orange zest	15 mL
¼ cup	freshly squeezed orange juice	60 mL
1¾ cups	spelt flour	425 mL
1 tsp	baking soda	5 mL
½ tsp	salt	2 mL
¾ cup	granulated sugar	175 mL
½ cup	vegan margarine, softened	125 mL
¼ tsp	almond extract	1 mL

Both orange zest and orange juice ensure that these muffins have ample citrus tones — a delicious complement to the nutty flavor of spelt.

Tip

When measuring flour, particularly spelt flour, be sure to spoon it into the measuring cup and level it off, rather than packing it down; this will keep these muffins light and tender.

Makes 12 muffins

- Preheat oven to 350°F (180°C)
- 12-cup muffin pan, greased

1. In a glass measure, combine milk and vinegar. Let stand for 5 minutes or until curdled. Stir in orange zest and orange juice.
2. In a medium bowl, whisk together flour, baking soda and salt.
3. In a large bowl, using an electric mixer on medium-high speed, beat sugar and margarine until light and fluffy. Beat in almond extract until blended.
4. With the mixer on low speed, beat in flour mixture alternately with milk mixture, making two additions of flour and one of milk, until just blended.
5. Divide batter equally among prepared muffin cups.
6. Bake in preheated oven for 20 to 25 minutes or until tops are golden brown and a toothpick inserted in the center comes out clean. Let cool in pan on a wire rack for 5 minutes, then transfer to the rack to cool.

Rhubarb Muffins

1½ cups	all-purpose flour	375 mL
1 cup	whole wheat flour	250 mL
2 tsp	baking powder	10 mL
1 tsp	baking soda	5 mL
1 tsp	ground cardamom	5 mL
½ tsp	salt	2 mL
2 tsp	finely grated orange zest	10 mL
¾ cup	freshly squeezed orange juice	175 mL
½ cup	unsweetened applesauce	125 mL
½ cup	agave nectar	125 mL
½ cup	vegetable oil	125 mL
1 tsp	vanilla extract	5 mL
2 cups	chopped rhubarb	500 mL
3 tbsp	turbinado sugar	45 mL

For sophisticated comfort, these tart-sweet muffins are hard to beat.

Makes 12 muffins

- Preheat oven to 350°F (180°C)
- 12-cup muffin pan, greased

1. In a large bowl, whisk together all-purpose flour, whole wheat flour, baking powder, baking soda, cardamom and salt.
2. In a medium bowl, whisk together orange zest, orange juice, applesauce, agave nectar, oil and vanilla until well blended.
3. Add the orange juice mixture to the flour mixture and stir until just blended. Gently fold in rhubarb.
4. Divide batter equally among prepared muffin cups. Sprinkle with turbinado sugar.
5. Bake in preheated oven for 21 to 26 minutes or until tops are golden brown and a toothpick inserted in the center comes out clean. Let cool in pan on a wire rack for 5 minutes, then transfer to the rack to cool.

Fresh Plum Muffins with Walnut Sugar Tops

Topping

1/2 cup	finely chopped walnuts	125 mL
2 tbsp	granulated sugar	30 mL
1/4 tsp	ground nutmeg	1 mL

Muffins

1 cup	whole wheat pastry flour	250 mL
1 cup	all-purpose flour	250 mL
2 1/2 tsp	baking powder	12 mL
1/2 tsp	ground cinnamon	2 mL
1/2 tsp	baking soda	2 mL
1/2 tsp	salt	2 mL
3/4 cup	vanilla-flavored soy yogurt	175 mL
1/2 cup	agave nectar	125 mL
1/4 cup	vegetable oil	60 mL
1 tsp	vanilla extract	5 mL
1 1/2 cups	diced firm-ripe plums	375 mL

These muffins would be terrific made with any type of stone fruit — peaches, nectarines, apricots — so feel free to substitute your summertime favorites for the plums.

Makes 10 muffins

- Preheat oven to 350°F (180°C)
- 12-cup muffin pan, 10 cups lined with paper liners

1. *Topping:* In a small bowl, combine walnuts, sugar and nutmeg. Set aside.

2. *Muffins:* In a large bowl, whisk together whole wheat pastry flour, all-purpose flour, baking powder, cinnamon, baking soda and salt.

3. In a medium bowl, whisk together yogurt, agave nectar, oil and vanilla until well blended.

4. Add the yogurt mixture to the flour mixture and stir until just blended. Gently fold in plums.

5. Divide batter equally among prepared muffin cups. Sprinkle with topping.

6. Bake in preheated oven for 20 to 25 minutes or until tops are golden brown and a toothpick inserted in the center comes out clean. Let cool in pan on a wire rack for 3 minutes, then transfer to the rack to cool.

Georgia Peach Muffins

1 cup	plain non-dairy milk (soy, almond, rice, hemp)	250 mL
1 tbsp	freshly squeezed lemon juice	15 mL
1 cup	all-purpose flour	250 mL
1 cup	whole wheat pastry flour	250 mL
2 tsp	baking powder	10 mL
1 tsp	baking soda	5 mL
1/2 tsp	ground cinnamon	2 mL
1/4 tsp	salt	1 mL
3/4 cup	packed light brown sugar, divided	175 mL
1/2 cup	vegetable oil	125 mL
1 tsp	vanilla extract	5 mL
1 1/2 cups	diced peeled firm-ripe peaches	375 mL
1/2 cup	chopped pecans, toasted	125 mL

As they bake, the chunks of golden peach meld and soften, seeming to exist expressly for these muffins.

Makes 12 muffins

- Preheat oven to 400°F (200°C)
- 12-cup muffin pan, greased

1. In a medium bowl, combine milk and lemon juice. Let stand for 5 minutes or until curdled.
2. In a large bowl, whisk together all-purpose flour, whole wheat pastry flour, baking powder, baking soda, cinnamon and salt.
3. Whisk 1/2 cup (125 mL) of the brown sugar, oil and vanilla into milk mixture until well blended.
4. Add the milk mixture to the flour mixture and stir until just blended. Gently fold in peaches.
5. Divide batter equally among prepared muffin cups. Sprinkle with the remaining brown sugar and pecans.
6. Bake in preheated oven for 18 to 22 minutes or until tops are golden brown and a toothpick inserted in the center comes out clean. Let cool in pan on a wire rack for 3 minutes, then transfer to the rack to cool.

Five-Spice Asian Pear Muffins

1 1/2 cups	all-purpose flour	375 mL
1/2 cup	whole wheat flour	125 mL
2 tsp	baking powder	10 mL
1 1/4 tsp	Chinese five-spice powder	6 mL
1/2 tsp	baking soda	2 mL
1/2 tsp	salt	2 mL
1/2 cup	granulated sugar	125 mL
1 cup	plain soy yogurt	250 mL
1/2 cup	unsweetened apple juice	125 mL
1/3 cup	vegetable oil	75 mL
1 tsp	vanilla extract	5 mL
1 1/2 cups	chopped peeled Asian pears	375 mL

These not-too-sweet muffins are moist, tender and innovative, but not remotely fussy.

Makes 12 muffins

- Preheat oven to 400°F (200°C)
- 12-cup muffin pan, greased

1. In a large bowl, whisk together all-purpose flour, whole wheat flour, baking powder, five-spice powder, baking soda and salt.
2. In a medium bowl, whisk together sugar, yogurt, apple juice, oil and vanilla until well blended.
3. Add the yogurt mixture to the flour mixture and stir until just blended. Gently fold in pears.
4. Divide batter equally among prepared muffin cups.
5. Bake in preheated oven for 20 to 25 minutes or until tops are golden brown and a toothpick inserted in the center comes out clean. Let cool in pan on a wire rack for 3 minutes, then transfer to the rack to cool.

Vanilla Pear Streusel Muffins

Streusel

2/3 cup	all-purpose flour	150 mL
1/3 cup	packed dark brown sugar	75 mL
1/2 tsp	ground cinnamon	2 mL
1/4 cup	vegan margarine, melted	60 mL

Muffins

2 cups	all-purpose flour	500 mL
2 tsp	baking powder	10 mL
1/2 tsp	baking soda	2 mL
1/2 tsp	salt	2 mL
2/3 cup	granulated sugar	150 mL
3/4 cup	plain non-dairy milk (soy, almond, rice, hemp)	175 mL
3/4 cup	plain soy yogurt	175 mL
1/3 cup	vegetable oil	75 mL
2 tsp	vanilla extract	10 mL
1 1/2 cups	diced peeled firm-ripe pears	375 mL

Looking for the perfect brunch muffin to impress some guests? These muffins have sophisticated flavors, but they are still a snap to make.

Makes 12 muffins

- Preheat oven to 375°F (190°C)
- 12-cup muffin pan, greased

1. *Streusel:* In a medium bowl, whisk together flour, brown sugar and cinnamon. Drizzle with margarine, tossing with a fork until crumbly. Refrigerate until ready to use.

2. *Muffins:* In a large bowl, whisk together flour, baking powder, baking soda and salt.

3. In a medium bowl, whisk together sugar, milk, yogurt, oil and vanilla until well blended.

4. Add the milk mixture to the flour mixture and stir until just blended. Gently fold in pears.

5. Divide batter equally among prepared muffin cups. Sprinkle with streusel.

6. Bake in preheated oven for 24 to 28 minutes or until tops are golden brown and a toothpick inserted in the center comes out clean. Let cool in pan on a wire rack for 5 minutes, then transfer to the rack to cool.

Agave Muffins

1 1/2 cups	all-purpose flour	375 mL
1/2 cup	whole wheat flour	125 mL
2 1/2 tsp	baking powder	12 mL
1/2 tsp	baking soda	2 mL
1/2 tsp	salt	2 mL
1 cup	plain soy yogurt	250 mL
1/2 cup	agave nectar	125 mL
1/4 cup	vegetable oil	60 mL

These simple muffins allow for the delicate floral notes of agave nectar to shine through.

Makes 12 muffins

- Preheat oven to 400°F (200°C)
- 12-cup muffin pan, lined with paper liners

1. In a large bowl, whisk together all-purpose flour, whole wheat flour, baking powder, baking soda and salt.

2. In a medium bowl, whisk together yogurt, agave nectar and oil until well blended.

3. Add the yogurt mixture to the flour mixture and stir until just blended.

4. Divide batter equally among prepared muffin cups.

5. Bake in preheated oven for 15 to 18 minutes or until tops are golden and a toothpick inserted in the center comes out clean. Let cool in pan on a wire rack for 5 minutes, then transfer to the rack to cool.

Tropical Fruit Muffins with Coconut Streusel

Streusel

⅓ cup	firmly packed light brown sugar	75 mL
⅓ cup	all-purpose flour	75 mL
¼ cup	vegan margarine, melted	60 mL
½ cup	sweetened flaked or shredded coconut	125 mL

Muffins

2 cups	all-purpose flour	500 mL
2 tsp	baking powder	10 mL
½ tsp	baking soda	2 mL
½ tsp	salt	2 mL
⅔ cup	granulated sugar	150 mL
¾ cup	plain non-dairy milk (soy, almond, rice, hemp)	175 mL
¾ cup	plain soy yogurt	175 mL
⅓ cup	vegetable oil	75 mL
1 tbsp	freshly squeezed lime juice	15 mL
1 tsp	vanilla extract	5 mL
1 cup	dried tropical fruit bits	250 mL

These showy muffins have much to offer: an assortment of tropical fruits, a vanilla-lime batter and crisp coconut topping.

Makes 12 muffins

- Preheat oven to 375°F (190°C)
- 12-cup muffin pan, greased

1. *Streusel:* In a small bowl, combine brown sugar and flour. Drizzle with margarine, tossing with a fork until crumbly. Stir in coconut. Refrigerate until ready to use.

2. *Muffins:* In a large bowl, whisk together flour, baking powder, baking soda and salt.

3. In a medium bowl, whisk together sugar, milk, yogurt, oil, lime juice and vanilla until blended.

4. Add the milk mixture to the flour mixture and stir until just blended. Gently fold in fruit bits.

5. Divide batter equally among prepared muffin cups. Sprinkle with streusel.

6. Bake in preheated oven for 18 to 22 minutes or until tops are golden brown and a toothpick inserted in the center comes out clean. Let cool in pan on a wire rack for 5 minutes, then transfer to the rack to cool.

Persimmon Muffins

1 cup	plain soy milk	250 mL
1 tsp	cider vinegar	5 mL
1 cup	quick-cooking rolled oats	250 mL
1 cup	whole wheat flour	250 mL
1 tsp	baking soda	5 mL
1/2 tsp	ground cardamom	2 mL
1/2 tsp	salt	2 mL
1/4 tsp	ground cloves	1 mL
1/8 tsp	ground nutmeg	0.5 mL
2/3 cup	packed dark brown sugar	150 mL
1/4 cup	vegetable oil	60 mL
1 tsp	almond extract	5 mL
1 1/2 cups	chopped firm-ripe persimmons	375 mL

Fragrant persimmons star in these muffins, inspired by a classic British steamed pudding.

Makes 12 muffins

- Preheat oven to 375°F (190°C)
- 12-cup muffin pan, greased

1. In a medium bowl, combine soy milk and vinegar. Let stand for 5 minutes or until curdled.
2. In a large bowl, whisk together oats, flour, baking soda, cardamom, salt, cloves and nutmeg.
3. Whisk brown sugar, oil and almond extract into milk mixture.
4. Add the milk mixture to the flour mixture and stir until just blended. Gently fold in persimmons.
5. Divide batter equally among prepared muffin cups.
6. Bake in preheated oven for 18 to 22 minutes or until tops are golden brown and a toothpick inserted in the center comes out clean. Let cool in pan on a wire rack for 5 minutes, then transfer to the rack to cool.

Mango Muffins with Cardamom Crumble

Crumble

1 cup	slivered almonds	250 mL
1/4 cup	packed light brown sugar	60 mL
1/2 tsp	ground cardamom	2 mL

Muffins

2 cups	all-purpose flour	375 mL
1 tsp	baking powder	5 mL
1 tsp	baking soda	5 mL
1 tsp	ground ginger	5 mL
1/2 tsp	ground cardamom	2 mL
1/2 tsp	salt	2 mL
3/4 cup	granulated sugar	175 mL
1 1/2 cups	vanilla-flavored soy yogurt	375 mL
1/3 cup	vegetable oil	75 mL
1/3 cup	unsweetened applesauce	75 mL
1 1/2 cups	diced firm-ripe mangos	375 mL

Makes 12 muffins

- Preheat oven to 350°F (180°C)
- 12-cup muffin pan, lined with paper liners

1. *Crumble:* In a small bowl, combine almonds, brown sugar and cardamom. Set aside.
2. *Muffins:* In a large bowl, whisk together flour, baking powder, baking soda, ginger, cardamom and salt.
3. In a medium bowl, whisk together sugar, yogurt, oil and applesauce until well blended.
4. Add the yogurt mixture to the flour mixture and stir until just blended. Gently fold in mangos.
5. Divide batter equally among prepared muffin cups. Sprinkle with crumble.
6. Bake in preheated oven for 20 to 25 minutes or until tops are golden brown and a toothpick inserted in the center comes out clean. Let cool in pan on a wire rack for 5 minutes, then transfer to the rack to cool.

Pineapple Lime Muffins

1 cup	all-purpose flour	250 mL
1 cup	whole wheat pastry flour	250 mL
¾ cup	large-flake (old-fashioned) rolled oats	175 mL
2 tsp	ground ginger	10 mL
1 tsp	baking powder	5 mL
1 tsp	baking soda	5 mL
1 tsp	ground allspice	5 mL
½ tsp	salt	2 mL
2 tbsp	ground flax seeds	30 mL
1 cup	vanilla-flavored non-dairy milk (soy, almond, rice, hemp)	250 mL
2 tsp	grated lime zest	10 mL
2 tbsp	freshly squeezed lime juice	30 mL
1 cup	packed light brown sugar	250 mL
½ cup	vegetable oil	125 mL
1	can (8 oz/227 mL) crushed pineapple, well drained	1

I've always been keen on pineapple, so developing a pineapple muffin I would like was no challenge. But I think this recipe — citrusy with lime, caramely with brown sugar — is one everyone will love.

Makes 12 muffins

- Preheat oven to 350°F (180°C)
- Blender
- 12-cup muffin pan, greased

1. In a large bowl, whisk together all-purpose flour, whole wheat pastry flour, oats, ginger, baking powder, baking soda, allspice and salt.

2. In blender, process flax seeds, milk, lime zest and lime juice for 1 minute or until thickened and frothy. Add brown sugar and oil; process for 2 minutes or until well blended and frothy. Stir in pineapple.

4. Add the pineapple mixture to the flour mixture and stir until just blended.

5. Divide batter equally among prepared muffin cups.

6. Bake in preheated oven for 25 to 28 minutes or until tops are golden brown and a toothpick inserted in the center comes out clean. Let cool in pan on a wire rack for 5 minutes, then transfer to the rack to cool.

Chocolate Avocado Muffins

¾ cup	all-purpose flour	175 mL
¾ cup	whole wheat flour	175 mL
¾ cup	unsweetened cocoa powder (not Dutch process)	175 mL
1 tsp	baking powder	5 mL
¾ tsp	baking soda	3 mL
¾ tsp	salt	3 mL
1	ripe Haas avocado, chopped	1
1 cup	brown rice syrup	250 mL
¾ cup	plain soy milk	175 mL
⅓ cup	vegetable oil	75 mL
1 tsp	vanilla extract	5 mL

Avocado replaces the eggs and most of the oil in a rich, chocolaty batter that turns out super-moist muffins.

Makes 12 muffins

- Preheat oven to 350°F (180°C)
- Blender
- 12-cup muffin pan, greased

1. In a large bowl, whisk together all-purpose flour, whole wheat flour, cocoa powder, baking powder, baking soda and salt.

2. In blender, process avocado, syrup, soy milk, oil and vanilla until blended and smooth.

3. Add the avocado mixture to the flour mixture and stir until just blended.

4. Divide batter equally among prepared muffin cups.

5. Bake in preheated oven for 22 to 27 minutes or until a toothpick inserted in the center comes out clean. Let cool in pan on a wire rack for 5 minutes, then transfer to the rack to cool.

Apricot Muffins

2 cups	all-purpose flour	500 mL
1 cup	yellow cornmeal	250 mL
2 tsp	baking soda	10 mL
1/2 tsp	salt	2 mL
2 cups	vanilla-flavored soy yogurt	500 mL
1 cup	agave nectar	250 mL
1/2 cup	vegetable oil	125 mL
2 tsp	finely grated orange zest	10 mL
1 tsp	vanilla extract	5 mL
1 cup	chopped dried apricots	250 mL
2 tbsp	turbinado sugar	30 mL

Orange zest and agave nectar amp up the flavor of these apricot muffins. The finishing touch? A sparkling sprinkle of turbinado sugar.

Makes 18 muffins

- Preheat oven to 350°F (180°C)
- Two 12-cup muffin pans, 18 cups greased

1. In a large bowl, whisk together flour, cornmeal, baking soda and salt.
2. In a medium bowl, whisk together yogurt, agave nectar, oil, orange zest and vanilla until well blended.
3. Add the yogurt mixture to the flour mixture and stir until just blended. Gently fold in apricots.
4. Divide batter equally among prepared muffin cups. Sprinkle with turbinado sugar.
5. Bake in preheated oven for 24 to 28 minutes or until tops are golden brown and a toothpick inserted in the center comes out clean. Let cool in pans on a wire rack for 3 minutes, then transfer to the rack to cool.

Fig Date Muffins

1 cup	pitted dates, chopped	250 mL
1 cup	dried figs, chopped	250 mL
1 1/2 tsp	baking soda	7 mL
1 cup	boiling water	250 mL
3/4 cup	all-purpose flour	75 mL
3/4 cup	whole wheat flour	75 mL
1/2 tsp	baking powder	2 mL
1/2 tsp	salt	2 mL
3 tbsp	ground flax seeds	45 mL
1/2 cup	packed light brown sugar	125 mL
1/4 cup	vegetable oil	60 mL
1 cup	chopped walnuts, toasted	250 mL

Dried fruit muffins are always crowd-pleasers wherever I take them, and these dark, moist muffins are no exception. The combination of time-honored ingredients — sweet dried figs, decadent dates and crunchy walnuts — will have your friends clamoring for the recipe.

Makes 12 muffins

- Blender
- 12-cup muffin pan, greased

1. In a medium bowl, combine dates, figs and baking soda. Stir in boiling water. Let stand for 15 minutes.
2. Preheat oven to 350°F (180°C).
3. In a large bowl, whisk together all-purpose flour, whole wheat flour, baking powder and salt.
4. In blender, process flax seeds and 1/3 cup (75 mL) water for 1 minute or until thickened and frothy. Add brown sugar and oil; process for 2 minutes or until well blended and frothy. Stir into date mixture.
5. Add the date mixture to the flour mixture and stir until just blended. Gently fold in walnuts.
6. Divide batter equally among prepared muffin cups.
7. Bake for 20 to 25 minutes or until tops are golden brown and a toothpick inserted in the center comes out clean. Let cool in pan on a wire rack for 5 minutes, then transfer to the rack to cool.

Date and Walnut Muffins

2 cups	pitted dates, chopped	500 mL
1 1/2 tsp	baking soda	3 mL
1 cup	boiling water	250 mL
1 cup	all-purpose flour	250 mL
1/2 cup	whole wheat flour	125 mL
1 tsp	ground cinnamon	5 mL
1/2 tsp	baking powder	2 mL
1/2 tsp	salt	2 mL
3 tbsp	ground flax seeds	45 mL
2/3 cup	packed dark brown sugar	150 mL
1/4 cup	vegetable oil	60 mL
1 tsp	vanilla extract	5 mL
3/4 cup	chopped walnuts, toasted	175 mL

Here, toasted walnuts cozy up with ever-so-sweet dates for an easy and delicious muffin that manages to be both new and familiar.

Makes 18 muffins
- Blender
- Two 12-cup muffin pans, 18 cups lined with paper liners

1. In a large bowl, combine dates and baking soda. Stir in boiling water. Let stand for 15 minutes.
2. Preheat oven to 375°F (190°C).
3. In a medium bowl, whisk together all-purpose flour, whole wheat flour, cinnamon, baking powder and salt.
4. In blender, process flax seeds and 1/2 cup (125 mL) water for 1 minute or until thickened and frothy. Add brown sugar, oil and vanilla; process for 2 minutes or until well blended and frothy. Stir into date mixture.
5. Add the flour mixture to the date mixture and stir until just blended. Gently fold in walnuts.
6. Divide batter equally among prepared muffin cups.
7. Bake for 24 to 28 minutes or until tops are golden brown and a toothpick inserted in the center comes out clean. Let cool in pans on a wire rack for 3 minutes, then transfer to the rack to cool.

Dried Cherry Corn Muffins

1 1/4 cups	plain soy milk	300 mL
2 tsp	finely grated lemon zest	10 mL
1 tbsp	freshly squeezed lemon juice	15 mL
1 1/4 cups	whole wheat pastry flour	300 mL
3/4 cup	yellow cornmeal	175 mL
3/4 tsp	salt	3 mL
1/2 tsp	baking soda	2 mL
1/4 tsp	ground allspice	1 mL
3/4 cup	mashed ripe bananas	175 mL
1/4 cup	vegetable oil	60 mL
1/4 cup	agave nectar	60 mL
2/3 cup	dried cherries	150 mL

The crunchy, subtly spicy corn muffin base showcases the tart-sweet intensity of dried cherries.

Makes 12 muffins
- Preheat oven to 375°F (190°C)
- 12-cup muffin pan, greased

1. In a glass measuring cup, combine soy milk, lemon zest and lemon juice. Let stand for 5 minutes or until curdled.
2. In a large bowl, whisk together flour, cornmeal, salt, baking soda and allspice.
3. In a medium bowl, whisk together bananas, oil and agave nectar until well blended. Whisk in milk mixture until blended.
4. Add the banana mixture to the flour mixture and stir until just blended. Gently fold in cherries.
5. Divide batter equally among prepared muffin cups.
6. Bake in preheated oven for 17 to 22 minutes or until tops are golden brown and a toothpick inserted in the center comes out clean. Let cool in pan on a wire rack for 3 minutes, then transfer to the rack to cool.

Almond Poppy Seed Muffins

1¾ cups	all-purpose flour	425 mL
2 tbsp	poppy seeds	30 mL
1 tbsp	baking powder	15 mL
½ tsp	salt	2 mL
¼ tsp	baking soda	1 mL
⅓ cup	packed light brown sugar	75 mL
¾ cup	plain non-dairy milk (soy, almond, rice, hemp)	175 mL
¾ cup	vanilla-flavored soy yogurt	175 mL
⅓ cup	vegetable oil	75 mL
1 tsp	almond extract	5 mL

Poppy seeds add a subtle crunch here, a foil for the brown sugar batter and almond fragrance.

Makes 12 muffins

- Preheat oven to 400°F (200°C)
- 12-cup muffin pan, greased

1. In a large bowl, whisk together flour, poppy seeds, baking powder, salt and baking soda.
2. In a medium bowl, whisk together brown sugar, milk, yogurt, oil and almond extract until well blended.
3. Add the yogurt mixture to the flour mixture and stir until just blended.
4. Divide batter equally among prepared muffin cups.
5. Bake in preheated oven for 20 to 25 minutes or until tops are golden brown and a toothpick inserted in the center comes out clean. Let cool in pan on a wire rack for 5 minutes, then transfer to the rack to cool.

Brown Sugar Pecan Muffins

2 cups	all-purpose flour	500 mL
2 tsp	baking powder	10 mL
½ tsp	baking soda	2 mL
½ tsp	salt	2 mL
¾ cup	packed dark brown sugar, divided	175 mL
¾ cup	plain non-dairy milk (soy, almond, rice, hemp)	175 mL
¾ cup	plain soy yogurt	175 mL
⅓ cup	vegetable oil	75 mL
1 tsp	vanilla extract	5 mL
1 cup	chopped pecans, toasted	250 mL

While these muffins appear modest, their nutty caramel flavor will draw everyone back for seconds and even thirds. Soy yogurt lends a subtle tang and extra tenderness to the overall texture.

Makes 12 muffins

- Preheat oven to 400°F (200°C)
- 12-cup muffin pan, greased

1. In a large bowl, whisk together flour, baking powder, baking soda and salt.
2. In a medium bowl, whisk together ½ cup (125 mL) of the brown sugar, milk, yogurt, oil and vanilla until well blended.
3. Add the milk mixture to the flour mixture and stir until just blended. Gently fold in pecans.
4. Divide batter equally among prepared muffin cups. Sprinkle with the remaining brown sugar.
5. Bake in preheated oven for 18 to 22 minutes or until tops are golden brown and a toothpick inserted in the center comes out clean. Let cool in pan on a wire rack for 3 minutes, then transfer to the rack to cool.

Toasted Almond Muffins

1¹/₂ cups	all-purpose flour	375 mL
¹/₂ cup	whole wheat flour	125 mL
2 tsp	baking powder	10 mL
¹/₂ tsp	baking soda	2 mL
¹/₂ tsp	salt	2 mL
¹/₃ cup	packed light brown sugar	75 mL
1 cup	plain soy yogurt	250 mL
¹/₂ cup	plain non-dairy milk (soy, almond, rice, hemp)	125 mL
¹/₃ cup	vegetable oil	75 mL
1 tsp	almond extract	5 mL
¹/₂ cup	sliced almonds	125 mL

Here, toasty almonds are framed by a scrumptious brown sugar batter that underlines their refined nuttiness.

Makes 12 muffins

- Preheat oven to 400°F (200°C)
- 12-cup muffin pan, greased

1. In a large bowl, whisk together all-purpose flour, whole wheat flour, baking powder, baking soda and salt.
2. In a medium bowl, whisk together brown sugar, yogurt, milk, oil and almond extract until well blended.
3. Add the yogurt mixture to the flour mixture and stir until just blended.
4. Divide batter equally among prepared muffin cups. Sprinkle with almonds.
5. Bake in preheated oven for 18 to 22 minutes or until tops are golden brown and a toothpick inserted in the center comes out clean. Let cool in pan on a wire rack for 5 minutes, then transfer to the rack to cool.

Whole Wheat and Walnut Muffins

1¹/₂ cups	whole wheat flour	375 mL
1 cup	all-purpose flour	250 mL
1¹/₂ tsp	baking powder	7 mL
1 tsp	baking soda	5 mL
¹/₂ tsp	salt	2 mL
1 cup	plain soy yogurt	250 mL
¹/₂ cup	plain soy milk	250 mL
¹/₃ cup	vegetable oil	75 mL
¹/₃ cup	dark (cooking) molasses	75 mL
1 cup	chopped walnuts, toasted	250 mL

Tender, moist and studded with toasted walnuts, these muffins are a perfect way to welcome any morning — but especially a chilly one.

Makes 12 muffins

- Preheat oven to 350°F (180°C)
- 12-cup muffin pan, greased

1. In a large bowl, whisk together whole wheat flour, all-purpose flour, baking powder, baking soda and salt.
2. In a medium bowl, whisk together yogurt, soy milk, oil and molasses until well blended.
3. Add the yogurt mixture to the flour mixture and stir until just blended. Gently fold in walnuts.
4. Divide batter equally among prepared muffin cups.
5. Bake in preheated oven for 24 to 28 minutes or until a toothpick inserted in the center comes out clean. Let cool in pan on a wire rack for 5 minutes, then transfer to the rack to cool.

Pumpkin Muffins

1 1/4 cups	all-purpose flour	300 mL
1/2 cup	whole wheat flour	125 mL
1 tbsp	baking powder	15 mL
2 1/2 tsp	pumpkin pie spice	12 mL
3/4 tsp	salt	3 mL
3/4 cup	granulated sugar	175 mL
1/2 cup	packed dark brown sugar	125 mL
1 cup	pumpkin purée (not pie filling)	250 mL
1/2 cup	vegetable oil	125 mL
1/3 cup	plain non-dairy milk (soy, almond, rice, hemp)	75 mL
1/4 cup	dark (cooking) molasses	60 mL
1 tsp	vanilla extract	5 mL

Embrace the flavors of autumn with these moist, delicious muffins. Pumpkin not only lends richness and color, but is also one of the healthiest ingredients you can keep on your pantry shelf.

Makes 12 muffins

- Preheat oven to 400°F (200°C)
- 12-cup muffin pan, greased

1. In a large bowl, whisk together all-purpose flour, whole wheat flour, baking powder, pumpkin pie spice and salt.
2. In a medium bowl, whisk together granulated sugar, brown sugar, pumpkin, oil, milk, molasses and vanilla until well blended.
3. Add the pumpkin mixture to the flour mixture and stir until just blended.
4. Divide batter equally among prepared muffin cups.
5. Bake in preheated oven for 18 to 22 minutes or until a toothpick inserted in the center comes out clean. Let cool in pan on a wire rack for 3 minutes, then transfer to the rack to cool.

Carrot Cake Muffins

1 cup	all-purpose flour	250 mL
1/2 cup	whole wheat flour	125 mL
2 tsp	baking powder	10 mL
1 tsp	ground cinnamon	5 mL
1/2 tsp	baking soda	2 mL
1/2 tsp	salt	2 mL
1/2 tsp	ground ginger	2 mL
1/4 tsp	ground nutmeg	1 mL
1/2 cup	packed light brown sugar	125 mL
1 cup	plain non-dairy milk (soy, almond, rice, hemp)	250 mL
1/3 cup	vegan margarine, melted	75 mL
1 tsp	vanilla extract	5 mL
2 cups	shredded carrots	500 mL
1/2 cup	dried currants	125 mL
1/2 cup	chopped walnuts or pecans	125 mL

Carrot cake is every bit as American as apple pie. Here, I use it as inspiration for a healthy muffin that is moist, heady with spices and just plain good!

Makes 12 muffins

- Preheat oven to 400°F (200°C)
- 12-cup muffin pan, greased

1. In a large bowl, whisk together all-purpose flour, whole wheat flour, baking powder, cinnamon, baking soda, salt, ginger and nutmeg.
2. In a medium bowl, whisk together brown sugar, milk, margarine and vanilla until well blended.
3. Add the milk mixture to the flour mixture and stir until just blended. Gently fold in carrots and currants.
4. Divide batter equally among prepared muffin cups. Sprinkle with walnuts.
5. Bake in preheated oven for 18 to 22 minutes or until tops are golden brown and a toothpick inserted in the center comes out clean. Let cool in pan on a wire rack for 3 minutes, then transfer to the rack to cool.

Whole Wheat Morning Glory Muffins

2 cups	whole wheat pastry flour	500 mL
2½ tsp	pumpkin pie spice	12 mL
2 tsp	baking powder	10 mL
½ tsp	baking soda	2 mL
¼ tsp	salt	1 mL
⅔ cup	packed light brown sugar	150 mL
½ cup	vegetable oil	125 mL
½ cup	carrot juice	125 mL
1 tsp	vanilla extract	5 mL
1	can (8 oz/227 mL) crushed pineapple, well drained	1
1 cup	finely shredded carrots	250 mL
½ cup	raisins	125 mL
½ cup	chopped walnuts or pecans, toasted	125 mL

Makes 12 muffins

- Preheat oven to 350°F (180°C)
- 12-cup muffin pan, greased

1. In a large bowl, whisk together flour, pumpkin pie spice, baking powder, baking soda and salt.
2. In a medium bowl, whisk together brown sugar, oil, carrot juice and vanilla until well blended.
3. Add the oil mixture to the flour mixture and stir until just blended. Gently fold in pineapple, carrots, raisins and walnuts.
4. Divide batter equally among prepared muffin cups.
5. Bake in preheated oven for 22 to 25 minutes or until tops are golden brown and a toothpick inserted in the center comes out clean. Let cool in pan on a wire rack for 5 minutes, then transfer to the rack to cool.

Zucchini Muffins

1 cup	all-purpose flour	250 mL
½ cup	whole wheat flour	125 mL
2¼ tsp	baking powder	11 mL
1 tsp	ground cinnamon	5 mL
½ tsp	baking soda	2 mL
½ tsp	salt	2 mL
¼ tsp	ground nutmeg	1 mL
⅓ cup	granulated sugar	75 mL
1 cup	plain non-dairy milk (soy, almond, rice, hemp)	250 mL
⅓ cup	vegetable oil	75 mL
1 tsp	vanilla extract	5 mL
2 cups	shredded zucchini	500 mL
1 cup	chopped pecans, toasted	250 mL

Makes 12 muffins

- Preheat oven to 400°F (200°C)
- 12-cup muffin pan, greased

1. In a large bowl, whisk together all-purpose flour, whole wheat flour, baking powder, cinnamon, baking soda, salt and nutmeg.
2. In a medium bowl, whisk together sugar, milk, oil and vanilla until well blended.
3. Add the milk mixture to the flour mixture and stir until just blended. Gently fold in zucchini and pecans.
4. Divide batter equally among prepared muffin cups.
5. Bake in preheated oven for 18 to 22 minutes or until tops are golden brown and a toothpick inserted in the center comes out clean. Let cool in pan on a wire rack for 3 minutes, then transfer to the rack to cool.

You know those gigantic zucchini your gardening friends "gift" to you at the end of the summer? Forget about using them as doorstops; shred them and make a bevy of these muffins (you can even re-gift some of them to the same friends).

Spiced Winter Squash Muffins

1½ cups	all-purpose flour	375 mL
2 tsp	baking powder	10 mL
¾ tsp	ground cinnamon	3 mL
½ tsp	salt	2 mL
¼ tsp	ground nutmeg	1 mL
¼ tsp	ground allspice	1 mL
½ cup	packed light brown sugar	125 mL
1	package (12 oz/375 g) frozen (thawed) winter squash purée	1
½ cup	unsweetened apple juice	125 mL
⅓ cup	plain non-dairy milk (soy, almond, rice, hemp)	75 mL
¼ cup	vegetable oil	60 mL

You know how wonderful zucchini is in a sweet morning muffin or bread; now it's time to make room for winter squash at the breakfast table. You can cook your own, but for convenience, look for packages of frozen squash purée in the frozen vegetable section of the supermarket.

Makes 12 muffins

- Preheat oven to 350°F (180°C)
- 12-cup muffin pan, greased

1. In a large bowl, whisk together flour, baking powder, cinnamon, salt, nutmeg and allspice.
2. In a medium bowl, whisk together brown sugar, squash, apple juice, milk and oil until blended.
3. Add the squash mixture to the flour mixture and stir until just blended.
4. Divide batter equally among prepared muffin cups.
5. Bake in preheated oven for 19 to 24 minutes or until tops are golden brown and a toothpick inserted in the center comes out clean. Let cool in pan on a wire rack for 3 minutes, then transfer to the rack to cool.

Raisin Bran Muffins

1 cup	all-purpose flour	250 mL
¾ cup	natural bran	175 mL
½ cup	whole wheat flour	125 mL
2 tsp	baking powder	10 mL
1 tsp	ground cinnamon	5 mL
½ tsp	baking soda	2 mL
½ tsp	salt	2 mL
½ cup	packed dark brown sugar	125 mL
1¼ cups	plain non-dairy milk (soy, almond, rice, hemp)	300 mL
⅓ cup	vegetable oil	75 mL
2 tsp	cider vinegar	10 mL
1 tsp	vanilla extract	5 mL
⅔ cup	raisins	150 mL

Loaded with plump raisins and whole grains, these muffins combine the best of great taste and great nutrition.

Makes 12 muffins

- Preheat oven to 400°F (200°C)
- 12-cup muffin pan, greased

1. In a large bowl, whisk together all-purpose flour, bran, whole wheat flour, baking powder, cinnamon, baking soda and salt.
2. In a medium bowl, whisk together brown sugar, milk, oil, vinegar and vanilla until blended.
3. Add the milk mixture to the flour mixture and stir until just blended. Gently fold in raisins.
4. Divide batter equally among prepared muffin cups.
5. Bake in preheated oven for 18 to 22 minutes or until tops are golden brown and a toothpick inserted in the center comes out clean. Let cool in pan on a wire rack for 3 minutes, then transfer to the rack to cool.

Sweet Potato Muffins with Dried Cranberries

¹⁄₂ cup	dried cranberries	125 mL
	Hot water	
³⁄₄ cup	all-purpose flour	175 mL
³⁄₄ cup	whole wheat flour	175 mL
2 tsp	baking powder	10 mL
1 tsp	ground ginger	5 mL
1 tsp	ground cinnamon	5 mL
¹⁄₂ tsp	baking soda	2 mL
¹⁄₂ tsp	salt	2 mL
¹⁄₃ cup	packed light brown sugar	75 mL
1 cup	plain non-dairy milk (soy, almond, rice, hemp)	250 mL
¹⁄₃ cup	vegetable oil	75 mL
1 tsp	vanilla extract	5 mL
1¹⁄₂ cups	shredded peeled sweet potatoes	375 mL

I am an avowed fan of all things sweet potato, so it was nothing but pleasure fashioning them into a vegan muffin. These have just the right balance of sweet, tart and spice, thanks to the additions of dried cranberries, ginger and cinnamon.

Makes 12 muffins

- 12-cup muffin pan, greased

1. In a small bowl, combine cranberries and enough hot water to cover. Let soak for 15 minutes. Drain well.
2. Preheat oven to 400°F (200°C).
3. In a large bowl, whisk together all-purpose flour, whole wheat flour, baking powder, ginger, cinnamon, baking soda and salt.
4. In a medium bowl, whisk together brown sugar, milk, oil and vanilla until well blended.
5. Add the milk mixture to the flour mixture and stir until just blended. Gently fold in cranberries and sweet potatoes.
6. Divide batter equally among prepared muffin cups.
7. Bake for 19 to 23 minutes or until tops are golden brown and a toothpick inserted in the center comes out clean. Let cool in pan on a wire rack for 5 minutes, then transfer to the rack to cool.

Best Bran Muffins

2¼ cups	bran cereal, such as All-Bran	550 mL
⅔ cup	packed light brown sugar	150 mL
1⅔ cup	plain soy milk	400 mL
½ cup	soft silken tofu	125 mL
⅓ cup	vegetable oil	75 mL
¼ cup	dark (cooking) molasses	60 mL
2 tsp	vanilla extract	10 mL
1 tsp	cider vinegar	5 mL
1¼ cups	all-purpose flour	300 mL
½ cup	whole wheat flour	125 mL
2 tsp	baking soda	10 mL
1½ tsp	ground cinnamon	7 mL
½ tsp	salt	2 mL
1 cup	raisins	250 mL

These bran muffins will impress everyone with how incredibly soft and moist they are. The secret ingredient? Soft silken tofu.

Makes 12 muffins

- Preheat oven to 400°F (200°C)
- Food processor
- 12-cup muffin pan, greased

1. In food processor, process half the bran cereal until finely ground. Transfer to a medium bowl and stir in the remaining cereal.

2. In food processor, process brown sugar, milk, tofu, oil, molasses, vanilla and vinegar until blended and smooth. Stir into cereal. Let stand for 5 minutes.

3. In a large bowl, whisk together all-purpose flour, whole wheat flour, baking soda, cinnamon and salt.

4. Add the cereal mixture to the flour mixture and stir until just blended. Gently fold in raisins.

5. Divide batter equally among prepared muffin cups.

6. Bake in preheated oven for 16 to 21 minutes or until a toothpick inserted in the center comes out clean. Let cool in pan on a wire rack for 5 minutes, then transfer to the rack to cool.

Morning Oatmeal Muffins

1½ cups	all-purpose flour	375 mL
¾ cup	large-flake (old-fashioned) rolled oats	175 mL
1 tbsp	baking powder	15 mL
1 tsp	salt	5 mL
¾ tsp	ground cinnamon	3 mL
½ cup	packed dark brown sugar	125 mL
1 cup	vanilla soy yogurt	250 mL
⅔ cup	vanilla-flavored non-dairy milk (soy, almond, rice, hemp)	150 mL
⅔ cup	mashed ripe bananas	150 mL
½ cup	vegetable oil	125 mL
⅔ cup	raisins	150 mL
2 tbsp	packed dark brown sugar	30 mL

These muffins were an unexpected favorite at a recent brunch potluck, with guests descending in droves while they were still warm in the basket.

Makes 12 muffins

- Preheat oven to 400°F (200°C)
- 12-cup muffin pan, lined with paper liners

1. In a large bowl, whisk together flour, oats, baking powder, salt and cinnamon.

2. In a medium bowl, whisk together ½ cup (125 mL) brown sugar, yogurt, milk, bananas and oil until well blended.

3. Add the yogurt mixture to the flour mixture and stir until just blended. Gently fold in raisins.

4. Divide batter equally among prepared muffin cups. Sprinkle with 2 tbsp (30 mL) brown sugar.

5. Bake in preheated oven for 25 to 30 minutes or until tops are golden and a toothpick inserted in the center comes out clean. Let cool in pan on a wire rack for 3 minutes, then transfer to the rack to cool.

Cinnamon Cracked Wheat Muffins

1/2 cup	bulgur (cracked wheat)	125 mL
1 cup	boiling water	250 mL
1 1/4 cups	plain soy milk	300 mL
2 tsp	cider vinegar	10 mL
1 cup	all-purpose flour	250 mL
1/2 cup	whole wheat flour	125 mL
2 1/2 tsp	baking powder	12 mL
1 1/2 tsp	ground cinnamon, divided	7 mL
1 1/4 tsp	salt	6 mL
3/4 tsp	baking soda	3 mL
1/3 cup	packed light brown sugar	75 mL
1/4 cup	vegetable oil	60 mL
1 tsp	vanilla extract	5 mL
3 tbsp	granulated sugar	45 mL

Don't be misled by the plain-looking appearance of these muffins: they really are fantastic. Bulgur has never tasted so delicious.

Makes 12 muffins

- 12-cup muffin pan, greased

1. In a small bowl, combine bulgur and boiling water. Let stand for 30 minutes. Drain off any excess water.
2. Preheat oven to 425°F (220°C).
3. In a medium bowl, combine soy milk and vinegar. Let stand for 5 minutes or until curdled.
4. In a large bowl, whisk together all-purpose flour, whole wheat flour, baking powder, 1 tsp (5 mL) of the cinnamon, salt and baking soda.
5. Whisk brown sugar, oil and vanilla into milk mixture until well blended.
6. Add the milk mixture to the flour mixture and stir until just blended. Gently fold in bulgur.
7. Divide batter equally among prepared muffin cups. In a small bowl, combine the remaining cinnamon and granulated sugar. Sprinkle over batter.
8. Bake for 16 to 20 minutes or until tops are golden brown and a toothpick inserted in the center comes out clean. Let cool in pan on a wire rack for 5 minutes, then transfer to the rack to cool.

Granola Dried Blueberry Muffins

1 cup	whole wheat flour	250 mL
1 cup	all-purpose flour	250 mL
1 tbsp	baking powder	15 mL
1 tsp	ground cinnamon	5 mL
1/2 tsp	salt	2 mL
1 1/2 cups	vegan granola, divided	375 mL
2/3 cup	packed light brown sugar	150 mL
3/4 cup	vanilla-flavored soy yogurt	175 mL
1/3 cup	plain non-dairy milk (soy, almond, rice, hemp)	75 mL
1/3 cup	vegetable oil	75 mL
2	large ripe bananas, diced	2
1/2 cup	dried blueberries	125 mL

Serve these granola muffins with more vanilla soy yogurt in a cup for a perfectly delicious, healthy breakfast.

Makes 12 muffins

- Preheat oven to 350°F (180°C)
- 12-cup muffin pan, greased

1. In a large bowl, whisk together whole wheat flour, all-purpose flour, baking powder, cinnamon and salt. Stir in 3/4 cup (175 mL) of the granola.
2. In a medium bowl, whisk together brown sugar, yogurt, milk and oil until well blended.
3. Add the yogurt mixture to the flour mixture and stir until just blended. Gently fold in bananas and blueberries.
4. Divide batter equally among prepared muffin cups. Sprinkle with the remaining granola and gently press into batter.
5. Bake in preheated oven for 18 to 21 minutes or until tops are golden brown and a toothpick inserted in the center comes out clean. Let cool in pan on a wire rack for 5 minutes, then transfer to the rack to cool.

Rise and Shine Fruit, Flax and Oat Muffins

1³/₄ cups	plain non-dairy milk (soy, almond, rice, hemp)	425 mL
1 tbsp	cider vinegar	15 mL
1 cup	large-flake (old-fashioned) rolled oats	250 mL
¹/₂ cup	bran cereal, such as All-Bran	125 mL
¹/₄ tsp	salt	1 mL
¹/₂ cup	boiling water	125 mL
1 cup	chopped mixed dried fruit	250 mL
¹/₃ cup	granulated sugar	75 mL
¹/₄ cup	ground flax seeds	60 mL
¹/₂ cup	vegetable oil	125 mL
1¹/₂ cups	whole wheat pastry flour	375 mL
1¹/₄ tsp	baking soda	6 mL
1 tsp	ground cinnamon	5 mL

If ever there was a reason to rise and shine, these muffins are it. They are packed with good-for-you ingredients, but what makes them stellar is their amazing taste.

Makes 12 muffins

- 12-cup muffin pan, greased

1. In a glass measuring cup, combine milk and vinegar. Let stand for 5 minutes or until curdled.
2. In a medium bowl, combine oats, bran cereal, salt and boiling water. Stir in milk mixture, dried fruit, sugar, flax seeds and oil. Let cool.
3. Preheat oven to 375°F (190°C).
4. In a large bowl, whisk together flour, baking soda and cinnamon.
5. Add the oat mixture to the flour mixture and stir until just blended.
6. Divide batter equally among prepared muffin cups.
7. Bake for 18 to 21 minutes or until tops are golden brown and a toothpick inserted in the center comes out clean. Let cool in pan on a wire rack for 5 minutes, then transfer to the rack to cool.

Maple Quinoa Corn Muffins

1 cup	quinoa, rinsed	250 mL
1 cup	yellow cornmeal	250 mL
3 tbsp	ground flax seeds	45 mL
1¼ cups	boiling water	300 mL
1¼ cups	plain non-dairy milk (soy, almond, rice, hemp)	300 mL
2 tsp	cider vinegar	10 mL
1¼ cups	all-purpose flour	300 mL
2 tsp	baking powder	10 mL
½ tsp	baking soda	2 mL
½ tsp	salt	2 mL
⅓ cup	pure maple syrup	75 mL

Makes 12 muffins

• 12-cup muffin pan, greased

1. In a large bowl, combine quinoa, cornmeal and flax seeds. Stir in boiling water. Let stand for 30 minutes.
2. Preheat oven to 375°F (190°C).
3. In a glass measuring cup, combine milk and vinegar. Let stand for 5 minutes or until curdled.
4. In another large bowl, whisk together flour, baking powder, baking soda and salt.
5. Whisk maple syrup into milk mixture until well blended. Stir into quinoa mixture until blended.
6. Add the quinoa mixture to the flour mixture and stir until just blended.
7. Divide batter equally among prepared muffin cups.
8. Bake for 23 to 26 minutes or until tops are golden and a toothpick inserted in the center comes out clean. Let cool in pan on a wire rack for 3 minutes, then transfer to the rack to cool.

One of my vegan friends is crazy for these not-too-sweet muffins and calls them "New World Order Muffins" because they are made with three ingredients — maple syrup, quinoa and corn — that originated in the Americas.

Amaranth Raisin Muffins

1 cup	raisins	250 mL
½ cup	whole-grain amaranth	125 mL
⅓ cup	ground flax seeds	75 mL
1½ cups	boiling water	375 mL
2 cups	whole wheat pastry flour	500 mL
2 tsp	baking powder	10 mL
1 tsp	ground cinnamon	5 mL
½ tsp	salt	2 mL
½ cup	agave nectar	125 mL
¼ cup	vegetable oil	60 mL
1 tsp	vanilla extract	5 mL
1 cup	chopped pecans, toasted	250 mL

Makes 12 muffins

• 12-cup muffin pan, greased

1. In a medium bowl, combine raisins, amaranth, flax seeds and boiling water. Let stand for 20 minutes.
2. Preheat oven to 350°F (180°C).
3. In a large bowl, whisk together flour, baking powder, cinnamon and salt.
4. Stir agave nectar, oil and vanilla into raisin mixture until well blended.
5. Add the raisin mixture to the flour mixture and stir until just blended. Gently fold in pecans.
6. Divide batter equally among prepared muffin cups.
7. Bake for 20 to 25 minutes or until tops are golden and a toothpick inserted in the center comes out clean. Let cool in pan on a wire rack for 3 minutes, then transfer to the rack to cool.

Amaranth is a tiny grain that dates back hundreds of years to the Aztecs in Mexico. It offers a particularly high-quality protein and is also high in fiber. What I love best about it, though, is that its toasty, nutty flavor makes it a delicious (and inexpensive) alternative to nuts in a wide range of baking recipes.

Dutch Spice Whole Wheat Muffins

1¹⁄₂ cups	all-purpose flour	375 mL
¹⁄₂ cup	rye flour	125 mL
1 tbsp	baking powder	15 mL
1 tsp	salt	5 mL
1 tsp	ground cinnamon	5 mL
1 tsp	ground ginger	5 mL
¹⁄₂ tsp	ground nutmeg	2 mL
¹⁄₂ tsp	ground cardamom	2 mL
¹⁄₄ tsp	ground cloves	1 mL
¹⁄₂ cup	packed dark brown sugar	125 mL
1 cup	vanilla-flavored soy milk	250 mL
¹⁄₃ cup	dark (cooking) molasses	75 mL

Nothing irks me more than a spice muffin, cookie or cake that has but a hint of spice. Not so with these muffins. They are intensely spiced and very moist. And they only get better with age, so try to resist eating too many at once.

Makes 12 muffins

- Preheat oven to 350°F (180°C)
- 12-cup muffin pan, greased

1. In a large bowl, whisk together all-purpose flour, rye flour, baking powder, salt, cinnamon, ginger, nutmeg, cardamom and cloves.
2. In a medium bowl, whisk together brown sugar, soy milk and molasses until well blended.
3. Add the milk mixture to the flour mixture and stir until just blended.
4. Divide batter equally among prepared muffin cups.
5. Bake in preheated oven for 24 to 28 minutes or until a toothpick inserted in the center comes out clean. Let cool in pan on a wire rack for 5 minutes, then transfer to the rack to cool.

Pumpernickel Muffins

1¹⁄₄ cups	rye flour	300 mL
1¹⁄₄ cups	all-purpose flour	300 mL
2 tsp	baking powder	10 mL
1 tsp	baking soda	5 mL
1 tsp	salt	5 mL
³⁄₄ cup	plain soy yogurt	175 mL
¹⁄₃ cup	plain non-dairy milk (soy, almond, rice, hemp)	75 mL
¹⁄₄ cup	dark (cooking) molasses	60 mL
¹⁄₄ cup	vegetable oil	60 mL
1¹⁄₂ tsp	instant espresso powder	7 mL
2 tbsp	caraway seeds (optional)	30 mL

Dark and delicious, these muffins top my list as an accompaniment for homemade soup.

Makes 12 muffins

- Preheat oven to 375°F (190°C)
- 12-cup muffin pan, greased

1. In a large bowl, whisk together rye flour, all-purpose flour, baking powder, baking soda and salt.
2. In a medium bowl, whisk together yogurt, milk, molasses, oil and espresso powder until well blended.
3. Add the yogurt mixture to the flour mixture and stir until just blended.
4. Divide batter equally among prepared muffin cups. Sprinkle with caraway seeds (if using).
5. Bake in preheated oven for 20 to 25 minutes or until a toothpick inserted in the center comes out clean. Let cool in pan on a wire rack for 5 minutes, then transfer to the rack. Serve warm or let cool.

Boston Brown Bread Muffins

1 cup	whole wheat flour	250 mL
1/2 cup	yellow cornmeal	125 mL
1 1/2 tsp	baking soda	7 mL
3/4 tsp	salt	3 mL
1/3 cup	packed dark brown sugar	75 mL
3/4 cup	plain soy yogurt	175 mL
1/2 cup	plain non-dairy milk (soy, almond, rice, hemp)	125 mL
1/3 cup	dark (cooking) molasses	75 mL
1/3 cup	vegetable oil	75 mL
1 cup	raisins	250 mL

Boston brown bread is a nostalgic favorite — my parents would buy cans of it to keep on hand for quick vegetarian lunches (they always partnered it with baked beans) for me and my siblings. I can attest that this muffin interpretation hits all the right notes.

Makes 12 muffins

- Preheat oven to 400°F (200°C)
- 12-cup muffin pan, greased

1. In a large bowl, whisk together flour, cornmeal, baking soda and salt.
2. In a medium bowl, whisk together brown sugar, yogurt, milk, molasses and oil until well blended.
3. Add the yogurt mixture to the flour mixture and stir until just blended. Gently fold in raisins.
4. Divide batter equally among prepared muffin cups.
5. Bake in preheated oven for 14 to 17 minutes or until a toothpick inserted in the center comes out clean. Let cool in pan on a wire rack for 5 minutes, then transfer to the rack to cool.

Irish Brown Bread Muffins

1 cup	plain non-dairy milk (soy, almond, rice, hemp)	250 mL
1 tsp	cider vinegar	5 mL
2 tbsp	vegetable oil	30 mL
1 1/2 cups	whole wheat flour	375 mL
1/2 cup	all-purpose flour	125 mL
1/4 cup	quick-cooking rolled oats	60 mL
2 tbsp	granulated sugar	30 mL
1 tsp	baking soda	5 mL
1/2 tsp	salt	2 mL
1/2 cup	dried currants	125 mL

With a hearty whole-grain flavor punctuated by sweet currants, these muffins are perfect at any meal of the day.

Makes 12 muffins

- Preheat oven to 425°F (220°C)
- 12-cup muffin pan, greased

1. In a glass measuring cup, combine milk and vinegar. Let stand for 5 minutes or until curdled. Stir in oil.
2. In a large bowl, whisk together whole wheat flour, all-purpose flour, oats, sugar, baking soda and salt.
3. Add the milk mixture to the flour mixture and stir until just blended. Gently fold in currants.
4. Divide batter equally among prepared muffin cups.
5. Bake in preheated oven for 15 to 20 minutes or until tops sound hollow when tapped and a toothpick inserted in the center comes out clean. Let cool in pan on a wire rack for 3 minutes, then transfer to the rack to cool.

Wheat Germ Banana Muffins

1¼ cups	whole wheat pastry flour	300 mL
¾ cup	wheat germ	175 mL
2 tsp	baking powder	10 mL
2 tsp	ground cinnamon	10 mL
½ tsp	baking soda	2 mL
½ tsp	salt	2 mL
⅓ cup	granulated sugar	75 mL
1 cup	vanilla-flavored soy yogurt	250 mL
⅓ cup	vegetable oil	75 mL
1 tbsp	freshly squeezed lemon juice	15 mL
1 cup	mashed ripe bananas	250 mL

I am particularly taken with banana baked goods of all varieties, largely for their homespun flavor and lack of pretense. This version is no exception. It's a perfect muffin for starting the day — and kids love it too.

Makes 10 muffins

- Preheat oven to 400°F (200°C)
- 12-cup muffin pan, 10 cups greased

1. In a large bowl, whisk together flour, wheat germ, baking powder, cinnamon, baking soda and salt.

2. In a medium bowl, whisk together sugar, yogurt, oil and lemon juice until well blended. Stir in bananas until blended.

3. Add the yogurt mixture to the flour mixture and stir until just blended.

4. Divide batter equally among prepared muffin cups.

5. Bake in preheated oven for 20 to 25 minutes or until tops are golden brown and a toothpick inserted in the center comes out clean. Let cool in pan on a wire rack for 5 minutes, then transfer to the rack to cool.

Multigrain Quinoa Muffins

½ cup	quinoa, rinsed	125 mL
⅔ cup	boiling water	150 mL
2 cups	whole wheat pastry flour	500 mL
½ cup	old-fashioned rolled oats	125 mL
2 tsp	baking powder	10 mL
1 tsp	baking soda	5 mL
1 tsp	ground cinnamon	5 mL
½ tsp	salt	2 mL
½ cup	unsweetened apple juice	125 mL
2 tbsp	ground flax seeds	30 mL
½ cup	packed light brown sugar	125 mL
1 cup	unsweetened applesauce	250 mL
¼ cup	agave nectar	60 mL
¼ cup	vegetable oil	60 mL
½ cup	dried blueberries	125 mL

Indigenous to the Andes, quinoa was called "the mother grain" by the Incas, who considered the plant sacred. And while much has been made of quinoa's nutritional properties, its nutty flavor in this recipe is a revelation.

Makes 18 muffins

- Blender
- Two 12-cup muffin pans, 18 cups greased

1. In a small bowl, combine quinoa and boiling water. Let stand for 20 minutes.

2. Preheat oven to 375°F (190°C).

3. In a large bowl, whisk together flour, oats, baking powder, baking soda, cinnamon and salt until blended.

4. In blender, process apple juice and flax seeds for 1 minute or until thickened and frothy. Add brown sugar, applesauce, agave nectar and oil; process for 30 seconds or until combined.

5. Add the apple juice mixture to the flour mixture and stir until just blended. Gently fold in quinoa and blueberries.

6. Divide batter equally among prepared muffin cups.

7. Bake for 18 to 23 minutes or until tops are golden and a toothpick inserted in the center comes out clean. Let cool in pans on a wire rack for 5 minutes, then transfer to the rack to cool.

Oat Bran Applesauce Muffins

1 1/2 cups	whole wheat pastry flour	375 mL
3/4 cup	oat bran	175 mL
2 tsp	baking powder	10 mL
1 tsp	ground cinnamon	5 mL
1/2 tsp	ground cardamom	2 mL
1/2 tsp	baking soda	2 mL
1/2 tsp	salt	2 mL
1/4 tsp	ground nutmeg	1 mL
1/2 cup	packed light brown sugar	125 mL
1 cup	unsweetened applesauce	250 mL
3/4 cup	vanilla-flavored soy yogurt	175 mL
1/4 cup	vegetable oil	60 mL
1/2 cup	dried cranberries	125 mL

There's no better partner for oat bran than applesauce. Here, they team up in a simple, but always satisfying, morning muffin. For added appeal, dried cranberries are stirred into the batter.

Makes 12 muffins

- Preheat oven to 350°F (180°C)
- 12-cup muffin pan, greased

1. In a large bowl, whisk together flour, bran, baking powder, cinnamon, cardamom, baking soda, salt and nutmeg.
2. In a medium bowl, whisk together brown sugar, applesauce, yogurt and oil until well blended.
3. Add the applesauce mixture to the flour mixture and stir until just blended. Gently fold in cranberries.
4. Divide batter equally among prepared muffin cups.
5. Bake in preheated oven for 25 to 30 minutes or until tops are golden brown and a toothpick inserted in the center comes out clean. Let cool in pan on a wire rack for 5 minutes, then transfer to the rack to cool.

Whole Wheat Biscuit Muffins

1 1/2 cups	whole wheat pastry flour	375 mL
1 cup	all-purpose flour	250 mL
4 tsp	baking powder	20 mL
3/4 tsp	salt	3 mL
3/4 cup	cold vegan stick margarine, cut into 1/4-inch pieces	175 mL
3/4 cup	plain non-dairy milk (soy, almond, rice, hemp)	175 mL

This whole wheat version of basic biscuits is made even easier by the use of a muffin pan. They are deliciously wheaty and substantial. A little bit of all-purpose flour in the batter keeps the muffins light in texture, while the non-dairy milk and margarine keep them soft.

Makes 12 muffins

- Preheat oven to 400°F (200°C)
- 12-cup muffin pan, greased

1. In a large bowl, whisk together whole wheat pastry flour, all-purpose flour, baking powder and salt. Using a pastry cutter or your fingers, cut or rub in margarine until mixture resembles coarse crumbs. Stir in milk until just moistened.
2. Divide batter equally among prepared muffin cups.
3. Bake in preheated oven for 16 to 19 minutes or until tops are golden and a toothpick inserted in the center comes out clean. Let cool in pan on a wire rack for 3 minutes, then transfer to the rack to cool.

Dark Chocolate Muffins

1½ cups	all-purpose flour	375 mL
½ cup	unsweetened cocoa powder (not Dutch process)	125 mL
1½ tsp	baking powder	7 mL
¼ tsp	baking soda	1 mL
¼ tsp	salt	1 mL
¾ cup	granulated sugar	175 mL
1 cup + 2 tbsp	plain non-dairy milk (soy, almond, rice, hemp)	280 mL
¼ cup	vegetable oil	60 mL
1 tbsp	cider vinegar	15 mL
1 tsp	vanilla extract	5 mL
3 oz	vegan bittersweet chocolate, chopped	90 g

Makes 12 muffins

- Preheat oven to 350°F (180°C)
- 12-cup muffin pan, greased

1. In a large bowl, whisk together flour, cocoa powder, baking powder, baking soda and salt.
2. In a medium bowl, whisk together sugar, milk, oil, vinegar and vanilla until well blended.
3. Add the milk mixture to the flour mixture and stir until just blended. Gently fold in chocolate.
4. Divide batter equally among prepared muffin cups.
5. Bake in preheated oven for 18 to 22 minutes or until a toothpick inserted in the center comes out clean. Let cool in pan on a wire rack for 3 minutes, then transfer to the rack to cool.

A double dose of decadent chocolate renders these muffins irresistible. They're amazing plain, but try them with a spread of peanut butter or raspberry jam, too.

Mocha Muffins

2 cups	all-purpose flour	500 mL
¼ cup	unsweetened cocoa powder (not Dutch process)	60 mL
2½ tsp	baking powder	12 mL
½ tsp	salt	2 mL
¼ tsp	baking soda	1 mL
¼ tsp	ground cinnamon	1 mL
¾ cup	granulated sugar	175 mL
¾ cup	vanilla-flavored soy yogurt	175 mL
½ cup	plain non-dairy milk (soy, almond, rice, hemp)	125 mL
½ cup	vegetable oil	125 mL
1 tbsp	instant espresso powder	15 mL
½ cup	vegan miniature semisweet chocolate chips	125 mL

Makes 12 muffins

- Preheat oven to 375°F (190°C)
- 12-cup muffin pan, greased

1. In a large bowl, whisk together flour, cocoa powder, baking powder, salt, baking soda and cinnamon.
2. In a medium bowl, whisk together sugar, yogurt, milk, oil and espresso powder until well blended.
3. Add the yogurt mixture to the flour mixture and stir until just blended. Gently fold in chocolate chips.
4. Divide batter equally among prepared muffin cups.
5. Bake in preheated oven for 18 to 22 minutes or until a toothpick inserted in the center comes out clean. Let cool in pan on a wire rack for 5 minutes, then transfer to the rack to cool.

Cocoa-cinnamon batter, chocolate chips and a shot of espresso add up to a handful of heaven for java junkies.

Chocolate Chip Coffeecake Muffins

Topping

1/2 cup	whole wheat pastry flour	125 mL
1/2 cup	firmly packed light brown sugar	125 mL
1/2 tsp	ground cinnamon	2 mL
1/4 cup	vegan margarine, melted	60 mL

Muffins

2 cups	whole wheat pastry flour	500 mL
2 1/2 tsp	baking powder	12 mL
1 tsp	ground cinnamon	5 mL
1/2 tsp	baking soda	2 mL
1/2 tsp	salt	2 mL
3/4 cup	granulated sugar	175 mL
3/4 cup	vanilla-flavored soy yogurt	175 mL
2/3 cup	vanilla-flavored non-dairy milk (soy, almond, rice, hemp)	150 mL
1/2 cup	vegetable oil	125 mL
1 tsp	vanilla extract	5 mL
2/3 cup	vegan miniature semisweet chocolate chips	150 mL

Friends and family will be throwing off the covers to ensure they get up in time for more than one of these muffins. Be sure to tuck one or more away for your afternoon coffee break.

Makes 12 muffins

- Preheat oven to 350°F (180°C)
- 12-cup muffin pan, greased

1. *Topping:* In a small bowl, combine flour, brown sugar and cinnamon. Add margarine, tossing with a fork until mixture is crumbly. Refrigerate until ready to use.

2. *Muffins:* In a large bowl, whisk together flour, baking powder, cinnamon, baking soda and salt.

3. In a medium bowl, whisk together sugar, yogurt, milk, oil and vanilla until well blended.

4. Add the yogurt mixture to the flour mixture and stir until just blended. Gently fold in chocolate chips.

5. Divide batter equally among prepared muffin cups. Sprinkle with topping.

6. Bake in preheated oven for 20 to 25 minutes or until tops are golden and a toothpick inserted in the center comes out clean. Let cool in pan on a wire rack for 5 minutes, then transfer to the rack to cool.

Mexican Chocolate Muffins

1¼ cups	all-purpose flour	300 mL
½ cup	unsweetened cocoa powder (not Dutch process)	125 mL
1 tsp	baking powder	15 mL
¾ tsp	ground cinnamon	3 mL
½ tsp	baking soda	2 mL
½ tsp	salt	2 mL
⅛ tsp	cayenne pepper	0.5 mL
½ cup	packed dark brown sugar	125 mL
⅔ cup	soft silken tofu	150 mL
⅔ cup	plain soy yogurt	150 mL
⅓ cup	vegetable oil	75 mL
½ tsp	almond extract	2 mL
½ cup	vegan miniature semisweet chocolate chips	125 mL

I find it extremely challenging to stop at just one of these spicy chocolate muffins. They are so simple to prepare, too.

Makes 12 muffins

- Preheat oven to 350°F (180°C)
- Blender
- 12-cup muffin pan, greased

1. In a large bowl, whisk together flour, cocoa powder, baking powder, cinnamon, baking soda, salt and cayenne.
2. In blender, process brown sugar, tofu, yogurt, oil and almond extract until blended and smooth.
3. Add the tofu mixture to the flour mixture and stir until just blended. Gently fold in chocolate chips.
4. Divide batter equally among prepared muffin cups.
5. Bake in preheated oven for 21 to 25 minutes or until tops are firm and a toothpick inserted in the center comes out clean. Let cool in pan on a wire rack for 3 minutes, then transfer to the rack to cool.

Chocolate Chip Cookie Muffins

1½ cups	all-purpose flour	375 mL
½ cup	whole wheat flour	125 mL
2 tsp	baking powder	10 mL
½ tsp	baking soda	2 mL
½ tsp	salt	2 mL
¼ tsp	ground cinnamon	1 mL
⅓ cup	packed light brown sugar	75 mL
⅔ cup	plain non-dairy milk (soy, almond, rice, hemp)	150 mL
⅔ cup	plain soy yogurt	150 mL
½ cup	vegan margarine, melted	125 mL
1 tsp	vanilla extract	5 mL
¾ cup	vegan miniature semisweet chocolate chips	175 mL

If you think the idea of chocolate chip cookies for breakfast is brilliant, these muffins are for you. They have the advantage of being more healthful than cookies, much less sweet and filling enough to propel you through the morning.

Makes 12 muffins

- Preheat oven to 400°F (200°C)
- 12-cup muffin pan, greased

1. In a large bowl, whisk together all-purpose flour, whole wheat flour, baking powder, baking soda, salt and cinnamon.
2. In a medium bowl, whisk together brown sugar, milk, yogurt, margarine and vanilla until blended.
3. Add the yogurt mixture to the flour mixture and stir until just blended. Gently fold in chocolate chips.
4. Divide batter equally among prepared muffin cups.
5. Bake in preheated oven for 18 to 22 minutes or until tops are golden brown and a toothpick inserted in the center comes out clean. Let cool in pan on a wire rack for 5 minutes, then transfer to the rack to cool.

Basic Sweet Muffins

2 cups	all-purpose flour	500 mL
2 tsp	baking powder	10 mL
1/2 tsp	baking soda	2 mL
1/2 tsp	salt	2 mL
2/3 cup	granulated sugar	150 mL
3/4 cup	plain non-dairy milk (soy, almond, rice, hemp)	175 mL
3/4 cup	vanilla-flavored soy yogurt	175 mL
1/3 cup	vegetable oil	75 mL
1 tsp	vanilla extract	5 mL

I call these "basic" muffins, yet they are everything but that. They are pure comfort, without being remotely stodgy. Use them as a template for creating countless variations of your own design, adding spices, dried fruits, nuts, seeds, herbs, extract — you name it. Or keep them simple and eat one straight up, with a cup of hot cocoa or tea.

Makes 12 muffins

- Preheat oven to 400°F (200°C)
- 12-cup muffin pan, greased

1. In a large bowl, whisk together flour, baking powder, baking soda and salt.
2. In a medium bowl, whisk together sugar, milk, yogurt, oil and vanilla until well blended.
3. Add the yogurt mixture to the flour mixture and stir until just blended.
4. Divide batter equally among prepared muffin cups.
5. Bake in preheated oven for 18 to 22 minutes or until tops are golden brown and a toothpick inserted in the center comes out clean. Let cool in pan on a wire rack for 3 minutes, then transfer to the rack to cool.

Jelly Doughnut Muffins

1 3/4 cups	all-purpose flour	425 mL
1 1/4 tsp	baking powder	6 mL
1/2 tsp	baking soda	2 mL
1/2 tsp	salt	2 mL
1/2 tsp	ground nutmeg	2 mL
1/2 cup	granulated sugar	125 mL
1 cup	vanilla-flavored soy yogurt	250 mL
1/3 cup	vegetable oil	75 mL
1/2 cup	seedless raspberry preserves	125 mL

Topping

1/4 cup	granulated sugar	60 mL
1 tsp	ground cinnamon	5 mL
1/4 cup	vegan margarine, melted	60 mL

These fabulous muffins require no explanation. Frankly, they are far more delicious than anything you could find at the local doughnut shop.

Makes 10 muffins

- Preheat oven to 350°F (180°C)
- 12-cup muffin pan, 10 cups lined with paper liners

Muffins

1. *Muffins:* In a large bowl, whisk together flour, baking powder, baking soda, salt and nutmeg.
2. In a medium bowl, whisk together sugar, yogurt and oil until well blended.
3. Add the yogurt mixture to the flour mixture and stir until just blended.
4. Divide batter equally among prepared muffin cups. Spoon 2 tsp (10 mL) preserves in the center of each cup (the preserves will sink as the muffins bake).
5. Bake in preheated oven for 20 to 25 minutes or until tops are golden and spring back when touched. Let cool in pan on a wire rack for 5 minutes, then transfer to the rack.
6. *Topping:* In a small bowl, combine sugar and cinnamon. Generously brush warm muffin tops with margarine, then sprinkle with cinnamon mixture. Let cool.

Double Ginger Muffins

1²/₃ cups	all-purpose flour	400 mL
¹/₃ cup	whole wheat flour	75 mL
2¹/₂ tsp	ground ginger	12 mL
2 tsp	baking powder	10 mL
¹/₂ tsp	baking soda	2 mL
¹/₂ tsp	salt	2 mL
¹/₃ cup	packed light brown sugar	75 mL
1 cup	plain soy yogurt	250 mL
¹/₂ cup	plain non-dairy milk (soy, almond, rice, hemp)	125 mL
¹/₃ cup	vegetable oil	75 mL
1 tsp	vanilla extract	5 mL
¹/₄ cup	minced crystallized ginger	60 mL

Ground ginger and crystallized ginger amp up the flavor of these muffins. Try serving them with fresh fruit, a delicious counterpoint to the peppery notes of the spice.

Makes 12 muffins

- Preheat oven to 400°F (200°C)
- 12-cup muffin pan, greased

1. In a large bowl, whisk together all-purpose flour, whole wheat flour, ground ginger, baking powder, baking soda and salt.
2. In a medium bowl, whisk together brown sugar, yogurt, milk, oil and vanilla until well blended.
3. Add the yogurt mixture to the flour mixture and stir until just blended. Gently fold in crystallized ginger.
4. Divide batter equally among prepared muffin cups.
5. Bake in preheated oven for 18 to 22 minutes or until tops are golden brown and a toothpick inserted in the center comes out clean. Let cool in pan on a wire rack for 3 minutes, then transfer to the rack to cool.

Jam Surprise Muffins

1¹/₄ cups	all-purpose flour	300 mL
1 cup	whole wheat flour	250 mL
1 tbsp	baking powder	15 mL
¹/₂ tsp	baking soda	2 mL
¹/₂ tsp	salt	2 mL
²/₃ cup	granulated sugar	150 mL
³/₄ cup	vanilla-flavored soy yogurt	175 mL
³/₄ cup	plain non-dairy milk (soy, almond, rice, hemp)	175 mL
¹/₃ cup	vegetable oil	75 mL
¹/₂ tsp	almond extract	2 mL
¹/₂ cup	seedless berry jam or preserves	125 mL

Caution: May require finger licking. It will come as no surprise that these muffins — although easily and inexpensively assembled with a short list of pantry staples — are a hit with anyone and everyone.

Makes 12 muffins

- Preheat oven to 400°F (200°C)
- 12-cup muffin pan, greased

1. In a large bowl, whisk together all-purpose flour, whole wheat flour, baking powder, baking soda and salt.
2. In a medium bowl, whisk together sugar, yogurt, milk, oil and almond extract until well blended.
3. Add the yogurt mixture to the flour mixture and stir until just blended.
4. Divide half the batter equally among prepared muffin cups. Spoon 2 tsp (10 mL) jam into the center of each cup. Top with the remaining batter.
5. Bake in preheated oven for 21 to 26 minutes or until tops are golden and firm to the touch. Let cool in pan on a wire rack for 3 minutes, then transfer to the rack to cool.

Peanut Butter and Jelly Muffins

1 cup	all-purpose flour	250 mL
½ cup	whole wheat flour	125 mL
¾ cup	large-flake (old-fashioned) rolled oats	75 mL
2¼ tsp	baking powder	11 mL
1½ tsp	baking soda	7 mL
¾ tsp	salt	3 mL
¾ cup	plain non-dairy milk (soy, almond, rice, hemp)	175 mL
½ cup	brown rice syrup or agave nectar	125 mL
⅓ cup	vegetable oil	75 mL
¾ cup	natural peanut butter, well-stirred	175 mL
¾ cup	mashed ripe bananas	175 mL
1½ tbsp	cider vinegar	22 mL
½ cup	strawberry jam or preserves	125 mL

Finally, PB&J in one neat package. In this whimsical muffin, a peanut butter batter is filled with a spoonful of strawberry jam before heading off to the oven.

Tip

Other natural nut butters, such as almond and cashew, can be used in place of peanut butter in these muffins.

Makes 16 muffins

- Preheat oven to 350°F (180°C)
- Two 12-cup muffin pans, 16 cups greased

1. In a large bowl, whisk together all-purpose flour, whole wheat flour, oats, baking powder, baking soda and salt.

2. In a medium bowl, whisk together milk, syrup and oil until well blended. Whisk in peanut butter, bananas and vinegar until blended.

3. Add the peanut butter mixture to the flour mixture and stir until just blended.

4. Divide half the batter equally among prepared muffin cups. Spoon 2 tsp (10 mL) jam into the center of each cup. Top with the remaining batter.

5. Bake in preheated oven for 20 to 25 minutes or until tops are golden brown and firm to the touch. Let cool in pans on a wire rack for 5 minutes, then transfer to the rack to cool.

Chai Latte Muffins

1 cup	vanilla-flavored non-dairy milk (soy, almond, rice, hemp)	250 mL
2 tbsp	loose black tea	30 mL
2 cups	all-purpose flour	500 mL
2 tsp	baking powder	10 mL
1 1/2 tsp	ground cinnamon	7 mL
1 1/2 tsp	ground cardamom	7 mL
1/2 tsp	ground ginger	2 mL
1/2 tsp	baking soda	2 mL
1/2 tsp	salt	2 mL
1/4 tsp	ground cloves	1 mL
2/3 cup	packed light brown sugar	150 mL
2/3 cup	plain soy yogurt	150 mL
1/3 cup	vegetable oil	75 mL
1 tsp	vanilla extract	5 mL

Scented with many of the spices of chai, these muffins are wonderful with hot black tea.

Makes 12 muffins

- 12-cup muffin pan, greased

1. In a small saucepan, bring milk and tea to a simmer over medium heat. Remove from heat, cover and let steep for 10 minutes. Strain through a fine-mesh sieve into a medium bowl, discarding tea leaves, and let cool.
2. Preheat oven to 400°F (200°C).
3. In a large bowl, whisk together flour, baking powder, cinnamon, cardamom, ginger, baking soda, salt and cloves.
4. Whisk brown sugar, yogurt, oil and vanilla into milk mixture until well blended.
5. Add the yogurt mixture to the flour mixture and stir until just blended.
6. Divide batter equally among prepared muffin cups.
7. Bake for 19 to 23 minutes or until tops are golden brown and a toothpick inserted in the center comes out clean. Let cool in pan on a wire rack for 5 minutes, then transfer to the rack to cool.

Gingerbread Muffins

2 cups	all-purpose flour	500 mL
1/2 cup	whole wheat flour	125 mL
1 tbsp	ground ginger	15 mL
1 1/2 tsp	baking soda	7 mL
1 1/4 tsp	ground cinnamon	6 mL
1/2 tsp	ground allspice	2 mL
1/2 tsp	salt	2 mL
1/4 tsp	ground cloves	1 mL
1/2 cup	packed dark brown sugar	125 mL
1/2 cup	vegetable oil	125 mL
2 tsp	vanilla extract	10 mL
1 cup	dark (cooking) molasses	250 mL
2 tsp	cider vinegar	10 mL
1 cup	boiling water	250 mL

Too many ginger muffins lean toward the soothingly plain; these are the opposite of that — they're spicy with an ample amount of ginger, as well as cinnamon, allspice and cloves.

Makes 16 muffins

- Preheat oven to 375°F (190°C)
- Two 12-cup muffin pans, 16 cups lined with paper liners

1. In a large bowl, whisk together all-purpose flour, whole wheat flour, ginger, baking soda, cinnamon, allspice, salt and cloves.
2. In a medium bowl, whisk together brown sugar, oil and vanilla until well blended.
3. Add the oil mixture to the flour mixture and stir until just blended.
4. In a large glass measuring cup, combine molasses and vinegar. Stir in boiling water. Slowly pour into batter, stirring until just blended.
5. Divide batter equally among prepared muffin cups.
6. Bake in preheated oven for 22 to 27 minutes or until a toothpick inserted in the center comes out clean. Let cool in pans on a wire rack for 3 minutes, then transfer to the rack to cool.

Tried and True Corn Muffins

2 cups	all-purpose flour	500 mL
1 cup	yellow cornmeal	250 mL
1 1/2 tsp	baking powder	7 mL
1 tsp	baking soda	5 mL
1/2 tsp	salt	2 mL
3 tbsp	granulated sugar	45 mL
1 cup	plain soy yogurt	250 mL
3/4 cup	plain non-dairy milk (soy, almond, rice, hemp)	175 mL
1/2 cup	vegetable oil	125 mL

Makes 12 muffins

- Preheat oven to 400°F (200°C)
- 12-cup muffin pan, greased

1. In a large bowl, whisk together flour, cornmeal, baking powder, baking soda and salt.
2. In a medium bowl, whisk together sugar, yogurt, milk and oil until well blended.
3. Add the yogurt mixture to the flour mixture and stir until just blended.
4. Divide batter equally among prepared muffin cups.
5. Bake in preheated oven for 17 to 20 minutes or until tops are light golden brown and a toothpick inserted in the center comes out clean. Let cool in pan on a wire rack for 3 minutes, then transfer to the rack. Serve warm or let cool.

As moist as cake beneath their golden crust, these crumbly treats are amazing when taken in either a sweet (think jam, molasses, peanut butter) or a savory (think soup, salad, tofu scrambles) direction, but they are also wonderful on their own.

Herbed Rye Muffins

1 1/4 cups	rye flour	300 mL
1/2 cup	brown rice flour	125 mL
4 tsp	baking powder	20 mL
3/4 tsp	salt	3 mL
3/4 cup	plain non-dairy milk (soy, almond, rice, hemp)	175 mL
1/4 cup	vegetable oil	60 mL
3 tbsp	brown rice syrup	45 mL
2 tbsp	minced fresh chives	30 mL
1 tbsp	minced fresh dill	15 mL

Makes 12 muffins

- Preheat oven to 375°F (190°C)
- 12-cup muffin pan, greased

1. In a large bowl, whisk together rye flour, brown rice flour, baking powder and salt.
2. In a medium bowl, whisk together milk, oil and syrup until well blended.
3. Add the milk mixture to the flour mixture and stir until just blended. Gently fold in chives and dill.
4. Divide batter equally among prepared muffin cups.
5. Bake in preheated oven for 22 to 26 minutes or until tops are golden brown and a toothpick inserted in the center comes out clean. Let cool in pan on a wire rack for 5 minutes, then transfer to the rack to cool.

In this easy and hugely versatile recipe, fresh herbs and rye flour are transformed into a boast-worthy muffin. And because you can vary the herbs by season — or even use dried herbs — they are muffins to be enjoyed year-round.

Rosemary Muffins

1½ cups	all-purpose flour	375 mL
¾ cup	whole wheat flour	175 mL
1 tbsp	granulated sugar	15 mL
2½ tsp	baking powder	12 mL
2 tsp	minced fresh rosemary	10 mL
½ tsp	salt	2 mL
⅛ tsp	freshly ground black pepper	0.5 mL
¼ cup	ground flax seeds	60 mL
1 cup	plain non-dairy milk (soy, almond, rice, hemp)	250 mL
¼ cup	vegetable oil	60 mL

The perfect soup partner, these fragrant muffins are as impressive and delicious as they are easy to make.

Makes 12 muffins

- Preheat oven to 375°F (190°C)
- Blender
- 12-cup muffin pan, greased

1. In a large bowl, whisk together all-purpose flour, whole wheat flour, sugar, baking powder, rosemary, salt and pepper.
2. In blender, process flax seeds and ½ cup (125 mL) water for 1 minute or until thickened and frothy. Add milk and oil; process for 30 seconds or until combined.
3. Add the milk mixture to the flour mixture and stir until just blended.
4. Divide batter equally among prepared muffin cups.
5. Bake in preheated oven for 20 to 24 minutes or until tops are golden brown and a toothpick inserted in the center comes out clean. Let cool in pan on a wire rack for 3 minutes, then transfer to the rack to cool.

Chipotle Red Pepper Muffins

1½ cups	all-purpose flour	375 mL
½ cup	yellow cornmeal	125 mL
2½ tsp	baking powder	12 mL
1 tsp	chipotle pepper powder	5 mL
1 tsp	ground cumin	5 mL
½ tsp	garlic powder	2 mL
½ tsp	baking soda	2 mL
½ tsp	salt	2 mL
2 tbsp	light brown sugar	30 mL
¾ cup	plain soy yogurt	175 mL
½ cup	vegetable oil	125 mL
¾ cup	chopped drained roasted red bell peppers, patted dry	175 mL

When mixed up with smoky spices and sweet roasted peppers, savory muffins become a delicious crowd-pleaser. There's enough chipotle here to make your lips just barely hum, but not so much as to overshadow the balancing act created by the other ingredients — garlic, cumin and a kiss of brown sugar.

Makes 12 muffins

- Preheat oven to 375°F (190°C)
- 12-cup muffin pan, greased

1. In a large bowl, whisk together flour, cornmeal, baking powder, chipotle powder, cumin, garlic powder, baking soda and salt.
2. In a medium bowl, whisk together brown sugar, yogurt and oil until well blended. Stir in roasted peppers.
3. Add the yogurt mixture to the flour mixture and stir until just blended.
4. Divide batter equally among prepared muffin cups.
5. Bake in preheated oven for 18 to 22 minutes or until a toothpick inserted in the center comes out clean. Let cool in pan on a wire rack for 3 minutes, then transfer to the rack. Serve warm or let cool.

Mediterranean Muffins

1½ cups	all-purpose flour	375 mL
¾ cup	whole wheat flour	175 mL
2½ tsp	baking powder	12 mL
¾ tsp	dried basil	3 mL
¾ tsp	dried oregano	3 mL
½ tsp	salt	2 mL
3 tbsp	ground flax seeds	45 mL
1 cup	plain non-dairy milk (soy, almond, rice, hemp)	250 mL
¼ cup	olive oil	60 mL
⅓ cup	chopped walnuts, toasted	75 mL
⅓ cup	chopped pitted kalamata olives	75 mL
⅓ cup	chopped drained oil-packed sun-dried tomatoes	75 mL

The labor in this recipe is minimal, and it pays tenfold (or more). The delectable (but healthy) result is great paired with soup, but one muffin is practically a meal unto itself.

Makes 12 muffins

- Preheat oven to 350°F (180°C)
- Blender
- 12-cup muffin pan, greased

1. In a medium bowl, whisk together all-purpose flour, whole wheat flour, baking powder, basil, oregano and salt.

2. In blender, process flax seeds and ½ cup (125 mL) water for 1 minute or until thickened and frothy. Add milk and oil; process for 2 minutes or until well blended and frothy.

3. Add the flax seed mixture to the flour mixture and stir until just blended. Gently fold in walnuts, olives and tomatoes.

4. Divide batter equally among prepared muffin cups.

5. Bake in preheated oven for 20 to 25 minutes or until tops are golden brown and a toothpick inserted in the center comes out clean. Let cool in pan on a wire rack for 5 minutes, then transfer to the rack. Serve warm or let cool.

Spinach Basil Muffins

3 cups	all-purpose flour	750 mL
1 tbsp	baking powder	15 mL
1 tbsp	dried basil	15 mL
1 tsp	garlic powder	5 mL
1¼ tsp	salt	6 mL
½ tsp	baking soda	2 mL
¾ cup	plain non-dairy milk (soy, almond, rice, hemp)	175 mL
¾ cup	plain soy yogurt	175 mL
½ cup	vegetable oil	125 mL
1	package (10 oz/300 g) frozen chopped spinach, thawed and squeezed dry	1

Here, I've pepped up my fail-safe savory muffin with a combination of spinach, basil and garlic.

Makes 18 muffins

- Preheat oven to 400°F (200°C)
- Two 12-cup muffin pans, 18 cups greased

1. In a large bowl, whisk together flour, baking powder, basil, garlic powder, salt and baking soda.

2. In a medium bowl, whisk together milk, yogurt and oil until well blended. Stir in spinach until blended.

3. Add the spinach mixture to the flour mixture and stir until just blended.

4. Divide batter equally among prepared muffin cups.

5. Bake in preheated oven for 18 to 22 minutes or until tops are golden and a toothpick inserted in the center comes out clean. Let cool in pans on a wire rack for 3 minutes, then transfer to the rack. Serve warm or let cool.

Cherry Tomato Muffins

2 cups	all-purpose flour	500 mL
2 tsp	baking powder	10 mL
1 1/2 tsp	dried basil	7 mL
1 tsp	baking soda	5 mL
1/2 tsp	salt	2 mL
1/4 tsp	freshly ground black pepper	1 mL
1 tbsp	granulated sugar	15 mL
3/4 cup	plain non-dairy milk (soy, almond, rice, hemp)	175 mL
3/4 cup	plain soy yogurt	175 mL
1/3 cup	olive oil	75 mL
1 cup	cherry tomatoes, quartered	250 mL

Makes 12 muffins

- Preheat oven to 400°F (200°C)
- 12-cup muffin pan, greased

1. In a large bowl, whisk together flour, baking powder, basil, baking soda, salt and pepper.
2. In a medium bowl, whisk together sugar, milk, yogurt and oil until well blended.
3. Add the yogurt mixture to the flour mixture and stir until just blended. Gently fold in tomatoes.
4. Divide batter equally among prepared muffin cups.
5. Bake in preheated oven for 18 to 22 minutes or until tops are golden brown and a toothpick inserted in the center comes out clean. Let cool in pan on a wire rack for 3 minutes, then transfer to the rack. Serve warm or let cool.

Delivering a lot of summer glamour for very little work, these gorgeous muffins find a perfect balance of tender, basil-flecked bread and sweet, fresh cherry tomatoes.

Sesame Scallion Muffins

1 1/2 cups	all-purpose flour	375 mL
1/2 cup	whole wheat flour	125 mL
2 1/4 tsp	baking powder	11 mL
1 tsp	baking soda	5 mL
1/2 tsp	salt	2 mL
1 tbsp	granulated sugar	15 mL
3/4 cup	plain non-dairy milk (soy, almond, rice, hemp)	175 mL
3/4 cup	plain soy yogurt	175 mL
1/4 cup	vegetable oil	60 mL
2 tbsp	toasted sesame oil	30 mL
1 cup	chopped green onions (scallions)	250 mL
2 tbsp	sesame seeds	30 mL

Makes 12 muffins

- Preheat oven to 400°F (200°C)
- 12-cup muffin pan, greased

1. In a large bowl, whisk together all-purpose flour, whole wheat flour, baking powder, baking soda and salt.
2. In a medium bowl, whisk together sugar, milk, yogurt, vegetable oil and sesame oil until well blended.
3. Add the milk mixture to the flour mixture and stir until just blended. Gently fold in green onions.
4. Divide batter equally among prepared muffin cups. Sprinkle with sesame seeds.
5. Bake in preheated oven for 18 to 22 minutes or until tops are golden brown and a toothpick inserted in the center comes out clean. Let cool in pan on a wire rack for 3 minutes, then transfer to the rack. Serve warm or let cool.

These muffins were inspired by the sesame-scallion pancakes at one of my favorite Chinese restaurants.

Chickpea Muffins with Indian Spices

1½ cups	whole wheat pastry flour	375 mL
½ cup	chickpea flour	125 mL
2 tsp	ground cumin	10 mL
2 tsp	garam masala	10 mL
1 tsp	baking powder	5 mL
1 tsp	salt	5 mL
½ tsp	baking soda	2 mL
⅛ tsp	cayenne pepper	0.5 mL
¼ cup	pumpkin purée (not pie filling)	60 mL
2 tbsp	toasted sesame oil	30 mL
2 tbsp	agave nectar	30 mL
1¼ cups	plain non-dairy milk (soy, almond, rice, hemp)	300 mL

Chickpea flour adds nutty flavor to this quick and savory supper bread. Pumpkin keeps the muffins moist, and a panoply of Indian spices makes them exciting.

Makes 10 muffins

- Preheat oven to 350°F (180°C)
- 12-cup muffin pan, 10 cups greased

1. In a large bowl, whisk together whole wheat pastry flour, chickpea flour, cumin, garam masala, baking powder, salt, baking soda and cayenne.
2. In a medium bowl, whisk together pumpkin, oil and agave nectar until well blended. Whisk in milk until blended.
3. Add the pumpkin mixture to the flour mixture and stir until just blended.
4. Divide batter equally among prepared muffin cups.
5. Bake in preheated oven for 18 to 22 minutes or until tops are golden brown and a toothpick inserted in the center comes out clean. Let cool in pan on a wire rack for 5 minutes, then transfer to the rack. Serve warm or let cool.

Jalapeño Corn Muffins

1 cup	all-purpose flour	250 mL
1 cup	yellow cornmeal, preferably stone-ground	250 mL
1 tbsp	baking powder	15 mL
1 tsp	ground cumin	5 mL
¾ tsp	salt	3 mL
3 tbsp	granulated sugar	45 mL
¾ cup	plain soy yogurt	175 mL
⅓ cup	plain non-dairy milk (soy, almond, rice, hemp)	75 mL
⅓ cup	vegetable oil	75 mL
1 cup	fresh or frozen (thawed) corn kernels	75 mL
2 tsp	minced seeded jalapeño pepper	10 mL

I'm at the point where I won't even consider eating my black bean chili without baking a batch of these muffins. They have just the right amount of heat, plus a bit of smoky flavor.

Makes 12 muffins

- Preheat oven to 375°F (190°C)
- 12-cup muffin pan, greased

1. In a large bowl, whisk together flour, cornmeal, baking powder, cumin and salt.
2. In a medium bowl, whisk together sugar, yogurt, milk and oil until well blended.
3. Add the yogurt mixture to the flour mixture and stir until just blended. Gently fold in corn and jalapeño.
4. Divide batter equally among prepared muffin cups.
5. Bake in preheated oven for 16 to 19 minutes or until tops are golden and a toothpick inserted in the center comes out clean. Let cool in pan on a wire rack for 10 minutes, then transfer to the rack. Serve warm or let cool.

Library and Archives Canada Cataloguing in Publication

Saulsbury, Camilla V.
  750 best muffin recipes : everything from breakfast classics to gluten-free, vegan & coffeehouse favorites / Camilla Saulsbury.

Includes index.
ISBN 978-0-7788-0249-5

  1. Muffins. I. Title. II. Title: Seven hundred and fifty best muffin recipes.

TX770.M83S29 2010   641.8'157   C2010-903252-7

Index